The Jewish Jesus

Revelation, Reflection, Reclamation

The Jewish Jesus

Revelation, Reflection, Reclamation

Edited by Zev Garber

Purdue University Press / West Lafayette, Indiana

Printed in the United States of America.

Library of Congress Cataloging-in-Publication Data

The Jewish Jesus : revelation, reflection, reclamation / edited by Zev Garber.

p. cm. -- (Shofar supplements in Jewish studies)

Includes bibliographical references and index.

ISBN 978-1-55753-579-5

1. Jesus Christ--Jewish interpretations. 2. Judaism--Relations--Christianity. 3. Christianity and other religions--Judaism. I. Garber, Zev, 1941-

BM620.J49 2011

232.9'06--dc22

2010050989

Cover image: James Tissot, French, 1836-1902.
Jesus Unrolls the Book in the Synagogue (*Jésus dans la synagogue déroule le livre*). 1886-1894.
Opaque watercolor over graphite on gray wove paper.
Image: 10 11/16 x 7 9/16 in. (27.1 x 19.2 cm).
Brooklyn Museum. 00.159.71. Purchased by public subscription.

Dedication

To the courageous and devoted essayists of this tome. Jews, who practice the faith of Jesus, and Christians, who believe by faith in Jesus. By the authority of Torah and Testament, they merge as one in proclaiming the Jewish Jesus and restoring his pivotal role in the history of Second Temple Judaism and beyond. The rest is commentary and controversy. Read and see why.

Contents

Introduction

Zev Garber

Though many articles, reviews, and books are not of one opinion on the life and time of Jesus, there is a general understanding in the dogma of the church and in the quests of the academy that the incarnate Christ of Christian belief lived and died a faithful Jew,[1] and what this says to contemporary Jews and Christians is the focus of this volume depicting Jesus in the context of Judaism and its impact on Jewish and Christian traditional and contemporary views of the other.

In the context of our time, Pope John Paul II challenged members of the Pontifical Biblical Commission to help Christians understand that the Hebrew Scriptures are essential to their faith (1997). That is to say, Catholic mysteries, including annunciation, incarnation, crucifixion, resurrection, and redemption are derived from the Hebrew biblical *Weltaschauung*. To speak of Jesus in the context of Judaism is affirmed by the church's acceptance of the Jewish Hebrew Bible as the Christian Old Testament, and this presents distinctive challenges to the visions of Judaism. When Jewish and Christian savants interweave the narrative and teaching of Jesus into the cultural and social life of first-century Judaism in the land of Israel under the rule of Caesar, they pinpoint the evolving Christology of Jesus believers, which conflicts with the viewpoints of the rabbis and jurisdiction of Rome. Second, Christians and Jews committed to reading scripture together are deeply motivated by an academic and reverential disposition toward rabbinic Judaism and the desire to correct the malign image of Jews and Judaism that emerges from erroneous readings of the Gospel sources. Arguably, *contra Iudaeos* biases happen when historicity (Pharasaic kinship of Jesus, Peter, and Paul) is conflated with apologetic ("give unto Caesar") and polemic depictions (Jews are a deicidal and misanthropic people), and theological innovation (Christ replaces Torah).

The desideratum is neither extreme skepticism nor full faith acceptance but rather a centralist position, somewhat contrary to an ecclesiastical tradition which teaches that truth is bounded and restricted to New Testament and early Christian *kerygma* (preaching) and *didache* (apologetics). Exploring the place of Jesus within Second Temple Judaism means to apply *drash* (insightful interpretation) to *peshat* (plain meaning of the text). Why so? Because Jesus the historical being, that is to say, Jesus before the oral and written traditions, is transformed and transfigured into a narrative character that appears in the canonized New Testament. The Jesus in narratology is a fluid figure of creative, idyllic, and dogmatic imagination, whose realness cannot be fixed in any given episode, teaching, or telling.

Thus, on reading the Gospel of John's account of Jesus before the Sanhedrin, the trial before Pilate, and the sentence of death, one may project that the Evangelist's Jewish opponents are the reason for the virtual negativity of the *Ioudaioi* towards Jesus in his teaching and trial. Also, the cry of the mob, "His blood be upon us and on our children" (Matt. 27:25) is neither an acceptance of guilt nor perpetual pedigree damnation for the death of Jesus but can be seen as an expression of innocence that says if we are not innocent of this man's blood then may the curse be fulfilled (see Acts 18:6 and *b. Sanh.* 37a).

Jewish-Christian Encounter

The ground rule for Christian-Jewish scriptural reading and discussion is simple but complex. Let the Christian proclaim core Christian dogma (Easter faith) and dicta (e.g., Jesus "the living bread that came down from heaven" [John 6:51] is the savior of Israel) without a hint or utterance of anti-Judaism. Likewise, the Jewish observant needs to be aware and sensitive about claims of Christian identity. The objective in the quest for the rediscovery, and possibly reclamation, by Jews of the Jewish Jesus is to penetrate the wall of separation and suspicion of "law and grace" and enable the believer in the Second Testament to appreciate the saga and salvation of Israel experientially in terms of Judaism, that is to say, in accordance with the teaching of Moses and the exegesis of the sages of Israel. Reciprocally, the follower of the Torah way learns the how and why of the Christian relationship to the Sinai covenant as presented in the Christian spirit of scriptural inspiration and tradition, a strong sign that the centuries-old "teaching of contempt" is not doable for Christians and Jews in dialogue, where a shared biblical tradition is the surest sign that the stumbling blocks of religious intolerance can be overcome. Take *lex talionis*, for example.

Three times the Pentateuch mentions the legislation of *lex talionis* (the law of retaliation, of an "eye for an eye" [Exod. 21:23-25; Lev. 24:19-20; Deut. 19:18-21]). Though the law of "measure for measure" existed in the ancient Near East, there is little evidence that the Torah meant that this legislation should be fulfilled literally except in the case of willful murder. "Life for life" is taken literally in cases of homicidal intention, and fair compensation is appropriate when physical injuries are not fatal. Equitable monetary compensation is deemed appropriate by the Oral Torah in the case of a pregnant woman whose unborn child's life is lost and when animal life is forfeited. Indeed, the Written Torah casts aside all doubts regarding the intent of the biblical *lex talionis* injunction: "And he that kills a beast shall make it good; and he that kills a man shall be put to death" (Lev. 24:21).

Rejecting the literal application of *lex talionis* puts an end to the mean-spirited charge that Judaism is "strict justice." Similarly, the words of Jesus on the Torah ("For truly, I say to you, till heaven and earth pass away, not an iota, not a dot, will pass from the law until all is accomplished" [Matt. 5:18]) beckon interpretation. Christian citing of Matthew 5:38-39a ("You have heard that it was said, 'an eye for an eye and a tooth for a tooth.' But I say to you, Do not resist one who is evil") to teach that "Jesus cancels the law of revenge and replaces it with the law of love" is wrong on two accounts:1) syntactically, the Greek text of Matthew 5:39 reads "and," not "but," thereby removing the onus of change; and 2) scripturally, the text in context (see Matt. 5:21-30, Jesus on murder and adultery) instructs not cancellation but affirmation of the commandments. Thus, Jesus, like the sages, focuses on the significance of the teaching and its cautionary warning about wrong doing in "thoughts, words, and deeds."

Nonetheless, there are significant differences on retaliation between Jesus and the Rabbis. In Matthew 5:38-39, Jesus addresses *'ayin tachat 'ayin* (eye for eye) in terms of personal revenge and related implementations, but the Rabbis' understanding is *mamon tachat 'ayin* (value of an eye), and this is seen as remedial justice for the guilty and concern for the injured. Also, a Christian interpretation of the scripture, "You shall love your neighbor as yourself" (Lev. 19:18) preceded by the prohibition, "You shall not take vengeance or bear a grudge," (Lev. 19:18) is the foundation of the Golden Rule: "In everything do to others as you would have them do to you; for this is the law and the prophets" (Matt. 7:12; see also Luke 6:31). However, the Jewish position is somewhat different. In Leviticus, "love your neighbor" is followed by, "You shall keep my statutes (*chuqqotai*, i.e., revelatory laws without applicable reason)" (19:19). In the rabbinic tradition, the covenantal partnership at Sinai represents the modus operandi to apply the love commandment, albeit taught in negative terms, "Whatever is hateful to you do it not to another."[2]

Participants in Jewish-Christian scriptural dialogue aim to show the interdependence of Jewish and Christian biblical traditions and do so by truncating the cultural, historical, psychological, religious, and theological differences between them. Some may see this and the absence of sustained critical discussion of texts and historical issues as major weaknesses, but I do not. There is something refreshing in connecting sentences to sentences, parts to whole, book to books. Spiritually informative, evocative in hermeneutics, less interested in critical scholarship that parses Jewish and Christian Scripture into strands and schools and more concerned with Torah and Gospels that instructs in moral values and fellowship; a religiously correct lesson for two sibling religions whose God is the author of all.

Testimony of Jesus[3]

There is a line of basic continuity between the beliefs and attitudes of Jesus and the Pharisees, between the reasons which led Jesus into conflict with the religious establishment of his day, and those which led his followers into conflict with the synagogue.

Two of the basic issues were the role of the Torah and the authority of Jesus. Rabbinic Judaism could never accept the Second Testament Christology since the God-man of the "hypostatic union" is foreign to the Torah's teaching on absolute monotheism. As the promised Messiah,[4] Jesus did not meet the conditions which the prophetic-rabbinic tradition associated with the coming of the Messiah. For example, there was no harmony, freedom, peace, or amity in Jerusalem and enmity and struggle abounded elsewhere in the land. This denied the validity of the Christian claim that Jesus fulfilled the Torah and that in his second coming the tranquility of the messianic age will be realized. As Rabbi Jesus, he taught the divine authority of the Torah and the prophets[5] and respect for its presenters and preservers,[6] but the Gospels claimed that his authority was equally divine and that it stood above the authority of the Torah. The disparity of the Jewish self and the Gentile other in the ancestral faith of Jesus is abolished in the new faith in Jesus: "There is neither Jew nor Greek, slave nor free, male nor female, for you are all one in Christ Jesus."[7] I see this testimony as a major point of contention between the Jesus way and the way of rabbinic halakha that ultimately led to the severance of the Jesus party from the synagogue. And this acquired new intensity after the passing of the Jewish Jesus and the success of Pauline Christianity.

'Ani Hu'/ I Am He: Seeking Unity in Diversity

No matter how composite the figure of the historical Jesus and how rudimentary the concept of the Christ event in the Second Testament, there can be no doubt that the Jewish and Gentile believers bestowed divine attributes and power upon Jesus and venerated him above all creatures. Such an attitude towards the person of Jesus as God incarnate led to conflict with the sages, who revered only Torah-from-heaven. This is illustrated in the exegetical dissimilarity between church and synagogue on how one is to submit to God's righteousness. Reading the nature of God's commandment (Deut. 30:11-14), the Apostle Paul comments that Christ is the subject of "Who will ascend into heaven? . . . Who will descend into the deep?" and confesses, "Jesus is Lord . . . in your mouth and in your heart"[8] is the justified salvation for all. For the sages, however, salvation is in believing and doing the commandments. "Surely, this commandment that I am commanding you today is not too hard for you . . . it is not in heaven,"[9] is the raison d'être of rabbinic Judaism. That is to say, the Torah is not in heaven, it is here and near so that Israel can hear "the blessing and the curse" and do the 613 Commandments[10] in order "to choose life"[11] and live.

The doctrine of the eternity of the Torah was axiomatic in Second Temple Judaism. It is implicit in verses that speak of individual teachings of Torah in phrases such as the following: "A perpetual statute throughout your generations in all your (lands of) dwellings" (Lev. 3:17) and "throughout the ages as a covenant for all time" (Exod. 3:16). Biblical (Proverbs, in which Torah equals wisdom), Apocryphal (the wisdom of Ben Sira), and Aggadic (Genesis Rabbah) traditions speak of the preexistence of Torah in heaven. Though the Talmud acknowledges the prerevelatory heavenly Torah, which the sages claimed was revealed to Moses at Sinai, it concentrates more on the Torah's eternal humanistic values. Indeed, the rabbinic mind speaks of two strains: revelation ("everything which a scholar will ask in the future is already known to Moses at Sinai"; see BT Menach. 29b) and the power of intellectual reasoning (as suggested in BT *Pes.* 21b, *Ketub.* 22a, *B.K.* 46b, *Chul.* 114b, *Nid.* 25a, *B.M.* 59b, and so forth). And by twinning the two dialectics, it appears, the sages taught more Torah than they received at Sinai.

Volatile are the arguments and disagreements between Petrine and Pauline Christians on issues of faith in Christ, with or without observance of the Torah on how to outreach to Gentiles.[12] On the other hand, the fallout is decisive and divisive in the disputations between the church and synagogue beginning with nascent Christianity, as John 8 seems to suggest. The destruction of Jerusalem and of the Second Temple was sufficient proof for believers in Christ that God had pronounced dire judgment upon his stiff-necked people and that the God of promises dispensed his countenance to those who accepted Jesus as Messiah. Hence, "Christ is the end of the law,"[13] in "(whose) flesh the law with its commandments and regulations"[14] are abolished. But Torah and its commandments are the matrix in which rabbinic Judaism was born, and it proved to be the mighty fortress to withstand danger of extinction from without (Rome) and from within (non-Pharisaic philosophies, including Jewish Christianity). Thus, in the rabbinic way, to despise an individual precept of the Torah is tantamount to rejecting the whole Torah; and this explains the measures taken by the synagogue, for example, the second century *Birkat ha-Minim* (prayer against Jewish sectarians inserted in the Eighteen Benedictions), to preserve its national and religious character in the face of adversity and catastrophe.

John 8 (indeed, throughout the Fourth Gospel) exemplifies disparate views of the Jesus party on the yoke of the Torah (temporary or eternal) and the separation of a specific Jewish Christian community in the late first century from the Jewish society to which its members had belonged and are now excluded by synagogue fiat. On the former, consider Jesus' words to the Samaritan woman at the well: "salvation is from the Jews. Yet a time is coming and has now come when the true worshippers will worship the Father in spirit and truth"[15] and on the latter, the intensity of conflict between the Jewish Christian community for which John was composed and the reigning religious authority is reflected in the hostile and vindictive language placed on the mouth of Jesus accusing his Jewish detractors of not accepting the truth, plotting to kill him, and being the children of the devil.[16]

In the long history of Christianity there exists no more tragic development than the treatment accorded the Jewish people by Christian believers based in part on the anti-Judaism in the Gospel of John. The cornerstone of supersessionist Christology is the belief that Israel was spurned by divine fiat for first rejecting and then killing Jesus. This permitted the apostolic and patristic writers to damn the Jews in the rhetoric of John 8, and more, to assign the worst dire punishment on judgment day. These are not words, just words, but they are links in an uninterrupted claim of antisemitic diatribes that contributed to the murder of Jews in the heartland of Christendom and still exist in a number of Christian circles today. How to mend the cycle of pain and the legacy of shame? The key is a midrashic (*peshat cum drash*) interpretation informed by an empathic and emphatic dialogue between siblings, Christian and Jew, individually and together.

Let me explain. It is a fact that church-synagogue relations turned for the better when the Second Vatican Council (1963-1965) issued the document *Nostra Aetate* (In Our Times), the first ever Roman Catholic document repudiating collective Jewish responsibility for the death of Jesus. In the Roman Catholic world, this inspired many dioceses and archdioceses to implement *Nostra Aetate* and to rid the anti-Jewish bias of Christian teaching. To illustrate, consider the sentiment of the Italian bishops to the Jewish community of Italy (March 1998): "For its part, the Catholic Church, beginning with Second Vatican Council—and thanks to the meeting of two men of faith, Jules Isaac and John XXIII, whose memory is a blessing—decisively turned in another direction [from teaching divinely sanctioned punishment of the Jews], removing every pseudotheological justification for the accusation of deicide and perfidy and also the theory of substitution with its consequent 'teaching of contempt,'[17] the foundation for all antisemitism. The Church recognizes with St. Paul that the gifts of God are irrevocable and that even today Israel has a proper mission to fulfill: to witness to the absolute lordship of the Most High, before whom the heart of every person must open."

Few can rival Pope John Paul II's papacy in ridding the Roman Catholic Church of antisemitism. He more than any predecessor has condemned "the hatreds, acts of persecution, and displays of antisemitism directed against the Jews by Christians at any time and in any place" (Yad Va-Shem, 23 March 2000). He has labeled the hatred of Jews as a sin against God, referred to the Jews as Christianity's "elder brother,"[18] with whom God's covenant is irrevocable, and established diplomatic relations with the State of Israel (1994). The Vatican documents, *We Remember: A Reflection on the Shoah* (1998) and *Confessions of Sins Against the People of Israel* (St. Peter's Basilica, 12 March 2000) are major milestones in the Roman Catholic Church's efforts to reconcile with the Jewish people. And, we might add, mainline Protestant denominations in the World Council of Churches, in different degrees, have done likewise.

I welcome this gesture of professing and confessing spoken in the spirit of *teshuvah* (repentance) from the largest member-church in the "body of Christ" and it bodes well for Jews to offer *teshuvah* (response) in kind. Jews must be true to their Torah, distinct from other sacred scriptures and religions. It is not the role of the synagogue to judge whether Jesus the Jew metamorphosed into the Christ of faith or that Jesus and the Christ are one and the same individual. Rather, Jews must do their homework and cleanse the people Israel of any conceived or perceived anti-Christian bias. Jews must see the Roman Catholic Church's altering attitude and action toward them as good omens done in the spirit of humility and contrition. Jews need to be reminded that the Roman Catholic Church views the encounter with Judaism and the Jewish people as an organic part of Christian penance. Indeed, Christianity is a legitimate dialogue partner in *tikkun 'olam,* endowing the world in peace, understanding, and unity.

Admittedly, dialogue at times creates unexpected friction, of a kind found in chronicles and hoary debates, if aggressively done for the purpose of settling a score. Progress, not regress in Christian-Jewish dialogue is only possible if old canards are exposed and reciprocal teachings of respect are encouraged. So proper dialogue on John 8 neither overlooks the harsh statements against the Jews and explains them in a setting in life of that time, nor allows misguided judgments of mean-spirited hermeneutics to pass by unchallenged, nor allows a conjunctional albeit controversial thought to go by untested. The "I am " of John 8:24, is such an example. It reveals an aura of divinity by Jesus because his words, "I am the one I claim to be," can be equated with God's identity to Moses, "I am that I am."[19] For the Christian divine, this can be interpreted as "I am" (God) is revealed in "I am" (Jesus). But the text continues, "He (God) said, 'Thus shall you say unto the children of Israel: I am has sent me (Moses) to you."[20] This can mean that God as God not God as Jesus is the absolute and sufficient revelation of the divine pathos for the Jewish people.

The significance attached to the name of God in the above midrashic discussion dispels illusion by illustration. The holiness, sanctity, and power of God's call are heard equally and necessarily differently by church and synagogue. One by Christ and the other by Torah. However, the completeness of God's name, meaning his essence and plan, is hidden in this world forever,[21] but in the fullness of time it will be made known: "Therefore my people shall know my name; therefore, on that day, that *'Ani Hu'* (name of God, the *shem ha-mmephorash)* is speaking: here am I."[22]

It is incumbent upon Jew and Christian together in dialogue and in action to bring that day speedily in our lifetime.

Case for Jesus the Jew

In the final paragraph of "Reflections on Jesus," a review essay by Zev Garber and Joshua Kulp on several books dealing with Jesus in the context of his time, the New Testament and Talmud,[23] I affirmed unashamedly that the modern Jew can identify with the faith and fate of Jesus but not faith in Jesus. I have no clue what Jesus would say but I proposed to Professor Peter Haas, Abba Hillel Silver Professor of Jewish Studies, Chair, Department of Religious Studies and Director, and Samuel Rosenthal Center for Judaic Studies at Case Western Reserve University, to convene a symposium on rediscovering the Jewish Jesus. So it was presented and so it was received. The three-day symposium on "Jesus in the Context of Judaism and the Challenge to the Church," hosted by the Samuel Rosenthal Center for Judaic Studies and managed brilliantly by Linda Gilmore,[24] took place at Case, 24-26 May 2009. The symposium presentations (Garber, Zevit, Moore, Basser, Fisher, Rubinstein, Bowman, Knight, Jacobs, and joined by Cook) were edited for publication in *Shofar* 28.3 (Spring 2010). Here they appear in a different format and increased word length. Additional chapters by Chilton, Schwartz, Ulmer, Kerem, Simms, Smerick, Mandell, and Magid complete this volume.

The articles in this volume cover historical, literary, liturgical, philosophical, religious, theological, and contemporary issues evolving in and around the Jewish Jesus. The contributors reflect on a plethora of issues on the Jewishness of Jesus and what this means to the steadfast articles of faith in Christ Jesus. They demonstrate that concerned and informed Jews and Christians together can assess dis/misinformation, monitor dissent, alleviate religious fears, and reassure that the covenantal mission of Torah and Gospel, historically honed by apologetics and polemics, has now become blessedly altered by academic quests and congenial interfaith dialogue.[25] In sum, the tradition has been enhanced by the acceptance of differences. The passionate dialogue over the Jewish Jesus has proven to be a blessing, not a curse. Indeed, the mosaic of articles by a seminal group of Jewish and Christian scholars has seized the teaching moment and developed an academically responsible agenda to learn and teach the Jesus narrative with academic savvy and with religious tolerance. One wonderful opportunity *B'Yameinu* (In Our Time) to lift the Cross of Calvary from the ashes of Auschwitz. So may it be done.

Zev Garber's opening plenary address on "Imagining the Jewish Jesus" postulated that the Easter faith without its Jewish historical context is unwieldy, or worse, a proven feeding ground for centuries-old Good Friday sermons that espoused anti-Judaism (replacement theology, conversion of the Jews) and anti-Semitism ("perfidious Jews and Christ killers"). A critical read of the Golden Rule, the Last Supper, and the Great Commandment in the context of Jewish exegesis showed how and why. Garber's methodology of reading Torah in the response of *na'aseh ve-nishma* ("We shall do and we shall hear [reason]"; Exod. 24:7) explained his *darshani* (interpret me) imperative in his analysis of scriptural readings.

Notes

1. For a selection of books dealing with the Jewishness of Jesus, see Harvey Falk, *Jesus the Pharisee: A New Look at the Jewishness of Jesus* (New York: Paulist Press, 1985); John Dominic Crossan, *The Historical Jesus: The Life of a Mediterranean Jewish Peasant* (San Francisco: HarperSanFrancisco, 1991); Trude Weiss-Rosmarin, *Judaism and Christianity: The Differences* (Middle Village, NY: Jonathan David Publishers, 1997); Geza Vermes, *The Changing Faces of Jesus* (New York: Penguin, 2000); Paula Fredriksen, *From Jesus to Christ: The Origins of the New Testament Image of Jesus*.2nd ed. (New Haven: Yale University Press, 2000); James Carroll, *Constantine's Sword* (Boston: Houghton Mifflin, 2001); Schalom Ben-Chorin, *Brother Jesus: The Nazarene Through Jewish Eyes*, trans. and ed. J. S. Klein and M. Reinhart (Athens, GA: University of Georgia Press, 2001); Amy-Jill Levine, *The Misunderstood Jew: The Church and the Scandal of the Jewish Jesus* (San Francisco: HarperSanFrancisco, 2006); Philip Sigal, *The Halakhah of Jesus of Nazareth According to the Gospel of Matthew* (Atlanta: Society of Biblical Literature/Brill, 2007); David Flusser, *The Sage from Galilee: Rediscovering Jesus' Genius* (Grand Rapids: Eerdmans, 2007); Oskar Skarsaune and Hvalvik Reidar, eds., *Jewish Believers in Jesus* (Peabody, MA: Hendrickson, 2007); Matthew Hoffman, *From Rebel to Rabbi: Reclaiming Jesus and the Making of Modern Jewish Culture* (Stanford, CA: Stanford University Press, 2007); Michael J. Cook, *Modern Jews Engage the New Testament: Enhancing Jewish Well-Being in a Christian Environment* (Woodstock, VT: Jewish Lights, 2008); John P. Meier, *A Marginal Jew: Rethinking the Historial Jesus*, vol. 4 of *Law and Love* (New Haven: Yale University Press, 2009); and Herbert Basser, *The Mind Behind the Gospels: A Commentary to Matthew 1-14* (Boston: Academic Studies Press, 2009).
2. The negative version of the Golden Rule suggests the frailty of subjective thinking, that is, "what is good for me, is good for you." The nonrational nature of *chuqqotai* supports this point of view.
3. My view on the historical Jesus is spelled out in Zev Garber, ed., *Mel Gibson's* Passion: *The Film, the Controversy, and Its Implications* (West Lafayette, IN: Purdue University Press, 2006), 63-69. Reprinted as chapter one in this book..
4. See also, among others, Matt. 26:62-64; Mark 14:60-62; Luke 22:60-70.
5. See also Matt. 5:17-20.
6. Matt 23:1-3a
7. Gal. 3:28. Also, 1 Cor. 12:13; Col. 3:11.
8. Rom. 10:6 commenting on Deut. 30:13-14
9. Deut. 30:11-12a
10. The Talmud states: "613 Commandments were revealed to Moses at Sinai, 365 being prohibitions equal in number to the solar days, and 248 being mandates corresponding in number to the limbs of the human body" (*Mak.* 23b). Another source sees the 365 prohibitions corresponding to the supposedly 365 veins in the body thereby drawing a connection between the performance of Commandments and the life of a person ("choose life"). The standard classification and enumeration of the *TaRYaG Mitzvot* (613 Commandments) follows the order of Maimonides (1135-1205) in his

Sefer ha-Mitzvot ("Book of Commandments," originally written in Arabic and translated several times into Hebrew).

11. Deut. 30:19
12. Galatians, for example, which I discussed in my paper, "How Believable Is the Allegory of Hagar and Sarah (Gal. 41)," given at the annual meeting of the National Association of Professors of Hebrew (NAPH), meeting in conjunction with the annual meeting of AAR-SBL, in Nashville, Tennessee, 18-21 November 2000.
13. Rom. 10:4a.
14. Eph. 2:15
15. John 4:22b-23.
16. John 8:31-59.
17. Term associated with Jules Isaac (1877-1963), French Jewish authority on antisemitism, who, in an audience with Pope John XXIII in 1960, persuaded the Holy Father to consider the errors of the Church's teachings on the Jews. Isaac's writings on *l'enseignement du mépris* played a key role in the declaration of *Nostra Aetate.*
18. Phrase introduced by Pope John XXIII.
19. Exod. 3:14
20. Ibid.
21. In the unvocalized Hebrew of the Torah, "this is my Name *l'lm*" can be read not as "forever" but "to be hidden." See Exod. 3:15b.
22. Isa. 52:6.
23. *Shofar* 27.2 (2009): 128-37.
24. Linda Gilmore's official title at Case is Manager of Interdisciplinary Programs and Centers but I call her "my Catholic angel." My admiration for Linda's managerial expertise was solidified in the spring 2005 semester when I taught at Case as the invited Rosenthal Fellow. Additionally, her Christian caring and concern that every "dot and tiddle" (see Matt. 5:17) of my Orthoprax Jewish ways be met is remembered with appreciation and respect.
25. On language violence in Jewish-Roman Catholic disputation, see Zev Garber, "Words, Words, Words," *Hebrew Studies* 48 (2007): 231-49.

Section 1

Reflections on the Jewish Jesus

The Jewish Jesus: A Partisan's Imagination

Zev Garber

My own approach to finding the historical Jesus in the text of the New Testament may appear to some as extreme. It seems to me that Mark, the earliest Gospel version on the life of Jesus compiled shortly after the destruction of the Second Jewish Temple by the Romans in 70 CE, contains authentic traces of the historical Jesus shrouded in repeated motifs of secrecy which are intended to obscure the role of Jesus as a political revolutionary sympathizer involved in the Jewish national struggle against Rome. When the Gospel of Mark is analyzed in its own light, without recourse to the special status which canonical tradition confers, it is less history and biography and more historiosophy and parable. It also features an astute polemic against the Jewish Christian believers in Jerusalem, whose influence diminished considerably following the fall of Jerusalem in 70 CE, and a clever apology to make early Christianity palatable for Rome by not identifying Jesus with the national aspirations of the Jews. The Markan account on the trial of Jesus and his execution, along with the portrait of a pacifistic Christ, are for the most part historically questioned by S. G. F. Brandon, who sees in these narratives attempts by the Gentile Church to win Roman favor by exculpating Pontius Pilate from his share in the crucifixion of Jesus.[1]

I agree. Regarding the Synoptic Gospels' (Mathew, Mark, Luke) account of Jesus before the Sanhedrin,[2] the trial before Pilate,[3] and the sentence of death,[4] the question of historical fairness intrudes into these accounts. Jesus is tried three times (the Sanhedrin night trial which found him guilty of blasphemy; the trial before Herod Antipas; the dawn trial before Pilate), and so which court condemned decisively Jesus?[5] Where in the biblical-talmudic tradition is blasphemy defined by claiming that one is the "Messiah the Son of the Blessed?"[6]

Leviticus 24:13-23 and Sanhedrin 7.5 proclaim that whoever curses God is guilty of blasphemy.[7] Rarely recorded are malediction and impious profanity by one who claims to be a messianic figure. True, Josephus recorded many messianic pretenders between 6-70 CE, but we have no record of any put to death. Bar-Kochba was called messiah by Akiba but tradition does not speak ill of either second-century hero. And no less a personality than Maimonides relegated the messianic doctrine to a secondary position among the articles of faith rendered in his name. Also, one guilty of blasphemy was stoned to death and not killed by crucifixion, as recorded by Mark.[8]

That Jesus was sympathetic to the Zealot cause may explain why the charges of sedition were not overtly denied by Jesus when asked, "Are you the King of the Jews?"[9] Other references support this view. One of the trusted disciples was Simon the Zealot.[10] The Zealot movement, rooted in the tradition of being "zealous for the Lord,"[11] arose in the Galilee in the first decade of the first century. It may be assumed that the child Jesus raised in Nazareth would have listened often to tales of Zealot exploits against the hated Romans and how many of the former died martyrs' deaths in a futile attempt to replace the bondage of Rome with the yoke of the "kingdom of heaven."[12]

These childhood experiences listened to in earnest and awe caused the adult Jesus to sympathize with the anti-Roman feelings of his people. Thus, the "cleansing of the temple" pericope is not to be read as anti-temple but rather as a critique of the temple functionaries who collaborated with Rome.[13] This episode appears to have coincided with an insurrection in Jerusalem during the period of Gaius Caligula (34-41), in which the Zealots appear to have been involved.[14] The famous question concerning tribute to Caesar has Jesus saying, "render to Caesar the things that are Caesar's and to God the things that are God's,"[15] thereby implying Jewish support of Roman fiscal and political policy. This is an assimilable position and it is very doubtful that the historical Jesus identified with it. Better to say, the Rome-based school of Mark coined Jesus' answer for it and guaranteed that Jesus and his fellowship were loyal to Rome and opposed to Jewish nationalism. This was a necessary survivor mandate for Gentile Christians living in Rome during and after the Zealot-inspired Jewish war against Rome.

The *ipsissima verba* of Jesus, recorded in Matthew 10:34, namely, "I have not come to bring peace but a sword," supports the militancy in the Jesus party mentioned in the Gethsemane tradition: Luke 22:35-38 portrays Jesus asking his disciples if they are armed and they reply that they are doubly armed. The size and arming of the arresting party "from the chief priests and the scribes, and the elders,"[16] can be cited as evidence of nationalist loyalty by Jesus. The unknown disciple who draws a word and cuts off the ear of the high priest's slave is identified in John's Gospel as Peter.[17]

Others say, the question of Jesus, "Have you come out against a robber with swords and clubs to capture me?,"[18] separates him from the Zealots. But can the parochial Jewish nationalism of Jesus be hidden in the image of the universal image of the Christ of peace? I think not. Yet Mark's anti-Jewish bias and pro-Roman sentiments inspired him to lay the guilt of Jesus in the hands of Jewish authorities. According to the Synoptic Gospels, Jesus was not an insurrectionist nor did he commit a crime deserving death by Roman law.[19] Later church narrative accepts this view without serious emendation and further presents Jesus as the "Prince of Peace." An early source of this tradition is the editorial note in Matthew 26:52. Here a post-70 CE Jewish Christian evaluating the ill-fated Jewish War declared in Jesus' name: "Put your sword back into its place; for all who take the sword will perish by the sword."[20]

A constant motif is the silence of the apostolic writings on matters pertaining to the political situation of the time. The Zealots of the period are essentially overlooked; episodes in which they are involved, as reported by Josephus and others, are not reported. Luke-Acts is silent about the identity and antecedents of James, Peter, and the other leaders of Jewish Christianity. Mark's theology prejudices the historical situation and declares that Jesus could not have involved himself in political nationalism and other contemporary issues. Later apostolic writers submissively follow the Markan line. How far theology distorts history is further shown by denigrating the Pharisees as the bitter opponents of Jesus.[21]

The received gospel tradition appears to suggest that the catastrophe of 70 CE and its aftermath was brought about by Jewish leaders who plotted Jesus' death, the Jewish mob who had demanded it, and the stiff-necked Jews who refused to follow the Jesus way. Also, the Jewish disciples do not know Jesus,[22] and it is the Roman centurion at the crucifixion who recognizes Jesus as the Son of God.[23]

Our thesis suggests that New Testament belief about "Who do the people say that I am?"[24] is more belief narrative than historicity. In my opinion, the genre of Christian Scriptures on the historical Jesus is expressed in the idiom of midrash. By midrash, I mean an existential understanding by man of his environment, history, and being. Its purpose is not to provide objective description of the world nor to relate objective facts, but to convey a particular cultural worldview rooted in a specific setting in the life of the people in a given historical moment (*Sitz im Leben*). Its content is doctrinal and ethical and its form is mythic. The very nature of midrash is an invitation to "demidrashize," that is, to decode the original form and make the content more meaningful for different time and clime. Indeed, the New Testament shows evidence of this. For example:

Given: Jesus returns in the clouds of heaven
Pauline: Shifts the emphasis of the failure of Jesus' return to the believer's present life.
Johanine: Achieves the same Pauline goal with its conception of eternal life here and now present to the faith, and of judgment as already accomplished in the world which Jesus brings.

My *Jewish* reading of Jesus in the Synoptic Gospels puts him in history and not in divinity. The Jesus of different Christologies could never find support in Judaism, since the God-man of the "hypostatic union" is foreign to Judaism's teaching on absolute monotheism. As the promised Messiah,[25] he did not meet the conditions which the prophetic-rabbinic tradition associated with the coming of the Messiah. Indeed, there was no harmony, freedom, peace and unity in the land of Israel—signs of the messianic age—and enmity and strife abounded everywhere. Not a false but failed Redeemer of the Jews, as witnessed by the words of the "King of the Jews" at the cross: *Eli, Eli, lama sabachthani* ("My God, my God, why have You *forsaken* me")?[26] Notwithstanding, he was a loyal son of Israel, whose commitment to the Torah[27]—albeit radical and reformist—and his remarks about the great Commandment[28] were steadfast and comparable to Pharasaic Judaism of the day.

Arguably, the great flaw in pre-Vatican II Catholic traditionalism (as depicted in Mel Gibson's movie, *The Passion of the Christ*) and Protestant fundamentalism in the teaching of the Easter faith is the heinous role played by the crowd, people, and Jews in the execution of Jesus. The cornerstone of supersessionist Christology is the belief that Israel was spurned by divine fiat for first rejecting and then killing Jesus. This permitted the apostolic and patristic writers and Protestant Reformers to attribute to Israel the mark of Cain and the evil of the Sodomites, and more, to assign the worst dire punishment on judgment day. These are not words, just words, but they are links in an uninterrupted chain of antisemitic diatribes that contributed to the murder of the Jews in the heartland of Christianity and still exists in a number of Christian circles today. How to mend the cycle of pain and the legacy of shame? The key is to separate the crucifixion of Jesus from the *contra Iudaeos* tradition by demystifying the composite Passion Narrative as taught and preached in ecclesiastical Christianity.

An illustration is in order. The nefarious words, "His blood be on us and on our children,"[29] seen by many as the scriptural flash point to the charge that Gibson's film is antisemitic, were composed in the 90s, a generation after the death of Jesus. And if the words are credible, then may they not be seen as composed by an anti-Zealot Jewish Christian writer who opposed the Jewish revolt against Rome and reflected on the wretched havoc on the Jewish people because of it? Similarly, to portray Pilate as meek, gentle, kind—a Jesus alter ego—that he cannot resist the aggressive demands of the Jewish mob to crucify Christ, is historically unfounded and not true.[30]

Finally, why the obsessive passion in Mel Gibson to portray endlessly the bloodied body of Jesus? May it not be this traditionalist Catholic's rejection of reforms advocated by Vatican Council II to present tolerantly the Passion of Jesus Christ? Whether conscientious or not, cowriter, director, and producer Gibson revises scriptural anti-Judaism in visual media. He does so by portraying overtly a corrupt Jewish priesthood, and especially the high priest, Caiaphas, a ferocious blood-thirsty Jewish mob, an effeminate Satan who hovers only among Jews, satanic Jewish children, and a complacent Roman leadership that does the bidding of Jews. The subliminal message: the destruction of Jerusalem and the Second Temple (the film's climactic and penultimate scene) is sufficient proof for believers in Christ that God has pronounced dire punishment upon old Israel and that he now dispenses his countenance to the new Israel, who accepts unhesitatingly Jesus as Lord and Savior. Hence, "Christ is the end of the law,"[31] in (whose) *flesh* the law with its commandments and regulations"[32] are abolished. Thus, to flagellate unceasingly the body of Jesus is to rid unmercifully Judaism from the body of Christ and provide salvation through the blood of Christ.[33] On Gibson's cross, replacement theology is reborn. And Satan and mammon laugh aloud, a bitter laugh.[34]

Discussion Questions

1. Explain the role of biblical criticism in understanding the historical Jesus.
2. In what way and to what degree does the claim that Jesus was a Jewish revolutionary ("Think not that I come to bring peace, but a sword," (Matt. 10:34) advance or impede the ecclesiastical belief that he was the "Prince of Peace"?
3. How does the scriptural Jewish Jesus counter Mel Gibson's cinematic Christ?

Notes

1. The writings of S.G. F. Brandon, the late professor of comparative religion at the University of Manchester, have influenced my thinking on Jesus as a nationalist sympathizer and a political revolutionary. See, in particular, his *Jesus and the Zealots* (New York: Charles Scribner's Sons, 1967). Also influential is Hyam Maccoby, *Revolution in Judaea: Jesus and the Jewish Resistance* (New York: Taplinger Publishing Company, 1981).
2. Matt. 26:57-75; Mark 14:53-72; Luke 22:54-71.
3. Matt. 27:11-14; Mark 15:2-5; Luke 2:3-5.
4. Matt. 27:15-26; Mark 15:6-15; Luke 23:17-25
5. See "The Trial of Jesus in Light of History: A Symposium," in *Judaism* 20.1 (1971): 6-74.
6. Matt 26: 63-65; Mark 14:61-65; Luke 22:67-70.
7. See Acts 6, where Christian tradition records that Stephen was guilty of death since he spoke "blasphemous words against Moses and against God" (Acts 6:7). See too Exod. 22:27; I Kgs. 21:10, 13 ("you have reviled God and king").
8. A brief description of the crucifixion is found in Matt. 27:33-44; Mark 15:22-32; Luke 23:33-43.
9. Matt. 27:11; Mark 15:2; Luke 23:3. See also, Mark 15:9, 12 and the charge against Jesus inscribed on the cross (Matt. 27:37; Mark 15:26; John 19:19).
10. See Matt. 10:14; Mark 3:18; Luke 6:15; Acts 1:3. In Matthew and Mark it is written, "Simon the Cananaean" (Zealot). Matthew's Jewish audience can understand the Aramaism, but Mark, who normally translates Aramaisms (e.g., Mark 7:34) into

Greek, purposely does not here. The writer of Luke-Acts, writing a generation after Mark, no longer sees the taint of political sedition about Jesus or is simply unaware of Mark's dilemma and unashamedly identifies Simon as a Zealot.

11. See the roles of Phineas (Num. 25:7-10), Matthias (1 Macc. 2:15-41), and Elijah (1 Kgs. 19:9-10) as zealot types.
12. "Blessed be His Name, whose glorious kingdom is forever and ever," recited in the Temple during the Day of Atonement services, was added by the Rabbis to accompany the opening verse of the *Shema* (Deut. 6:4). Since the period of Gaius Caligula (34-41), Roman emperors demanded from their subjects divine respect. The loyalist Jew (religious, nationalist) who rejected did so at the penalty of death. He submitted to the rule of God alone whom he proclaimed in "Hear O Israel, the Lord is our God, the Lord alone," and followed by the above doxology.
13. Mark 11:15-19; Matt. 21:21; Luke 19:45-48.
14. A reference to Pilate's ruthless suppression of the rebellion may be found in Luke 13:1.
15. Mark 12:17; Matt. 22:21; Luke 20:25.
16. The episode of Jesus taken captive is found in Mark 14:43-52; Matt 26:47-56; Luke 22:47-53.
17. Mark 14:46; Matt. 26:51; Luke 22:50; John 18:10.
18. Mark 14:48; Matt. 26:55; Luke 22:52.
19. Matt. 27:23; Mark 15:14; Luke 23:22.
20. Also, Luke 22:50. A similar message is associated with national restoration and rebuilding the Second Temple (515 BCE) in Zech 4:6, which is later linked to the synagogue service of Chanukkah by the Rabbis in order to play down the militancy of the Maccabean victory and state imitated by the ill-fated revolt against Rome.
21. The word Pharisees occurs over a hundred times in the New Testament (29 times in Matthew; 12 times in Mark; 27 times in Luke; 19 times in John; 9 times in Acts; and one time in Phillipians). There is ample fodder in these references to portray Pharisaism as sanctimonious, self-righteous, hypocritical, petrified formalism, and a degraded religious system corroded by casuistry. The bitterest tirade against the Pharisees is found in Matt. 23.
22. See Mark 8:27-33; Matt 16:13-23; Luke 9:18-22. The Petrine blessing found in Matt. 16:17-19 was added by a Jewish Christian to offset Mark's rebuke of Peter (The Jerusalem Church) as Satan by Jesus (Mark 8:33).
23. Matt. 27:54; Mark 15:39; Luke 23:47.
24. Matt. 16:13; Mark 8:27; Luke 9:18
25. See, among others, Matt 26:62-64; Mark 14:60-62; Luke 22:66-70.
26. Matt. 27:46; Mark 15:34. Emphasis added.
27. Matt. 5:17-20
28. Similar quotes can be found in Matt. 22:37 = Mark 12:30 = Luke 10:27 – Deut 6:5; Mark 12:29 – Deut 6:4; Matt 23:39 = Mark 12:31 = Luke 10:27b – Lev 19:18; Mark 12:33, see also I Sam 15:22.
29. Matt. 27:25. In *The Passion*, these words are heard in the original Aramaic but deleted in the English subtitles.
30. Philo Judaeus wrote about Pilate's "endless and intolerable cruelties"; this was no doubt why he was recalled to Rome in 37.
31. Rom 10:4a
32. Eph 2:15. Emphasis added.

33. Adversely, blood fixation by Jews is not associated with suffering, torture, and death but with birth, hope, and life. Consider the Ezekielian verse recited at the circumcision rite linking the birth of a Jewish male child (potential Messiah) with the birth of Jerusalem; "I (Lord God) said to you: 'In your blood, live.' Yeh, I said to you, 'in your blood, live.'" (Ezek. 16:6)
34. *Forbes* magazine (July 2004) announced that *The Passion* grossed more than $970 million, $370 million domestically and $600 million plus worldwide.

The Kabbalah of Rabbi Jesus

Bruce Chilton

Why speak of Kabbalah, and then link that to Jesus? The "Kabbalah," as that term in commonly used, refers to a movement of Jewish mysticism from the twelfth century through the Renaissance (in its initial flowering).[1] Its focus was on the mystical union with God, in a way analogous to the paths advocated by Christian mystics such as Julian of Norwich and Johannes Eckhart. Its character included an intellectual discipline, literary focus on the precise wording of the Torah, and even an academic rigor in the description of the divine spheres into which the initiate was to enter with great care. What relation might that have to a rabbi of the first century from Galilee, whose attainments did not include the ability even to write, and whose on references to the Hebrew Bible were so imprecise—and meditated through oral Targumim[2]—as to indicate he was illiterate?

Although Kabbalah indeed can be used with a restrictive meaning, its underlying orientation is nothing other than the approach of God's *merkabah*, the heavenly chariot throne from which divine power and wisdom emanated for the ordering of all creation. The conception of that *merkabah* is much more ancient, profoundly rooted in the theology of Israel, than the development of kabbalistic techniques during the Middle Ages. Indeed, the ascent to the divine throne is older than Israel itself.

From Mesopotamia, from the twenty-third century BCE and the fifteenth century CE, stories are told of kings and courtiers entering into the palace of heaven and receiving visions and empowerment there.[3] Israel learned these royal traditions from Babylonia and converted them into prophetic authorization, especially during the time of Ezekiel (in the sixth century CE). Ezekiel himself related his classic vision of the throne of God as a chariot, a *merkabah*, and what is usually called *merkabah* mysticism derives from his vision (in Ezek. 1). After Ezekiel, the book of Daniel (chapter 7) detailed this vision further (during the second century BCE). And by the time of Jesus, the book of Enoch, found in fragments in Aramaic at Qumran, had taken that tradition further.[4]

The book of Genesis says of Enoch only that "he walked with God, and he was not" (Gen. 5:22). This disappearance is taken as a sign that Enoch enjoyed a vision by ascent into the multiple heavens above the earth, and was authorized to relate its wisdom to Israel, indeed to act as an intermediary to the angels who had disobeyed God. From Ezekiel, through Daniel and Enoch and on to John and Jesus, there is a growing tradition, a *kabbalah* (something received),[5] which reflects a deep commitment to the disciplined practice of the vision of God's throne. The fragments of Enoch at Qumran are found in Aramaic, which suggests that the book was used, not just by the Essenes (who tended to guard their sectarian documents in Hebrew), but by a wider audience, which included the Essenes.[6] In fact, the book of Enoch is also quoted at a later stage in the New Testament, so that there can be no doubt of its widespread use. Another work found in Hebrew at Qumran and widely attested elsewhere, the book of Jubilees, also presents Enoch as a figure of revelation: he himself knows the Torah later communicated to Moses by angelic communication.

The development of these traditions is obviously not independent: there is a successive building and borrowing from one to the other. The ascent to the divine throne was an aspiration that was "received" or "taken," one source from others. To "receive" or to "take" in both Aramaic and Hebrew is expressed by the verb *qabal*, from which the noun *qabbalah* is derived, and the noun is used in both Mishnah and Talmud to refer to ancient tradition, including the Prophets and the Writings within the Bible of Israel (as distinct from the Torah).[7] Now what is *qabal*ed might be any sort of authoritative tradition, but it is tradition concerning the *merkabah* that is our concern here. When Paul wishes to underline that authority of his teaching concerning the Eucharist, he says, "For I received from the Lord what I also delivered over to you," and he goes on to speak of both Jesus last meal with his followers and its significance and correct observance (1 Cor. 11:23-33). The sources of Paul's authority include what he learned from primitive Christians (especially Peter, see Gal. 1:18), but more importantly what he calls the *apokalupsis*, the uncovering, of Christ Jesus (Gal. 1:12): "For I want to inform you, fellows, of the message of triumph messaged by me, that it is not by a person. For I neither received it from a person, nor was I taught, but through an uncovering of Messiah Jesus." That disclosure occurred in a supernatural realm, the third heaven, the paradise to which Paul on another occasion says he was snatched up, where he was told unutterable wisdoms (2 Cor. 12:1-4)[8].

Such language is not merely formal or rhetorical; it is also a matter of spiritual practice and personal experience. Paul is attesting, at the generative moment of his identity as an apostle and thereafter, that the vision of the divine throne to which the risen Jesus had been elevated was at the heart of his own consciousness. There is no trace of Paul's famous tendency toward argumentation here: the practice of ascent is simply taken to be understood among those who first heard his letters. The assurance of Paul that this ascent was a self-evident aspect of his authorization invites us to look back, to seek traces of the power of the *merkabah* in the experience of Jesus. Those traces are perhaps most plain in Jesus' baptism, and in what that reception of the holy spirit produced in him. That takes us back to Jesus' association with John called the "immerser" (the *baptistes* in Greek, from the verb *baptizomai*, which means, "immerse").

Many people came to John for this immersion, most often on the way to the Temple along the well-established path of pilgrimage that followed the Jordan Valley. Once they arrived at the base of the mount of the Temple in Jerusalem itself, they would be confronted by a bewildering array of differing kinds of purification—of varying degrees of expense—and every pilgrim would have to negotiate passage up the triple gate. But even before arrival there, enthusiastic pilgrims wanted to know themselves as part of Israel, the people of God. Immersions such as John's provided them with a sense of confidence and integrity. From the writings of Josephus, we know that John was not the only such figure; Josephus refers to his own study with another immerser, named Bannus.[9] Pilgrims' local *miqveh* (immersion pool, if they even had access to one) might not correspond to the Pharisaic design, and would be much less luxurious than those of the Sadducees, less elaborate than those of the Essenes. But John offered them purification in God's own water collected from natural sources ("living waters"), and the assurance that this was the science of Israel's true purity. Then what they faced in Jerusalem was less daunting; the claims and counter claims of various factions would be put into perspective by the confidence what one had already been purified by God's own living waters.

Immersion, for John, was no once for all act, as in later Christian baptism. In the practice of the primitive Church, after the resurrection, believers felt that they received the spirit of God when they were immersed in the name of Jesus. That conviction became possible after the resurrection, stemming from the belief that Jesus was alive and at the right hand of God, so as to be able to dispense divine spirit. In Peter's speech at Pentecost (the Magna Charta of baptismal theology), Jesus, having been exalted to the right hand of God, receives the promise of the holy spirit from the father and pours it out on his followers (Acts 2:33). Once received by a Christian, that spirit did not come and go. Subsequent immersion could not top up a lack of spirit. A Christian lived in the power of God's spirit; its influence might increase or decrease, but the fact of its presence was irrevocable. But in John's practice, as in Judaism as a whole, purification was a routine requirement, and people might return to John many times, and they naturally engaged in many forms of purification other than John's, whether in their villages or at the Temple. Impurity was a fact of life, and therefore so was purification. But John was there in the wilderness to attest the natural, living water provided by God would achieve acceptability before God, provided that immersion was accompanied by repentance.[10]

But for the *talmidim* of John, this continual immersion—as well as the immersion of others—was more than a matter of simple repentance. Within that activity, there was also an esoteric meaning. John conveyed a definite understanding of the final significance that his purification for Israel offered. The sources are plain: for John, immersion brought one to the point that one could understand what God was about to do with Israel. As John himself expressed it, immersing oneself in water prepared one to receive the spirit of God himself, which was to drench all Israel with its sanctification. The key to John's preparation for God himself lies in the wording attributed to him, "I immerse you in water, but he himself will immerse you in holy spirit" (Mark 1:8; see Matt. 3:11; Luke 3:16).

Within the context of Christianity after the resurrection, those words are fulfilled by what the risen Jesus endows the believer with; but that assumes Jesus' identification with God at that point, because only God himself can give of his own spirit. Within the context of John the immerser, however, what is at issue is the purification that prepares the way for divine spirit. The link between purification with water and the vindicating presence of God's spirit is explicitly made in the book of Ezekiel, the same book that is the *locus classicus* of the *merkabah* (Ezek. 36:22-27):

> Therefore, say to the house of Israel: So says the Lord, the LORD: Not for your sake am I acting, house of Israel, but for my holy name, which you have profaned among the peoples you came to. I will sanctify my great name, although profaned among the peoples among whom you have profaned it, and the peoples will know that I am the LORD, says the Lord, the LORD, when I am sanctified among you before their eyes. I will take you from the peoples, and gather you from all the lands, and bring you to your land. I will sprinkle on you clean waters and cleanse you from all your uncleanness and from all your idols I will cleanse you. I will give you a new heart and a new spirit I will put in you midst, and remove the heart of stone from your flesh and give you a heart of flesh. My spirit I shall put in your midst and I will make you walk according to my statutes and keep my judgments and do them.

The close and causal connection between water and spirit here has led to the insight that we have here an important Scriptural precedent of John's immersion.[11] Everything that divided Israel, that prevented itself from realizing the full promise of the covenant, was to be swept away by the power of the spirit. Those who were urged to repent, the pilgrims of Israel and their companions, were told of the impending judgment which the coming of God's spirit necessarily involved. After all, God's spirit proceeded from his throne, the source of all true judgment.

John practiced a *kabbalah* of envisioning the throne of God, which backed up his practice of immersion. He and his *talmidim* saw the spirit of God before his throne, ready to drench Israel, just as communal Israel was drenched in the waters of purification. The careful discipline of these *talmidim*, their repetitive, committed practice, their sometimes inadequate diet and exposure to the elements all contributed to the vividness of their visions of God's throne. It was suggested some years ago by John Allegro that the ingestion of psychotropic mushrooms was a part of this discipline.[12] While the influence of herbs and grasses, as well as mushrooms, on people's psychological state cannot be discounted, the greater influence of these visions was the *kabbalah* itself, its intentional recollection and envisioning of the throne of God. From Qumran, a fragment praises God as the apex of a heavenly panoply: "He is God of gods of all the heads of the heights and king of kings for all eternal councils."[13] The foundation of *kabbalah* is putting the intent of the mind into envisaging the heavenly throne.

Jesus' skill in this vision made him one of John's most prominent *talmidim*, but it also lead to Jesus' break with John. The Gospels all relate the baptism of Jesus in a way that adumbrates baptism in early Christianity. But they also refer to the particular vision of Jesus, which not every baptized Christian could or did claim (Matt. 3:13-17; Mark 1:9-13 Luke 3: 21-22):

> Matthew 3:13-17
> [13] Then Jesus arrives from Galilee at the Jordan to John to be immersed by him. [14] Yet John prevented him, saying, I have need to be immersed by you, and do you come to me? [15] Jesus replied, and said to him, Permit it now, for so it is proper for us to fulfill all righteousness. Then he permitted him. [16] Yet when Jesus had been immersed, at once he ascended from the water, and look: the heavens were opened, and he saw God's spirit descending as a dove, coming upon him. [17] And look: a voice from the heavens, saying: This is my son, the beloved, in whom I take pleasure.
>
> Mark 1:9-13
> [9] And it happened in those days that there came Jesus from Nazareth of Galilee and he was immersed in the Jordan by John. [10] At once he ascended from the water and saw the heavens splitting and the spirit as a dove descending upon him. [11] And a voice came from the heavens: You are my son, beloved; in you I take pleasure.
>
> Luke 3:21-22
> [21] But it happened when all the people were immersed, and Jesus was immersed and praying, the heaven were opened [22] and the holy spirit descended upon him in bodily form as a dove, and a voice came from heaven, You are my son, beloved; in you I take pleasure.

As Jesus was immersed for purification, he came to have an increasingly vivid vision, of the heavens splitting open, and God's spirit coming upon him. And a voice: "you are my son, beloved; in you I take pleasure." Each of these elements is resonant with the Israelite *kabbalah* of the divine throne.

The heavens are viewed as multiple, hard shells above the earth, so that any real disclosure of the divine must represent a rending of those firmaments. But once opened, Jesus' vision is not of ascending through the heavens, as in the case of Enoch, but of the spirit, as a dove, hovering over him and descending. That image is a vivid realization that the spirit of God at creation once hovered over the face of the primeval waters (Gen.1:2), as a bird. The bird was identified as a dove in rabbinic tradition, and a fragment from Qumran supports the association.[14] The spirit, which would one day come to Israel, in Jesus' vision was already upon him, and God took pleasure in him as a "son." The term "son" itself appears extremely frequently in the Old Testament, in order to speak of the special relationship between God and others. Angels can be called "sons of God," Israel is referred to as a divine son (most famously in Hos. 11:1), and the Davidic king can be assured by divine voice, "You are my son, this day have I begotten you!" (Ps. 2:7). All these are expressions, not of a biological relationship, but of the direct revelation that God extends to certain people and angels. Jesus claims that he is of their spiritual lineage within his embrace of John's *kabbalah.*

Jesus' vivid experience within his practice of John's immersion, a persistent vision occurring many times, may be contrasted with a story about Hillel, an older contemporary of Jesus. He readily accepted a convert to Judaism and taught, "That which you hate, do not do to your fellow: that is the entire Torah, while all the rest is commentary thereon" (see Shabbath 31a).[15] Jesus took a similar point of view (Matt. 7:12; Luke 6:31) that is known as the golden rule. The same Hillel was held in such high esteem that he was thought worthy to receive the holy spirit. That estimate appears all the more exalted, but also strangely wistful, when it is borne in mind that the rabbis held that the spirit had been withdrawn since the time of the last prophets of scripture. These motifs are drawn together in a rabbinic story:[16]

> Until the dead live, namely Haggai, Zechariah, and Malachi, the latter prophets, the holy spirit has ceased from Israel. Yet even so, they made them hear *bath qol.* An example: the sages gathered at the house of Guria in Jericho, and they heard a *bath qol* saying, There is here a man who is predestined for the holy spirit, except that his generation is not righteous for such. And they put their eyes on Hillel the elder, and when he died, they said of him, Woe the meek man, Woe, the faithful disciple of Ezra.

With the withdrawal of spirit until the prophets live again, God's favor is made known by an angelic echo, a *bath qol* (daughter of a voice). But the poignancy of this story is that, for all Hillel's merit, the spirit itself is withheld. Jesus' approach to the *merkabah* by means of John's *kabbalah* had opened the revolutionary prospect that the gates of heaven were open again for the spirit to descend upon Israel.

Initially, Jesus' special vision of the *merkabah* was a victory for John. He even referred to Jesus as "the lamb of God that takes away the sin of the world"

(John 1:29; see also 1:33, 36). That phrase is attributed to John the immerser in the Gospel according to John, in a passage that serves as a commentary on the meaning of Jesus' baptism. For the readers of John, in the period after the temple was destroyed in 70 CE, that evoked a picture of Jesus as replacing sacrifice. But the earlier meaning was more humble, and directly rooted in John's movement of baptismal forgiveness. He designated Jesus as a student or *talmid* who, young as a lamb, also wiped away so much sin that God's own spirit could be felt as present within him. Jesus success as a baptist, an active immerser of other people, is also attested in John's Gospel (John 3:22, 26). The Gospel subsequently attempts to correct that plain statement, by saying it was Jesus' *talmidim*, rather than Jesus himself, who baptized (John 4:1-3). But that is double anachronism: Jesus did not yet have his own *talmidim*, and he was not yet independent of John.

The fourth Gospel, like the Synoptics, would prefer to forget that Jesus himself engaged in baptism. For them, the basic pattern was that John prepared the way by his baptism, and that Jesus followed as what was being prepared for. But, as a *talmid* of John, Jesus' personal activity as an immerser was natural; that is why it is attested in the Gospel according to John (3:22, 26; 4:1). Jesus' success is such that it is brought to John the immerser's attention, who says in a stoic manner, "he must increase, and I must decrease" (John 3:30). But the tensions went much deeper than that remark can conceal. John's Gospel also speaks of a battle concerning "purification" (John 3:25), evidently involving John and Jesus. That was at the heart of John's program, and attests the break, which became all but inevitable.

Open antagonism developed between John and Jesus, as Jesus moved out of John's home ground of the Jordan into settlement areas. He was baptizing more people than John, and he began to assert that the people coming to cleanse themselves with John were in fact already clean. In Jesus' mind, repentance alone cleanses, so that Israelites who have repented can claim access to God, divine forgiveness, and divine support. The basis of Jesus' activity was his own experience while being himself immersed. He intensified, extended, and generalized John's teaching of the *merkabah*.

The practice of fellowship in meals, especially the *kiddush*, often celebrated, then and now, on the eve of the Sabbath, became more than a matter of happenstance in Jesus' activity at this time. Once he had celebrated makeshift feasts with hungry pilgrims. Now he actively sought out people in their hamlets and villages and towns around the Jordan, and accepted hospitality from them in advance of immersing them. He was their guest, but he was also an itinerant rabbi,[17] known by his association with John to offer purification. As he joined in the meal of *kiddush*, Jesus or the elder host of the meal, would speak of the sanctification of God, who for Jesus was the *Abba* of all who turn to the source of Israel's blessing. In this reference to the *Abba* of Israel and his sanctification, major elements of the prayer Jesus later taught his own *talmidim* were taking shape, and being brought together:

> Abba, your name will be sanctified,
> Your sovereignty will come.

At this stage, the prayer was not a form of words, but a thematic approach to God closely associated with the *kiddush* of God's sovereignty. What was being celebrated was not only the dawn of the Sabbath on its eve, but also the dawn of the manifestation of God's glory.

Another case where stories concerning divine voices find resonance in the New Testament is the transfiguration (Matt. 16:28-17:8; Mark 9:1-8; Luke 9:27-36a):

> 28 Amen I say to you that there are some of those standing here, such as
> will never taste death until they see the one like the son of man coming
> in his kingdom. 1 And after six days Jesus takes Rock and James and John
> his brother and brings them up to a high mountain privately. 2 And he was
> transmuted before them and his face shone as the sun, and his clothing be-
> came white as the light. 3 And look: there was seen by them Moses and Eli-
> jah, speaking together with him. 4 Rock answered and said to Jesus, Lord, it
> is fine for us to be here; if you wish, I shall build here three lodges: one for
> you and one for Moses and one for Elijah. 5 While he was still speaking, look:
> an lustrous cloud overshadowed them, and look: a voice from the cloud,
> saying, This is my son, the beloved, in whom I take pleasure: hear him. 6
> The students heard and fell on their faces and were exceedingly frightened. 7
> Jesus came forward and touched them and said, Be raised, and do not fear! 8
> They lifted up their eyes and saw no one but him, Jesus alone.

> 1 And he was saying to them, Amen I say to you that there are some here of
> those standing, such as will never taste death until they see the kingdom of
> God having come in power. 2 And after six days Jesus takes Rock and James
> and John along and brings them up to a high mountain privately: alone.
> And he was transmuted before them 3 and his clothing became gleaming,
> very white, as a launderer on the earth is not able to whiten. 4 And there was
> seen by them Elijah with Moses, and they were speaking together with Jesus.
> 5 Rock answered and says to Jesus, Rabbi, it is fine for us to be here, and we
> shall build three lodges: one for you and one for Moses and one for Elijah.
> 6 For he did not know what he should answer, because they were terrified. 7
> And there came a cloud overshadowing them, and there came a sound from
> the cloud, This is my son, the beloved: hear him. 8 Suddenly looking around
> they no longer saw anyone with themselves but Jesus, alone.

> 27 But I say to you truly, there are some there of those standing, such as will
> never taste death until they see the kingdom of God. 28 Yet it happened after
> these words, about eight days, taking Rock and John and James he ascended
> into the mountain to pray. 29 And it happened while he prayed the appear-

> ance of his face was different and his garments flashed out white. [30] And look: two males were speaking together with him, such as were Moses and Elijah, [31] who were seen in glory speaking of his exodus, which he was about to fulfill in Jerusalem. [32] Yet Rock and those with him were weighed down with sleep. But becoming alert, they saw his glory and the two males standing with him. [33] And it happened as they were being separated from him, Rock said to Jesus, Master, it is fine for us to be here, and we shall build three lodges: one yours and one Moses' and one Elijah's (not knowing what he was saying).) [34] But while he was saying this there came a cloud and overshadowed them, and they were afraid when they entered into the cloud. [35] A voice came from the cloud, saying, This is my son, the chosen: him hear. [36] And when the voice came, Jesus was found alone.

The narrative structure is reminiscent of Moses' ascent of Sinai in Exodus 24. At the close of that story, Moses is said to ascend the mountain, where God's glory, as a cloud, covered it (24:15). The covering lasted six days (24:16), which is the amount of time between the transfiguration and the previous discourse in both Matthew (17:1) and Mark (9:2). After that time, the Lord called to Moses from the cloud (Exod. 24:16b), and Moses entered the glory of the cloud, which is like a devouring fire (24:17-18). Earlier in the chapter, Moses is commanded to select three worshippers (Aaron, Nadab, and Abihu) together with seventy elders, in order to confirm the covenant (24:1-8). The result is that just these people (24:9) see the God of Israel in his court (24:10) and celebrate their vision with a meal. The motifs of master, three disciples, mountain, cloud, vision, and audition recur in the transfiguration.

Other details in the presentation of the story cohere with Exodus 24. Matthew 17:2 uniquely refers to Jesus' face shining like the sun, like Moses' aspect in Exodus 34:29-35. In more general terms, Mark's reference to the whiteness of Jesus' garments also establishes a heavenly context. A variation in Luke is more specific and more interesting. Luke puts a distance of eight days, rather than six, between the previous discourse and the transfiguration. Although that has baffled commentators, in rabbinic interpretation that variation is meaningful. In the f Pseudo-Jonathan (Exodus 24:10-11), Nadab and Abihu are struck by God, because their vision contradicts the principle that "man will not see God and live" (Exod. 33:30). But their punishment (narrated in Num. 3:2-4) is delayed until the *eighth* day.

In this heavenly vision two figures of rabbinic tradition who were understood not to have tasted death, Moses and Elijah, also make their appearance. Elijah, of course, is the primordial prophet of the *merkabah*. Elijah's *talmid*, Elisha, sees Elijah taken up into the heavens and God's "chariot of fire and horses of fire" (2 Kings 2:11). (The term for "chariot" here is *rekhev*, simply the masculine form of the feminine *merkabah*.) At least from the time of Josephus, Moses was also held to have been taken up alive into the heavenly court.[18] Taken together, then, Elijah and Moses are indices of Jesus' access to the heavenly court. Peter's apparently inept suggestion to his rabbi, of building "lodges," also corresponds to the enclosure for God's glory on earth which Moses is commanded to build in the chapters of Exodus after chapter 24. Taken as a whole, the transfiguration at its generative moment attests Jesus introduction of his *talmidim* to a vision of the divine throne comparable to his own at his baptism.

Jesus' conscious framing of a *kabbalah*, an approach to the divine *merkabah* for himself and for his own *talmidim*, naturally includes an understanding of his own identity. Who is it that can offer this approach? Luke's presentation of what Jesus had to say in a synagogue at Nazareth, the first village he knew, provides a precise indication of just this self-consciousness. Luke's Gospel also presents a clear-eyed profile of Jesus as Messiah by means of reference to the book of Isaiah, as we shall see. Throughout, Luke prepares us for the meaning of Jesus' messianic status by a fairly straightforward enhancement of an element in the commonly Synoptic account of Jesus' baptism. All three Synoptics have Jesus propelled by the spirit into the wilderness, in order to be pressed to the limit by Satan (Matt. 4:1; Mark 1:12; Luke 4:1), and Matthew and Luke both include three itemized temptations at this point (Matt. 4:1-11; Luke 4:1-13). In all three, the sense is conveyed that one's possession of the spirit of God in baptism brings one into conflict with the primordial source of resistance to that spirit.

But Luke's articulation of that necessary resistance to the spirit is the most fulsome and explicit (Luke 4:1-2):

> [1] But Jesus, full of holy spirit, returned from the Jordan, and was being led by the spirit in the wilderness [2] forty days, tested by the devil.

The repeated reference to the spirit here makes all the more emphatic the uniquely Lukan insistence that Jesus was "full of holy spirit," and that expression proves to be key in the unfolding motifs of this section of the Gospel.

Again, after the story of his temptations,[19] Luke alone has Jesus return "in the power of the spirit into Galilee" (Luke 4:14). There can be no question, then, but that at this paradigmatic moment, as Jesus commences his public activity, the issue of the spirit is uppermost in the reference to Jesus' divine identity within Luke. The inauguration of this activity takes place—only in Luke—by means of an appearance in a synagogue in Nazareth, where his citation of the book of Isaiah is pivotal (Luke 4:14-30):

> [14] And Jesus returned in the power of the spirit into Galilee. And news went out into all the surrounding land concerning him. [15] He himself was teaching in their synagogues, glorified by all. [16] And he came into Nazara, where he had been nurtured, and he entered according to his custom on the day of the Sabbath into the synagogue. [17] And he arose to read and there was delivered to him a scroll, of the prophet Isaiah. He opened the book and found the placed where it was written, [18] The Lord's spirit is upon me, forasmuch as he

> anointed me to message triumph to the poor. He delegated me to proclaim release to captives and recovery of sight to blind, to dispatch the broken with release, [19] to proclaim an acceptable year of the Lord! [20] He rolled the scroll, gave it back to the assistant, and sat. And of all, the eyes in the congregation were staring at him. [21] But he began to say to them that: Today this scripture has been fulfilled in your ears! [22] And all attested him and marveled at the words of grace that proceeded out from his mouth, and they were saying, Is he not Joseph's son? [23] And he said to them, You will by all means say this comparison to me: Physician, heal yourself! As much as we heard happened in Capernuam, do also here, in your own country! [24] But he said, Amen I say to you that no prophet is acceptable in his own country. [25] Yet in truth I say to you, There were many widows in Elijah's days in Israel, when the heaven was shut three years and six months, as a great famine came on all the earth, [26] and to none of them was Elijah sent, except to Sarepta of Sidon, to a widow woman. [27] And there were many scabby people in Israel while Elisha was prophet, and none of them was cleansed, except Naaman the Syrian.[28] And all in the synagogue were filled with rage when they heard this; [29] they arose and threw him out, outside of the city, and led him to an edge of the mount on which they city was built, so as to hurl him down. [30] But he went through their midst and proceeded.

A great deal in this passage models the ideal activity within synagogues and worship more generally which both Luke and Acts portray, but the focus on the spirit is the crux of the whole.

The agreement of this passage with the overall structure of Luke-Acts has supported the finding that it had been synthesized by the editorial work that went into those two documents. And the utility of the passage within Luke-Acts cannot reasonably be denied. The entire pericope, from verse 14 until verse 30 in Luke 4, sets up a model—of reading scripture in a synagogue, enjoying some success but then violent rejection, a rejection that leads to a turning to non-Jews—which corresponds to the experience of Paul and Barnabas in the book of Acts, especially at Pisidian Antioch (that is, Antioch in Asia Minor, not on the Orontes) in Acts 13:13-52.[20] Together, Luke 4 and Acts 13 set out a pattern for the Church of Luke-Acts. The name "Antioch" is a key to the importance of the latter passage, just as the verb "to anoint" in the former passage is profoundly evocative. The two are as if violins in an orchestra set at a quaver distance, at which one instrument causes the other to resonate. For Luke-Acts, Paul and Barnabas resonate with the purpose, program, and authorization of Jesus himself.

The words cited from Isaiah begin, "The Lord's spirit is upon me, forasmuch as he anointed me." Here, then, is the specification of how the spirit has been with Jesus since the moment of his baptism. The spirit represents his anointing. In Greek, as in Hebrew and Aramaic, the term "messiah" means most basically "anointed one." This etymology is of more than academic interest, because the very verb used here (*khrio*) associated itself in the ear of a Greek speaker with the term "messiah" or "Christ" (*khristos*). Jesus is Messiah because the spirit is upon him, and the text from Isaiah becomes an itinerary of his activity.

Just here, however, the dissonance between Jesus' own typical activity and the text of Isaiah 61, cited by Luke, becomes evident. The simple facts are that Isaiah 61:1-2 refers to things Jesus never did, such as releasing prisoners from jail, and that Jesus did things the text makes no mention of, such as declaring people free of impurity (see Matt. 8:2-4; Mark 1:40-45; Luke 5:12-16). This dissonance is in all probability not a Lukan creation, because the pattern of the Gospel is to make the correspondence to the Septuagint in biblical citations as close as possible. As the text stands, moreover, a change from any known form of the biblical text results in a lost opportunity to relate directly to the activity of Jesus, as well as introducing an element of greater dissonance. The phrase "to bind the broken of heart" is omitted from the citation, and wording similar to Isaiah 58:6, a reference to setting the oppressed at liberty, has been inserted.

Although Luke's Gospel presents the wording—evidently inspired from Isaiah—as a routine reading in a synagogue, it evidently was not so in the tradition prior to Luke. Jesus' "citation" is no citation at all, but a freer version of the biblical book than could have been read. The wording of the passage in the Old Syriac Gospels (in a language closely related to Jesus' indigenous Aramaic) is freer still:

> The spirit of the Lord is upon *you*,
> on account of which he was anointed *you* to message triumph to the poor;
> And he has sent me to preach to the captives release, and to the blind sight
> —and *I* will free the broken with release—
> and to preach the acceptable year of the Lord.

The oddities Luke preserves are present, together with what has been homogenized in Luke: the radical change in pronouns.[21] By speaking these words, Jesus portrays himself as responding to a divine charge: "The spirit of the Lord is upon you, on account of which he was anointed you to message triumph to the poor." Then he emphatically accepts that charge: "And he has sent me to preach to the captives release, and to the blind sight—and I will free the broken with release—and to preach the acceptable read of the Lord." Both the charge and the emphatic acceptance are produced by the signal changes in pronouns, which are italicized above. They are part and parcel of a conscious alteration of the language taken from the book of Isaiah, an alteration that voices the text in a way that makes it akin to the baptismal *bath qol* and the *bath qol* at the transfiguration.

The alteration is typical of Jesus' style of employing scripture, especially the book of Isaiah (and especially in a targumic form). His aim was to use the scripture as a lens of his own activity of behalf of God, such that the wording focused on how God was active in what he said and did, without suggesting a complete fit between the text and what Jesus referred to. The scripture was a guide to the experience of God in the present, but that experience was more important than the text, and could be used to refashion the text. This passage from Luke brings us to the wellspring of Jesus' understanding of himself in messianic terms. He declared that his anointing with the spirit of God empowered and constrained him to act on God's behalf.

Scholarship has been deflected from a due appreciation of this passage. The identification of Jesus as Messiah has been freighted with the assumption that the term "messiah" must be understood with a specific political, priestly, or prophetic meaning in order to be employed. Because Jesus cannot be associated directly with any such program, it is routinely denied that Jesus applied the term to himself.[22] Clearly, the association of Jesus as Messiah with the spirit gained currency after and as a consequence of the resurrection, as we have already seen. But its currency is very difficult to explain, as Marinus de Jonge points out, if "Jesus himself avoided this designation and discouraged his followers from using it."[23] Some consistent usage of messianic language would likely have been in the background of Jesus' teaching for the term to have emerged as the primary designation of Jesus. In that Luke's Gospel was composed in Antioch around 90 CE in a community in which both Greek and Aramaic were spoken, it is a likely source among the Synoptics for indicating what this background may have been. The tight connection between the spirit of God and the verb "anoint," as in Jesus' reference to Isaiah 61 in Luke 4, provides us with just the indication that fills out the picture of the development of early Christian usage. Anointed by the spirit of God, Jesus' viewed himself as enacting and articulating the claims of God's sovereignty ("the kingdom of God"). His teaching indeed does not spell out the content of being "Messiah" by means of a precise program drawn from biblical or pseudepigraphic literature, but it does relate the spirit to his own activity, and in Luke 4 that relationship involved explicitly messianic language.

But the Lukan presentation is precisely what makes the form of the "citation" of Isaiah 61 all the more surprising. As a Lukan invention, the reference would have accorded with the Septuagint. Indeed, the Old Syriac Gospels provide an insight into the shape of the reference to Isaiah 61 by Jesus before it was partially accommodated to the Septuagint within the Lukan presentation. The fractured reference to Isaiah 61 focuses Jesus' messianic identity on the issue of the spirit, and that was the point of departure for the development of primitive Christian messiology, and therefore of Christology in the proper sense.

Luke provides us with a centered view of Jesus' Christology, focused on the spirit of God. Within the recent study of Jesus, two discarded pictures of his Christology have emerged again, and I would suggest in closing that they are likely to be discarded again. The first stresses the undoubted importance of the political challenge to the identity of Israel within the first century. Jesus then becomes the "Davidic messiah," a ruling figure who sets up his throne in association with the Temple.[24] This, despite the portrayal of Jesus in the Temptations as rejecting a picture of such rule, and despite his own rhetorical question, "How do the scribes say the messiah is David's son?' (Mark 12:35, together with Matt. 22:42; Luke 20:41). That question assumes a tradition of identifying the Messiah and the ben David, but it also—and obviously—refutes it.[25] Any messianic theology inherently involved a political dimension, but to make that dimension the only index of meaning runs against the grain of Jesus' contention that Davidic and messianic claims were not simply identifiable. Another view, derived ultimately from Albert Schweitzer's picture of Jesus as a failed apocalyptist, imagines Jesus as personally taking on himself all the conditions of the covenant with Israel, in a desperate attempt to get God to fulfill the covenantal promises.[26] This, despite the fact that the term "covenant" within sayings of Jesus only appears in a single case, in what seems to be a liturgical addition to the meaning of the cup of wine in the context of his last meals in Jerusalem.[27] Peter and Paul were undoubtedly theologians of this covenant, because they had directly to face the issues of who was and was not of the people of God. Jesus, however, does not appear to have confronted that question in covenantal terms.

But once Jesus' approach to the *merkabah*, on the basis of his endowment with spirit, is seen to be the pivot of his experience and his program of activity, his care in defining how he was and how he was not Messiah acquires its sense. His messianic identity was a function of his self-consciousness and the awareness of his *talmidim* that his *kabbalah* offers the vision of God in his glory because divine spirit makes that vision possible.

Discussion Questions

1. How may one critically locate Jesus' spiritual practice within the development of Judaism, both before and after his time?
2. Which influences were most powerful in Jesus' personal development?
3. What conflicts emerged as a consequence of Jesus' teaching?

Notes

1. See Gershom Scholem, "Kabbalah," *Encyclopedia Judaica* (Jerusalem: Keter, 1972), 489-653 and *Origins of the Kabbalah*, trans. Allan Arkush (Princeton: Jewish Publication Society and Princeton University Press, 1987); and the fine introduction of Joseph Dan in *The Early Kabbalah*: The Classics of Western Spirituality (New York: Paulist, 1986), 1-41. Among many more recent works, reference should be made to Ithamar Gruenwald, *Apocalyptic and Merkavah Mysticism* (Leiden: Brill, 1980); Moshe Idel, *Kabbalah. New Perspectives* (New Haven: Yale University Press, 1988); David Halperin, *The Faces of the Chariot. Early Jewish Responses to Ezekiel's Vision,* vol. 16 of *Texte und Studien zum Antiken Judentum* (Tübingen: Mohr, 1988); Peter Schäfer, *The Hidden and Manifest God. Some Major Themes in Early Jewish Mysticism:* SUNY Series in Judaica: Hermeneutics, Mysticism, and Religion, trans. Aubrey Pomerance (Albany: State University of New York Press, 1992); Elliott R. Wolfson, *Through a Speculum that Shines: Vision and Imagination in Medieval Jewish Mysti-*

cism (Princeton: Princeton University Press, 1994) and *Circle in the Square. Studies in the Use of Gender in Kabbalistic Symbolism* (Albany: State University of New York Press, 1995).

2. See Bruce Chilton, *A Galilean Rabbi and His Bible. Jesus' Use of the Interpreted Scripture of His Time* (Wilmington: Glazier, 1984), also published with the subtitle, *Jesus' Own Interpretation of Isaiah* (London: SPCK, 1984).
3. See Bernhard Lang, "Die grosse Jenseitsfahrt," *Paragana* 7.2 (1998): 24-42, 32.; Stephanie Dally, *Myths from Mesopotamia* (Oxford: 1989), 182-87; James D. Tabor, "Heaven, Ascent to," *Anchor Bible Dictionary*, ed. David Noel Freedman, Gary A. Herion, David F. Graf, John David Pleins, and Astrid B. Beck (New York: Doubleday, 1992), 391-94.
4. The tradition on which the book is based clearly emerged prior to the book of Daniel, but Enoch continued to be expanded for centuries; see Matthew Black, *The Book of Enoch or I Enoch,* vol. 7 of *Studia in Veteris Testamenti Pseudepigraphia* (Leiden: Brill, 1985); Michael Langlois, *Le premier manuscit du livre d'Hénoch. Étude épigraphique et philologique des fragments araméens de 4Q201 à Qumrân* (Paris: Cerf, 2008).
5. At a much later stage, this mystical tradition was formalized into the academic complexity of the Medieval Kabbalah, which was a learned and intellectual movement.
6. For an introduction and translation, see E. Isaac, "1 Enoch," *The Old Testament Pseudepigrapha*, ed. J. H. Charlesworth (Garden City: Doubleday, 1983), 1.5-89.
7. See the article appended to Scholem's, *Encyclopedia Judaica* (Jerusalem: Keter, 1972), 653-54, in which Cecil Roth remarks in respect of Scholem's essay (referred to as the "previous entry"), "Today the term Kabbalah is used for the mystic and esoteric doctrine of Judaism (see previous entry). The mystical connotation is unknown in the Talmud."
8. See Victor Paul Furnish, *II Corinthians,* translated with introduction, notes, and commentary. *The Anchor Bible* (Garden City: Doubleday, 1984), 542-45.
9. See Josephus's *Life* 11. For my discussion of John, Bannus, and their methods of purification as related to Jesus, see Bruce Chilton, *Jesus' Baptism and Jesus' Healing. His Personal Practice of Spirituality* (Trinity Press International, 1998); "Yochanan the Purifier and His Immersion," *Toronto Journal of Theology* 14.2 (1998): 197-212; "John the Purifier: his Immersion and his Death," *Teologiese Studies* 57.1-2 (2001) 247-67; "John the Baptist: His Immersion and his Death," *Dimensions of Baptism. Biblical and Theological Studies*, Journal for the Study of the New Testament Supplement Series 234, ed. Stanley E. Porter and Anthony R. Cross, (Sheffield: Sheffield Academic Press, 2002), 25-44.
10. See Joan Taylor, *The Immerser. John the Baptist within Second Temple Judaism: Studying the Historical Jesus* (Grand Rapids: Eerdmans, 1997).
11. See Otto Böcher, "Johannes der Täufer," *Theologische Realenzyklopädie* 17 (1988): 172-81. This insight, suggested to me by Bernhard Lange, is worked out more fully in Chilton, *Jesus' Baptism and Jesus' Healing.*
12. John Allegro, *The Sacred Mushroom and the Cross. A Study of the Nature and Origins of Christianity within the Fertility Cults of the Ancient Near East* (Garden City: Doubleday, 1970). His suggestion that "Jesus" was simply a name for a mushroom assured Allegro a frosty reception, and his attempt to see Jesus as entirely mythical (indeed, hallucinatory) reads as a desperate attempt not to place him within historical context. More recently, see Carl A. P. Ruck, Blaise Daniel Staples, and Clark Heinrich, *The Apples of Apollo. Pagan and Christian Mysteries of the Eucharist* (Durham: Carolina Academic Press, 2001), reviewed in: *The Classical Bulletin* 78.2 (2002): 261-63.

13. The fragment was found in the fourth cave from near Qumran (its designation is 4 Q403 frg. li). E. Glicker Chazon of Hebrew University in Jerusalem showed me a copy.
14. See Dale C. Allison, "The Baptism of Jesus and a New Dead Sea Scroll," *Biblical Archaeology Review* 18.2 (1992): 58-60.
15. The cleverness of Hillel's response to the request of the convert to be taught the Torah while he stood on one foot is manifest in the next sentence, "Go and learn it!" That is, he insists that the summary does not replace the commentary. In that regard, see Matt. 5:17.
16. Tosefta Sotah 13:3. For a discussion, see Chilton, *Profiles of a Rabbi. Synoptic Opportunities in Reading about Jesus,* Brown Judaic Studies 177 (Atlanta: Scholars Press, 1989), 77-89.
17. See Chilton, "Rabbis," *Dictionary of New Testament Background*, ed. Craig A. Evans and Stanley E. Porter; Downers Grove: InterVarsity, 2000), 1145-53; *Rabbi Jesus. An Intimate Biography* (New York: Doubleday, 2000); "Jesus, A Galilean Rabbi," *Who was Jesus? A Jewish-Christian Dialogue*, ed. Paul Copan and Craig A. Evans (Louisville: Westminster John Knox, 2001), 154-61; "Review Essay: Archaeology and Rabbi Jesus," *Bulletin for Biblical Research* 12.2 (2002): 273-80; "Master/Rabbi," *Encyclopedia of the Historical Jesus*, ed. Craig A. Evans (New York and London: Routledge, 2008), 395-99.
18. See Josephus, *Antiquities* 4.326. For further discussion, see Chilton, "The Transfiguration: Dominical Assurance and Apostolic Vision," *New Testament Studies* 27 (1980): 115-24.
19. The story of itemized temptations is the contribution of the source called "Q"; for an account of the contents of "Q," see Chilton, *Pure Kingdom. Jesus' Vision of God.* Studying the Historical Jesus 1 (Eerdmans: Grand Rapids and London: SPCK, 1996), 107-10.
20. I have worked out this correspondence in some detail in *God in Strength. Jesus' Announcement of the Kingdom.* Studien zum Neuen Testament und seiner Umwelt 1 (Freistadt: Plöchl, 1979), 123-56.
21. For a full discussion, see Chilton, *God in Strength*, 157-77.
22. See Marinus de Jonge, *Early Christology and Jesus' Own View of His Mission: Studying the Historical Jesus* (Grand Rapids: Eerdmans, 1998), 98-106 for a cautious and skeptical assessment of this denial.
23. De Jonge, *Early Christology,* 101.
24. For a sophisticated argument to this effect, see Richard A. Horsley, *Sociology and the Jesus Movement* (New York: Crossroad, 1989), 105-45.
25. See Chilton, "Jesus ben David: reflections on the Davidssohnfrage," *Journal for the Study of the New Testament* 14 (1982): 88-112.
26. For this neo-orthodox rereading of Schweitzer, see N. T. Wright, *Jesus and the Victory of God* (Minneapolis: Fortress, 1993).
27. For a full discussion, see Chilton, *A Feast of Meanings. Eucharistic Theologies from Jesus through Johannine Circles:* Supplements to *Novum Testamentum* 72 (Leiden: Brill, 1994), 75-92.

The Amazing Mr. Jesus

James F. Moore

I was initially surprised by the focus of this volume, not that it was unimportant but that it was a subject treated so thoroughly already. In addition, there is the question about what is gained by thinking about a Jewish Jesus or about the Jewish context for understanding Jesus. Much of what can be said is likely to lead us where others have already gone and treated much more thoroughly. That is, we would find that Jesus is rather unremarkable in many ways. He was not especially distinctive in his teaching as best as we can tell. Thus, a Jewish Jesus would be yet another Jewish teacher, perhaps with insight, but little of anything especially new.

Of course, the rationale for such a discussion hinges on the fact that as much as we recover the Jewishness of Jesus, he is remarkable for our discussion because he is the focus of Christian teaching. Reconnecting Jesus with his Jewish context is naturally a major necessary task for any Christian theologian if there is to be some hope for authentic dialogue. Even so, there is no clear benefit for Christians to do so, in terms of their theologies, other than to gain additional insight into the meaning of Jesus' teaching. Some of us have tried to move this discussion forward by thinking of Jesus in the midrashic tradition and to accept Jacobus Schooneveld's reading that Christians regard Jesus as the "Oral Torah." If we are not merely to return to a form of supersessionism in this claim, we must read Jesus back into context, the Jewish context, which allows him to return to the discussion on the tradition of Oral Torah.

But then we are left with a puzzle since Jesus fits in the Jewish history no doubt but there is much disagreement about where he fits. Christians have variously thought of Jesus as among the Zealots, or among the Essenes, or among the

Pharisees (that is, the rabbinic tradition). None of this is clear and each of these possibilities produces a variety, a plurality of possibilities. Each also produces a view of Jesus that is quite different even in conflict with other alternatives. So the puzzle remains for us. What is gained by doing this?

I add yet another issue for us in that recovering the Jewish Jesus somehow forces us to think about this Jewish context in a post-Shoah framework. While Jesus fit some kind of first-century Jewish context, that story is no longer fully viable by itself, especially not for Christians. We can hardly speak of Jesus as a Jew now without realizing that the ones who have claimed Jesus as their Oral Torah were the ones who fostered or allowed the great destruction of European Jewry in the last century. It is this problem which has captured my energies as a Christian theologian and was at the heart of Roy Eckardt's work especially seen in his *Reclaiming the Historical Jesus*. That work is very interesting in many ways, perhaps particularly because of his revised view of the resurrection narrative.[1]

So I was drawn into these various lines of thought as I began to construct an idea for this conference. In the end, I cannot actually deal with all of these questions, but I believe that I might get close to something valuable if I turn my attention to materials that have not fared well as a source for either the search for the historical Jesus or for the Jewish context of Jesus. I decided to think about the miracle stories, what I have captured somewhat lightly with the title—"The Amazing Mr. Jesus." I came to this point because of the thinking I had regarding the many efforts that have already contributed to this literature but also because of an interesting, provocative, and profound comment made by Haim MacCoby at the first Oxford Remembering for the Future conference back in 1988.[2] He said, as a way of opening his paper presentation, that Jews would have little problem with Christians and Jesus in particular if Christians would just give up the resurrection. I am sure he knew that this would provoke response and that there was little likelihood that the Christians present would accept his suggestion. The remark was rather a way of pointing to the real dividing issue between us. A Jesus who is for Christians the Oral Torah can be a potential bridge. A Jesus who performed miracles and was raised from the dead seems to be a major dividing line. But can we talk of a Jewish Jesus without considering this challenge? And what if we did this seriously, that is, think of Jesus as amazing, the miracle worker in a Jewish context. That will take some doing, as we consider the history of thinking about the historical Jesus as contrasted with the Christ of faith (as Martin Kaehler spoke of this in his classic text). So this is my aim, with a full realization that this may lead us nowhere except toward knowing the line of difference. But this may lead us somewhere even if not exactly where we might expect. I will try this as a midrash, a post-Shoah midrash, which surely will be different from the approaches I have attempted thus far over the years.

The History of the Quest

It would be a challenge to recount the whole story of the various quests for the historical Jesus, but some effort to think about these attempts, especially as they link to the way scholars (mostly Christian) have thought about miracles is needed. The initiation of thinking about historical settings for the Biblical narratives coincided with the development of history as a discipline in its own right during the nineteenth century. There were those who thought that such studies could substantiate the unique, and therefore, superior status of Christianity by historical evidence. The long search through the century actually ended with a statement of fundamental failure in the classic text by Albert Schweitzer in which he claimed that the actual Jesus was an apocalyptic prophet whose vision for the world and himself ended in failure with the crucifixion. His conclusion was that the remainder that was useful was the ethical teaching of Jesus, which meant finally the teaching that basically matched the same ongoing development of rabbinic thought. Of course, such a judgment leaves the miracles out of this useful remainder since they were judged to be constructions of the early church designed especially to defend the credibility of Jesus in a predominantly Hellenistic world. This includes the resurrection, which would, by the writings of Rudolf Bultmann, become a claim available only in the existential encounter of faith. It would be outside of history. In addition, this first quest set the stage for thinking about the miracles in a Hellenistic and not a Jewish context. This was surely already in the thought of both Friedrich Schleiermacher and David Strauss, who both wrote lives of Jesus in the nineteenth century, even if they were striking in their contrast.

This treatment of the miracle stories dominates much of the work that has been done on the historical Jesus among Christian scholars. The assumption that the context for understanding the meaning of the gospel narratives is the Hellenistic world of the early church has broken the connection between the Jewish Jesus and the context of his life and the postresurrection view of Jesus that was confessed in the early church. In addition, the miracle stories are seen as "outside of history" and thus can be only symbols of meaning often taken to be affirmations of the power of Jesus or the authority of Jesus or the messianic claims connected to Jesus. All of this opens the door for the exclusivist, supersessionist views of the early church, or so it seems.

Jewish Views

All of the above stands in stark contrast with what has become the various views about miracles that can be found in Jewish tradition. Indeed, Jewish scholars have also participated in the historical-critical reading of sacred texts, but the tradition relating to miracles seems quite different. There seems to be three different views, perhaps related, that can be explored further so that we can talk about a Jewish context.[3] First, the rabbinic tradition has viewed miracles as inside of history and have managed to reconcile this with reason by claiming that the central miracles of the tradition are not opposed to nature but are planned by God in creation. What seems miraculous in the telling actually can have natural explanations but are planned by God for God's purposes in creating nature as such.

Jewish tradition—at least early rabbinic interpretations—seems to accept that miracles are common and not unusual. Thus, they do not really need explanation and are also of minor importance. They do point to something but are much more signs of God's activity, the meaning of which can be found developed more fully in the whole narrative. Thus, miracles must be taken as part of the larger story in order to discover exactly what it is that the narratives intend to claim.

Finally, there are miracle narratives that take on special importance for Jewish tradition, most central of which are the miracles associated with the Exodus. These miracles are signs of God's power, God's authority, and God's redemptive promises. The focus shifts from the humans involved to the work of God, and when humans claim too much importance, as with Moses, they are set straight by God.

Given these three readings of miracles, the contrast with what has been a Christian view in the various quests for the historical Jesus are obviously clear. Perhaps that is the point, that Christianity becomes very different and the miracle stories are simply a good way to see that difference. However, this volume aims to think about the Jewish context for understanding Jesus, and I now move to consider what that might mean if we read the miracles in Jewish context (views that are likely to have been available to Jesus and his contemporaries). We make a slight jump here to attempt to think not about the Hellenistic setting of the early church but the Jewish setting of Jesus and read the miracles in that light.

A New Kind of Midrashic Reading

I apologize beforehand to all those who do historical-critical work. I am not intending such a detailed and careful study of the texts as that would demand, and if I were to do this, I may find alternative conclusions than what I am prepared to suggest. I am rather approaching these texts and this question by using the midrashic model that I have employed now for close to twenty years. This approach begins with the assumption that the Christian scriptures and particularly the words of Jesus are a midrash on the tradition, especially on the Torah. I move to a new stage of this reflection by treating not just the words of Jesus but events attributed to Jesus' life. We will see where this leads us. My assumptions include a post-Shoah midrash in that I begin by assuming a dialogical approach that anticipates a response. In addition, we assume that any interpretation is tested by taking account of the fact that the Shoah is now a critical component of our stories, Jewish and Christian, although in different ways.

I begin the process in this paper by looking at a text from Numbers 20 and connecting this text to Matthew 14:13-21. The two stories are clearly linked in my judgment, and we might see that the texts from Jesus' life also presume connections to stories about Elijah and Elisha as well, a point that may have some significance for our reading. I will begin with a brief reflection on Numbers 20 noting what I believe are key points for our purposes. I will then take up the narrative from Matthew (notably a narrative that appears in all four Christian gospels), which will likely lead me back to the text from Numbers. All of this will require a reflection in the end that is post-Shoah.

Numbers 20

The account in Numbers 20 is similar to a text in Exodus 17, and a thorough reading would lead us to explore these connections. My aim though is to give an account of the Jewish context for Jesus, and this may only be a pattern that is suggestive. Thus, further work will be needed to explore all the possibilities. In addition, my aim has always been to create a sense of a plurality of possible meanings and not to assume that any one reading is likely to be the best. In the end we can sift through the options for what cannot possibly be acceptable to our post-Shoah dialogue. Thus, we focus on Numbers 20 which carries an interesting set of possibilities because it follows the strange text of the "Red Heifer."[4] Our attention is drawn here to the story of the rock at Meribah and what is said to be the context and result of what takes place there.

Briefly, I note that the text suggests a quarrel between the people and the leaders (Moses and Aaron) which is not different from the complaints of earlier episodes (such as that which brings about the discovery of the mysterious "manna" in the desert.) The people are thirsty and take the occasion to complain about being led to such a desolate place and such a grim possible end. Troubled by this, Moses and Aaron retreat to the tent, where they are met with the presence of God, who instructs them to take the rod and before the assembly to order the rock to produce water. Moses proceeds to do this, except that he says that "we shall get water for you out of this rock." Then Moses raises his hand and strikes the rock twice with the rod causing, water to flow.

We are familiar with this story and likely with the variety of interpretations that have emerged. Above all, the story includes the anger of God, which falls on both Moses and Aaron for not trusting fully in God's promise. Aaron dies that day and Moses dies before he can enter the promised land. Those deaths are clearly connected with the passing of leadership to a new generation, just as those who enter the land are also a new generation from the one that complained in the desert and built the golden calf. All of these aspects are important for the story; yet our interest is to think about the interpretation of the miracle.

Returning to a Jewish Context

The very interesting text from Numbers leaves us with so many options for further thought that I simply note that I am narrowing my approach to setting a Jewish context for the miracle stories of Jesus. I claimed above that one key rabbinic view of miracles has been that God set these miracles at the time of creation. Thus, they cannot be outside of nature and, thus, outside of history. All of this seems to fit the Numbers text as these are the very miracle accounts that were in the minds of the rabbis who offered this summary interpretation. However, we note that there are basic philosophical problems that emerge with the implications of this view. The view suggests that there was a plan in creation that anticipated the occasions for miracles in history. To claim such a plan seems to suggest that God planned the historical context that set the stage for the miracles. But this would mean that the details—the quarrelsome people, the sin of Moses and Aaron such as it may have been, the death of the leaders, and so on—were all part of this plan. Otherwise the full extent of the activity of God would not have been clear. So the miracle may have been in history as part of a planned creation, but the implications say more than we might wish to claim about God (and God's apparent control of history).

The resolution here seems to be in the way the rabbis see nature as flexible. That is, the potential for the miracle is present in nature but this does not mean a set pattern of historical events or some super-control of history. The Jewish context seems to view God as active in history in a planned way but that human choices still create history that God must respond to. The meaning of this narrative then must be derived from the context of what is the necessity for response and what are the implications for the future. I will return to this point after I consider the text from Matthew.

The second rabbinic view, that miracles are common and do not deserve special attention, is also useful in reading the Numbers text since the point of the text is not the miracle as such but rather the broader theme of trust in God's promises. This point will also be useful in treating the narrative from Matthew. On the other hand, the point does not discount the level of skepticism that arises from modern views of miracles and leads rather to a sense that miracles are symbolic and not historical at least in their meaning. This point does seem to match the trend in Christian scholarship and must be considered more fully. I will do this, however, as part of a post-Shoah and not a modernist reading of the texts.

The final view that miracles are signs of God's activity is fitting for this text and makes sense of the whole narrative. Of course, we need to decide exactly what is signaled. Surely it is too simplistic to suggest that it is merely the idea of provision in time of need. That claim will be severely tested by a post-Shoah reading. The point must be larger and connected to the broader view of divine activity. We will see how this links to the Matthew text.

I make one last point since it may be of some value. There is at least one direct reference in Christian scripture to Numbers 20 and this can be found in 1 Corinthians 4:10 where the writer (Paul?) refers to the rock of Meribah as a figure of the Christ. We see that this becomes a reference to a postresurrection view of the Christ and yet can play into our treatment of a Jewish context for this midrash.

Matthew 14

The text in Matthew 14 tells the story of Jesus' feeding of the 5000. I choose Matthew somewhat randomly, although there is some general consensus that Matthew may have been a Gospel written for a generally Jewish audience (i.e., members of the Jesus group who were from Jewish background). The story also includes a moment of crisis (people gathered to hear Jesus teach who had followed Jesus to a "deserted place"). The idea is that these people were not prepared to find food. The disciples were quarreling insofar as they assumed the people should be sent away. Another factor was that this narrative follows (in Matthew) the death of John the Baptist, who represented in this Gospel a sign of God's activity calling for repentance. Thus, this is a turning point in the story. It is followed by a series of miracle stories as well, but we focus on this one story in which Jesus simply instructs the disciples to bring the food available (five loaves of bread and two fish) to him. He looks to heaven and blesses the bread, brakes the bread and gives it to the crowds. All are described as eating, and the result is that all are satisfied with twelve baskets left over.

There is nothing particularly unique about this narrative, either in Jesus' story or in Jewish history. It is certainly no more remarkable than the water coming from the rock in Numbers 20 even though the story is told as a remarkable event. What is notable is that Jesus does not make much of this event and simply dismisses the crowds. That is, it is not made to be a miracle performed by him to draw attention to him but rather is written as pertaining to the activity of God. In this way, the story fits well the received tradition, and much in the Gospels suggests that Jesus does not want the miracles to be seen otherwise. If we begin with an assumption that miracles are not rare, then this story is more easily understood within a Jewish context than as a way of impressing a Hellenistic world of the early Church.

The story does seem to suggest an image of the Last Supper meal and in that sense is set into a larger context of meaning. That supper was a preamble to Jesus' death as the striking of the rock was a preamble to the death of Moses and Aaron. If we think of the Jewish understanding of God's activity as part of a plan set in creation, then we can see this story as part of history and not outside of it, not ahistorical, insofar as it is God's history. This point may help us see a midrash on Numbers 20 to which we can return. The key point is that the Gospel will view Jesus' death as part of God's plan and not as a punishment. This will be a key for us.

Of course, the central issue is the larger meaning of these events, which now becomes critical, since I have set this as a midrashic reading in connection with Numbers 20. The larger meaning there is surely the entry into the promised land and in Matthew the meaning is the events of the crucifixion and resurrection. But since the story is a preamble, we can view it as a midrash on Numbers 20. The point in both cases is redemption (and not just the immediate feeding or giving of water). The central meaning is that God will provide, a meaning that is clear in Numbers and surely also obvious in Matthew. The issue becomes how we read this provision now which is a post-Shoah question and not merely a hermeneutical question.

Of course, we do not need the Jesus narrative to provide this meaning to the rabbinic tradition. We can simply state that the story seems thoroughly Jewish, certainly fitting a Jewish context, and is read more authentically, I contend, as part of the inherited Jewish tradition, Jesus' proper religious context. What is important if we see this as a representation of the Jesus story is that the issue of how to move forward from a point of occupation is again a critical issue for Israel in Jesus' time. Perhaps this is a reaffirmation of the tradition in that the notion that God will provide was under some question when Israel was under the power of the Romans. But we may gain more in allowing Matthew to be a midrash to seek some interpretation for Numbers 20. That is what I turn to now by returning to Numbers.

A Midrash: Returning to Numbers 20

\We hardly need the feeding of the five thousand to interpret Numbers 20. There is an entire tradition of interpretation that offers various alternative meanings. But we can think of the story as midrash and see where that leads us. I am particularly struck by the problem that remains a puzzle for the rabbis. There does not seem to be a reasonable warrant for the death of Moses and Aaron in the text of Numbers 20. The text seems to say that the pride of striking the rock rather than trusting God's promise, especially failing to announce this to the people, was sufficient reason to bring on Aaron's death and to deny Moses entry to the promised land. However, the rabbis do not seem convinced about this. The failure appears to be minimal, certainly not deserving such punishment. The arguments offered seem to show the struggle to accept this as a picture of the God of Israel. It seems similar to the struggle that the rabbis had with the punishment brought on Job, the righteous one. As part of a created plan, the result seems to fail. We are left searching for a meaning in the larger purposes of God.

The idea that the striking of the rock, however, does not seem to warrant punishment if this is symbolic of God's redemptive plan as seems to be the case in Numbers. Moses is surely unjustly treated if denied this end simply for a moment of arrogance. Perhaps we can find in Matthew a midrash that can lead us to another conclusion. Jesus also dies as a result of his work not to see the full fruits of his work. This was, indeed, the sad conclusion by Albert Schweitzer when he saw the apocalyptic vision of Jesus go unfulfilled with his crucifixion. This can make sense in a Jewish context only if the death is seen as necessary for the redemption of the people.

Schweitzer could not see this in Jesus' death and thus decided that what remained was Jesus' teaching. But perhaps this is the point. The people of Israel could not move forward claiming the covenant and its promise as long as Moses and Aaron remained. The people had to be formed around new leadership to prepare the way for a future. Thus, the death of Moses is not punishment but is rather necessary for the redemptive future of the people. Moses is not so much punished for his arrogance as he clearly must step back for the full activity of God to be recognized apart from Moses. That is the full reason, perhaps for the death of Moses. This also is the case for Jesus, who must die so that the people can fully take up his teaching and not merely be dependent on him. This seems to be the point of this story and is noted by the immediately following story about Peter and whether Peter has the trust to "do it on his own."

So the issue is one of continuing leadership and the capacity for the people to take on their own agency as a covenant people. This seems also to be the central point of Numbers 19-20.[5] Such a message leads us back to the need for a post-Shoah reading that can test this interpretation in the light of our Shoah history.

A Post-Shoah Midrash

This will have to be a beginning reflection since moving to such a post-Shoah interpretation requires looking at a number of details in the texts and also needs to be done in dialogue. However, I will think about the possible reading I have suggested at this point in terms of a post-Shoah consideration. Above all, our reflections will take on the claim that any vision of the long picture begins with a trust in God's promise to provide. I will look closely at the argument that Roy Eckardt offered as to why he changed his view about the resurrection as part of this post-Shoah midrash.

The idea that God provides, even in a long range view, comes under heavy skepticism in a post-Shoah theology. This is especially problematic for Christians who neither can claim the role of victim nor claim any real evidence of massive Christian resistance or rescue during the Shoah. Thus, for Christians, the idea that God provides cannot be much comfort nor can it be so easily applied to Christians as Christians. Of course, there are many Christians who do continue to live with this trust, but this surely means that it is done, for most, without any real test of the kind represented by the Nazi destruction of European Jews. For this reason, the argument that Eckardt uses in his book co-authored with Alice

Eckardt, *Long Night's Journey into Day*,[6] seems appropriately to respond to the Shoah challenge. He argues that, "No past event, however holy or divine, can ever redeem the terror of the present. Only a future event can do this."[7]

In his later book, Eckardt argues another point which seems to thoroughly revise his position described above. Eckardt is influenced by the writing of Paul van Buren and is led to claim a historicity for the resurrection. The need to claim a bodily reality matches the need for Christians to affirm a relationship with Jesus while maintaining a belief in the Christ. Here we see difference come forward fully as he says, "For is not Jesus, the Jewish Hasid from the town of Nazareth, loose again in the social world, amidst all the anguish and all the joy of human events?"[8] This is surely not a future event that Eckardt spoke about in 1982. But this is precisely, despite his efforts to moderate supersessionist positions, a return to a Christian reading of Jesus and not to the Jewish Jesus. To claim that Jesus is a Jewish Hasid seems to do little to take fully seriously the Jewish context.

There is more to be worried about here. The claim that Jesus is in any sense released in the social world seems to deny that this Jesus as a Jew would surely have found himself in Auschwitz had he roamed the world of Nazi Europe, as I presume is the claim made here. This would mean that the very Christological claim for a faith rooted in the resurrection is surely undermined by the fact of Auschwitz as our story. Or do we seek a second resurrection? Surely Eckardt was correct to begin with: only a future event will do and this puts Jesus back into the Jewish context.

Now I have moved us in that direction already by pushing the discussion back behind the dogmas, to speak of Mr. Jesus. This means that the death of Moses and the death of Jesus as necessary for redemption for Jews and Christians, respectively, now is met with a clear pause. Can we say the same about the deaths of six million (indeed, even 11 million)? The miracle stories of Numbers and Matthew must now be seen in this light. This means that even more than _ would argue, morality must be seen as after Auschwitz, to use an idea developed by Peter Haas.[9] This morality is one in which death is no longer seen as a necessity for the redemption of the people. It is a brute fact of human history, but it is not so viable as a cornerstone of our vision. As I argued some time ago, this morality must now be seen in our agency (indeed, the agency of the people as I argued earlier) to resist and to rescue.[10] This becomes the meaning of water from the rock and the feeding of the hungry. Only a present event will do.

Discussion Questions

1. Why does Judaism need to seek the Jewish roots of Jesus?
2. How does Christianity require a Jewish Jesus in a post-Auschwitz world?
3. What does this new search for the Jewish roots of Jesus contribute to Jewish-Christian relations?

Notes

1. Roy A. Eckardt, *Reclaiming the Jesus of History* (Minneapolis: Fortress Press, 1992), 213-17.
2. Maccoby, Haim. "Antisemitism and the Christian Myth," in *Remembering for the Future,* vol. 1 (NY: Pergamon Press, 1988), 836-43; Jacobus Schoneveld, "Torah in the Flesh," in *Remembering for the Future,* vol. 1 (NY: Pergamon Press, 1988), 867-78.
3. The following is extracted from an analysis of miracles in Millgram, Abraham, ed. *Great Jewish Ideas.* (Washington, D.C.: B'nai B'rith, 1964), 225-26.
4. See readings of this text in Joseph Edelheit, "The Messy Realities of Life: A Rereading of Numbers 19 and 20," in Jacobs, Steven, ed., *Maven in Blue Jeans: A Festschrift in Honor of Zev Garber* (West Lafayette, IN: Purdue University Press, 2009): 28-34 and James F. Moore, "Dialogue as Praxis: A Midrashic Reading of Numbers 19-20 and Hebrews 9," in Jacobs, Steven, ed., *Maven in Blue Jeans: A Festschrift in Honor of Zev Garber* (West Lafayette, IN: Purdue University Press, 2009), 49-55.
5. See James F. Moore, "Dialogue as Praxis: A Midrashic Reading of Numbers 19-20 and Hebrews 9," in Jacobs, Steven, ed. *Maven in Blue Jeans: A Festschrift in Honor of Zev Garber* (West Lafayette, IN: Purdue University Press, 2009), 49-55.
6. See Roy A. Eckardt and Alice Eckardt, *Long Night's Journey Into Day* (Detroit: Wayne State University Press, 1982).
7. Eckardt and Eckardt, *Long Night's Journey*, 150.
8. Eckardt, *Reclaiming the Jesus of History*, 217.
9. See Peter Haas, *Morality After Auschwitz* (Philadelphia: Fortress Press, 1988).
10. James Moore, *Christian Theology after the Shoah* (Lanham, MD: University Press of America, 1993).

Jesus the "Material Jew"

Joshua Schwartz

Introduction

To speak today of "Jesus the Jew" is commonplace. Jesus, son of Joseph and Mary, residents of Nazareth, was born a Jew, lived as a Jew and died as one. But what kind of Jew was he? During the course of the years, scholarship has helped us understand much about his life and his basic teachings and not a small amount of work has been done on the Jewish context of his life and teachings. However, much less attention has been paid to the physical and material realities surrounding the everyday life and teachings of Jesus. The "academic" Judaism of Jesus is often a "literary" Judaism, short on material culture and archaeology, although attempts have been made recently to focus on "Jesus archaeology."[1] Less work, however, has been devoted to material culture and realia, or in the words of Marianne Sawicki: "Until recently, studies of Jesus have paid surprisingly little attention to the land, regarding it merely as a kind of stage or neutral platform supporting the events told in the Gospels. . . . Anyone who wants to know about Jesus must seek him on his native turf, in his own land and landscape."[2] This is easier said than done, however, or as stated by Peter Richardson: "It is difficult to use realia in Galilee, Judea, and South Syria in descriptions of the rising of the Jesus movement, in part because no realia can certainly be associated with it in these early stages."[3] "Christian archaeology" is still very monument oriented and still expends much energy on actively seeking archaeological confirmation of the New Testament, focusing on the "big" issues, and not the micro issues of everyday life.[4] Thus, the material life and culture of Jesus is perforce the material life of Jesus the Jew.

But how can that material life be determined? Surprisingly, there is not agreement about the composition of "material culture." There are those who stress landscape with material culture being a segment of one's physical environment shaped by humans. Others stress artifacts seeing material culture as the totality of artifacts in culture, including remnants left behind from the physical world. The former would seem to reflect the quote of Sawicki above. The latter might be identified with archaeology, but it is not. Material culture and archaeology are related but not the same. To both of these views it is possible to add liberally from the theories (and sometimes jargon) of the world of social sciences forming satellite and subviews including issues of caste, kinship, and gender.[5]

It is also not easy to determine just what makes up "Jewish" material culture as opposed to material culture of the Jews. Thus, the material life of the Jews in Hellenistic-Roman Palestine was not that much different that that of their non-Jewish neighbors, both in terms of urban and rural life. What was different related to "Jewish" aspects of everyday life or *halakha* and included such ethnic and religious material markers as *mikvaot*, or stone vessels, both relating to purity, the wearing of fringes on a four-cornered garment, or the use of religious paraphernalia such as "Sabbath lamps." There might also have been some minor differences in agricultural procedures and perhaps in agricultural tools and implements. Certain types of burial, such as secondary burial, might be an indicator of Jewishness, animal bone profiles that lack pig and aniconic decoration, without human or animal figures, might also be (negative) Jewish material markers.[6] Are we to look then for Jesus and the Jesus movement to be frequenting *mikvaot* or using stone implements? Did they wear fringes on their garments? Could we even tell them apart from any other Palestinian Jew of the time in terms of their material culture and everyday life? For our purposes, what we seek is material culture of the Jews and here and there some "Jewish" material culture. Both of these would probably have also served as the material framework for Jesus and his followers.

While even the "historical Jesus" may have lived at times in an apocalyptic world,[7] his images and thought used a language of everyday life in Roman Palestine. His teachings and parables mention stone vessels, lamps and flasks, pots, utensils, vineyards and towers, coins, and swords, among other items. Understanding the realia of his world, Jewish or not, is of the highest priority in re-creating his social world and this in turn can help us understand his spiritual. What I cannot do, however, in this article is to deal with the corpus of spatial imagery in the Gospels, or even in Q. The explication of individual verses or motifs must be studied elsewhere. My work at present serves simply as background.[8]

The material world of Jesus was not just limited to artifacts and land. Jesus was peripatetic and is reputed to have visited certain sites in Palestine such as Nazareth, Cana, Bethsaida, Capernaum, Jericho, and Jerusalem. What would he have found in these sites in terms of everyday life and how would all this have impacted upon "Jesus the Jew"? How would his religious life have intersected with the material culture of the sites which he visited? How would his physical surroundings, Jewish or otherwise, have influenced him?

To answer all these questions would also probably be an endeavor of a lifetime. What I can attempt to do here is briefly to describe the material reality with which Jesus might have come in contact, allowing for a better understanding of the world in which he functioned and taught. As most of this was done in the Galilee, I shall try to relate as much as possible to that region, but I shall not be restricted to the Galilee as Jesus was not. As there is also no proof that Jesus entered the Galilean cities of Sepphoris or Tiberias, and in fact the only real city that he spent time in was Jerusalem, I shall limit my discussion to the rural sphere.[9] However, as stated above, my work here is a drop in the bucket and at best can give only a taste, both in terms of content and of bibliography.[10]

A Framework for Study: Limitations and Reality

What are the parameters of study to describe the material world of Jesus? In an ideal world the study framework of the material culture of the first century CE would be all encompassing of everyday life (and death). Palestinian society of that time was both rural and urban, but Jewish society was mostly rural. A discussion of rural society would relate to settlements and their components, for example, houses, courtyards, utensils, and the aspects of everyday life with which they were associated, agriculture (crops, implements and labor), work and labor in general, roads, and even harbors. A study of urban society—and the Jews after all were also found in the cities of Palestine—would include much of what was just mentioned from an urban perspective as well as such usually urban, but not always, phenomena as bathhouses, markets and fairs, and synagogues. Both sectors were not monolithic in terms of population. There were upper class and lower class, rich and poor, and various economic and social permutations of these with their variations in material life. Nor was there an iron wall between rural and urban; distances were relatively short and events and developments in one sphere might impact on the other. The archaeology of the rural and urban spheres might have been somewhat different, but apparently the material culture and everyday ethnic and religious lives were similar and this was the case not only in Galilee, but also in Judaea.[11]

While the depictions of Jesus in the Gospels are mostly in the rural sphere, some of his followers had urban backgrounds of sorts and in any case, the relatively short distances between rural and urban allowed for a diffusion of material culture from one sphere to another and if not in a physical sense, at least certainly in a virtual sense in terms of knowledge. In that ideal study framework it would also be necessary to concentrate on local manifestations of material culture, that is, of Judaea, Samaria, Peraea, and Galilee. Also, due to interregional migrations, "local" might have been just as interregional (or not). As mentioned above, I make do here with providing background information in order to understand some of the aspects of the material world of Jesus.

Finally, the issue of time frame is also critical. It would certainly be ideal if there were enough sources on all matters which could clearly depict the material culture of Jesus' times. However, this is not the case. Can a tradition dating to the second century CE about this or that utensil depict the material reality of a century before? The fact is that changes in material culture in general in the ancient world progress at a very slow pace. *La longue durée* reigns in the ancient material world. Thus, some of our comments may be dependent on reality described in rabbinic literature, which while it postdates the times of Jesus, is still probably dependable in general regarding material culture.[12]

Rural Life

Settlements

Most Jews in first century Palestine lived in villages of various sizes.[13] Some may have lived in isolated large manor houses or farms, but not many, and the few that did were not in the Galilee. Most of these rural villages were also fairly homogenous and monolithic in terms of their ethnic, social, and religious composition but it would not be correct to postulate a uniform "peasant" model, as it were, and social differentiation should not be totally ruled out as an option in the rural sphere. Relatively speaking, a low level of building existed in this sphere and in private homes it would be unusual to find dressed stones, capitals, or colored mosaics, although there were some exceptions. Household "high design" did not much exist here. We shall discuss homes in somewhat more detail below. The quality of life in these settlements was probably not high. There were in general few public buildings although the larger rural settlements might have had synagogues or a school building. While there might have been some Hellenization or Romanization in such settlements, it would probably have been more in the nature of politics than of culture or architecture

Courtyards and Houses

Village life for men, women, and children often revolved around the courtyard, usually reached by passing through narrow streets and alleys.[14] It is the courtyard which often provides the means for understanding the relationship between public and private space in the village. Allegiance might often have been more to one's (family) courtyard (being one's neighborhood) than to the village itself. There was constant tension here between the open courtyard life and the quest for at least some degree of privacy, the latter accomplished usually through the construction of partitions or fences within the courtyard. These physical changes might also have been necessary due to changes in family demographics or on account of changes in the dynamics of courtyard possessions. Often it was not clear who owned what and tension between neighbors was not uncommon.

In addition to residences, the courtyard might have contained dovecotes, chicken coops, storage facilities, cisterns, toilets, a primitive sewer system, and perhaps a shop. Life in the courtyard was boisterous and loud with laundering, cooking, baking, grinding, and often eating occurring there. Outdoor life in the courtyard was communal. This was also a common play area for children, and various animals, when not grazing, might have also wandered about the courtyard, sometimes serving as children's pets.[15] Courtyards were often locked at night, but there was generally always a coming and going with ultimately little privacy and little quiet. It is not difficult to understand why doors of private residences entered from a courtyard were often kept locked, requiring one to knock to gain entry.[16] Sometimes the courtyards were of a more "internal" nature, signifying that they were not "public" space and this also allowed for greater degrees of privacy.

Different types of houses were constructed in the courtyards. While I shall discuss houses within the framework of a rural setting, it should be remembered that the line of demarcation is not always absolute between rural and urban, at least regarding domiciles, although a higher level of Romanization was to be found in urban residential architecture. It is also important to remember that a house and its attendant space is more than a just a "container" for basic human activities, but rather reflects an "architectural language" which can shape society as well as reflect that society. Also, house décor can provide clues as to the nature of life in a particular house.

Eyal Baruch has distinguished six principal types of homes based on architectural function: common courtyard house, front courtyard house, atrium house, peristyle house, manor house, and farmhouse.[17] The common courtyard house is the most widespread and continues trends in architecture from the Hellenistic period. It had a square or rectangular floor plan, a central courtyard surrounded by rooms from all or some of its wings, and usually common walls with other residential structures. The plan of the front courtyard house was generally the same except for the front courtyard. The two courtyard houses, the type Jesus would have come in contact with, were on the lowest socioeconomic level. Then came the farmhouse, but as I mentioned, it not generally found in Galilee. The Roman house, an urban phenomenon, in all its forms, was on the highest level.

One of the striking features of "Jewish" domiciles was the large number of *mikvaot* or ritual baths found in these houses, in spite of the fact that there were often numerous public *mikvaot* nearby, in the settlement itself or in adjacent fields. While these are clearly religious and ethnic markers, the house *mikvaot* reflect a desire for private observance of ritual purity as opposed to a more public expression in a public *mikveh*.[18]

Baruch has also shown us that despite a well-developed communal organization in many of the rural villages, the residences were for the most part built in the same style and level of construction. There were no significant signs of social gaps. Baruch sees this as reflecting a cultural perspective that sees the display of personal wealth in a negative manner. If there was surplus wealth, it would have been invested in public buildings such as synagogues, with these providing a leveling mechanism within Jewish village society.[19] Jesus would probably have not been opposed to a view that looked askance at displaying signs of personal wealth and he might even have been in favor of a system of rural leveling mechanisms. Would he have supported the synagogue as an expression of that leveling?

It is obviously impossible here to deal with all component parts of all the types of houses and I shall make reference only to major components.[20] Some houses had a gate house or anteroom. External windows seem to have been problematical, since they might have weakened the walls, but internal windows were built to provide light and air. In spite of this, natural sunlight probably did not suffice and it was necessary to find other modes of lighting. The oil lamp was the most common solution. Some were portable and some were hung from the ceiling. Restrictions on kindling fire on the Sabbath required the construction of slow-drip lamps and other types of "Sabbath lamps." These too served as clear ethnic and religious functional markers.[21]

The more simple houses were of the one-room variety and might have been divided into upper and lower parts. Those who could manage it constructed additional rooms. This new space, and the division of space, was a function of social structure and rank, gender, and age, as well as of practical functionality. There might have been a *traklin*, the rabbinic version of the Roman *triclinium*, serving as dining room for family or formal meals. Reclining on couches, diners ate food that was placed on different types of tables, some individual, low and round with three legs. This does not mean that diners always dined in Hellenistic style and perhaps often did not. Archaeological evidence from Gamla seems to indicate that residents would have gathered around one or two shared dishes, using a single small bowl or saucer.[22] The food might have been prepared in a kitchen or in oven areas in the house, but a good deal of food preparation and cooking took place in the courtyard.[23]

Behind the *traklin* there was often a *kiton* or bedroom, with or without a curtain or partition, and often serving all family members. The size of the room determined sleeping arrangements and furniture, whether a bed with a wooden frame, mattresses, and pillows, or a sleeping mat.[24] Additional domestic furniture was rather limited. Sometimes there were chairs, stools, and seats of various kinds. Sitting or sleeping (without at least a mat) on the floor was considered a sign of abject poverty.[25] There might also have been various types of chests, boxes, and cupboards for storage.

Bathing rooms and indoor privies were not to be found in rural villages, although they did exist in homes of the wealthy in the urban sphere. The same is true for basements, although there were often more simple storage areas in village houses, and some houses had their own water cisterns. Some houses also had a second storey, which would have been reached by a staircase from the outside. The roof of a house was usually flat, providing more living space if necessary and served as a work area. Some of the activities that took place in the courtyard might have been transferred to the roof allowing for more privacy.

Khirbet Qana

As mentioned above, Jesus lived in, visited or passed through numerous sites in Palestine and perhaps not all were mentioned in the Gospels. While in the rural sector there was much that was standard, clearly each village or site had its own individual and sometimes even unique personality. Obviously I cannot describe all the rural sites associated with Jesus. I shall make do with one example, Khirbet Qana, associated with New Testament Cana (John 2:11; 4:46; 21:2 with 1:43-45).[26]

Khirbet Qana is located on a hundred-meter hill on the north side of the Beth Natufa valley eight kilometers south-southwest from Sepphoris and within sight of modern day Nazareth Illit. This site should not be confused with modern day Kefr Kanna near Nazareth and on the Sepphoris-Tiberias road, and which became associated with Jesus only in the Middle Ages. It is always important to remember, as pointed out above, that distances in Palestine between various cultural, economic, and social spheres are relatively short, and while Jesus might be associated for the most part with rural life, urban life was only a short distance away, although it cannot not be insignificant that no Gospel source has him visiting a Galilean city.

Cana persisted through several occupation stages with few major changes. As a hillside village its plan was set by considerations of access and topography and the first century settlement seems to have had little in the way of formal planning. The main access road was from the east, but road connections with other towns are uncertain. Cana was unwalled when Jesus knew it, and this was the case in most Galilean villages Jesus would have visited, such as Capernaum and Chorazin. Terms such as *agora* and *forum* are inappropriate for villages like Cana. There might have been a commercial area, though, in the northeast.

The town core was a fairly packed hilltop with houses, streets, and lanes organized in some form of regularity. There were a number of large public cisterns there. Cana had several industrial areas. Much of the industry was related to agriculture, although there might have been some glass-blowing activity. It is possible that there was some neighborhood and housing differentiation. Some of the houses were terrace houses without courtyards, while others were of the courtyard variety described above. Some had two stories. Walls were constructed in rough masonry rubble with few dressed stones. Cana had at least one public *mikveh* and a number of apparently Jewish tombs have been uncovered around the site, but all were 200-400 meters away in keeping with purity concerns. A public building whose chronology is not yet clear and perhaps existed already in the first century CE could have been a synagogue or study house. Other villages were not that different.

Utensils

In addition to the basic furniture found in the Jewish houses or courtyards and described above, one would have found in them also implements, vessels, utensils, and equipment of sundry types for various purposes.[27] While few houses had kitchens, as mentioned above, there seems to have been a good deal of cooking and eating going on and thus many of the utensils in the Jewish home were related to these basic activities. The Jewish housewife had a well-stocked kitchen and in this she was no different than her non-Jewish neighbors and often they bought the same utensils from the same suppliers.[28] As we shall see below, changes in household assemblages, and such did occur, at least in Galilee, might reflect social and political change.

Certain aspects were, however, unique to the Jewish kitchen. Stone ware was popular among Jews because it was not susceptible to ritual purity and some vessels, such as the wide-necked, bulbous *meyham*, used for heating water, could be stacked on another *meyham* or on a pot-bellied, round-bottom cooking pot in order to keep it contents warm over the Shabbat.[29]

There were also various types of stoves available. The most common was the *kirah*, a single, hollow compartment allowing air to circulate through top holes on which pots or pans could be placed. They could be portable or permanent and sometimes a number were joined together. The best were made of metal or stone and might be status symbols.

The most common cooking vessel was the pot-bellied cooking pot, which came in various sizes, allowing for easy stacking. Long use would have caused them to be blackened by fire. There were also various types of casseroles for stewing and steaming. Various types of frying pans were also common. Food was served in bowls and platters of different sizes and shapes, some shallow some deep, and were made of metal, glass, clay, or wood.

Liquids, and especially wine, were stored in sealed storage jars, in a wine cellar, if one was available. A vent hole would allow for minimal amounts to be poured out, but larger amounts could have been poured through a funnel. The wine would be poured into a decanter and then into clay pitchers. It was not drunk neat and had had to be diluted with water. The wine was drunk in a cup which in Jewish society was often personal and reflected social position. The rich drank from clear colorless glass and the poor from colored glass.

We have no way of knowing which utensils or implements Jesus used in Galilee, but what he did use in the first century reflected changes in lifestyle in Galilee and these changes went beyond pottery and reflected changes in the political atmosphere.[30] Thus, from the second century BCE and throughout the first century BCE, people in Galilee, Jews and non-Jews, set their tables with imported red-slipped plates and bowls and lit their homes with imported mold-made lamps. These might well be defined as luxury items. There was much use of narrow-mouthed cooking vessels and wide-mouthed casseroles, popular in Greek cuisine, and this implied that Greek cuisine had become commonplace in Galilee for both Jews and non-Jews. On top of all this, at this time there was even some interior wall painting and stucco decoration in Jewish sites such as Yodfat and Gamla.

It is unlikely that any of this would have made much of an impression on Jesus, since at the end of the first century BCE and continuing into the first century CE, while non-Jews continued to import these wares, the Jews stopped. Galilean Jews set their tables exclusively with locally manufactured, small, undecorated buff-colored saucers and white chalk vessels and lit their homes with wheel-made local knife-pared lamps. Why did the demand for specific objects cease in Galilee? Adele Berlin sees this as a declaration of anti-Romanization on one hand and an expression of Jewish self-identity on the other. Local Jews made a political statement of solidarity and affiliation with a traditional, unadorned, Jewish lifestyle as well as demonstrated a unified opposition to the Roman presence. That "Jewish lifestyle" also seems to be in keeping with an allegiance to *halacha* and purity. Did Jesus and his followers read their Galilean wares (as well as their simple Judaean stoneware) in this manner? Did they express anti-Roman feelings and Jewish patriotism with every meal? Obviously this cannot be proven, but Berlin's views do add a fascinating interpretation to mundane activities of (Jewish) life.

Modes of Production

Agriculture

Agriculture was the main sphere of production in Roman Palestine, and it affected the lives of everyone, whether as consumers or producers.[31] Consumption was not just a matter of survival but impacted upon Jewish life, whether at weekday meals or at Sabbath or holiday meals. An entire order of the Mishnah, *Zeraim*, relates to agriculture, cultivation and consumption of produce, and even if the Mishnah postdates Jesus, it is likely that there was not much change regarding major aspects of agricultural law or modes of production and consumption during the Second Temple and Mishnah periods. *La longue durée* also reigns supreme here.

In any case, though, Josephus can give us a good indication of agricultural life during the first century CE. The best general statement regarding Jewish life and agriculture is found in *Against Apion* 1.60: "Now we do not inhabit a country with a coast, nor are we keen on trade or on the mixing with others which results from it. Rather our cities have been built inland, far from the sea, and since we live on good terrain, we work it thoroughly."[32]

In his description of the land of Israel in *War* 3.35-58, Josephus provides information about the state of agriculture in various regions of Palestine. The soil of the Galilee was rich and fruitful and replete with many types of trees (3.41-43). The Peraea was less fertile than Galilee and much of it was desert, but there were fertile tracts which allowed for the cultivation of olives, grapes and date-palms (3.45-47). Judaea and Samaria were fruitful with an abundance of trees, but also had excellent grass for grazing (3.48-50).

Josephus also provides more local descriptions. Thus, regarding the Valley of Gennesar along the northwestern coast of the Sea of Galilee (also known the "Lake of Gennesar") Josephus (*War* 3.516-521) tells us that it was so fertile that even opposite varieties grew there all year round, such as, walnuts which required a cold climate, figs and olives which required a more temperate one and palms which required hot air. Other crops such as grapes were also found there. Jesus would have spent much time in and around this area. Jesus would have also been familiar with the fertile Jericho plain (*War* 4.459-475), the breadbasket of Judaea.[33]

In addition to the crops mentioned above by Josephus, it is also important to mention the grains grown in Palestine. Wheat was the most important crop and barley was also popular, especially in southern regions. Spelt was also grown and bread of various forms was the universal dietary staple. There were also more than twenty types of legumes, such as lentils, green beans, and *ful* grown in Palestine, popular among the poor in the form of porridge or as a grain substitute. Grapes mentioned above were an important cash crop, but wine consumption was not usually excessive in Jewish society, although wine was supposed to be a part of the festive, holiday, or religious meal. In addition to figs, pressed or otherwise, and dates, often in the form of cakes, one could also find carobs, pears, apples, peaches, nuts, and pomegranates. Many people also maintained small vegetable gardens for private use.[34]

Grazing: Animals and Diet

The crops above provided a basic diet, and even a rich one for some. In addition to the agricultural produce mentioned above, there were additional modes of production for the farmer. There was a good deal of sheep grazing in Palestine, most of it in Judaea and a small amount in Galilee, and later rabbinic dicta possibly forbade the raising of sheep in Galilee while allowing it to continue in Judaea and adjacent desert areas. The sheep not only provided a good deal of wool, but also were a source of meat. A farmyard might also have had a cow or two, providing milk or cheese and there might also have been chicken coops. Both animals obviously also served as a source of meat, as did doves that were raised in underground columbaria.[35]

Another important component of the ancient diet in Palestine was fish. Then, as today, fish was often part of the Sabbath meal and was eaten more often than meat. Fish were caught both along the Mediterranean Sea and the Sea of

Galilee. The former fishermen were often non-Jews, the latter were mostly Jewish and they provided for the needs of the Jewish population. While the capital of this industry was Tiberias, it was extremely popular all along the basin of the Sea of Galilee, as we learn from numerous sources of the New Testament.[36]

While it is of course impossible to know what constituted the basic diet of Jesus and his followers, there is no reason to assume that it was any different than the norm described above. A safe bet would be along the lines of bread, fish, fresh or salted, olive-oil, (watered down) wine, and perhaps the occasional additional fruit or vegetable.

Field Work

Farm work was not easy.[37] Much time was spent plowing. The first two plowings in the summer and fall after the first rain, respectively, prepared the land to absorb water, air, and seeds. The third plowing was deep and right before seeding, usually of winter grain and the final plowing covered the seeds, after the land had further been prepared for sowing through fertilization. The metal funnel-shaped plowshare, with a sharp point, cut into the earth. It was connected to a sharp wooden tailpiece, which was attached to the knee. The knee was connected to a long pole attached to the yoke, and another pole placed on the neck of an ox or cow. Hoeing and weeding kept the planted area free of weeds.

Harvesting with a short handled sickle would have occurred in late spring and was backbreaking. The small piles of grain were gathered into larger stacks and transported to the threshing floor, which could be public or private. Threshing separated kernels from husks, consisting of chopped straw and chaff. The work, done in public threshing floors, was an ecological hazard, even by ancient standards, and could not be done near a settlement. Little was wasted, though, and leftover straw was used to feed animals or made into compost. Some settlements also had flour mills.

Grapes and olives were of course for the most part not eaten raw but consumed as wine and oil. Both were produced in presses. Various systems of weights, levers and presses, and crushing basins existed. Most olive presses were also public or community property. Wine presses might be public or private. The juice was stored in vats and after the first fermentation it was stored in jars in a cool place until it became wine concentrate. There can be no doubt about the fact that Jesus and his fellows would have been familiar with the nitty gritty of all of this.[38]

Most of the agricultural work was done by the farmer himself, sometimes with the help of immediate family or, if additional help was needed, with a permanent or temporary worker. There were also specialized workers such as vegetable growers, date-palm planters, fig pickers, threshers, and drivers, who helped the farmer when necessary. Most of the work, of course, was done locally. When it came time to sell the produce, the farmer usually marketed the produce himself, but there were exceptions and in more developed regions in terms of economy, there was more division of labor even in these agricultural fields.[39]

Fishing

Fishing was no less physically exacting, although it was not as time consuming.[40] A telling description is found in Matthew 13:47-48: "The kingdom of heaven is like a net that was thrown into the sea and caught fish of every kind; when it was full, they drew it ashore, sat down, and put the good into baskets but threw out the bad." This would have been done with a trammel net or a series of such nets, pulled along by a boat, perhaps similar to the "Jesus Boat" discovered in 1986, and pulled back in concert with those on shore. There were also smaller casting nets and one could also cast a hook (Matt. 17:27). While Jesus of Nazareth may not have known much about fishing, it is likely that Jesus of Capernaum and its environs would have picked up quickly on all this.[41]

Crafts, Industry and Services

While most people in the rural sphere were involved in agriculture, it was not the only way to make a living.[42] There were different forms of crafts and industry found in both village and city. I shall stress those related to the rural sphere and in any case, they could often be found both in both the rural and in the urban spheres.

There were a number of industries in Palestine which were of importance, such as textiles, pottery, glass, and perhaps paper. As we saw above, stoneware was also produced and stones were quarried for construction. Some of the production was for local needs, some regional, and some might have even been appropriate for export.

The most important industry was probably the textile industry and the most important areas within this were the cultivation of flax and subsequent production of fibers and the grazing of sheep and production of wool. The textile industry also made use of cotton and silk. The labors included weaving, dying, washing, and sewing. A good deal of this work was specific to women and there was often much more to it in terms of larger issues of gender and sexuality, certainly beyond the tedium of these everyday labors.[43] Men involved in the textile industry might have come into more contact with women than was normally the case in everyday life and this could have caused problems.

Many of the utensils of everyday life were of pottery. They would have broken easily and have been difficult to clean, but the raw materials to produce new ones were easily found and labor was cheap. Broken pottery, at least of the local variety, could be tossed aside because it was far more convenient to buy new cheap local pottery than to repair old broken utensils. In the Galilee, for instance, one could have bought kitchen and dining pottery from Kefar Hanania, the boundary point between Lower and Upper Galilee, or storage jars from Asochis (Shihin) in the Lower Galilee.[44] There were, of course, also imported wares, as I mentioned above, but the vast majority of pottery in use in Jewish society was local.

While it is impossible to know how familiar Jesus and his circle were with the intricacies of the labors and industries just described, they were so common and so local, that it is impossible to think that they were not familiar with the basic workings of these industries. They certainly enjoyed the garments and utensils that would have been produced. They would have been less familiar perhaps with the workings of the glass industry, connected with the coast or with cities, but we saw above that this industry might have existed in Cana and Jesus might have known of it. It is likely, though, that they were not overly familiar with the less extensive industries such as the metal industry and the papyrus industry. Rabbinic literature also mentions numerous other occupations such as leather workers, plasterers, shoemakers, blacksmiths, perfumers, builders, ditch-diggers, and carpenters. While some would have been undertaken only in the cities, these laborers would also have been found in larger villages. There was also much business in death with artisans preparing ossuaries at workshops or working on funerary art.

Jewish settlements also offered various services. Most villages probably had a public bathhouse, although there were also private ones. There would have been a public lavatory. One could find perhaps a doctor, blood letter, scribe, and slaughterer, who served also as butcher. There might also be washer men (or washer women). While cities had a higher standard of living, those living in Jewish settlements, mostly rural, enjoyed a relatively high level of services.

Clothing and Jewelry

An important aspect of material life is the clothes that make the man or woman.[45] There is no doubt that garments, individual or even uniform, might be identity markers and today the study of clothing is considered vital for the understanding of society. The question, however, is whether there was any distinctive dress that could be described as an ethnic or religious identity marker. Was there Jewish dress or did the Jews dress similar to their non-Jewish neighbors?

There were two distinctive types of Jewish clothing: the *tsisit* or fringes attached to the four corners of a male's outer garment, and the *tefellin* or phylacteries, the leather containers strapped to one's arm and head containing excerpts from the Bible. Matthew reports Jesus speaking to a crowd and his disciples and accusing the Pharisees of various kinds of ostentation in religious practice.[46] "They make their phylacteries broad and their fringes long" (Matt. 23:5). While this supposedly describes just the Pharisees, it is they who go to extremes, as it were, and there is no reason to assume that only the Pharisees dressed like this. In fact it is possible that Matthew depicts Jesus himself wearing fringes (Matt. 9:20; 14:36) and it is likely that he and his circle also wore phylacteries on those occasions when other Jews did.[47] The only other significant Jewish clothing marker would not be visible to the eye and that was refraining from wearing (and weaving) garments made of flax and wool because of the prohibition of "mixed kinds."

Differences in clothing and style probably reflected differences in socioeconomic standing and not ethnicity. Clothes were a status symbol in Jewish society. Husbands were supposed to provide for their wives in terms of at least basic clothing and more if they could. Apart from the "Jewish" apparel mentioned above, there were not many differences in dress between Jews and non-Jews. Ancient authors provide no sources that Jews, men or women, were recognizable in their dress.[48] Men and women wore an outer garment or mantle (*talit*), with only the men attaching fringes. Underneath both men and women would wear a tunic (*haluq-kutonet*) and one might wear a number of them. The woman's tunic was usually longer that that of the man and might reach the ankles or feet. A strip of cloth could serve as a belt and the length and width was adjusted to allow the folds to serve as a purse. Underneath one wore some type of underwear or loincloth, but this was not always the case for men. Both men and women wore different types of caps and headdresses, sometimes veiled in the case of women. In Jewish society, children dressed basically in the same manner as "small adults." All of the above depended of course on having the means to make or buy clothing. The poor were often relegated to wearing rags.

Clothing was not the only external status marker. Those who could afford it (men, women, and children), wore jewelry, although this was more popular among women, both in villages and cities,[49] and cosmetics of all kinds were popular among those who could afford it. One gets the impression that physical appearance was important and care was taken when possible to improve it.

Death

The final stage of material life was death and there was much that can be learned about life from the mechanics of passing over, as it were.[50] There were field tombs, shaft tombs (or dug out) tombs, *loculi* or rock-cut tombs, tombs with *arcosolia* (bench-like apertures with arched ceilings hewn along the length of wall), ornamental tombs and monumental tombs. One of the most popular modes of burial was in burial caves. From an external courtyard, the body would be brought into an internal one and placed in niches (*kochim*) carved in the cave. After a year what was left of the body would be placed in internment receptacles such as ossuaries or wooden coffins and the niche could be used again. The tomb might contain inscriptions and funerary art. Often a large stone was placed at the entrance of the tomb to prevent unlawful entry. Just about every step of the funeral and burial procedure, as well as the subsequent mourning had meaning regarding religion, social, and economic status.

The monumental and most ornate tombs were discovered in and around Jerusalem and they are the exception rather than the rule, even if they make the most prominent remains. Most tombs of the times of Jesus were of the various rock-cut varieties, as indeed was the tomb of Jesus in Jerusalem.[51] There were also many shaft and field tombs. The tombs of first century CE Galilee, as of Judaea, apart from Jerusalem and its environs were of the simpler varieties.

Conclusion

The material life of Jesus and his early followers was the material life of a Jew, and mostly a rural Jew. For the most part there was nothing unique in this and the everyday life of the Jews was not that different than that of their non-Jewish neighbors. However, occasionally religion, ethnicity, and even politics resulted in change and there is no reason to assume that Jesus diverged in these matters from his Jewish neighbors.

His life and teachings evolved in the material milieu described above, and while it is impossible to reconstruct all aspects of Jesus' everyday life, his words and teachings can be better understood through a better understanding of the material world in which he functioned.

Discussion Questions

1. To what extent was the everyday life in Roman Palestine Jewish?
2. Describe an average material day of Jesus and his followers in Roman Galilee.
3. Bring examples of New Testament teachings and traditions that reflect on everyday life in Galilee.

Notes

1. See, for example, James H. Charlesworth, ed., *Jesus and Archaeology* (Grand Rapids: Eerdmans, 2006). See especially Charlesworth, "Jesus Research and Archaeology: A New Perspective," in *Jesus and Archaeology*, 11-63 and the bibliography cited there.
2. Marianne Sawicki, *Crossing Galilee: Architectures in the Occupied Land of Jesus* (Harrisburg: Trinity Press International, 2000), 3, 7.
3. Peter Richardson, *Building Jewish in the Roman East*, in Supplements to the *Journal for the Study of Judaism* (Waco: Baylor University Press, 2004), 74.
4. Kim Bowes, "Early Christian Archaeology: A State of the Field," *Religion Compass*, 2/4 (2008): 575-619. Most work relates to structures and their relationship to other structures. While this is not totally devoid of material culture, the studies themselves express little interest in that field.
5. On all of this see Joshua J. Schwartz, "The Material Realities of Jewish Life in the Land of Israel c. 235-638, " in *The Cambridge History of Judaism*, vol. 4, *The Late Rabbinic Period*, ed. Steven T. Katz (Cambridge: Cambridge University Press, 2006), 431-33. Limitations of space prevent me from expanding further on methodological issues. See also in detail Sawicki, *Crossing Galilee.*
6. Schwartz, "Material Realities" 453-56 and bibliography. See also Jonathan L. Reed, *Archaeology and the Galilean Jesus: A Re-examination of the Evidence* (Harrisburg: Trinity Press International, 2000).

7. Christopher Rowland and Christopher R.A. Morray-Jones, *The Mystery of God: Early Jewish Mysticism and the New Testament*, Compendia Rerum ad Novum Testamentum 12 (Leiden: Brill, 2009).
8. See, for instance, "Q's Spatial Imagery in a Galilean Context" in Reed, *Archaeology*, 189-95. Agricultural metaphors pervade Q. Whether or not this proves a Galilean provenance for Q cannot be discussed here.
9. See Sean Freyne, *Galilee and Gospel: Collected Essays* (Boston: Brill, 2000), 71. Jesus was not necessarily anti-city and pro-village, although he was critical of certain ideas related to the city. It cannot be coincidence that the Gospels do not have Jesus in either Tiberias or Sepphoris, cities not that far from his Galilean stomping grounds. It should also be clear that I do not relate to Capernaum and similar settlements as cities. The lively scholarly discussion as to the level of urbanization of the Galilee is beyond the purview of this survey.
10. An excellent survey of both archaeology and material culture in the Galilee can be found in Zeev Weiss, "Jewish Galilee in the First Century CE: An Archaeological Perspective," in Daniel R. Schwartz, *Flavius Josephus, Vita: Introduction, Hebrew Translation, and Commentary* (Jerusalem: Yad Ben-Zvi, 2007), 15-60 (Hebrew).
11. Weiss, "Jewish Galilee," 43.
12. Schwartz, "Material Realities," 432-33.
13. Schwartz, "Material Realities," 433-34; Weiss, "Jewish Galilee," 18-20. See also Peter Richardson, "Khirbet Qana (and other Villages) as a Context for Jesus," in Charlesworth, *Jesus and Archaeology*, 120-44. See also Zeev Safrai, *The Economy of Roman Palestine* (London: Routledge:1994), 39-99.
14. Schwartz, "Material Realities," 434-35.
15. On children's play, see Joshua Schwartz, "Jew and Non-Jew in the Roman Period in Light of Their Play, Games, and Leisure-Time Activities," in *God's Word for Our World, Biblical Studies in Honor of Simon John De Vries*, ed. J. Harold Ellens, Deborah L. Ellens, Rolf P. Knierim, and Isaac Kalimi (London: Clark, 2005), 128-40. On animals in the courtyard see Joshua Schwartz, "Dogs in Ancient Jewish Rural Society," in *The Rural Landscape of Ancient Israel*, ed. Aren M. Maeir, Shimon Dar and Zeev Safrai (Oxford: British Archaeological Reports, 2003), 127-36.
16. See Reed, *Archaeology*, 159 on primitive locks on houses in Capernaum.
17. My discussion on houses is based mostly on Eyal Baruch, *The Dwelling House in the Land of Israel during the Roman Period: Material Culture and Social Structure* (PhD diss., Bar-Ilan University, 2008) (Hebrew). A revised version will be published as a monograph by Yad Ben Zvi.
18. Others see the private *mikvaot* as reflecting wealth. See Richardson, "Khirbet Qana."
19. Avraham Faust and Eyal Baruch, "The Synagogue and the Rural Jewish Community in the Period of the Mishnah and Talmud: Financing the Construction and Maintenance of Synagogues as a Leveling Mechanism," *Cathedra* 116 (2005): 49-66 (Hebrew). Needless to say, it is impossible to talk in terms of absolutes. See Richardson, "Khirbet Qana."
20. Schwartz, "Material Realities," 436-39.
21. Hanan Eshel and Dina Avshalom-Gorni, "A Stand for a Sabbath Lamp from Hurvat Uza," *Atiqot* 29 (1996): 57-61.
22. Andrea M. Berlin, *Gamla I: The Pottery of the Second Temple Period, The Shmarya Gutmann Excavations, 1976-1989* (Jerusalem: Israel Antiquities Authority, 2006), 140.

23. There were very few indoor kitchens in the Roman East. On an indoor kitchen in Qatzrin see Ann Killebrew and Steven Fine, "Qatzrin: Reconstructing Village Life in Talmudic Times," *BAR* 17 (1991): 51,55.
24. Joshua Schwartz, "Material Culture and Rabbinic Literature in Late Antique Palestine: Beds, Bedclothes and Sleeping Habits, " in *Continuity and Renewal: Jews and Judaism in Byzantine-Christian Palestine*, ed. Lee I. Levine (Jerusalem: Yad Ben Zvi, 2004), 191-209 (Hebrew).
25. Joshua Schwartz, "'Reduce, Reuse and Recycle'—Prolegomena on Breakage and Repair in Ancient Jewish Society: Broken Beds and Chairs in Mishnah Kelim," *Jewish Studies Internet Journal* 5 (2006): 147-80, http://www.biu.ac.il/JS/JSIJ/5-2006/Schwartz.pdf.
26. Our discussion is based on Richardon, "Khirbet Qana." For a good discussion of public and private space in Capernaum see Reed, *Archeology*, 148-60.
27. Schwartz, "Material Realities," 439-41; Weiss, "Jewish Galilee," 45-48.
28. Much, but not all, of the kitchen work and cooking would have been "women's work." A full discussion of gender- specific labor is impossible within the space restrictions of this study. On women in the kitchen see Judith Hauptman, "From the Kitchen to the Dining Room: Women and Ritual Activities in Tractate *Pesahim*," in *A Feminist Commentary on the Babylonian Talmud: Introduction and Studies*, ed. Tal Ilan, Tamara Or, Dorothea M. Salzer, Christina Steuer, and Irina Wandrey (Tübingen: Mohr Siebeck, 2007), 109-26. See also Tal Ilan, *Mine and Yours are Hers: Retrieving Women's History from Rabbinic Literature*, Arbeiten zur Geschichte des Antiken Judentums und des Urchristentums 41 (Leiden: Brill, 1997), 227-33 for more examples of "women's work" (raising children, food preparation, spinning and weaving, bewailing the dead, hairdressing, and inn keeping).
29. See, however, Weiss, "Jewish Galilee," 47-48 for other theories. Berlin does not deny that this should be seen as an ethnic marker, but she also sees it as a matter of local pride in using local Jewish wares as opposed to imported non-Jewish utensils. See Andrea M. Berlin, "Romanization and Anti-Romanization in Pre-Revolt Galilee," in *The First Jewish Revolt: Archaeology, History, and Ideology*, ed. Andrea M. Berlin and J. Andrew Overman (London: Routledge, 2002), 57-73. This preference was also in keeping with preferences of Jews in Judaea and Jerusalem.
30. This is based mostly on Berlin, "Romanization" and , "The Pottery as Evidence for Life at Gamla," in Berlin, *Gamla I*, 133-56.
31. Schwartz, "Material Realities," 441-43.
32. The translation is that of John M. G. Barclay, *Against Apion, Translation and Commentary Volume 10, Flavius Josephus, Translation and Commentary, edited by Steve Mason* (Leiden: E. J. Brill, 2006). Available at http://pace.mcmaster.ca/york/york/showText?book=1&chapter=1&textChunk=nieseSection&chunkId=60&text=apion&version=english&direction=&tab=&layout=english
33. Joshua Schwartz, "On Priests and Jericho in the Second Temple Period," *Jewish Quarterly Review* 79 (1988): 23-48.
34. Schwartz, "Material Realities," 442; Safrai, *Roman Palestine*, 104-62.
35. Safrai, *Roman Palestine*, 165-82.
36. Ibid., 163-65.
37. Schwartz, "Material Realities," 443-45. The classic study on farming and agricultural technique is still that of Yehuda Feliks, *Agriculture in Eretz-Israel in the Periods of the Bible, Mishnah and Talmud*, rev. ed. (Jerusalem: Reuven Maas, 1990) (Hebrew).

38. Eventually, some of the labors associated with the presses would take on importance in Christian symbolism. See Joshua Schwartz, "A Holy People in the Winepress: Treading the Grapes and Holiness," in *A Holy People: Jewish and Christian Perspectives on Religious Communal Identity,* Jewish and Christian Perspectives 12, ed. Joshua Schwartz and Marcel Poorthuis (Leiden: Brill, 2006), 39-51. See also Joshua Schwartz, "The Wine Press and the Ancient Judaeo-Christian Polemic," *Thelogische Zeitschrift* 49 (1993): 215-28; 311-24.
39. See Hayim Lapin, *Economy, Geography, and Provincial History in Later Roman Palestine*, Texts and Studies in Ancient Judaism 85 (Tübingen: Mohr Siebeck, 2001).
40. R. Alan Culpepper, *John: The Son of Zebedee, The Life of a Legend* (Columbia: University of South Carolina, 1994), 7-15.
41. Sawicki, *Crossing Galilee*, 183 mentions an indigenous fishing industry there. Reed, *Archaeology*, 144 writes of "fishing opportunities" to supplement the diet of local inhabitants.
42. The part of the discussion is based mostly on Safrai, *Roman Palestine*, 188-219.
43. See Miriam B. Peskowitz, *Rabbis, Gender, and History*, Critical Studies in Jewish Literature, Culture and Society 9 (Berkeley: University of California Press, 2007).
44. Weiss, "Jewish Galilee," 19-20, 45-46.
45. Schwartz, "Material Realities," 449-52.
46. Closely related to clothing is the issue of gesture and material culture. See, for example, Steven G. Matthews, "The Instantiated Identity: Critical Approaches to Studying Gesture and Material Culture," paper presented at the Theoretical Archaeology Group conference, University of Glasgow, Scotland, 17-19 December 2004.
47. Yehudah B. Cohn, *Tangled Up in Text: Tefillin and the Ancient World* (Providence: Brown University Press, 2008), 109-11.
48. Shaye J. D. Cohen, *The Beginnings of Jewishness: Boundaries, Varieties, Uncertainties* (Berkeley: University of California Press, 1999), 30-34.
49. Ziyona Grossmark, *Jewelry and Jewelry Making in the Land of Israel at the Time of the Mishnah and Talmud* (PhD diss., University of Tel-Aviv, 1994) (Hebrew).
50. Amos Kloner and Boaz Zissu, *The Necropolis of Jerusalem in the Second Temple Period* (Jerusalem:Yad Ben-Zvi and the Israel Exploration Society, 2003) (Hebrew); Rachel Hachlili, *Jewish Funerary Customs, Practices, and Rites in the Second Temple Period* (Leiden: Brill, 2005).
51. I refer to the Tomb of the Holy Sepulcher. I make no attempt to adjudicate regarding recent discoveries such as the Talpiot Jesus Tomb. See James Tabor, "The Talpiot Jesus Tomb," in his April 9, 2007 posting in his blog *The Jesus Dynasty* (http://www.jesusdynasty.com/blog/2007/04/09/the-talpiot-jesus-tomb-an-overview). On the controversial James ossuary, see Uzi Dahari "Final Report of the Examining Committees for the Yehoash Inscription and James Ossuary" (http://www.antiquities.org.il/article_Item_eng.asp?module_id=&sec_id=17&subj_id=175&id=266). This is the final and official report of the Israel Antiquities Authority of the State of Israel.

Jesus Stories, Jewish Liturgy, and Some Evolving Theologies until circa 200 CE: Stimuli and Reactions[1]

Ziony Zevit

People tell stories, stories about friends, enemies, heroes, and whatnot. Stories play social roles. They can connect people or separate them. Well-told stories can compel people to think about their implications. In societies not given to abstract thinking, stories convey implicit philosophies, theologies, and world-views. They are also the embryonic source of explicit philosophies, theologies, and worldviews

During the first century of the Common Era Jews told stories about biblical figures, sages such as Rabbi Akiba, and about Jesus. Judging from extant texts, the stories tended to be short and punchy, self-standing, and not necessarily connected thematically or sequentially. Story-tellers in Eretz Israel did not create complex plots or long legends about their spiritual heroes.

Independent Jesus stories circulated widely in communities of early Christians before and long after the canonical Gospels were composed. They were told casually, though some may have been used formally in early eucharistic settings to remind people what they were celebrating. Good stories, whether historically accurate or not, attracted an audience, triggered discussions, and created the interest that drew potential converts into conversations with disciples. Stories could answer questions, salve doubts, convince.[2] They could, of course, also raise questions.

Jesus Stories

Jesus stories and their interpretations created an intellectual-cultural frame within which believers created lives of Christian significance. Each story made a point that could trigger discussions about the life, death, and resurrection of Jesus, about his parables and instructions, and about their importance and relevance. Tellers of tales cast their stories into this or that form, combining them as they saw fit, tailoring them for a particular audience of fellow Jews, the folks with whom they shared wine and meals, with whom they prayed and, perhaps, frequented a study house, the folks with whom they argued and debated.

Since it is unlikely that so intelligent a man as Paul would have attacked Christians as a religious activist with little or no knowledge of their beliefs and stories, scholars conclude he must have known at least some Jesus stories that he found disturbing (Gal 1:13; 1 Cor. 15:9). He may have heard his first stories from Christians in Tarsus as well as from their detractors. His repertoire would have grown in the bustling markets of Jerusalem through discussions with like-minded Pharisees and on the Temple Mount with anti-Christian Sadducees. What he learned led him to consider Christians enemies of Judaism, or at least inimical to what he considered proper, essential beliefs, and he was willing to make their lives miserable.

Despite his opposition to Christians, one subset of their Jesus stories eventually worked its power on him, and Paul came to faith through inner conversion (Acts 9:1-7, 22:6-11; Gal 1:15-17).[3] His experience transformed the significance of what he had once held to be true and important, disturbing part of his worldview. Beliefs that he may have condemned as falsehoods before he set out for Damascus to persecute Christians he came to experience as truths. At first, the transformed Paul, writing around 50-60 CE, may not have known a broad panoply of Jesus stories, but he most likely learned many more after his conversion during his three-year stay in Damascus with the Christian community and then later during subsequent visits to Jerusalem.[4] They helped support and rationalize his faith.

The gamut of Jesus stories may have brought many Jews to associate with and join Christian groups. For most, becoming a Christian would have been a slow process best described as ecclesiastical conversion. Such conversion was the end result of an extended socialization process influenced and stimulated by many factors in addition to knowing Jesus stories: personal-psychological, familial, political, sociological, and intellectual.[5]

Paul himself distinguishes between stories that he did not tell the Corinthians—what he describes as "testimony (in Greek, *marturion*) of God" types—and "Christ and him crucified" types. Because the crucified and resurrected Christ was the beginning of all that was important for Paul, he preferred them in his own work (1 Cor. 2:1-4).[6] His eschatology lay at the beginning of his theology and he would have it no other way.[7] For him, this was the primal, essential belief, the first axiom.

In *First Letter to the Corinthians*, Paul writes: "For since, in the wisdom of God, the world did not know God through wisdom, God decided through the foolishness of our proclamation, to save those who believe. For Jews demand signs and Greeks desire wisdom, but we proclaim Christ crucified, a stumbling block to Jews and foolishness to Gentiles, but to those who are the called, both Jews and Greeks, Christ the power of God and the wisdom of God" (1 Cor. 1:21-24). Paul speaks about the crucified and resurrected anointed one. He refers to Jesus as the anointed one, *christos*, that is, messiah, but not as God, *theos*. His rhetoric attempts to skate a fine line and to not cross over into what many Jews of his day might have considered the range of the absolutely intolerable. Sometimes he fails.

His comment about the Jews supports the following interpretation: Jews wanted signs or proofs that Jesus was divine or divinely sent, and there were missionaries who provided them with a message based on such stories. What Jews didn't get—the stumbling block—was that belief in Jesus could save them, belief in the Jesus who died, rose from the dead, appeared to and conversed with people, and then ascended to heaven. So far as most Jews were concerned, according to Paul's experience, death and resurrection stories did not provide convincing signs and proofs. In other words, only one type of story conveying only one part of the Christian narrative was a stumbling block, not all of the stories conveying other messages.

Failing to build conventicles or congregations among Jews using the stories that he considered essential because they were the ones to which he had responded, Paul left his fellow Jews to others (Acts 11:19) and took his teachings to gentiles (Acts 18:1-11). One indicator of Paul's abject failure among Jews is that sometimes they reacted violently to his teachings. In 2 Corinthians 11:24, Paul writes: "Five times I have been flogged by the Jews forty lashes minus one. Three times I was beaten with rods. Once I was stoned." The first punishment that he lists, thirty-nine lashes—see, Deuteronomy 25:3—suggests that the punishment was meted out by local Jewish courts that found him guilty of some offense against another Jew or against a community. The context of the statement in 2 Corinthians 11 indicates that the quarrels may have been due to Paul's insistence on teaching the Jesus that he wished to proclaim through the stories that he preferred (2 Cor. 11:1-5).

The canonical Gospels, all composed after Paul, are replete with the types of stories that Paul did not tell. In the first centuries of the church, they continued to attract the attention of Jews and to bring about the ecclesiastical conversion of some.

Jesus Stories among Rabbinic Jews

Two stories reflecting a second century Jewish milieu preserved in the Tosefta illustrate Jewish awareness of these stories. The first tells about a man, Bar Damma, who was bitten by a poisonous snake. A certain Jacob of Kefar Sana came to heal him in the name of Yeshua son of Pantera (Jesus). Rabbi Ishmael prohibited the healing on the grounds that one might not heal in the name of Jesus. Bar Damma claimed that he could provide acceptable arguments for healing in the name of Jesus but died before he could present them (Tosefta Hullin 2:22).[8]

The second tells about Rabbi Eliezer ben Hyrkanus who had been tried on charges of *minut* (heresy) and found innocent. Dismayed over his experience, he was depressed, until one day his student, Rabbi Akiva, asked him: "Perhaps one of the *minim* [heretics] said a word of *minut* [heresy] to you that pleased you?" Eliezer suddenly recalled, "When I was walking in Sepphoris, I met Jacob of Kefar Sikhnin and he said a word of *minut* in the name of Yeshua son of Pantera and it pleased me (Tosefta Hullin 2:24). By recovering the forgotten event, Eliezer understood that his experience was a fit punishment for his moment of inappropriate pleasure. Although it is unclear from the story in its various versions exactly what justified the accusation of *minut*, the story does illustrate that in the second century, the tension lines drawn by Paul had thickened into incipient borders. There was a growing edginess within the rabbinic community about Jewish Christians and their beliefs, particularly since Gentile Christians shared the same beliefs.[9]

Both Rabbi Ishmael and Rabbi Eliezer were familiar with Jesus stories, and Eliezer admitted to finding something useful in them. Bar Damma, bitten by the snake, was aware of *halakhic* objections to being healed in Jesus' name, but clearly thought such a healing could be effective, most likely on the basis of Jesus stories. Moreover, he apparently had marshaled arguments that he believed could convince Ishmael that such a healing was permissible, if not required, on *halakhic* grounds. Additionally, the healer is not discredited in the story by being referred to as a *min*. He was most likely a specialist who appropriated the best "medicine" available, no matter its source. Acts 19:13 refers to Jewish exorcists who healed in the name of Jesus. The formula cited there, "We exorcise you by the name of Jesus whom Paul preaches," suggests that they were coasting on Paul's belief, not on their own; but if it worked, they used it.

If the healer, Jacob from Kefar Sana, is the same person who shared a teaching of *minut* in the name of Jesus with his friend Rabbi Eliezer, the rabbinic story informs us that in the second century Palestinian Jews conversed quite openly about Jesus and his teachings, even if it was thought somewhat dicey.

In 1935, R. T. Herford pointed out that *minut* in rabbinic parlance did not necessarily refer to people who studied and discussed questionable teachings, but came to refer specifically to those Jewish Christians who had come to equate Jesus with God.[10] (What they thought about him as a messiah was less important.)

Since Paul indicates which of his claims about Jesus were deemed unlikely by most Jews of his ken, this study undertakes to determine 1) which stories were not "stumbling blocks," at least early on, 2) which claims about Jesus would not necessarily have raised Jewish eyebrows at all, and 3) how some stories might have led Jews to equate Jesus with God.

Predications about God in Jewish Liturgy

The preliminary section of the Jewish morning service, *Birkhot Hashachar*, contains a series of benedictions sharing a common introduction. Each concludes with a different predication about God. The introduction is "Blessed are you, Lord our God, king of the universe."[11] The concluding sections presented below are followed by parentheses in which I indicate the poetic, prophetic, or psalmodic passage that appears to have inspired the benediction:

1. who gives the rooster understanding to distinguish between day and night (Job 38:36)
2. who did not make me a gentile
3. who did not make me a slave
4. who did not make me a woman (or, in an alternative tradition: who made me according to his will)
5. who opens (the eyes) of the blind (Ps. 146:8; Isa. 35:5-6)
6. who clothes the naked
7. who releases the bound (Ps. 146:6-8)
8. who straightens the bent over (Ps. 146:6-8)
9. who spreads out the earth upon the waters (Ps. 146:6-8?)
10. who provided for my every need (Ps. 146:6-8)
11. who firms a man's footsteps (Ps. 37:23; 1 Sam. 2:9a)
12. who girds Israel with might (*gevurah*). (Ps. 65:7; 93:1)
13. who crowns Israel with splendor (Isa. 62:3)
14. who gives strength to the tired (Isa. 40:29)

Originally, individuals recited these blessings at home, as part of an extended private liturgy.[12] When awakened by the rooster's crowing, they recited the first benediction. Then, according to a *baraita*—a Tannaitic teaching not found in the Mishna but cited in the Gemara—in tractate Berachot 60b, benedictions were recited as they opened their eyes, dressed, got out of bed, stood on the floor, put on sandals, took a step, fastened their outer garment with a belt, put on a head cover, and the like.[13] Through these benedictions, quotidian acts became choreographed prayers. They proclaimed a practical theology of active presence, of divine imminence and involvement.

Composed originally in Pharisaic circles between the late second and the first century BCE, their extant articulation is due to Tannaim, rabbinic teachers of the first and second centuries CE. Their inclusion in the formal liturgy of the morning service of the synagogue, however, is not datable earlier than the medieval period, ca. 500 CE.[14] Most of their predications about God are composed in phrases and idioms drawn from the Bible as was the practice in Pharisaic and later Tannaitic prayers. It is important to observe that predications 2, 3, 4, and 6 are not connected to biblical verses.

Predications 2, 3, and 4 do not reflect biblical-based concerns and so the absence of a relevant passage is unsurprising. Through them, the individual Jew expresses pride in his identity as an individual and in his social status. Both their formulation and justification are discussed by sages who inherited them as givens and were therefore compelled to justify their presence in the liturgy (j. Ber 9:2; b. Menach 43b-44a).[15] They reflect attitudes and concerns typical of Levantine Hellenistic and Roman values, but are explained in apologetic sources as expressions of thanks for having being made as a free, male Israelite obligated to fulfill the maximum number of divine commandments (b. Menach 43b; tos Ber 6:18).[16] Indirectly, they attest to a belief in divine determination of an individual's ethnicity, gender, and social status before birth.

Paul's polemical statement against some early form of these very benedictions in Galatians 3:28 indicates that they were well known in the mid-first century CE: "There is no longer Jew or Greek, slave or free, male or female; for all of you are one in Christ Jesus."[17]

Although predication 6 may allude to the garden of Eden story wherein God manufactures leather tunics for Adam and Eve (Gen. 3:10, 21), I have been unable to find source for its actual wording.

A comparison of the language of all the predications with their adduced sources reveals that people who knew large swatches of the Bible by heart and who could free-associate their way through its texts composed the benedictions, thereby formulating elements of a shared common, Jewish theology. It is worthwhile observing that most of the verbs are in the present tense.

Additional expressions of common theology are found in the central core of the morning service, in fact, of every contemporary service, in a prayer called variously *Shemoneh Esreh*, "the Eighteen Blessings," or *Amidah*, "The Standing Prayer," or *Hattefillah*, "The Prayer."[18] The origins of this prayer go back to the Hasmonean period but it may have been cast into its extant form in the time of Gamliel II, a *tanna* of the second century CE who, until he was deposed, attempted to impose an intrusive orthodoxy on Yavnean scholars.[19] The second benediction of this longish prayer has been referred to as *Gevurot* since the *Tannaitic* period (see m. Rosh Hashanah 4:15). This term translates loosely as "God's mighty deeds" and is an appropriate title for its description of God's activities.[20] This benediction contributes to the list of predications but also repeats some from the earlier list.

15. sustaining and providing the wherewithal for the living (in grace) (Ps. 145:15-16; 2 Sam. 19:33)
16. resurrecting the dead (in abundant mercy) (1 Sam. 2:6)[21]
17. supporting the fallen (Ps. 3:6; 145:14, see predication 8)
18. healing the sick (Ps. 103:3)

19. freeing the bound (Ps. 146:7, see predication 7)
20. maintains and fulfills his faith/promise/covenant for those sleeping in the dust (Dan. 12:2)[22]

The language of the final predication is drawn from Daniel 12:2 that refers to some distant period of time when the divine messenger Michael will be present at a judgment: "And many of those sleeping in the earth-dust, *ʾadmat ʿapar*, will rise; some for eternal life and some for eternal reproach and contempt."[23]

The main theme of this section of the *Shemoneh Esreh* is resurrection, mentioned twice overtly in predications 16 and 20 and less obviously in predication 15.[24] Considered together, 15-16 and 20 may be interpreted as referring to God who sustains life, resurrects the dead, and maintains his promise to those not yet resurrected.[25]

The other themes in predications 17-19 that break the resurrection sequence may have been inserted by someone who thought that he was either clarifying what constituted resurrection, or who understood predication 18, "making live the dead," to refer to those so sick that they were thought of as dead already. This would have not made the final predication appear redundant.[26] What is significant, however, is that the language of these, like most of the fourteen predications adumbrated above, is also drawn from Scripture.

The 20 predications of both lists describe part of the complex character of the deity addressed by Jews after 250 BCE as *Adonay*, "My Lord."[27] It is to him that Jews directed their petitions, fully expecting a positive response, but not always receiving it. From the second century BCE, as reflected in much of the pseudepigraphic literature, and certainly after the destruction of the Second Temple, he was considered more universal than local, more transcendent than imminent, though available to those who called out to him. They held his characteristics to be eternal and unchanging—in a vague, Neoplatonic sense—and real. That is, they did not flatter him by ascribing characteristics in the hope that he actually could achieve changes in the various areas covered by the descriptions; rather, the characteristics were abstractions based on recorded events.[28] Expressed by participles in a nominal sentence, the predications of the *Gevurot* declare that what God did in the past he continues to do in the present. His presence in the world is indicated by his ongoing, active involvement in these matters. The predications reflect a counter-tendency, a reaction by many in parts of self-transforming Judaism to the distancing of God reflected, for example, in the theology of the Qumran community and in the persistent copying and translating of pseudepigraphic texts. This counter-tendency eventually became deeply rooted in early rabbinic Judaism, and normative to it.

Additionally, as Ephraim Urbach pointed out, by the second century CE, visible attestations of the powerful deeds listed in *Gevurot* were understood to be manifestations of God's self-revelation in the world for the benefit of all people, not only Jews. Indeed, in rabbinic parlance, God was referred to as *baʿal gevurot*, master of *gevurot*, the Hebrew equivalent of Greek *dynamis*, power or authority.[29]

Although the language of the predications was drawn almost exclusively from Isaiah and Psalms, God was believed to have earned these predications because of past performances. Illustrations can be found for most of them in biblical narratives.

The statements listed above as 2, 3, 4 are less predications about God than expressions of thanksgiving concerning postbiblical civics. We would not expect to find them in biblical narratives. Predications 12 and 13 are too vague to be connected to a particular narrative. That leaves 5-11 and 14-20, a total of 14 predications. Some of these are identical: numbers 7 and 19, 10 and 15, and 16 and 20 are the same, while 8 and 17 also appear similar. This reduces the number of unique predications to 11. Most of these refer to stories in which God or an agent with divine authority acts on behalf of a person:

Tanakh Stories Justifying the Predications

1. who gave the rooster understanding to distinguish between day and night

According to Job 38:26, this refers to some primeval event unmentioned elsewhere in the Bible. The word, rendered "rooster," is sometimes rendered "human mind" or the like, to overcome the awkwardness of this benediction. The verse in Job remains poorly understood.

5. who opens (the eyes) of the blind

God uncovered Balaam's eyes and he saw an angel (Num. 22:31).

Elisha prayed to God that he open the eyes of his servant so that the servant could see the supernatural horses and chariots of fire that would protect them from an Aramean raiding party sent to capture him (2 Kings 6:15-17). After God blinded the Arameans with light, Elisha led them to Samaria and prayed that the Arameans eyes be opened (2 Kings 6:18-20).

Both stories use verbs from the root *p-q-ch* as the benediction. There are, however, no stories of someone blind from birth or permanently blinded by accident being healed.

6. who clothes the naked

God made proper outer garments for the naked Adam and Eve and dressed them (Gen. 3:21). He also addressed Israelite needs during the wandering period. Israel did not lack for new clothing or sandals in the wilderness because what they had never wore out (Deut. 8:4; 29:4).

7 (and 19). who releases the bound, prisoners

It is possible to cite some stories such as those of how Joseph prospered in prison and was then released (Gen. 39:19-23; 41:14), how Samson (Jude 16: 25) and Jeremiah (Jer. 37:15-38:13) were released from prison but these can only be figurative examples.

8 (and 17). who straightens the bent over

I am unable to connect this verse with any story without bending the story beyond exegetical recognition.

9. who spreads out the earth upon the waters

This phrase appears to refer not only to a primeval event, but also to the fact that God controls the waters totally and subjects them to his will. In mythopoeic language God walks on the back of the personified or metaphorical sea and controls it (Hab. 3:15; Job 9:8; 38:8-11,16).

A few stories indicate his control over water. God changed water to blood in Egypt (Exod. 7:19-20) and split the waters at the Yam Suf during the Exodus using the wind (Exod. 14:21); he also divided the Jordan for Joshua, the ark and the Israelites (Josh. 4:7, 14, 18, 22-23) and Elijah (2 Kings 2:8).

He arranged for water to come forth from a rock on more than one occasion (Exod. 17:5-6; Num. 20:7-11; Judg. 15:19).

10 (and 15). who provided for my every need

God provided a meal on top of the mountain for Moses, Aaron, Nadab, and Abihu and seventy elders of Israel. They sat opposite him and saw him (Exod. 24:1, 9-11).

God provided quail and manna for all the Israelites in the wilderness (Exod. 16:13-35).

Ravens fed Elijah at God's command (1 Kings 17:4-6) and God supplied a miraculous supply of flour and water for the widow in Zarephath who fed Elijah (1 Kings 17:7-16).

Elisha provided a miraculous supply of oil (2 Kings 4:2-7) and fed a multitude on his own authority, without prayer and without God's help (2 Kings 4:42-44).

11. who firms a man's footsteps.

Perhaps this alludes to a miracle reported in Deuteronomy 8:4 (and Neh. 9:21) whereby Moses pointed out to the people that during their wanderings, "your garment did not wear out and your foot did not swell up" and Deuteronomy 29:4, "and your sandal did not wear out on your feet."

14. who gives strength to the tired

In Deuteronomy 25:18, Moses described the Israelites as tired and exhausted when they left Egypt and were attacked by the Amalekites. In the description of the battle against the Amalekites at Rephidim, God miraculously enabled the tired Israelites to defeat them (Exod. 17:8-13).

The divine spirit strengthened Samson at different places under varying circumstances (Jude 13:25; 14:6, 19; 15:14; 16:28-30).

16 (and 20). resurrecting the dead

God hearkened to Elijah's prayer and made a dead boy live (1 Kings 17:17-24).

Elisha prayed to God and then lay over the body of the Shunemite's son (as did Elijah in the abovementioned story) and the boy revived (2 Kings 4:32-37).

A dead man tossed into Elisha's tomb was resuscitated immediately when his corpse touched Elisha's bones (2 Kings 13:21).

Second Maccabees, written in the first half of the second century BCE, contains a number of relevant references to resurrection. Men executed for refusing to eat pork proclaimed their belief that they might be raised from the dead to an everlasting renewal of life (2 Macc. 7:9, 14, 21). They also believed that lost limbs would be restored after death to those who had been dismembered in life so that the dead would be resurrected whole (2 Macc. 7:11; 14:46 [the death of Razis]).

18. healing the sick

Abraham prayed to God on behalf of Abimelech and his household, and then God healed him, his wife and female slaves so that they bore children (Gen. 20:17-18).

God was responsible for Sarah's pregnancy (Gen. 21: 1-2). He was believed to be the one who allows pregnancy to occur (Gen. 30:2).

God healed Moses' leprous arm (Exod. 4:7) and later Miriam's leprosy (Num. 12:10-15).

Naaman, the Syrian general healed from leprosy, understood that it was God who healed him and to God that thanks were due (2 Kings 5:9-15).

God caused and cured Ezekiel's dumbness (Ezek. 3:26-27; 33:22 and see also 24:27) and caused and cured Nebuchadnezzar's madness (Dan. 4:21-34)

Jesus Stories Corresponding to the Predications

Similar predications may be made about Jesus on the basis of his "mighty acts" narrated in Gospel stories. Many of these, not all, are reported multiple times, and although some are redacted versions of the same story, many are different stories about the same type of mighty act.[30] Originating as isolated stories eventually used to interest potential converts, many may have achieved this objective. I do not argue that the Gospel writers, who collected stories that they liked and cast them into the particular forms in which we know them, worked with a list of accepted predications. I propose that Jews telling and hearing the individual stories in the second century processed them through a list of predications available to them in the liturgy.

The following list is based on the essential *res gestae*, and not on any particular ideological redaction of the core story as reflected in any individual Gospel.[31]

1. who gave the rooster understanding to distinguish between day and night

No Jesus story parallels this predication, but the story of Peter's denial connects him with roosters crowing (Mark 14:30, 66-72; Matt. 26:34, 69-75: Luke 22:34, 56-62; John 18:17-27).

5. who opens (the eyes) of the blind

Jesus heals the blind (Mark 8:22-26; 10:46-52; Matt. 9:27-31; 15:29-31; 20:29-34; Luke 18: 35-43; John 9:1-41).

6. who clothes the naked

No stories connect to this predication. Readers may infer that Jesus clothed the man possessed by Legion since Gospel accounts mention that "the man was clothed and in his right mind" (Mark 5:15; Luke 8:27, 35). However, since Luke alone refers to the fact that when possessed, the man had worn no clothes, reference to his clothing after the exorcism (unmentioned in Matt. 8:28-34) may have been understood as an external sign of the person's new state of mind.[32]

7 and 19. who releases the bound

Jesus releases the demons, Legion, from a man who could not be restrained in chains. At the request of the demons, he sends them into a herd of swine that run into the sea and are drowned (Mark 5:1-20).

Jesus releases the bent over woman who was bound by Satan (Luke 13:10-17)

8 and 17. who straightens the bent over; supports the fallen

Jesus heals a paralytic who gets up from his bed and walks (Matt. 9:1-8).

Jesus straightens the bent over woman (Luke 13:10-17).

9. who spreads out the earth upon the waters

Jesus calms a storm on the sea showing that he controls wind and waters (Mark 4:35-41; Matt. 8:23-27; Luke 8:22-25).

Jesus walks on the waters, showing that he can subdue and control them (Mark 6:45-51; Matt. 14:22-23; John 6:16-21).[33]

The same control is illustrated by the miracle at the wedding in Cana where he turned water into wine (John 2:3-11). Referred to as "the first of the signs" it alludes to the first plague in Egypt through which God revealed his ability to change the nature of what was perceived as naturally unchanging.

10 and 15. who provided for my every need; sustaining, providing the wherewithal for the living

Jesus feeds multitudes (Mark 6:30-44; Matt 14:13-21; 15: 32-39; Luke 9:10-17; John 6:5-14) and is responsible for large catches of fish (Luke 5:1-11; John 21: 1-14).

11. who firms a man's footsteps (paralytics and cripples)

Jesus heals a paralytic who gets up from his bed and walks (Mark 2:1-12; Matt. 8:5-13; 9:1-8; 11:5). He heals a lame man who then walks (John 5:2-9).[34]

14. who gives strength to the tired

No story connects to this predication.

16 and 20. resurrecting the dead; maintaining his faith for those sleeping in the dust

Jesus raises the daughter of Jairus, a synagogue elder, but claims that she was just sleeping (Mark 5:21-43; Matt. 9:18-26; Luke 8:40-56).

Jesus revives a dead man being carried to his funeral at Nain (Luke 7:11-17).

Jesus raises Lazarus from the dead after he had been entombed four days (John 11:17-44).

18. healing the sick

Jesus heals sick, possessed, and lepers often (Matt. 4:23-25; 8:1-4, 5-13, 14-15, 16-17): lepers (Mark 1:40-45; Luke 17:11-19); epileptics (Mark 9:27; John 4:46-54); deaf-mutes (Mark 7:31-37); fever (Mark 1:29-31); bleeding woman (Mark 5:24-34); dropsy (Mark 3:1-6; Luke 14:1-6); possessed (Mark 7:24-30; Matt. 12:22-23; 15:21-28; Luke 11:14).

This category, *healing the sick*, is problematic in that healings involving exorcisms lack parallels in the Tanakh (Matt 7:22, etc.; Mark 1:21-28; 9:38-40; 16:17; Luke 4:31; 9:49-50; 10:17). Some have parallels in rabbinic literature where stories are told about rabbis invoking God's name to get rid of demons. Tanakh parallels might not be expected since this particular healing specialty appears to have developed only in the Hellenistic era and rabbis are numbered among its practitioners.[35] Consequently, nothing in the exorcism stories per se would have necessarily made Jews think of Jesus as divine; rather, it would have reinforced his association with other healers, be they rabbis or not, practicing the same art and gifted with the same skill.

Profiling Jesus: An Explicit List of Predications in Matthew and Luke

Something like what is posited in the preceding section as an explanation for how and why some Jews may have understood that Jesus was God is observable in Matthew and Luke.

In both, John the Baptizer sends messengers to inquire of Jesus: "Are you the one who is coming or should we expect another?" (Matt. 11:3; Luke 7:19). Jesus responds obliquely: "Go and tell John the things you hear and see. The blind see and the lame walk, the lepers are cleansed and the deaf hear, the dead are raised up and the poor have good news preached to them" (Matt. 11:4-5 and Luke 7:22). In paraphrase, this would be, "Of course I am the one. Haven't you noticed all these interesting phenomena associated with me?" The fact that the story is presented in these two Gospels alone indicates that it derives from the Q tradition and predates the Gospels.[36] This is a matter of importance for the discussion in the next section of this study.

In Matthew's account, Jesus is referring to healing stories reported earlier in the Gospel: leper (8:2-3), paralytic (9:2-7), resurrection (9:24-23 [though Jesus says that the little girl was sleeping]), blind person (9:27-23). The order of healings which are intended to inform John that yes, he, Jesus is the one, differs from the one listed by Jesus and does not include the healing of a deaf person.[37] In Luke, the healings antecedent to Jesus' response are the following: healing a fever (4:38-40), leprosy (5:12-13), a paralytic (5:24-25), and resurrection (7:12-15). Absent from Luke's list are healings of a blind person and a deaf one. Given only a partial congruence between deeds reported as performed and deeds claimed indicates that the Gospel writers did not feel compelled to illustrate every one of Jesus' claims, even though their point was that he was the one.

Jesus' response in the literary context of both Gospels suggests that only a few individual predications required demonstration and that they were to be considered sufficient as he made a case on his own behalf. His deeds did not have to match all of the predications in order that he be recognized as the coming one. What is remarkable in the parallel narratives is that Jesus' list of accomplishments is not presented as a fulfillment story. Perhaps, that is why it was not necessary for all the healings to have been included in the narrative. But, if so, why have Jesus refer to them at all in a somewhat boastful manner?

In his recent Matthew commentary, Herbert Basser argues cogently that Jesus' answer reflects a known list of predications that defined a human savior and that this list predates the Gospels.[38] The profile to which the story claimed at least partial congruence is found in Isaiah 35:5-6: "then the eyes of the blind will be opened and the ears of the deaf will be unstopped; then he who limps will leap like a stag and the tongue of the dumb sing." and in Isaiah 61:1: "The Spirit of the Lord God is on me. Because the Lord God anointed me to preach good news to the poor." Implicitly, the list drawn from statements in Isaiah reflects a theology of divine deliverance through a divinely appointed agent. This differs from the list of predications about God himself that have been this study's main focus.

Comprehending Jesus Stories through a Jewish Liturgical Filter

Prayer books containing the liturgy were first developed sometime after the eighth century when the number of liturgical texts grew and the texts became lengthier and more complicated. Prior to that, Jews knew the list of essential prayers and blessings by heart. In the second century, that list included the *Birkhot Hashachar* and the *Shemoneh Esreh*. Consequently, Jews in the second century hearing the many Jesus stories of the nonstumbling block variety could easily have constructed a theological syllogism after filtering them through their liturgy.

Since Jesus stories narrate that Jesus did what liturgy states God does, and since Scripture teaches that God did in the past what the liturgy declares he continues to do, then Jesus must have been a manifestation of God on earth. However, insofar as God was in the heavens at the same time that Jesus was on earth, then there were two distinct, divine presences in the cosmos at one and the same time. In certain Jewish circles this may have been considered *minut*, in others, odd thinking; and in still others, something interesting, worthy of additional consideration.

Some Jews in the latter half of the first century familiar with Jesus stories may already have understood some of these stories as illustrating a binitarian equivalence without the liturgical lens. They could have reached such a conclusion on the basis of the full text that was only quoted partially to establish a profile in the Q material incorporated into Matthew 11:4-5 and Luke 7:22 (discussed in the preceding section). Gentiles working with Greek translations could have reached the same conclusion.

The verse immediately before Isaiah 35:5-6, cited above, reads: "Say to the anxious, 'Be strong. Do not fear. Behold your god! Vengeance comes, requital. God, he will come and save you.'" The text in Isaiah continues with the citation used in the Gospels, "then the eyes of the blind will be opened." Jews knowing their Isaiah and grasping the allusion in a Q form of the story would have recognized the incomplete citation out of context. By recontextualizing the abbreviated citation, they would have understood that Jesus referred to himself as an ongoing theophany of the God of Israel, an active divine presence on earth parallel to that of God in heaven, and they could have shared their binitarian understanding with others.

Most people would not have not thought through the implications of the Q story or of the Jesus stories because most people are not systematic thinkers. Others, who may have grasped or intuited the implications may not have been bothered by them, comprehending in some way that theological knowledge is complicated, full of logical contradictions, and hardly worth worrying about. Yet others of more rational bent may have come to view binitarian (or bitheistic) explanations as problematic when presented with a question such as "How, then, do you explain 'Hear O Israel, the Lord our God, the Lord is one'"?

The issue may have come to a head in some Christian circles by the second half of the first century.

Jesus as Divine in the Gospels (60-120 CE)

Judging from their compositions, the Gospel writers felt that their imagined audiences required an education not only in the "Christ and him crucified" types of stories, but also in "Jesus-God" stories.

The Gospel writers, however, had additional concerns beyond the possible binitarian implications of Jesus stories.[39] Nourished by conceptualizations of deity molded in Hellenistic broth, their individual understandings of God and of the nature of Jesus were more complicated than Jewish or pagan ones could be. They had to confront Hellenistic notions gaining popularity in the first and second centuries that no matter their names, all gods were real and concerned in one way or another with all people; and what is more, local names were merely labels for the same known deities.[40] Gospel writers were concerned that the facticity of particular events be recognized and that the uniqueness of Jesus, who was not to be dissolved in the broth, be acknowledged by readers of their redacted collections of stories.

On the one hand, they had to express their new ideas by reshaping conceptions from their pre-Christian past, and on the other, they had to address objections to their claims that might come from pagans and Jews. To do so they had to present their theses, ignore or refute objectionable ideas, and reshape others by adding to the stock of Jesus stories. The Gospel writers were not philosophical theologians, but rhetorical storytellers. Rhetoricians have objectives. The Gospel writers have to be imagined as self-designated teachers motivated by dissatisfaction with some state of affairs who wrote with the specific intent that their edition of Jesus stories right matters and keep others from thinking improperly.

The following paragraphs address how and why each preprogrammed his readers to interpret the Jesus-God stories in a particular way. Their different interpretative strategies moved the stories beyond Paul's explicit claims about them.

The first sentence of Mark informs readers that Jesus was different from all people: "The beginning of the good news of Jesus Christ, the Son of God" (1:1). Mark, does not, however, expound on the significance of his statement because he intended his Gospel to be a mystery about the nature of Jesus.

Following the tympanic introductory sentence, Mark narrates that the adult Jesus came from the Galilee and was baptized by John, and that as he emerged from the water "he saw the heavens torn apart and the Spirit descending like a dove on him. And a voice came from heaven, 'You are my beloved son with whom I am well pleased.'" This spirit immediately drove Jesus into the wilderness where Satan tempted him unsuccessfully.[41] Some time later, after John was arrested, Jesus returned to the Galilee and began to preach (Mark 1:11-14).

Mark 1:10 reveals that something unique happened to Jesus at his baptism, but leaves details of the dovelike descent of the Spirit unclear. The divine utterance is recognizable as a standard adoption formula on the basis of its usage in the Hebrew Bible and in Mesopotamia. The significance of the formula is that at that moment of their utterance, the words "you are *my* son" changed the status of Jesus. But, since the Gospel is neither a Hebrew document of pre-exilic Israel nor a product of the ancient Near East, but of Israel in late antiquity and the Greco-Roman Near East, the phrase need not be construed as an adoption formula. The complete utterance might mean no more than Jesus was his "son" even prior to the baptism, and that what pleased he whose voice was heard was that Jesus had finally embarked on his predestined journey by undergoing baptism. Mark left this matter unsettled.

As a consequence of his baptism experience, Jesus, now inspirited permanently, was suddenly endowed with an awareness of who he truly was and how his life was scripted. The brief mention of the spirit compelling his activities signaled to Mark's audience that all that followed in his story was significant and deserving of close attention: the words of Jesus, his behavior and his deeds.

But, within the framework of Mark, Jesus' self-understanding was his private secret. Only the evangelist, Jesus, and the readers knew the secret—otherwise they would not be reading the story—but nobody else in the world of the narrative itself was aware of it.

Mark informs his readers that throughout his career, even though Jesus did and said things that should have enabled his disciples to discern who he was, they had a difficult time doing so. After rebuking the storming wind, Jesus asked his disciples, "Why are you afraid? Do you still have no faith?" All they could mumble among themselves is "Who then is this, that even the wind and the sea obey him?" (Mark 4:41 and see 6:49). In Mark 8:29, Peter finally figures it out and declares in the presence of the disciples, "You are the Messiah," Jesus, acknowledges the correctness of this deduction by ordering the disciples not to tell others. Nowhere does Jesus explain to them what the designation "Messiah" meant in his particular case.

In chapter 9, Mark relates that after witnessing his transfiguration and Jesus' conversing with Elijah and Moses, God informed three of his disciples from an overshadowing cloud, "This is my beloved son, listen to him" (Mark 9:7). Having come close to the truth about Jesus' nature rationally when they guessed "Messiah," and having been informed by a divine voice about Jesus' nature, the disciples are finally aware of who he is. Moreover, in this scene, Mark clarifies that what sounded at his baptism was not an adoption formula, but something that a pleased father uttered about his son. At the moment the Gospel solved one mystery, it presented another.

Again Jesus ordered them to tell nobody what they had seen "until after the Son of Man had risen from the dead" (Mark 9:2-13). Although the disciples were puzzled by what Jesus meant—a dense lot, those disciples, whose lack of understanding must have brought smiles to the lips of Mark's audience—they kept silent. The rest of Mark consists of more clues intended to clarify Jesus' reference to rising from the dead, a mystery clarified only in the story of the first Easter in Mark 16.

The traditional end of Mark narrates how after the resurrected Jesus gave final instruction to his disciples, "Lord Jesus . . . was taken into heaven and sat down at the right hand of God" (Mark 16:19). A position befitting the beloved son. This conclusion of Mark's inductive approach resulted in a view of Jesus imagined above as one that Jews may have reached about Jesus' nature after considering the implications of Jesus stories.

The authors of Matthew and Luke were impatient with Mark's inductive method of instructing readers about Jesus' nature. Moreover, they may have objected to Mark's lack of clarity with regard to the time that Jesus acquired his divine nature: at birth or after baptism. In their birth narratives, Matthew and Luke taught that a particular child was conceived purposefully by the Holy Spirit who had determined a special destiny for that child. According to these Gospels, Jesus, born of the Holy Spirit, was divine from birth, and divinely appointed to fulfill a role in saving his people from the consequences of their own sins (Matt. 1:20-21; Luke 1:35-45; 2:10, 26, 29-30).

Matthew and Luke teach explicitly at the beginning of their respective narratives that a particular child was conceived and bore the character of his divine origin from birth. Consequently, there is absolutely no ambiguity in what the phrase, "this is my beloved son" means in the baptism stories of Matthew 3:1-17 and Luke 3:1-21. The fact that God was presented as his father literally in Matthew 1:20-21, and in a somewhat more ambiguous sense in Luke 1:34-36; 2:49-50, offset any possible thought that Jesus was tainted with original sin as were all men according to the teachings of Paul that antedate the Gospels.[42]

Mark's secret is never a secret in Matthew and Luke. Consequently, readers of Matthew and Luke knew to look for signs while reading and to follow the characters in the Gospels who regularly figure out that there is something special about Jesus, grasping it intuitively. In all three Gospels, the divine man is the unanointed anointed one, but there is much more to him than a title. His "divine" ancestry provided him with supra-natural, divine powers illustrated in many stories.

No Jesus stories illustrate personal, individual traits or virtues such as loyalty, steadfastness, charity, or piety. The stories about Jesus were not intended to present him as one whose character could be emulated by those hearing them. If anything, they create a gulf between the hearers and Jesus. What he was capable of doing no mere man could do. The stories do present, however, role models to be emulated. The characters with whom Matthew and Luke, and, sometimes, Mark intend their audiences to identify are the people in the stories who see Jesus, who listen to him or hear about him and thereby come to recognize his true divine nature, and to believe in him at some level.

Those hearing the Gospels were supposed to listen to the narrative voice guiding them, see what the crowds described saw and hear what they heard. They were supposed to identify with Jesus' audiences and even with his confused disciples. The Gospel writers intend that their own audience respond, as did the pious and even the questioning characters in their compositions, in faith and with understanding.

There is no possibility of confusion, though, in the Gospel of John. This Gospel's famous opening verses introduce a top-down story, declaring unmistakably the incarnation of *theos*, not the en-theosing of the carnate: "In the beginning was the Word and the Word was with God, and the Word was God. He was in the beginning with God. All things came into being through him, and without him not one thing came into being" (John 1:1-3a). The introduction associates the Logos with God on the one hand and identifies it as God on the other. A few verses later, John identifies the Logos with Jesus: "and the Word became flesh and lived among us, and we have seen his glory, the glory as of a father's only son, full of grace and truth" (John 1:14).[43] John understands Jesus as God become human, not playing human. Moreover, he teaches that Jesus-God was a preexistent divine figure who was "in the beginning with God" (John 1:2). In responding to the question, "Have you seen Abraham?" Jesus says, "Truly, I tell you before Abraham was, I am" (John 8:58), and in a prayer, he says, "now, glorify me, Father, with yourself with the glory that I had with you before the cosmos existed" (John 17:5).

Incapable of explaining the mechanics of how the Word that was God became flesh, though it happened, John dispenses with a sticky, problem-filled birth narrative. Even Jesus, as portrayed by John, avoids a query requiring that he deal with the question of incarnation. Jews ask themselves in his presence: "Is not this Jesus, the son of Joseph, whose father and mother we know? How can he now say, 'I have come down from heaven'?" In response, Jesus ignores their questions and delivers a sermonette about the Father that hinges on a verse in Isaiah 54:13, "And they shall be taught by God." John recognizes that Jesus dodged the question and reports that dissatisfied with his response, "many of his disciples turned back and no longer went about with him" (John 6:41-71).

No unsafe metaphors for him. John came to close doors on speculation, not open them.

Elsewhere, as in the Gospel's opening lines, John equates Jesus and God. In a discussion with Jews in the temple, John has Jesus say "The Father and I are one" (John 10:30), and in a discussion with Philip, he says, somewhat testily, "Have I been with you all this time Philip and you still do not know me? Whoever has seen me has seen the Father. How can you say, 'Show us the Father?' Do you not believe that I am in the Father and the Father is in me?" (John14:8-10).[44] The last citation discloses John's comprehension that though some distinction is to be made in accident between Jesus and God, there is no distinction in essence. Translated into a theological term, John attempts to collapse binitarian arguments by arguing that there are two aspects to the single whole that is God.

This element in John's thought has been traced back easily to Ben Sirah's "Praise of Wisdom," composed at the beginning of the second century BCE. The poem narrates that Wisdom, formed by God before time in the beginning to exist forever, is sent by him to dwell in Israel (Sirah 24:3-12, and see Prov. 8). In the poem, Wisdom shares her teachings with her people. In John, although the Logos become Jesus did likewise, John erased the distinction between God and Jesus. In John, Jesus is an avatar of God.

When examined through John's theo-Christology around 100-120 CE, the difficulties that the synoptic Gospels had in clarifying and expressing Jesus' divine nature as revealed through what he reportedly did and said disappear. Despite many loose ends discernable in John's nonsystematic attack on binitarianism, the Gospel advances a theological argument to which teachings, stories, and apothegms of the Synoptics could be accommodated and through which they could be understood.

One of the many functions of the birth narratives was to make quite clear to even the most dense of readers that binitarianism was not a valid way of viewing the relationship between Jesus and God. According to Mark, Matthew, and Luke, Jesus was divine but not exactly God, Godly but not quite God. Matthew said it most boldly, he was God's son, filled with God. John, however, with no reference to the Synoptics, addressed the binitarian conception that emerged from Jesus-God stories in terms of a cosmos within which time collapsed so that Jesus-God was ubiquitous in time and immanent in all places. Consequently, binitarianism could only be explained as a perceptional error, a faulty two-dimensional view of a three-dimension reality.

This explanation of the Gospels reads them as formal, instructional documents and interprets their organization and presentation of material as part of a curriculum. Although this is how contemporary readers encounter Jesus stories, the preceding analyses of how Jews in the second century CE interpreted them outside of a Gospel context assumes that the relevant stories were usually free floating, and not coordinated in any particular way, even after the Gospels were written.[45]

Conclusions

Stories such as those considered above, preserved in the Gospels but told individually without the explicit "divine Jesus" theology, would neither have offended nor tested the credulity of many Jews, and might have convinced them that Jesus was divine simply because he had done in the past what they said that God did every day. Properly told, the stories could cohere cognitively with what Jews thought God to be doing in the world. These stories would not have been stumbling blocks for them because they had no commitment to their implications. Jews would have "gotten" the points of these stories immediately whether they considered them credible or not.[46]

Additionally, for many Jews, particularly those who thought themselves still living in the biblical age, there would have been nothing overly strange about the idea of God assuming human form and being among people. Stories premised exactly on that appear in the Hebrew Bible. For example, in Genesis 18, God is one of three strangers who visit Abraham, wash their own feet, recline in the shade of a tree, and dine on soft veal. He converses with both Abraham and Sarah, and then haggles with Abraham over the fate of righteous people in Sodom.

In Exodus 24:9-11, Moses, Aaron, Nadab, Abihu, and seventy elders ascend and "see the God of Israel: under his feet there was the likeness of sapphire, like the sky for purity. Yet he did not raise his hand against the heads of the Israelites; they beheld God, and they ate and drank."

From scripture, Jews knew that when it was God's desire that they do so, people could see him.[47] Consequently, they would have had no problem dealing with the binitarian implications of the Jesus stories had they thought in theological categories. Binitarianism would not have been problematic because they knew from the Bible that God came and went at his will and could assume human shape and mass at his will. But, even if God had become Jesus and done these things, that was long before their own time. Christianity may have appeared attractive to them, but not compelling.[48]

But why, then, was "Christ and him crucified" a stumbling block?

1) The idea of individual resurrection was not new. Biblical passages supporting the idea have been discussed above. Belief in its reality and broad based efficacy runs through the martyr stories in 2 Maccabees. By the first century CE, many people who considered themselves pious and faithful believed that they would be resurrected. These views are defended at great length in 4 Maccabees dated to the first century, a composition contemporary with the Gospels.[49] Consequently, Paul's repeated claim in Acts that he is teaching resurrection as a common belief is valid (Acts 23:6; 24:15; 26:8, 23).[50] What was difficult for Jews would have been Paul's teachings about who would be deserving of resurrection.

2) Reading Paul through the eyes of the post-Pauline Gospels created additional difficulties. There was no precedent in Tanakh for the death and resurrection of God, the epochal claim of Christians, and the creative, generative core of Christian beliefs. Neither was there a developed precedent for the death and resurrection of the Messiah.[51] The closest that Jewish texts could provide was their descriptions of God's self-willed absence from Israelite affairs and his retreat from their care, when he "hid his face." There was thus no comparable story whose authority might support the claim.

Some Jews in the second century CE, at the margins of rabbinic influence, may have accepted the veracity of Jesus stories in some general way. Of these, some or many may have become ecclesiastical converts.

Among those particularly open to the binitarian implications of the Jesus stories may have been people familiar with traditions about human savior figures of the past such as Adam, Enoch, also known as the angel Metatron (who was also identified, sometimes, with God), and Melchizedek, who had been transported to the heavenly realm where they filled important roles, exercising great power along with God. A large body of pseudepigraphical literature about these individuals circulated in Palestinian Jewish circles by the second century BCE and is partially preserved in a few Qumran texts as well as in the Apocrypha. Citations from and allusions to these traditions in rabbinic and New Testament literature attest to their broad dissemination.[52] The binitarian impulse generated by these texts was common in Judaism and did not necessarily lead to the consideration of Christianity as its legitimate expression.[53] Some such Jews, however, may have accepted Jesus stories and allowed for his uniqueness, perhaps even his messiahship, but with an a priori surety in their individual resurrection would have felt no need to join resurrectionist communities. Theirs was a Christianity based on a Jesus who was both God and God returned to teach and provide new instruction for his people.

Theirs was not necessarily a faith concerned with his death and resurrection. They may have thought that resurrectionist communities did not offer them anything that they did not possess already either individually or as members of the Jewish people.[54] Groups of such Jews may have joined together, developed their own interpretations of Jesus' life and death and created communities such as the Ebionites and Elkeseites that would be deemed heretical by Christians in later centuries.[55]

A few, however, hearing the stories, may have accepted the idea of the divine Jesus as understood by the Gospel writers and their followers along with the truthfulness of the unparalleled stories of his death and resurrection in their own era—but before their own time—as interpreted by Paul. These would have become converts of the type that Paul liked, converts by inner conviction.[56] They would have been those who understood Paul to be teaching—though he would not have expressed it as did they—that a particular type of faith enabled one to share the death of the resurrected Messiah-God.[57]

Most, however, like Rabbi Eliezer ben Hyrkanus, may have considered some of the stories interesting and worth talking about with their friends, even as they sensed that they were expressions of *minut*. By the beginning of the third century, with the dynamic spread of Christianity and a sharpening sense of orthodoxy in Palestinian rabbinic circles, *minut* began to shift its meaning from the questionable thoughts of a Jew to a combination of thoughts and actions such as eating nonkosher meat (b. Avoda Zarah 26b).[58]

Most Jews did not become Christians because they did not accept the validity of the Christian narrative testifying to salvivic miracles in their own age.[59] For them, the Hellenistic world was a new age, significantly different from that of the Hebrew Bible and its narratives. Some, however, may have believed that they were still living in the wondrous biblical age and could not fathom why unique events should not occur in their own lifetimes. These may have been more open to the Christian message.

It was against them that a dictum preserved in the Talmud was directed. In response to the question, "Why is Esther compared with the morning star?" the following answer is given: "To teach you that just as the morning star is the end of every night, (the story of) Esther is the end of all miracles" (b. Yoma 29a). This teaching maintained that the age of great miracles had ended in the days of Esther during the period of Persian world dominion.[60]

Discussion Questions

1. The importance of Jesus was gauged differently by individuals and groups after his death. How did the following view him: Paul? Early rabbinic groups? Authors of the Gospels?
2. How did different types of Jewish preknowledge affect Jewish understandings of Jesus?
3. What problems did binitrarian theology pose for Jews? For Christians?

Notes

1. This study is expanded from "Jesus, God of the Hebrew Bible," *Shofar* 29:1 (2010): 14-32, which focused on why some Jews may have been attracted by claims made about Jesus in certain types of stories and why, despite accepting some, they chose not to join Jewish-Christian communities. In addition to augmenting discussion there, this study analyzes how Jewish comprehensions of the nature of Jesus may have stimulated questions for which the birth narratives were appropriate responses. Additionally, it describes the different strategies embraced by Gospel writers in shaping their responses.
2. Many of the stories referred to below from the Tanakh and from the Gospels may be described as *legenda*, a term used originally to describe a genre of medieval stories about saints. They all have simple outlines: a description of the situation requiring a remedy, a request for help, and a description of the deed. See, Ziony Zevit, *The Religions of Ancient Israel: A Synthesis of Parallactic Approaches* (London: Continuum, 2001), 489-91.
3. For descriptions of dramatic conversion experiences and their underlying bases, see the classical study of William James, *The Varieties of Religious Experience: A Study in Human Nature* (New York: Penguin, 1985), 193-208, 212-17, 236-43.
4. Georgia M. Keightley, "Christian Collective Memory and Paul's Knowledge of Jesus," in *Memory, Tradition, and Text: Uses of the Past in Early Christianity*, ed. Alan Kirk and Tom Thatcher, vol. 52, Semeia Studies (Atlanta: SBL, 2005), 129-31.
5. Albert I. Gordon, *The Nature of Conversion* (Boston: Beacon Press, 1967), 2-3.
6. Some manuscripts of First Corinthians read "mystery" (Greek, *mysterion*) rather than "testimony" here. See critical commentaries.
7. William B. Davies, *Paul and Rabbinic Judaism,* 3rd ed. (London: SPCK, 1970) 285-88; E. P. Sanders, *Paul and Palestinian Judaism: A Comparison of Patterns of Religion* (London: SCM Press, 1977), 442-47.
8. Peter Schäfer suggests that by the middle of the second century, in certain circles the name of Jesus was considered one of the most powerful divine names that could be invoked. See, *Jesus in the Talmud* (Princeton, NJ: Princeton University Press, 2007), 57-59.
9. Schäfer considers the various versions of the stories and suggests that the charge was brought because Eliezer associated with Christians or those sharing Jesus' teachings and was willing to apply one of them in a halachic discussion. See Schäfer, *Jesus in the Talmud*, 41-45.
10. Robert T. Herford, "The Problem of the Minim," in *Jewish Studies in Memory of George A. Kohut*, ed. Salo Baron and Alexander Marx (New York: Alexander Kohut Memorial Foundation, 1935), 362-69.
11. *Lord* translates Hebrew *Adonay* that replaced pronunciations of the tetragrammaton, YHWH, in Torah reading and prayer ca. 250-200 BCE.
12. Dalia Marx, "The Morning Ritual in the Talmud: The Reconstitution of One's Body and Personal Identity through the Blessings," *HUCA* 77 (2006): 103-29.
13. The order of blessings in b. Ber 60b differs from that cited above that is common in contemporary prayerbooks and lacked # 2-4. Too much may not be made of this since much in the fixed order of contemporary liturgy owes its origin to the printing press.
14. Lawrence A. Hoffman, *The Canonization of the Synagogue Service* (Notre Dame: University of Notre Dame Press, 1979), 128. Some penitential and apotropaic motifs

of *birchot hashachar*, not included in this discussion, are attested in sectarian scrolls from Qumran. See Moshe Weinfeld, *Early Jewish Liturgy: From Psalms to the Prayers in Qumran and Rabbinic Literature* (Jerusalem: Magnes Press, 2003), 196-97, 203-13 (Hebrew).

15. Marx, "The Morning Ritual," 125-26.
16. In defending the formulation of the benediction referring to women, R. Judah points out that women are not obligated to fulfill as many commandments as are men (tos Ber 6:18).

    B. Menach 43b mentions other formulations of these benedictions used during the Tannaitic period: who made me an Israelite (used in the Sephardic ritual); who did not make me a woman; who did not make me a boor. (The latter formulation is found also in the j. Berach 9: 2.) Tos. Ber 6:18, cites R. Judah attempting to support the statements by referring to passages for two of the alternative formulations: 1) Isa. 40:17, "all the gentiles are like nothing before him," (and by implications who would want to be born a gentile); 2) M. Avot 2:5 presents the aphorism "a boor does not fear sin," implying that nobody would want to be born a boor.
17. On these three benedictions, see Joseph Tabory, "The Benedictions of Self-Identity and The Changing Status of Women and of Orthodoxy," *Kenishta* 1 (2001): 107-38.
18. The final words of the expression "our God and *God of our fathers*" in the first benediction of the *Shemoneh Esreh* appear to be redundant. Binyamin Katzoff explains them as becoming prominent liturgical statements in Eretz Israel during the fourth century CE as a Jewish response to primarily gentile Christian claims that they, rather than Jews, were God's chosen people and that they had inherited Israel's relationship with God. See "'God of our Fathers': Rabbinic Liturgy and Jewish Christian Engagement," *JQR* 99:3 (2009): 316-20. I would add that the phrase functioned as an assertion of ethnic self-identity against Christians who viewed themselves as a deracinated religious community. (Katzoff's conclusion to this point is less direct. See pp. 321-22.)
19. Louis Finkelstein, "The Development of the Amidah," *JQR* 16 (1925): 2. The rabbinic authority for such a conclusion is a *baraita* in b. Meg 17b. Other traditions suggest that it was first composed in the late pre-exilic or Persian periods (b. Ber 33a; b. Meg 17b). These references may be to the time of its earliest formulations. See Ismar Elbogen, *Jewish Liturgy, A Comprehensive History* (Philadelphia: The Jewish Publication Society/The Jewish Theological Seminary, 1993), 25, 201-03. This version of Elbogen is based on the original 1913 German edition and the Hebrew edition of 1972 edited by Joseph Heinemann et al. that incorporated material introduced by Elbogen into subsequent editions along with Heinemann's own notations based on his own research up to 1972. For a critique of Finkelstein's research, see p. 393, note 1 and pp. 395-96, note 4.
20. An earlier form of *Gevurot* evolved into part of a Christian liturgy known as the "Apostolic Constitutions." See Kaufmann Kohler "The Origin and Composition of the Eighteen Benedictions with a Translation of the Corresponding Essene Prayers in the Apostolic Constitutions," *HUCA* 1 (1924): 412-14. Although Kohler's identification of the underlying prayer as Essene is doubtful in terms of what has been learned from the Dead Sea Scrolls, its Jewish nature and origin is fairly certain.

    The Apostolic Constitutions exist only in a fourth century C.E. Christian version, but research indicates that it originated as a first century CE Jewish composition. See David A. Fiensy, *Prayers Alleged To Be Jewish: An Examination of the*

Constitutiones Apostolorum (Chico, CA: Scholars Press, 1985) 143-48. For a summary of Jewish elements in early Christian liturgy, see Abraham Z. Idelsohn, *Jewish Liturgy and Its Development* (1932; repr., New York: Schocken Books, 1967), 301-08.

21. On the basis of manuscripts and various references to this and the following predication in rabbinic discussions, Louis Finkelstein determined that the adverb *chesed*, grace, in this predication and *rachamim rabbim*, abundant mercy, in the following one were added in the Middle Ages; therefore, they are not addressed in the following discussion. See Louis Finkelstein, "The Development of the Amidah: Appendix I," *JQR* 16 (1925): 143-54. See also the short form of the *gevurot* in the Eretz Israel version of the benedictions found in the Cairo Genizah where the adverbs are missing in Richard S. Sarason, "The Persistence of Penitential Prayer in Rabbinic Judaism," in Mark J. Boda, Daniel K. Falk, Rodney A. Werline, eds., *Seeking the Favor of God,* vol. 3 of *The Impact of Penitential Prayer Beyond Second Temple Judaism* (Atlanta: SBL, 2008), 20.

    The additional words were based on the hendiadys in Zech. 7:9; Isa. 63:7, 44:8; Jer. 16:5.

22. For a theological analysis of the Gevurot with its emphasis on resurrection within the structure of the complete prayer, see Reuven Kimelman, "The Daily 'Amidah and the Rhetoric of Redemption," *JQR* 79.2-3 (1998-99): 182-86.

23. On Dan. 12:1-3, the clearest, but not only, reference to resurrection. See Jon L. Levenson, *Resurrection and the Restoration of Israel* (New Haven: Yale University Press, 2006), 181-200. On the contemporary Jewish rejection of belief in resurrection though it is part of a prayer repeated three times a day, see pp. 1-22. For the notion of the resurrection, see also Isa. 26:19: "Let your dead live, your corpses rise. Wake and sing, dwellers of dust."

24. Which of these "almost synonyms" in English captures the sense intended by the Hebrew authors depends on their conceptions of death. In the pre-exilic period, it is possible that death was conceived as something happening to people on earth that resulted in their translation to Sheol where they continued an after-death existence in desiccated bodies but with each personality intact. See, Ziony Zevit, "The Two-Bodied People, Their Cosmos, and The Origin of the Soul," in *Maven in Blue Jeans: Festschrift in Honor of Zev Garber*, ed. Steven L. Jacobs (Purdue University Press, 2009), 465-69.

    Conceptions of what happened after death most likely changed significantly in the post-exilic period, and then again during the Greco-Roman period, during which the *Shemoneh Esreh* was composed. With each different conception of death, the idea of what revivication or resurrection accomplished changed also.

25. It is uncertain what predication 16 means. Translated literally, "makes live the dead," when compared to predication 20 could lead to the conclusion that the liturgy declares that the resurrection of some may already have occurred and that it is an ongoing process rather than a future event.

26. See Elbogen, *Jewish Liturgy*, 39 for a discussion of these phrases.

27. This sobriquet remains in use to this day.

28. We cannot speak of a Tanakh canon at this point in time, since canonization, understood as an official act performed by an authoritative body, did not occur in the first century CE even though the Torah, Psalms, and most of books in the Former and Latter prophets circulated as collections and comprised, at least part of, the Jewish scroll-shelf. See, Ziony Zevit, "The Second-Third Century Canonization of the

Hebrew Bible and Its Influence on Christian Canonizing" in *Canonization and Decanonization: Papers Presented to the International Conference of the Leiden Institute for the Study of Religions (LISOR), Held at Leiden 9-10 January 1997*, ed. Arie van der Kooij and Karel van der Toorn (Leiden: Brill, 1998), 133-60.

29. Ephraim E. Urbach, *The Sages—Their Concepts and Beliefs* (Jerusalem: Magnes Press, 1975), 86-96 (and the accompanying notes in volume 2, the footnote volume).
30. B. L. Blackburn provides a verse-specific breakdown of the multiple attestations of Jesus' miraculous activities broken down by sources and genres. See "The Miracles of Jesus," in *Studying the Historical Jesus: Evaluations of the State of Current Research*, ed. Bruce Chilton and Craig Evans (Leiden: Brill, 1994), 356-57. See also the detailed analyses in Marvin Meier, *A Marginal Jew*, vol. 2 (New York: Doubleday, 1994), 618-45.
31. The standard solutions proposed for the Synoptic Problem—the Griesbach Hypothesis, the Two-Source Hypothesis, or variations based on proto-Gospels or the schools of Matthew and Luke—are beyond the scope of my interest in this study. I do, however, use the siglum Q when referring to stories and dicta reported in Matthew and Luke exclusively.
32. I thank an anonymous colleague who directed my attention to this element in the Legion story following my presentation at the annual meeting of the Catholic Biblical Association in Omaha, Nebraska (August, 2009).
33. The Gospel stories about Jesus and the sea have more in common with Canaanite myths about the Baal-Yam conflict than with passages from the Tanakh that draw from the same myths. This idea is developed in the context of other pericopes dealing with the control of chaos by Foster R. McCurley, *Ancient Myths and Biblical Faith: Scriptural Transformations* (Philadelphia: Fortress, 1983), 58-60.
34. These are variants of the same story.
35. See Meir Bar Ilan,"Exorcism by Rabbis: Talmudic Sages and Magic [Hebrew]," *Da'at* 34 (1995): 17-35 and references in note 3. This is available online at http://faculty.biu.ac.il/~barilm/mag.html.

    Paula Fredriksen suggests that the exorcism traditions are most likely historical: "Jesus as exorcist, healer (even to the point of raising the dead), and miracle worker is one of the strongest, most ubiquitous, and most variously attested depictions in the Gospels. All strata of this material—Mark, John, M-traditions, L-traditions, and Q—make this claim. This sort of independent multiple attestation supports arguments for the antiquity of a given tradition, implying that its source must lie prior to its later, manifold expressions, perhaps in the mission of Jesus himself. See *Jesus of Nazareth, King of the Jews: A Jewish Life and the Emergence of Christianity* (New York: Knopf, 1999), 114.
36. Joseph A. Fitzmyer presents cogent arguments for the priority of the incident in Matthew, but notes that it is constructed from Q material. See *The Gospel According to Luke (I-IX)* (Garden City, NY: Doubleday, 1981), 662-63.
37. Such a story was available to Matthew in Mark 7:31-37 had he wanted everything to line up perfectly.
38. Herbert Basser, *The Mind Behind the Gospels* (Boston: Academic Studies Press, 2009), 264. I thank Prof. Basser for his observations when we discussed this matter in May 2009 as well as for his emails with additional information in June 2009.

    See also É. Peuch, "*4Q Apocalypse messianique*" in *Émile Peuch, Discoveries in the Judaean Desert XXV: Qumran Grotte 4, xviii* (Oxford: Clarendon Press, 1998),

10—A broken text refers to freeing the bound, opening the eyes of the blind, etc., and includes a line "and mighty acts that never were Adonay will do as he said."

39. See, Jeffrey S. Siker, "Abraham, Paul and the Politics of Christian Identity," *Jewish Studies Quarterly* 16 (2009): 61-62.
40. Arthur D. Nock, *Early Gentile Christianity and Its Hellenistic Background* (New York: Harper & Row, 1964), 8-11.
41. The text of Mark is overly precise, suggesting that the evangelist is alluding to stories already familiar to his audience: "He was in the wilderness forty days, tempted by Satan; and he was with the wild beasts and the angels waited on him" (Mark 1:13). In the absence of preexistent stories, it is the type of passage that invites midrashic expansion to clarify details of his encounters with Satan, the beasts, and the angels.
42. Paul, however, did not originate the notion that humanity was tainted with primal sin owing to events in Eden. This idea appears in Hellenistic Jewish sources from the second century BCE on. See Frederick R. Tennant, *The Sources of the Doctrine of the Fall and Original Sin* (1903; repr., New York: Schocken Books, 1968), 106-247.
43. On the origin, development, and application of Logos theology to Jesus, see the recent study of Daniel Boyarin, *Border Lines: The Partition of Judaeo-Christianity* (Philadelphia: University of Pennsylvania Press, 2004), 89-111 and the relevant literature cited there.
44. Raymond E. Brown suggests that the New Testament identifies Jesus as God infrequently and that wherever such predications occur—John 1:18, 20:28; Rom. 9:5; Heb. 1:8, 2 Peter 1:1—the passages are difficult and tend to occur in hymns or doxologies. He takes this as an indication that the title "God" was more quickly applied to Jesus in liturgical formulae than in narrative or epistolary literature. See, *The Gospel According to John (i-xii)* (Garden City, NY: Doubleday, 1966), 24.
45. Schäfer argues that the Gospel of John, the most anti-Jewish of the Gospels, was known to Amoraim, Jewish teachers of Babylon (modern Iraq) cited in the Babylonian Talmud. Some form of his Gospel or, at least, of its stories and interpretation of events was known to them since they provide some of the most truculent counter-stories that refute the Gospel's versions on specific points. See *Jesus in the Talmud*, 122-29.
46. An evaluation of the types of stories that Jews told about Jesus stories is found in Schäfer, *Jesus in the Talmud*. As Schäfer shows, some of these were counter-stories, Jewish retorts to various claims made about Jesus by Christians. He emphasizes that the Jewish stories are unimportant for historical Jesus studies, but of major significance for the study of Jewish-Christian relationships from the second through the seventh centuries.
47. On the topic, see James Kugel, *The God of Old: Inside the Lost World of the Bible* (New York: The Free Press, 2003), 5-36; Esther J. Hamori, *When Gods Were Men: The Embodied God in Biblical and Near Eastern Literature* (Berlin: Walter de Gruyter, 2008), 1-128.
48. Binitarianism emerged as a serious theological problem in rabbinic circles when sages comprehended that Jewish Gnosticism, Enochic Literature, and early Jewish-Christian metaphysics raised the issue of multiple authorities in heaven. That topic, however, is beyond the scope of this paper.
49. Daniel R. Schwartz suggests that 2 Maccabees should be read as presenting the following themes in order: sin + divine punishment + martyrdom + triumph. Sin is reflected by Hellenization (ch. 4) and divine punishment (4:16-17) in attacks on

Jerusalem and decrees against Jewish religious practice (5:1-6:1). The martyrdom stories of chs. 6-7 appear to set the stage for the military successes and triumphs in ch. 8-15. See his concise presentation in "Foils or Heroes? On Martyrdom in First and Second Maccabees," *AJS Perspectives* (Spring 2009): 10-11. To this I add that the theme of belief in resurrection accompanies the martyrdom stories.

50. According to the author of Acts, Paul tailored his message out of conflicting, vague notions about resurrection to each particular Jewish audience in order to get them through the door. See, Davies, *Paul*, 299-306. For evolving ideas about resurrection from the fifth through the first centuries BCE, see the texts collected in George W. E. Nickelsburg, *Resurrection, Immortality and Eternal Life in Intertestamental Judaism*, Harvard Theological Studies 26 (Cambridge: Harvard University Press, 1972) and Nickelsburg's synthesis on pp. 174-76.

51. 4 Ezra, a composition of the first half of the second century CE does refer to a messianic son of God who will appear and die after 400 years (4 Ezra 7:26-29). This attests to the notion in Jewish circles; but aside from the cursory mention, no other information is provided in the text. See Nickelsburg, *Resurrection*, 172. There must have been more to this tradition, but contemporary scholars do not know what it was.

52. James H. Charlesworth, "Messianology in the Biblical Pseudepigrapha," in *Qumran-Messianism*, ed. James H. Charlesworth, Hermann Lichtenberger, and Gerbern S. Oegma (Tübingen: Mohr Siebeck, 1998), 29-36; Gerbern S. Oegma, "Messianic Expectations in the Qumran Writings," in Charlesworth et al., *Qumran-Messianism*, 81-82; Gary Anderson, "The Exaltation of Adam and the Fall of Satan," in Gary Anderson, Michael Stone, and Johannes Tromp, eds., *Literature on Adam and Eve: Collected Essays* (Leiden: Brill, 2000), 85-87, 96-108; F. L. Horton, *The Melchizedek Tradition: A Critical Examination of the Sources to the Fifth Century A.D. and in the Epistle to the Hebrews* (London: Cambridge University Press, 1976), 74-79; P. S. Alexander, "From the Son of Adam to Second God: Transformations of the Biblical Enoch," in *Biblical Figures Outside the Bible,* ed. Michael E. Stone and Theodor A. Bergren (Harrisburg, PA: Trinity Press International, 1998), 87-122; Birger A. Pearson, "Mechizedek in Early Judaism, Christianity, and Gnosticism," in M. E. Stone et al., *Biblical Figures Outside the Bible*, 176-202; Igor R. Tantlevskij, *Melchizedek Redivivus in Qumran?* (Krakow-Mogilany: Enigma Press, 2004), 9-15, 22-26.

53. On Jewish binitarianism, see Boyarin, *Border Lines*,120-25, 134-45. Boyarin's analyses are significant in that they enable us to see how small the gap may have been between Jewish binitarianism and some early Christian beliefs. Just as some of the rabbis dealt with it through deft eisegesis and clever rhetoric, so too did Gospel writers.

54. For example, in 4 Ezra, a composition of the first century CE, God refers to the Messiah as his son (though in what sense is unclear), who will die. His death would be followed by a period of judgment lasting seven years, during which all would be resurrected, righteous and unrighteous so that they could be judged and assigned their ultimate destiny (4 Ezra 7:28-43).

55. See, Jean Daniélau, *The Theology of Jewish Christianity*, vol. 1 (London: Darton, Longman & Todd/ Henry Regnery, 1964), 55-85.

56. Samson H. Levey has argued that Simeon ben Zoma, a sage active during the first half of the second century, became a Jewish Christian on the basis of metaphysical speculations. Although Levey's views won few adherents when published almost forty years ago, they should be reevaluated in the light of changed comprehensions

about the dynamics of the relationships between Jews, Jewish-Christians, and Gentile-Christians in the early centuries of the church (see, e.g., Boyarin, *Border Lines*, 143). See S. H. Levey, "The Best Kept Secret of the Rabbinic Tradition," in *The Text and I: Writings of Samson H. Levey*, ed. Stanley F. Chyet, South Florida Studies in the History of Judaism 166 (1972; repr., Atlanta, GA: Scholars Press, 1998), 38-45.

57. See the extensive discussion of what was new in Paul vis-à-vis some common, a priori Jewish theological notions by E. P. Sanders, "Convenantal Nomism Revisited," *Jewish Studies Quarterly* 16 (2009): 23-55, but on this specific point, see pp. 52-55.
58. Boyarin, *Border Lines*, 54-63.
59. Alexander Gutman, "The Significance of Miracles for Talmudic Judaism," *HUCA* 20 (1947): 401-02. Gutman suspects that the increasing deprecation of postbiblical miracles in rabbinic sources may have been precipitated by Christian Jewish claims about the authenticity of miracles associated with Jesus (pp. 404-05). See also, Karel van Der Toorn, *Scribal Culture and the Making of the Hebrew Bible* (Cambridge: Harvard University Press, 2007), 233-64.
60. Among identifiable groups who considered themselves to be living in some continuation of the "Tanakh Age" the Qumranites (ca. 100 BCE-100 CE), Enochic Jews (ca. 200 BCE-500 CE?) and Nazarenes (200-400 CE) may be listed. For a summary of evidence bearing on the last named group, see Ray A. Pritz, *Nazarene Jewish Christianity: From the End of the New Testament Period Until Its Disappearance in the Fourth Century* (Jerusalem: Magnes Press, 1988), 108-11.

Avon Gilyon (*Document of Sin*, b. Shabb. 116a) or *Euvanggeleon* (*Good News*)

Herbert W. Basser

The questions I want to explore are complex. 1) Was Jesus a good Jewish boy with some constructive critiques of the status quo—so that today he would be just another blogger in the ilk of *vosizneias.com*? Was he executed by Rome for his anti-Rome sentiments? In short he was not anything like a "Christian"? Or, 2) was he a rebel trying to destroy the foundations of old Jewish life so he could begin a new sect of righteousness?

Let us look for a moment at the reception of Jesus in Jewish society. Although there were exceptions, the vast majority of Jews could not and many still cannot utter his name at all. Even when circumlocutions were used—for example, *oto ish*, *ha-talui*, *yoshka pandira*—they were generally followed by an imprecation. While Maimonides did not detest Christianity as much as he abhorred Islam, still he could not mention the name of Jesus without cursing that his bones should rot.[1] It was generally understood by all Jews, enshrined in the Talmud and the words of Jewish commentators, that Jesus and his disciples were executed by the sages of the Great Court for high crimes and misdemeanors in leading Jews astray—not in the least by deifying himself but far more importantly by preaching an end to Torah observance as ordained by what they came to know as the Oral Law. In short, he was getting others to ignore the authority of ancestral laws and so threatened to undermine Judaism. Another version has it that his disciples were secretly to be sure—really agents of the high court who purposely challenged the Oral Law so as to clearly separate Judaism from Christianity. Sid Z. Leiman has written and lectured on this phenomenon.[2] According to this version, Christian adherence to the traditional law might have been a liability. Here was a group that seems to have jumped over the abyss. Some Jews did and do espouse various notions of divine intermediaries, divine agents, and emanations. They might have addressed prayers to them akin to the controversial but widely recited *slichot* prayer addressed to the *midat rachamim* (something like "the angel of mercy") as channels to the Godhead mythically described by various attributes such as justice or kindness. But Jesus was not just "the Word made flesh." For Christians, in his own being he was deserving of worship and was worshipped as God's junior partner or more. According to Jewish views, a group practicing such idolatry while still adhering to *halakhic* practices would threaten Judaism far more than a group that rejected *halakhic* practices. On the other hand, a doctrine that made the Law passé was not such welcome news either but was preferable to remaking the Law in Christian terms.

Let us now examine a more practical issue. Can the teachings of Christianity in any way make room for the people of Israel as eternal Jews? Christians preached a theology of sonship and liminality: a new world not yet quite arrived but no longer that world demanding Jewish practices. I have read Karl Barth and am not certain of his final stance. He seems to have had a more open attitude towards Jews than most. Frank Talmage, my colleague and in many ways my teacher, understood that Barth does not allow for Christian teachings to have damned the Jew but rather blames Jewish doctrine for their own suffering.[3]

We have looked briefly at Jewish views of Christianity and Christian views of Judaism almost at their most benevolent. I now want to look at how a Jew might best understand Jesus. I see Jesus as a wonder worker and faith healer—a *baal shem* to use an anachronism—a Jew, blessed with many talents. Through a series of unfortunate events, at least unfortunate from my perspective, Jesus was soon pictured to serve the needs of Christian evangelism, as a divine agent who uprooted promises made to the people of Israel and replanted these promises in the Gentile nations. As a case in point, I suggest that Jesus's parables are dramatized by the narratives that creatively interpret these parables. I refer to Matthew's dramatic presentation of his shared Q sources. To my mind the parables (Matt. 13:3-23; Mark 4:2-20; Luke 8:4-15) of the sower and the burning of the weeds are about the Jewish inability to hear Jesus—unlike the Gentiles.

The parables of the tiny mustard seed and its growths and also those of the yield of loaves from a small amount of dough have to do with the theme of abundance from very little, from next to nothing, in the new kingdom.

These parables are followed in the Gospels, for example, Matthew 13 and 14, by Jesus being in demand in Gentile towns while in his own hometown he is shamefully rejected—in consequence of the first set of parables. Then, Jesus feeds thousands with much food from a measly two loaves and a fish—prefigured by the second set of parables. So the simple Gospel message is the Jews, the children of Abraham, Isaac, and Jacob are to end up cast out of the kingdom, burned like stubble while the poor and meek of the nations inherit the kingdom and its ever abundant riches. The Gospels portray a state of existence for its own story occurring between two worlds or two kingdoms, this world and the next. For Jews, this divide in that time frame is untenable, for ultimately, Easter and Passover are not compatible.

But how might Jews make sense of Jesus? In 1925, Harry A. Wolfson published a piece entitled "How the Jews will reclaim Jesus" and republished it in 1962 in the last issue of the *Menorah Journal*. This is where I first saw it. Wolfson regarded Jesus as neither a prophet nor a messiah but as a Galilean sage in the great tradition of Torah learning promulgated by the Pharisees. Wolfson forecast that in the future Jesus would occupy that place in the annals of Jewish historians. At around the same time, Joseph Klausner[4] produced his monumental work on Jesus, almost in the same lens as Geiger had in a previous generation. Klausner saw Jesus as a Jewish failure who rejected living a Jewish life under Rome in favor of living for the coming kingdom. Yet, Jews needed hope in national redemption and Gentiles had no interest in his legal teachings. So his message was lost on the simple peasants to whom he preached his impractical ideals. In the end he is pictured as bitter and angry. For Geiger, Jesus was the reformer model whose message was realized in the reform movement Geiger belonged to. For the Jews of the late nineteenth and early twentieth century, the Jewish background of the Gospels is blatant—the language and idiom though Greek easily reverts into the Hebrew-Aramaic language of the midrashim and Talmuds. Less well known, the world of the artist reclaimed Jesus in a more striking way. We find "Uri Zvi in Front of the Cross" in 1922. It is the suffering Jesus, the suffering Jew, that the artist reclaims and not the sage. The model is already found in Marcus Antokolsky's sculpture *Ecce Homo* (1873), where Jesus is depicted with peyos-sidelocks and a yarmulke. My own work, between the lines to be certain, suggests that the real but now historically invisible Jesus could find audiences in synagogues because he would have been at home with Wolfson in the great yeshiva of Slobodka.[5]

This subtle undertone has not gone entirely, to put it mildly, without its critics from many corners. I have tried to show that the only reason the Gospels preserve anything of Jesus' legal arguments is that they must have a base in early apostolic memory and that these legal arguments have been reworked to heap scorn on the Pharisees and by extension on observant Jews. My sharpest critic is Steven Katz, who claims that Jesus must have had some personal messianic pretensions, or what was his group all about?[6] And that Jesus' arguments against the Pharisees show us a Jesus who rejects all such manner of teaching and has not been layered in the Gospels. Many have told me that Pharisees were only one of many sects of Jews then and had no particular distinction, especially in the Diaspora. But Acts 23:6 knows that Pharisees were common in the Diaspora and so Luke, its author, has no hesitancy in claiming that Paul told the Sanhedrin in his trial that he was a Pharisee and the son of a Pharisee, someone therefore who believed in *tehiyat hametim*: the resurrection of the dead.

Consider the following as indicative of my methods to show the Jewish background to the Gospels, a background undermined by the Gospel writers when it suited their purposes.

Matthew 10:24-25

A student is not above his teacher, nor a slave above his master. It is sufficient for a student to be like his teacher, and the slave like his master. If they call the master of the house "Beelzebub," how much more will [they so slander] the members of his household!

I explain how every syllable here resonates with material that in sum could only be found in talmudic or midrashic sources: The members of the household (Hebrew, *bnei bayit*; see Gen. 15:3) are the servants, the slaves and the attendants. "It is sufficient for a slave to be like his master" was a popular saying that appears over a dozen times in the rabbinic literature (Sifra Lev. [parashat 3] *behar* ch. 4, B Berakhot 58b, Bereishit Rabba 49:2 [ed Theodor-Albeck],[7] as well as the near parallels in Shemot Rabba 42:5, and Tanhuma Genesis, *lekh lekha* 23). Here Jesus uses this saying, but in the form of a well-known legal argument ("sufficient" meaning "ample" for legal argument). Technically the argument is called, literally, "an argument of sufficiency to discover an unknown premise that will be clarified from a known premise" (in Hebrew, *dayo lavo min hadin lihiot kenadun*). A tradition from Sifra Baraita de Rabbi Yishmael 1:3 (and B Baba Batra 111a) shows us how the argument was used by the rabbi:

> How should we apply the principle of kol vehomer? [We need to consider] "And God said to Moses: If her father had spat in her face [an exaggerated way of saying if a woman's father was totally annoyed with her behaviour] would she not carry her shame for 7 days?" (Num. 12:14a). All the more if the Shekhinah was totally annoyed with her should she not be locked away for 14 days? [But God indicated to Moses] that conclusions based on comparing punishments of greater and lesser cases are sufficiently cogent to warrant punishments no more severe than those applied to the original cases [and so He told him] Let [Miriam] be shut out of the camp seven days and afterwards she may be brought back. (Num. 12:14b)

The logic of what Jesus says in Matt 10:24-25 is as follows: because it is beyond any reasonable expectation that a student should ever be shown more respect than his teacher then if it should happen that a teacher is besmirched, it can only follow that his student is to be besmirched in the same fashion. The vocabulary and method of expression is completely part of talmudic culture and unintelligible in any other culture.

What is the nature of the Gospels in respect to its conceptions of Jews and what in them can be rightfully attributed to Jesus? The quest for the historical Jesus occupies a huge corpus of investigation examining criteria to make decisions concerning what gospel traditions are historically accurate and which might be additions reflecting later interests of the Church. Some think the scant material about Jesus in the authentic works of Paul, perhaps our earliest witness to the Jesus tradition, may shed light on the problem. The quest is now said to be in its third phase: phase 1, Jesus as founder of moral ethical movement; phase 2, Jesus as a literary construct of sayings (credible) and narrative (not credible); and now phase 3, Jesus as Jew within the context of his Jewish environment. I have for the most part remained dubious if such theories can lead us anywhere useful. Nevertheless, I have reasons to believe that there are at least three themes that we can ascribe to the historical Jesus: 1) he was a faith healer; 2) he was a preacher who was obsessed with the notion of the coming of the *eschatn*; and 3) he saw himself as instrumental in leading a new movement regarding the concept of faith and strict teachings about behavior. Even the somewhat antinomian Paul can refer to "teachings of the Lord" that he received and passes[8] on, much as Moses received Torah and passed on.[9] There is no Christian document of first century date that will undermine this modest summation.

Where does this leave us? It leaves us with the same historical dilemma we face regarding the character we call Israel Baal Shem Tov: Moshe Rosman discounts the stories in *Shivhei haBesht* as historical while Immanuel Etkes affirms most of them, including the reports of miracles and knowledge of events in far off places as they were occurring.[10] It leaves us with the same historical dilemma facing the teachings of the Kabbalistic doctrines that first surface in writing around the twelfth and thirteenth centuries: Moshe Idel argues they are very original oral Jewish teachings that date back to antiquity, while Gershon Scholem sees the doctrines as foreign to Judaism and which entered Judaism from Christian heretical teachings such as Gnosticism in the twelfth century. Without entering into details, the evidence for all sides of these arguments suggests that a purely positivistic approach will not satisfy the criteria sufficiently to explain the rapid rise of new religious movements if we completely ignore the testimony of their proponents.

In sum, while Rosman considered the Gospels to be analogous to *Shivhei haBesht*, both appearing about 55 years after the death of their respective heroes, he claimed that the stories of the *Besht* were as reliable as the Gospel stories. Etkes maintained the integrity of most of the *Besht* stories with an array of persuasive arguments. If we reverse Rosman's point of similarity and accept Etke's affirnmation of *Besht* stories we could, by Rosman's analogy, also affirm many of the miracle stories in the NT. We might also see the rise of Christianity in terms of the rise of Hasidism and its schisms.

That said, and taking into account Otto Rank's notion that the birth of a hero in ancient writings required certain events to have occurred that marked him as a hero, I want to examine a few aspects of Gospel accounts that might lead us back to considering who the historical Jesus was. I discuss the accounts of Jesus' birth as based on Rank's *topos* and nothing more. I need to begin my historical quest with the realization that the Gospels do not always preserve their sources accurately as I will soon demonstrate. On the other hand, in some instances, it can be shown that Pharisaic/anti-Pharisaic debates actually reflect the rhetoric of early first century Jewish accounts of debates and may contain historical foundations. Let's get down to basics:

The rhetorical features of these Gospel debates are seen to be:

1. Statement of opponent's analogous legal practice as a question: "Is not this your practice in similar cases to our discussion."
2. Conclusion: Therefore you must agree with me to be consistent.

In close detail we see what is being addressed:

a. Something indeed looks problematic and in general your position is right.
b. Here by analogy is why this case is an exception.
c. Understood conclusion: We can now both agree.

The Pharisaic-Sadducean argument in Mishna Yadaim 4:5 echoes this form precisely. The Sadducees complain about a strange Pharisaic purity concern. Rabbi Yochanan ben Zakkai asks them if they do not revere the bones of their own revered high priest more than they would a donkey's bones and then provides the argument that they must likewise agree with a Pharisaic practice that was challenged. Here we have the ideal form of argument. This is the form of debate—a form used in Jesus' debates with the Pharisees.

The next piece of the puzzle is to demonstrate that the NT preserves material that completely undermines the scholarly consensus concerning the development of something commonly called "Rabbinic Judaism" or the doctrine of the dual torahs to use Jacob Neusner's expression. It is commonly held that Second Temple notions and terminology gave way to something now called rabbinization: a newly proclaimed doctrine of an oral law passed down from Sinai to court elders, complex hermeneutics and the development of a body of rabbinic enactments to supplement biblical writings. But Matthew's Jesus argues with Pharisees over the correct application of rabbinic enactments, although they would have been called something else in regards to purity issues—he calls them, as others did, the traditions of the fathers or elders.[11] Furthermore, this Jesus uses the step-by-step exegesis of extraordinary complexity to make points—an exegesis most would want to see as *amoraic* if not later. What I am saying is that no one would invent such convoluted forms if they did not exist in the apostolic tradition and it is hardly likely they were easily understood. The pointer seems to swing towards Jesus himself—or why preserve these things when there are simpler ways to make the same point. In short, some features we call rabbinic are likely earlier than we care to admit, and what we call Gospel invention is likely more authentic than we should care to acknowledge. We need to appear sophisticated, nuanced, and critical, but in so doing we may be missing large chunks of reality that could shed light on Christian origins and what we call rabbinic culture.

We also need to acknowledge the mutual animosity of Jews and Christians in the first century, although it is not politically correct. But I cannot accept that these hatreds are all in-house. The supersessionist message is the major teaching of the NT with little exception. The theological differences, while there, are only minor. These are not in-house Jew versus Jew debates, as many pretend, but debates concerning the view of Christianity as needing neither high priest nor Jewish scribe. But the methods of exegesis of Jews and Christians remain almost identical, although the messages are not compatible.

The Jews (i.e., their Torah) have been superseded by the Gentiles (i.e., their hope) as the chosen people of God, and he redeems the latter from sin and eternal death. The question I pose is: why are the documents so heavily laden with authentic Jewish idioms and concepts if their audience is so predominantly Gentile? Put another way—do the documents at all reflect anything that Jesus did or said, and if so, how much? What charge did Jews level at early Christians about 20 years after the death of Jesus? Let us see how Luke pictures the scene. He writes that Paul is told what Jews are saying about him and his movement:

> Acts 21:21
> And they are informed of thee, that thou teachest all the Jews which are among the Gentiles to forsake Moses, saying that they ought not to circumcise their children, neither to walk after the customs.

The vulnerability of Diaspora Jews "which are among the Gentiles" is a concern of the Talmudic teachers: in Babylonian Talmud Berachot 59a we find, "When God remembers his children living in distress among the nations, he drops tears into the great sea, its sound is heard from one end of the earth to the other and this produces tremors." Jews from the first century and on uses the phrase, "children who live among the Gentiles," to mean Jews in the Diaspora who are prone to abandon God's laws and covenant. And it was these people whom Paul and other missionaries were said to prey upon. At least Luke, one of these missionaries, knows this charge.

My evidence for claiming that the Gospels reworked their original legal sources to heap scorn on the Jews and the laws of the Pharisees (which by the way is assumed as normative in the sources I am about to cite) is evident in both Jewish and Gospel materials. Let me cite one example from Matthew 12:11-12 in illustration of the point. Jesus is called upon to defend his healing of someone's withered arm on the Sabbath. "He said to them, 'Which person from among you who has a single sheep, would not grasp it and lift it out, should it fall into a pit on the Sabbath! Now, how greatly does a human being surpass a sheep! So it is permitted to do good on the Sabbath.'"

The second sentence does not follow from the first. The first assumes that everyone is lax in the law "which one of you who has a single sheep (and nothing else for support) would not hesitate to grasp it and lift it"—a forbidden act under any circumstance. But the next sentence assumes such a scribal *tiltul* (seizing and lifting) prohibition is legally permitted in certain cases of alleviating an animal's pain and then can be subjected to a legal exegesis: how greatly does a human being surpass a sheep! Conclusion, one can heal people on the Sabbath.

What has Matthew or his source done? He made it seem, perhaps inadvertently—through a slight change of "any sheep" to "a single sheep" (since animal suffering trumps scribal rules)—that Jews transgress their own laws. But if so, how does this argument help Jesus? What can we learn about a legal principle from those who break it—nothing at all. It does not take much thought to realize the passage has not been rendered faithfully to what Jesus must have said, namely, that one relieves pain for any animal on the Sabbath even if scribal law is transgressed (and the rabbis know this as evidenced in b Shab 128b). He then properly concluded that one is allowed to save a sheep from a pit and disregard a rabbinic (to use an anachronism) injunction in accomplishing this to save the animal from pain and not because of self-serving purposes. How much more so can one heal people on the Sabbath. Also, the form of "how much more so" is common in arguments permitting healing on the Sabbath. "Now we can argue that if circumcision, which concerns setting just one of the 248 limbs of a man, is done on the Sabbath, so the whole body of a man all the more so can be set right." Sifra Tazria 1:11 and John 7:21-24 are near parallels.

The historicity of actual debates between Christian and Jews over legal matters should not be doubted. It is the only reason I can think of to explain why the Gospels bother with them, for the Christian evidence shows us any manner of dismissing Jewish law from Paul onwards. Jewish sources of a slightly later period concur. A brother and sister from an eminent Pharisaic family come before a Christian legalist for a decision. This story in the Talmud Shabbat 116b (translation based on ed. Soncino)[12] shows that Jews believed self-serving interests governed the attitude of Christians towards Jewish law.

> Imma Shalom, R. Eliezer's wife, was R. Gamaliel's sister (second century). Now, a certain philosopher lived in his vicinity, and he bore a reputation that he did not accept bribes. They wished to expose him, so she brought him a golden lamp, went before him, [and] said to him, "I desire that a share be given me in my [deceased] father's estate." "Divide",ordered he. Said he [R. Gamaliel] to him, "It is decreed for us, Where there is a son, a daughter does not inherit." [He replied], "Since the day that you were exiled from your land the Law of Moses has been superseded and another book given, wherein it is written, 'A son and a daughter inherit equally.'" The next day, he [R. Gamaliel] brought him a Lybian ass. Said he to them, "Look at the end of the book, wherein it is written, I came not to destroy the Law of Moses nor to add to the Law of Moses, and it is written therein, A daughter does not inherit where there is a son." Said she to him, "Let thy light shine forth like a lamp." Said R. Gamaliel to him, "An ass came and knocked the lamp over!"

In this regard it is useful to note objections against the possible historicity of the story raised by Maren R. Niehoff,[13] since she assumed the word gospel—*evangelon*—is not found in the first century. But of course the Gospel of Mark 1:1 refers to his work by this term and Paul uses it in Romans 2:16. This by no means exhausts its NT usages. That such ambivalence over new/old law existed in terms of teachings attributed to Jesus need not surprise.

The term "philosopher" refers to a Christian sage in other places in the Talmud and midrash as well: in Gen. R. 11:7, Rabbi Hoshaya is confronted with the question of why men are not born circumcised if God prefers that. He answers the philosopher and in this conversation the Christian uses the Syriac word *shtutha* in reference to its Christian usage of "shamefully offensive" exactly as it appears in the *Didascalia Apostolorum*: "Also wear shoes on your feet which were designed to arouse *shtiutha* . . . You shall not allow the hair of your head to grow long. and you must not injure the edges of your beard" (Codex Harris 4a). The point is that we have a legal issue, perhaps verbatim, where Christian law is observed but Jewish law not. According to Abraham Epstein's exhaustive study, later sources have tended to translate original Syriac phrasings of the pristine tradition into Hebrew.[14]

One more example will suffice: the Jewish Christian philosopher here is bothered that Jews claim Christians are rebellious when in fact it is they who negate the law of love. The Jew responds that Christians can be called lawless because they can be called atheists. The precise sense of the passage is ambiguous but that much we can surmise. The Jew's arguments centers on the Christian's acceptance of the last half of the Ten Commandments. He apparently wants to show them they do accept at least part of the Law and that is sufficient to justify the claim, on their own terms, that since many Christians break these rules they are rightly called lawless and atheists. The passage goes as follows:

> Tosefta *Shevuot* 3:6:
>
> Hanania ben Kinai explains: [Scripture states:] "[A person who sins and deceives God] and negates his fellow." (Leviticus 5:21; in some biblical versions, Leviticus 6:1).
>
> [This means] a person does not negate his fellow unless he has already diminished his Root (i.e. he is an atheist).
>
> Once Rabbi Reuven delivered a [Sabbath] homily in Tiberius and a philosopher challenged him. He said to him—Who is always rebellious (i.e., lawless)? He replied to him—The one who denies the One who created him (i.e., you are rebellious and also atheists.)
>
> He said—How so?
>
> He replied to him: [We all agree upon] "Honor your father and your mother, do not kill, do not commit adultery, do not steal, do not give false witness,

> do not covet your neighbor's possessions." Now [Leviticus 5:21 champions concord and claims] a person cannot negate a [social] rule (Heb: *davar*) without diminishing the Root. In fine, a person does not go to perform a transgression unless he has already denied the One who commanded it.

The tie between Leviticus 5:21 and the social commandments of the Decalogue in Christian thought is attested as early as the beginning of the second century. Pliny, in a letter to Trajan, refers to the major Christian rite being an oath to abstain from theft, robbery, adultery, and breach of faith—not to deny a deposit which was claimed. This testimony ties together Leviticus 5:21 and Decalogue teachings. The Tosefta has probably preserved, albeit in fragmented form, the essence of a Christian oath as part of the Toseftan commentary to Leviticus 5. There is no reason to suspect that the story is a fictitious story on the part of the editor.

From Jewish and Christian and Roman sources we can establish that legal matters were a key issue in the break of Christian communities and Jewish ones in an early period that stretched into the second century. Perhaps we will not be far wrong that Jesus himself was a faith healer and wonder worker, much like Israel Baal Shem Tov in the eighteenth century, who was familiar with Jewish learning but did not make it the central tenet of his relationship with God. At some point it might have been possible for Hasidim to have broken free of their learning tradition but the rabbinic way of life was too entrenched to lose it. Christianity attracted a strong following amongst Gentiles and so faith in the divinity of Jesus came to dominate the movement and those texts were preserved while the legal ones, now pointless, were of not much interest to the Gentiles at large.

What then remained for Christians to claim about Jews? They rendered Jewish learning and Jewish law as the road leading to evil and the path of Satan. In my forthcoming commentary to Matthew I go through the steps from the birth of Jesus to show how the Gospel is shaped by a Jewish Jesus tending the lost sheep of Israel who reject him. Eventually Jesus says that God will replace the Jews and another nation. Once destined to be rejected, the Gentiles will be chosen in their stead. The stone the builders rejected will become the cornerstone. So reads Matthew 21:42, and the sentiment seems widespread and is echoed in Luke 21:24. A similar motif is to be found as early as Paul. Romans 11:25 speaks of the Jews being frozen in their opposition to Christian doctrine, to some extent, and unable to perceive the reason. That reason is to make room for the Gentiles in the ancient divine promises that are now at a remove from the Jews. Just as Pharaoh's heart was frozen against accepting God's will, so is the Jewish mind. The Gentiles now will be brought to the promised redemptions. This is the basic format of NT teachings, and at its worst, the Jews are rendered sterile, their synagogues houses of Satan (Rev. 2:9-10) and the blood of Jesus eternally on their heads (Matt. 27:25), as scribes preaching Christ replace the Jewish ones rejecting him (Matt. 23:24).

Jews are often outraged by my citing evidence that supports the early Christian claims detailing the vehemence of Jewish expressions of anger and outright hatred, including officially composed curses, against the fledgling Christian religion. Christians may be angered by my claim that the official churches within a decade or so after Jesus sanctioned their saints and evangelists to stop at absolutely nothing within reach to delegitimatize Judaism. The canon of Christianity is rooted in the hatred of Jewish beliefs and practices and as such forms a powerful polemic against Torah-centered culture and substitutes in its stead a Jesus-salvation centered culture.

An American, Larry Proctor, took out a US patent (number 5,894,079, 13 April 1999) on Mexican yellow beans, which he named after his own wife. For every pound of beans anyone in the world sells, this American pirate charges 8 cents US. The Mexicans are angry and refuse to recognize the patent on their own beans. The matter came before the courts and to this date the issue seems to be bogged down in them. In the same way, first-century Christians claimed to have a patent on the very text of the Jewish Bible, its meaning, and the Jewish God. The Jews who had received the text and guarded its every word for centuries were outraged by this act of piracy. There and then began a war which continues in various ways to this very day, for it was in this milieu of strife and discord that Christians put together their foundational documents and thereby preserved this animus as an indispensable part of Christianity. Some may live in denial of it, but even so, the text has touched them no less as they struggle, in vain, to excuse contemporary Jews from the accusations.

Every Semitic religion, whether pagan or monotheistic, understood some relationship between the law dictated by the gods and the happiness of mankind. Judaism, more than any other, formalized the doctrine in promulgating a concept of covenant. Paul denied the efficacy of this covenant of the law after the death of Christ, and that became the major tenet of Christianity—if the law had an efficacy still, then Christ died for nothing. The Jews of course agree—yes, that is correct, Christ's death cannot abrogate the law. Paul, who styled himself as the "Apostle to the Gentiles," strove to prove his points through using the rhetoric of Rabbis and Pharisees to deny their own belief system. Let us see take one example and see how the Rabbis dismissed Paul's claim. Paul is famous for his notion that one is safeguarded from perdition through faith but not through good works. The word for "saved" in Paul's terminology is "justified." There was one early Christian writer, James, who opposed Paul, and Luther charged him as being a heretic.

Undoubtedly, this sentiment was a throwback to the original Jesus cult, which quickly lost its hold on the Christianity that developed in the two decades following the death of Jesus. Let us begin by looking at a passage from the prophet Isaiah, likely the most oft-quoted prophet in Christian literature.

Isaiah 42:21 reads "The Lord is pleased for the sake of his righteousness (*tsidko*); He will magnify the law and make it powerful." This verse is rendered by the Rabbis in Mishnah *Makkot* 3:16, apparently as an answer to Pauline theologies: "God wanted to justify (*le-zakot*) Israel, therefore he enlarged for them Torah and Commandments. This is as Scripture states: The Lord is pleased for the sake of his righteousness" (Isa. 42:21).

This is the precise paraphrase of *Targum Isaiah* 42:21 (1949): *le-zaka'utei yisra'el; yerabei le-avdei oray'tei* ("to justify Israel He increased the workers of His Law"). A variant reading gives us "the works of his law." A Qumran document (4QMMT) refers to "some of the works of the law," and it may simply be that Targum Isaiah utilizes a well known phrase.

When we consider the rabbinic Targum to Isaiah and its restatement in Mishnah *Makkot* in view of Christian contexts, we are struck by the impression that the last two *mishnayot* in *Makkot* (showing that God justifies__ *yizkeh lo*__ the one who avoids "theft and adultery" and justifies their children until the end of time) address sectarian attacks on the Judaism of the sages. Early Christians were concerned with some ethical laws (yet disregarded most, if not all, ritual laws) of the Bible. Early Christians specifically mentioned the sins of theft and adultery, as Pliny noted in his letter to Trajan concerning Christians.

What I have tried to show is that the sources agree on the major issues. Jews and Christians were divided by the efficacy of the covenant and its legal requirements. Jesus himself had not entertained any such notions, nor had his disciples. He was not a reformer or a rebel, but a faith healer and wonder worker who anticipated divine intervention in history to save Jews—if Jews would only be more stringent in their observances and its ethical base teaching mercy and kindness. He was executed by Rome because he was firm in his conviction that the Messiah was knocking at the door and therefore was considered dangerous as John the Baptist had been. Much of the kosher Gospel material concerning Jesus appear to be based on original Jesus reports: the miraculous, the legal teachings, the social critiques, the millenarianism, the manner of expression, and the frustrations, although the sources have been painted over with a thick layer of nonkosher fat.

When we consider the Gospel of John, the matter is entirely different. Here we are faced with a fully divine Jesus who is the visible face, in the flesh, of God. We are also faced with a high Christology that sees Jews as children of Satan (John 8:41). So the Gospels have a Jewish undercoat covered over with layers and more layers of hostile materials. This is not to be seen necessarily as nefarious. All groups define themselves in their literatures as above and over all others who they are not, whose tenets they eschew, and whose religious claims they perceive as threatening. The move from there to physical and political violence may not be as predictable as one would think. It depends on the moral tolerance of the group and a host of other factors. Teaching contempt about others is one thing, denying people the opportunity to practise things we find contemptible is another, and physically abusing them is still another. Of course, it would be better not to teach contempt but that is not how religious and political identity is usually fashioned. The suffering Jew is symbol to the non-Jew of God's vengeance, the domineering Christian is symbol to the Jew of the rod of chastisement. Between these close words lies an inseparable gulf of religious vision. The same is true of *Avon Gilyon* and *Euvanggeleon*.

This is what I think.

Discussion Questions

1. Is there any point to Jewish schools teaching about the New Testament and if so, what should they teach?
2. If Jesus were to appear today would he pray in a church or in a synagogue?
3. How can we make sense of the thoroughly Jewish legal materials in the New Testament and the very strong anti-Jewish message?

Notes

1. See Moses Maimonides, *Epistle to Yemen*, ed. Abraham S. Halkin (New York, 1952), iii-iv (English version).
2. See Sid Z. Leiman, "The Scroll of Fasts: The Ninth of Tevet," *JQR* 74 (1983): 174-95.
3. See Frank Talmage, *Disputation and Dialogue* (Hoboken: KTAV, 1975), 378.
4. Joseph Klausner, *Jesus of Nazareth: His Life, Times, and Teachings* (Boston: Beacon, 1964).
5. See Herb Basser, *The Mind Behind the Gospels* (Boston: Academic Studies Press, 2009).
6. For Katz's position and my reply see Herb Basser, "Katz's Agenda, Chilton's Agenda, Basser's Agenda," *Review of Rabbinic Judaism* 4, no. 2 (2001): 330-43.
7. *Midrash Bereshit Rabbah*, ed. Julius Theodor and Chanoch Albeck (1903-1929; repr., Jerusalem: Wahrman Books, 1965).
8. 1 Cor. 11:23.
9. Mishna Avot 1:1.
10. Moshe Rosman, *Founder of Hasidism: A Quest for the Historical Ba'al Shem Tov* (Berkeley: University of California Press, 1996), ch. 9; Immanuel Etkes, *The Besht: Magician, Mystic, and Leader* (Waltham, MA: Brandeis University Press, 2005), 223.
11. Matthew 15:1-20.
12. *Shabbath,* trans. H. Freedman, The *Babylonian_Talmud; seder Mo'ed,* trans. and ed. Rabbi I. Epstein. London, The Soncino Press, 1938.
13. Maren R. Niehoff, "*Creatio ex Nihilo:* Theology in *Genesis Rabbah* in Light of Christian Exegesis," *Harvard Theological Review* 99.1 (2006): 37-64.
14. Abraham Epstein, *Kitve Avraham Epshtain,* ed. A. M. Habermann, *Mi-Qadmoniyot ha-Yehudim*, vol. 2 (Jerusalem: Mossad ha-Rav Kook, 1950-1957), 345.

Psalm 22 in Pesiqta Rabbati: The Suffering of the Jewish Messiah and Jesus

Rivka Ulmer

Psalm 22 is cited in several critical New Testament passages; by comparison, Psalm 22 is rarely cited in rabbinic literature. In particular, Psalm 22 is used as an expression of personal suffering by the New Testament writers in the crucifixion scenes that recount the suffering of Jesus. In rabbinic literature, Psalm 22 is also cited as relating to the afflictions of a Jewish Messiah. The major rabbinic passage addressing the subject of a suffering Messiah is found in Pesiqta Rabbati, a rabbinic homiletic work that contains numerous messianic passages, as well as four entire homilies that present apocalyptic messianic visions, which mainly focus upon Messiah Ephraim (Pesiqta Rabbati 34, 35, 36, 37). The major premise of this chapter is that the unique character of these passages in Pesiqta Rabbati is based upon an ideological inversion of Jesus. This depiction in Pesiqta Rabbati responds to the Christian view that Jesus was the only messianic figure who suffered and died in pain while bringing salvation to the righteous. This rabbinic text demonstrates that there will be a Jewish Messiah who fulfills the same paradigm.

In the Hebrew Bible, Psalm 22 is a Psalm of lament in the first person singular that voices this persona's claim of being abandoned by God while seeking a divine response.[1] This Psalm is a composition that dramatizes the speaker's suffering.[2] The speaker, who is understood to be King David, expresses his feelings of abandonment as he recounts the times that God has listened and intervened on behalf of his ancestors; he is grieved that God is not listening to him or to Israel. The individual cited in this Psalm has been identified in several different ways and this transformation and its rereferencing opens the lemmata in the Psalm to personal, communal, and liturgical usage.[3] Psalm 22 may be divided into several sections: addressing God directly (2-3); recalling previous deliverances (4-6, 10-11); the depiction of adversarial behavior (7-9, 13-14, 17-19); description of extreme pain (15-16, 18); and prayers appealing for help (12, 20-22). Additional sections include God's kingship being recognized by the nations. All of these sections provide language for messianic and apocalyptic narratives. The semiotic feature of this open and widely applicable text has enabled midrashic texts to proffer different savior figures that occupy the position of King David. Furthermore, the sections of this Psalm provide a script for a hagiography or historical salvation narrative.

Psalm 22 is rarely cited or referred to in Jewish literature of the Second Temple period. A few traces that may have utilized Psalm 22 in regard to a salvific figure are found in the pseudepigraphic texts of *Joseph and Aseneth,* particularly in some of the manuscripts, and in *Wisdom of Solomon.*[4] In the confession of Aseneth (*Joseph and Aseneth* 12:9-11), a lion is mentioned, which is thought to be similar to Psalm 22:14.[5] In my opinion it is more significant that Aseneth refers to her ascetic behavior by invoking the dryness of her mouth and a potsherd, which derives from Psalm 22:16:

> And lo, for seven days and seven nights I have neither eaten bread nor drunk water; and my mouth is dry like a drum and my tongue like horn, and my lips like a potsherd, and my face is shrunken, and my eyes are failing as a result of my incessant tears. (JosAs 12:8)

Psalm 22:16 is referenced as Scriptural proof of suffering, which reappears in the Christian and Jewish sources discussed below. This interpretation of Psalm 22 is not found in extant Jewish texts before the era of Christianity.[6] The interpretation of Psalm 22 was augmented in rabbinic literature after Christian interpretation made it applicable to Jesus. Another pseudepigraphic text, *Wisdom of Solomon*, may have some affinities with Psalm 22:9 and Psalm 22:20. The texts from the Dead Sea also contain Psalm 22, especially certain lemmata in the *Hodayot*, genres of praise or teaching. Heike Omerzu states that primarily the lament portion of Psalm 22 is found when the Psalm serves as a possible hypotext.[7] This occurrence is significant, since both New Testament and rabbinic literature also focus upon the lament section.

Two fragments[8] containing Psalm 22:17, "For dogs surround me; the assembly of the wicked encircle me; they seize my hands and my feet like a lion," were discovered among the documents from the Dead Sea. In the first fragment (4Q88=4QPs[f]), the word translated as "like a lion" is not preserved. In the second fragment (5/6HevPs), the last letter of the term appears to be a somewhat elongated letter י (*yod*), almost appearing like the letter ו (*vav*). Thus, the reading of this word would be either כארי (*ka'ari*) or כארו (*ka'aru*), respectively. These two renditions of the term[9] have been the focus of much controversy, because Christians understand the key word as "pierced" and apply it to Jesus on the cross.[10] The word *ka'aru* has been construed to read כרו (*karu*), which has the meaning "[they] dug" (e.g., Gen. 26:25) or "they pierced." However, this verb is never used in the context of "piercing" in the Hebrew Bible. A comparison of the versions reveals a major discrepancy in the renditions of the term in different hypo-biblical texts.[11] The lemma, "they seize my hands and my feet like a lion," Psalm 22:17 (Christian numbering: 22:16), has been translated as "they pierced my hands and my feet," one of the verses most frequently referenced by Christians when claiming that the crucifixion of Jesus was foretold.

The different renditions in the above texts may have compelled the initial creators of rabbinic texts to base their arguments on one reading convention, "like a lion," which then became crystallized in the Masoretic text of the Hebrew Bible. Christians, beginning with some Church Fathers,[12] selected "they pierced" from among the Greek traditions and versions of the biblical text in order to create a consistent text base, which was utilized in their fulfillment interpretations. This reliance upon divergent texts in the Christian and Jewish traditions, the Hebrew Bible, the Septuagint, or a mixture of both, greatly contributed to the schism of Christianity and rabbinic Judaism.

Psalm 22 is rarely cited in tannaitic literature, and this avoidance may suggest a reaction against the Christian use of this Psalm. Some of the traditions of Pesiqta Rabbati, later discussed at length, reflect tannaitic strata, which would render them approximately contemporaneous to New Testament texts. In particular, a messianic passage in Pesiqta Rabbati 36:9[13] utilizes the term "the rabbis taught," which may refer to a tannaitic teaching.[14]

Prior to the attestation in the New Testament, there is no evidence of Psalm 22 being used in a Jewish messianic context. This Psalm became the preferred focus of Christian fulfillment interpretation in regard to the dying Christian Messiah, while in Judaism single lemmata from the Psalm began to be viewed as having salvific potential, culminating in describing the affliction of a Jewish Messiah.

Since the Hebrew Bible ascribes Psalm 22 to King David, this Psalm is applicable to the messianic figure that according to Jewish tradition is a descendant of King David. Jewish interpretations of the Psalm identify the individual in the Psalm with a royal figure, alternatively interpreted as King David, King Hezekiah, or Queen Esther. In Christianity, the savior figure in Psalm 22 is Jesus. This usage shows a correlation of this Psalm with prayers by other individuals, who are either royal or messianic or both. The personal pronoun "I" referring to David in the Psalm is thus understood to be uttered by another figure.

Additionally, Psalm 22 was transformed by the Church Fathers from a text indicating the affliction of an individual into a messianic Psalm. The early Church Fathers were contemporaneous to tannaitic literature.[15] Justin Martyr (ca. 100-165 CE) *Apol.* 35[16] writes:

> And again in other words, through another prophet, He says, "They pierced My hands and My feet [Ps. 22:17], and for My vesture they cast lots." [Ps. 22:19]. And indeed David, the king and prophet, who uttered these things, suffered none of them; but Jesus Christ stretched forth His hands, being crucified by the Jews speaking against Him, and denying that He was the Christ. And as the prophet spoke, they tormented Him, and set Him on the judgment-seat, and said, Judge us. And the expression, "They pierced my hands and my feet," [Ps. 22:17] was used in reference to the nails of the cross which were fixed in His hands and feet. And after He was crucified they cast lots upon His vesture [Ps. 22:19], and they that crucified Him parted it among them.

Judith Lieu makes a convincing case that Justin Martyr was probably the first to claim that this entire Psalm referred to Jesus (*Dial.* 99).[17] The purpose of Justin's interpretation was to demonstrate that Jesus asked to be saved from death and that he became a human being in his suffering, as well as to identify Jesus' adversaries. Justin's Jesus was aware of the suffering that he would incur; Justin furthermore identified the adversaries of Jesus as Jews, thus lending additional personae to the unfolding drama in Psalm 22 from a Christian polemical perspective.[18] In Justin, we probably have the first traceable Christological interpretation of Psalm 22, as applied to Jesus in the New Testament.[19]

Animal Imagery in Psalm 22

Psalm 22 refers to numerous animals that serve as salient metaphors[20] for the suffering or the endangerment of King David. Most of the animals mentioned refer to a world filled with dangerous adversaries: *For dogs surround me; the assembly of the wicked encircle me; they seize my hands and my feet like a lion* (Ps. 22:17). The lemma "assembly," translated as "synagogé" in the Septuagint, made the verse applicable to "synagogue", that is, the wicked Jews encircled Jesus in the polemic mind of the early Christians. Christians needed to dissociate themselves as a distinct group from Judaism. Furthermore, "For dogs surround me" is cited in all the Gospel narratives relating to the suffering Jesus.

The dog motif is also referred to in midrashic interpretation. Since animals in apocalyptic and other texts often refer to kingdoms or nations, this could be the case in midrash. In Babylonian Talmud, Megillah 15b, King Ahasuerus of Persia is interpreted as the "dog" in Psalm 22:21; this identification occurs in the prayer of Esther. Furthermore, the hosts of Ahasuerus are called "bulls" (Ps. 22:13), and the sons or descendants of Haman are described as "strong bulls of Bashan" (Ps. 22:13). When Esther is raped by Ahasuerus, she refers to him as a "lion" (Ps. 22:14), as in the following text:

> Babylonian Talmud, Megillah 15b: *And stood in the inner court of the king's house* (Esther 5:1f.) R. Levi said: When she reached the chamber of the idols,

> the Divine Presence left her. *She said, My* God, *My* God, *why have You forsaken me?* (Ps. 22:2) Is it possible that You punish the inadvertent sin like the presumptuous one, or one done under compulsion like one committed willingly? Or is it because I called [Ahasuerus] "dog," as it says *Save my soul from the sword, my only one from the power of the dog?* (Ps. 22:21) She immediately retracted and called him "lion," as it says. *Save me from the lion's mouth* (Ps. 22:22).

Queen Esther occupies the paradigmatic position of a savior figure who pronounces lemmata from Psalm 22 to invoke God's help in her personal plight as well as in the rescue of the entire Jewish population. In an interpretation by R. Judah (2nd century) of the term *ka'ari* (Ps. 22:17) found in Midrash Tehillim 22, Esther claims that she was made to appear repulsive. However, R. Nehemia derives *ka'ari* from a Greek loan-word χαρά ("gladness"); thus, Esther in this understanding is joyful. Explaining a critical term by referring to a similar sounding word in another language is a common midrashic technique. Lemmata from Psalm 22 are also utilized to describe actions of Israel's enemies. The lion as an adversary is also found in 1 Peter 5:8, which refers to the devil. The dog motif does not only show the mortal threat to the body, but also a threat of idolatry. While in the New Testament dogs are Jesus' adversaries, in rabbinic texts "dogs" in Psalm 22 are endangering the continuation of Judaism. This exemplifies the divergent focus in interpretations of Psalm 22.

The interpretation of the verse *Save my soul from the sword, yehidati [my only one] from the power of the dog* (Ps. 22:21) does not only focus upon the lemma "dog," but also upon "my only one." Genesis Rabbah 46:7 (see Sifre Deuteronomy 313) contains an interpretation relating this Psalm to the *Aqedah*, the sacrifice of Isaac. Rabbinic hermeneutics situate Psalm 22:21 in the context of sacrificing a son. *Your only son* (Gen. 22:12) is implied and juxtaposed to *my only one* (Ps. 22:21); the text states God said to Abraham: "I give merit to you, as if I had asked you to sacrifice yourself and you did not refuse it." *My only one* in this case would indicate that God recognized Abraham's willingness to sacrifice his son. In another midrash, Numbers Rabbah 17:2, a lemma from Genesis *Your only son*, referring to Isaac, is changed to "your soul," proof-text is Psalm 22:21. The ram sacrificed saves not only Isaac, but also Abraham. These passages show a nexus between Psalm 22:21 and Isaac, the "only son" of Abraham. The problematic passage in Genesis which ignores Abraham's other son, Ishmael, is clarified through this interpretation of Psalm 22:21. The second part of the verse containing the dog motif is implied. The dog motif could refer to the biblical Moloch who required child sacrifice,[21] which rendered child sacrifice as an idolatrous practice.

Whereas the lion is a symbol of strength and royalty, and the dog a symbol of meanness and idolatry, the worm is viewed as the humblest of creatures in ancient texts. Israel is considered humble before God; there is a connection between the abundant love of God and the humility of the Jewish people. The reference to a worm as a metaphor for people is also found in Isaiah who compares the Jewish people to a worm.[22] In Psalms 22:7 King David uses this metaphor as he writes about the plight of his people. Babylonian Talmud, Hullin 89a, states that God said to Israel that He loved them because even when He bestowed greatness upon them, they humbled themselves before Him. One example of a humble person cited is King David; the proof-text is "But I am a worm, and not a man" (Ps. 22:7). In contrast to the positive quality of humility, this metaphor illustrates the humiliation of the dehumanized body as the sufferer endures great pain. In a messianic context, the final moments of a Messiah are indicated by this animalistic state of suffering like a worm. Clement of Rome[23] cited the lemma from Psalm 22:7 as having been spoken by Jesus:

> *First Epistle to the Corinthians* 16: And again He saith, "I am a worm, and no man; [Ps. 22:7] a reproach of men, and despised of the people. All that see Me have derided Me; they have spoken with their lips; they have wagged their head [Ps. 22:8], [saying] He hoped in God, let Him deliver Him, let Him save Him, since He delighteth in Him [Ps. 22:9]."

However, this lowly status is reversed and the Messiah is transformed into a godlike or royal position, when he is elevated to lead Israel.

Psalm 22 (LXX Ψ 21)[24] and the Crucifixion of Jesus

The explicit use of Psalm 22:2 in the Gospels is found in the crucifixion scene, Matthew 27:46 and Mark 15:34.[25] Matthew and Mark describe Jesus' agonizing plea from the cross:

> And at the ninth hour Jesus cried with a loud voice, "Eli/Eloi, Eli/Eloi, lama sabachthani?" (Ηλι ηλι λαμα σαβαχθανι) which means, "My God, my God, why have You forsaken me?"

The beginning words of Psalm 22:2 appear in a transcription of the Hebrew-Aramaic before being translated into Greek. Jesus speaking in Hebrew-Aramaic lends authenticity to the rendition of his last words; the utterance of last words is comparable to numerous deathbed scenes in postbiblical literature.[26] Matthew and Mark situate this citation at the climactic moment just before Jesus' death. In the Greek rendition Matthew is closer to the Hebrew version, whereas the Greek translation of this lemma from Psalm 22:2 found in the Gospels differs from the Septuagint translation of the same verse. The Gospel version of the lemmata of Psalm 22:2 is closest to the Targum of Psalms.[27] The New Testament has *sabachthani* in the sentence spoken by Jesus instead of *azavtani* in the Hebrew Bible. The problem has long been recognized whether *sabachthani* has the same meaning as *azavtani*. The verb *azavtani* derives from *azav* (to abandon, forsake, leave), whereas the word *sabachthani* of the Gospels is not extant in early Jewish texts. The closest Hebrew-Aramaic term would be the artificial construct *z^e^vahtani*. The term *sabachthani* could possibly be derived from *zavah* (to sacrifice, slaughter [a sacrificial animal]), which is found in the Hebrew Bible and rabbinic literature,[28] but not in the form indicated by the Gospel passage (*z^e^vahtani*). This artificial construct is not found in ancient Jewish texts; no sacrificial animal speaks about itself. Based upon the association with *zavah*, the phrase could be rendered as "My God, my God, why have You sacrificed me?" If this rendition is correct, one could speculate that using *sabachthani* in the two Gospels was designed ostensibly to depict the scene of the Passion as a sacrificial offering,[29] relating it to the Passover sacrifice. Utilizing the lemma from Psalm 22:2 as "sacrificed or slaughtered" in the Christian Scriptures would connect the term to Isaiah 53:7, which has been applied to the death of Jesus. The "suffering servant" in Deutero-Isaiah would be slaughtered in the future as a sacrifice: *He was oppressed and afflicted, yet he did not open his mouth; he was led like a lamb to the slaughter, and as a sheep before her shearers is silent, so he did not open his mouth* (Isa. 53:7).

"My God, my God, why have You forsaken me?" (Matt. 27:46; Mark 15:34) is attributed to David in Psalm 22:2. The writers of the Gospels understood that David's words concerning his own situation applied to Jesus' suffering and were an expression of abandonment. In a rabbinic text that may be tannaitic this crucial lemma of the Psalm is used in entreating the mercy of God. Mekhilta, Shirata 3: *My* God, *my* God *why have You forsaken me* (Ps. 22:2) explains the lemma "My God (*eli*)" as signifying the measure of mercy (*middat ha-rahamim*) of God. This text in the Mekhilta is consistent with rabbinic typological interpretation: whenever God is referred to as "El" it signifies God's compassionate nature, judging people by God's measure of mercy.[30] For example, Psalm 22:2 appears as Esther's prayer in her attempt to save the Jews of Persia from destruction.[31] The affliction voiced in the Psalm is utilized to evoke the suffering of the Jews in Persia. This suffering is reversed by divine intervention in response to Esther's prayer.

Midrash Tehillim 22 contains the most extensive treatment of Psalm 22 and the savior figure Queen Esther. Among other scenes of the history of the Jewish people, this midrashic text depicts Moses and the Israelites during the exodus at the Red Sea, as well as King Hezekiah and the prophet Isaiah during the siege of Jerusalem. The midrashic interpretation of the first two verses of Psalm 22 emphasizes the salvation of the Jewish people. The lemma in Psalm 22:16 "my strength כחי" is read as "my palate, throat" (through metathesis rendering חכי). Psalm 22:16 is applied to Queen Esther in this midrash, when it states Esther has a dry "throat" due to a severe fast, and secondly, when it is interpreted that she was coerced to renounce the Oral and the Written Torah. This passage weaves together the question of who would offer praises to God, if Israel were to be destroyed. The lemma *My* God, *my* God, *why have You forsaken me?* is subjected to deconstruction, whereby each segment is related to different human experiences during the process of fasting. The verse is mapped upon the three different days of Esther's fast. Her piety is expressed in self-inflicted suffering, similar to the fasting of Aseneth (JosAs 12:8). Whereas the pain of fasting and the dry throat is self-inflicted in Judaism, in the Christian context the lemma from Psalm 22 is used to express the pain inflicted by the Roman government.

Additional Significant Lemmata from Psalm 22 in New Testamental and Rabbinic Interpretation

In addition to direct quotations of Psalm 22, there are numerous allusions to this Psalm in the New Testament,[32] for example: *All those who see me mock me; they move the lip, they shake their head, saying, He trusted on the Lord that He would save him; let Him save him, seeing He delights in him* (Ps. 22:8-9). Matthew, Mark, and Luke utilize the identical theme to describe the actions of Jesus' enemies in their Passion narratives: mocking him, shaking their heads at him, and telling him to save himself, since he claimed to be the son of God (Matt. 27:39-44; Mark 15:29-32; Luke 23:35-39). This adaptation of biblical lemmata is an illustration of midrashic writing with Scripture in the New Testament. In particular, Origen, *De Principii, Anima* 8:1[33] views this entire Psalm as a Passion narrative:

> And in the twenty-second Psalm, regarding Christ—for it is certain, as the Gospel bears witness, that this Psalm is spoken of Him . . . .

In all four Gospels—Matthew 27:35; Mark 15:24; Luke 23:34, and John 19:23-24—the casting of lots and the division of Jesus' garments correspond to verse 19 of the Psalm:

> Then the soldiers, when they had crucified Jesus, took his garments and made four parts, to every soldier a part; and also [his] coat: now the coat was without seam, woven from the top throughout. They said therefore among themselves, Let us not rend it, but cast lots for it, whose it shall be: that the Scripture might be fulfilled, which says, *They divide my garments among themselves and cast lots for my raiment.* These things therefore the soldiers did (John 19:23-25).

The Gospel of John claims this verse was a prophetic passage and was fulfilled by the soldiers dividing Jesus' clothes into four parts and casting lots for his tunic; John cited the Psalm from the Septuagint as a proof-text for the narrative. This is another example illustrating how Christianity has adapted David's words to be applicable to Jesus, Psalm 22:19: *They divide my garments among them and cast lots for my clothing.* The Gospels develop the metaphors and scenes concerning Jesus' garments at the crucifixion by contextualizing the Psalm in the passion.

Justin Martyr, First Apology. 38, expanded the narrative before the canonized New Testament came into existence:

> And again, when He says, "They cast lots upon My vesture, and pierced My hands and My feet [Ps. 22:19, 17]. And I lay down and slept, and rose again, because the Lord sustained Me." And again, when He says, "They spake with their lips, they wagged the head [Ps. 22:8], saying, Let Him deliver Himself." [Ps. 22:9] And that all these things happened to Christ at the hands of the Jews, you can ascertain. For when He was crucified, they did shoot out the lip, and wagged their heads [Ps. 22:8], saying, "Let Him who raised the dead save Himself."

The previous verse, Psalm 22:18, is critical to understanding the co-text of Psalm 22:19. The person whose clothes were being divided is described as counting his bones, while those who are taking his garments are staring at him. This starving man is so emaciated that his bones are visible. The "voice" here is still King David, as it is throughout the Psalm, and he uses the act of taking and dividing his garments as a metaphorical reference to the desires of his enemies to take away his mantle of royalty and make it their own. In Christianity, the savior figure that is substituted for King David in Psalm 22 is Jesus.

Psalm 22:19 has a very different connotation in rabbinic texts; the garments are the possessions of God that are divided among the nations. Esther Rabbah 1:13 states that Israel was punished and her sovereignty was taken away and given to the nations of the world. In the future, when Israel repents, God will take the kingship away from the nations and restore it to Israel; the proof-text is Obadiah 1:21: *Then saviors shall come to Mount Zion to judge the mountains of Esau, And the kingdom shall be the Lord's.* As commented upon earlier, Psalm 22 has the semiotic feature of an open text, which leads to multiple identities of its metaphors and personae and the actions described in the Psalm can have multiple applications. In midrashic texts, different savior figures may be substituted; in the corresponding exegetical move a hagiography or historical salvation narrative is construed.

Liturgical Usage

Liturgically, Psalm 22 is part of the commemorative service of Purim in Judaism[34] and is part of the Good Friday liturgy in Christianity. Traces of a liturgical usage of Psalm 22 and its interpretations presenting a salvific figure are found in rabbinic homiletical texts, such as the Esther Midrash in the Babylonian Talmud, Midrash Tehillim, and Pesiqta Rabbati. This liturgical usage should be viewed as occurring within the cultural transfer and the cultural migration of ideas between Judaism and Christianity. The application of critical lemmata of Psalm 22 to Esther and Messiah Ephraim in homiletical texts is possibly a critical, post-New Testament reaction to its Christian application to Jesus. With regard to liturgical usages of Psalm 22, it is significant that the Psalm is part of Esther's prayer, as well as the prayer of a righteous man (Babylonian Talmud, Yoma 29a).

In these two instances the prayer setting involves an individual under enormous stress. Several midrashic passages interpreting Psalm 22 may have been reflective of the liturgy of the synagogue. Menn[35] notes that the opening passages, *petihot* (proems) in Midrash Tehillim are homiletic introductions to Scriptural passages read liturgically in the synagogue service. Psalm 22:1-2 serve as introductory verses, so-called *petiha-verses*, in most of these proems. For example, Esther is the "deer of the dawn," the midrashic transposition of the Hebrew letters change "deer" (איילת) into Esther's "strength" (אילותי) (Ps. 22:20). There may have been liturgical occasions for the use of Pesiqta Rabbati,[36] which contains scripted homilies as well as blessings (for example, Pesiqta Rabbati 37:9).

Pesiqta Rabbati

The Pesiqta Rabbati homilies contain numerous midrashic reinterpretations of messiahs that rely upon the messianic passages in the Hebrew Bible, which are key passages in the Christian "fulfillment theology," as evident in Justin Martyr:

> *First Apology.* 38: And that these things did happen, you can ascertain from the Acts of Pontius Pilate. And we will cite the prophetic utterances of another prophet, Zephaniah [recte: Zech.], to the effect that He was foretold expressly as to sit upon the foal of an ass and to enter Jerusalem. The words are these: "Rejoice greatly, O daughter of Zion; shout, O daughter of Jerusalem: behold, thy King cometh unto thee; lowly, and riding upon an ass, and upon a colt the foal of an ass." [Zech. 9:9][37]

Zechariah 9:9 is applied to the Messiah in Pesiqta Rabbati 34,[38] a homiletic midrash that describes the messianic age. It is based upon the Haftarah reading of the fifth Sabbath of Consolation after the Ninth of Av, Zechariah 9:9: "Rejoice greatly, O daughter of Zion! Shout, O daughter of Jerusalem! Behold, your King is coming to you; He is just and having salvation, lowly and riding on a donkey, a colt, the foal of a donkey."

> Pesiqta Rabbati 34:8
>
> *Just and redeemed is He* (Zech. 9:9)—[this is] the Messiah who justifies [the] judgment [received by] him for the sake of Israel while sitting in the house of affliction [prison]. And if he is called "just" [*tsaddiq*], why is he called "redeemed [saved]"? Because he justified the judgment [received by] him because of them. He said to them: You are all doomed, nevertheless, you will all be redeemed [saved] through the compassion of the Holy One, Blessed be He.
>
> *Afflicted and riding on a donkey* (Zech. 9:9)—that is the Messiah, why is he called "afflicted"? Because he was afflicted during all those years in prison and because the transgressors of Israel laughed at him [Ps. 22:8].

> *Riding on a donkey* (Zech. 9:9)—because of the transgressors. The one who does not have any merit will go and receive the merit of the Fathers in God's presence. The Holy One, Blessed be He, will shield them through the merit of the Messiah in a straight way, and He saves you, as it is written: *They shall come weeping, and with supplications will I lead them; I will make them walk by the rivers of waters in a straight way, where they shall not stumble; for I am a Father to Israel, and Ephraim, he is My firstborn* (Jer. 31:9).

The above homily is the first in a succession of messianic homilies in Pesiqta Rabbati. This section establishes that verses utilized by Christians in respect to Jesus, were used by Jews regarding the fulfillment of the verse by a Messiah named Ephraim. What is particularly troubling in the above text is the implication that Ephraim, the firstborn of God, is used in a messianic rabbinic context, although it is clear in the Hebrew Bible that Ephraim refers to Israel. The messianic interpretation of Psalm 22 transpires in Pesiqta Rabbati 36 and 37.[39] In Pesiqta Rabbati 36 this Psalm is cited in a homily based upon *Arise, shine for your light has come! And the glory of the LORD is risen upon you* (Isa. 60:1). This is a Haftarah reading for the sixth Sabbath of consolation after *Tisha` b'Av* (the Ninth of Av).

Pesiqta Rabbati, like other rabbinic texts, connects the personal distress of the individual in Psalm 22 with a specific figure. This is made possible by the rich metaphoric language of the Psalm that, from a linguistic perspective, enables its application to other figures. In this homily, Pesiqta Rabbat 36, it is claimed that King David composed Psalm 22 on behalf of the "son of David," the Messiah who would suffer for the sins of others. This narrative includes the dynamics of the critical relationship between the individual savior and the righteous ones. The Messiah's future triumph is recounted in Pesiqta Rabbati 36:3, which cites Psalm 89:23, 24, 26. The midrashic passage furthermore follows the inscribed narrative of Psalm 22, a progression of abandonment, threat, suffering, and divinely initiated restoration. The Psalm, therefore, provides the matrix of the messianic narrative in this rabbinic homily; similar to the New Testament Passion, the rabbinic Messiah narrative is anchored in Scripture.

> Pesiqta Rabbati 36:4
>
> [God] began to talk about the terms with him [Ephraim], saying to him: In the future the sins of those that have been hidden with you will bring you under an iron yoke. They make you like a calf whose eyes grow dim; and they will choke your spirit with [your] yoke; and because of their sins your tongue will stick to the roof of your mouth (Ps. 22:16) Are you willing [to endure] this?
>
> The Messiah said in [God's] Presence: Will this suffering [last] for many years?

> The Holy One said to him: By your life and the life of My head! I have decreed for you a week [seven years]. If your soul is saddened, I will immediately banish them [the sinful souls hidden with you].
>
> [The Messiah] said in His presence: Master of the universe, I will take this upon myself with a joyful soul and a glad heart, provided that not one [person] in Israel perish; [that] not only those who are alive should be saved in my days, but that also those who are dead, who have died since [the days] of the first human being up until now should be saved [at the time of salvation] in my days {ed. pr.: but also the aborted ones};[40] [including] those who You thought to create, but who were not created. Such [are the things] I desire, and for this I am ready to take [all this] upon myself. {ed. pr.: At the same time, the Holy One blessed be He, will appoint for the Messiah the four creatures who will carry the Messiah's throne of glory.}

The above text commences with: "In the future the sins of those that have been hidden with you will bring you under an iron yoke." Thus, the Messiah Ephraim will suffer for the sins of others. Also, all "souls" will be saved. As an aside, it should be noted that Ephraim is also known as the son of Joseph in other texts; it is not coincidental that the Jewish Messiah is called the son of Joseph, since Jesus on one level was "a son of Joseph." In Pesiqta Rabbati 36 Ephraim is referred to as the true Messiah, which connects him to the concept of triumph over the nations. It is obvious that there can only be one true Messiah and this passage can be viewed as a reaction to the concept of a Christian Messiah. The inequities of humanity will cause Ephraim's tongue to cleave to the roof of his mouth based upon Psalm 22:16.[41] Christian authors understood this lemma as referring to Jesus' silence at his trial or his thirst while being crucified.[42] This "thirst," as noted above, may be a trajectory of Aseneth's fast. In Pesiqta Rabbati God predicts a period of suffering of a "week," which is apocalyptic language referring to a seven-year period. After this period the Messiah will scream and implore God to end his suffering, since his flesh and his spirit cannot endure it any longer. The following passage also describes the suffering of the Messiah Ephraim.

> Pesiqta Rabbati 36:6
>
> During the week [seven year period] when [Ephraim][43] comes, they will bring iron beams[44] and they will put them on his neck until the Messiah's body is bent. He will scream and weep and his voice will rise up to the height [of heaven]. He will say in His presence: Master of the universe, how much can my limbs endure? How much my spirit? Am I not but flesh and blood? It was this moment that David lamented, saying: *My strength is dried up like a potsherd* (Ps. 22:16). In that hour the Holy One says to them {ed. pr.: him}: Ephraim, My righteous Messiah, You have already accepted [this suffering] since the six days of Creation. Now your suffering is like My suffering, since

> the day on which wicked Nebuchadnezzar destroyed My Temple and burnt My sanctuary, and exiled My children among the nations of the world, by your life and by the life of My head! I have not sat on My Throne. And if you do not believe, see the dew that is upon My head, *My head is filled with dew, [My locks with the drops of the night]* (Cant. 5:2). In that hour, [the Messiah] will say in His presence: Master of the universe, now my mind is at rest, for it is sufficient for the servant to be like his Master.

> Rabbi Levi said: In that hour when the Holy One says to the congregation of Israel: *Arise, shine for your light is come* (Isa. 60:1), [Israel will] say: Master of the universe, in the future You lead us. At that hour the Holy One will turn around and acknowledge [it] and say to her [Israel]: My daughter, you spoke well, as it is said: *My beloved speaks and says to me, [Arise, my love, my beautiful one, and come away]* (Cant. 2:10).

The above passage emphasizes the suffering of Ephraim; his suffering was determined at the time of creation. Psalm 22:16 is used as a proof-text when the Messiah complains about his suffering; he is comforted by God. The passage relies upon tropes describing God, who suffered because His Temple was destroyed. This passage is set forth within the larger interpretation of Psalm 36:10: *You are the fountain of life*, which was understood as God being the source of resurrection. Cant. 5:2 mentions "dew" on God's head, which in rabbinic texts indicates resurrection.[45] This messianic portrait presents the Messiah as God's light; this light is hidden until the end of time when it will shine for Israel.[46] This narrative in Pesiqta Rabbati evolves as a tale told by the *darshan* (the composer of the homily) about the Messiah; the ideas about the Messiah in Pesiqta Rabbati 36 define the Messiah's suffering and the tasks he will fulfill at the end of time. When the Messiah will reveal himself as a king, every Israelite will have multiple disciples from the nations.

The earliest medieval rabbinic text that appears to cite this Pesiqta Rabbati material is found in Moshe of Narbonne (eleventh century), also referred to as Moshe Ha-Darshan (the preacher). He presents a dialogue in which the Messiah is asked by God, if he accepts his suffering:

> Midrash Bereshit Rabbati, Gen. 1:3: Your eyes will not see light, but your ears will hear the great reprimand of the nations of the world. . . your tongue will cleave to the roof of your mouth [Ps. 22:16], your skin will stick to your bones [Ps. 22:18], and your body will be worn out from distress and moaning.

The passage appears as a commentary on Genesis 1:3; he focuses upon the lemma "light." He alludes to Psalm 22 and Isaiah 53, the Suffering Servant passage, cited as proof that the Messiah will suffer.

Another medieval rabbinic work is Yalqut Shim`oni; in Tehillim 686, which is one of the few late passages describing a suffering Messiah, Shimon Ha-

Darshan refers to a suffering son of a king. The king is understood to be God; and the entire passage is a commentary on Psalm 60:1-3, which mentions a victory of King David. The passage is probably purposefully elliptical. The term "commit" may also be translated as "rolling something" [to God] or "to throw a burden" [onto God].[47]

> *He committed himself [gol] unto the Lord*] [Ps. 22:9] through a parable of a king's son: They made him carry the heavy end of the beam [cross-beam]. His father looked and saw him. He said to them: Let me have anything you wish and I will carry it. Thus said the Holy One, Blessed be He, throw *[gol]* your sins onto Me and I will carry them.

Some medieval rabbinic passages, as well as citations in the Christian work Pugio Fidei (by Raimundus Martinus, c. 1280), reflect the idea of a suffering Messiah, who is carrying the sins of Israel. Arnold Goldberg[48] and Michael Fishbane[49] relying upon Goldberg, contend that Pugio Fidei[50] contains excerpted passages from Pesiqta Rabbati 36. In my opinion, they are only partially correct, since a close look at the section under discussion in Pugio Fidei reveals a conflated text based upon both Pesiqta Rabbati 36 and 37, as well as the above cited text by Moshe of Narbonne.

> Pugio Fidei, 598: Those who are hidden with you, their sins will bend (bring) you under a heavy yoke; your eyes will not see light, your ears will hear great taunts from the nations of the world [Ps. 22:7-8], your nose will smell stench, your mouth will taste bitterness, your tongue will stick to the roof of your mouth [Ps. 22:16], your skin will shrink on your bones [Ps. 22:18], your soul will expire with lamentation and sighs.

Azariah de Rossi (sixteenth century), in Me'or Enayim , chapter 19,[51] suggested the passages of the suffering Messiah were added to Pesiqta Rabbati under Christian influence in the Middle Ages. It is indeterminate as to when this engagement with Christianity transpired, since Pesiqta Rabbati has material from the first, third and fifth centuries and was subsequently edited in the Middle Ages.

The editio princeps of Pesiqta Rabbati (Prague, 1653 or 1657) has the most extensive quotations from Psalm 22; as discussed earlier, this Psalm had been critical in early Christian fulfillment theology. The earlier Parma Manuscript (MS 3122, thirteenth century) cites Psalm 22:16 and may allude to other lemmata from Psalm 22; however, it quotes verses mainly from Lamentations to provide Scriptural proof for the Messiah. Nevertheless, the verses from Lamentations support the arguments made by the text, because they are very similar to Psalm 22. We could have a case of Scriptural referentiality or unmarked intertextuality in the Parma manuscript of Pesiqta Rabbati. This is typical of midrash which often follows the sequence of events in a biblical text without citing the entire passage. Regarding the Christian references or their inversion in Pesiqta

Rabbati's suffering Messiah narrative, we find that this rabbinic text interacts with references and allusions from the cultural sphere. Vernon Robbins noted that a text interacts "with traditions that are 'cultural' possessions that anyone who knows a particular culture may use."[52]

The hidden Jewish Messiah relates to a preexistent heavenly being, resplendent, majestic, and sitting on the Throne of Glory. Similarly, the Christian description of Jesus, occasionally referred to as the "Word" (John 1:1, 14), claims the Christian Messiah was with God at the beginning of creation. The concept of the hidden Messiah continues in mystical midrashic literature, such as Midrash Konen, depicting a concealed Messiah residing in the Garden of Eden.[53]

In these sections of Pesiqta Rabbati we find reinterpretations of Christian tropes reflecting the transformation from a heavenly Messiah to an earthly Messiah, who eventually will return at the end of time. The Messiah in Pesiqta Rabbati 36 combines elements of apocalypticism and this-worldliness. After victory in an apocalyptic battle, the Messiah is depicted as standing on the roof of the Temple (Pesiqta Rabbati 36:9).[54] This is one of the most difficult messianic passages in Pesiqta Rabbati; it is indeterminate whether this passage reflects thoughts existing prior to the destruction of the Second Temple (70 CE by the Romans) or implying the destroyed Temple will be rebuilt when the Messiah comes. However, I think it is significant this passage is presented as tannaitic, which would place it in close temporal proximity to early Christianity, when the Jerusalem Temple was still standing.

The task of Ephraim in Pesiqta Rabbati is to redeem Israel; his deeds are anchored in biblical lemmata, which he fulfills. In rabbinic hermeneutics this fulfillment amounts to an actualization of lemmata. The text contains dialogues between God and satan, and between God and the angels of the nations. Ultimately, the Messiah triumphs over satan. The nations ask a series of questions regarding the Messiah. This construction of responding to the questions of gentiles allows the *darshan* to present his version of the Jewish Messiah in response to the Christian Messiah. The question and response format probably points to ongoing polemic between the two groups.

The epithet משיח צדקינו (Pesiqta Rabbati 36 and 37) can be understood in two ways: "our true Messiah" or "Messiah of righteousness;" this epithet also appears in the *siddur*, the prayer book. Since a similar phrase concerning the Messiah is found in Revelation 3:14 and 19:11, "faithful and true," we may have a rhetoric of redemption here; both traditions claim their Messiah as the "True One." As Reuven Kimelman has shown, there was such rhetoric in the *Amidah* (the Eighteen Benedictions).[55]

Pesiqta Rabbati 37 continues the interpretation of Isaiah commenced in Pesiqta Rabbati 36; this serialized interpretation may be due to the consecutive utilization of the two homilies on different Sabbaths of Consolation. Pesiqta Rabbati 37, based upon the lemma *Rejoicing I will rejoice* (Isa. 61:10) שוש אשיש, contains repetitive, serialized, almost liturgical benedictions. Messiah Ephraim is represented as the son of God. Pesiqta Rabbati 37 describes the Messiah sitting in prison and the nations of the world attacking him and offering him nothing but contempt. Messiah Ephraim is prepared for his mission and dressed in special garments by God. In contrast to Jesus, Ephraim's garments are not stolen or divided. Several lemmata of Psalm 22 are applied to the Messiah and the battles at the end of days; we find Psalm 22:7-8, 22:14-15 and 22:16, 18 cited as proof-texts, as well as numerous allusions to this Psalm. In the following three consecutive passages the Messiah is recognized by the resurrected Patriarchs of Israel:[56]

> Pesiqta Rabbati 37:2: This teaches that in the future, in the month of Nisan, the Fathers of the World [Patriarchs] will arise and say to him: Ephraim, our righteous [true] Messiah, even though we are your fathers, you are greater than we are, because you suffered [for] the iniquities of our children and terrible ordeals came upon you, such as did not come upon earlier [generations] or later ones. For the sake of Israel you [experienced] anguish, derision, and mockery among the nations of the world [Ps. 22:7-8]. *You sat in darkness* (Micah 7:8) and gloominess, and your eyes saw no light, and your skin cleaved to your bones [Ps. 22:18], and your body was as dry as a piece of wood; and your eyes did not see light, and *your skin is shriveled on your bones* (Lam. 4:8) [Ps. 22:18], and your body was dried up like wood and your eyes grew dim from fasting—your *strength is dried up like a potsherd* (Ps. 22:16)—all these [afflictions happened] on account of the iniquities of our children. It is your will [to benefit] your children through that goodness, which the Holy One will bestow upon Israel. It may be because of the utmost anguish, which you did suffer on their account in prison, that your mind is displeased with them. He said to them: Fathers of the World, all that I have done I have done only for your sake and for the sake of your children and for your honor and the honor of your children that they will benefit from the goodness which the Holy One will bestow upon Israel. They said: Ephraim, our righteous Messiah, may your mind be at rest, since you put to rest the mind of your Creator and our minds.

> Pesiqta Rabbati 37:3: R. Simeon b. Pazzi[57] said: In that hour the Holy One will raise the Messiah up to the heaven of heavens, and will shroud him in [something] of His splendor because of the nations of the world, because of the wicked Persians. He [God] said to him: Ephraim, My true Messiah, be the judge of these and do with them as your soul desires, for the nations would long have been destroyed by you in an instant had not My mercies been exceedingly mighty on your behalf, as it is said: *Is Ephraim My dear son? Is he a darling child? [For whenever I speak of him, I earnestly remember him still; therefore My inward parts are troubled for him; in mercy I will have mercy upon him, says the Lord]* (Jer. 31:20).

> Pesiqta Rabbati 37:4: [Why does the verse mention] twice mercy: *In mercy I will have mercy upon him* (Jer. 31:20)? One mercy refers to the hour when he is in prison, since the nations of the world will gnash their teeth, wink their eyes, nod their heads, open their lips, as is said: *All those who see me mock me; they move the lip, they shake their head* (Ps. 22:8); {ed. pr.: *My strength is dried up like a potsherd; and my tongue cleaves to my jaws; and you lay me down in the dust of death* (Ps. 22:16).} They roar at him like lions and fancy devouring him [Ps. 22:14], as it is said: *All our enemies have opened their mouths against us.* (Lam. 3:46).{ed. pr.: *A predatory and roaring lion* (Ezek. 22:25) *I am poured out like water, and all my bones are out of joint; my heart is like wax; it is melted in the midst of my bowels* (Ps. 22:15). And they roar at him like lions and fancy devouring him [Ps. 22:14], as it is said, *All our enemies have opened their mouths against us. Fear and the pit have come upon us, desolation and destruction* (Lam. 3:46-47)}. *In mercy will I have mercy upon him* (Jer. 31:20)—[referring to] the hour when he [Ephraim] leaves the prison, since the nations of the world will despise him. There is not one kingdom or two or three kingdoms that will come upon him, but one hundred and forty kingdoms will encompass him. The Holy One will say to him: Ephraim, Messiah of my righteousness do not be afraid of them, because all of them will die from the breath of your mouth, as it is said: *and with the breath of his lips shall he slay the wicked* (Isa. 11:4).[58]

The date mentioned in the above narrative is Nisan; this is the month during which Passover occurs, the feast of redemption from Egypt. Elijah is expected to announce the arrival of the Messiah in Nisan. The 14th day of Nisan is the biblical Passover, when the Israelites slaughtered a lamb and used its blood for protection. They left Egypt the following evening, the 15th of Nisan, to begin the Exodus. As a memorial to this event, the Feast of Unleavened Bread begins on this day and is celebrated for seven days, suggestive of the seven days of God's master plan. According to John 19:14, Jesus was crucified the day before the Passover celebration, precisely when the lambs were slaughtered. In Jesus' day, by tradition of the elders (John 18:28), the Passover meal was observed on the 15th of Nisan. According to Mark 14:12-16, Jesus had the Passover meal with his disciples and was put on the cross the next morning, the day of Passover. It is speculation that the month of Nisan appears in these messianic passages in Pesiqta Rabbati in response to the death of Jesus. According to Rabbi Joshua, the world was created in Nisan and the Patriarchs were born in Nisan.[59] Pesiqta Rabbati connects the idea of creation to the final redemption and resurrection, independent of any Christological references.

Conclusion

A Psalm of suffering (Psalm 22) is applied to the Messiah Ephraim in Pesiqta Rabbati and a narrative of salvation is created. The explication of biblical lemmata as narrative is a hermeneutic approach of some midrashic texts; this is often the case in homiletic works that create a narrative for the listeners. Pesiqta Rabbati contains the rabbinic crystallization of creating a descriptive narrative of a Jewish Messiah through Psalm 22 and its metaphors of distress. Allusions to this Psalm are deeply embedded in the Pesiqta Rabbati narrative. This narrative is part of a hagiography,[60] slightly resembling other narratives of martyrs in rabbinic texts. Additionally, the messianic narrative is somewhat similar in construction to the Jesus narrative in the Gospels and the extra-testamental writings of the Church Fathers. Pesiqta Rabbati applies Psalm 22 to support the concept of Messiah Ephraim's suffering for humanity; in the New Testament, lemmata from this Psalm are applied to the Passion.[61] The Psalm provides biblical language and the dramatic script for the description of suffering for the Jewish and Christian Messiah. In Pesiqta Rabbati a remarkable interpretation emerges: the Messiah suffers for the sins of Israel and of the world; God makes an agreement with the Messiah to be afflicted for the sake of the sinners.

After a period of suffering, followed by his humiliation and the final eschatological battle, the Messiah is involved in the Final Judgment and the resurrection of the righteous. Other rabbinic texts interpret lemmata in order to combine Psalm 22 and the *Aqedah*, the Sacrifice of Isaac.

While the direct influence of the Christian interpretation of Psalm 22, referring to the suffering Jesus on the cross, upon the Jewish interpretation in Pesiqta Rabbati is an open question, the midrashic interpretation may be a polemic reaction to the Christian interpretation. The evidence for the Christian connection between Psalm 22 with Jesus on the cross predates this Psalm's association with the Messiah in Judaism. In both traditions, the Psalm is identified with a central figure bringing about final salvation at the end of days. Psalm 22 is critical to the Christian fulfillment theory, culminating in the Christological interpretation of that Psalm. The Jewish response to a suffering Messiah inverts the Christian interpretation by making Psalm 22 applicable to a future Messiah, Ephraim.

Psalm 22 became critical to early Christians, possibly because it provided the narrative structure for an unfolding drama of a suffering person who is saved. Certain aspects of the Psalm connect it to traditions concerning a son of God, an heir of David, a servant of the Lord, a prophet, a righteous person; these aspects provided the potential conduit for Psalm 22 to become essential among early Christians. Psalm 22 was hermeneutically constructed by early Christian Bible interpretation to claim this Psalm should be read as a prophetic text about a Davidic heir, namely Jesus. In contrast, the rabbinic interpretation in Pesiqta Rabbati applies the suffering of King David in Psalm 22 to the future Messiah Ephraim (son of Joseph), who is not viewed as a descendant of King David.

Discussion Questions

1. What particular terms in Psalm 22 had radically different trajectories in Jewish and Christian interpretations?
2. How could Queen Esther fulfill the suffering savior figure in Psalm 22?
3. In what ways is interfaith dialogue inspired or hampered by divergent interpretations of the same biblical text?

Notes

1. Psalm 22 (based upon the Masoretic Text):
   1. To the chief Musician, according to "Deer of Dawn," a Psalm of David.
   2. My God, my God, why have You forsaken me? Why are You so far from helping me, from the words of my loud complaint?
   3. O my God, I cry in the daytime, but You do not hear; and in the night, and I have no rest.
   4. But You are holy, O You who are enthroned on the praises of Israel.
   5. Our fathers trusted in You; they trusted, and You saved them.
   6. They cried to You, and were saved; they trusted in You, and were not disappointed.
   7. But I am a worm, and not a man; scorned by men, and despised by the people.
   8. All those who see me mock me; they move the lip, they shake their head, saying,
   9. He trusted on the Lord that he would save him; let Him save him, seeing He delights in him.
   10. But You are He who took me out of the womb; You made me hope when I was upon my mother's breasts.
   11. I was cast upon You from the womb; You are my God from my mother's belly.
   12. Do not be far from me; for trouble is near; for there is none to help.
   13. Many bulls surround me; strong bulls of Bashan surround me.
   14. They open wide their mouths at me, like a ravening and a roaring lion.
   15. I am poured out like water, and all my bones are out of joint; my heart is like wax; it is melted in the midst of my bowels.
   16. My strength is dried up like a potsherd; and my tongue cleaves to my jaws; and You lay me down in the dust of death.
   17. For dogs surround me; the assembly of the wicked encircle me; they seize my hands and my feet like a lion.
   18. I can count all my bones; they look and stare at me.
   19. They divide my garments among them, and cast lots for my clothing.
   20. But You, O Lord, be not far from me; O my strength, hasten to my help.
   21. Save my soul from the sword; my only one from the power of the dog.
   22. Save me from the lion's mouth; for you have answered me from the horns of the wild oxen.
   23. I will declare Your name to my brothers; in the midst of the congregation will I praise You.
   24. You who fear the Lord, praise Him; all you the seed of Jacob, glorify Him; and fear Him, all you the seed of Israel.
   25. For He has not despised nor loathed the affliction of the afflicted; nor has He hidden His face from him; but when he cried to Him, He heard.

26. My praise shall be of You in the great congregation; I will pay my vows before those who fear Him.
27. The humble shall eat and be satisfied; those who seek Him shall praise the Lord. May Your heart live for ever!
28. All the ends of the world shall remember and turn to the Lord; and all the families of the nations shall worship before You.
29. For the kingdom is the Lord's; and He is ruler over the nations.
30. All the fat ones of the earth shall eat and worship; all those who go down to the dust, and he who cannot keep alive his own soul, shall bow before Him.
31. Their seed shall serve Him; it shall be told of the Lord to the coming generation.
32. They shall come, and shall declare His righteousness to a people that shall be born, that He has done this.

2. Theodor Lescow, "Psalm 22 und Psalm 88: Komposition und Dramaturgie," *Zeitschrift für die Alttestamentliche Wissenschaft* 117 (2005): 217-31.
3. Fritz Stolz, "Psalm 22: Alttestamentliches Reden vom Menschen und neutestamentliches Reden von Jesus," *Zeitschrift für Theologie und Kirche 77* (1980): 129-48.
4. See Heike Omerzu, "Die Rezeption von Psalm 22 im Judentum zur Zeit des Zweiten Tempels," in Dieter Sänger, ed., *Psalm 22 und die Passionsgeschichten der Evangelien* (Neukirchen Vluyn: Neukirchener Verlag, 2007), 33-76. The date of *Joseph and Aseneth* is disputed, it derives probably from the first century CE, see John Collins, "Joseph and Aseneth: Jewish or Christian?" *Journal for the Study of the Pseudepigrapha* 14 (2005): 97-112, who confirms that this work originated in Egyptian Judaism, before the revolt under Trajan.
5. I disagree with this premise because the "lion" in this passage has definite Egyptian connotations.
6. Mark G. Vitalis Hoffman, *Psalm 22 and the Crucifixion of Jesus* (PhD diss., Yale University, 1996), 320, expresses a similar idea. Catherine Brown Tkacz, "Esther, Jesus, and Psalm 22," *Catholic Biblical Quarterly* 70 (2008), 709-28; 714, n. 27 refers to the literature that contends that Psalm 22 was first applied to Esther and then later to Jesus.
7. Omerzu, "Die Rezeption," 58.
8. James Sanders, *The Psalms Scroll of Qumran Cave 11 [11QPs[a]]* (DJD 4) (Oxford: Clarendon, 1965).
9. Kristin Swenson, "Psalm 22:17 Circling around the Problem Again," *Journal of Biblical Literature* 123 (2004): 637-48. The Greek translation "they dug my hands and feet" led to the Christian interpretation "they have pierced my hands and feet" (638); Swenson concludes that the consonantal text "proffered by the Masoretes" is the best. James R. Linville, "Psalm 22:17B: A New Guess," *Journal of Biblical Literature* 124 (2005): 733-44; 739, suggests "picked clean," since the ancient versions presuppose a verb in this passage.
10. Gregory Vall, "Psalm 22:17B: The Old Guess," *Journal of Biblical Literature* 116 (1997): 45-56. Michael Barré, "The Crux of Psalm 22:17c: Solved Long Last?" in Bernard F. Batto and Kathryn Roberts, eds., *David and Zion: Biblical Studies in Honor of J.J.M. Roberts* (Winona Lake, IN: Eisenbrauns, 2004), 287-306; 305 views 17b and 18a as interconnected and based upon cognate languages; he suggests the reading: "hands go lame" and "bones intone a funeral lament," which would preserve the chiastic structure of the Psalm.

11. See the appendices in Hoffman and the table in Conrad R. Gren, “Piercing the Ambiguities of Psalm 22:16 and the Messiah's Mission,” *Journal of the Evangelical Theological Society* 48 (2005): 283-99, 292.
12. A treatise concerning the early Christian interpretation is found in Justin Martyr, *Dialogue with Tryphon* 103.8; 99-107.
13. In this chapter I cite from Rivka Ulmer, *A Synoptic Edition Of Pesiqta Rabbati Based Upon All Extant Hebrew Manuscripts And The Editio Princeps*, vol. 1 (Atlanta: Scholars Press, 1997);vol. 2 (Atlanta: Scholars Press, 1999);vol. 3 and index (Lanham, MD: University Press of America, 2002); repr. vols. 1-3, 2009. All English translations are by Rivka Ulmer. The symbol [] indicates additions by the editor or allusions to verses; the symbol {} indicates textual variants.
14. The problem of fictitious baraitot was recognized by Louis Jacobs, “Are there Fictitious Baraitot in the Babylonian Talmud?” *HUCA* 42 (1971): 186-96.
15. Judith M. Lieu, “Justin Martyr and the Transformation of Psalm 22,” in Charlotte Hempel and Judith M. Lieu, eds., *Biblical Traditions in Transmission*, Supplement Journal for the Study of Judaism (Leiden: Brill, 2006), 195-211.
16. Phillip Schaff, *Ante-Nicene Fathers*, vol. 1 (Peabody, MA: Hendrickson, 1994), 174-75.
17. Lieu, “Justin Martyr,” 197.
18. Naomi Koltun-Fromm researched this development in “Psalm 22's Christological Interpretive Tradition in Light of Anti-Jewish Polemic,” *Journal of Early Christian Studies* 6 (1998): 37-57, 55.
19. Lieu, “Justin Martyr,” 209.
20. Philip Nel, “Animal Imagery in Psalm 22,” *Journal of Northwest Semitic Languages* 31 (2005): 75-88, 81.
21. See 2 Kings 3:21-27; 2 Kings 16:1-4; 2 Kings 21:1-8; 2 Kings 23:4-11.
22. *Fear not, O worm of Jacob, the number of Israel; “I have helped you,” says the Lord, and your redeemer, the Holy One of Israel* (Isa. 41:14); Bildad the Shuhite, one of Job's friends, utilizes the same comparison: *How much less, man, who is a worm, and the son of man, who is a maggot!* (Job 25:6).
23. Philip Schaff, *The Apostolic Fathers* (Peabody, MA: Hendrickson, 1994), 9.
24. It should be noted that the numbering of Psalms is slightly deviant in the Septuagint; for example, superscriptions are not part of the numbering in the LXX.
25. Stolz, “Psalm 22, ” 146, lists the distribution of the lemmata of Psalm 22 in Mark.
26. The Testaments in the Pseudepigrapha.
27. For further details, see Esther Menn, “Nor Ordinary Lament: Relecture and the Identity of the Distressed in Psalm 22,” *Harvard Theological Review* 93 (2000): 301-41, 330.
28. Among the multitude of examples, see Mekhilta, Pisha, 4; Mishnah, Menahot 7:6; Babylonian Talmud, Pesahim 70b.
29. *Targum Yonathan* has *Eli, Eli, m^{e}tul mah sh^{e}vaqtani*. The verb *sh^{e}vaqtani* derives from the Aramaic *sh^{e}vaq* [leave, forsake]. The Greek text is not precise or consistent in its transliteration from Aramaic; it is therefore remotely possible that the Aramaic *sh^{e}vaqtani* could have become *sabachthani* in the process of transliteration.
30. For example, Midrash Sekhel Tov, Shemot 15, cites Psalm 22:2; see also Yalqut Shim`oni Beshallah, 244.
31. Menn summarized some of the rabbinic interpretations of single lemmata from Psalm 22 in the rabbinic corpus; see also Brown Tkacz, who views Queen Esther as a female messiah, 710-11.

32. A table of the passages is found in Hoffman, 392.
33. Philip Schaff, *Fathers of the Third Century: Tertullian, Part Fourth; Minucius Felix; Commodian; Origen, Parts First and Second* (Peabody, MA: Hendrickson, 1994), 287.
34. Ismar Elbogen (tr. Raymond Scheindlin), *Jewish Liturgy: A Comprehensive History* (Philadelphia: The Jewish Publication Society, 1993), 110-11.
35. Menn, "Nor Ordinary Lament," 318.
36. Ulmer, *A Synoptic Edition,* xix-xxii.
37. Phillip Schaff, *Ante-Nicene Fathers,* vol. 1 (Peabody, Mass.: Hendrickson, 1994), 174-75.
38. Cited in Yalqut Shim'oni, Zephaniah 567.
39. Pesiqta Rabbati 36 is partially cited in Yalqut Shim'oni, Isaiah 494, 499 and Pesiqta Rabbati 37 in Yalqut Shim'oni Jeremiah 515.
40. Ed. pr. (editio princeps) refers to the first printed edition.
41. Hoffman, *Psalm 22,* 165, draws attention to the variant readings in early biblical translations, including throat, larynx, and jaws.
42. Hoffman, *Psalm 22,* 360.
43. The text has "ben David," although it continues with Messiah Ephraim. This may indicate the conflation of messianic ideas in Pesiqta Rabbati; alternatively, it may be due to one of the numerous scribal errors in the Parma manuscript.
44. In Rev. 19:15 the messianic figure returns to rule with "an iron rod;" this term is symbolic of power. Pesiqta Rabbati applies the term to the power of the government. In Psalms of Solomon the messianic figure is a king in the image of David (Ps. Sol. 17:21); he will smash the gentile oppressors of Jerusalem with an iron rod.
45. See Rivka Ulmer, "Consistency and Change in Rabbinic Literature as Reflected in the Terms 'Rain' and 'Dew,'" *Journal for the Study of Judaism* 26 (1995): 55-75.
46. The Messiah as the light of the world is found in Babylonian Talmud, Shabbat 116b; similar in Genesis Rabbah 2:4.
47. Dörte Bester, *Körperbilder in den Psalmen*, FAT, 2, 54; (Tübingen: Mohr/Siebeck, 2007), 57.
48. Arnold Goldberg, *Erlösung durch Leiden: Drei rabbinische Homilien über die Trauernden Zions und den leidenden Messias Efraim (Pesiqta Rabbati 34.36.37),* Frankfurter Judaistische Studien, 4 (Frankfurt am Main, 1978), 261; and *Ich komme und wohne in deiner Mitte: Eine rabbinische Homilie zu Sacharja 2,14 (Pesiqta Rabbati 35),* Frankfurter Judaistische Studien, 3 (Frankfurt am Main, 1977).
49. Michael A. Fishbane, "Midrash and Messianism: Some Theologies of Suffering and Salvation," in Peter Schäfer and Mark Cohen, eds., *Toward the Millenium: Expectations from the Bible to Waco* (Leiden: Brill, 1998), 57-71.
50. Benedikt Carpzov, ed., *Raimundus Martinus, Pugio Fidei* (Leipzig: Johannis Wittegau, 1687, facsimile repr. Farnborough: Gregg Press, 1967), 416.
51. *Me'or Enayim* (Vilna, 1863-66, repr. Jerusalem: Maqor, 1970), 250; Joanna Weinberg, ed., *Azariah de' Rossi Meor Eynaim: The Light of the Eyes. Translated from the Hebrew* (New Haven: Yale University Press, 2001). This work may be a partial response to Christian polemics against rabbinic ideas.
52. Vernon K. Robbins, *Exploring the Texture of Texts: A Guide to Socio-rhetorical Interpretation* (Valley Forge, PA: Trinity Press, 1996), 58. For example, a diegetic allusion is mentioned in Luke 1:1.
53. "The fifth chamber: [this is where] Messiah ben David, Elijah and the Messiah Ephraim dwell. Elijah holds his head and allows it to rest on his chest. He encour-

ages him and says to him: Bear the torment and judgment of your Lord while He punishes you for the sin of Israel, for Scripture says: *He is pierced for our rebellions, crushed for our transgressions* (Isa. 53:5) until the time when the end arrives. Every Monday, Thursday, Shabbat, and festival day the ancient Patriarchs, Moses, Aaron, David, Solomon, the entire royal line, the prophets and the pious ones come to greet him [the Messiah] and to weep together with him. They express gratitude to him and say to him: Bear the judgment of your Lord, *for the end has almost arrived, and the chains which are on your neck will be broken off* and you will go forth in freedom." Jellinek, *BHM*, 2:29.20-33 (trans. Rivka Ulmer), similar in 2:50.5-9. Here Isa. 53:5 is applied to the Jewish Messiah.

54. In Matt. 4:5, it is the devil who placed Jesus on the pinnacle of the Temple; Pesiqta Rabbati 36:9 may reflect a process in which an element of another culture is incorporated, but changed, which then results in an inverted response to the apocalyptic forces of evil in its reference to the Messiah on the roof of the Temple.
55. Reuven Kimelman, "The Literary Structure of the Amidah and the Rhetoric of Redemption," in Dever, W.G. and Wright, J.E., eds., *The Echoes of Many Texts: Reflections on Jewish and Christian Traditions. Essays in Honor of Lou H. Silberman*, BJSt 313 (Atlanta: Scholars Press, 1997), 171-218.
56. The dialogue between the Fathers and the Messiah is cited in Pirqe Mashiah (*BHM* 3:73, based upon Pesiqta Rabbati).
57. Third-century Babylonia.
58. See Yalqut Shim`oni, Isaiah 56: "This is the light of the Messiah, as is written in Psalm (36:10): *In Your light, we see light.*"
59. Babylonian Talmud, Rosh Ha-Shanah 11a.
60. Rivka Ulmer, "The Contours of the Messiah in Pesiqta Rabbati," Paper presented at the Association for Jewish Studies Conference, Los Angeles, December 21, 2009.
61. The opening words are cited in Matt. 27:46 and Mark 15:34.

Section 2

Responding to the Jewish Jesus

What Was at Stake in the Parting of the Ways between Judaism and Christianity?

Richard L. Rubenstein

In this chapter, I will explore the question of what was at stake culturally, religiously, and psychologically in the parting of the ways between Judaism and early Christianity. Since the issues involved are multifaceted, I have chosen to focus primarily on religious sacrifice. I believe that this issue exhibits simultaneously elements of both continuity and discontinuity between the two traditions.

Let us begin with the narrative of the *Aqedah* in Scripture (Gen. 22:1-19). As is well known, on one of the holiest days of the Jewish religious calendar, the second day of Rosh Hashanah, the reading from the Torah deals primarily with the *Aqedah* in which Abraham is unconditionally commanded, "Take your son, your favored one, Isaac, whom you love, and go to the land of Moriah, and offer him there as a burnt offering on one of the heights that I will point out to you." (Gen. 22:2)

This is a story of an aborted infanticide demanded by God. According to the eminent Jewish scholar, the late Shalom Spiegel, "the primary purpose of the Akedah story may have been only this: to attach to a real pillar of the folk and a revered reputation the new norm—abolish human sacrifice, substitute animals instead."[1] It would appear that most, but by no means all, modern Jewish scholars agree with Spiegel.

There is, however, a minority opinion persuasively expressed by Harvard's Jon Levenson that "Gen. 22:1-19 is frighteningly unequivocal about YHVH's ordering a father to offer up his son as a sacrifice." [2] I share that opinion. Although Shalom Spiegel was my teacher at the Jewish Theological Seminary, I must respectfully disagree with him.

An important reason for this difference of opinion is that there are verses in Scripture in which the divine command to sacrifice the firstborn male appears to be unconditional. For example, Exodus 13:1-2 stipulates: "The Lord spoke further to Moses, saying, "Consecrate to Me every first-born; man and beast, the first issue of every womb among the Israelites is Mine." Exodus 22:28-29 reads, "You shall not put off the skimming of the first yield of your vats. You shall give Me the first-born among your sons. You shall do the same with your cattle and your flocks: seven days it shall remain with its mother; on the eighth day you shall give it to Me." In neither verse do we find a mitigating qualification.

Elsewhere in Exodus, Scripture does call for a surrogate offering to take the place of and redeem the male child: "And when the Lord has brought you into the land of the Canaanites . . . you shall set apart for the Lord every first issue of the womb: every male firstling that your cattle drop shall be the Lord's. But every firstling ass you shall redeem with a sheep; if you do not redeem it, you must break its neck. And you must redeem every firstborn male among your children." (Exod. 13:11-13)

There is also evidence in Scripture that child sacrifice was not only practiced in Israel, perhaps as late as 500 BCE, but that it may very well have been part of the official cultus rather than a pagan intrusion. The most intriguing hint that such might indeed have been the case occurs in the words of the Prophet Ezekiel who depicts YHVH as mounting a crescendo of accusations against "Jerusalem" that culminates in the following condemnation: "You even took the sons and daughters that you bore to Me and sacrificed them to those [images] as food.—as if your harlotries were not enough, you slaughtered My children and presented them as offerings to them" (Ezek. 16:20-21).

Moreover, there is a very strange passage in Ezekiel in which the prophet apparently admits that the rituals he abhors were actually practiced by men and women who regarded them as an authentic expression of Yahvism: "I gave them laws that were not good and rules by which they could not live: When they set aside every first issue of the womb, I defiled them by their very gifts—that I might render them desolate, that they might know that I am the Lord (Ezek. 20:25-26).

Ed Noort, a Dutch scholar, has called this passage "the most peculiar sentence on the role of torah (sic) in the Hebrew Bible," noting, "it is YHVH himself who provides the laws leading to death instead of life. He allows Israel to taint itself by the sacrifice of the firstborn."[3] Ezekiel's depiction of YHVH giving Israel "laws leading to death" is consistent with Noort's view that in contemporary scholarship, "The picture of the black-and-white oppositions between Baalism and Yahwism has disappeared." [4]

We may be able to learn a good deal about child sacrifice in ancient Israel from ancient Carthage. Founded as a colony of the Phoenician city of Tyre, with which Judah and Israel had important commercial and religious contacts in ancient times, there was apparently a close affinity between Israelite and Phoenician or Canaanite culture." [5] Ancient writers such as Kleitarchos, Agathocles,

Diodorus Siculus, Plutarch, and the Christian theologian Tertullian (ca. 160-ca. 220) all testify to the practice of child sacrifice in the realm of Carthage. In December 1921, the largest cemetery of sacrificed infants in the ancient Near East was discovered at Carthage, now a resort suburb of the city of Tunis.[6] There are similar, smaller Phoenician sites in Sicily, Sardinia, and Tunisia.

In the 1970s, archaeologists Lawrence E. Stager and Samuel R. Wolff excavated an area in the city of Carthage estimated to be no less than "between 54,000 and 64,000 square feet" that they called the "Carthaginian Tophet." They estimate that as many as 20,000 funerary urns containing the bones of young children were deposited at the site between 400 BCE and 200 BCE or approximately one child sacrifice every three days.[7] Mixed in with children's bones in some of the urns, they also found urns containing the charred bones of lambs and kids. They concluded that the "burned animals were intended as substitute sacrifices for children."[8] I should, however, note that a minority of scholars challenge the notion that live children were sacrificed at Carthage and argue that the literary evidence for such sacrifices was nothing more than a blood libel spread by foreign antagonists.[9] Nevertheless, the scholarly consensus is that the literary and archaeological evidence point overwhelmingly to the practice of child sacrifice. We should also note that although such sacrifices were religiously motivated, they did serve a sociological function of population control, much as abortion and infanticide have in other cultures.

There would thus seem to be a clear connection between lambs and kids in the Carthaginian urns and the ram that takes the place of Isaac in the *Aqedah* (Gen. 22:13), as well as the lamb required for redemption in place of the Israelite firstborn in Exodus 34:19-20 where God is depicted as declaring: "Every first issue of the womb is Mine, from all your livestock that drop a male as firstling, whether cattle or sheep. But the firstling of an ass you shall redeem with a sheep; if you do not redeem it, you must break its neck. And you must redeem every firstborn among your sons. None shall appear before Me empty-handed." Similarly, there would seem to be a connection between the Carthaginian surrogate animals and the Passover lamb in Exodus 12-13. Thus, Scripture depicts God as commanding the Hebrews to place "some of the blood" of the lamb on doorposts of their houses and declare: "I will go through the land of Egypt and strike down every firstborn . . . , both man and beast; and I will mete out punishments to all the gods of Egypt, I the Lord. And the blood on the houses where you are staying shall be a sign for you: when I see the blood I will pass over you, so that no plague will destroy you when I strike the land of Egypt." (Exod. 12:12-13) As with the *Aqedah* ram, the Passover lamb is a substitute offering in place of the Hebrew firstborn. The blood provides the evidence of the substitution.

As noted above, most modern Jewish scholars have held that the fundamental lesson of the *Aqedah* was that the sacrifice of the firstborn was no longer required and that an animal was an acceptable surrogate. Such a judgment may reflect a cultural bias in which religion is seen as evolving from the lower to higher forms. Thus, nineteenth-century Reform Jewish thinkers tended to eliminate traditional prayers for the restoration of the Jerusalem Temple and its Scripturally ordained rituals of animal sacrifice because they regarded prayer as a "higher" and more "spiritual" form of worship than bloody animal sacrifices. Nevertheless, Stager and Wolff inform us that there was no retreat from human sacrifices in Carthage over the centuries. On the contrary, they report that the proportion of human to animal bones found in the urns were far greater in "the fourth and third centuries BCE, when Carthage had attained the height of urbanity," than in the earlier centuries. Moreover, the inscriptions on the monuments reveal that a far greater proportion of the bones were of children of noble and prosperous families rather than of "common Carthaginians." They also remind us that the Phoenicians were among the most highly civilized and cosmopolitan people in the Mediterranean.[10] Let us recall that Hiram, King of Tyre, sent architects, stone masons and other workmen, as well as cedar wood, to Solomon for the construction of the First Temple of Jerusalem.

An important reason for the persistence and even the increase in human sacrifice may have been the thought that if animal sacrifices were efficacious, how much more efficacious would an even more precious offering, the sacrifice of the beloved child, be.

Moreover, Judaism never entirely rejected the idea that God demands the sacrifice of the firstborn son. However we evaluate the existence of child sacrifice in ancient Judah, Israel, Canaan, and the colonies of Canaan-Phoenicia, it is evident that we are dealing with a God who demands the death of children. In reflecting on the issue of child sacrifice in Judaism and Christianity, Levenson comments, "the mythic-ritual complex that I have been calling 'child sacrifice' was never eradicated; it was only transformed."[11] A prime example of that transformation is the *pidyon ha-ben* ritual in fulfillment of the commandment already noted: "You shall redeem all the firstborn of your sons. None shall appear before Me empty-handed." (Exod. 34:20) In the ceremony, the father presents his firstborn son to a *cohen* or hereditary priest on the thirtieth day after his birth whereupon the priest asks the father, "Which do you prefer, your son or your money?" The father declares that he prefers his son and presents the *cohen* with five silver dollars, the symbolic equivalent of five biblical shekels, in order to "redeem" his son. The priest accepts the coins with the ritual formula, "This (the coins) in place of that (the child). This in exchange for that."

I have personally described the *pidyon haben* ceremony for my firstborn son, Aaron, in an autobiographical work.[12] To make my point, I included an outrageous fantasy about the ritual. Instead of saying, "I want my son," I imagined myself as saying, "I want my money. God can have the boy." The response totally disorients the *cohen* because he knows that in the Bible whatever is employed to "redeem" the child is actually the surrogate for the life of the child, just as the ram substituted for Isaac in the *Aqedah*. When I participated in the ceremony, I had no such thoughts. The fundamental purpose of the ceremony was subliminally to acknowledge and deflect our infanticidal tendencies. In its own way, that motive is also operative in Christian for it is Christ, the Son, who is sacrificed so that others may be redeemed. Nevertheless, in retrospect, I understood that at some level the ritual recognized that the subterranean power of the infanticidal impulse had never entirely disappeared. Today, the ceremony is a happy family occasion and few, if any, participants are aware of its older significance.

Not only does Jewish tradition continue the *pidyon haben* ceremony to this day, but, as we have seen, on one of Judaism's holiest days, Jews are reminded that the death of their ancestral patriarch's firstborn son was only averted as a result of the patriarch's unconditional obedience to God's terrible command. Thus, Scripture depicts an "angel of the Lord" telling Abraham: "Do not raise your hand against the boy, or do anything to him. For now I know that you fear God, since you have not withheld your son, your favored one, from Me." (Gen. 22:12) There follows a second angelic address. Abraham is told: "All the nations of the earth shall bless themselves by your descendents, because you have obeyed my command." (Gen. 22:18) Not only has the sacrifice has been averted because of Abraham's unconditional obedience, but God's covenant has been bestowed on him and his descendants because of that same obedience." Moreover, Abraham's obedience was matched by that of his son. Scripture depicts Isaac as asking his father, "Here are the firestone and the wood; but where is the sheep for the burnt offering?" And Abraham said, "God will see to the sheep for His burnt offering, my son." Scripture then reports, "And the two of them walked on together." (Gen. 22:7-8) indicating thereby their complete unity of resolve.[13] Some traditions refer to the "ashes of Isaac" and claim that Abraham performed the sacrifice but that Isaac was resurrected.[14] Thus, the twelfth century poet, Rabbi Ephraim ben Jacob of Bonn (b. 1132), depicted Isaac as imploring Abraham :

> Bind for me my hands and my feet
> Lest I be found wanting and profane the sacrifice.
> I am afraid of panic, I am concerned to honor you,
> My will is to honor you greatly.[15]

Abraham then prepares the fire and wood of the sacrifice "in their right order" after which:

> With steadfast hands he slaughtered him according to the rite,
> Full right was the slaughter.

The poet then tells of Isaac's resurrection and of Abraham's determination to complete the sacrifice:

> Down upon him fell the resurrecting dew, and he revived.
> (The father seized him (then) to slaughter him once more.
> Scripture, bear witness! Well-grounded is the fact:
> And the Lord called Abraham, even a second time from heaven.

At that point, the ram appears "in a nearby thicket."

Because of the Crusader massacres of Jews in the Rhineland during Rabbi Ephraim's lifetime, the poem had a special poignancy. At the time, many Jewish fathers did slaughter their children. When the Crusaders swept through Bonn, Mainz, Wurms, and other communities on their way to the Holy Land, they gave Jews the choice of death or conversion. In those days, the Jews preferred to die and frequently slaughtered their children to prevent them from being overcome by a moment of weakness.

As noted above, most modern Jewish commentators see the lesson of the *Aqedah* as YHVH's rejection of human sacrifice. Nevertheless, so eminent a religious authority as the late Rabbi Joseph B. Soloveitchik, arguably the most important Orthodox thinker of twentieth-century America, rejected that view:

> Abraham implemented the sacrifice of Isaac not on Mount Moriah but in the depths of his heart. He gave up Isaac the very instant God addressed Himself to him and asked him to return his most precious possession to its legitimate master and owner. Immediately, with no arguing or pleading, Abraham surrendered Isaac. He gave him up as soon as the command "and offer him there for a burned offering" (Gen. 22:2) was issued. Inwardly, the sacrificial act was consummated at once. Isaac no longer belonged to Abraham. He was dead as far as Abraham was concerned. [16]

According to Soloveitchik, because of Abraham's willingness to slay his son and the fact that he experienced the full horror of the sacrifice the very instant the command was given, "there was no need for the physical sacrifice" and the animal became an acceptable substitute. Soloveitchik further comments that had Abraham not "immediately surrendered Isaac, had he not experienced the *Aqedah* in its full awesomeness and frightening helplessness, God would not have sent the Angel to stop Abraham from implementing the command. Abraham would have lost Isaac physically." [17]

Thus, Soloveitchik clearly refutes the notion that the purpose of the *Aqedah* narrative was to demonstrate that God's rejection of the actual sacrifice of Isaac. Soloveitchik's interpretation is consistent with Scripture which clearly states that not only was Isaac's sacrifice averted because of Abraham's unconditional obedience, but God's covenant was bestowed on Abraham and his progeny because of that very same obedience (Gen. 22:15-18).

Let us now turn more directly to Jesus. Whatever narrative divergences exist between the four canonical Gospels, they are at one in depicting the death of Jesus as occurring during the Passover season. Mark, in all probability the oldest Gospel, offers the following description of the beginning of the public career of Jesus:

> In those days Jesus came from Nazareth in Galilee and was baptized by John in the Jordan. Immediately coming up out of the water, He saw the heavens opening, and the Spirit like a dove descending upon Him; and a voice

came out of the heavens: "You are My beloved Son, in You I am well-pleased. (Mark 1:9-11; see Matt. 3:17, Luke 3:22, 2 Peter 1:17).

Levenson sees echoes of Isaac's role in the *Aqedah* in Jesus' designation as God's beloved Son, but there is great irony in this designation. To be God's beloved son or even the beloved son in the Israelite-Canaanite-Phoenician religion complex is no promise of enduring felicity. All too often the fate of the beloved son was to endure a supreme sacrificial test or worse. In Carthage, noble families often sacrificed that which was most precious to them, their child, as a gift to the goddess Taanith or the god Baal Hammon. Moreover, at a very early stage, the infant Christian community came to believe that the suffering servant of Isaiah 52:13-53:12 was linked to the idea of Jesus as God's beloved Son. This helped to transform the crucifixion from a weapon of painful death to an assurance of eternal life.[18] Isaac, Isaiah's suffering servant, and Jesus must all submit to a terrible confrontation with death to please their heavenly Father.[19]

At the first meeting of Jesus and John the Baptist, the Fourth Gospel depicts the Baptist as declaring: "Behold, the Lamb of God who takes away the sin of the world!" (John 1:29). These words have been incorporated into the Latin Mass as *Agnus Dei qui tollis peccata mundi*, "an image that foreshadows the coming Passion."[20] In reality, this double identification of Jesus as Son of God and Lamb of God may not indicate a real difference inasmuch as the term Son of God may also point to Jesus' role as the sacrificial victim.

There may be some question concerning the historical veracity of John's version of the meeting between the Baptist and Jesus. However, because John depicts Jesus as a stranger who descends from a heavenly realm for a temporary earthly sojourn, historical details concerning Jesus' earthly activities were of less concern to him than to Mark, Matthew, and Luke. Hence, at least in the narrative concerning the involvement of Jewish authorities in Jesus' death, Paula Fredricksen argues that John may preserve more of the historical details than do the later gospel writers.[21]

The earliest written narrative about Jesus, the letters of Paul, identifies Jesus as the Paschal Lamb. Paul was not only at home in Jewish custom, but the symbolism and mood of Passover is present in 1 Corinthians where Paul calls Christ "our Passover," and uses the Jewish custom of cleansing the home of all leaven before the Passover festival as a metaphor for the moral self-cleansing of the Corinthian Church (1 Cor. 5:6-8).[22] Paul's First Letter to the Corinthians is also the oldest extant Christian document about the Lord's Supper.[23] Although Paul left no systematic exposition of the meaning of the Eucharist, he does discuss the Lord's Supper at some length in two passages in that epistle. In these passages he refers to the Lord's Supper in connection with his efforts to deal with problems that arose in Corinth in his absence. Warning Corinth's believers against immoral and idolatrous behavior, Paul writes:

> Is not the cup of blessing which we bless a sharing in the blood of Christ? Is not the bread which we break a sharing in the body of Christ? Since there is one bread, we who are many are one body; for we all partake of the one bread . . . You cannot drink the cup of the Lord and the cup of demons; you cannot partake of the table of the Lord and the table of demons. (1 Cor. 10:16-21)

In the next chapter, Paul writes:

> For I received from the Lord that which I also delivered to you, that the Lord Jesus in the night in which He was betrayed took bread; and when He had given thanks (*eucharistéō*), He broke it and said, "This is My body, which is for you; do this in remembrance of Me." In the same way He took the cup also after supper, saying, "This cup is the new covenant in My blood; do this, as often as you drink it, in remembrance of Me." For as often as you eat this bread and drink the cup, you proclaim the Lord's death until He comes. (1 Cor. 11:23-26.)

In its written form, Mark's account of the Lord's Supper (Mark 14:12-26) is a few years later than Paul's, but it probably reflects the same oral tradition utilized by Paul. Although Paul's account differs somewhat from Mark's in detail, there is a fundamental agreement that suggests that the primitive church preserved a well-defined memory of Jesus' last meal with his disciples in which he identified the bread and wine with his own body and blood. By so doing, Jesus opened the possibility of the development of a sacrificial ritual centering in his own person. Nevertheless, Jesus' Last Supper is not yet a meal in which Jesus himself is the sacrificial victim. During the Last Supper, Jesus declared to his disciples, "I tell you solemnly, I shall not drink any more wine until the day I drink new wine in the kingdom of God" (Mark 14:25). These words would indicate that the Last Supper was primarily a feast of leave-taking and hopeful anticipation. Jesus looked forward to the time when be would once again eat in fellowship with his disciples "in the kingdom of God." It is the consensus of scholarly opinion that Jesus' promise refers to the future messianic feast that the Messiah will enjoy with the faithful when all is accomplished.

It is very likely that Jesus' promise to return corresponded with his disciples' deepest yearning. They were aware of the terminal threat that hung over their master's life and it was by no means certain that the group could maintain itself without him. By virtue of the absolutely unique impact Jesus had upon his followers, he simply could not be replaced. In all likelihood, his words of confident assurance that he would return reflected his intuitive understanding of what his loss would mean to them.

Oscar Cullmann has commented that the meals shared by the disciples immediately after Jesus' death were initially meals of joy and thanksgiving rather than sorrowful commemorations of the crucifixion.[24] According to Acts, the disciples "continued to meet every day in the Temple and, breaking bread at home, they ate their meals with joy and simplicity" (Acts 2:46). If the meals they shared had a distinctly sacrificial character, emphasizing the consumption of the body and blood of the risen Christ, it is unlikely that they would have continued to meet "every day in the Temple" where the traditional Jewish sacrifices were offered.

Perhaps the most helpful way of understanding the evolution of the Eucharist is to be found in Oscar Cullmann's distinction between the earliest sacred meals, at which the disciples ate with Christ, and the later Lord's Meal, at which Christ was eaten.[25] The joyful meals of fellowship at which the risen Christ was present to his disciples were meals in which the disciples either ate with Christ or anticipated eating with him at the messianic feast. However, there came a time when hopeful anticipation of Christ's return predominated over the feeling of his presence. The sources depict Christ as present immediately after the Resurrection, but, within a short time, the disciples are left to carry on their work without him. It is at this point that their longing for his return must have intensified. That longing is powerfully expressed in the Eucharistic liturgy preserved in the *Didache*, which most scholars date no later than 150 and many date much earlier. As the sacred meal concludes the leader prays: "Let his Grace (i.e., Christ) draw near, and let the present world pass away." The congregation replies: "Hosanna to the God of David." Leader: "Whoever is holy, let him approach. Whoso is not, let him repent." The congregation concludes with the *Maranatha:* "O Lord, come quickly. Amen."[26]

The Didache's version of the Eucharist rests upon Jesus' assurance to his disciples that he would not drink wine again until he did so in God's kingdom. This version expresses the note of anticipation and expectation we have already noted in the earliest forms of the Christian sacred meal. Nevertheless, there is a limit to the human capacity for unrequited yearning. Ultimately, men must choose either to abandon the object of yearning and reinvest their emotional energy elsewhere or to find a way to rejoin the lost object.

That way was found through identification with Christ. Throughout his life, Paul saw humanity's fundamental problem as: how can we achieve the right relationship to our Creator? Before conversion his response was the classical Jewish answer: human beings achieve the right relationship by obedient submission to the will of God. That submission was why normative Judaism has always been the religion of Torah and its authoritative interpreters. After conversion, Paul found another way to achieve an acceptable relationship to God: identification with Christ. Identification is therefore a crucial category in which both the religious and the psychological worlds intersect in the experience of Paul and his spiritual heirs.

I am indebted to the scholarship of Albert Schweitzer for much of my understanding of the role of identification in Paul's thought and religious experience.[27] Before Schweitzer, Protestant New Testament scholarship tended to read

Paul through the eyes and experience of Martin Luther, stressing the centrality of the doctrine of justification by faith. Schweitzer maintained that the doctrine of justification by faith, while undoubtedly of great importance, was less central to Paul's thought than his "Christ mysticism" and his eschatology. Instead of regarding Paul as an opponent of Judaism, as earlier Protestant scholars tended to do, Schweitzer interpreted him as a loyal Jew who was convinced that the risen Christ had initiated the messianic age.[28] According to Schweitzer, Paul understood the kind of existence baptized Christians enjoyed in the messianic age to be literally that of corporeal solidarity with the glorified, immortal body of the risen Christ. He asserted that the fundamental conception of Paul's Christ mysticism is that the elect and Christ partake of a common bodily identity.[29] This identification is expressed most graphically in Paul's exclamation that, having been crucified with Christ, it is no longer he who lives but Christ who lives in him (Gal. 2:20). Paul described Christians as having "clothed themselves" with Christ, by which he meant that Christ was their new, heavenly body rather than new apparel (Gal. 3:27; Rom. 13:14; see 11 Cor. 5:3, 4; Eph. 4:24; Col. 3:10).

According to Paul, in baptism Christians identify with both Christ's death and his resurrection. Thus, in Romans 6:3-4 Paul writes: "Are you ignorant that when we were baptized in Christ Jesus we were baptized in his death? In other words, when we were baptized we went into the tomb with him and joined him in death, so that as Christ was raised from the dead by the Father's glory, we too might live a new life" (Rom. 6:3, 4). And, in Colossians 2: 12: "You have been buried with him, when you were baptized; and by baptism, too, you have been raised up with him through your faith in the power of God who raised him from the dead."

The notion that at baptism Christians enter a new life, actually true life for the first time, was central to his thinking. He contrasted the convert's pre-Christian existence, at best a kind of living death that ends in actual death, with his Christian life, which was in the process of becoming life as it was intended by God before the sin of Adam, life devoid of the related curses of sin and mortality (1 Cor. 15:21-2; Rom. 5:12-15). Paul repeatedly described the baptized Christian as *en Christo*, "in Christ," and he insisted that *en Christo* the Christian became a new man. He wrote to the Corinthians, "For anyone who is in Christ, there is a new creation" (11 Cor. 5:17). So radically is the Christian's identity transformed by his existence in Christ that Paul could assert of his own postbaptismal identity: "I have been crucified with Christ, and I live now not with my own life but with the life of Christ who lives in me" (Gal. 2:19).

Paul frequently used the metaphor of stripping off the old and putting on the new to describe the dying of the old self and rebirth in Christ (Eph. 4:22-24: Col. 3:9; see Rom. 13:12, Col. 2:12). The new self the Christian acquires annuls both the old self and the premessianic world. All of the crucial distinctions that have cursed mankind are ended, at least in principle, with baptism: "All baptized in Christ, you have clothed yourselves in Christ, and there are no more distinctions between Jew and Greek, slave and free, male and female, but all of you are one in Christ Jesus" (Gal. 3:27-28; see 1 Cor. 2:13). If the term "rebirth" is absent from the undisputed letters of Paul, the spiritual and psychological reality of the Christian's experience as newly and truly born pervades his thought.

In order to understand Paul's theology, in the middle decades of the twentieth century Christian scholars such as W. D. Davies, Robin Scroggs, and C. K. Barrett studied the relevance of rabbinic speculation concerning Adam. Scroggs, in particular, has pointed to the importance of both rabbinic and apocryphal speculation (if indeed the two tendencies can be separated) concerning the fall of Adam for an understanding of Paul's interpretation of Christ's role as "the last Adam" who reverses the condemnation brought upon the race by the first Adam. According to Scroggs, rabbinic tradition maintained that 1) before sinning, Adam enjoyed royal prerogatives over all of creation: Just as God is king on high, Adam's original destiny was to be king below; 2) Adam originally possessed superlative wisdom, far greater than that of the angels; 3) Adam was truly made in the image (*eikon*) of God. Adam therefore resembled God himself rather than the angels, who were originally inferior to him; 4) Adam possessed a glorious nature. The ball of his heel outshone the sun. Adam thus partook of the very glory of God insofar as was possible for a created being; and 5) Adam possessed cosmic dimensions and was reduced to the size of mortal men only after his disobedience.[30]

Scroggs' categories summarize conveniently and accurately rabbinic speculation about Adam before the fall. I concur with his estimate of the significance of these speculations: the rabbinic-apocryphal picture of Adam before the fall resembles that tradition's image of what man will be like in the world to come. The deathless, glorified, felicitous existence enjoyed by prelapsarian Adam is the kind of existence that awaits the righteous in the world to come. Adam originally enjoyed the kind of existence God intended all men to savor. When the corruptions of the present era are finally undone, Adam's progeny will be restored to the felicitous existence their primal father was meant to enjoy. Although there is an elusive and an ambiguous character to rabbinic speculation concerning the world to come, which makes it exceedingly difficult to assert that any doctrine represents the rabbinic consensus, it would seem that there was at least agreement that the dead would be resurrected and that those found acceptable by God would enjoy some kind of bliss. My caution in suggesting more than this reflects the admonition implied in the well-known saying of R. Johanan, a second-century Palestinian teacher: "R. Johanan said: Every prophet prophesied only for the days of the Messiah, but as for the World to Come (i.e., the last age after the final judgment of humanity), 'Eye has not seen nor ear heard what God has prepared for those who wait for Him.' (Isa. 64:4)" (Berakhoth 34b). It is possible that Johanan's comment reflected a rabbinic reaction to the increasingly successful Christian movement. Nevertheless, there was a link in rabbinic myth between the felicity that awaits the righteous and the immortality lost by Adam at the fall. The rabbis frequently utilized the term *gan ʿeden,* the garden of Eden, to refer to the paradise to come. Even the English language cannot avoid a certain linguistic concurrence in this ideal—the same word is used for both the paradise to be regained and the paradise lost. Although no single rabbinic reflection on the world to come can be taken as authoritative, there is one statement by Rab, a third-century Babylonian authority, which may be relevant to our study of Paul. According to Rab,

> The World to Come is not like this world. In the World to Come there is neither eating nor drinking; there is no begetting of children or business; no envy or hatred or strife; but the righteous sit enthroned with their crowns on their heads and enjoy the lustre of the *Shekhinah*, as it is written, 'And they beheld God, and ate and drank' (Exod 24:11)—they were satisfied with the radiance of God's *Shekhinah*; it was food and drink to them. (Berakhoth 17a)

This saying resembles Jesus' reply to the Sadducees concerning the marital status of a woman who had successively married several brothers according to the law of levirate marriage. Jesus said: "When they rise from the dead men and women do not marry; no, they are like the angels in heaven" (Mark 12:24; see Matt. 22:30, Luke 20:34-36). Behind the sayings of Johanan, Rab, and Jesus, it is possible to discern a common conviction that the order of things as we know it offers few hints concerning existence in the age to come. As we shall see, Paul shared this conviction (see 1 Cor. 15:46-50).

The supreme importance of obedience in biblical religion was graphically illustrated by Herman Melville in *Moby Dick* in Father Mapple's sermon in which the preacher describes the sin of Jonah Ben Amittai:

> As with all sinners among men, the sin of the son of Amittai was his willful disobedience of the command of God—never mind what that command was, or how conveyed—which he found a hard command. But all the things that God would have us do are hard for us to do. . . . And if we obey God, we must disobey ourselves; and it is in this disobeying ourselves, wherein the hardness of obeying God consists.[31]

Some argue that Father Mapple's God is the God of an especially rigid form of Calvinism and not the true God of biblical faith.[32] Nevertheless, Father Mapple is correct when be observes that in biblical religion man's primary duty is to subordinate his own inclinations to the will of God.

But, have we not heard of the salvific virtue of obedience before? Did not Scripture tell us that Abraham was relieved of his obligation to sacrifice because of his obedience? Let us recall the words of the first Angel of God: As Abraham lifts the knife to slay Isaac, the Angel calls to him and tells him not to slay the boy, "For now I know that you fear God, since you have not withheld your son, your favored one from me" (Gen. 22:12). In his comment in the authoritative Jewish

Study Bible on the term "fear of God" as it is used here, Jon Levenson writes that "in the Tanakh, the 'fear of God' denotes an active obedience to the divine will."[33] It is because of his obeying God and disobeying himself that the covenant is bestowed on Abraham and his progeny. Moreover, this act of radical obedience is shared by Isaac who offers no resistance. Concerning father and son Scripture repeats "And the two of them walked together" (Gen. 22:8).

Paul's belief that the world had been transformed, at least for those who are "in Christ," arose from his unshakeable belief in Christ's resurrection. Like his rabbinic teachers and contemporaries, such as Rabban Gamaliel, Paul did not see human mortality as necessarily rooted in human biology. On the contrary, they saw human mortality as originating in the disobedience of humanity's original progenitor, Adam. However, unlike the rabbis, after Damascus Paul became convinced that the related flaws in creation, mortality, human disobedience, and the subjugation of the cosmos to the elemental powers were in the process of being overcome. He expressed that conviction in many places. Those most relevant to our issue are his reflections on the first and last Adam in Romans 5 and 1 Corinthians 15. In Romans 5 Paul begins with a reflection on the origin of death. "Well, then, sin entered the world through one man, and through sin death, and thus death has spread through the whole human race because everyone has sinned" (Rom. 5:12).

Few passages in the New Testament have been commented upon as extensively as this. As we have seen, Paul's twin assertions that death is the result of sin and that sin entered the world "through one man" are entirely in keeping with the speculations of his Jewish contemporaries. Romans 5:12 rests in the final analysis upon the authority of Genesis 3:17-19. In this passage in Romans Paul seems to hold that men die because they replicate Adam's sin, not because of Adam's sin. However, Paul's Jewish contemporaries could not have agreed with Paul as he continued his reflection on the two Adams: "Adam prefigured the One to come, but the gift itself outweighed the fall. If it is certain that through one man's fall so many died, it is even more certain that divine grace, coming through one man, Jesus Christ, came to many as an abundant free gift" (Rom. 5:15).

The "abundant free gift" that comes through Christ is, of course, an end to mortality. In this verse Adam is depicted as the antitype of Jesus.[34] Just as the fruit of Adam's sin is death, so through Christ's superlative righteousness many will receive "divine grace" as "an abundant free gift" (Rom. 5:16). Paul elaborates on this theme in the next verse: "If it is certain that death reigned over everyone as the consequence of one man's fall, it is even more certain that one man, Jesus Christ, will cause everyone to reign in life who receives the free gift that he does not deserve, of being made righteous." The undeserved "free gift" that Christ makes available is the opposite of the penalty brought upon mankind by his antitype. Adam brings death; Jesus brings eternal life.

Paul also describes Christ as reversing the "condemnation" brought about by Adam and bringing instead "'justification" (Rom. 5:16). Justification has a very explicit meaning for Paul. When God justifies the unworthy sinner, he pronounces a verdict of acquittal upon him and bestows upon him the gift of eternal life. From the time of Martin Luther until the beginning of the twentieth century, Protestants have tended to regard the doctrine of justification by faith as the heart and center of Paul's theology. I do not wish to enter the debate on this issue save to say that I believe one aspect of the doctrine of justification by faith must remain central to any interpretation of Paul: We must not lose sight of the decisive importance of eternal life as the fruit of God's justification of the sinner as understood by Paul. In Romans 6:23, Paul contrasts the fruits of sin and justification: "For the wage of sin is death; the free gift of God is eternal life in Christ Jesus." Adam paid the price of sin; through Jesus the unearned gift of justification is bestowed.

The centrality of eternal life as the fruit of justification is emphasized with great force in Paul's discussion of Adam and Christ in 1 Corinthians 15. Scroggs has observed that the themes of Romans 5:12-21 and 1 Corinthians 15 "are related but not identical.'" In 1 Corinthians 15 Paul's primary interest is to render credible to the skeptical Corinthians the Christian hope that those who are "in Christ" will ultimately be resurrected as was Jesus. By resurrection Paul meant the resurrection of the body, as did his Jewish contemporaries. Apparently there was considerable skepticism in Corinth concerning the future resurrection of the bodies of the dead even among those who believed in Jesus' resurrection. Paul confronted this skepticism by arguing that "Christ has In fact been raised from the dead as the first fruits (*aparche*) of all who have fallen asleep." (1 Cor. 15:20). According to Jean Héring, the word *aparche* is almost synonymous with the Hebrew *arrabon*, which is an earnest or a deposit. Paul's meaning is that Christ's resurrection anticipates the resurrection of his followers, who will some day share his glorious destiny.

Having asserted that resurrection awaits the believer, Paul returned to the theme of the first and last Adam: "Death came through one man. Just as all men die in Adam, so all men will be brought to life in Christ" (1 Cor 15:21-22). Paul's emphasis in 1 Corinthians is on the perfected, eternal life that awaits the believer in Christ. We cannot go into Paul's understanding of the kind of perfected bodily existence in Christ the resurrected will enjoy, save to say that Christ's resurrected nature is that of a *soma pneumatikon*, a "spiritual body," and that the spiritual body is for both Paul and the rabbis not immaterial. Paul also tells us that "Flesh and blood cannot inherit the kingdom of God, and the perishable cannot inherit what lasts forever." (1 Cor 15:50) When the transformation occurs, all things will be changed. The perishable world will be redeemed. Death, corruption, and demonic domination will be forever defeated.

Paul's assertions about Christ's extraordinary power to redeem man and the cosmos leads to the question of why Christ alone had the superlative merit to be "the first fruit of all who have fallen asleep" as well as the fount of eternal life for a resurrected humanity. In an important sense, both Paul and his Jewish contemporaries were convinced that disobedience was the only sin and that all other sins derived from that one offense. Since Judaism regarded all of the commandments as expressions of God's will, every commandment presented men with the agonizing choice of obedience or rebellion against the all-wise and all-powerful Father. It made no difference whether a commandment was opaque to human understanding. It was a supreme act of arrogance for a man to judge for himself what to obey and what not to obey. It could in fact be argued that obedience to seemingly irrational or inconsequential commandments was of greater import than obedience to commandments whose purpose could be clearly understood. The real issue was whether a man submitted to or rebelled against his Creator. Furthermore, the Creator was always in the right since the very structure of reality was the fruit of his will. In biblical religion a man who decides for himself which of God's commandments he will obey puts himself in God's place, asserting the priority of his own judgment over God's. He judges what God alone can judge and, by so doing, arrogates to himself a preeminence God alone rightfully possesses.

There is no place in this system for the modern ideal of the autonomous man who regards his own actions as entirely within his ethical competence. Paul asserts that Adam committed the paradigmatic sin of biblical religion, disobedience. He held that because of Adam's disobedience in not fulfilling a single commandment death entered the world. By contrast, Christ alone of all men was so perfectly obedient that he even regarded his own life as of no account whatsoever against the majestic framework of God's wisdom. As Paul regarded Adam as the paradigmatically sinful man, he saw Christ as the only truly righteous man. For Christ's obedience extended even to the extraordinary agony of death as an unblemished innocent on the cross. Although Paul offers many suggestions as to why Christ's death brought about the liberation of humanity from the consequences of Adam's sin, he is most explicit in asserting that Christ was a "life-giving spirit" because of his obedience: "As by one man's disobedience many were made sinners, so by one man's obedience many will be made righteous" (Romans 5:19).

In his first letter to the Corinthians, Paul reminded the church that he had handed on to them the good news that he had received: "I taught you what I had been taught myself, namely that Christ died for our sins" (1 Cor. 15:3). This is one of the earliest statements of the Christian *kerygma*. It has often been interpreted as a reference to Christ's death as a vicarious atonement for the sins of mankind. There can be little doubt that Paul maintained that Christ's death was sacrificial in character (Rom. 3:21-28; 5:1-2; 1 Cor. 5:7). Nevertheless, even if we accept the thesis that Paul regarded Christ's death as a vicarious atonement, we have yet to identify the superlative merit possessed by Christ that made such atonement possible. Others died without so fortunate an outcome; what was unique about Jesus? Paul answered that question in the passage we have cited, Romans 5:19: Christ's merit consisted in his superlative obedience. Christ, in his innocence, had more justification for rebellion against the fate meted out to him than any other man. Nevertheless he submitted in perfect obedience to unmerited death on the cross. According to Paul, Christ alone was unblemished by any trace of rebellion against the Father.

Paul's logic was in keeping with that of his Jewish contemporaries. There was a prevalent Jewish speculation that were a man totally without sin—that is, perfectly obedient—he would not be condemned to death.[35] Unlike his Jewish contemporaries, Paul was convinced that there was one such man, Christ, and that the merit of his flawless obedience was sufficient to bestow life on others as well as himself.

According to Paul, had Christ been tainted with even a trace of sinfulness, the powers to whom dominion had fallen after Adam's transgression would have been within their legitimate right in claiming Christ as their victim. Under the Law, their Law, the wages of sin are death. Happily for mankind, the cosmic powers did not recognize Christ as the sinless obedient Son of God. Christ permitted them to exceed their proper sphere when they condemned him to crucifixion. By his perfect obedience to the Father's wise and mysterious plan, Christ tricked the "rulers of this age" (*hoi archontes tou aiōnos toutou)* (1 Cor. 2:8), and thereby deprived them of their dominion over mankind. Christ thus reversed what Adam had sadly initiated.

Paul saw this union of Christ and Christian as a true unity. The church is more than a collection of individuals united by common belief and hope. The church is literally the body of Christ, and Christians are "living" members of that body (Eph. 5:30). To be a member of the church is to share a common identity with Christ. Paul asked the Corinthians rhetorically, "You know surely that your bodies are members making up the body of Christ. (1 Cor. 6:15). This is no mere figure of speech. Later in 1 Corinthians Paul illustrates the meaning of the Christian's existence in Christ by analogy with the human body: "Just as a human body, though it is made up of many parts, is a single unit because all these parts, though many, make one body, so it is with Christ (1 Cor. 12:12-13). "Now you together are Christ's body; but each of you is a different part of it" (1 Cor. 12:27). Bishop John A. T. Robinson has observed that the body Paul has in mind here is not that of "a supra-personal collective" but of a single, concrete individual.[36]

Once Christ's physical departure had finally become a reality, the forces that made for a Christian's identification with him were overwhelming. Christ had become the heart and center of the disciples' lives both in this world and for the world to come. As we have noted, identification with Christ gave Christians the means of achieving the most crucial of all relationships, the right relationship with the God who held the destiny of their souls in the balance. Identification with Christ provided Christians with their most awesome hope, hope for a way out of mortality; it also provided them with a primary community, the church, in which their fears, hopes, and aspirations could be shared. Christ was simply too important to lose or even to remain a distant object of yearning. A way had to be found to assure the primitive church that Christ was a present reality, as he had been in those first days after the Resurrection.

There was more than one way in which Jesus could be present at the sacred tables of the primitive church. He could be, as he had been, with them in spirit; he could also be with them concretely as both food and feeder. Jesus' action in offering bread and wine with the words, "This is my body; this is my blood," contain the implicit message, "I am the food as I am the feeder." If it was no longer possible for Christians to share food with Jesus, it was inevitable that they would find in these words a way to be with him in body.

By construing the bread and wine of their sacred meal as the body and blood of Christ, Christians resorted to the oldest, most effective, and most crudely physical way of becoming one with the beloved object, physical incorporation. The Eucharist was a literal acting out of the basic Christian strategy for achieving the right relationship with the Father in Heaven, identification with the beloved Son, whom Paul in one place calls the "first born of many brothers." (Rom. 8:29) By finding a way to overcome the gap that separated the bereft disciples from Christ, a way that was rooted in the most archaic, nonverbal, sensuous strategies of the human organism, the primitive Christians preserved both the integrity of their community and its redemptive message. They were also able to cope with the inevitable tension between the Christian proclamation of hope fulfilled and the Christian reality of hope deferred. By partaking of what they regarded as the true substance of the risen Christ, they periodically became "one body" with his immortal glory and anticipated sharing in it completely at the end of days. At the same time, they prepared themselves for the rhythm of life in which the assurance of redemption was constantly countered by the harsh realities of the Roman Empire.

It is precisely the crudely physical aspects of the Lord's Meal, in which Christ is both food and feeder that constitute its overwhelming power. Wherever this rite has been taken seriously, and wherever the real presence of Christ in the elements of the Lord's Meal has been asserted, Christendom has had an incomparable way of expressing through religious ritual its deepest conscious and unconscious yearnings concerning human morality, kinship, and mortality. In 1 Corinthians 10, Paul's insistence that Corinthians who participated in the Eucharist must abstain from pagan cultic banquets is an example of the way sacrificial rituals have been utilized for the purpose of moral and religious control. Since no man may partake of the sacrifice if, in the eyes of God, so to speak, he is morally or ritually unfit, the sacrifice itself acts as a barrier against improper behavior.

The worst offense in sacrificial religion is to partake of the sacrifice when one is morally or ritually unworthy. This is beautifully expressed in Psalm 24: "Who shall ascend unto the mountain of the Lord: or who shall stand in his holy place? He that hath clean hands and a pure heart; who hath not lifted up his soul in vanity nor sworn deceitfully" (Ps. 24:3-4). One ascends the mountain of the Lord to partake of the sacrifice. The psalmist defines with utmost simplicity the conditions under which such participation is appropriate. Another side to this definition is the implicit warning against standing "in his holy place" unless one has "clean hands and a pure heart."[37]

We have noted that Paul regarded the believer as having literally consumed Christ's body. Because of the "spiritual" nature of the risen Christ's glorious body, there has been some confusion on this point. However, if we bear in mind the comments of Héring and Käsemann that for Paul the spiritual is not immaterial but "the substance of resurrection corporeality," we will understand that in the Lord's Meal the Christian becomes united with the body of Christ, which he or she regards as the only true body. Since Christ is no longer subject to decay or death, he alone truly exists as God intended existence before the sin of Adam.

Within a few years after Paul's death, Ignatius of Antioch declared that when the communicant partakes of the bread and wine of the Eucharist he partakes of the "medicine of immortality, and the sovereign remedy by which we escape death and live in Jesus Christ forever more."[38] For Paul, when Christians participated in the Eucharist, their identification with the risen Christ was just as tangible and concrete as were the older forms of consuming the sacrificial victim, whether human or animal. There was, however, an important difference: the older victims were consumed either in the process of being slaughtered or after having been slaughtered. Christ alone is consumed after he had passed through slaughter and had been resurrected to enjoy the only truly incorruptible existence. Christ alone was therefore the sacrificial victim par excellence to whom no harm can come.

There is much more that can be written of the Lord's Meal, but even with this brief account, the dialectic of continuity and discontinuity between Judaism and Christianity should be clear. Without such sacrificial elements in Judaism as God's claim on the firstborn, the redemption of the firstborn, the aborted sacrifice of Isaac, the substitution of the ram for Isaac, the paschal lamb, and the sprinkling of the blood of the Lamb to redeem the Israelite firstborn from the slaughter visited upon the Egyptian firstborn, it is difficult to imagine Christianity arising as it did. Some new religion might have arisen from the turmoil visited upon first-century Judaism, but it is hardly likely that it would have assumed the forms that it did. Similarly, without the exegetical training Paul received from his rabbinic teachers, it is difficult to see how he could have arrived at his views of Jesus and his salvific role.

What is certain is that the paths taken by Judaism and Christianity to achieve the all-important relation with God became radically distinct. Even in its mystical forms, Judaism rejected union with God. One could achieve a certain proximity to the Divine Glory but one could never become one with it through identification. Given its strict dietary laws, it would have been unthinkable for Jews to consider themselves at one with God through an act of consumption, yet this is precisely how believers achieve that all-important identification within the Christian tradition. One of the most important aspects of the dietary laws was the strict taboo on the consumption of the blood of an animal, yet in the Eucharist it is Christ's blood that is offered to the believer as "the medicine of immortality."

It is easy to see how mutual understanding was difficult, if not impossible, between the adherents of the two traditions. There is in Christianity no substitute for Christ and his mediating role between God the Father and humanity. This was clearly understood by the author of the Fourth Gospel who depicts Jesus as saying in the synagogue of Capernaum:

> I tell you the truth, unless you eat the flesh of the Son of Man and drink his blood, you have no life in you. Whoever eats my flesh and drinks my blood has eternal life, and I will raise him up at the last day. For my flesh is real food and my blood is real drink. Whoever eats my flesh and drinks my blood remains in me, and I in him. Just as the living Father sent me and I live because of the Father, so the one who feeds on me will live because of me. This is the bread that came down from heaven. Your forefathers ate manna and died, but he who feeds on this bread will live forever. (John 6:53-58)

John also depicts Jesus as saying: "I am the way, and the truth, and the life; no one comes to the Father but through Me" (John 14:6).

These passages have been criticized as supersessionist and radically exclusivist, but they do indeed express the foundational conviction of Christianity that salvation, the fruit of the right relation with God, comes only through Jesus Christ. By contrast, while the rabbis believed in the Resurrection, they were much more concerned with the kind of life Jews would live in the here and now. Hence, their promises about the world to come were considerably vaguer and they were far more concerned with how a community, especially a community under threat, could sustain itself in this world. Hence, they saw Christianity's assurance of eternal life as promising too much as the Christian world came to see the Jewish insistence on Torah obedience as the path to a right relation with God as offering too little.

Although the comparison is not explicit in Paul's extant writings, his insistence upon Christ as the perfect atonement for the sins of mankind suggests that for Paul, as well as for those early fathers of the church who explicitly take up the comparison, Isaac's aqedah is an aborted Golgotha. They depict Jesus as the perfect Isaac and Isaac as lacking the capacity to redeem humanity because he did not really die on his wooden pyre.

I should like to suggest that Christianity brings to manifest expression much that remains latent in Judaism and that this spells out the fundamental difference in the religious strategies of the two traditions. Although I have not been able to find the source, the difference was spelled out long ago in the following observation: What is *latet* (latent) in Judaism is *patet* (patent or manifest) in Christianity.

Thus, Jesus' atoning death at the Passover season effects a convergence of redemptive themes: Jesus is the perfect lamb; he is also the perfect Isaac. For Paul, his sacrifice is alone efficacious. Like the Law, Isaac anticipates redemption but can not achieve it. Jesus dies for all men's sins, but most especially for the sin of Adam. Jesus accepts death in order to undo the totality of God's infanticidal hostility toward sinful, errant humanity from the moment of Adam's first catastrophic disobedience to the small disobediences of ordinary men in Paul's own era.

As I conclude this essay, I might ask: why was it so important to identify Jesus with the Passover lamb? Why would no other sacrifice do? The simple answer is that, unlike the other sacrifices offered in the Jerusalem Temple, the Passover lamb had already served as a vicarious surrogate, if not for all of Israel, at least for the firstborn of Israel at the time of the exodus from Egypt. As such, it performed the same function as the ram of the *Aqedah*. It was deemed an acceptable substitute for sinful human beings. As a surrogate, the lamb is offered to God in place of—or could it be as if it were a human being. Could it be that at a very early time in the history of Israel's Semitic ancestors a human being was offered where at a later moment a lamb was offered as a substitute? Let us not forget the pervasiveness of human sacrifice in Phoenician Carthage that continued to be offered until the Romans put a stop in 146 BCE to it by destroying Carthage.

If indeed such were the case, the identification of Jesus with the paschal lamb would constitute a resurfacing of a very archaic sacrifice. Moreover, if one reads the biblical commandments concerning the original Passover sacrifice, its archaic character becomes apparent. Thus, in the Exodus account:

> on the tenth of this month each of them shall take a lamb to a family . . . Your lamb shall be without blemish, a yearling male; you may take it from the sheep or from the goats. You shall keep watch over it until the fourteenth day of this month; and all the assembled congregation of the Israelites shall slaughter it at twilight. They shall take some of the blood and put it on the two doorposts and the lintel of the houses in which they are to eat it. They shall eat the flesh that same night; they shall eat it roasted over the fire, with unleavened bread and with bitter herbs. Do not eat any of it raw, or cooked in any way with water, but roasted—head, legs, and entrails—over the fire. You shall not leave any of it over until morning; if any of it is left until morning, you shall burn it. (Exod. 12:3-10)

Let us also bear in mind that the injunction to offer up the First Born which we cited earlier, "Consecrate to Me every first-born; man and beast, the first issue of every womb among the Israelites is Mine." Exodus 13:2 is given in connection with the Passover sacrifices.

Addendum

Sigmund Freud's Myth of the Primal Crime

I have argued that, at least in the Christianity of Paul of Tarsus and the author of the Fourth Gospel, eating the body and the blood of the Son of God is the fundamental act of sacred worship. At first glance, such an idea would appear to violate the canons of common sense. Nevertheless, this form of worship has been maintained for two millennia by the majority of religious men and women throughout the Christian world. If Paul did not originate this conception of Christian worship, he was among the first to assert its truth.

In the twentieth century, Sigmund Freud, a far less believing Jew than Paul, argued that the Lord's Supper, as understood by Paul, was in fact a dramatic reenactment of the moral crisis with which religion, morality, and human society had their beginnings and that there was a profound psychological truth embedded in these ideas.[39] Freud's attempt to reconstruct the origins of religion through the myth of a primal parricide is enormously enlightening without necessarily being literally true.[40]

Briefly stated, Freud argued that before human religious and social institutions developed as we know them, men dwelt in small hordes consisting of the father, his harem, and some of the younger male offspring. The older male had exclusive sexual possession of the harem, which consisted of all the females in the group. His sexual rights were maintained by aggression against his own male offspring, whom he reckoned to be potential rivals. In Freud's narrative there was at this time no incest taboo. Chiefly by expulsion, but also by infanticide and castration, the father prevented the sons from displacing him.

According to Freud, the expelled sons were driven by sexual need to find a way to gain access to the forbidden females. They did so by banding together and murdering their father. Nevertheless, in spite of their envious hatred of the father, there was much about him that they admired and wished to emulate. Although the young men sought the father's riddance, they also wanted to be like him, enjoying especially his sexual privileges. Inevitably, the contradictory emotions of hatred and love were comingled in the first parricide.

Elsewhere, I have noted that there is a cannibalistic aspect to all acts of identification insofar as the object we prize is taken into and becomes a part of us.[41] The crudest form of becoming one with an object is to consume it. For Freud, the primal crime of humanity was the sons' cannibalistic devouring of their father so that they might simultaneously rid themselves of him, become like him, and take sexual possession of his females.

Since love and hate were comingled in the original act, the sons were incapable of feeling entirely gratified with their victory. On the contrary, Freud maintained that their feelings of guilt were so strong that they were driven to deny to themselves that the father was actually dead or that they had actually committed the crime. This only made matters worse. By denying their parricide, the sons could neither cancel their unconscious memory of the deed nor their fear of their victim's retaliatory aggression. According to Freud, denial led the sons to ascribe such extraordinary power to their earthly father that he became for them the Father in heaven. As a result, the sons were condemned to unending obedience to the dead father's will as their way of assuaging their fear of his retaliation. Freud's implicit definition of God is both paradoxical and compelling: The heavenly Father is the first object of human criminality. Men feel compelled to obey his "law" because of their fear that he will retaliate against them.

Though the transgression was never forgotten, the sons were unable consciously to admit their deed. Hence, they were inwardly compelled to repeat the act in dramatic form. The repetition took the form of the archaic totem sacrifice, which Freud regarded as "perhaps mankind's oldest festival." Normally, the totem animal was regarded as sacrosanct, but on certain festival occasions the entire tribe was compelled to slaughter, consume, and mourn the very animal that they revered as the tribal ancestor. According to Freud, the totem animal was in reality a surrogate for the murdered father. He pointed to many examples of animals that were identified with heroes, ancestors, and gods.

In dreams, poetry, religious symbolism, myth, and individual neuroses, a similar process of identification continues to this day. One of the most beautiful examples of this kind of identification in the history of art can be seen in the great van Eyck altarpiece in Ghent, "The Adoration of the Mystic Lamb," in which all of the figures are turned reverently toward the central figure, the mystic lamb, who is of course Christ, "the lamb of God."

The totem sacrifice was both a reenactment and a confession of the unconsciously remembered deed. Remorse and self-assertion were comingled in the reenactment, as love and hate had been in the original deed. The totem sacrifice also offered the possibility of "deferred obedience" to the murdered father. The sons quickly learned that they could not indulge in unrestricted sexual license with the slain father's women without grave conflict among themselves. Hence, they imposed the incest taboo on themselves, ascribing it to the will of the father who in their minds had become all-powerful. Having committed parricide to acquire the women, the sons voluntarily imposed the father's sexual taboos upon themselves in order to maintain group cohesion and fraternal solidarity. No man could partake of the totem sacrifice, thereby repeating symbolically the original deed, if he were guilty of violating the newly instituted tribal taboo against incest.

The totem sacrifice became the focal point of tribal memory, solidarity, and morality. Freud did not dismiss lightly the oft-proclaimed confession that we are all miserable sinners. According to Freud, the original basis of social solidarity was criminal complicity in the unconsciously remembered parricide. All who partook of the sacrificial animal were regarded as of one substance with both the victim and the other members of the tribe.

Freud's interpretation of the substantial solidarity of those who eat together was partly dependent upon the work of the Scottish scholar, W. Robertson Smith (1846-1894).[42] Freud cited an example Smith had given of the Bedouin custom that renders a stranger inviolable for a certain period of time after he has eaten with them. As long as the food remains within his body, the Bedouins regard the stranger as having shared a common substance with them and hence not to be harmed.

The idea that people who share a meal partake of a common bond persists to this day even in secularized forms. Few acts are as hostile as the refusal to break bread. Paul's vigorous opposition to Peter when he withdrew from table fellowship with Gentile Christians at Antioch indicates that be understood the extent to which the act of sharing a common meal is a profound expression of human solidarity (Gal. 2:11-16). This intuition is explicit in Paul's statement that "though there are many of us, we form a single body because we have a share in this one loaf" (1 Cor. 10:17). The loaf to which Paul referred was, of course, the bread of the Lord's Supper, the body of Christ.

Moreover, the act of ingesting is perhaps one of the oldest ways in which we confront our environment. Long before living organisms develop the faculty of visual perception, they must consume a portion of their environment. Eating also partakes of the oldest expression of love: The mother gives of her own substance when she feeds the child. Originally, the beloved object, food, and the feeder are one to the infant. In totemic sacrifice they become one again. When a god is consumed, he is both food and feeder. Those who partake of his substance become one with him, as do Christians with Christ in Holy Communion.

Freud rejected the theory that the sacrificial victim is a gift of the worshiping community to its god. He regarded the sacrifice as gift as a later development that arose after the institution of private property. Instead, he stressed the perennial centrality of the Communion sacrifice as the decisive religious act. His view conflicts with certain rationalizing and moralizing tendencies within both Judaism and Protestantism that regarded sacrifice as a "primitive" anticipation of more "advanced" expressions of religious worship such as personal prayer. Freud's emphasis was, however, by no means foreign to Roman Catholicism, which has always stressed the real presence of the body and blood of the Christ in the sacrificial elements of the Mass.

Freud saw the difference between Judaism and Christianity in terms of the "return of the repressed," namely, what was latent or repressed in Judaism had became manifest in Christianity, for example, the Lord's Supper. From a Freudian perspective, the sacrificial reenactment of the primal crime had been transformed in Judaism into a system of animal sacrifices. Admittedly, apart from the Passover lamb and the Redemption of the First Born ritual, the Hebrew sacrificial system contained few overt traces of the surrogate character of animal sacrifices. Nevertheless, as we have seen, extensive knowledge of Canaanite and other

Near Eastern sacrificial systems tends to corroborate the hypothesis that many of the biblically ordained animal sacrifices had their roots in human sacrifice.[43]

Freud argued that the archaic sacrifice of a divine-human victim was finally revived in Holy Communion. He maintained that Christ had redeemed man psychologically from the "burden of original sin" by laying down his own life in payment of the primal crime. According to Freud, mankind's "original sin" was not Adam's eating the apple. The biblical tradition censored a far graver offense, parricide. Had men been guilty of the lesser crime, Freud contended, God would have been depicted as requiring a far less severe punishment, in accordance with the measure-for-measure principle. Christ's atoning death points back to an archaic blood guilt.[44]

Freud also maintained that by offering himself on the Cross, the slain "Son" took the place of the originally murdered "father" as the object of human adoration. As a result, son-religion (Christianity) took the place of father-religion (Judaism). As a sign of the displacement of the father by the son, the totem feast was revived, but now the community of brothers (i.e., the church) ate the body and blood of the son rather than that of the father or his animal surrogate. The ritual permitted the brothers to identify with the son in the most concrete way, by eating his substance. It also repeated the primal crime in a novel form: By his prefect atonement, the Son had done in his way what the oldest group of brothers had done in theirs—he had displaced the Father. Freud therefore concluded that the Eucharist was "essentially a fresh elimination of the father, a repetition of the guilty deed.[45]

I believed Freud erred when he interpreted Christianity as a religion in which the Father is once again displaced. No such displacement takes place in Pauline Christianity. As noted, the Jewish strategy of obedience to the Father has been altered to identification with the perfectly obedient older brother as Christianity's way of achieving a right relationship to the Father. Nevertheless, the fundamental issue remains the same in both traditions: How do men and women achieve the right relationship with the Father? According to Paul, Christians achieve the relationship of perfect obedience to the Father through identification with the perfectly obedient Son. We are therefore compelled to seek a somewhat different understanding of Holy Communion than that suggested by Freud, although our explanation will be along Freudian lines. Insofar as Holy Communion is a symbolic repetition and confession of the original parricide, by offering his body to the disciples in the Communion meal, Christ pays once again the price of the original crime on their behalf as their surrogate. However, while Christ's sacrifice permits a dramatic repetition of the crime, by partaking of Christ in the Eucharist, Christians also identify with his perfect obedience in accepting a death he did not deserve because he was wholly without sin.

Christ is thus truly a mediating figure. He mediates between the brothers and the Father by offering the Father an obedience even unto death of which the brothers are incapable, and by taking upon himself God's punishment for the brothers' disobedience. He mediates between the Father and the brothers by allowing the brothers to become one with him rather than the Father, thereby freeing them from the temptation to commit the worst of all crimes, deicide against the Father, a crime they can freely ascribe to the Jews, who have repressed the memory of the primal crime.

Freud's primal crime myth has been dismissed by some scholars as unfounded speculation by a man who overstepped the limits of his own competence.[46] Even Freud admitted that the myth was a "just so" story.[47] Nevertheless, although his attempted reconstruction can hardly be taken as factual, Freud deepens our understanding of the Christian religious revolution, of which Paul was perhaps the decisive exponent after the crucifixion of Jesus, and helps us to understand its extraordinary emotional power.

Both Freud and Paul accepted the doctrine of "the fall of man." Both agreed that human history began with an act of primal rebellion against the Father. Both saw Christ's fundamental role as that of undoing the consequences of the primal rebellion. In Paul's narrative, Christ's role as the last Adam is to reverse the sin of the first Adam. Both Paul and Freud regard the Lord's Meal as the way the believer becomes one with the elder brother (Christ). Both take very seriously Christ's "real presence" within the elements of the Lord's Meal, although for Freud, Christ's presence is only psychologically "real." Both Paul and Freud, for very different reasons, regard the Jewish strategy of obedience to the Father as futile, and both see Christ as uncovering a deeper level of the meaning of God's controversy with man, which Judaism had repressed.

There were, of course, major areas of disagreement between Freud and Paul, the most important being Freud's conviction that the Christian solution to mankind's religious problem was ultimately as illusory as was the Jewish solution. Nevertheless, I believe there is much value in Freud's midrash or myth. In the spring semester 2009, I taught a course on "The Age of the Enlightenment" at my university. When taken literally, Paul's doctrines, such as becoming one with Christ in the Lord's Meal and Christ as the last Adam undoing the sins brought upon humanity by the first Adam, were regarded by the Enlightenment with considerable skepticism. Yet, as noted above, these ideas and their accompanying rites made sense and were believed by millions for two thousand years. Freud's midrash or myth shows that there are profound psychological truths embedded in these beliefs and practices and that they have enabled men and women, both Jewish and Christian, each in his or her own way, to overcome the destructive intra-familial temptations that were so painfully evident even in such advanced civilizations as the Carthaginian, Canaanite, Phoenician, and Hebrew civilizations before the reforms of Josiah (649-609) and the "discovery" by his temple priests of the "scroll of the Law."

Discussion Questions

1. According to Professor Jon Levenson, the mythic-ritual complex in the ancient Middle East referred to as "child sacrifice" was never eradicated; it was only transformed. How did rabbinic Judaism and Christianity, each in its own way, transform the ritual of child sacrifice?
2. At the first meeting of Jesus and John the Baptist, the Fourth Gospel depicts the Baptist as declaring: "Behold, the Lamb of God who takes away the sin of the world!" (John 1:29). These words have been incorporated into the Latin Mass as *Agnus Dei qui tollis peccata mundi*, thereby pointing to Jesus' role as both the Son of God and the "true" Passover lamb. How does this double identification point to Jesus' role as the supreme sacrificial victim in Christianity?
3. According to Professor Shalom Spiegel, the primary purpose of the aqedah story (Gen. 22:1-19) may have been to attach to the revered patriarch Abraham, the establishment of a new religious norm, namely the abolition of human sacrifice and the substitution of animal sacrifice instead. Professor Jon Levinson strongly disagrees. He writes, "Gen. 22:1-19 is frighteningly unequivocal about YHVH's ordering a father to offer up his son as a sacrifice." With which scholar do you agree and why?

Notes

1. Shalom Spiegel, *The Last Trial*, trans. Judah Goldin (New York: Schocken Books, 1969), 64.
2. Jon D. Levenson, *The Death and Resurrection of the Beloved Son* (New Haven: Yale University Press, 1993), 12; unless otherwise stated, the New Jewish Publication Society (NJPS) translation of the *Tanach* is used for Biblical texts.
3. Ed Noort, "Child Sacrifice in Ancient Israel: The Status Quaestionis," in Jan N. Bremmer, ed., *The Strange World of Human Sacrifice* (Leuwen: Peeters Publishers, 2006), 112-13.
4. Noort, "Child Sacrifice," 104.
5. Levenson, *The Death and Resurrection*, 20.
6. Malcolm W. Browne, "Relics of Carthage Show Brutality Among the Good Life," *New York Times*, September 1, 1987, http://www.nytimes.com/1987/09/01/science/relics-of-carthage-show-brutality-amid-the-good-life.html?pagewanted=all, accessed May 17, 2009.
7. Lawrence E. Stager and Samuel R. Wolff, "Child Sacrifice at Carthage-Religious Rite or Population Control?" *Biblical Archaeology Review* 10, no. 1 (January-February, 1984): 31-51. http://members.bib-arch.org/publication.asp?PubID=BSBA&Volume=10&Issue=1&ArticleID=2&UserID=4722, accessed May18, 2009.
8. Stager and Wolff, "Child Sacrifice."
9. See M'hamed Hassine Fantar, "Were Living Children Sacrificed to the Gods? No," *Archaeology Odyssey* 3, no. 6 (November-December 2000), http://members.bib-arch.org/search.asp?PubID=BSAO&Volume=3&Issue=6&ArticleID=11&UserID=0&., and Joseph Greene and Lawrence E. Stager, "An Odyssey Debate: Were Living Chil-

dren Sacrificed to the Gods? Yes." *Archaeology Odyssey*, 3, no. 6 (November-December 2000).

10. Stager and Wolff, "Child Sacrifice."
11. Levenson, *The Death and Resurrection,* 45.
12. I describe the *pidyon ha-ben* ceremony in detail in Richard L Rubenstein, *Power Struggle: An Autobiographical Confession* (New York: Charles Scribner's Sons, 1974), 112-13.
13. See Levenson, *The Death and Resurrection,* 133-40.
14. See Levenson, *The Death and Resurrection,* 298-99.
15. A translation of the poem is to be found in Spiegel, *The Last Trial,* 143-52.
16. Joseph B. Soloveitchik, David Shatz, Joel B. Wolowelsky, and Reuven Ziegler, eds., *Abraham's Journey: Reflections on the Life of the Founding Patriarch* (New York: K'TSAV, 2008), 11-12.
17. Soloveitchik et al., *Abraham's Journey.*
18. Levenson, *The Death and Resurrection,* 200-01.
19. Levenson, *The Death and Resurrection,* 202.
20. Paula Fredricksen, *From Jesus to Christ,* 2nd ed. (New Haven: Yale University Press, 2000), 20.
21. Fredricksen, *From Jesus,* 204.
22. Richard L. Rubenstein, *My Brother Paul* (New York: Harper and Row, 1972), 91.
23. Jean Héring, *The First Epistle of Saint Paul to the Corinthians,* trans. A. W. Heathcote and P. J. Allcock (London: Epsworth Press, 1962), 115.
24. Oscar Cullmann, *Early Christian Worship*, trans. A. Stewart Todd and James B. Terrence (London: SCM Press, 1962), 10-15.
25. Cullmann, *Early Christian Worship*, 19.
26. *Didache*, trans. Maxwell Staniforth, in *Early Christian Writings: The Apostolic Fathers* (Harmondsworth, Middlesex: Penguin Books, 1968), 231-35.
27. Albert Schweitzer, *The Mysticism of Paul the Apostle,* trans. William Montgomery (London: A &C Black, 1953); see also W. D. Davies, "Paul and Judaism Since Schweitzer," in Davies, *Paul and Rabbinic Judaism: Some Rabbinic Elements in Pauline Thought* (New York: Harper Torchbooks, 1967), vii-xv.
28. Schweitzer, *The Mysticism of Paul*, 52-74.
29. Schweitzer, *The Mysticism of Paul*, 116-25.
30. Robin Scroggs, *The Last Adam: A Study in Puline Anthropology* (Philadelphia: Fortress Press, 1966), 46-50.
31. Herman Melville, *Moby-Dick* (New York: Bantam Books, 2003), 57-58.
32. Henry A. Murray, "In Nomine Diaboli," in *Melville*, ed. Richard Chase (Englewood Cliffs, NJ: Prentice-Hall, 1962); originally published in *The New England Quarterly* 24, no. 4 (December 1951): 435-52.
33. Jon D. Levenson comment on Genesis 22:12 in *The Jewish Study Bible*, ed. Adele Berlin and Marc Zvi Brettler (New York: Oxford University Press, 2004), 46.
34. There is some scholarly debate concerning the meaning of "the One to come." According to C. K. Barrett, "the One to come" is the eschatological Christ who will be fully revealed at the Last Day. See C. K. Barrett, *From First Adam to Last* (London: A & C. Black, 1962), 92-119.
35. See`Louis Ginsberg, *The Legends of the Jews*, vol. 5 (Philadelphia: Jewish Publication Society, 1909-13), 128-131, n. 142; Richard L Rubenstein, *The Religious Imagination* (Indianapolis: Bobbs-Merrill, 1968), 43-47.

36. John A. T. Robinson, *The Body: A Study in Pauline Theology* (London: SCM Press, 1952), 51.
37. Shalom Spiegel, "Prophetic Attestation of the Decalogue: Hosea 6:5. With Some Observations on Psalms 15 and 34," *Harvard Theological Review* 27, no. 2 (April 1934): 105-44.
38. Ignatius (of Antioch), Ignatius: Epistle to the Ephesians, in *Early Christian Writings: The Apostolic Fathers*, ed. and trans. Maxwell Staniforth and Andrew Louth (London: Penguin, 1987), 66.
39. Sigmund Freud, *Totem and Taboo,* trans. James Strachey (New York: Norton, 1962).
40. Richard L. Rubenstein, *The Religious Imagination* (Indianapolis: Bobb-Merrill, 1968), 1-21.
41. Rubenstein, *The Religious Imagination*, 8-9.
42. See W. Robertson Smith, *The Religion of the Semites: The Fundamental Institutions* (New York: Meridian Press, 1956).
43. On Canaanite sacrifice, see also Theodore H. Gaster, "The Service of the Sanctuary: A Study in Hebrew Survivals," in *Melanges Syrien offert á M. R. Dussaud* (Paris: Geuthner, 1939), 577-82; Roland de Vaux, *Ancient Israel: Its Life and Institutions,* trans. John McHugh (New York: McGraw-Hill, 1961), 438-46.
44. Sigmund Freud, *Moses and Monotheism*, trans. Katherine Jones (New York: Alfred A. Knopf, 1939), 174, and *Totem and Taboo,*154.
45. Freud, *Totem and Taboo,* 155.
46. See A. L. Kroeber, *American Anthropologist,* New Series 22 (1920), 48-55.
47. Sigmund Freud, *Group Psychology and the Analysis of the Ego* (New York: Norton, 1989), 69.

The Jewish and Greek Jesus

Yitzchak Kerem

The purpose of this article is to contrast the actual Jewish Jesus with a Hellenized Greek-speaking Eastern Orthodox Jesus as he is perceived, reinterpreted, and reconceived from the writings of the apostles and early Christianity. While little is known about the actual Jewish Jesus, a lot is known about the portrayal of Jesus in early Christian literature. Unique will be the presentation of Jesus as an icon of Hellenization and a Greek-speaking Christian (Eastern) Orthodox perspective.

In replicating the Hellenized Roman Empire, where the emperor was idealized as God, but his wife human, and a mystical secretive religion was emerging, the disciples of Jesus portrayed him as the son of God and his mother as the divine. Influenced by Hellenism, Jesus was the by-product of the search for a new deity. The Gospels and the initial primitive church incorporated Platonic philosophy and science, which they brought from Egypt and Babylon, but also adopted the oriental cult and in Greece the priests remained simple officials of the rites, guardians of the shrines, and performers of religious acts. In this diasporic scenario, early Christianity was formulated and gained impetus. In the spirit of Rome and Cicero, a state religion was needed. In Asia Minor paganism had worn out, and there was a need to create new gods. Oriental mysticism tinged by Hellenism had to be overcome by the disseminators of the new Christianity, and the latter borrowed from local cults in Greece and Asia Minor the image of a Saint based on local heathen deities. Christmas Day was originally the birthday of the Sun-God, baptism and communion were based on heathen cult worship within Hellenism.

The Jewish Jesus

Jesus was a Galilean Jew, who spoke some form of Hebrew or Aramaic, and only knew enough Greek to get by. He probably was born in Nazareth[1] and not Bethlehem, which was an invented birthplace made up by disciples to connect him to an ancient prophecy and actualize his messianic role based on descent from the royal Davidic dynasty with its Bethlehem birthplace origins from the Biblical characters Naomi, Boaz, Ruth, Peretz, and others. At any rate, he grew up in Nazareth and the Galilee. At the end of his life, when he had moved to Judea and professed "in his public ministry," he returned to the Galilee to visit his family, friends, and colleagues.[2]

The closest one can get to the personality of Jesus, in light of no archeological or historical sources, is to analyze the Jew of the Galilee during his life and under Roman rule, which had the most mixed population in Israel consisting of Jews, Phoenicians, ancient Arabs, pagans, Syrians, and Greeks. The Galilean Jews were more informal than those of Judea. The Galileans were `less bound by rules and regulations, more spontaneous, less learned and more poetic, less legalistic and more lyrical. Certain customs and ceremonies of theirs differed from Judea. Their language was not as accurate nor as pure as in Jerusalem, which the men of the latter attributed to lack of good teachers and to indifference.[3] However, they did have their illustrious Jewish scholars, but Galileans were more noted for emphasizing Aggada over Halakha, and caring more for the poetic, ethical, and spiritual interpretation of the Bible than its legalistic commentary. Galileans were industrious, brave, and courageous and produced heroes and martyrs in the struggle of Jewish emancipation from oppressive Roman rule. According to Enelow, the Jewish Galileans "were a temperamental people, according to the Talmud, excitable and enthusiastic, capable of profound hate as well as of ardent love and devotion."[4] Simultaneously, the Jewish Galileans learned tolerance from living under Greek and Roman rule, needed to use Greek speech to speak with their rulers, and needed to familiarize themselves with Roman behavior; whether in court practices, legal doctrine, riddles, athletics, architecture, market practices, or general customs.

In this Galilean spirit and environment, Jesus grew up and developed. Jesus was a man of changing moods: he was loving, but also temperamental, lyrical, not legalistic, moral, and in a spirit of nonconformity, he sought to establish a new way in Judaism. He would not intentionally break Jewish law, but he sought a more spiritual and flexible framework for Jewish tradition. He was a Pharisee, albeit denouncing this stream continuously, but attended its schools and synagogues where he prayed, learned, and preached. He scorned the Hellenized aristocratic Sadducees in Jerusalem; feeling they abused temple ritual, and blemished the holiness of the temple with their intrigues, ambitions, rivalries, and corruption. He clearly revolted against the Sadducees and denounced their pompous and hypocritical temple practices.[5] Jesus was not an Essene, did not live in isolation or in a desert commune, and mingled with his people when he left the Galilee and was found in Jerusalem.

Jesus showed no sign of straying from Judaism. He was certainly circumcised, unlike the Greeks, who despised the practice. Some Jews reversed the circumcision through the operation of epispasm for reasons of embarrassment or in desire to Hellenize,[6] but this was not part of the milieu of Jesus. Later, after the time of Jesus, the disciple Paul led the path to the abandonment of circumcision and most Jewish laws of *kashrut*.[7] The Jewish prototype of Jesus opposed such outward customs as the practice of wearing tefillin all day long or wearing the extra-wide tefillin popular in his day, but similarly eventually the Jews abandoned such customs. The Jewish Jesus of his time most certainly was circumcised, would have required it of all male Jews, and would have abided laws of kashrut.

Through the Gospels, disputes involving fasting, Sabbath observance, the role of women, and rules of purity between Jesus and the Pharisees come to the forefront. While the Gospels, influenced in their early Christian polemic against Judaism, may distort Jesus to opposing fasting, tolerating adultery, differing on divorce, disagreeing on Sabbath observance, or being a disobedient son according to Jewish law, these issues represent some problems that Jesus had with Pharisee law. On the other hand, he opposed the Zealots in their ardent intolerance for breaking Jewish law. Jesus, while still holding basic Pharisee tenants of Jewish law, did differ in his compassion for fellow men, women, and children, exhibited tolerance, may have sought a more liberal interpretation on many issues of observance under Jewish law, and tended toward messianism.[8]

Jesus was not known to have officially been a scribe, but as a rabbi; being called *rabi* (my teacher, master). According to the scholar Geza Vermes, Jesus `acknowledged the law of Moses as the foundation stone of his Judaism.[9] Amongst those in his inner Christian circles, he was addressed as "Lord" *(ha'adon)* a term of high self-awareness and not a sign of a deity.[10] He, or his father, was portrayed as working as a carpenter; a profession in which its people had the reputation for being learned.[11]

First-century Judaism included a belief in the afterlife, the expectation of a messianic coming, a desire for liberation from Roman rule, growing tendencies toward atonement, and a closening of the individual to God.[12] Most Jews of the period believed ardently in afterlife and yearned to merit "eternity in the World to Come."[13] Jesus was arrested and put to death for his opposition to Roman rule. Jews were willing to lay their lives down in order not to transgress Jewish law, and not to offend God, who would give them afterlife. The prophets prophesized for not only the Messiah, but also the afterlife in the world to come as God would award for those who waited for him.[14] Jews did not suffice with temple sacrifices in service to God, but sought an individual personal relationship, and repentance was a common doctrine to first-century Judaism and early Christianity. Some Dead Sea sects saw repentance as a deviation of divine will and predestined destiny, of paths of light and darkness, and would have opposed those who sought repentance as a path to increased closeness to God and sought an individualist spirituality. In first-century Judaism, such opposition was carried out in treacherous acts of violence and murder between Jewish sects and streams, and this is the part of the background of Jewish hostility toward those like Jesus who diverted from perceived norms and who differed theologically from any other given Jewish sect.

Pontius Pilate hated Jews, and in his ten-year governorship of Judea, "he crucified Jews for the slightest suspicion of revolt."[15] Jesus, the Jew, was one of many Jews suspected of rebelling against Roman rule.

After the crucifixion of Jesus, Schiffman noted:

> the early church developed as a group of Jews who came to see the messiah in the person of Jesus. There is no question by that early Christians were influenced by the apocalyptic trends which we have seen in the Second Temple literature. The basic teachings of Jesus and his community are described in the excerpts from the Gospel of Mark from the New Testament. Jesus preached the social message of Pharisaic Judaism in an environment in which Roman oppression had led to poverty and degradation for many. On some ritual matters, he differed with the Pharisees, the most prominent legal authorities of the day, yet he and his early followers remained observant Jews. [16]

Jesus, according to the apostles, preached to crowds in the Galilee and Jerusalem.[17] This is a continuation of Jewish expectations of messianism, a more personal dialogue with God than the Pharisees in their legalistic approach would recognize, and if he did meet with the masses, this would be a threatening sign to Roman authority. Jesus as portrayed by the early apostles was a teacher, healer, and prophet.[18] Most of Jesus' followers were poor, and he is portrayed as someone sensitive to the poor and supportive of them.

The tongue of the disciples and adherents of Jesus was primarily Greek, and in that late-pagan and early Christian domain the image of Jesus, the martyr, personified, culturally and theologically was formulated. Jesus is the common Greek form of Joshua. In his day, Jesus' name was pronounced Yeshua (meaning "salvation" from Hebrew. In ancient Jewish literature, the name was referred to as Yeshu, a form of Galilean pronunciation).[19] Symbolically, Jesus, or Yehoshua, was named after the military leader, Joshua, who captured Jericho and led the Jewish people after the death of Moses. According to the eminent Israeli researcher David Flusser, Jesus (Yeshua) was one of the most common names of his time. Jesus' father was Joseph and his brothers were James, Joses, Judah, and Simon (Mark 6:3). James is the anglicized form of the Hebrew and Greek name Jacob. Joses is short for Joseph, the name of the father of Joseph. Assuming that the firstborn received the name of the living father (in accordance with Romaniote late Second Temple or Byzantine Jewish Greek tradition, as well as other Eastern and Iberian Jewish naming traditions predating Ashkenazi Jewry, which does not name after the living father) Joses would be the eldest, and not Jesus. According to Luke (2:41-51), Joseph was still alive when Jesus was twelve and during their annual pilgrimage trip to Jerusalem, where Jesus stayed on at least for three days to study with teachers in the temple.[20] Jesus' mother was Mary, the Greek Maria (Matt. 1:16) in the Greek New Testament, or the Hebrew Miriam, the latter being a popular name given from the sister of Moses. In the books of Matthew and Luke of the Christian New Testament, the Virgin Mary bore Jesus; while the Jewish Jesus/Yehoshua was the son of Joseph/Yosef and Mary/Miriam. According to Luke 2:4, Jesus' family journeyed to Bethlehem only for the census, Jesus was born, and then the family returned to Nazareth. According to Matthew 2:23, the family resided in Bethlehem before the birth of Jesus and settled in Nazareth only after returning from Egypt. Both Gospels in different ways trace Jesus via his father Joseph back to King David. They both also tell of the birth of Jesus from the Virgin Mary. According to Flusser, neither genealogy from Jesus to David is convincing, and there are tensions (paradoxes) between the paternal lineages and the virgin birth version without a human father; leaving the impression that the genealogies were composed ad hoc in order to prove descent from David.[21]

Jesus lived in Nazareth for about thirty years. According to Luke 3:23, Jesus was baptized by John in 27-28 or 28-29 CE. According to the first three Gospels, his public ministry was for not more than a year between his baptism and crucifixion.[22]

Jesus' brother John "died for his faith in his brother,"[23] being murdered by a Sadducean high priest. His mother and brothers moved to Jerusalem after the crucifixion, and joined the apostles there (Acts 1:14). His brothers later converted to the Christian faith and their wives were accepted into the congregations of the followers.

Jesus spoke of himself as the "Son of Man," and the early church associated him with the prophecy of the "coming of an angelic Son of Man" in Daniel 7:13.[24] To the Jew, *bar-nasha*, "Son of Man" carried with it the messianic vision of this verse from Daniel.[25] A Gentile reading of the verse sheds light on an angelic "Son of Man" with divine heavenly power who comes to lead an eternal messianic kingdom:

> In my vision at night I looked, and there before me was one like a son of man, coming with the clouds of heaven. He approached the Ancient of Days and was led into his presence. He was given authority, glory and sovereign power; all peoples, nations and men of every language worshiped him. His dominion is an everlasting dominion that will not pass away, and his kingdom is one that will never be destroyed. (Daniel 7:13; New International Version).

The Gospel Mark described Jesus as divinely appointed to establish God's rule on earth; diverging from a normative Jewish view as simply an ordinary man to an apocalyptic figure. In Mark 1:10-12 Jesus as the Son of Man proves his ability to provide a miracle, and uses his Godly powers to enable a paralyzed man to overcome sin to get up and walk:

> But to convince you that the Son of Man has authority on earth to forgive sins—he turned to the paralyzed man—I say to you, stand up, take your bed, and go home, And he got up, and at once took his bed and went out in full-view of them all, so that they were astonished and praised God. "Never before," they said, "have we seen anything like this."[26]

The Greek viewed "Son of Man" as the opposite of anything beyond a human figure; something conveying purely human origin and metaphysical status; thus, the first generation of Christians dropped the term and it disappears from the New Testament except for the line in Daniel 7, "one like unto the Son of Man" in order to avoid confusion and misunderstanding.[27]

Harris Lenowitz notes that Jesus was one of several Jewish messiahs of this time, that he was a Jewish messiah, and atypical as a Jew in his time in changing the social order, undermining rabbinical authority, and not as a messiah of salvation, but one who exploited expected betrayal and disaster. The list of other Jewish messiahs include Yehuda or Theudas (Judas), Menachem, the son of Yehuda known as the "Galilean," and Simon (Shi'mon), the son of Giora.[28] These messiahs are referred to as kings, leaders, and messiahs in texts between 6 and 70 CE. These Galilean rebels, like Jesus, rebelled against the Romans, but they used military means or were crowned leaders. Theudas, in 45 CE, attracted many followers, as he intended to split the waters of the Jordan River[29] and the Roman reaction was to order their horsemen to behead him.

Messianism was definitely in the air during the lifetime of Jesus. In 35-36 CE, when either Jesus was still living or already executed, a Samaritan messiah wanted to show his believers the holy vessels buried on Mount Gerizim. Armed masses herded around this messiah, and when seeing this rebellious behavior, the Romans attacked the Samaritan messiah and killed many of the followers. Around 56 CE, there was a Jewish messiah in Egypt, coined by Josephus Flavius as the "Egyptian Prophet," who had 30,000 followers and called them to amass on the Mount of Olives in Jerusalem and to wait for his order for the walls of the city to fall, and who afterward forced the Roman forces to surrender, He promised that when he ruled, he would become the messiah who would bring back independence to Judea and expel the Roman authority.[30]

Lenowitz categorized Jesus as an anti-Roman leader and a prophet within a Jewish context, and not as the Christian Messiah, but one of many Jewish messiahs throughout history. He noted:

> The social programs of the northern prophets from the eighth century BCE on had held that the conduct of the wealthy and the powerful brought disaster upon them and that the conduct of the poor and powerless assured their

> righteousness. Jesus went farther than this. He insisted that one could not be powerful or rich and be righteous, nor could one be powerless and poor and be unrighteous. A person found guilty of a crime by a court that was itself a criminal body was innocent; the poor were impoverished by a social structure that dispossessed them. Jesus was also unlike other messiahs in his apparent disinterest in developing a program for gaining power against malign political authorities (those in Rome) or for governing his kingdom when it came. In fact, his desire to be put to death in Jerusalem, in itself unique among Jewish messiahs, brings together precisely these two peculiarities of his. It would seem that he expected betrayal and disaster and sought to make use of the expectation, if not to bring it about.[31]

Lenowitz further depicts Jesus as not a king, but a prophet, one opposed by Pharisee rabbinic circles. He added, "For some Jews, he (Jesus) has become the true messiah precisely because he does not lead a military force against Rome in his attempts to establish the Kingdom of God. After his death at the hands of the Romans, he continues to perform acts—miracles, particularly miraculous cures—that were the central element of his life as messiah."[32] Lenowitz controversially includes Jesus as a miracle worker even before his resurrection in a Jewish context; whereas most Jews do not view the Jewish Jesus as a miracle worker, nor his resurrection as part of the Jewish Jesus, but a recreated Christian image. Lenowitz added that after his death by the Romans, the miracles he performed gave witness to him not being dead, even before the resurrection or the second coming; also a departure from a conventional Jewish perspective.

While contemporary Jews regard Jesus as a Jewish man with an unclear agenda, part of his Jewish image was as a revolutionary against the Romans and as a self-regarded messianic figure with a small but fervent following. Yehuda Adler notes that while Jesus was half nude, wretched, and on the stake he provided compassion to the barren women that in the coming days would be lauded during the great rebellion against Rome. Adler also notes that previously Jesus told his followers he did not come for peace, but for the sword, in order to separate people from their fathers, daughter from mother, and daughter-in-law from mother-in-law: "In these dramatic moments, in his last walk, Jesus already did not hide his clear intention to mount a miraculous rebellion against the Roman Empire, in his belief from all the days of his life that he is the longed-for messiah, redeeming the Jewish people from Roman captivity."[33]

En route to Jerusalem for the Passover pilgrimage, Jesus and his followers were taunted by the Samaritans. Still enduring tension when passing with his small entourage into Jericho and attracting a big crowd, a blind man observing his passing said, "Jesus, son of David," referring to him as the Messiah.[34] Not wanting to arouse suspicion, detection, possible arrest, or violent resentment, his followers tried to silence the blind man and to keep secret Jesus' status as Messiah. In Matthew 20:29-31 the incident is depicted as follows:

> As they were leaving Jericho he was followed by a huge crowd. At the roadside sat two blind men. When they heard that Jesus was passing by they shouted, "Have pity on us, Son of David." People told them to be quiet, but they shouted all the more. "Sir, have pity on us; have pity on us, Son of David."[35]

Robert Wolfe expresses certainty that Jesus viewed himself as Messiah, but that this must be analyzed within the existing Jewish organizations and ideologies of his time. He expands on this theory:

> This recognition has given rise to a large literature devoted to such themes as "Jesus the Zealot" or "Jesus the Essene." What needs to be remembered here is that all four "gospels" were written, in Greek, many decades after the events which they purport to recount. They were written by the followers of Saint Paul, a quarrelsome individual who did not get along well with the original followers of Jesus Christ. No one knows or will ever know properly how much accurate "history" the gospels recorded and how much sheer fable they invented. But of one thing we can be fairly certain: Jesus Christ must have claimed to be the Messiah. . . . But this claim is so central to Christianity that it is highly unlikely that it was invented by Paul and his followers. It may be that Jesus and his followers used some term other than "Messiah" to designate the awaited Redeemer described by Isaiah and others, but there is every reason to assume that the belief in Jesus Christ as "the Messiah" started with his original followers and was based on the words and actions of Jesus himself. So if we want to situate Jesus within the spectrum of the Jewish tendencies of his day, the obvious point of departure is among groups the concept of the Messiah was particularly important. As we have seen, groups were invariably those who were dissatisfied with the way the temple was being run. Jesus too expresses this dissatisfaction in the New Testament.[36]

The Last Supper was a Greek symposium-like banquet held somewhere discretely on Mount Zion the night before the Passover gathering on the Temple Mount, the day Jesus was arrested by the Romans and then executed. This would have been attended by Jesus and his small group of followers sometime in the early part of the 30s CE. The Passover seder was a post-70 CE creation in response to the destruction of the Second Temple and the cessation of sacrifices. The full Passover seder emerged over centuries. Jesus and his followers never practiced any seder of any kind, and efforts to resurrect the visual imagery of the actual Last Supper have no correlation to the Passover seder.[37] Matthew, Mark, Luke, and John or their disciples may have attended an early Passover seder or some of the first features of that commemorative meal celebrating the exodus from Egypt, but the analogies between drinking wine at the Last Supper and the four cups of wine and other customs at the Passover seder do not hold credibility since the Passover seder was formulated centuries later; thus grossly recreating the nature of the Last Supper.

According to Moshe Bazes, that Roman governor Pontius Pilate acted[38] freely and on his own to arrest Jesus, who he considered a dangerous insurgent. Thus Jesus, by this account, was not betrayed and informed on to the Romans by the Jews. Pilate had a long record of hate and cruelty against the Jewish people.

The Greek Christian Jesus

Based on the Christian perception of Christ, an image cultivated throughout two millennium, Jesus Christ is claimed to be God, the Creator of the cosmos, the one and only by which mankind can enter into heaven. In the early Christian viewpoint, somewhere after Jesus began personally identifying and communicating with God, as the creation of the latter and in his image, he took on the personification of God, became God the creator, and the one who would carry on the messianic role and enable mankind to reach heaven. The writings of the apostles portray Jesus in an ahistoric relationship with God. While the Jews negated Jesus as Messiah, and, with the exception of Josephus, did not mention him as part of the first century, the disciples and followers found in Jesus a moral leader and often a messianic figure, while the Jewish Jesus may have viewed himself as a teacher and reformer living in a time of great internal Jewish tension and oppression under Roman rule.

Josephus identified Jesus as a Jewish sage of his time. Christians later distorted the passage about Jesus in Josephus Flavius's *Jewish Antiquities* (18:63-64), written in Greek in 93-94 CE, more than sixty years after the crucifixion, to say, "about this time there lived Jesus, a wise man—if indeed one ought call him a man." According to Flusser, it was precisely this intervention that "guaranteed the authenticity of Josephus's" statement that Jesus was "a wise man."[39] Furthermore, the Greek word for "wise" shares a common root with the Greek term "sophist," which in that time was a positive designation. Josephus coined two other Jewish sages as sophists, and he used this term regularly to refer to prominent Jewish sages.

The Last Supper on Mount Zion in Jerusalem is a Greek adaptation of the symposium to the meal Jesus and his disciples ate together before his arrest.

> The sermon goes on to talk of Jesus' sending "another paraclete" (Greek, ἄλλο Παράκλητον), a «Spirit of Truth» that will «testify about» Jesus. Paraclete comes from the Koine Greek word παράκλητος (paraklētos, "one who consoles, one who intercedes on our behalf, a comforter or an advocate"). When the dogmatic definition of the Trinity became necessary in the 3rd century, the passage became central to the arguments about the role of the Holy Spirit. Arguments about the *Filioque*, which partly caused the East-West Schism between the Roman Catholic Church and the Eastern Orthodox Church, centered around this verse. In some sectors of the early Jesus movement the paraclete was considered a more human figure, and, in the

> 2nd century, Montanus claimed that he himself was this paraclete that had been promised.[40]

Jesus was the first paraclete, the consoler, comforter, or helper, coming to assist his disciples; but more central to the term is that as paraclete Jesus is the Holy Spirit in the Holy Trinity, the triangle consisting of the messenger between how God is revealed and God's role in salvation. In the Trinitarian theology, the paraclete or the Holy Spirit is the third person of the Trinity and provides guidance, support, and consolation to people. Titles synonymous to the Holy Spirit are "Spirit of Truth," "Giver of Life," and "Lord of Grace." In rabbinical tradition in the Talmud, the παράκλητος was the advocate or intercessor who saved another when summoned to court to face capital punishment. Today in modern Hebrew in Israel, the praklit (פרקליט), is the government prosecutor.

Christianity was based on the New Testament, meaning in Latin "a new covenant," which came from the Greek interpretation of Jeremiah 31. Jeremiah prophesized that "God would renew the destroyed country of Israel with a new covenant was [sic] re-understood as a prophecy of Jesus' incarnation."[41] The early church advanced the theory of the new covenant; but not Jesus. However Jesus led an apocalyptic movement, not just a movement for educational social reform. Segal shows a view of apocalyptism in the classical Biblical sense and its modern context, which is also applicable to Jesus' adaptation of the term:

> Until recently, apocalyptism was defined solely by the literary apocalypses, especially the Book of Daniel in the Hebrew Bible and the Revelation of Saint John in the New Testament. Apocalyptism, coming from the Greek verb meaning to "disclose," "uncover," or "bring the light," has always implied the revelation of the secret of the coming end of time, apocalyptic books have in common the violent end of the world and the establishment of God's kingdom. . . . As opposed to holding an optimistic view of progress, which moves toward the final goal by slow approximations, apocalypticists are totally impatient with the corrupt present, seeing it as a series of unprecedented calamities. Usually, the "end of days" is viewed as a sudden, revolutionary leap into an idealized future state, when the believers will finally be rewarded for their years of suffering, while their oppressors and the other evil infidels will be justly punished.[42]

Initially the concept of the messiah was strange to Hellenism and materialistic and pagan-believing Greek society. This Jewish concept was based on the *mashiach*, "the anointed one." In Hebrew Jewish ritual, when a man was inaugurated into a divinely sanctioned official position, such as a king, prophet, or priest, he was appointed to his function by having oil poured over his head. When the term was translated to Greek and became *christos,* it had little context or frame of reference.[43] Athletes oiled their bodies before competition, but winners of races, like those in the ritual Olympics, were crowned with branches of shrubs and bushes, as was the custom in Greek tradition. With the exception of the burial of Jesus, where he was luxuriously groomed, the concept is overlooked in the New Testament. A Greek convert to early Christianity had to learn from a Christian the meaning of the "messiah," since it was a foreign concept to Hellenism.

In contrast to Catholicism, which sought to replace Judaism and erase as much of it as possible, and then became dominant and far reaching, the Greek Orthodox Church and all of its Eastern Orthodox affiliates retained some facets of Judaism, such as the Jewish calendar, fasting, canonization, codification of the Bible, and mysticism. However, they shared general Christian animosity toward the Jews for the death of Jesus, accused the Jewish Judas for betraying Jesus, and in general took out their wrath against the Jews in prayer and in violence against the Jews on Easter for their allegation that the Jews killed their lord and salvation, Jesus.

In the Apostles and throughout the New Testament, written initially in Greek, when Jesus speaks, he does so in Greek. A fable, of which there are many, revolving around a humanist and altruistic Jesus, is conveyed in Greek. The image of Jesus can be misconstrued as an elite Hellenized Jewish resident (and Sadducee) of Jerusalem as opposed to a simple and marginal reformer in the Galilee, who was a Pharisee and opposed teaching Jewish law and theology to non-Jews. In the Gospels, Jesus warns his followers to be wary of the "leaven of the Sadducees" as well as that of the Pharisees.[44] In actuality, the Jewish Jesus, like the prophets, gave a fresh interpretation of the laws governing spiritual life and a new meaning and purpose of religion, but Christianity created him as the Messiah for a new religion.

The Christian Jesus was a spiritual novelty in an Asia Minor, where new markets and manufactures were emerging at the time. In Matthew 23:15-26, Jesus criticizes the Pharisaic legal practices, disapproves of their proselytism, and views negatively their distinction between diverse forms of oaths and their emphasis on tithes and purifications. There is no historical evidence for or against this, and in general one does not know how much of the writings of the apostles represent historical reality. In Matthew 15, Jesus attacks the Pharisaic "tradition of the elders." Based further on Matthew 16:14, the Jews who admired Jesus considered him as prophet probably because he performed many miracles, another highly contentious phenomenon lacking historical proof. The new Christian disciples revered Jesus as a healer, for his humility, and as a teacher. In reconstructing the image of Jesus as a cornerstone of the new Christian religion, the character of the Jewish Jesus was misconstrued and reinvented, but in light of the lack of historical proofs, the extent of the recreation of the former Jewish Jesus into the Christian Jesus can not be assessed and quantified.

Seltzer demonstrates that there was belief in Jesus before Paul attempted to convert Jews and pagans to early Christianity, but he also notes how the disciple utilized their prayers and proclamations:

> The main area for Paul's activity as a Christian missionary was Asia Minor and Greece, where Jewish communities had been in existence for some time. However, Paul was not the originator of diaspora Christianity. Even before he became active among Christians in the early 40s, Jews and gentiles in such cities as Damascus and Antioch had already begun worshiping Jesus as "Lord" (*Kyrios*) and Christ (the Greek translation of the Hebrew *mashiah*, anointed). Paul apparently made use of prayers and proclamations already formulated by these groups for baptismal initiation and the Lord's Supper, the central rites of the nascent movement. But Paul drew drastic and radical conclusions from Jesus' crucifixion and resurrection—conclusions that were a major factor in furthering the spread of Christianity beyond the Jewish orbit.[45]

Saul of Tarsus, the Apostle Paul, was significant in creating the doctrine that Jesus was the expected messiah of the Jews, but created a new faith around the image of Jesus.[46]

The eminent researcher Haym Maccoby deduced from Paul's Epistles that Paul invented the idea of the Last Supper (the Greek *kuriakon deipno*, meaning Lord's Supper) and added to it the cannibalistic pagan elements of remembering Jesus by breaking bread to symbolize eating his body and drinking wine to symbolize drinking his blood. The Eucharist (its initial meaning was "blessing") at first was a Jewish custom where at the beginning of the meal bread was blessed, broken, and given to eat, and the wine was drunk as the last blessing at the end of the Grace after meals. Paul claimed that he received the details of the Last Supper from the Lord Jesus himself, in a revelation by the latter after his death about how the latter instituted the Eucharist. Since Paul wanted Jesus to be considered the creator of Christianity, he said that Jesus created the Eucharist. Paul wanted to create a new religion, so he incorporated a popular pagan custom where worshippers eat part of the body of the god to enhance belief in that god. Paul did not want to be considered the founder of the new religion, so he gave the omnipotent mystical role to Jesus to credit him with founding the new faith. In order to give credence to the new religion and show its magical mystical side, Paul claimed that he received the revelation personally from the Lord Jesus: "at the Last Supper, Jesus gave instructions about the institution of the Eucharist."[47] Maccoby notes that the Eucharist ceremony was not observed the Jerusalem church, but only by those churches coming under the influence of Paul, and he was the only source for the institution of the Eucharist. The three Synoptic Gospels do not associate Jesus with instituting the Eucharistic rite, but instead depict Jesus as performing a ceremony which in the aftermath was made to be the basis of the Eucharistic rite. Afterward, John did not include the Eucharist in his portrayal of the Last Supper, but noted the institution as part of Jesus' preaching. All the Gospels included the Eucharistic rite in the life of Jesus, but he himself was unfamiliar with it. Maccoby adds that the early church fathers were so embarrassed by Paul's expression, "the Lord's Supper," that they replaced it with the name "Eucharist," which had Jewish, rather than pagan associations.[48]

Maccoby strongly shows the shock of the Eucharist idea for the Jews:

> John shows himself well aware of the shocking character of the Eucharistic idea in Jewish eyes when he portrays even the disciples as offended by it, and some of them as so alienated that "they walked no more with him." What John is describing here is not the shock felt by Jewish hearers of Jesus (for Jesus never expressed any Eucharistic ideas) but the shock felt by hearers of Paul when he grafted on to the practice of Christianity a rite so redolent of paganism, involving a notion of incorporation of the godhead by a product with strong overtones of cannibalism.[49]

Early Christianity used the motif of Jesus as the son of God. A pre-Hellenistic and early Hellenistic variation of the biblical story of Reuben, son of Jacob, and Bilha, where Reuben moves his bed into the tent of his father's concubine and loses his right to a double inheritance when accused of infidelity, depicts "the mutual curse by which the Fallen Angels bound themselves; the man-devouring giants begotten by them; the dire punishment of the celestial transgressors by God."[50] An early Christian reading would label Reuben, the son of God, coming to the daughter of man. While this makes little sense in modern logic, it is noteworthy how the early Christian conceptualized the term "Son of God," and to see how the early Christians elevated Jesus to divine status.

Noteworthy also are the Ebionites and early Greek-speaking Christians and how they contributed to the image of Jesus:

> The descendants of the original followers of Jesus Christ, who became known as Ebionites, maintained themselves as a small sect for some time and then dissolved. They are today forgotten, except as they are pictured in the New Testament, a compilation of Greek language tracts put together by Saul of Tarsus and the Christians. In these tracts, the insistence of the Ebionites that Jesus Christ had been "the" Messiah is given an entirely new significance. It becomes the basis for a pseudo-cannibal ritual in which Christians are enjoined to pretend to eat the flesh and drink the blood of Jesus Christ in order to attain unto eternal life. From the rank of "Messiah," the New Testament promotes Jesus to the rank of "Son of God," the better to enjoin pretending to eat his flesh and drink his blood.[51]

The Ebionites spoke Aramaic, while the Paul and his followers spoke Greek. For the first three centuries of Christianity, the known documents are in Greek and it was the Greeks who popularized Christianity; they used the Greek language, in Egypt, Syria, and Turkey and later expanded their proselyte activities and influence in Greece and Rome. After 70 CE, the Ebionites settled in Jordan and had little further influence, but they retained Mosaic law, as opposed to the Greek Christians. The Christians of the second and third centuries CE condemned the Ebionites as heretics for the Ebionite custom of pretending to eat the flesh and drink the blood of their deceased leader Jesus.[52]

Both the Ebionites and later the Greek-speaking early Christians claimed that Jesus had magical powers.[53] The Christians added the claim that Jesus was the "Son of God" to further his supernatural image.

Another view of Jesus, formulated in the New Testament and based on the Greek term κήρυγμα (*kérugma*), is the Greek term in the New Testament for preaching (or proclaiming, announcing, or crying). Jesus is portrayed in the New Testament as entering synagogues to preach or proclaim and reading from the book of the prophet Isaiah, an analogy to proclaiming Jesus as Messiah based on the interpretation from the book of Isaiah. However, basically, the New Testament portrayed Jesus as proclaiming the good news to the poor, the blind, and the captive. Jewish Christianity viewed Jesus' combined role as the healer, miracle worker, teacher, prophet, and messiah as much more important than the plain risen Lord of the kerygma. In the initial Hellenistic Christian congregations, founded by Greek Jews and comprised mainly of non-Jews, the idea of Jesus as the risen Lord of kerygma evolved to the state where "redemption through the crucified and risen Christ became the heart of preaching."[54]

According to the Christian biblical scholar, Charles Harold Dodd, the ancient kerygma contributed to the belief that "by virtue of the resurrection, Jesus has been exalted at the right hand of God as Messianic head of the new Israel."[55] Kerygma not only was a means, but it was an end, and it always closed with an appeal for repentance, an offer for forgiveness, and the promise of salvation. Followers were lured into the new religion with an offer of forgiveness for sin in the spirit of Jesus and the present of the Holy Spirit. Forgiveness for sins was not connected in the early church to the death of Jesus, but his whole life, death, and resurrection. Furthermore, the Jerusalem kerygma did not include Jesus' intervention on behalf of the sins of the new converts, but Paul entered this later. Hence, the kerygma did lead to replacement theory, which diverts from the Jewish Jesus, but the initial "resurrected" Jesus did not replace God in pardoning sins.

Dom Gregory Dix claims that after the crucifixion of Peter in Rome, the apostles presented Syriac (a middle Aramaic prevalent across the Fertile Crescent) documents of the New Testament and Hellenic influence ceased:

> That astonishing leap from one world to another was the achievement of the *single* "Apostolic" Christian generation, between the crucifixion of Jesus in Jerusalem and the crucifixion of Peter in Rome. And it is only after that leap has been accomplished that the Gentile Churches produced the most substantially and obviously "Syriac" documents of the New Testament—the Gospels—as the record of that Jewish-Christian *κήρυγμα* which had brought them in their own Christian being. If there is any "process" observable in the

> composition of the Gospels it is a process of "translations" rather than one of "adaptation." Strictly speaking, there is no more "Hellenism" thought in them (so far as we can discover) than there was in Jesus Himself. We have to recognize this fact. The Gospels present purely Syriac, not Hellenic, ideas, even though they are written in Greek, and for a Greek and Gentile public. They are, broadly speaking, the authentic record of Jesus Himself, of what He said, and did and what was in historical fact. But they are also the proof of His continuous directing power in this hurricane process of Christian expansion across the alien Greek world in a single generation, because they are also the essence and product of what the Gentile churches believed and preached at the end of that prodigious and swift expansion. Otherwise they would not be as they are. [56]

While the above depiction by a Protestant monk may be more theological than historical and negates the above depictions of the strength of Greek texts and Hellenism in early Christianity, and adds a bit of later Latin preeminence in Christianity which may not be appropriate for a Greek-dominated primitive church, he does add the element of the Aramaic influence in early Christianity that went beyond the Ebionites and Jordan.

According to Christian tradition, one of the initial twelve disciples of Jesus, the Jew Judas Iscariot, was lured to betray Jesus for a sum of money—thirty pieces of silver (Matthew 26:14-16). Adler quotes the Evangelists Matthew, Mark, and Luke and the French scholar Renan, who notes that Judas handed Jesus over to the Romans with the identifying signal of one kiss. According to Mark, the high priests were looking for a crafty way to arrest Jesus and they did not want to do it on the Passover holiday or the Passover feast, but the night before, in order to avoid a riot by the public. However, Adler differs with them in that he claims that Judas handed Jesus over to the Romans, not aggressively or in exchange for bribery, but out of love and admiration.[57] There are scholars who surmise that Jesus went along with the plot willingly or even initiated it in order to be remembered as the martyr and even Messiah.

The story of Judas' betrayal of Jesus, according to the scholar Hyam Maccoby, was part of an attempt to fill in the biography of Jesus in a way that Paul never attempted, and various details were imported from historical traditions of the Jerusalem church, but mainly the followers of Paul sought a narrative to re-create the image of Jesus as divine sacrifice.[58] Maccoby provides lengthy background and details to put this assertion further into proper historical context.

Jesus appointed Judas Iscariot as treasurer of the disciples, and there was another disciple, Judas, whose loyalty was not questioned. Jesus knew that Judas Iscariot intended to betray him, and based on numerous accounts mentioned in the Gospels, at the Last Supper, Jesus handed him a piece of bread dipped in wine, stating that the person receiving that piece would betray him.[59] After Judas Iscariot signaled Jesus and he was arrested by the Roman soldiers, the former had regrets, returned the money to the temple priests, and tried to commit suicide. Judas as a Jew was one of Jesus' people, but he betrayed him. Judas the disciple betrayed Jesus, but so did the Jews on a communal level. Nowhere in the Gospels is Judas specified to represent the Jewish people as a whole,[60] but he is a symbol by virtue of his name as the Jew, and historically, he is blamed for Jesus' death, and Christian followers have shown virulent animosity toward the Jews in association with Judas and as a people who opposed Christianity and rejected their belief in the messianic Jesus.

Judas is the Greek form of the name for Yehudah, Judah, the son of Jacob, and the progenitor of the great tribe of Judah, to which King David belonged and named his kingdom. The messiah Ben David was to come from this tribe. Judas was chosen "for a diabolic role, as part of the anti-Semitic campaign within the Pauline Church, which had cast the Jews as people of the devil and enemies of the incarnate God."[61] Not only was Judas selected to represent the betrayal of Jesus by his fellow Jews, who refused to recognize him as the Messiah, but the betrayal fell on all twelve of the original disciples. Peter, who was chosen by Jesus to be the stalwart of his kingdom, was rebuked the most in the Gospels:

> Not only does he deny Jesus thrice on the night of his imprisonment (though he does not desert him as the other disciples do); he has also had a serious quarrel with Jesus at the time of the Salutation (see Mark 8:32-33, Matthew 16:21-23). When Jesus revealed his imminent sacrifice, Peter failed to understand the need for Jesus' crucifixion and "rebuked" him for predicting it. On this occasion, Peter was harshly addressed by Jesus as "Satan" (Mark 8:33, Matthew 16:23).[62]

According to Maccoby, "During this period leading up to the composition of the Gospels, the incipient anti-Semitism found in Paul's Epistles developed into a full-blown indictment of the Jewish people as the rejecters, betrayers, and finally murderers of Jesus."[63] Maccoby shows, in a passage of one of Paul's Epistles, an anti-Jewish diatribe accusing the Jews of killing the Lord Jesus:

> You have fared like the congregations in Judaea, God's people in Christ Jesus. You have been treated by your countrymen as they are treated by the Jews, who killed the Lord Jesus and the prophets and drove us out, the Jews who are heedless of God's will and enemies of their fellow-man, hindering us from speaking to the Gentiles to lead them to salvation. All this time they have been making up the full measure of their guilt, and now retribution has overtaken them for good and all. (1 Thessalonians 2:14-16)[64]

Maccoby signifies the above passage as the Jews being the victims of typical Hellenistic anti-Semitism, whereby the Jews are accused of being "enemies of their fellow-men" in the writings of the Hellenistic Alexandrian writers, Apion and Manetho, and the Roman writers, Tacitus and Seneca. Maccoby further explains Hellenistic anti-Semitism by noting that the above authors portrayed the

Jews as being doomed for expulsion from the land and blamed them for their guilt, sins, and killing of prophets, culminating in their killing of Jesus. After the Jewish War against Rome, which ended in military defeat and the destruction of the Second Temple, the Pauline Church disclaimed all Jewish connections, denied that Jesus was a rebel against Rome, and instead asserted that Jesus rebelled against Judaism, "thus throwing the entire blame for the crucifixion of Jesus on the Jews."[65] The Pauline anti-Jewish positions are established in the Gospels and Acts. The first of the Gospels, Mark, probably written in Rome at the time of the Jewish War, voices vehement hostility against the Jews and concludes with the proclamation of the divinity of Jesus by a Roman centurion (Mark 15:39), "contrasting theRoman faith with Jewish treachery."[66] Maccoby notes the depiction of Jesus and the Jews by Mark's Gospel:

> Mark's Gospel is written in a tough, colloquial Greek. It portrays Jesus as a Galilean wonder-worker, who is the Son of God, and knows that he must suffer on the Cross. It gives a graphic and laconic version of the Passion story, portraying the Jews as Jesus' chief enemies, and is blind to the obsolescence of their religion. It ends abruptly with the "empty tomb," and gives no account of resurrection appearances.[67]

In Mark 14:10-11, Judas Iscariot's betrayal of Jesus is described as follows:

> Then Judas Iscariot, one of the Twelve, went to the chief priests to betray him to them. When they heard what he had come for, they were greatly pleased, and promised him money; and he began to look for a good opportunity to betray him.

The gnostic influence assists in explaining the origin of the role of Judas in Jesus' betrayal. Gnosticism means "knowledge" in Greek, and the gnostics were those who knew the secrets that could bring salvation.[68] For gnostics, a person was saved by knowing the secrets of the world—who the true god or gods were. The material world was not home for gnostics; they were trapped in their bodies of flesh and needed to find the way to heaven. For Christian gnostics (most gnostics were not), Christ brought this secret knowledge, and he revealed the truth to his followers, thus setting them free. According to Christianity, one true God created the earth, but according to the gnostics, there were other gods beside the one who created the earth, and he was inferior to the others. In light of the earth's multiple physical disasters, the gnostics believed that salvation only came from those who knew how to escape from this world. Ehrman elaborates on some gnostic teachings on Jesus:

> Some gnostics taught that Christ was an aeon from the realm above—that he was not a man of flesh and blood, but that he came from above only in the apparatus of human flesh. He was a phantom who took the appearance of flesh to teach those who were called (i.e., the gnostics), who have the

> spark within the secret truths they need for salvation. Other gnostics taught that Jesus was a real man, but that he did not have a typical spark of the divine within. His soul was a special divine being who came from above to be temporarily housed within the man Jesus, to use him as a conduit through which to reveal the necessary truths to his close followers. In this understanding, the divine element came into Jesus at some point of his life—for example, at his baptism, when the Spirit descended upon him—and then left him once his ministry was over. This would explain why, on the cross, Jesus cried out "My God, my God, why have you abandoned me?" It was because the divine element within him had left prior to his crucifixion, since, after all, the divine cannot suffer and die."[69]

For the Christian gnostics, the Christ is this divine revealer of the truths of salvation and this reincarnated phantom had literally forsaken Jesus (or left him behind). "After Jesus' death, though, he raised him from the dead as a reward for his faithfulness, and continued through him to teach his disciples the secret truths that can lead to salvation."[70]

According to Irenaus, the gnostic Cainites believed that the God of the Old Testament was not the true God, but the ignorant creator of the world from whom they needed to escape. Thus, all the men in Jewish and Christian history who stood against God, like Cain, the men of Sodom and Gomorrah, and later Judas Iscariot, were those that had witnessed the truth and understood the secrets needed for salvation. The Cainites were extreme in their opposition to the Old Testament God. They opposed anything God commanded, and supported anything forbidden. In doing the opposite, they ignored the Sabbath, ate pork, and committed adultery in order to show their freedom from the God of the Old Testament. The Cainites viewed Judas as the only disciple of Jesus who understood his message and did according to what Jesus wanted, "turning him over to the authorities for his crucifixion. Judas was thus seen as the ultimate follower of Jesus, one whose actions should be emulated rather than spurned. For he was the one to whom Jesus had delivered the secret knowledge necessary for salvation."[71]

In the gnostic Gospel of Judas from the second century CE, Jesus challenges the twelve disciples to see who is perfect and capable of salvation. Only Judas is capable of standing. He has the same divine spark that Jesus has. Only Judas knows the true identity of Jesus—not a mere mortal from this world alone, but from the immortal realm of Barbelo, who according to Serbian gnostics, is one of the primary divine beings in the perfect realm of the true God. Since Judas correctly perceived Jesus' character, the latter took him aside to teach him the "mysteries of the kingdom," the secret knowledge necessary for salvation. Jesus assured Judas that he would attain salvation, but grieve in the process, since he would be rejected by the twelve disciples and be replaced. In the New Testament Book of Acts, when Judas dies, he is replaced by Matthias. Judas can reach salvation, while the other apostles are concerned about their God, the creator god of the Old Testament, whom both Jesus and Judas can transcend.[72]

In the Gospel of Judas, Judas has a vision of being stoned by the twelve disciples, and he sees a house, which he wants to enter. Jesus tells Judas that no one born to mortals can enter the house and that it is reserved for the holy. Judas, who has a divine spark within him, will be allowed to enter once he has left his mortal flesh. He is to surpass the other twelve disciples, will come to rule over them, and be far superior than all in the material world once he has reached salvation based on the secret knowledge that Jesus will reveal. The revelation comprises "a great and boundless eternal realm: of the truly divine beyond this world and far above the inferior deities who created the material existence and humans. Numerous superior divine beings came about long before the gods of this world; El (God of the Old Testament), his helper Nebro (also called Yaldabaoth) who is defiled with blood and whose name means 'rebel,' and Saklas, meaning 'fool.'"[73]

In summarizing the Gospel of Judas, Jesus taught Judas that salvation was attained not by worshipping the God of this world and accepting his creation, but rather by denying this world and rejecting the body that binds man to the world. "That is the ultimate reason why the deed that Judas performs for Jesus is a righteous act, one that earns him the right to surpass all others. By handing Jesus over to the authorities, Judas allows Jesus to escape his own mortal flesh to return to his eternal home."[74]

Conclusion

Jesus was a Galilean Jew who was associated with rebellion against oppressive Roman rule, had a group of disciples, and scorned Hellenistic Sadducee practices and abuses in the holy temple. He was considered a threat not only to the Roman regime, but possibly by the Jewish high priest and other priests. While being a devout practicing Jew, his emphasis laid in helping society and creating a new unique path in Jewish society, and his activities diverted from legalistic Pharisee streams.

Messianism was definitely in the air in the Jewish society seeking liberation from the Romans, and Jesus and his disciples were exposed to such thought, but geared their activities toward salvation. Wolfe goes as far to claim that Jesus viewed himself as the Messiah and Lenowitz takes the Gospels literally to the point where he depicts Jesus as one of many Jewish messianic figures and a miracle worker. The lineage of Jesus does not tend to lie in line with the Davidic dynasty and the composition of his family—his parents and siblings—suggest a conventional structure and little room for supernatural relationships. Ahistoric theories of both the living Jesus and Judas emulating divine redemption and taking on godly tasks were presented.

The Greek Jesus was an image of Jesus established postmortem by the Gospels, later disciples, and as the Christian church evolved. Sometime between the death of Jesus and the activism of Paul of Tarsus in disseminating Christianity to the Jews and pagans of Asia Minor, the disciples and early church created a messianic Jesus, including a symbolic resurrection and evolution into divine status and mission. Paul added to the image of the crucified Jesus and used the motif of the traitor Judas to blame the Jews for the betrayal of Jesus in leading the path for a new religion. Paul succeeded through preaching and galvanizing the Greek-speaking society of Asia Minor and Greece to adopt Christianity, created a wedge between Judaism and Christianity, and flamed the polemic between Judaism and the newly emerging Christian religion. Not only did he demonize the Jews, but he also led to the split between the Jews and the Christians and cast out the Jewish practices and theological aspects from the newly emerging religion. He succeeded in recruiting numerous Greek pagans and took on the challenge of explaining the new religion in terms unknown to them. Early Christianity borrowed pagan concepts to create the Eucharist ceremony, a symbolic mixing and eating of the blood and flesh of Jesus. The Aramaic-speaking Ebionites introduced the idea of the messianic Jesus and advocated the belief of the mixing of his blood and body in order to advance his eternal life.

And finally, the gnostic Cainites provided the theoretical background for the resurrection of Jesus and his departure from his body in order to become the new eternal god needed for salvation. Judas, the betrayer, was a necessary agent to bring about crucifixion, thus enabling Jesus to break out of his body in order to reach heaven.

Discussion Questions

1. Was Jesus in his day considered a rebel, a messianic figure, or a unique reformer within Judaism?
2. Did Jesus create a messianic role for himself or did his disciples and the Gospels recreate an image of him as a divine reincarnation?
3. How did paganism and Hellenism influence the formulation of ceremonies like the Eucharist?
4. Was the image of the traitor Judas a byproduct of early church antagonism toward Judaism or was it implanted to strengthen the new theology from Jesus, himself, and afterward?

Notes

1. David Flusser, who researched Jesus for most of his life, agrees with this assumption. See David Flusser, *Jesus* (Jerusalem: The Magnes Press, The Hebrew University, 1997), 27.
2. Hyman G. Enelow, *A Jewish View of Jesus* (New York: New Bloch Publishing, 1931), 32.
3. Ibid., 34.
4. Ibid., 35.
5. Ibid., 41.

6. Stephen M. Wylen, *The Jews In The Time Of Jesus, An Introduction* (Mahwah, NJ: Paulist Press, 1996), 90-91.
7. Ibid., 91.
8. Helmut Merkel, "The Opposition between Jesus and Judaism," in *Jesus and the Politics of His Day*, ed. Ernest Bammel and C. F. D. Moule (Cambridge: Cambridge University Press, 1984), 129-144.
9. Geza Vermes, *The Religion of Jesus the Jew* (Minneapolis: Fortress Press, 1993), 189.
10. Flusser, *Jesus*, 32.
11. Ibid., 33.
12. Wylen, *The Jews In The Time Of Jesus*, 92-93.
13. Ibid., 93.
14. Talmud Berakhot 34b.
15. Moshe Bazes, *Jesus The Jew—The Historical Jesus, The True Story of Jesus* (Jerusalem: Alpha Press, 1976), 53-54.
16. Lawrence H. Schiffman, *Texts And Traditions, A Source Reader for the Study of Second Temple and Rabbinic Judaism* (New York: Ktav Publishing, 1998), 370.
17. Wylen, *The Jews In The Time Of Jesus*, 172.
18. Shaye J. D. Cohen, *From The Maccabees To The Mishnah, Second Edition* (Louisville: Westminster John Knox Press, 2006), 116.
19. Flusser, *Jesus*, 24.
20. Ibid., 29.
21. Ibid., 25.
22. Ibid., 27.
23. Ibid., 35.
24. Alan F. Segal, *Rebecca's Children, Judaism and Christianity in the Roman World* (Cambridge: Harvard University Press, 1986), 78.
25. Dom Gregory Dix, *Jew and Greek, A Study in the Primitive Church* (Westminster, England: Dacre Press, 1953), 77.
26. *The Oxford Study Bible, Revised English Bible with the Apocrypha* (Oxford: Oxford University Press, 1992), 1306.
27. Dix, *Jew and Greek*, 78.
28. Harris Lenowitz, *The Jewish Messiahs, From the Galilee to Crown Heights* (New York: Oxford University Press, 1998), 25-28.
29. Jehuda Adler, *Jesus—Jew and Rebel* (Tel Aviv: Hadar, 1997), 21. (Hebrew)
30. Ibid.
31. Lenowitz, *The Jewish Messiahs*, 35.
32. Ibid., 33.
33. Adler, *Jesus—Jew and Rebel*, 12.
34. Jehuda Adler, *Jesus, Who Are You?* (Tel Aviv: Hadar, 1986), 51. (Hebrew)
35. *The Oxford Study Bible*,1290.
36. Robert Wolfe, *The Origins Of The Messianic Ideal* (New York: J-Rep, 2003), 94-95.
37. Michael J. Cook, "Christian Appropriation of Passover: Jewish Responses Then and Now," *Jewish History and Thought*, vol. 5 (New York: Hunter College, 1998), 49-63.
38. Bazes, *Jesus The Jew*, 34.
39. Flusser, *Jesus*, 30.
40. "Last Supper," Wikipedia, http://en.wikipedia.org/wiki/Last_Supper.
41. Segal, *Rebecca's Children*, 68
42. Ibid., 69-70.

43. Ibid., 64-65.
44. Cohen, *From The Maccabees,* 143.
45. Robert M. Seltzer, *Jewish People, Jewish Thought, The Jewish Experience in History* (Upper Saddle River, NJ: Prentice Hall, 1980), 234.
46. Wolfe, *The Origins*, 53.
47. Hyam Maccoby, *The Mythmaker, Paul And The Invention Of Christianity* (New York: Harper and Row, 1986), 110-18.
48. Ibid., 116.
49. Ibid., 115.
50. Elias J. Bickerman, *The Jews in the Greek Age* (Cambridge: Harvard University Press, 1988), 206.
51. Wolfe, *The Origins,* 54.
52. Ibid., 55.
53. Ibid., 56.
54. Flusser, *Jesus,* 20.
55. Charles Harold Dodd, *The Apostolic Preaching and its Developments: Three Lectures with an Eschatology and History* (London: Hodder and Stoughton, 1936), chap. 1.
56. Dix, *Jew and Greek,* 3-4.
57. Adler, *Jesus, Who Are You?*, 66-67.
58. Hyam Maccoby, *Judas Iscariot and the Myth of Jewish Evil* (New York: The Free Press, 1992), 26.
59. Ibid., 2.
60. Ibid., 5.
61. Ibid., 29.
62. Ibid.
63. Ibid., 27.
64. Ibid.
65. Ibid., 27-28.
66. Ibid., 28.
67. Ibid., 34.
68. Bart D. Ehrman, "Christianity Turned on its Head: The Alternative Vision of the Gospel Judas," in *The Gospel of Judas from Codex Tchacos*, ed. Rodolph Kasser, Marven Mayer, and Gregor Wurst (Washington DC: National Geographic, 2006), 77-120.
69. Ibid., 87-88.
70. Bart D. Ehrman, *Misquoting Jesus, The Story Behind Who Changed the Bible and Why* (New York: HarperCollins, 2005), 171.
71. Ehrman, "Christianity Turned on its Head," 89-90.
72. Ibid., 97-99.
73. Ibid., 99-100.
74. Ibid., 101.

Jewish Responses to Byzantine Polemics from the Ninth through the Eleventh Centuries

Steven Bowman

Jesus has presented a difficulty for Greek-speaking Jews for the past two millennia. To paraphrase the Greek-Jewish scholar Asher Moissis: the Athenians killed Socrates and no one blames them; the Jews are wrongly accused of killing Jesus and the world hates them.[1]

This essay is primarily concerned with the Christian-Jewish "dialogue" in tenth- to eleventh-century Byzantium or, more accurately, with several Jewish responses to Orthodox polemics and propaganda. It will focus mainly on two literary texts that were internal and integral to the memory of Jewish identity and one midrashic text that provides a clear response to some Byzantine theological arguments. The Christian dominating and the Jewish dominated discussion about Jesus, arguing mostly from biblical sources, revolves around two facets of the Christian claim: 1) was Jesus indeed divine or human, a question that was partially resolved by Orthodoxy with the defeat and banishment of Arianism after a century of intense theological debate and persecution and the apparent defeat of Gnosticism, and 2) was Jesus "the" or "a" Christ, the latter claim partially and occasionally accepted by some Jews as long as they were permitted to practice their Judaism as the Epistle to the Hebrews stressed. A cursory background of the following eight centuries is requisite for understanding the length and depth of the Jewish experience in Byzantium, which effected developments in the Latin West.

The first apostles preached the resurrected Jesus to a highly acculturated community of Jews and polytheists scattered throughout the eastern Mediterranean and Aegean Seas. Their message was rejected by the core of the synagogues in which they preached; however, those on the fringe, the so-called Phovoumenoi or God-Fearers (see Mal. 4:2), as well as perhaps those Jews by birth or conversion less educated or those prone to rebel against the system of a temple-directed Judaism, or others for various (philosophical, mystical, acculturist or assimilationist, etc.) reasons, received the message sympathetically. When Paul began his missionary travels—perhaps within a decade or so of Jesus' execution by the Roman authorities in Judea, he offered two elements of leniency to encourage Gentiles and assimilating Jews by birth to accept his message. First was an expansion of Jesus' teaching that what God created cannot pollute and thus the biblical laws of kashrut—let alone the ongoing Pharisaic embellishment of them—were not necessarily applicable to non-Jews. Later he substituted the Deuteronomic metaphor of "circumcision of the heart" for the Genesis commandment of "circumcision of the flesh" and thus literally established a new emphasis in the Jesus message, now preaching faith in the resurrection and its salvation rather than adherence to the Mosaic discipline of practice. The conflicting interpretations of biblical proof texts and the competition between preachers and poets, later halakhists and theologians, would define popular and scholarly dialogue throughout the subsequent Byzantine period.

By the fourth century Jews were being put under restraint in the political, legal, economic, social, and religious expression of their Roman citizenship. These restrictions would be concretized as a collective body of Jewry law in the code of Theodosius II, promulgated in 438, which formally recognized the inferiority of the Jewish collective, now bereft of its centuries-old institution of a patriarch or nasi who had represented the dispersed Jews religiously and politically to the imperial government.[2] Palestina had already been divided into three distinct provinces and the promised land was in the process of becoming a Christian Holy Land replete with monumental government-financed pilgrimage structures: churches, monasteries, hostels, hospitals, tourist shops, resettled army veterans, and so on.[3] The mission to convert the Jews became more aggressive and synagogues suffered a fate similar to pagan temples, although in the case of the permitted religion of Judaism a compensatory plot of land occasionally replaced the confiscated (by consecration) synagogue complex. The sixth-century Code of Justinian broadened sanctions against Jews and redefined Judaism as a superstition, one stage below characterization of it as a heresy, the latter a preliminary step to being outlawed, as was the fate of the Samaritans. Justinian also designated, in his notorious novella 146 (553 CE), what Jews should believe about angels, resurrection of the dead, and other topics central to an evolving Christian orthodoxy in addition to outlawing the oral tradition or *deuterosis*. He also reinstituted a selective policy of forced baptism that was to characterize imperial policy toward Jews within the empire in succeeding centuries. This imperial policy and the problem of ecclesiastical support for it would form the basis for the Jewish status in Byzantium, however stringently or leniently it might be enforced by the government.

The succeeding seventh to tenth centuries frame the continuing competition with the Jews and thus shape their response that we examine below. The external attacks on the truncating Byzantine Empire encouraged, if not forced, emperors to resurrect the Hellenizing policies of Antiochus IV and forcibly baptize Jews in order to establish a united front against these new enemies. The church, however, refused to accept forced converts—in its eyes a violation of the voluntary requirement for conversion to salvation in Christ—and rejected the validity of such baptisms; even so, ecclesiastics continued the well-developed tradition of polemic and disputation with Jews.[4] Nonetheless, in times of crisis, the theological contempt by a religion that appropriated the claims and sources of its progenitor was a necessary part of the propaganda aimed at the different *ethni*, in particular, the ongoing mission to the Slavs, whose support was necessary to the survival of the empire. The persecutions of the seventh to tenth centuries, by Heraklios, Leo the Isaurian, Basil the Macedonian, and Romanos Lekapenos, were each rescinded in turn, but the legacy of ecclesiastical anti-Jewish propaganda—sometimes virulent, on occasion congenial—continued throughout the millennium of Byzantium and was to underlie the hostility of Byzantium's heirs: the Russian Orthodox Church and its czar through to the demise of that Orthodox Christian empire in the twentieth century.

While periodic New Testament and church father "tolerance" was rare, at least until the empire adopted Christianity and attempted to make orthodoxy the only official religion, there was no persecution of Jews that could parallel the hysteria of the Catholic Visigoths and their spiritual descendents in inquisitorial Spain. A recent Hebrew University of Jerusalem dissertation attempts to place the Orthodox Christian texts of the seventh to eleventh centuries in the context of the Islamic military and theological challenge to Christianity. The Byzantine response to this new and threatening reality which spawned or supported a bevy of heterodox sects is reflected, according to this thesis, in the polemical literature against Jews. These treatises and dialogues focused mainly on Jesus, the Trinity, biblical commandments, supersession based on Christian victory, and Jews as "infidels."[5] The Byzantine theologians had to struggle to counter the Muslim claim of God's blessing to them as witnessed in their acquisition of Jerusalem, a claim that the church had made as part of its supersessionist argument against Judaism. The theological responses argued were not too convincing to Jews, however, who sympathized with Islamic monotheism and its tolerance to dhimmis.[6] In our context the Byzantine argument for Jesus was restricted, as Roly Zylbersztein shows, to a Christian interpretation of biblical verses, drawn primarily from Psalms, while one anonymous text relies on verses from the Torah, the latter perhaps reflecting an audience of converted Jews, whether willingly or unwillingly. Some of the favored texts were Psalms 2 and Psalms 110 (both drawn from the Epistle to the Hebrews), Proverbs 8, 24-25; Psalms 72; and Psalms 118:26-27, among others.

I focus, however, in this essay on the internal Jewish response to Byzantine imperial and ecclesiastical aggression. Those Jews forced by circumstances to react and respond to the Christian arguments had to do so cautiously, as their Hebrew commentaries and midrashic literature were likely subject to the danger of examination by apostates (no evidence for this however is extant as it was the case in the Latin world from the thirteenth century on). Jewish wags could occasionally affect a naiveté, as when they were quoted in a spurious (but nevertheless enlightening) text from fifth- and ninth-century Syriac traditions to query the emperor why they should be castigated as Christ-killers ("god-slaying synagogue" is the common pejorative) when the Council of Chalcedon argued that Jesus was crucified as a human and not as a god. Moreover, he had to die before he could effect the miracle of resurrection. In our own day we have all read Nikos Kazantzakis's sympathetic reading of Judas, about whose fate the Gospels and later Christian sources are ambivalent. Indeed, the newly discovered Gnostic Gospel of Judas anticipated Kazantzakis.[7] Numerous other inconsistencies have been the grist for nineteenth- and twentieth-century polemics and apologetics between Protestants and Catholics, between secularists and religious, and in the past few generations between Jews and Christians. In 2007 Lena Einhorn, a sober Swedish investigator and a critically trained MD and PhD, assembled a skeptical documentary that challenges blind faith with the measured observations and occasional speculations of a trained doctor.[8] Religious and secular skepticism have complicated the Jesus issue for our times, despite increasing Jewish scholarly interest in the Jesus phenomenon and its overlap with the Dead Sea Scrolls and Gnostic texts.

To return to Byzantium, the infamous parody of the Gospels known as *Toldoth Yeshu*—a product perhaps of late antiquity[9] that has annoyed the church more for its Jewish origin than for its conflation of many diverse Christian traditions—had its impact in successive centuries before the emergence of detailed Jewish responses to Christian interpretations and manipulations of biblical verses by Latin literate scholars in Western Christendom from the twelfth century on.[10] Evidence has yet to emerge that the *Toldoth Yeshu* tradition had any direct impact in Byzantium during our period of inquiry.

In Byzantine southern Italy, still maintaining its Byzantine cultural base long after its political loss to the empire, there are extant several important responses to the Christian argument which had their own influence on the development of the Ashkenazi polemics of the later Middle Ages.

During the middle third of the tenth century—the date of one manuscript is 953 but it may be the copyist's date—there appeared a seminal text in exquisite Hebrew detailing the history of the Second Temple period. The book is known as *Sepher Yosippon* (in Modern Hebrew *Sefer Yosifun*) after its alleged author Yoseph ben Gurion, a mistaken alias for Flavius Josephus. Actually, the author is more accurately designated as Mar Ploni, an anonymous nonrabbinic scholar fluent in Latin and Hebrew, secular in his outlook, an historian in his critical methodology, and perhaps also a trained physician, or at least well read in medical texts. He was not a Talmudist and perhaps was somewhat restricted to his expertise in the Hebrew Bible and its language, possibly having only a passing familiarity with the expanding influence of the Babylonian Talmud, which only reached Byzantine Italy in perhaps the ninth or tenth century. (The Mishna and the Palestinian rabbinic tradition were well known in Byzantium among the periodically harassed rabbinic teachers and learned lay men and women.) The author's Hebrew reflects the renaissance of the Hebrew language in southern Italy beginning in the later eighth century and certainly well developed by the new immigrants to southern Italy who have left us an important corpus of Hebrew epitaphs in Venosa and elsewhere throughout Apulia.[11] The author was innovative in his style and language, to which he contributed many neologisms and phrases that have been revived by Eliezer Ben Yehuda (see his *Dictionary and Thesaurus of the Hebrew Language*).

Sepher Yosippon has two stages of development. The first is the tenth-century autograph (some scholars opt for a late -ninth-century composition) that is mostly extant in one manuscript that has been reconstructed in the scholarly edition of David Flusser.[12] In other words, the authentic *Sepher Yosippon* was obscured from popular and even scholarly view for nearly a millennium, despite the plethora of chapbooks, citations, plagiarisms, translations and reeditions, all based on the following second stage. The second stage saw a series of interpolations by successive copyists in the eleventh century that produced a considerably expanded text, rediscovered, collated and edited in the mid-fourteenth century by the young Balkan scholar Yehudah ibn Moskoni, as he calls himself,[13] and printed in Istanbul at the beginning of the sixteenth century; this edition remained the basis for the popular versions until the twentieth century and is still in widespread use as the major source for the (religious) Jewish memory of the Second Temple period. This latter text in its many versions was superseded, at least for modern Jewish historical scholarship, by the translation into Hebrew of Flavius Josephus's *Bellum Iudaicum* or *Jewish War* in 1923 by I. N. Simhoni.[14]

The attitude toward Jesus differs in both versions of *Sepher Yosippon*. But first some background. The Greek Josephus was preserved by the Orthodox Church as a semi-sacred history of Israel—the Church identified itself as the New Israel—which fortuitously mentioned Jesus.[15] This tradition may well have contributed to the sanctification of Josephus himself in the canon of Orthodox Christian saints. There is little doubt that the mention of Jacob (aka James *pace* James I of England), brother of Jesus, in book 20 is not authentic. The so-called Testimonium Flavianum, which recognizes Jesus as the Messiah (χριστος), has been critiqued by scholars since the sixteenth century and is now generally considered as an interpolation in whole or in part sometime between Origen, who does not mention such a text in his oeuvre, and Eusebius, the polymath Arian biographer of Constantine who is considered the likely candidate for this pious fraud.[16] In the fourth century Josephus was translated into Latin (usually attributed to Rufinus d. ca. 410-11) and sometime in the late fourth or early fifth century Josephus's *Jewish War* was partially rewritten as an anti-Jewish treatise, known today as Pseudo-Hegesippus, but was considered for over a millennium and a half by many Christians as the *ipsissima verba* of Josephus to his own people.[17] The anonymous author of Pseudo-Hegesippus[18] heavily annotated his treatise with Christian exempla and filled it, in good Latin rhetorical and historical tradition, with homespun speeches carefully choosing what he would include from Josephus to strengthen his argument that the Jews deserved the loss of temple and capital and perpetual exile for their role in the death of Jesus the Christ.[19] Yehudah ibn Moskoni, the fourteenth-century editor and collator of the expanded *Sepher Yosippon*, refers to his discovery in Rome—perhaps in the papal library—of two versions of Josephus, which he calls *Hegesippus maior* and *Hegesippus minor*, the latter manuscript dated 586.[20]

Let us return now to the tenth century where our anonymous Hebrew scholar happens upon these two versions of Josephus and the Vulgate translation by Jerome of the Bible and various Apocrypha. Here was the history of his own people, a history practically unknown save to the few who read Christian sources, since the rabbis had eschewed history and had excluded nearly all Hellenistic Jewish literature (except for Daniel and Esther and a few Maccabean period psalms) from their biblical canon. Enthralled, entranced, and fascinated by this discovery, he determined to make this history available to his own people in their own ancestral language, the newly revived Hebrew of the contemporary midrashic texts being written in Byzantium and Baghdad.[21]

Reading additional books, such as Orosius against the pagans and other Christian and ancient historians, and cognizant perhaps of the tenth-century interest in historiography in Byzantium and among the Lombards in southern Italy that would soon blossom in the Ottonian renaissance, he wrote what David Flusser calls the only real history produced in the Middle Ages. That is to say, a study of the ancient past based on sources and manuscripts, without relating it directly to his contemporary reality. And interestingly enough, he came to the same conclusions as the nineteenth- and twentieth-century historians of the Second Temple period using the same sources.

So what does the tenth-century historian of *Sepher Yosippon* write about Jesus? Virtually nothing, overtly. That will be the brief of the above-mentioned eleventh-century Italian interpolators of his text. Yet there are broad hints and allusions in *Sepher Yosippon* that gave guidance to the hacks that expanded his text with their polemics.

Like Josephus, the author of *Sepher Yosippon* commingles Roman and Jewish history. His first chapter updates the family of nations in Genesis 10 to his contemporary tenth century and provides one of the earliest geo-ethnic surveys of the new tribes who would form the basis for modern European nations.

Perhaps his most interesting contribution is to list the Rus (the Scandinavians who founded Kiev) among the Teutonic descendents of Yaphet, an identification clearly contradicting modern attempts to link them with Slavs. His second chapter is a lengthy treatment of the antiquities of Rome, much of it drawn from epitomes and legends that he found perhaps in the environs of the Bay of Naples where he likely read his Josephan and other manuscripts in the newly established library of the ruling duke. In this chapter he provides a creative interpretation to the sobriquet Edom that Jews had long attached to the persecuting Roman Empire and its church. He weaves a tale of Zepho ben Eliphaz, the grandson of Esau of Edom, that incorporates the story of Hercules and Caius, the cattle-stealing monster of Virgil's *Aeneid*, in the career of the progenitor of the Roman monarchy—the deified Zepho-Saturnus. So much for Roman polytheism and the Roman deification of the emperor, which the author of *Sepher Yosippon* demystifies on two historical levels by a tongue-in-cheek use of Rome's own classical traditions and satirically claims a Semitic origin for the ancient Roman state.

When the author reaches the reign of Tiberius he finds his way well lit by Josephus and Pseudo Hegesippus. We begin with the scandals that afflict the chaste wife Paulina, a devotee of Isis, seduced by one of the Roman athletes who bribes a priest of Anubis to convince the Roman matron that the god wishes to conjoin with her. She informs her husband, and he and all her neighbors bless her over this divine choice. The athlete, disguised as the god, enthuses her for the whole night. On the morrow she returns home to another round of blessings. Later he, somewhat arrogantly, approaches her at home and asks for a rematch, this time without divine disguise. Shocked and insulted, she complains to her husband at the violation of her chastity, and the husband in turn appeals to the emperor, who punishes the priests with death and destruction of the temple, but punishes the horny jock merely with banishment. *Sic semper Italia!* "There were many scandals such as this in the days of Tiberius," Josephus concludes. Pseudo-Hegesippus, in turn, takes up Josephus's hint at Mary's conjoining with God and cites the appropriate Gospel praises of Mary: "Blessed art thou among all women." This intertext helps to Christianize Josephus's story. In his expanded rewriting of his source the author of *Sepher Yosippon* sharpens his wit by making the athlete a chariot driver—they were the superstars of Byzantine sports—and emphasizes the verses from Luke 1, 28, and 42 that Pseudo-Hegesippus had alluded to in his rewriting of Josephus' version of Paulina's Affair. His intertext thus serves the purpose of parodying Pseudo Hegesippus and restoring Josephus's story to a Jewish discourse. The author further expands the story with his acerbic quill that reflects his delight in the comedic style he found scattered throughout the biblical text, in particular the sardonic wit of the Book of Judges. No Hebrew reader would miss his allusions to the Immaculate Conception and the virgin birth.

Several other instances in *Sepher Yosippon* allude to Jesus, although even more obliquely. Recently I examined his rewriting of the attempted suicide of Herod as a mock *aqedah*.[22] I shall have more to say about *Sepher Yosippon* and the *aqedah* tradition in a moment. In this scene the author has Herod attempt to kill himself with a *ma'akheleth*. Indeed, this special term for a ritual knife appears three times in his story and, in addition, appears with another liturgical term, albeit also in a secular vein—he uses *letaher* (Levitical term for "purify") as a verb to peel the apple with the *ma'akheleth*. The author's use of such ritual terms recalls the *aqedah,* where the word *ma'akheleth* first appears (Gen. 22), as well as the Levite's ritual butchering of his *pilegesh* at the end of the Book of Judges. But here, in a clearly secular scene, the anointed king Herod, *eo ipso* a messiah, attempts suicide just as another "king of the Jews"—Jesus—also considered a messiah, committed suicide. The traditional Jewish reading of the Gospels does not invoke any justification for Jesus' or his apostles' argument that he had to fulfill the prophecies of the messiah's death in order to be resurrected.

In another reference to the *aqedah* that the author found in his source, he uses the opportunity to respond to the Christian appropriation of the *aqedah.* In a response to Pseudo Hegesippus' Christianization of Elazar ben Anani's final speech at Metzadah, the author of *Sepher Yosippon* cleanses the text of his source's theology and anti-Jewish venom and restores the biblical theme, but with his own twist. Pseudo-Hegesippus creates a speech for Eleazer extolling a neo-Platonic vision that immortality in death is preferable to slavery. In a clear allusion to Jesus he inserts: "But did not thus father Abraham instruct you, who taught through his one son, [that] his [fate] was not to be death but immortality, if he was sacrificed for his religion."[23] The beginning of the Latin text of this speech recalls The First Epistle of Peter (2:9) in the New Testament. The author of *Sepher Yosippon* reverts in his version to the original source of Peter's epistle and restores the language of Exodus (19:6). Then he recasts the Abraham reference thus: "Understand what your father Abraham did, who took his only son to offer him up to God and did not think in his heart that he would kill him, rather he thought and knew that he would keep him alive."[24] So, while Pseudo-Hegesippus slipped in his allusion to the immortality of Jesus, the author of *Sepher Yosippon* of necessity broke the chain of logic in the list of Christianized examples that the Latin text brought: Abraham and his son, Josiah and Pharaoh Necho, Abel and Cain, and rejects having Isaac killed.[25] Thus the author of *Sepher Yosippon* cleansed his Christianized source, returning the speech to the Jewish belief in Abraham's trust in God for his son's survival.

The question is, where did this idea of altering his source originate? Was it another instance of the author's creative imagination, of which there are numerous examples in *Sepher Yosippon*? Or perhaps did it stem from his wide reading in Hebrew and Latin sources that proliferated in the highly developed intellectual climate of southern Italy? We may suggest a candidate for such a source which, in turn, would widen the intellectual range of our anonymous author and shed some light as well on a unique midrash from southern Italy known to modern scholars for over a century and a half but only recently becoming the subject of scholarly research.

It is not necessary here to rehearse the well-known Christian reading of the *aqedah* as a prefiguration of the crucifixion of Jesus already adumbrated in Hebrews 11:17-19. Rather, I shall look at a Byzantine Jewish response to this tradition, so strongly entrenched in the church and its broader ecclesia. Recent studies of the *midrash aggadat bereshit* (easily accessible in the mid-nineteenth-century edition of Adolph Jellinek, *Beth Hamidrash* IV) date this interesting collection of sermons to late ninth- or tenth-century Byzantine south Italy.[26]

Midrash is too difficult and complex a discipline and methodology to rehearse here; however, the uniqueness of midrash *aggadat bereshit* necessitates a brief journey into its homiletics which reflects in sufficient examples the response of this creative south Italian *darshan* to the vicissitudes of Byzantine imperial oppression and ecclesiastical propaganda.[27] We should recall with respect to the Orthodox Church in Byzantium that it was the official Department of Religion and hence had to follow the dictates of the Imperator et Pontifex Maximus who was *eo ipso* the head of the church or rather superior to the bishops and their heads the patriarchs.[28] If the proposed dating of *aggadat bereshit* is accurate, then it likely falls within the generation of the persecution and forced baptisms of Basil the Macedonian, which the church rejected.[29] An early pericope in the midrash may well refer to this persecution.

> This is what Scripture says: I say, "Keep the king's command and because of God's oath do not be terrified" (Eccles. 8:2-3). The Holy Spirit said to Israel: I make you swear that if a kingdom makes decrees over you, you shall not rebel against it in respect of anything that it decrees over you; but if it decrees over you to abolish the Torah, the commandments or Sabbath, do not obey them. This is what is written: I say, "Keep the king's command"—in respect of anything that it (the kingdom) needs. But because of the oath of God do not be terrified; go from his presence . . .—as did Hananiah, Mishael and Azariah when Nebukhadnezar erected the statue.[30]

It is true that this admonition follows two rabbinic principles—*dina demalkhuta dina*—regarding obeying the government in power—and *yehareg ve'al ya`avor*—regarding the specifics of the rabbinic principle concerning martyrdom in the face of forced conversion. Even so, given the dating of this midrash, the admonition of the statement is quite strong in the general context of the author's arguments in support of circumcision.[31]

An important text in the Orthodox-Jewish debate is Psalm 110:1, one of the many verses argued by the church to buttress its Jesus theology: "The Lord says to my lord, 'Sit at my right hand.'" *Aggadat bereshit* begins its polemical response with the verse from Daniel 3:25:

> And the wicked Babylonians say that he has a son, as is stated: "And the fourth has the appearance of a son of gods." The Holy One said: Wicked ones! As if it were written: " the appearance of a son of God" (sing.)! If it

> were written thus, then you would have had an excuse to say so. But this is not written, rather: "the appearance of the son of gods (plur.)—those are the angels, who are called sons of gods. Apart from that, if it were not said about them, the one who said the thing was he not one of yours? Nebukhadnezar, was he not one of yours? He was a Babylonian!" When he was punished, did he not say the truth? Thus it is stated: "Nebukhadnezar said, Blessed be the God of Shadrach, Meshach, and Abednego" (Dan. 3:28). He did not say, god forbid: "who has sent his son," but: "who has sent his angel" (Dan. 3:28). Therefore: "'pi-shnaim' shall be cut off and perish."[32]

Teugels duly emphasizes the uniqueness of this text with no known parallels in the midrashic (primarily *tanhuma*) tradition that the author relied on. This point was already noted by Leopold Zunz in the nineteenth-century who emphasized that this pericope was an open polemic against Christian theology.[33] The *darshan* systematically applies Psalms 110:1 to Abraham, thus countering the orthodox claim that it refers to Jesus. With regard to Daniel 3:25, which the church applied to Jesus as well, the author gives his literal reading of the text, which is quite different from the theological reading of the church. Compare, for example, the Septuagint version with the English:

> 3:92 ἰδοὺ ἐγὼ ὁρῶ ἄνδρας τέσσαρας λελυμένους περιπατοῦντας ἐν τῷ πυρί καὶ φθορὰ οὐδεμία ἐγενήθη ἐν αὐτοῖς καὶ ἡ ὅρασις τοῦ τετάρτου ὁμοίωμα ἀγγέλου θεοῦ

> GrDn 3:92 He answered, "Look, I see four men loose, walking in the midst of the fire, and they are unharmed; and the aspect of the fourth is like a son of god!"

> Other versions, however, have quite specifically υιώ θεόυ [i.e., "son of god"] instead of the more literal midrashic reading of the Septuagint αγγέλου θέου [angel (or messenger) of god]. The Aramaic of Daniel 3:25 clearly reads: *veraivai di reviaya damai levar elohin* [i.e., son of gods].[34] Clearly then the Greek and Hebrew texts as well as their respective commentaries set up an irresolvable impasse that precluded dialogue between Byzantine Christians and Jews. Is it any wonder then that the Jews were at a disadvantage when the official position was based on a variant text that provided a defective translation in their eyes? Theology may be argued, proof texts may be challenged, but a translated word is as methodologically invalid as recourse to a miracle, and rabbinic Judaism did not accept miracles as proof for an argument.[35]

Chapter 31 of *aggadat bereshit* rehearses the *aqedah*, the binding of Isaac recounted in Genesis 22, which the church had applied to Jesus in its theology of prefiguration. The midrash confronts the Christian prefiguration of the *aqedah* directly and has God say:

> "Nor did it enter my mind" (Jer. 19:5)—that Abraham would slaughter his son even though I commanded him from my mouth and said to him "[Please] take your son . . . (Gen 22: 2)!" [Kakh na ... *ag. br.* 31]—yet it never entered my mind that he would slaughter him. Therefore: "I will not violate my covenant" (Psalm 89:35).[36]

This text thus becomes a key polemical response to the Orthodox tradition of prefiguration and was likely known directly or otherwise by the contemporary author of *Sepher Yosippon*. This text too appears to be a unique Byzantine Jewish response to the Christian argument. Indeed, as noted, recent scholarship claims that most of this midrash is an anti-Orthodox polemic.[37] The author of this passage was surely aware of the corresponding passage in *Midrash Tanhuma* (*Behukotai* 7 [p. 203a]) in his listing of Abraham, Yiphtah (Jephthah), and Mesha, king of Moab, the latter two of which the author of *Sepher Yosippon* ignores in his speech, since it is not in his source. *Midrash Tanhuma* is usually dated to the late eighth or ninth century, that is, a possibly somewhat earlier contemporary to *aggadat bereshit*, although the chronology of these later midrashim has yet to be fixed by scholars.[38] Recall again *Sepher Yosippon*'s response to Pseudo-Hegesippus: "Understand what your father Abraham did, who took his only son to offer him up to God and did not think in his heart that he would kill him, rather he thought and knew that he would live."

The *darshan* ends his sermon on the *aqedah* with another anti-Christian polemic:

> "When he came to slaughter him, the Holy One immediately felt compassion and cried: 'Do not lay your hand on the boy'" (Gen. 22:12). R. Abin said in the name of R. Hilkia: "Foolish is the heart of liars who say that the Holy One has a son. Now concerning the son of Abraham: when he saw that he came to slaughter him, he could not see him in pain, but immediately cried: 'Do not lay your hand on the boy.' Had He had a son, would He have abandoned him, and would He not have overturned the world and turned it into chaos? Therefore Solomon says: 'There is one and there is no second, he does not have a son or brother'" (Eccles. 4:8). "And because of this love for Israel, he calls them 'his sons,' as is stated: 'Israel is my firstborn son'" (Ex. 4:22).[39]

Aggadat bereshit ends with a chapter emphasizing messianic themes and martyrdom, the latter using Psalm 44:23, Job 13:15, and Psalm 116:13, among others. The *darshan*'s last anti-Christian statement that may allude to Jesus is the following:[40]

> "Isaac called Esau [euphemism for Christians] his firstborn, and I call Jacob 'my firstborn son'" (Exod. 4:22). "The primogeniture of Isaac was cancelled, and that of Jacob was established. Isaac loved Esau, as it is stated: 'Isaac loved Esau'" (Gen. 25:28); "but I love Jacob. The love of Isaac was cancelled and the love of Jacob was established. How much have the Nations of the World

> labored to put hatred between him and me? But they cannot abolish it, as is stated: 'Many waters cannot quench love'" (Song 8:7). "These are the nations, who are likened to waters, as is stated . . ." (Isa. 17:12). "And not only this, but how many [peoples] have killed Israelites, to make them leave the Holy One. But the community of Israel says to them: 'I cannot renounce him, as is stated: "My inmost being yearned for him"'" (Song 5:4). "My soul failed me when he spoke" (Song 5:6.). "Since he spoke at Sinai, my soul listened, and see, my heart is sick for him, as is stated: 'For I am sick with love'" (Song 2:5).

The above comments point out the methodology of the Jewish midrashic response to the Christian midrashic (later theological) reading of the biblical verses already initiated by Jewish authors in the New Testament. The standard Jewish response was to translate the texts literally from the Hebrew if the Greek translation did not fit their counterargument and to buttress the argument with a bevy of ancillary verses. This method gave to the Jews in their constant interface with Byzantine preachers and lay people the requisite verses to counter the barrage of Christian theological interpretations meant to convince them that the Old Testament, now superseded politically by the New Testament, prophesied about Jesus in so many of its verses.

Aggadat bereshit is only one of the many midrashim (in the broadest sense including apocalypses, chronicles, legal treatises, histories, etc.)[41] ascribed to a Byzantine provenance by modern scholars. Available since Jellinek's edition of the mid-nineteenth century, it has not yet been exploited by Jewish historians, let alone known to Byzantinists. A systematic study of these neglected gems is a desideratum, both the printed editions and the many manuscripts and fragments now being identified by scholars. One question for historians that is particularly germane to our survey is: to what Orthodox polemic is the author of the midrash replying and from what sources is he drawing his response? A contemporary one or the rich tradition of Christian invective against Judaism or the extensive campaign of the Orthodox Church to convert Jews by honey rather than by force as was the policy of the state during the Middle Byzantine period from Justinian's successors through Heraklios (seventh century) to Romanos Lekapenos (tenth century)?[42]

The better understanding of the discourse of these Byzantine polemics offered by Zylbersztein's analysis may allow future researchers to date the responses of these Hebrew midrashim or at least to contextualize them within the ongoing challenges that each religious culture posed to the other. A case in point is the polemic of Nestor the Priest. The modern editors show it to be based on the *Qissat Mujadalat al-Usquf*, an anonymous Judeo-Arabic polemic against Christianity (indeed the earliest Jewish anti-Christian text extant) written perhaps in Egypt or at least in an east Mediterranean milieu and undatable (editor suggests a plausible date around the middle of the ninth century).[43] The Hebrew Polemic of Nestor the Priest is a reworked and expanded version based on the Arabic and is first mentioned by Jacob ben Reuben in his anti-Christian polemic *Milhamot Ha-Shem* (*The Wars of the Lord*, dated 1170 and written in northern Spain or Provence). The editors suggest that the translation was produced earlier in Andalusian Spain; however, a Hebrew version might well have been done or the Arabic text even known in southern Italy or Sicily. In any case, at some point the text moved eastward to a Greek-speaking milieu, where numerous Greek glosses were added.[44] It is evident from the two manuscripts with Greek glosses (dated 1578 and 1493, the latter copied in Canea, Crete) that they were based on independent texts of unknown date. Hence the text of Nestor's polemic is not necessarily germane to this paper but definitely does belong to the latter stages of the Byzantine Romaniot experience.[45]

History is interdisciplinary in its methodology and must exploit all the specialized ancillary disciplines that contribute new knowledge and new techniques of evaluation to comprehend the periods and the trends whose stories it is creating. The recent development of Byzantine studies and its subdiscipline of Byzantine Jews, among other specialized fields, have broadened our understanding of this major third culture of the medieval period and have pointed out the extent to which Constantinople and Baghdad were the twin foci of the period rather than Rome, London, or Paris as promoted by the weltanschauung of nineteenth-century historiography. As the twelfth-century Benjamin of Tudela noted in amazement, "there is none like it [Constantinople] in the world except Baghdad, the great city of Islam." So, too, a broader knowledge of the discussions about Jesus in the major cultures of the medieval period, both scholarly and polemical, will enlighten the modern dialogues that were so obfuscated by past political and theological controversies before these were superseded by the rediscovery of the apocalyptic literature, the Jewish background of the New Testament, the Dead Sea Scrolls, and a touch of tolerance.

In the eleventh century a number of hack interpreters interpolated a series of tales and expansions into the terse and beautifully crafted tenth-century *Sepher Yosippon*. Like other pieces of Hebrew prose, *Sepher Yosippon* was treated as a midrash, that is, an "open text," to be continuously expanded at the whim of the copyist;[46] incidentally, the book suffered from that designation and is dismissed in recent times by numerous Talmudists, literary scholars, and historians as a children's book, as evidenced in the vocalized edition that recently appeared in Jerusalem.[47] Fortunately for us, this expanding *Sepher Yosippon* corpus from the eleventh century on contains a very early Greek version of Pseudo-Kallisthenes's fourth-century novel about Alexander the Great, a hitherto unknown Byzantine chronicle, and a description—perhaps eye witness—of the crowning of a tenth-century Saxon emperor, among other miscellany. But where the wags found an opening, there they included various tales and traditions about Jesus, some based on *Toldoth Yeshu* traditions, others elaborating on hints in the Talmud, and some perhaps drawn from Christian apocrypha and polemics. More apropos to my discussion in this paper, these interpolations do not belong to

Byzantine tradition until the longer version of *Sepher Yosippon* was compiled by the young Balkan scholar Yehudah ibn Moskoni in the mid-fourteenth century. Following its publication by Ibn Yahya in the sixteenth century, this compilation became the most popular version, serving as the model for the many later editions in Hebrew, Yiddish, and other modern translations.

Thus there came to be two traditions of Jewish responses to Christianity during the later Middle Ages (post-twelfth century). The one was *Sepher Yosippon* in its various versions throughout Christian and Muslim lands. The second was, primarily in Western Christendom, detailed scholarly polemics against Christian interpretations of biblical verses, most deriving from earlier midrashic tradition, such as the *yelamdenu* and *tanhuma* texts, that had characterized Palestinian and Byzantine midrashim. Later in the thirteenth century, Western Christian attacks on the Talmud would generate a different apologetic response. Recall that in the sixth century, Justinian had interdicted the oral tradition—which he called *deuterosis*. The Latin Catholic church began to carry out its anti-Talmudic campaign only in the thirteenth century through the new Office of the Inquisition established by Pope Gregory IX in the 1230s, just a few years prior to the trial and burning of the Talmud in Paris. One should note that the Justinian Code was already reintroduced and taught in western Europe by the twelfth century.[48] To date, I have not seen any reference to Justinian's Novella 146 in modern discussions of the inquisitional trial of the Talmud in Paris.[49]

Let us turn now to the second text that I mentioned at the beginning of my paper. We have already discussed *Sepher Yosippon* in its tenth- and eleventh-century incarnations. The second literary text is the *Scroll of Ahima'az ben Paltiel*, known as *Megillat Ahima'az*, written in the mid-eleventh century in Capua by a clever poet in the makama style (rhymed prose) as a history of his ancestors in Byzantine Oria.[50] This hilltop city, located midway between Tarentum and Bari, was the hub of a liturgical revolution through its excellence in *piyyut* compositions that only within the last generation has been shown to be at the base of the Ashkenazi synagogue tradition of *piyyutim*.[51] Ahima'az had wit and style and used these rhetorical tools in his response to ninth-century Byzantine aggression against the Jews of southern Italy. Let me note in passing that modern scholarship has numerous studies on the Scroll of Ahima'az despite its having been "lost" for over eight centuries and only fortuitously discovered in the late nineteenth century, about the same time as the "lost" Hebrew Chronicles of the Crusades. Regrettably, practically none of the scholars of these two sets of texts has put them in the context of *Sepher Yosippon*: Ahima'az for the historical consciousness of tenth- to eleventh-century Italy, and *Sepher Yosippon* for its influence on the Hebrew Chronicles of the Crusades, in particular *Sepher Yosippon*'s adumbration of *kiddush hashem*.[52]

The Scroll of Ahima'az preserves faithfully the culture and superstitions of ninth-to tenth-century Jews and Christians in southern Italy and is so delightful and valuable a read that it deserves a modern English version—perhaps blank verse would suffice. Let me choose a few examples of the author's response to Byzantine Christians.

The sixth-century emperor Justinian was a builder par excellence. His contemporary historian Procopius dedicated one of his many books to his constructions: churches and fortresses in particular, the former still represented by Hagia Sophia in Istanbul and the foundations of the recently discovered Ta Nea Church in Jerusalem. It was about the former that Justinian quipped: "Solomon, I have outdone you!" To which Ahima'az replied in his recapitulation of the disputation between Rav Shephatiah and Basileus Basil: *vesha'alu mibinyan beit hab'hirah umibinyan hatumah asher Sophia keruah b'ey zeh armon nikhnas yoter mammon*[53] ("Scriptures show that David and Solomon expended more funds than you"). Basil admits defeat, and invites Shephatiah, who exorcises and captures the devil in his daughter (based on a Talmudic tale, but Basil did not have a daughter), and the king revokes his decree of forced baptism of the Jews in Italy as he had promised Shephatiah.[54] It is a matter of interest and somewhat perplexing that Byzantine Jewish commentaries on the Bible do not, so far as scholarship has discovered, comment on Ezekiel's detailed description of the temple in chapters 40-48.[55] Any discussion of this lacuna will have to focus on Byzantine pride in its great churches. Ahima'az, we should note, was no longer subject to Byzantine control in eleventh-century Capua.

Ahima'az's ridicule of an arrogant Byzantine official, his delight in the magical way that Rav Shephatiah overcame his astronomic miscalculation that otherwise would have necessitated his conversion, his use of Talmudic stories to return good for the evils exacted in Byzantium, and his messianic colophon are informative but not particularly germane to a paper on Jesus. His *golem* (perhaps here understood as a zombie) story in which the corpse of a young man was resurrected by the insertion in his arm of a parchment with the Ineffable Name of the Lord that resulted in his dissolution into dust upon its removal is more than just a hint at the *Toldoth Yeshu* tale of Jesus acquiring the correct pronunciation of the Ineffable Name to practice his magical tricks. Jews were careful not to blaspheme the holy family openly, at least in circumstances where a sensitive Christian environment was quick to avenge any perceived, let alone actual, insult. Already in the fifth century Jews had ceased to burn Haman in effigy on a cross during Purim, while Christians until recent times continued to stone Jewish houses on Easter.[56] It was not until the twelfth century before Karaite authors in Byzantium would answer Byzantine Christian taunts with their own.[57]

And whatever his exact date, whether twelfth or fifteenth century, Meyuhas ben Eliahu in his biblical commentary responded directly to the Byzantine and general Christian interpretation of Genesis 49:10: *lo yasur shevet miyehudah . . . ad yavo shiloh* ("the scepter shall not depart from Judah . . . until Shilo comes [again?]"). Christians still interpret s*hiloh* to be a prophecy for Jesus as evidenced in the many churches that bear the name Shiloh. Meyuhas, however, identifies *shilo* as Shlomo (King Solomon) by an apt manipulation of the atbash (A=T B=Sh) substitution code which of course is found elsewhere in the Tanakh.[58]

The tenth and part of the eleventh centuries in Byzantium were perhaps the high point of medieval Jewish self-pride and confidence. True, there was a brief persecution of the Jews under Romanos Lekapenos, but as a counterbalance there was the strong voice of Hasdai ibn Shaprut in the Umayyad Caliphate in Spain, who sent a veiled warning to Constantinople about the persecution of the Jews and the continued presence of the still powerful Khazar Kaganate, where many Byzantine Jewish scholars took refuge, albeit now in its eleventh hour with the about to be Christianized Rus lurking over their shoulder.[59] And the powerful Fatimid Caliphate with its recent acquisition of Jerusalem meant that, except for occasional Byzantine pressures and developing Italian competition, the Mediterranean was still united by the Radhaniyyah, those long-distance merchants and diplomats who would soon be superseded by the Italian city-states. It was a sunlit period for the Jews, so much so that in the early 960s a letter from the Rhineland of Ashkenaz reached Jerusalem asking whether the messiah had come. "No need to answer regarding coming of the Messiah," was the reply. "Nor," the respondent added, "do we refrain from praying on the Mount of Olives on every holiday."[60]

Finally, in this "messianic" context, there is need to mention an extant chronology of rulers representing the four kingdoms in the messianic vision of Daniel that ends with the fourth year of the reign of the Emperor Nikephoros Phokas (963-969), nearly contemporary to the aforementioned correspondence with Jerusalem.[61] Nikephoros was a successful general who defeated the Abbasids and retook Crete and part of Syria, thus initiating what modern scholars call the Byzantine Crusades.[62] The author of this text was well researched in extant chronicles and familiar with imperial politics and gossip; he evidences no hostility toward these "kings of Rome" nor does he reference anything Jewish. This Byzantine reconquest initiated an era that encouraged Jewish migration into the recently reconquered Anatolian peninsula, followed by a new period of peace and prosperity for Byzantine Jews lasting until the end of the empire in the mid-fifteenth century (save for a brief spate of persecution in the rump state of Nicaea during the fragmentation of the empire by the Fourth Crusaders in the early thirteenth century).[63] Religious animosity increased in inverse proportion to the new imperial protection of its Jewish minorities.[64] Notwithstanding the final gasps of overt Byzantine persecution, *Sepher Yosippon* is emblematic of this shift in the Jewish global position and represents a new stage in the emergence of a proud national heritage that would buoy up Jews for the next millennium until the resurrection of a Jewish state in a final defiance of the Christian Roman legal and theological opposition to the settlement of Jews in Jerusalem.[65]

Those ancient oppositions and controversies are still manifest in our own times, albeit masked in the expanding dialogues (however creative and illuminating and occasionally healing) over Jesus carried out in many forums and unknowingly obfuscated in the contemporary ideological languages of politics and history. If Jesus were indeed "king of the Jews," as the Romans charged him in his execution, who then are his legitimate heirs to Jerusalem, Judea, and Israel, the land promised to his ancestors by the God of Abraham, Isaac, and Jacob and recognized by the apostles of Jesus and even Allah and Muhammad in the Qur'an (see Surahs 5:21 and 17:104)? The Jewish scholars of Byzantine southern Italy in the tenth to eleventh centuries have left us a resounding answer to the challenges posed by their successor religious cultures.[66]

Discussion Questions

1. What verses were central to the Byzantine Orthodox polemic against Judaism?
2. How did historical events affect the argument between the two religions?
3. What is the range of texts and the methodology involved in midrash?

Notes

1. See Steven Bowman, "The Contribution of Asher Raphael Moissis," *Studies in Bibliography and Booklore* 12 (1979): 25-27. My paraphrase is from the opening essay in his *Helleno-Ioudaikai Meletai* (Athens, 1958), 7, where he plays on the words "the Greeks . . . 'collect' . . . while the Jews 'pay.'" Moissis was a lawyer and an intellectual who probed the history of the Jews in Greece in a number of seminal essays during the middle third of the twentieth century.
2. Texts in Amnon Lindner, ed., *The Jews in Roman Imperial Legislation* (Detroit: Wayne State University Press and Israel Academy of Sciences 1987); see Steven Bowman, "Jews in Byzantium" in *The Cambridge History of Judaism*, vol. 4 of *The Late Roman-Rabbinic Period* (Cambridge, 2006), 1035-52 and bibliography. The 1930s classic of James Parkes, *The Conflict of the Church and the Synagogue* (London: Soncino Press, 1934) is still worth reading for its usefulness and influence on successive scholarship. A recent informative read is Martin Goodman, *Rome and Jerusalem: The Clash of Ancient Civilizations* (London: Allen Lane, 2007).
3. For a more critical view, see Günter Stemberger, *Jews and Christians in the Holy Land. Palestine in the Fourth Century* (Edinburgh: T&T Clark, 2000), and the more recent argument of Moshe Gil, *And the Roman Was Then in the Land* (Tel Aviv: Hakibbutz Hameuhad, 2008) (in Hebrew) for the survival of a majority Jewish population in Palestine through the end of the first millennium, when it was destroyed or dispersed by the Crusaders.
4. Samuel Krauss, *The Jewish-Christian Controversy from the Earliest Times to 1789,* ed. William Horbury (Tübingen: J.C.B. Mohr/Paul Siebeck, 1996).
5. Roly Zylbersztein, "Byzantine Views on the Jews: Studies in Polemical Discourses in the Byzantine Empire from the Beginning of the Seventh Century through the Eleventh Century" (PhD diss., Hebrew University of Jerusalem, 2007). For the last stage of Byzantine history see Steven Bowman, "Two Late Byzantine Dialogues with the Jews," *The Greek Orthodox Theological Review* 25, no. 1 (1980): 83-93.
6. Even though the restrictions on dhimmis (Christians and Jews) are easily traceable to the restrictions on Jews encoded by Theodosius's and Justinian's legal experts. In any case, numerous Christians and Jews were accepting Islam.

7. See Yaron Dan, "On the Jewish-Christian Controversy of the Fifth Century—A Jewish Response to the Council of Chalcedon," *Zion* 45 (1980): 154-57, xiv (Eng. summary) and Steven Bowman, "Survey of Recent Scholarship in Hebrew on Byzantine Subjects (1970-1984)," *Byzantine Studies* 13 (1986), 43. Among the burgeoning bibliography on Judas, see Marvin Meyer, *Judas: The Definitive Collection of Gospels and Legends about the Infamous Apostle of Jesus* (New York: HarperCollins, 2007).
8. Lena Einhorn, *The Jesus Mystery. Astonishing Clues to the True Identities of Jesus and Paul* (Guilford, CT: The Lyons Press, 2007).
9. Even though its first historical citation appears in the letters of Agobard and his student Emilo in their early ninth-century Carolingian condemnations. For texts, see Samuel Krauss, *Das Leben Jesu nach jüdischen Quellen* (Berlin: S. Calvary, 1902).
10. See Ya'akov Deutsch, "'Toldoth Yeshu' in the Eyes of Christians" (Phd diss., Hebrew University of Jerusalem, 1997).
11. See Cesare Colafemmina, "Hebrew Inscriptions of the Early Medieval Period in Southern Italy" in *The Jews of Italy. Memory and Identity*, ed. Bernand D. Cooperman and Barbara Gavin (Bethesda: University Press of Maryland, 2000).
12. David Flusser, *The Josippon* (*Josephus Gorionides*), rev. ed. (Jerusalem: The Bialik Institute, 1981). I do not want to discuss here the scholarly edition of *The Arabic Josippon* by Shulamit Sela, 2 vols. (Jerusalem: Ben Zvi Institute, 2009) and her critique of Flusser's edition.
13. He signs his autograph as Judah known as Leon son of Moses known as Moskoni, i.e., Moskoni is the secular designation of his father's name and not a family name as in modern scholarship.
14. Reprinted in 1964. *Toldoth milhemet hayehudim im haromaim*, published by Masada Press established by Yosef Brenner in 1906, who coined the phrase '*aharonim al hahomah*' (perhaps an adaptation of the French tradition of "mounting the barricades"?). See citation in Hannan Hever, *Paytanim vebiryonim* (Poets and Zealots. The Rise of Political Hebrew Poetry in Eretz-Israel) (Jerusalem: Bialik Institute, 1994), 171.
15. See Steven Bowman, "Josephus in Byzantium," in *Josephus, Judaism and Christianity*, ed. Louis Feldman and Gohei Hata (Detroit: Wayne State University Press, 1987), 362-85 with further bibliographical references.
16. See discussion and bibliography in Louis Feldman, *Josephus: A Supplementary Bibliography* (New York: Garland, 1986). Also see the many comments by Feldman in Feldman and Hata, *Josephus, Judaism, and Christianity* and Feldman and Hata, *Josephus, the Bible and History* (Detroit : Wayne State University Press, 1989).
17. Now in the modern edition of Vincente Ussani, ed., *Hegesippi qui dicitur historiae libri V* (Vienna: Hölder-Pichler-Tempsky, 1932).
18. Hegesippus was a second-century Christian historian to whom medievals erroneously ascribed this text.
19. Albert A. Bell, "Josephus and Pseudo-Hegesippus," in Feldman and Hata, *Josephus, Judaism, and Christianity*, 343-61. This is a more accessible summary of Bell's detailed analysis in his 1977 University of North Carolina PhD dissertation "An Historiographical Analysis of *De Excidio Hierosolymitano*."
20. Steven Bowman, "Dates in Sefer Yosippon" in *Pursuing the Text: Studies in Honor of BenZion Wacholder on the Occasion of his Seventieth Birthday*, ed. John C. Reeves & John Kampen (Sheffield: Sheffield Academic Press, 1994), 349-59. The *minor* here no doubt is Pseudo-Hegesippus while the *maior* is the Latin Josephus.

21. I emphasize the word "history" here since the author, as Flusser has demonstrated, reintroduced Josephus's model of sober history writing to subsequent generations of Jewish scholars.
22. Steven Bowman, "Aqedah and Mashiah in Sepher Yosippon," *European Journal of Jewish Studies* 2 (2008): 21-43.
23. Adapted from the online translation of Ps. Hegesippus, translated from the Latin into English, 2005, by Dr. Wade Blocker, available on the web at Roger Pearse, ed., Early Church Fathers—Additional Texts, http://www.ccel.org/ccel/pearse/morefathers/files/.
24. Flusser, *The Josippon*, vol. 1, 424, ll. 19-20.
25. My thanks to Yael Feldman for her insights on the implications of this shift. Here we might note in passing that *Bereshith Rabbah* does have Isaac die only to be resurrected, surely under the influence of fourth-century Christian preachers in Palestine where this option is listed among numerous others by the Jewish editor of that midrash. See S. Giora Shoham, *Valhalla, Calvary & Auschwitz* (Cincinnati: BCAP, 1995), s.v. "Isaac."
26. Studies by Lieve M. Teugels, *Aggadat Bereshit* (Leiden: Brill, 2001) and Ezra Kahalani, "Aggadat Bereshit. Introduction, Proposal for a Critical Edition and Discussion of its Content and Structure" (PhD diss., Hebrew University of Jerusalem, 2003), who summarize older literature that comments on the plethora of Greek and Latin lexeis in the text. However, many of these lexeis are available in early Palestinian rabbinic literature and hence are not useful for dating purposes, although they may well signify provenance. It is well known that there was a direct link from Byzantine Palestine of the classical midrashic period to Byzantine southern Italy of the later midrashic period and continuous contact between these two areas during the ninth to eleventh centuries. The text, it should be noted, does not necessarily represent orally delivered sermons.
27. For the latter polemics see Zylbersztein, "Byzantine Views on the Jews." A considerable number of learned Jewish communities with halakhists, *darshanim*, and *payyetanim* flourished in Apulia from the ninth to eleventh centuries. The *locus classicus* for this center was the obscure medieval laudatory statement "From Bari shall go forth Torah and the word of God from Otranto," only fully revealed through the modern discovery of the Scroll of Ahima'az. The imperial law codes are available in Amnon Lindner, ed. and trans., *The Jews in Roman Imperial Legislation* (Detroit: Wayne State University Press, 1987).
28. Earlier scholars have debated this reality within the framework of "Caesaropapism," a decidedly western misinterpretation of an oriental phenomenon. King David is a better model for the Byzantine tradition. See J. B. Bury, *A History f the Later Roman Empire* (Chicago: Aries Publishers, 1974), 49-50, although he ignores the biblical precedent.
29. See Joshua Starr, *The Jews in the Byzantine Empire, 641-1204* (Athens: Verlag der "Byzantinisch-Neugriechischen Jahrbücher", 1939) for sources; note that the eleventh-century *Scroll of Ahima'az* still castigates that emperor for his persecution.
30. Lieve M. Teugels, *Aggadat Bereshit* (Leiden: Brill, 2001), 22. See I Maccabees, preserved in the Orthodox Bible, for the persecution of Antiochus IV. Maccabees was a central text in the Byzantine Church and a Hebrew translation of I Maccabees was made in southern Italy in the late ninth century. The sentiment is drawn from early rabbinic texts, e.g., *Shir hashirim rabbah*. The call to *kiddush hashem* (albeit not by

this name) appears in the Byzantine Jewish tradition of southern Italy in the ninth to eleventh centuries. See also Teugels, *Aggadat Bereshit*, 29 C.

31. See chapters 16 and 17 in Teugels, *Aggadat Bereshit.*
32. Translation from Teugels, *Aggadat Bereshit*, 85-86. Babylonian is one of author's euphemisms for Byzantines. *Pi-shnaim* is the darshan's play on Zechariah 13:8 where he cites R. Berakhiah: The Holy One said, "The mouth (*peh*) that says they are two (*shnaim*) shall be cut off and perish." The standard English versions use the singular, as do some of the Greek versions. Psalm 110 was a key text in Byzantine polemics, in many of which the "Jew" accuses his interlocutor of blasphemy for claiming that God had a son. See Zylbersztein, "Byzantine Views on the Jews," 68-71.
33. *Hadrashoht batorah*, 394 n. 39 as noted by Ezra Kahalani, "Aggadat Bereshit. Introduction, Proposal for a Critical Edition and Discussion of its Content and Structure" (PhD diss., Hebrew University of Jerusalem, 2003). Kahalani stresses that about 50% of the text consists of mainly independent creations of the author who was an exegetical teacher rather than just an anthologizer.
34. To any *darshan* the phrase "son of gods" might well resonate with *bene haelohim* (Genesis 6) who were understood to be angels if not just *nephilim*. One Byzantine Jewish commentator, Meyuhas ben Eliahu, parsed *bene elohim* as *bene yavan*, i.e., Greeks. See *Bereshit Rabbah* (Warsaw, 1867), *Parashat* 26:8.
35. This is part of the polemical argument of Nestor the Priest in the outdated version of J. D. Eisenstein, *Ozar Wikuchim* (New York, 1928), 310-15. See the critique of Eisenstein's texts in the scholarly edition of Daniel J. Lasker and Sarah Stroumsa, *The Polemic of Nestor the Priest* (Jerusalem: Ben-Zvi Institute, 1996), 1:95. Vol. 2 presents the Judeo-Arabic and Hebrew versions of the texts and introductions.
36. Translation slightly adapted from Teugels, *Aggadat Bereshit*, 98. Kahalani's own assessment in his introduction is: "the author of AB is a preacher possessed of literary and homiletical creativity" who redesigns homilies created from earlier sources.
37. The south Italian milieu reflects the local Islamic challenge to Byzantine sovereignty and an awakened Jewish self-confidence. In general, Jewish responses were more aggressive until the thirteenth century.
38. See Moshe David Herr, "Tanhuma" in *Encyclopedia Judaica* 15, cols 794-96. The textual tradition of Tanhuma is still not fixed. See Mauro Perani and Günter Stemberger, "A New Early Tanhuma Manuscript from the Italian Genizah: The Fragments of Ravenna and their Textual Tradition," *Materia Giudaica* 10 (2005): 241-66. The Italian Genizah consists of Hebrew fragments recycled by Renaissance bookbinders now being recovered by Mauro Perani.
39. After Teugels, *Aggadat Bereshit*, 100. The anti-Christian material is omitted from the Warsaw edition of 1876. Solomon Buber, editor of the 1876 edition, adds specifically anti-Christian readings from the Bodleian Ms. Opp. Add.8vo.35 (better known as Ms. Oxford 2340). The translation is from Teugels, 100 n. 395: R. Abin said in the name of R. Hilkia: There are those among the Nations of the World [here a euphemism for the Byzantines] who say that the Holy One had a son. And what about the son of Abraham? When he came to the hour of the Akedah, he cried out and said: "Do not lay your hand on the boy" (Gen. 22:12). And if he had a son, would he have left him to his murderer on his cross, and would he not have overturned the world because of him? And concerning him, Solomon says: "here is one and there is no second, he does not have a son" (Eccles. 4:8). And you do not find for The Holy One [a son] but Israel, as is stated: "Israel is my firstborn son" (Exod. 4:22), and it is stated:

"Let my son go that he may worship me" (Exod. 4:23), and it is stated: "You are the children of the Lord your God" (Deut. 14:1).

40. Teugels, *Aggadat Bereshit*, 248.
41. See Steven Bowman, "Sefer Yosippon: History and Midrash," in *The Midrashic Imagination: Jewish Exegesis, Thought, and History*, ed. Michael Fishbane (Albany: State University of New York Press, 1993), 280-94.
42. Ahima'az does describe the tactics of the Emperor Basil in his attempt to convert his ancestor Shephatiah of Oria: first the carrot, then the bribe, and lastly the stick. Byzantine merchants and clergy usually preceded the army into new territories.
43. Daniel J. Lasker and Sarah Stroumsa, *The Polemic of Nestor the Priest*, vol. 2, 15 (English version), 9 (Hebrew version). The dating of *aggadat bereshit* may necessitate a revision of this claim, although it is a collection of sermons rather than a sustained polemical treatise.
44. Lasker and Stroumsa, *The Polemic of Nestor the Priest*. The editors record another scholar's opinion that the Greek dialect may be from Crete (p. 32 note 91). This seems logical since one text was copied in Crete.
45. For another late polemic see Bowman, *Jews in Byzantium*, document 111 and notes there.
46. See the comments of Shulamit Sela, introduction to *The Arabic Josippon*, vol. 1 (Jerusalem: The Ben Zvi Institute, 2009).
47. The efforts of David Flusser to produce and publicize the Hebrew Yosippon have been useful; however, most of his essays are still in Hebrew. The folklorist at Tel Aviv University, Eli Yassif, has explored numerous facets of medieval Hebrew literature and has integrated the Yosippon into his overall analysis of the material. See his *The Hebrew Folktale: History, Genre, Meaning*, trans. Jacqueline S. Teitelbaum (Bloomington: Indiana University Press, 1999).
48. See Charles M. Radding and Antonio Ciarelli, *The "Corpus iuris civilis" in the Middle Ages: Manuscripts and Transmission from the Sixth Century to the Juristic Revival* (Leiden: Brill, 2007) and review by Wolfgang P. Mueller in *Speculum* 83 (2008): 1026-27.
49. See texts collected and translated by Solomon Grayzel, *The Church and the Jews in the XIIIth Century*, vol. 1, rev. ed. (New York: Hermon Press, 1966); vol. 2, ed. Kenneth R. Stow (Detroit: Wayne State UP, 1989).
50. Edited and annotated by Benjamin Klar, *Megillat Ahimaaz. The Chronicle of Ahimaaz, with a collection of poems from Byzantine Southern Italy and additions* (Jerusalem, 1974). A rough translation into English was provided by M. Salzman, *The Chronicle of Ahimaaz* (New York, 1924); English selections in Joshua Starr, *The Jews in the Byzantine Empire 641-1204* (Athens, 1939).
51. Through the efforts of Yona David, Ezra Fleischer, and other scholars. See in general Cecil Roth, ed., *The World History of the Jewish People*, vol. 9 of *The Dark Ages* (New Brunswick: Rutgers University Press, 1966) and Bowman, "A Survey of Recent Scholarship in Hebrew," 62-65.
52. See Yael Feldman, "'The Final Battle' or 'A Burnt Offering'?: Lamdan's Masada Revisited," *AJS Perspectives* (Spring 2009): 30-32. That entire issue is devoted to "Martyrdom through the Ages." A discussion of the Byzantine milieu is in Shmuel Shepkaru, *Jewish Martyrs in the Pagan and Christian Worlds* (Cambridge University Press, 2006). See also Isaiah M. Gafni and Aviezer Ravitzky, eds., *Sanctity of Life and Martyrdom. Studies in Memory of Amir Yekutiel* (Jerusalem: Zalman Shazar Cen-

ter for Jewish History, 1992) (in Hebrew). There was an enormous outpouring of scholarship on the theme in Israel during the mid-1990s, particularly in The Historical Society of Israel Quarterly *Zion*. For further bibliography, see Steven Bowman, "Twelfth-Century Jewish Responses to Crusade and Jihad," in *Crusaders, Condottieri, and Cannon. Medieval Warfare in Societies Around the Mediterranean*, ed. Donald J. Kagay and L. J. Andrew Villalon (Leiden: Brill, 2003), 417-38.

53. "They queried in which—the Chosen House or the Impure Building called Sophia—was invested more money."
54. The story is well rehearsed by Yehudah ibn Shmuel, *Midrashe Geulah,* 2nd ed. (Tel Aviv: Bialik Institute, 1968), 239, in the course of his extended historical commentary on the tenth-century apocalypse *Hazzon Daniel,* which summarizes Byzantine political treatment of Jews during the iconoclastic and posticonoclastic periods. For additional bibliography, see Steven Bowman, "A Review of Recent Articles in Hebrew on Byzantine Scholarship," 54-57 for details of Reuben Bonfil's critical study "'The Vision of Daniel' as a Historical and Literary Document," *Zion* 44 (1979): 111-47 (in Hebrew; Eng. summary xv-xvi).
55. Gershon Brin, "Outline of The Newly Published Byzantine Biblical Exegesis," *Shai le-Sara Japhet. Studies in the Bible, its Exegesis and its Language*, ed. Moshe Bar-Asher et al. (Jerusalem: The Bialik Institute, 2007), 157-71 (Hebrew section) and Richard C. Steiner, "The Byzantine Biblical Commentaries from the Genizah: Rabbanite and Karaite" in the same volume (Eng. section), 243-62, esp. 261. The relevant sources are edited and translated by Nicholas de Lange, *Greek Jewish Texts from the Cairo Genizah* (Tübingen: Mohr/Siebeck, 1996).There were relevant midrashim however, e.g., "The Throne and Hippodrome of King Solomon."
56. *Cecil Roth*, "The *Eastertide* Stoning of the Jews and its Liturgical Echoes," *Jewish Quarterly Review* 35, no. 4 (1945): 361-70.
57. Zvi Ankori, "Peraqim be-mishnato ha-meshihit shel Yehudah Hadassi ha-Qara'i le-qevi'at ha-nusah shel 'nifla'ot ha-mashiah' be-'Eshkol ha-Kofer," *Tarbiz* 30 (1961): 186-208. Byzantine *paytanim* were more aggressive in their responses to Christian attacks. See Leon J. Weinberger, *Jewish Hymnography. A Literary History* (London: The Littman Library of Jewish Civilization, 1998), chaps. 4-5 and his earlier editions of Byzantine *piyyutim.*
58. For codes, see Michael Fishbane, *Biblical Interpretation in Ancient Israel* (Oxford, 1985); for Meyuhas, see Joshua Starr, *Jews in the Byzantine Empire 641-1204* (Athens, 1939) and the alternative date offered by Israel Ta Shma, *Studies in Medieval Rabbinic Literature*, vol. 3 of *Italy & Byzantium* (Jerusalem: The Bialik Institute, 2005) (in Hebrew). See A.W. Greenup and C.H. Titterton, eds., *The Commentary of Rabbi Meyuhas B. Elijah on the Pentateuch. Genesis* (London, 1909). Rabbi Dr. Michael Katz of Yeshiva University has published the latter books of Meyuhas's commentary on the Torah.
59. Jacob Mann, *Texts and Studies in Jewish Literature*, vol. 1 (1931; repr. New York: Ktav, 1972), 10-14; Norman Golb and Omeljan Pritsak, eds. and trans., *Kazarian Hebrew Documents of the Tenth Century* (Ithaca, NY: Cornell University Press, 1982).
60. A. Z. Aecoly, ed., *Jewish Messianic Movements* (Jerusalem: The Bialik Institute, 1956), 1:133-34. My comments here supersede those in "Aqedah and Mashiah in Sepher Yosippon."
61. Text edited by Ad. Neubauer, *Medieval Jewish Chronicles and Chronological Notes*, vol. 1, 2nd ed. (Oxford, 1887; Jerusalem, 1967), 185-86; commentary in Stephen Gero,

"Byzantine Imperial Prosopography in a Medieval Hebrew Text. Language of Work," *Byzantion* 47 (1977): 157-62.

62. See Zvi Ankori, *Karaites in Byzantium* (Jerusalem: The Weizmann Science Press of Israel, 1959), ch. 3. For a detailed treatment of Nikephoros' campaigns, see G. Schlumberger, *Un empereur byzantiin au dixième siècle* (Paris, 1890).
63. See Ankori, *Karaites in Byzantium,* chapter 3 and following note for the thirteenth-century persecution.
64. See Steven Bowman, *The Jews of Byzantium, 1204-1453* (1985; repr. New York: Bloch Publishing, 2000), 28-30.
65. See Steven Bowman, "'Yosippon and Jewish Nationalism," *Proceedings of the American Academy for Jewish Research*, vol. 61 (1995), 23-51.
66. See for the Palaeologan period, Steven Bowman, "Hebrew as a Second Language in Byzantium" in *Acts XVIIIth International Congress of Byzantine Studies (Moscow 1991)* (Shepherdstown, WV: Byzantine Studies Press, 1996), 84-92.

A Meditation on Possible Images of Jewish Jesus in the Pre-Modern Period

Norman Simms

> Look and behold, O Lord, what we are doing to sanctify Thy Great Name, in order not to exchange You for a crucified scion who was despised, abominated, and held in contempt in his own generation, a bastard son conceived by a menstruating and wanton mother.
>
> —R. Yom Tov Lipman Heller, Mainz, 27 May 1096[1]

Conceptions of Jesus exist in rabbinical legal discourses, polemics, and commentaries of the Middle Ages. They come in the course of discussion among rabbis who experienced or were speaking in the name of those who had experienced various persecutions in the times of the early church. They are imagined in times of stress and confusion when formal trials against the Talmud and other sacred writings necessitated the formalization of defensive arguments against the charges made that, on the one hand, the rabbinical texts slandered the person and family of Jesus and the primitive Christian community, and on the other, that Talmudic stories really confirmed the truth of the New Testament and the ecclesiastical interpretation of the Old Testament. These conceptions and illustrations of Jesus, more negative than positive, exist from time to time as well in *responsa* literature and other documents in which European Jews had to confront the reality of an overwhelming hegemonic Christian world, a world of formal church iconography and liturgy that spilled out of cathedrals and monasteries on to the streets and into the marketplaces, a world of popular and local cults, rituals, and shrines at almost every turn and in every nook and cranny of the landscape through which Jewish men, women, and children walked. Even when not overtly hostile to Jews and Judaism, these Christian depictions of the Savior at various times in his life—from miraculous birth through childhood and maturity and on through his death on the cross and resurrection—signaled an opposition to all that made Jewish life meaningful and spiritual.

Unlike today, when a post-Reformation Christianity exists in an increasingly secularizing if not already post-Christian Europe, the notion of Jesus and his family as Jews, of his earliest disciples and supporters as children of Israel, and of his main lessons and teaching exempla as derived from or at least analogous to rabbinical teachings—all those Christian icons would be viewed negatively as triumphalist, replacement imagining, where at best Jews could be tolerated only as living proofs of a connection between the old Israel and the God of the old dispensation and the purified new Israel and the Christ in a Trinity of the new revelation and order. But attitudes in the fourteenth and fifteenth century were quite different on both sides of the divide between Christians and Jews. Nevertheless, this little meditation will examine something other than the fear, rage, and resentment medieval Jews would surely have felt in England and other Western lands of Christendom when they looked within, thought about, or wrote about the central character in that other religion. Instead it is (even more speculatively) about a few texts which seem, on the face of it, and within long critical tradition, at the very heart of Christian piety—sometimes texts that, precisely because they do not express official clerical views and merely seek to entertain, articulate the unquestioned and pure essence of common beliefs.

Thus, the images of Jesus to be dealt with here have no explicit or even implicit polemical function. They do not even focus on the standard icons of piety and affirmation of belonging to the body of the church and the state. Rather, they take those images for granted and then, for reasons I shall elucidate, make them appear in ways which would seem otherwise impossible to conceive without some lens of anguished Jewish experience or prior Jewish mentality of grief and loneliness. They are images distorted on the surface by the masks of the narrators or fictional characters who are made to speak or enact them in circumstances that mark these personae as limited in their understanding, comical in their failure to engage properly with the noble and faithful figures around them, and satirical in their voicing of condemned and sinful heresies. Beyond these superficialities to put the audience and the censorious officials of governance and rectitude behind them, however, there is another dimension of Jewish shaping at work in such imaginings of Jesus as abused and injured infant, as decomposing and stinking corpse, and as untrustworthy pretender at miracle working and moral comforting. None of this can proved for certain.[2] There are no documents to call on. There are no confirming examples outside the texts themselves. All here works by indirection, implication, and effect.

Of course, were we living in a strictly rational and well-principled world,[3] there is no way that Jesus should or could have appeared in rabbinical writings of the medieval period in Europe—other than as either an oblique character in polemics meant to prepare the Jewish community for confrontations in the great Talmudic debates in France and Iberia or as a bizarre, ludicrous and threatening figure in more secular or entertainment literature. The truth is, as I discovered over three decades when I was writing about Geoffrey Chaucer and the *Gawain*-Poet, both of whom may have had Jewish backgrounds a generation or two before their time, and who at times in their literary texts directly confronted the issue of their relationship to the God of the Gentiles: there were themes and images developed in Jewish tradition to deal with the dominant and pervasive presence of Christian narratives and iconography.

Indeed, despite our modern liberal misgivings, we do find a limited range of specific references in the rabbinical writings—*piyyutim*, martyrological narratives, and exegetical discussions—to the Christian worship of Christ in such repulsive terms as "the crucified bastard son," "the dead one," "the green slime" and "the putrid corpse,"[4] or sometimes the "bastard son of the bleeding one."[5] A church, to such pained and angry people, was "a tomb for their idol" or "an edifice of idolatry,"[6] and baptismal water was "their evil water," but above all it was the crucifix that was "the abomination,"[7] "the image of jealousy," or even just *semel ha-qin'ah*, "the filth"[8] that they cried out in disgust and hatred.[9] Such startlingly grotesque language indicates that the whole myth of the dying and resurrecting savior was, to Jewish thought and taste, often more than a theological absurdity—it was a horrible, ghoulish threat to their very being.

However, theological rejections aside, along with polemical scorn, it would have been well-nigh impossible for Jewish communities to have lived in close proximity, no matter how tinged with threats and dangers, without being influenced in other ways. For just as Christian myth and Roman Catholic cult permeated the majority group's European culture for nearly fifteen hundred years, infusing virtually every facet of cultural, social, public, and domestic and intimate life—to the point where it was inconceivable to think or feel outside of such influence, let alone articulate other thoughts and feelings—there is little chance that Jews, at least beyond their self-conscious statements of belief and practice—could have escaped this phenomenon altogether.

For the most part, until the formation of locked ghettos and pales of settlement, Jews were not hermetically sealed from Christian society. In many ways—thanks to commercial dealings and political negotiations, along with shared aesthetic and cultural tastes—Jews interacted with their *goyish* neighbors. When possible (and sometimes when clearly not possible), Jewish men and women tried to dress like their neighbors, to play and engage socially with these others, sometimes to the point of sexual alliances and marriage if not concubinage, to imitate their architecture and furniture, and to worship in similar styles and with analogous gestures, music, and intentions. Insofar as the figure of Jesus, as well as his mother, disciples, saintly followers, and priestly imitators, permeated all these facets of European life, the iconography of Christ seeped into the Jewish unconsciousness—and was sometimes partly recognized and welcomed, albeit with occasional cautionary words and signs.

But while the image that most springs to mind in our modern minds is that of Jesus the adult, Jesus the crucified Savior on the cross—not least because of the great Renaissance and Baroque paintings that fill our museums and imaginations—we also can remind ourselves of the other common image, that of baby Jesus in his mother's arms. Of course, these were anything but rare pictures for the medieval imagination, and therefore likely to be well-known by Jews who could see them everywhere, carved into buildings, embroidered into tapestries, painted on frescoes, and described in the words of priests and friars haranguing the blinded men and women of the old dispensation to convert or else—or else suffer in the bottommost pit of unending perdition, be forced into humiliating exile, or be killed on the spot. Hence, for a Jew, it would be hard, if not impossible, to see in these images love, mercy, and forgiveness, let alone justice and salvation. They are frightening and grotesque pictures of a world gone mad, a world in which biblical cautionary prophecies are distorted into threats of punishment and descriptions of imminent danger. We hardly have any record of how real Jews reacted. We do have fantasy accounts of what Christians assumed were Jewish responses: desecrations of the Host, ceremonials of child murder in imitation of the original crucifixion, and other supposed celebrations of Jewish perfidy and malevolence. Occasionally we read a passing mention of a member of the Jewish community who could not control himself and threw mud at an ecclesiastical procession or sullied the icon or banner being paraded through the streets. Such an event would be a disaster for the Jews in that town, as punishment would be swift and collective. Rabbinical authorities would themselves be nearly at their wits' end to control young hotheads from letting loose in such a way. But aside from such small-scale, individual acts of symbolic rebellion, there are no historical cases where Jews collectively and conspiratorially performed any of these iconoclastic and blasphemous acts.[10]

None, that is, except in literary form, and even then usually in oblique and coded manners. It may be that during the anti-Jewish riots in northern France and the Rhineland during the first and second Crusades there were communities who responded with *Kiddush ha-Shem* in the way some of the rabbinical chroniclers and martyrlogical hymn writers describe, that is, with attempts by fathers and mothers to sacrifice their own children rather than seem them forcibly converted and taken away to be brought up as Christians, deeds performed not only in defiance of the crusaders' zeal and the local mob's judeophobia, but actions appropriating the images of Christ's willing death on the cross and of the healing power of the sacramental blood.[11]

The usual assumption of religious historians is that they are dealing with intelligent, sophisticated, and educated people, when, in fact, the great bulk of experience affirms that we usually have to deal with not very bright, crude, and uneducated people. Hence, the small elites for whom literature was written and performed took a special delight in knowing that they could understand what most of their contemporaries could not.

For those small Jewish audiences, secretly hidden among a large Christian society where their rabbinical knowledge and ways of thinking and feeling were not easily recognized and would be very dangerous if exposed, there was a peculiar piquancy in finding means to express their darkest inner feelings and communicate secrets between themselves. Moreover, the very circumstances of their isolation, state of anxiety, and sense of superiority meant that they did more than understand the world and the knowledge carried down by tradition differently; it meant they also knew aspects of the world that the others could not know or understand and therefore their traditions could navigate through the ocean of what was generally known, codified into institutions, and internalized as common sense with a very different mentality and technology of knowledge. At the same time, we have to remember that medieval Jews often lived amidst and did business with not only the elites—that is, princes, priests, professional lawyers, physicians, and rich burghers—but also to a greater extent the uneducated laborers in the towns and serfs in the villages. How ignorant is ignorant? In 1848 in a *Report on Wales*, a school inspector recalls how he went to a rural school close to a town of about five thousand:

> I then called up a larger class, most of whom had recently come to the school. Three girls repeatedly declared they had never heard of Christ, and two that they had never heard of God. Two out of six thought Christ was on earth now, three knew nothing about the crucifixion . . . their minds were perfect blanks.[12]

This is precisely the kind of ignorance that the church began to address at the Second Lateran Council at the end of the twelfth century, prompting calls for parish priests to be literate and ordinary lay folk to be instructed in the basics of the faith. The educational imperative stands behind the directives to create the great Corpus Christi plays as a way of reaching a population beyond the grasp of formal education. These ecclesiasts also called on artists to decorate churches, especially stained glass windows, with a visual correlative of these elementary teachings. It was also this large cultural blank in popular knowledge which Chaucer mocks in *The Canterbury Tales,* where some of his pilgrims, such as the Miller, know only so much of Scripture as they have gleaned from the pageant plays performed in the streets of English towns.

We may say, then, that if ordinary Christians for the most part had almost no sophisticated knowledge of their own religion, Jews may not have had a better understanding—but they did have a different apprehension. And, because of the periodic persecutions and the waves of pressure to abandon their ancestral faith, rabbinical educators tried to ensure that their congregants were armed with responses to the forced sermons and the overwhelming saturation of

Christian conversionist iconography that were becoming common in the High Middle Ages.

But rather than examine these putative actions—to me, they seem more like fantasy and myth than actual occurrences, attempts after the fact to rationalize what actually happened—I want to turn to another set of Christian images that appear in crypto-Jewish writing of the fourteenth and fifteenth centuries. These are images of Jesus as a newborn baby, as an infant in the arms of his mother Mary, and as an innocent child among many who were massacred by Herod the Great on New Year's Day.

The three texts I will look at—some of which I have dealt with in the past extensively and will not try to reproduce the annotations adduced there but only a few new sources—are *Sir Gawain and the Knight of the Green Chapel* (which I take from the poem itself as the correct title), Chaucer's *Prioress's Tale* from *The Canterbury Tales*, and *The Second Shepherds' Play* in the Wakefield Cycle. None of these works are normally considered to be Jewish in any sense by literary and cultural historians, and I only contend that their "authors" (already a problematical term) may have been crypto-Jews or their mostly assimilated Christian children.

The Many Circumcisions of *Sir Gawain* of "Qa'milot" or Camelot

> ...the tendency of holy war is to turn inwards . . . the appeal [of] introspective violence appears to have had for lay men and women . . . the failure of the church leaders to control public emotion.[13]

In a book I wrote about the Middle English alliterative poem known usually as *Sir Gawain and the Green Knight*,[14] I argued that the protagonist in the Arthurian adventure, the nephew of the renowned King of Camelot, named Gawain or Wawain, represents from an obscured and distorted perspective the crypto-Jews who were still in England after their expulsion in the last decade of the previous century. Though Gawain's quest to save the honor of the court and the Knights of the Round Table is steeped in ancient mythologies and folklore, this adventure also has about it qualities that make sense only if seen as part of a Jewish midrashing of private history, the individual lives of the few men and women who remained after 1290. Like Chaucer himself,[15] these secret Jews—and their Judaism may have been more or less hidden from themselves—at the same time that they wished to be an assimilated, integrated component in the dominant, and indeed, the only society, which was Christian, feudal, and profoundly troubled by its own political and social ambiguities, they also felt themselves uncomfortable in its belief system, alienated from its ideals and values, and threatened by the ambiguities in the otherwise hegemonic state to which they belonged.

Though it does not loom over the alliterative poem in any explicit way, the figure of Jesus Christ is nevertheless present. The first long section of the Middle English alliterative romance is set during a twelve-day Christmas season and the next three sections of various lengths during the following year, with the high points in each part of the poem culminating on New Year's Day, the Feast of the Circumcision, which was also celebrated as the Feast of Fools, in commemoration of the Massacre of the Innocents. Rather than the adult Christ in his passion, crucifixion, and resurrection, this Christmas adventure has as its subtext the birth and *brit millah* of baby Jesus.

The quest Gawain undertakes on behalf of Arthur and the Knights of the Round Table to find the Knight of the Green Chapel on the next New Year's Day and receive in turn a beheading (as he had given this Green Man in Christmas mumming costume at Camelot) moves him from a recognizable, if pseudo-historical, landscape in southwestern England across the more fantastic dreamland of Celtic Wales and eventually into the bizarre and unexpected mirror world at his quest's end. Though he assumed he would meet the challenger at the Green Chapel, Gawain first confronts a refracted series of images in the Castle of Hautdesert, at once a double of Camelot itself and a strange shimmery apparition that rises up out of the mists on Christmas Eve to confront Arthur's favorite nephew. Each day begins here with an increasingly humiliating and soul-confusing temptation scene, when the host's wife, the illusive, elusive, and allusive Lady Bertilak, seeks to break his protective armor of virtue, *courtoisie,* and loyalty to Arthurian ideals, including his determination to perform the agreed-upon beheading game. Gawain seems to parry successfully the wife's advances but he succumbs when she offers him her green girdle, which will protect him from sudden bloody death provided he keeps the gift a secret. Because of its sexual associations—the girdle is at once an archaic apotropaic, as Gawain assumes, but also a signifier of female's sexuality and fertility and a surrogate of the foreskin removed in circumcision—the would-be virtuous knight fails to trust in his Christian faith, to uphold the laws of guest-honor by avoiding gratuitous hints of adultery with Bertilak's spouse, and to play by the rules of the subsidiary bargain undertaken with the host to exchange prizes won during the day.

The whole episode in the Castle of Hautdesert, moreover, provides a lens through which to see the nature of his original testing begun in Camelot since, though unexpected, it mirrors the beheading game played out at the Green Chapel on New Year's morning, and thus clarifies the real ordeal through which Gawain passes in order to rescue the honor—the "name," *ha-shem*—of Arthur and his fellows of the Round Table. At the testing ground, which is neither a chapel in the sense of a Christian place of worship nor green in any of the symbolic codes known to Gawain and the "Arthur books" referred to by the Lady in her probing of the young knight's essential identity, the beheading does not take place. This echoes the all-important Jewish account of the *Akeda*, the Binding of Isaac, in which the father's hand is stayed from slaying his son, a scriptural passage read out from the Torah on the Jewish New Year. Hence, in the alliterative poem there is a sudden opening up and illumination of the abyss between Gawain's nominal Christmas-Christian quest and his covert-Jewish confirmation, his combined *brit* and *bar mitzvah*. How so? Rather than an *imitatio christi*, this New Year's game reproduces and displaces the young knight's circumcision with a "nik on the nek" and three small drops of blood. The green girdle, worn under his armor and behind his shield—one side of which faces outward his pentangular virtues of courtly Christian honor and another side which faces inward an icon of the Virgin Mary and her five sorrows—becomes an outward sign. This occurs, not as the Knight of the Green Chapel tells Gawain of his success in the quest but, rather, as Gawain tells himself and then the court upon his return, "a badge of shame." The ambiguity may be seen as deeper still, for the green girdle is spoken of in a calque of the scriptural designation of circumcision as an *ot ha brit*, a sign of the covenant, or *brit milah*, the covenant of the word, an undertaking that is *qa-milot*, like the words spoken between God and Moses and then Moses and the children of Israel in receiving the Tablets of the Law (the *luchot ha-brit*), here rendered as the now redefined site of the Round Table, with some manipulation of sounds to match the articulation in French and Celtic, Camelot, *qa'milat* and Bertilak, *luach ha-brit*.

In this midrashic optic, Sir Gawain moves in and out of focus. The hero is a Jew, a Christian, then back and forth, and perhaps also, as so often in this poem, a combination of the two—as was Jesus, whose first shedding of blood marked him through circumcision as a Jew and then in the second, on the cross, as a Christian. Though the green girdle can emblemize Gawain's achievements on behalf of the Round Table knights back in Camelot and then be re-imagined into the sash of the Order of the Garter with its motto of "Honi soyt qui mal [y] pence" that has been editorially appended to the conclusion of the poem, for the hero himself the girdle is a "token of untrawth." This phrase may be glossed superficially as "a sign of his disloyalty," that is, his failure to live up to the pentangular virtues on the front of his shield—his slippage into lying to the host about his winnings in the exchange game, and hence his lack of loyalty to the rules of *courtoisie*, as well as his diminished faith in the way he accepts the lady's girdle to protect himself from what he should confront boldly as a Christian knight. It may also, we suggest, be understood in at least two other ways: first, as a reminder to himself that he has "lacked a little" in the quest and therefore must beware of overwhelming pride in his new-found celebrity at court, a noble acquisition of Christian humility still missing among the Round Table Knights; and second, an indication that, ironically, Gawain is a crypto-Jew, having been secretly circumcised into the old Law, and so, like Christ himself, whose *brit milah* is celebrated on New Year's Day (The Festival of Fools), he too has and will continue to suffer inwardly on behalf of the Arthurian court.

But in addition to the drops of blood exuded during the *brit milah* and the ribbons that flowed from his wounds into the chalice of eucharistic salvation, there was also the blood of his mother who, as a virgin, continued to menstruate during pregnancy, marking her vagina and uterus as sacred places. Hence, when Gawain arrives at the unexpected Castle of Hautdesert, that high and empty manifestation of confused identities, he confronts what seems like two separate women, Lady Bertilak, young and beautiful but childless and perhaps virginal in spite of her seductive gambits, which makes her, in a sense, the dark double of the ambiguously virtuous Gaynor or Gwenor (Guenevere) and an unnamed old hag, perhaps a version of Morgan La Fee, Arthur's incestuous sister, certainly a type of the female beyond menstruation and childbearing; that is, two figures at either extreme of the Blessed Virgin Mary. In another sense, these two women at Hautdesert stand to one another as *Ecclesia* and *Synagoga* in Christian iconography, females who were once twin sisters but whose theological history pulled them into opposing camps, *Lady Holy Church,* though born from the heart of Judaism, remaining youthful, insightful, and chaste, and *Old Dame Synagogue,* necessary for the conceptualization of the new religion, becoming haggard, blind, corrupt, and sterile.

Matching these ambivalent and mismatched icons at Bertilak's castle there are more deeply ambiguous and more occulted images at the Green Chapel. A feature of the natural landscape, from one perspective, the rocky declivity, that is, "nobot an olde cave," is also, from another point of view, an ancient tumulus, a place once sanctified by the old and worn-out religion, and yet also the devil's oratory, figuratively, the site of the Green Man's testing of Gawain. As the young knight Gawain draws close, his guide leaves him, and he dismounts to approach on foot, noting, as he peers down into the deep valley and the stone mound, that it is covered with rotting greenery, a stream divides around it, and there is a strange opening into the unknown darkness. On the one hand, this scene is reminiscent of the fairy mound in John Keats's "La Belle Dame Sans Merci," where the innocent knight is lured in and kept an indefinite period of time—locked in the wasteland of his own sterile desires. On the other hand, it is the forbidden location of female sexuality, rotten, deceptive, and dangerous. But just as the beheading game turns out to be a playful gambit under the control of the genial host in the mumming costume of a Green Man who demands in reality no more of the young man than he can give—as when God backed off from his dire words against Cain when the first murderer said "It is more than I can bare"—so too the secret opening into life and death in the female body proves illusive, elusive, and allusive: no more than the flesh and blood of nature, not easily gained or demonically attractive, and signifying the complexities of love, law, and faith that an honest man with a proper education can comprehend.

The Oral Fantasies of the *Prioress's Tale*

> We have heard it said about concentration camp life, that if the person of the age of 12 was with a mother or father or older brother or sister, he or she could remain the child that could in some way be cared for or protected. On the other hand, if she or

> he were left without a family member, the child became an adult overnight, having sole responsibility for his or her own survival.[16]

When literary historians wish to point to evidence of anti-Semitism, they zero in almost immediately on the tale told by the Prioress[17] because it seems so obviously to be based on the blood libel—Jews murder little Christian boys to obtain the blood they need to make matzoh for Passover and thus re-enact to their fiendish delight the crucifixion. These critics also make much of the Chaucerian nun's gleeful and vicious reiteration of a hymn to the Blessed Virgin Mary that drips with Jew hatred. In one very important sense, of course, these modern writers are correct: the fictional Prioress in *The Canterbury Tales* is a manifestation of medieval Judeophobia. However, in another sense—no less significant, I will argue, and have shown in my book *A New Midrashic Reading of Chaucer*—these modern critics are wrong insofar as there is no easy slide from what the Prioress says to what the author felt or intended, either as a *persona* for the author or as an historical person in his own right. For as soon as we examine the tale closely and compare it to the standard models of the genre of miracle-tales-against-the-Jews that Miri Ruben investigates in her book,[18] it becomes evident that Chaucer's version is extremely different in concept and execution. Such mythic paradigms as the blood libel and the ritual murder do not occur at all, and the focus shifts from a mythic event to a rather more shoddy affair, wherein the inhabitants of a Jewish street in an Asian city react to a young boy's singing of a hymn to the Virgin Mary as he passes through on his way to school. The Prioress, to be sure, slanders the Jewish killers for their collective guilt and historical propensity to hate Christians, instigated as they are by the devil himself, but behind all this Chaucer the poet purges the tale of its purported elements of anti-Christian ceremony and implication. At the same time, as both part of her fantasy displacement of the abuse on to the Jews and her attempt to garner spiritual kudos by her un-Christian rage against these monstrous people, the Prioress also identifies (by psychological over-determination) with the young martyr in her tale and envisions him and herself as the infant Jesus at his mother's breast.

For this reason, an even closer reading of the *Prologue to the Prioress's Tale* in association with this story, told supposedly to celebrate a miracle of the Blessed Virgin, reveals aspects of the female narrator's own anything but pious or saintly personality—her background history, her current circumstances, and her intentions in telling the miracle of the murdered boy to the other pilgrims en route to Canterbury—that provide explanations for her apparent vicious but highly personalized anti-Semitism and for her unconscious utilization of traditional doctrinal *topoi* to express painful and humiliating features of childhood abuse. It thus becomes clear that Geoffrey Chaucer, rather than himself being a hater of Jews, seeks, if not to exonerate them from all crimes they are accused of, whether the ancient charge of deicide itself or of ritual desecrations and murders in the present, then at least to provide extenuating circumstances, provocations, and mitigating conditions.

It is indeed the oral fixation in the Prioress's singing and especially in her personal asides to the other pilgrims that hint towards such abuse in her girlhood, an interference by some older male adult who forces her to perform an unbearable, incomprehensible act, something that she now reconstructs, first in palatable terms as the maternal nursing of mother Mary on the Christ child, and later, in more repulsive, rejected language as the foul deed upon the young chorister by the demonic Jews—

> For nought oonly thy laude precious
> Perfourmed is by men of dignitee,
> But by the mouth of children thy bountee
> Parfourmed is, for on the brest soukynge
> Sometyme shewen they thyn heriyinge. (*Prioress's Prologue*, 455-59)

The oblique, probably unconscious construction of her repressed memory continues a few dozen lines later:

> . . . I ne may the weighte nat susteene;
> But as a child of twelf month oold, or lesse,
> That kan unnethes any word expresse,
> Right so fare I . . . . (*PP*, 483-86)

Thus, in this unnamed Asian Muslim city, populated by both Christian and Jewish minorities, the fictional crime is committed in reaction to the child's obsessive, and probably tuneless, chanting of *Alma redemptoris*—a Latin hymn he memorizes but cannot construe out of Latin—

> Nought wiste he what this Latyn was to seye,
> For he so young and tender was of age.
> But on a day his felawe gan he preye
> T'expounden hym this song in his langage,
> Or telle hym why this song was in usage;
> This preyed he hym to construe and declare
> Ful often tyme upon his knows bare. (*Prioress's Tale*, 523-29)

The posture on his knees begging the older boy to let him into the mystery of the hymn may be construed along the lines of a double entendre of oral sexual abuse, perhaps, if Alain de Lille's *De planctu naturae* is correct, common in all-male church schools.

But perhaps most telling of all, the crime and its aftermath indicate the Prioress's obsession with orality and filth, and thus hint towards the redemption she seeks from her own sense of violation and helplessness as a child in the bloody retribution she calls down upon the Jews. For it is when the "litel child" sings "[t]wies a day" walking to and from school through the Jewish quarter a chant which the Jews abhor as "again [their] laws reverence," that they conspired the "homicide." One of their number undertakes the task, and then, having murdered the boy, they throw his body into "a privee place," down an "aleye" and into "a pit." This site is also called "a wardrobe . . . Where as thise Jewes purgen here entraille" (*PT*, 572-73). One need only recall Yeats's poem about the paradox—derived from Augustine—about the place of love (in a woman) being also the place of excrement to follow the unconscious but traditional logic of the *Prioress's Tale*.

After his bloodied corpse is thrown into the common privy, the child continues to sing his hymn, as though his spirit were transformed into the very words and melody of the song he could not understand in a rational sense. Even when the local Abbot and other priestly assistants bring his body to the church and lay him out on a bier for the entire congregation to adore, the singing persists. The Abbot requests in the name of the Holy Trinity that the boy explain why his voice continues after death.

> "My throte is kut unto my nekke boon,"
> Seyde this child, "and as by way of kynde
> I should have dyed, ye, longe tyme agon.
> But Jesu Crist, as ye in books fynde,
> Wil that his glorie laste and be in mynde,
> And for the worship of his Mooder deere
> Yet may I synge O Alma loude and cleere. (*PT*, 649-55)

After some further explanations, all told in a literary and theological language quite beyond the child's capacity, but clearly indicative of the Prioress's interjection of her own feelings into the miraculous corpse's words, he concludes by saying that the Blessed Virgin, once he had begun to sing, "leyde a greyn upon my tonge" (*PT*, 662). Once we are alerted to the kind of coded language the narrator uses to shape the story and the boy's miraculous singing, each detail begins to unburden itself of its ambiguous depths and psychological secrets. If we recall, for instance, that "neck" in Latin is *cervix,* then the transference of the description of the crime from the cut to the throat—and we have to recall, too, the climactic moment in *Sir Gawain and the Knight of the Green Chapel*, when the hero receives the "nik in the nek" from the Green Man—to the sexual violation of the young girl who would grow up to be the Prioress. The "greyn upon my tonge" has been taken by many critics to be the eucharistic wafer, or some mystical or mythical equivalent in the discourses of saints' legends concerned with liturgical magic. But if this "greyn" is, rather, a seed, a drop of semen, then the image of the unconsciously recalled abuse can be seen. In addition, again recalling the deeper significances of the alliterative Gawain poem, the "green" seed can also be taken as an allusion to the putrid matter of the failed resurrection—and hence to the persistent pain, humiliation, and rage in the memory of the child rape at the core of the narrator's character. The "anthem" of *Alma redemptoris* will only cease, the murdered boy's corpse claims only when "from my tonge of taken is the greyn"

(*PT*, 665). That action performed by the Abbot, the child gives up the "goost" and, amidst general tears and lamentation, the body is finally buried "in a tombe of marbul stones cleere" (*PT*, 681).

In this way, normal filler lines, such as "There may no tonge expresse in no science" (*PP*, 476), "til he koude by rote" (*PT*, 545) take on a new valency in support of this hint at oral rape of the female infant. As the fountain or source of sweetness, milk and mercy, Mary—at one with her breasts, her maternal embodiment of Christian love—suckles, not only her own child, Jesus, but all those other lost and hungry souls who seek consolation from the profound sorrows and discomfort they feel from their own infancy.

In Chaucer's poem, then, the Jews who conspire to murder the chorister, in a sense, recapitulate the physical act of oral rape on the (self-)infant(alized) Prioress, to be sure. But perhaps more painful in memory for the now grown woman is the fact that the person who should have most protected her was her mother. This ambiguity is indicated in the poem by the casual way in which the little boy's mother behaves when he fails to return home in the evening after school.

> This poure wydwe awaiteth al that nyght
> After hir litel child, but he cam noght;
> For which, as soone as it was dayes light,
> With face pale of drede, and bisy thought,
> She hath at scole and elleswhere hym sought. (*PT*, 586-90)

The whole night goes by without her making any effort to find her son. Certainly in the morning, she is said to be distraught and searches everywhere, before she finally enters the Jewish quarter. There she asks everyone she meets on the street "To telle hire if hir child wente ought forby" (*PT*, 602). It is not until much later, however, when other Christians pass through this Jewry and hear the song being sung by the corpse, that the body is discovered and, following that, the authorities, Christian and Islamic, are called for. On the one hand, it is interesting to note that neither the mother nor the other Christian folk from the start assume that the missing child must be a victim of foul play by the Jews, something that the Prioress would do because of her disposition to treat the children of Israel as creatures of the devil, and which, moreover, the genre of Mary miracle tales on the Continent would make evident throughout; so that Chaucer's version points towards a problematic relationship between the Prioress and her literary sources. On the other hand, her telling of the miracle tale and her reasons for telling the narrative seem be distorted by the peculiarities in her personality and by the uniqueness of her personal history. Then, following a day of despair and fruitless searching, divine grace intervenes to point the mother in the right direction:

> . . . but Jhesu of his grace
> Yaf in her thought inwith a lityel space

> That as in that place after her sone she cryde,
> Where he was casten in a pit bisyde. (*PT*, 603-06)

It would seem then that neither she nor anyone else heard the corpse singing in the Jewish quarter of the city until Jesus—not Mary, please note—put it into her mind. Given the logic of the genre of Marian miracle tales, the singing should be taken as divinely inspired, but the failure of the Mother of Mercy to be the active agent in this transformative event emerges as striking, as is the delayed sentimental concerns of the boy's own biological mother.

To confirm this breakdown in the Prioress's desire to sing her own song to entertain the Canterbury pilgrims and to display her piety and firm devotion to the Blessed Virgin, we need to go back to Chaucer's *General Prologue*, where the fictional character is introduced in a quite satiric vein. All her virtues form an unsteady amalgam—and a contradictory mishmash—of courtly and religious ideals. Much is made by Chaucer the Pilgrim, as critics have long noted, in her social pretentiousness and false sentimentality. Still, it is important to note how the details take on significance in the light of her subsequent *Prologue* and *Tale*. In them, the stress on matters concerning mouth and throat move inwards from external descriptions to emotional and psychological signs, from her singing through her nose and her meticulousness about dabbing away sauces from her lips to her manner of speaking French, not after the Continental way but "After the scole of Stratford atte Bowe" (*General Prologue*, 125).

Questions have often been raised concerning the appropriateness, under canon law, of her presence on the pilgrimage itself. Less has been indicated about her vocation as a nun. Why has she not adjusted to the rules of her order, in terms of obedience, poverty, and chastity? Her very name, the courtly commonplace "madame Eglentyne," is discordant with her religious calling. The wild rose, woodbine, has its place in erotic romances because of its clinging, embracing characteristics. But even the name hides in its syllables allusions to the *glans*, the *glent,* and the *tyne* of sexual congress: copulative organs, sweaty processes, and exhausting consequences.

If not a sincere spiritual calling, her profession in a convent belongs to motivations that must be either social and political (including financial, as when daughters were sent to avoid awkward or dangerous marital alliances) or personal (including an aversion to marriage or a desire for a quiet, contemplative, and learned life). Yet her own decision, distinct from those made for her by her family, would entail inner needs to avoid courtly rituals, marriage, and even private intimacies. Her own *Prologue*, furthermore, suggests that she has been sent to a religious house to get away from embarrassing memories—not just the unconscious and untenable anxieties and rage discussed above: domestic problems of a dysfunctional family, in which she is scapegoated or, as it is now put in more clinical terms, elected as the surrogate sufferer. She would herself, we may also venture to guess, have preferred to be out of such a household where she was abused and where, it seems, her mother either denied the interference or was collusive in its performance. Eglentyne's attitudes towards sexuality and towards spirituality are thus fraught with almost unmanageable contradictory emotions—and given a chance, as here on the pilgrimage, when she can display herself as "al . . . conscience and tender herte" (*GP*, 150), she reveals what her whole life has been constructed to conceal. Her obsessive wish to be suckled at the breast of the Virgin is at one with her self-image as Jesus suffering at the hands of the Jews. Only in this way she can she find some temporary relief from her inner demons.

Masked Judaism on the Moors in the *Second Shepherds' Play*

> Such a severe critique should not remain unanswered, because it is by the confrontation of sometimes irreconcilable points of view that our perception of past events makes progress.[19]

There is no question among literary historians that the Jewish characters presented on the stage of medieval towns and cities were usually caricatures and typologies; nor do these critics deny that some playwrights, such as the so-called Wakefield Master developed social and comic routines based on the way in which ordinary English men and women suffering from natural (such as famines and plagues) and political or economic disasters could be compared to and then identified with Jews who lived before the coming of Christ—that is, to the already caricatured types seen in the New Testament and the ideologically driven interpretations of the Hebrew Bible (tendentiously called an "Old Testament"). Indeed, the satiric motif in these medieval spectacles was developed so far as to suggest that contemporary England seemed to be like a world in which the Savior had not yet appeared. These homiletic, comic, and satiric elements could be carried into the plays depicting the incarnate life of Jesus as well, although in such popular plays something more than allegorical devices was involved. We need to see what this "more" consists in before it is possible to deal with the occluded and probably misperceived presence of the "Jewish Jesus" in these plays.

To begin with, there would be a separation between those Old Testament stage-Jews who were in the process of becoming Christian because of their favorable attitude towards Jesus and those other Jews who, imagined as obstinate, perfidious, and blind, by refusing to recognize the messianic signs in Jesus' words and deeds, were already perceived to be embodiments of the anti-Jewish figures in medieval iconography and folklore. But beyond this, one finds not only an ambiguity and sometimes even a neutrality about Jews and Judaism, insofar as these manifestations mark the matrix in which the scheme of salvation was historically worked out, but also a questioning of the negative stereotypes.[20] Sometimes for the sake of dramatic tension, tied to a theological point, the stereotypes were reversed, as when Satan and his henchmen attempt to thwart the plot of the crucifixion once they realize that the consequence will be their own undoing. In such plays, too, the figure of Christ, still living within a Jewish community and operating according to the Mosaic law, nevertheless displays hesitation at fulfilling his prophetic destiny on the cross and has anxious doubts about his disciples' inability to comprehend the mysteries he attempts to disclose to them.

Like this ambiguously conceived Jesus, other stage-Jews seen in the mystery plays may nevertheless be enacted in ways other than the negative stereotypes and devilish farcical scenarios. This is not only because there are "good" Jews who will in time "become" Christians, either through the perfection of their figural roles or by their participation in the transformative events of Jesus' life as a messianic preacher, but also because they represent on the public stage attitudes and mentalities which match the moral and spiritual ambiguities and anxieties of an English society in transition. Those Israelites who are then seen to be acting out their traditional roles as accusers and deniers receive positive responses from the audience since they make salvation possible and are, at worst, the inadvertent agents of divine justice and mercy; while at best, their Jewishness is perceived as a necessary component of the Christian story. And yet, my argument adds another component to the story, namely, that for some members of the Christian community—whether as playwrights, actors, or simply as audience—the hesitations and worries belong to their own private histories as the children or grandchildren of forced or voluntary converts from Judaism. Leo Strauss remarks in this regard that while "it was sufficient in the Christian countries for a Jew to convert to Christianity and then . . . cease to be a Jew. . . . Yet it was not quite easy even then."[21]

Continuing awareness by a few secret and confused Jews—full of self-doubts and anxiety, to be sure—of their ancestral Jewish identity in England has more than emotional or sentimental (or even somatic)[22] causation. There is also an intellectual aspect. Ways of reading and interpreting texts, as well as esoteric knowledge in family traditions, including what would seem to the Christian outsider as peculiar interests, were also involved in the preservation of Jewishness in England during those centuries where Jews and Judaism were not allowed a legal status. If we recall, as we must, that prior to the expulsions at the end of the thirteenth century, England had been not only a participating part of the northern French Jewish cultural zone but also an intellectual center in itself well-known for philological studies, which included the verbal manipulations that are associated with Jewish mysticism, or Kabbalah,[23] including the writings of R. Elhanan b. Yaqar, author of a mystical commentary on the key kabbalistic text *Sefer Yetsira*,[24] and a mystical circle, the *Hug ha-Keruv ha-Meyuhad*, in London,[25] then we should not be surprised if this knowledge did not totally disappear in the subsequent centuries, kept alive, if not actively and accurately by rabbinical scholars, then at least subversively in fragments of memory, distorted through slowly shifting attitudes and feelings about the Holy Scriptures. Specific content—the morals and spiritual themes of medieval Judaism—might be dissipated much faster than habits of mind, eye, and hand, as it were: ways of reading, analyzing, and applying these rabbinic modes of interpretation. These intellectual methods and practices divorced from the content and values could be taken as tolerable within Christianity, so that they would at worst be seen as peculiarities—eccentricities and exotic novelties—and at best as insights into the text, useful preaching *exempla*, and dramatic expositions of essential truths. By reading texts closely and carefully, dividing passages up on the basis of sound and syllable combinations, and integrating kabbalistic, folkloric, and legendary characters and events, the Jewish reader, or rather Judaizing Christian—lay or clerical—could put new focus on the meaning of the Scriptures or their application to daily life. Yet, as with the more affective side of this fuzzy Jewishness, the intellectual elements would always be suspicious both to the more conventionally minded old Christians and to the thinker or writer himself. Self-doubt and uncomfortableness are the hallmarks of the persons we are concerned with, and it is both of these qualities that seem to appear in the plays.

The example we shall examine here is that of Mak the Sheepstealer in the Wakefield *Second Shepherds' Play*.[26] Like the other characters in this fifteenth-century Yorkshire Nativity Play, Mak and his wife are Jewish men and women living on the eve of the incarnation, still suffering under the old dispensation, and longing for the coming of a Savior. Mak, however, is at once an outsider to the local community, distrusted, suspected of thievery and other crimes, and yet also familiar and tolerated, and perhaps even liked by the other shepherds Coll, Gyb, and young Daw. He is spoken of in terms that associate him anachronistically with the devil, and is therefore assigned in the play—but only indirectly and implicitly by the shepherds—a conventionally theological role as forerunner of Christ's spiritual and moral enemies in the medieval church. He represents particularly those who Judaize in their legalisms and need for "signs." He also personifies those false shepherds, the dishonest clergy, who steal from their congregations, both the "goods" of the parish and the trustworthiness of the Eucharist through their confused recital and performance of the Mass, their garbled teachings in sermons, and their uncharitable example to the flock. At the same time, those anachronisms that constitute his depiction on the pageant of the cycle drama seem to signal his role as one of the foolish folk who most require the coming of the Word into the world as a flesh and blood Lamb.

Perhaps further, more than anyone else in the mystery play, Mak prefigures Christ himself, who comes into the world like a thief in the night. After all, following the hint of his wife Gyll (= Guile), it is Mak who inscribes the space of the little day star and sacred meal which will be the ritual road to salvation. In playing so many complementary and contradictory roles, however, Mak does more than manifest and confirm Christian typological history. He also, albeit inadvertently, enacts "one of the great paradoxes of Jewish existence," as a modern thinker has said: "The consciousness of history becomes so intense that it abolishes the consciousness of time."[27]

In these ambiguous and anxiety-ridden roles, Mak does not draw to himself what would be normal and indeed the whole point of his representation: that is, the hatred and fear associated with the conventional stage Jew who is the enemy of Christ and Christianity. While the three other shepherds seem destined to pass out of their current stage of expectations to move into the place of Christian salvation, Mak remains in a locus of Jewish expectations, troubled and confused by the nature of the world he must inhabit. He is, along with his wife, still waiting for a messiah to be born. For him, the play remains in this ambiguous and unsettled spiritual and chronological position, and he does not proceed with the other shepherds to adore the Virgin Mary and her Son. Like the Jews who once lived openly in England and later lay hidden from view, either practicing Judaism in secret, as the Marranos did in later centuries in Spain and Portugal, or hidden inside their new Christian identities and perhaps only partly aware at most of strange, untoward feelings that made them uncomfortable with themselves and their neighbors, there is no messiah come into the world, no relief from external dangers and inner anxieties.

Mak first comes on stage following the entry of the two elder and one younger shepherds, each complaining of the weather, of the exploitation of southern landlords, of the difficulty of supporting crabby wives and howling infants, and even of their own selfishness to one another. He enters the scene dressed in long-pipe sleeves reminiscent of the hated agents of absentee oppression and speaking lines of numerical enchantment: "Lord, for thy naymes vij, that made both moyn and starnes / Well mo then I can neuen, thi will, Lorde, of me tharnys" (ll. 190-91). Whatever else these lines may signify in preparing for his own complaints against the world, they are more than suspiciously like the kabbalistic incantations to the secrets of the Holy Name in meditations on *Bereshit*, Genesis. As Ephraim Karnarfogel points out, the Jews of northern France and England were influenced both by the Tosafist rationalists who followed in the wake of Rashi's school and to a lesser degree by the new school of *Hasidut Ashkenaz*, German Piety, and displayed an "interest in using Divine or angelic names for incantations and prayers."[28] In Mak we find little of the emphasis on self-denial or even self-affliction "cultivated and valued by the German Pietists not as ends unto themselves, but as means of fulfilling the hidden Will of God, securing atonement, or achieving future rewards."[29] The sufferings common to him and the Yorkshire-like shepherds on the moor outside of Wakefield are identified by the play implicitly as the birth pangs of the Christian Messiah; they are, however, not relished as exercises in piety. Nevertheless, the lingering fascination with mystical techniques remains a sign towards a latent Jewishness in Mak.

It is not clear whether or not Mak's words are heard or understood by the three other shepherds who recognize him through his disguise, when on all their behalf, Coll asks "Who is that pypys so poore?" (195). Speaking in a false southern accent Mak seeks their compassion, but in a complaint that is quite distinct from those pronounced by the three shepherds in the first movement of the play. His words, comic though they are in their immediate context, where he is pretending to be a stranger in their midst, have a metaphysical dimension their analysis of the world's injustices lacked, except by the most abstractive of interpretations. Says Mak:

> Wold God ye wyst how I fore!
> Lo, a man that walkys on the moore,
> And has not all his wyll. (196-198)

He wishes these Yorkshire men knew how he felt and fared, and could appreciate what it was like to be a man who has no real place in society and no ability to act by his own will. His complaint, in other words, is not simply of bad weather, economic injustices, or nagging families: he is suffering from both an existential *anome*—lost and lonely, no fixed identity in the world—and a spiritual crisis—feeling cut off from a deity whom he cannot conjure up using the fragments of secret and sacred lore he can barely recollect.

The three shepherds find his whole stance patently absurd, and ask why, when he pretends to be a landlord's yeoman, he is being "so qwaynt" and playing the "saynt"? They only move towards threatening violence when he tries to bluff out this pretence of social and economic importance. Mak, of course, is absurd. Nevertheless, his foolishness embodies roles that Jews played before the expulsions at the end of the thirteenth century, above all of assuming, against the reality of their status in medieval English society, that they were free agents who could serve the king and the landlords through their commercial and financial abilities. In the light of what happened after 1290, Mak seems a preposterous outsider who is nothing less than a parasite on the society and a danger to its good order. But seen in the perspective of the play as acting his part on the cusp of the transformation from the Jewish to the Christian dispensation, Mak's pretences and anxieties mark the sad and confused state of the world grasping for meaning and stability. When he begins to talk in his own voice and in response to the sympathetic queries from the shepherds about how he and his family are faring, Mak is seen to be one more victim of the failing world order, and his pains, like his audacious criminal acts—stealing the sheep and trussing it up as though it were his newborn son—actually push the age towards its transformation into the lifetime of Jesus Christ and the *saeculum* of the church. If he and his wife are punished by the shepherds when their silly trick is discovered, it is by having Mak tossed in a blanket, a fairly mild folk correction of transgressive behavior, not a violent ejection from the local community. That exclusion appears in a more subtle form precisely in the fact that neither Mak nor Gyll are included in the angelic address nor do they participate in the adoration of the Virgin Mother. The silence of this separation from the Christian community in itself bespeaks the implicit possibility of subsequent acceptance, particularly in their prefigurative parody of the holy family; and thus in the social cohesiveness of the domestic home, they should have foreshadowed their own role in those aspects of the Nativity Play's depiction of the moral and spiritual lessons of Mary and baby Jesus' powerful iconic presence on stage. Yet have they been positioned for salvation within the Corpus Christi?

In a powerfully subversive way, as Leo Strauss remarks, "The Jewish people and their fate are the living witness for the absence of redemption. This, one could say, is the meaning of the chosen people; the Jews are chosen to prove the absence of redemption." And here Strauss cites as his proof text, "one of the oldest prayers of our liturgy," according to Morris Silverman,[30] *Aleinu leshabeiach*, "It is our duty to praise the Lord,"[31] which contains the key lines:

> He has not made us like the nations of other lands, and He has not placed us like other families of the earth, since He has not assigned to us a portion as to them, nor a lot as to all their multitude. (For they worship vain things and emptiness, and pray to a god which cannot save.) But we bend the knee and bow in worship and acknowledge thanks before the supreme King of kings, the Holy One blessed be He, Who stretched out the heavens and laid the foundations of the earth, the seat of Whose honor is the heavens above . . . there is none else . . . .

This ancient prayer was the virtual anthem of Jewish martyrs during the Middle Ages, a song of defiance against idolatry and an assertion of pride in the monotheistic faith, which leads towards the messianic wish: "May all the inhabitants of the world perceive and know that unto Thee every knee must bend, every tongue vow loyalty."[32]

Could any Englishman or woman, let alone Mak the sheep stealer, have conceived of such a thing in England in the late fourteenth or fifteenth century when the Wakefield play was performed? It seems impossible. And yet what else does Mak say when he comes on stage? As noted earlier, he wishes he could praise the Lord with his seven mystical names, this God who created the moon and the stars. In this allusive manner, Mak articulates and then can be seen to incarnate the political and metaphysical propositions that he belongs to a different breed of people, that he and Gyl constitute a family apart, and that for these reasons he walks alone on the moor. Though he seems to parody the language of religious inclusion, redemption, and compassion, his words do not ring true, either to the shepherds or to the original audience; and yet—in spite of all this—Mak is not rejected, and so his particular witness is confirmed. Daw (= David) the youngest shepherd says in the final words pertaining directly to Mak in the play:

> We will nawther ban ne flyte
> Fyght nor chyte,
> But haue done as tyte,
> And cast hym in canvas. (625-28)

Though no one at the time could have conceptualized the problematic of this profound mystery of the Jewish witness to nonredemption in the midst of a

Christian celebration of the redemption of the incarnate Christ, the embodiment of that new testimony, Mak, is not at all subject to *rish'us*, the vicious hatred of the Jews that was experienced in the Middle Ages.[33] Indeed, Daw's words explicitly reject that response, which is normal in so many other medieval mystery, miracle, and morality plays. Such leniency suggests that perhaps more than just a sense of Christian charity, as rendered by the affective worship of the late Middle Ages, is displayed as a way of honoring the compassionate heart of the Virgin Mary, whose figure dominates the pageant on which the Wakefield *Secunda Pastorum* is performed; there could be a sense that men and women like Mak, whose ancestors were once Jews, remained or came to England as Jews, and though strictly outsiders, still are tolerated within the community—and their presence understood as troubled souls.

Conclusion

The examples I have given here do not come from the rabbinical corpus or from the specifically polemic writings of Jews confronted by pseudo-debates about the Talmud called by ecclesiastical and monarchic authorities in order to expose the weakness of Judaism in regard to Christianity. To have done so would have been to enter into a very different kind of argument concerning Jewish attitudes to Christianity. Rather, the texts chosen for discussion come from that small but often powerful collection of works by secret Jews who felt called upon to respond in a concealed manner to the dominance of Catholic piety and religiosity in which they lived and pretended to believe and participate in. Such responses do not present systematic theological doctrine either in favor of Jewish concepts or against church dogma or practice—but they enacted and embodied ripostes that teased and subverted the official persons and actions they imitated.

It may be that in some of the instances chosen here these distorted images of Jesus are so lacking in subtlety it is a wonder that Christian authorities did not recognize what was happening and took measures to remove these offensive texts and characters. For these "Judaized" images of Jesus depicted him sometimes as a child, sometimes as a preaching and miracle-working saint, sometimes as a zombie-like corpse on the cross or sometimes as a ghost wandering outside the tomb from which he has supposedly risen. How could fifteenth-century Christian audiences, even when more faithful than learned, have missed out on the negative qualities discussed above? Were the authors super-subtle ("pharisaic") crypto-Jews seeking to subvert or mock their supposed fellow religionists?[34] Perhaps, as David Nirenberg suggests in a review of Yirimiyahu Yovel's latest study of Marranos, *The Others Within*,[35] the Catholic Church in the late Middle Ages prior to the stresses of the Reformation actually was diverse and flexible enough within itself to accommodate a fairly wide range of perceptions and hence to tolerate—in the sense in which one comes to tolerate a disease or toxic substance—ideas and speculative depictions of the very heart of sacrality beyond which more modern versions of Christianity (stemming from sixteenth-century Protestantism and Counter-Reformation Catholicism) could not stand—and perhaps surprisingly to enjoy or at least learn from the seemingly radical and heretical.

Even given the very critical stance taken by Nirenberg in regard to Yovel and other recent writers' suggestions of a substantial anti-Christian Jewishness infiltrated into Catholic nations after the waves of forced conversion, ethnic cleansing, and punitive attacks on Jewish communities from the late thirteenth century onwards in England, France, and other parts of western Europe, it is more likely, however, that there were indeed several varieties of pseudo-Christians living and working under the very noses of church and civil authorities; and these individuals—very few in number, but nevertheless well placed, given their education and experience—took a degree of pleasure in and gained some kind of psychological relief from mocking the public icons of Jesus. In this meditation, I have given three examples from Middle English literature and drama, but, who knows, perhaps if we widened our study, we could find similar subversion and taunting in iconography, architecture, tapestry, and other forms of visual art, as well as in instrumental music and choral singing.

Discussion Questions

1. Why and how did medieval crypto-Jews express their ambiguous fears and anxieties about Jesus and the Passion story?
2. What was there about these often perverse and obscene images of Jesus that made them invisible or acceptable to Catholic readers and audiences?
3. How do crypto-Jews differ in these attitudes to Christianity from rabbinical authors in the Middle Ages?

Notes

1. Cited from A. M. Habermann, "The Religious Poems of Rabbi Yom Tov Lipman Heller," *Licvud Yom Tov*, ed. J. L. Mymon (Jerusalem, 1956) by Simha Goldin, *The Ways of Jewish Martyrdom*, trans. Yigal Levin, trans. and ed. C. Michael Copeland (Turnhout, Belgium: Berpols, 2008), 97.
2. In my other studies, such as *Sir Gawain and the Knight of the Green Chapel*, I have added several other dimensions to these texts. I have suggested that because of their illegal and anomalous position in Christian society, secret and quasi-Jews were more sensitive to and sometimes able to discern by Talmudic logic the mythic origins and folkloric relics of pre-Christian Europe. Their profound discontents and sense of deracination also gave them insights—not always consciously, of course—into the psychological and oneiric mysteries of their fears, anxieties, and longings.
3. An undergraduate student—of course, he was non-Jewish, as I never see Jewish students here at the farthest fringes of the Galut—once asked me what Jews thought about Jesus Christ. He may have been leading up to a conversionist spiel or perhaps he was really curious. But at least, unlike most who have no curiosity at all and can-

not even find a word in their vocabulary for Jew, speaking of "a Jewish" (not even able to add the noun that goes with the adjective) or "a Judaism sector," he knew the J word. What could I answer? I said: "Usually, they don't." He looked sad and confused, so I added: "Well, as much as you do about Santa Claus." Then, since he didn't walk away and might have been trying to comprehend what was just said—and there was that look in his eyes, the one that comes when the students are suddenly confronted by ideas they have never come across before (here in New Zealand perhaps there are no ideas they ever come across despite four or five years in university), that rolling back of the eyes, that nervous fluttering of their lashes, and then when I knew he was about to say something like: "Run that by me again, please," I went on: "Jesus has nothing to do with Judaism." So far as—"should I have said "we" or "I"? I chose the easier option—"I am concerned, Jesus is not and never was real in the historical sense." At that, the student walked away. But was this the right way to have answered him? When I read through the resumés for this conference and looked closely at the many papers sent by Zev Garber and his friends, all of which take very seriously the historical and theological questions concerning Jesus and the Jews, it seems that perhaps I shouldn't be so glib.

4. Goldin, *The Ways of Jewish Martyrdom*, 122.
5. Goldin, *The Ways of Jewish Martyrdom*, 114.
6. Goldin, *The Ways of Jewish Martyrdom*, 143.
7. Goldin, *The Ways of Jewish Martyrdom*, 190.
8. In a fourteenth-century poem by Peretz Yehiel cited by Susan L. Einbinder, *No Place of Rest: Jewish Literature, Expulsion, and the Memory of France* (Philadelphia: University of Pennsylvania Press, 2009), 149.
9. Goldin, *The Ways of Jewish Martyrdom*, 114-15.
10. Norman Simms, "Moving Through Time and Space: Memories, Midrash and Trauma" *Australian Journal of Jewish Studies* 16 (2002): 223-37.
11. Norman Simms, "The Unspeakable Agony of *Kiddush ha-Shem*: Forced Jewish Infanticide during the First and Second Crusades," *The Medieval History Journal* 3, no. 2 (2000): 337-62
12. Cited by John Ruskin, "Lecture II.—Lilies: Of Queens' Gardens" in *Sesame and Lilies*," (London: Collins' Clear-Type Press, n.d. [1904]), 141.
13. Jonathan Riley-Smith, "Christian Violence and the Crusades," in *Religious Violence Between Christians and Jews: Medieval Roots, Modern Perspectives*, ed. Anna Sapir Abulafia (Houndsmith: Palgrave, 2002), 5.
14. Norman Simms, *Sir Gawain and the Knight of the Green Chapel* (Lanham, MD: University Press of America, 2002). The text I am referring to here is that compiled by Christine Franzen for the Department of English, Victoria University (Wellington, NZ, 1993) of *Sir Gawain and the Green Knight*.
15. If Chaucer himself was not a crypto-Jew two or three generations from ancestral conversion, then he would have come across such people in his father's wine business in the dock area of London and on his official diplomatic missions to the Continent. Once alerted to their presence and insights, he may have used his status at court to speak with men and women in the *Domus conversorum*, where many refugees from persecutions and expulsions sought a temporary rest before entering normal society.
16. Eva Engel, "Child Survivors Report Outline," abstract presented on 28 January 2009 by Sydney Child Holocaust Survivors Group in Sydney, NSW, Australia.

17. Larry D. Benson, ed., *The Riverside Chaucer* (Oxford University Press, 1988); this is now the standard student edition based on F. N. Robinson's classic 1933 edition of *The Works of Geoffrey Chaucer.*
18. Miri Rubin, *Gentile Tales : The Narrative Assault on Late-Medieval Jews* (Philadelphia, PA: University of Pennsylvania Press, 2004).
19. Antoine Capet, review of James Renton, *The Zionist Masquerade: The Birth of the Anglo-Zionist Alliance 1914-1918* (New York: Palgrave Macmillan, 2007) on H-Albion (March, 2009) at http://www.h-net.org/reviews/showrev. php?id=24250 distributed on EEJH (East European Jewish History) by B.G. Dobbs on 16 May 2009, eejh@ yahoogroups.com.
20. Norman Simms, "Mrs Noah's Secret: A Psychohistorical Reading of the Chester Cycle Third Pageant" *Parergon* 14, no. 2 (1997): 15-28.
21. Leo Strauss, "Why We Remain Jews: Can Jewish Faith and History Still Speak to Us?" in *Leo Strauss: Political Philosopher and Jewish Thinker*, ed. Kenneth L. Deutsch and Walter Nicgorski (Klanham, MD: Rowman & Littlefield, 1994), 43-80.
22. Somatic causation here refers to a psychohistorical approach to the problem of continuing deep memories of traumatic events in which the pain is so deeply internalized it cannot be evoked as either image or verbal statement but nevertheless remains as a bodily phenomenon and can thus influence childrearing practices through several generations, in spite of formal or informal education and adult activities. For example, see Norman Simms, "Passion, *Compotatio, Rixus*, and the Shameful Thing: English Guilds and the Corpus Christi Cycles," *Mentalities/Mentalités* 11, no. 2 (1997): 45-60; and "Medieval Guilds, Passions and Abuse" *The Journal of Psychohistory* 26, no. 1 (1998): 478-513.
23. Ephraim Kanarfogel, *Peering through the Lattices: Mystical, Magical and Pietistic Dimensions in the Tosafist Period* (Detroit: Wayne State University Press, 2000), 10, 46. 79.
24. Kanarfogel, *Peering through the Lattices*, 191 and n. 4.
25. Kanarfogel, *Peering through the Lattices,* 56, n. 65. See also 171-72, where this mystical group is associated with the great Spanish poet and exegete Avraham Ibn Ezra who visited England in the twelfth century.
26. A. C. Cawley, ed., *The Wakefield Pageants in the Townley Cycle* (Manchester: Manchester University Press, 1958), "4. *Secunda Pastorum*," 43-63.
27. Leon Wieseltier, *Kaddish* (New York: Knopf, 1998), 353.
28. Kanarfogel, *Peering through the Lattices*, 29. The *Aleynu* prayer was the subject of discussion in texts attributed to R. Judah he-Hasad, R. Isaac of Corbeil, and other German Pietists in this same period (Kanarfogel, 87, 179, 182).
29. Kanarfogel, *Peering through the Lattices*, 34.
30. Morris Silverman, ed., *High Holiday Prayer Book* (Hartford, CT: Prayer Book Press, 1951), 159.
31. Strauss, "Why We Remain Jews," 327.
32. Silver, *High Holiday Prayer Book,*160.
33. Strauss, "Why We Remain Jews," 349.
34. Norman Simms, "Satanic Midrashim: Or, The Abuse of History," *Mentalities/Mentalités* 21, no. 1 (2007): 32-47.
35. David Nirenberg, "Unrenounceable Core," a review of Yirimiyahu Yovel, *The Others Within: The Marranos: Split Identity and Emerging Modernity* (Princeton, NJ: Princeton University Press, 2009), in *London Review of Books* (23 July 2009): 16-17.

Typical Jewish Misunderstandings of Christ, Christianity, and Jewish-Christian Relations over the Centuries

Eugene J. Fisher

Introduction

I have spent a large portion of my professional life since I finished my coursework at New York University's Institute of Hebrew Studies in 1971 educating my fellow Christians on the Jewishness of Jesus, of his teachings, and of Christianity down through the ages. My dissertation analyzed the treatment of Jews and Judaism in Catholic religious education materials, a study I was happy to share with the publishers a few years later in a program co-sponsored with the Anti-Defamation League, which resulted, I am even happier to say, in a number of improvements in Catholic textbooks. My first book[1] briefly summarized my dissertation and presented chapters on understanding Jesus and his teaching in its Jewish context, as well as the events leading up to his crucifixion by the Romans. Such themes have been central to my writing and to the programs I organized while staffing Catholic-Jewish Relations for the US Conference of Catholic Bishops from 1977-2007. I was therefore as delighted as was Zev Garber when I read Amy-Jill Levine's wonderfully written and insightful work on the topic to which I have devoted so much of my life,[2] and I reviewed it just as positively as he did, feeling it has distilled a generation of the work of both Jewish and Christian scholars for the education of generations to come. A percentage of these scholars are represented in this volume and I am greatly honored to have been invited to be among them.

Since the topic of this collection is well within the area in which I have done so much work, one might ask why I have chosen, in essence, to turn the topic around 180 degrees and address the challenge not so much to my Christian as to my Jewish colleagues. It's a good question. Part of the reason lies in the fact that I have spent my life in dialogue and deeply believe that dialogue is a two-sided affair of sharing, probing, and coming to a deeper understanding not only of the other, but of one's own traditions and beliefs as well. Part, too, is a habit of doing this that I picked up at New York University, where I was often the only non-Jew in a class full of Jewish graduate students and rabbis,[3] pretty much the only time in my life when I have been uncontested in how I interpret Christianity!

In my three years at New York University, I often encountered misunderstandings about Christianity and Christian beliefs, not only from my fellow students but from the professors as well. Interestingly, over time, a pattern began to emerge in these misunderstandings. The Jewish Jesus, I discovered, is not only misunderstood by Christians, as Levine rightly documents and rebuts, but the Christian Jesus, and Christianity itself, are rather systematically misunderstood by educated Jews. This is not to suggest a parallel in any sense to the polemical anti-Judaic and anti-Jewish diatribes within Christian history that begin with the very Fathers of the church as early as the second century of the Common Era. Nor were they the product of the medieval apologetics with which Jewish teachers sought to protect their students from over-zealous Christian missionaries.

Pondering on this phenomenon, as I ended up doing for a paper in a course on the classic work, *Hovoth ha Levavoth* by Bahya Ibn Pakuda, a work I understood better than the rabbis in the class because it was written, albeit in Hebrew, in the philosophical language of medieval scholasticism (and I was fresh from a Catholic seminary, having majored in philosophy, by which they meant scholastic philosophy at the time), and putting it all together with what I had learned in other courses, the outline of the pattern and its historical origins began to emerge for me. What resulted was, in fact, the first article I ever published in the then nascent field of Jewish-Christian studies, *Typical Jewish Misunderstandings of Christianity*,[4] which I will here reprise and update before moving on to the related topic of our mutual misunderstandings of our shared history. The aim of this paper, it should be understood, is neither rebuttal nor exhaustive analysis. Rather, it is a position paper, offering examples of these misunderstandings and a possible explanation for their popularity even today, some 45 years after the Second Vatican Council historic statement, *Nostra Aetate*, revolutionized Catholic and to some extent most Christian attitudes toward and understandings of Jews and Judaism.[5]

The Making of a Myth

The categories which I shall offer as those underlying much of modern Jewish scholarship in its attitude toward Christianity have their roots in nineteenth-century Germany. For it was the German academic community which fused Hegelian idealism and social Darwinism into a philosophical language tool for the analysis of scripture, religion, and history. It was German-Jewish scholarship which reacted with the Science of Judaism (*Wissenschafte des Judentuums*), utilizing that same tool for its own apologetic. Both groups saw history in terms of the Hegelian stages of thesis, antithesis, and synthesis. The former posited Christianity as the ultimate stage in world history. With some, like Hegel himself, it was specifically Christian Germany which was the pinnacle of human evolution. Since this approach not so implicitly denigrated Judaism to the level of a vestigial anachronism, the latter reacted by placing prophetic ethics at the pinnacle of human achievement.[6] This view, however, logically reduced Christianity and implicitly Western civilization to the level of an aberrant offshoot from normative Judaism.

The symbol of the Christian branch of this polemic has become Julius Wellhausen,[7] who saw the temple priesthood and later Talmudic legislation as corruptive of the original, nobly primitive, prophetic ethical monotheism, in need of purification and renewal, which came in the form of Christianity. The main target of such romantic, pseudo-scientific theorizing, of course, was not Judaism but Roman Catholicism, with its hierarchical priesthood, dogmas, and volumes of canon law. Indeed, the dim view of Scripture studies by the Catholic Church until Pius XII's groundbreaking encyclical, *Divino Afflante Spiritu* (1943), opened up modern biblical methodologies to Catholic scholars.[8]

The reaction of the freshly emancipated Jews of Germany was even more dramatic. Eager to prove their mettle, the Jewish intellectuals began a movement that was to become the *Wissenschaft des Judentuums*. It took its name from the Society for the Culture and Science of the Jews, founded in Berlin in 1819 by Eduard Gans, Moses Moser, and Leopold Zunz.[9]

In the first volume of the journal of this society, there appeared an essay by Immanuel Wolf setting the tone for all that followed.[10] Wolf maintained that the "religious idea" of Judaism is the key to the interpretation of Jewish history. Though pummeled into isolation by the vicissitudes of the Galut, the Jew has survived "for the sake of this idea which must be admitted to be of the essence of humanity itself." The nationalistic implications of this reaction to German nationalism are important for the understanding of the growth of Zionism, whether the political variety of Herzl or the cultural form celebrated in the works of Ahad Haam and Martin Buber. On the opposite pole are the "Germans of Mosaic persuasion," the early reluctance of American Judaism to embrace Zionism,[11] and (curiously enough) the popularity of Buber's existential mysticism.

Nachman Krochmal (1785-1840), in his *Guide for the Perplexed of Our Time*, assumed the dialectical cycle of Hegel as the dynamic of history. While each culture seeks a particular idea, he argues, Judaism alone seeks the absolute idea. Hence Judaism alone has been able to break the cycle of birth and decay to which all other cultures are prey.

In 1835, Abraham Geiger launched the *Journal of Jewish Theology*, using its pages to develop his notion of a Jewish "genius for religion" embodied in the ethics of the prophets. Since the Science of Judaism founded the Jewish identity upon its ethical excellence, it was in that sphere that Judaism had to be established as superior. Successive Israeli governments and its Supreme Court have over the years echoed this notion, using it as a rationale for the rejection of capital punishment save in the sole case of Adolf Eichmann, the man in the glass booth, despite the extreme provocations of terrorism.[12]

Although European Judaism gradually broke out of the Hegelian mold through the works of such existentialists as Shestov, Buber, and Rosenzweig, the nature of the debate with Christianity had become so firmly established that the shift in attitude became more one of terminology than of basic understanding. It is important to note that the questions raised by the Science of Judaism, their direct contact with Christianity, were limited mainly to the sphere of German Protestantism. (Indeed, Reform Judaism patterned much of its change on the model of the German Lutheran Church.) Unfortunately, then, many of their views were one-sided.[13] Either Protestant doctrine was viewed as normative, or Protestant polemics against Catholicism were rather uncritically swallowed whole. What was and is missing in much of the Jewish understanding of Christianity is a sense of the complexity of Christian belief, the variety of practice, and the nuances and historical contexts which alone can give flesh to the bare bones of doctrine.[14]

A Modern Jewish Myth

The context and tone of the Jewish-Christian dialogue has changed over the centuries. Rabbi Henry Siegman of the then Synagogue Council of America (now the National Council of Synagogues, minus the Orthodox), for example, wrote that "the arguments (against dialogue) rarely reveal the deep-seated fears which underlie the reservations and objections raised by religious traditionalists."[15] The major fear, as Rabbi Siegman saw it, is "the fear of conversionary motives imputed to the Church." More recently, at the June 25, 2009 meeting of the United States Catholic Conference and the representatives of the Orthodox Union and Rabbinical Council of America, David Berger, head of the Jewish Studies Department at Yeshiva College, New York City, cited "grave" concerns of some in the Jewish community about the "Note on Ambiguities Contained in Covenant and Mission," which was prepared by the US Conference of Catholic Bishop's Committees on Doctrine and Ecumenical and Interreligious Affairs as an attempted clarification of a statement issued by the Conference's own dialogue with the National Council of Synagogues in 2002. "Orthodox Jews can tolerate any Christian view on the necessity of faith in Jesus Christ as savior of all, but they cannot agree to participate in an interfaith dialogue that is a cover for proselytism," Berger said.[16]

Rabbi Siegman's reasoning was much the same then as Professor Berger's today. There is nothing intellectually or morally offensive about the desire to convert and there is nothing in the Jewish character or history which would lead one to believe "that Jews might in fact be converted to the Christian faith as a result of these interreligious conversations" (96-97). Siegman went on to note the seriousness of the charges of Christian implication in the Shoah made by many Christians as well as Jews, Siegman concluded: "And yet, those who nevertheless believe in the possibility—even the necessity—of dialogue, do so because the Church speaks with many voices. There are men within the Church today who are deeply sensitive to the implications of the Holocaust and to whom we should apply the Talmudic directive *haba leather messayin oto*" (98-99).

My own point is not that history does not confirm the Jewish fears concerning the treachery of the church towards Jews over the centuries, for it certainly does. Rather, I would argue that what is needed is a deeper awareness of the complex reality of Christian belief and practice such as that manifested by Siegman. Because the history of Christianity is practically coterminous with the history of Western civilization, no single generalization can define the "essence" of Christianity beyond its core, creedal beliefs. Just as pluralism is necessary for the working of a democracy, so a pluralism of insight is necessary for the understanding of the multifaceted phenomena we call "Christianity."

It was precisely this fact that the Science of Judaism, trained in the oversimplifications of the Hegelian dialectic, found most difficult to grasp. And it is just this point that remains the greatest obstacle to the understanding of Christianity by many Jewish thinkers. (Indeed, most Christians, enwrapped in the demands of their own sectarian interests, likewise find it difficult to view this complex reality as complex. We must all learn to perceive reality, each other and ourselves, in shades of gray, not simple black and white.)

Pre-Haskalah Judaism had a different approach in its polemic against Christianity than does modern Judaism. The medieval Jewish apologist, Isaac b. Abraham of Trokki (1533-1594) strove, in classical Hebrew style, to demonstrate the superiority of his own faith "with a minimum of diatribe" in his work, *Hizzuk Emunah* (Faith Strengthened). On the Christian dictum that love, even of one's enemies, is the only way to break the self-escalating circle of violence and hate, Isaac comments that Jews are also prohibited from hating their enemies:

> Matthew 5:43: You have heard that it has been said, "Love your neighbor and hate your enemy." Truly, you also see in this verse that Matthew has made a false statement, for nowhere in the Pentateuch or the Prophets have we found the statement that you shall hate your enemies. On the contrary, it is written in Exodus 23:4-5: "If you see your enemy's ox or his ass going astray, you shall surely bring it back to him again."[17]

A more recent Jewish apologist, Dr. Trude Weiss-Rosmarin, of blessed memory, took a much more aggressive approach to the same text. She maintained that the Christian ethic is here both unreasonable and unnatural:

> It is true that Jesus demanded, by going beyond the letter of the Jewish law and without asking into consideration human nature, "love your enemies and pray for your persecutors" (Matt 5:44). However, of what avail is this teaching if its promulgator also taught: "If anyone comes to me without hating his own father and mother . . . he cannot be a disciple of mine" (Luke 14:26)? Jewish law *does not* command that one love his adversary for this would be unnatural. It does, however, command to refrain from wreaking vengeance upon him and to assist him moreover in an emergency, for this is to be expected of a human being.[18]

The criterion for the validity of a religion has become, is no longer conformance to divine revelation but "naturalness." Note that Dr. Weis-Rosmarin subtly equates the active notion of returning love for hate with the passive notion of not resisting evil at all. I know of no Christian denomination which advocates total passivity in the face of evil. Rather, the point among Christian pacifists is that it is impossible to defeat evil and hatred by becoming evil and hate-filled oneself. One can see the difficulties of generalizations such as Dr. Weis-Rosmarin's when one considers that pacifism is itself a minority position within the churches.

The approach often taken to the discussion of asceticism among Jewish scholars offers us another striking example of the myth in action. Extremes are set up, with care taken to place Judaism securely in the "reasonable" center. Christianity, then, is relegated to the "otherworldly" pole.[19] Ahad Haam, whose popularity and influence as a writer are well attested, made of this technique an art. He posited a prophetic and Pharisaic golden mean between the extremes of the Sadducees and the Essenes, that is, between "the sovereignty of the flesh and its annihilation."[20]

Ahad Haam's opening definition of asceticism is of significance: "the psychological tendency to . . . turn from the pleasures of the world with hatred and contempt, and to regard every material good thing of life as something evil and degraded, to be avoided by him who cares for his soul's health" (139). Note again the implication of mental illness. What at times occurs in our modern dialogues is, I believe, reflective of such views as Haam's. The very term, "asceticism" tends to conjure up, on the Jewish side, images of flagellation and starving monks. Since the emotional nuances of the term are not the same for Christians, necessarily, the result can be a heated discussion that leads nowhere.

If the Jewish scholar begins by defining asceticism (and hence Christianity) from its extreme, it follows that for him or her it becomes impossible to admit of an ascetic trend within "normative Judaism." (This term itself, of course, represents a vast over-simplification of a complex reality.) For to admit a valid ascetic trend within Judaism would be the same as admitting an extremist, world-hating viewpoint as part of that heritage.

The contrast between the approach of Ahad Haam and that of the medieval philosopher, Bahya ibn Pakuda, is illustrative of the impact of the Haskalah on

Jewish thinking. Bahya begins with a morally neutral definition of asceticism and then establishes its extremes. For him there exist good and bad forms of asceticism, higher and lower, general and specific. The level on which an individual is counseled to engage in ascetic practices depends upon his character and potential.

> General abstinence is that which is practiced to improve our physical condition and keep our secular affairs in good order . . . Specific abstinence is that kind which Torah and Reason indicate for the welfare of our souls in the world to come . . . The plain meaning of abstinence is that kind which Torah and Reason indicate for the welfare of our souls in the world to come . . . The plain meaning of abstinence is bridling the inner lust, voluntarily refraining from something that is in our power and which we have the opportunity to do—the abstinence being due to an obligatory motive.[21]

Because he does not include his value judgment in his definition, Bahya is able to embrace certain modes of ascetic practice, with the proper *kavanah* (intention), as morally acceptable and authentically Jewish. Ahad Haam, on the contrary, makes explicit the fact that he is defining a theological doctrine, not an ethical practice. The doctrine of course is not a Christian but a Manichean one. Unfortunately, many today erroneously ascribe it to Christianity.

> Asceticism, so defined, is not a descriptive term for certain outward practices, but a name for the inner spring of conduct which prompts those practices; and thus we exclude all those phenomena which have (only) an external similarity . . . A man may renounce pleasure and yet not deserve the name of ascetic, because he . . . only refrains in order to avoid danger to his health . . . but true asceticism, as I have said, is that which has its source in hatred and contempt for the flesh.[22]

Ascetic practices and doctrines have always existed within Judaism, though usually within stricter limits than in the Christian tradition. The "wise scholar" (*talmid chaam*), according to the Talmud, for example, is one who studies not less than eighteen hours a day, a demand which would leave little time for "pleasures of the world." Fasting, on certain occasions, has been approved and practiced throughout Jewish history. And mortification of the body was even seen (after prayer and intensification of the performance of the *mitzvoth*) as a substitute for the temple sacrifice—and, thus, clearly connected with atonement in a salvific sense. R. Sheshet prays (Ber. 17a):

> Lord of all beings, it is manifest in Your sight that at the time when the Temple was in existence, a man might sin and bring an offering, and though nothing was sacrificed from it save only its fat and its blood, nevertheless atonement was made for him. Now I have observed a fast, and my fat anblood have been reduced. May it be Your will that my fat and blood which have been reduced be regarded as though they had been offered before You on the altar, and grant me Your favor.

On the other hand, the discussion of the rabbis concerning the Nazirites reveals an opinion that extreme asceticism could actually be a sin against the body for which atonement must be made.[23]

There is a controversy today over whether or not Bahya was "ascetic." As we have seen, the resolution should be simple and straightforward. It is the emotional nuance of the term itself, and its involvement in the anti-Christian apologetic which gives heat to the discussion.

The argument from the Jewish side, when stripped of particulars, usually runs like this: Christianity is ascetic because it is other-worldly, and is based on the notion that faith alone, irrespective of one's actual, physical deeds, is necessary for salvation. The latter statement, of course, equates a certain interpretation of the thought of Luther with that of all Christians. The argument goes on to conclude that Christianity maintains that belief in a set of intellectual propositions (dogmas) can save humanity from its sinfulness. These beliefs, it is asserted, go back to Paul, not Jesus (who was really not such a bad guy, but a good Jew whose teachings Paul distorted). Paul of Tarsus was more Greek in his thinking, this argument runs, than he was Jewish (Gamaliel notwithstanding). As Matthew V. Novenson has recently pointed out: "Scholars in Jewish studies, who give due attention to Jesus of Nazareth as a data point on the graph of early messianic phenomena, typically do not adduce Paul in this connection, sit it was, after all, the self-styled apostle to the Gentiles who launched a movement that in late antiquity increasingly became something other than, if not opposed to Judaism."[24] Novenson cites Harris Lenowitz to this effect: "Often thought the most successful messianic movement in Judaism, Christianity achieved it power and endurance largely by abandoning the goals and society of Jesus and his disciples following his death . . . Christianity in fact ceased to be a messianic movement and became instead a revitalization movement."[25] Michael J. Cook, in his otherwise excellent volume, *Modern Jews Engage the New Testament*, which I have highly recommended, also suffers from this anti-Pauline syndrome.[26] The catch phrases ensuing from such a reduction of Christianity to a stereotype of itself are the tradition of the Prophets, "uncorrupted by Hellenism," and so on.

There is truth to the argument. Leslie Dewart, for example, in *The Future of Belief*[27] has convincingly shown the pervasiveness of Hellenistic philosophy from the patristic period through scholasticism. The claim, however, cannot be made of the New Testament or of recent theological developments, in the same proportions. The view of Christianity sketched above remains myth, not reality.

Examples of Common Misconceptions

Prof. Eliezer Berkovits has written that "Christianity is an other-worldly religion. It has no use for this world and no respect for it."[28] So convinced was he of the acceptance of this sweeping statement by the readership to whom he wrote that he offered it without evidence of any kind. The statement, however, would come as a great shock to the authors of the *Constitution on the Church in the Modern World* of the Second Vatican Council.

The bishops of the Council would be even more surprised to learn that, according to Christianity, the world is "corrupt" and humanity unredeemed. These statements represent denials of the incarnation and the validity of the redemption. Both are fundamental heresies so far as the church is concerned. Yet Berkovits felt he could make the charges without feeling the slightest need for any documentation. "According to the compromise," he wrote, "salvation applies only to the individual soul, the inner man; the world, history, remains unredeemed." Berkovits then refers to a view which he ascribes to Kierkegaard. "Faith is absurd because it is and must be outside of history. From the Christian point of view, all history is Fall and all culture Fall into history" (80). Here we have it, the myth in a nutshell! The Second Vatican Council, however, gives quite a different picture:

> The joys and hopes, the grieves and anxieties of the people of this age, especially those who are poor or in any way afflicted, these are the joys an hopes, the grieves and anxieties of the followers of Christ . . . That is why this community realizes that it is truly linked with humanity and its history by the deepest of bonds. . . Therefore this council focuses its attention on the world of humanity . . . that world which is the theater of human history, and the heir of human energies, of human tragedies and triumphs; that world which the Christian sees as created and sustained by its Maker's love, fallen indeed into the bondage of sin yet emancipated now by Christ.[29]

Clearly, there is a communication gap between us.

Despite the reality, myths such as that presented by Berkovits persist in the Jewish community. Martin Buber wrote of the difference between *pisis* and *emunah*, the former implying a sterile faith in a solely intellectual set of propositions, the latter being he involvement of the whole person, in the context of his or her history and community, with God. Guess which concept, for Buber, represents the Christian position?

Christianity speaks with many voices. Unfortunately, despite the fact that Buber perfected the theory and art of dialogue, he listened only to a few of them. The ogre is of course St. Paul, whose "Hellenized" dogmatism perverted the essentially Jewish teachings of Jesus:

> I can connect the Pauline doctrine of faith only with a peripheral Judaism, which was actually "Hellenistic." If we consider the Synopic and Johannine dialogues . . . we immediate see that Paul's doctrine was procured at the expense of the plain, concrete and situational-bound dialogicism of the original man of the Bible, who found eternity not in the super-temporal spirit but in the depth of the actual moment. The Jesus of the genuine tradition still belongs to that, but the Jesus of theology does no longer.[30]

Though he denounces Hegel, Buber was trained to the German methodology. He does to Scripture here just what Wellhausen did to it; he eisegetes into it the theological presuppositions of his own thought. He plugs a personalist existentialism into the areas which Wellhausen filled with Hegelian idealism. Buber takes his view of Christianity from the perspective of northern European Protestantism. The results are similar to what would happen if a Christian were to analyze Judaism from the perspective of the Karaites and Franz Rosenzweig.[31]

David Rudavsky followed the pattern set by Buber when he wrote: "Many believe that if Jesus' preaching had not been infused with extraneous elements by Paul, Christianity, like Hasidism, might have remained within the fold of Judaism."[32] The element of truth in this statement obscures its oversimplifications.

A further dynamic needs to be mentioned here. There is a tendency in some to infuse Christian doctrine with ideas actually belonging to such pseudo-messiahs as Shabbetai Zevi. In this view, St. Paul's doctrine is seen as the equivalent of that of Nathan of Gaza, the "theologizer" of Shabbetai's movement. Again, Luther's *fortiter pecca* (sin bravely) somehow loses its conclusion, "and believe more bravely still" and becomes identified with the Shabbatean notion of the holiness of sin. Nathan's formulation maintains two justifications for Shabbetai Zevi's psychological weaknesses and excesses. First, since the messianic age has presumably arrived, all are saved and it is impossible for them to sin no matter what they do. Second, by committing evil one is not really sinning but plunging into the evil in order to wrest from it the divine sparks of the Shechinah which have been entrapped in the shells of evil since the primal cataclysm of creation.[33] Neither of these rationalities, however, has any analogies within Christianity.

That Luther's rhetorical commandment means something entirely different from the way it is taken in Jewish circles is obvious as soon as one puts it back into a Christian context. Dillenberger and Welch comment:

> This is the assertion that God's mercy is continuous and inexhaustible. At the same time, where forgiveness does not issue in new life, it is doubtful that it is actually forgiveness . . . It was from such a perspective that Luther asserted 'sin bravely, yet believe more bravely still.' This is not a counsel to sin; it is the recognition that life involves sin, that at no point can humanity completely escape it. It is a counsel against those who are so afraid of sin that they refuse to act or participate freely in the events of life.[34]

Paul's lengthy condemnations of sins of every sort are famous for their passion and detail. And that his view of the messianic age was far different from that of Nathan of Gaza is seen from the fact that he, like rabbinical Judaism following the demise of the Bar Kochba revolt (in which Rabbi Akiba proclaimed Bar Kochba to be the Messiah), strives earnestly to dissuade his followers from the idea that the Day of the Lord had come or would come in the foreseeable future (e.g., 2 Thess. 2:12). Paul's ethic is maximalist, not minimalist. Freed from the bondage of sin through Jesus' resurrection, humanity must now assume the responsibility that goes along with freedom.

A note on Luther's much maligned doctrine of justification by faith alone is in order, since many Jews ascribe it to all of Christianity. Dillenberger and Welch sum up the doctrine by stressing the fact that for Luther good works (not indulgences) are a *sine qua non* for justification. What Luther had in mind was to stress the constant mercy of God and to destroy the "merit badge" system in which one strives to pile up more "good deeds" on the scale of judgment than evil ones. Such "quantative calculations" were repugnant for Luther.

John Calvin stated in his *Institutes of the Christian Religion* that "they who are justified by true faith prove their justification, not by barren and imaginary resemblance of faith but by obedience and good works" (III, xxvii, 12). Clearly, Christian thought has once again been somewhat manhandled to serve an apologetical purpose. The reality is far more complex than it may appear at first glance.

The various misunderstandings are too numerous to discuss in detail in the present paper. Some are merely amusing, for example the charge that Mary functions as a mother goddess within Roman Catholicism, or that Christianity is polytheistic (and hence pagan) because of the doctrine of the Trinity. The Trinity, I believe, can best be understood by Jews through the lens of Jewish mysticism which, for example adumbrates ten *sephiroth* (emanations of God) from the *En Sof* to the Spirit in the world. More serious is the notion that Christians have placed mediators between the direct communication of God and humanity—that is, Christ, the priesthood, and the Blessed Mother. This posits on to all of Christianity a stereotype of Catholicism once popular among Protestants.

I have attempted in this section merely to introduce the idea that there is more under the surface of "Christian unity" than would appear from the outside. The differences between us should be clearly seen and delighted in by all persons of faith. They are a sign of the ever-abiding mystery and infinite intricacy of God's creation.

Augustine and the Jews

Many Jews tend to lump Augustine in with other Fathers of the church, such as Chrysostum, as simply one more example of the patristic teaching of contempt against Judaism and Jews. They are unaware of the crucial role played by St. Augustine in the survival of the Jews in Christian Europe in the centuries after the church gained political power at the time of the Emperor Constantine. Of all of the non-Christian religions that existed in the fourth century CE, Judaism alone was allowed to maintain its ancient status as *religio licita*, a legally recognized religion.

It was Augustine's brilliant theology that established the theological base on which the popes over the centuries drew to defend the rights of Jews to freedom of worship and freedom to practice their religion. Much of his theology was developed in opposition to the anti-Judaism theologies of virtually all other Christian thinkers of the period.

Even many of those who are aware of the revolutionary nature of Augustine's thought and its positive influence on papal policy over the centuries are not aware of how he reached his unprecedented (save for St. Paul) conclusions about the Jews. His thinking about the Jews actually had a role in his overall defense of orthodox Christianity against the chief heresies of his time. Those who have such a view will be disabused of it by the brilliant new study by Paula Frederikson.[35]

Augustine was a convert to Catholicism from Manicheanism. This Christian heresy taught, among other things, that the body (and everything physical or "carnal") was evil, and only the soul (and spiritual realities) was good. One extreme of this thought was to be found in that of Marcion, a gnostic "dualist" who taught that there were two distinct gods. The Old Testament God of justice and vengeance demanded of the Jews blood sacrifices and carnal practices such as circumcision and resting on the Sabbath; the New Testament God was concerned with love, mercy, and the spirit. The coming of Jesus represented the defeat of the evil God of the Old Testament, so Marcion concluded that the church should destroy all of its books, and even many New Testament books that Marcion and the later Manichees felt to be "too fleshly, too Jewish," and thus evil.

Augustine the convert preserved for the church much of its sacred Scripture. To him, at stake were the very nature of Christ as incarnate Son of God and the very nature of the sacraments, especially the Eucharist, as a physical sign in which Christ is fully present, not only spiritually but also physically.

Augustine's understanding of "the redemption of the flesh" in the incarnate Christ also led him to his startling (for the time) defense of the Jews and of the continuing right of the Jews to worship as God told them to do in their Scripture. God, for Augustine, did not lie to the Jews. What he told them to do must forever be acknowledged as God's will, which Jews must faithfully observe until the end of time.

But unlike many Christian thinkers—then and now—Augustine did not see the observance of God's will for Israel and the Christian observance of God's will for humanity in Christ as an either/or proposition. The Jewish Way, God's Way for the Jews, did not, could not, given the nature of God as Truth, become an evil or wrong way with the revelation of the New Way.

While the Jews may have killed Jesus as their ancestors killed the prophets, Augustine does not proceed to belabor them with the charge of "deicide." Rather, he states that they have on them the mark of Cain, which of course is God's mark, setting the Jews aside, for all time, as God's to deal with. No humans can attempt to do violence to the Jews or try to force the Jews to convert without risking the wrath of God. Treating them justly and with love would make the Christian faith shine brightly for them.

Jewish-Christian Relations over the Centuries

Pope St. Gregory the Great, in establishing the first legislation in the now Christian-dominated Roman empire, accepted the theology of Augustine on the Jews and established the precedents in canon law that made the papacy in many ways over the centuries the the protector of the Jews. Through the early Middle Ages until the first Crusade in 1096 resulted in the massacre of upwards of ten thousand Jews, relations between Jews and Christians were in the main peaceful. It was only beginning with the twelfth century that the anti-Jewish themes and persecutions which we today think of as the basic model of Jewish-Christian relations, such as distinctive and demeaning clothing, the ghettos, the blood libel charges, the expulsions, the Inquisition, Passion Plays, and pogroms began to occur. And even then such tragedies and anti-Jewish preaching and violence were not endemic throughout Christian Europe, but ebbed and flowed in different times and places. It was not always and everywhere as bad for the Jews as it was in those places and times when it was at its worst. And even in the massacres of 1096, the local bishops of the Rhineland valley tried to save their Jews from the huge mob that went rampaging along, having missed the boats of the actual first Crusade and wanting to go overland to Jerusalem. The Catholic king of Hungary, learning of the massacres that marked the mob's progress, gathered his army and destroyed the self-styled Crusaders when they approached his borders.[36]

The "lachrymose" view of the history of Jews among Christians severely oversimplifies that long, complex history. Yet in all too much of Jewish education, both in the US and in Israel, what is typically taught to Jewish students is: "Jesus was a good guy. Paul was a bad goy. The Christians got power and persecuted the Jews, always and everywhere and everywhen. The Crusades happened. Then the Inquisiton, blood libels, and pogroms. Then there was the Holocaust. Then the British Christians would not let us into Palestine. But we persevered and Israel and America saved us." This is about as valid as the old joke summarizing Jewish feasts: "They tried to kill us. They failed. Let's eat." But not as funny. And it fails utterly to begin to explain how the Jews over the centuries within Christendom survived often enough, and often enough thrived.

Jonathan Elukin in *Living Together, Living Apart: Rethinking Jewish-Christian Relations in the Middle Ages*[37] joins a distinguished list of Jewish historians such as Yosef Yerushalmi, Marc Saperstein, Michael Signer, and David Berger in presenting a fuller and more balanced account of Jewish history with all its shades of gray. He issues a conscious challenge to much of the Jewish historiography on the relations between the Jewish minority and the Christian majority in the Middle Ages. He rightly notes that the tendency to view the relationship as everywhere and always what it was at its worst in some places and at some times is a vast generalization which leads to an inability to explain both Jewish survival in the period and the continuing choice of numerous Jewish communities to stay within Christendom even when expelled from a particular country or region within it. The view of many that, following the First Crusade, Christian Europe became nothing other than an unremitting "persecuting society" against Jews and Judaism fails, he argues, to account for the continuing vitality and continual return of Jews to areas that had expelled them, or worse.

During the early Middle Ages, Jews and Christians interacted relatively peacefully within the context of a legal structure that allowed the Jews freedom of worship, a legal status accorded to no other non-Christian religious group following the ascendancy of Christianity in the Roman Empire in the fifth century. Elukin tracks the situation of Jews and their interactions with Christians in Minorca, Merovingian Gaul, Italy, and Visigothic Spain, noting the roles of St. Augustine and Pope St. Gregory the Great in enacting that vision into canon law making the popes through history the primary protectors of the Jews. Yosef Yerushalmi, in a brilliant article rebutting what I call the "straight line method" of leaping from St. John's Gospel to Auschwitz with nary a stop in between, makes the point that it was precisely because the popes, as the court of last appeal, did so often intervene to protect Jews over the centuries, that they held (and mostly still hold—another misunderstanding!) the expectation that European Christians would do the pope's bidding during the Holocaust.[38] In reality, of course, the last time a pope thought he could make a European ruler act as he wished by issuing a simple fiat was, well, Henry VIII, who divorced Catherine of Aragon anyway. Stronger statements by Pius XII might well have motivated more Catholics (surely not Lutherans or Orthodox or neo-pagans such as the Nazis) to act to save Jews, but it would not have stopped the Nazi machine of genocide. So there is much room to criticize the decision of Pius to maintain a public silence for the sake of being able to save Jews hidden in Catholic institutions in Rome and throughout Europe. But not to demonize him. Or, at this point, to sanctify him. That should wait at least until the rest of the Vatican archives for the period are released for scholarly review and study.

One must note the normality of Jewish-Christian interaction commercially and socially, but also religiously, since the two communities shared a common liturgical culture based on Scripture which made them aware even of each other's hymns, so that they could sing them together. The Jewish community of Venice contracted with a Catholic musician to write music for them that is still heard today. Efforts to entice or force Jews to convert came and went with individual bishops and local nobility, and even at different times in these bishops' lives.

The Carolingian period was marked by an attempt to establish a uniform Christian culture on the disparate areas of the empire. Representations of Jews in Christian polemics were relatively mild. Jews were seen as Pharisees, not Israelites, so offered no challenge to the Carolingian claim to be in continuity with the ancient kings of Israel. Again, as in the early Middle Ages, Jews were able, with enterprise and flexibility, to weather the storms of occasional violence and create and maintain thriving communities in Christian Europe.

The High Middle Ages, which can be defined as the period from the middle of the eleventh to the middle of the thirteenth centuries, saw a great rise in the population of Europe, victories over Muslims, movements to reform monasteries and church life, and the development of new and varied "Christian identities," which, in turn gave more room for the persistence of Jewish identities. Jews and Catholic biblical scholars conversed over the sacred texts. Disputations showed that Jews could understand Christian discourse well enough to debate it. This was the period of "the discovery of the individual" or "the discovery of the self," in which spiritual introspection came to the fore. Again, the dynamic of individual spirituality allowed room for Jewish spiritual differences.

Violent language against and violent attacks on Jews, however, culminated in the great expulsions up to the end of fifteenth century. For example, walled areas of cities were often originally created for the Jews in order to protect them from Christians coming out of churches and Passion Plays during Holy Week. Only in later centuries were these turned into areas to keep Jews in, and they became the ghettos. The word "ghetto" itself comes from the Italian "giotto," or foundry, and was simply the Jewish quarter of Venice. Tourist maps in Venice to this day give the location of the "Giotto Vecchio" and the "Giotto Nuovo." The latter is an island with one bridge, which could be closed and guarded at night. Italy, or at least the papal states, in fact, was the only country in Western Europe not to expel its Jews in the period.

With regard to verbal violence, it might be noted that similar charges of murdering children, cannibalism, desecrating the host, being agents of the devil, and depicting Jews as feral animals were commonly made in the period of many other groups than Jews: Cathars, Waldensians, Mongols, Muslims, and others. So the question is raised, in a period when anticlericalism was quite popular, as to whether the general lay populace of Europe would have taken such high clerical rhetoric literally.

Elukin, in chapter six of his book, argues that the expulsions were not inevitable outcomes of the ancient Christian teaching of contempt against Jews and Judaism, but discrete, individual acts of various monarchs, sometimes motivated by religious zeal, but most often motivated by the economics of ridding the monarchs and the nobility of debts to Jews. And, going through a country by country analysis of England, France (the most ambivalent and convoluted of all), Spain, Germany, and Italy (where the few expulsions lasted at most a decade), he notes that only the expulsion from Spain was "final." For the rest of Western Europe, Jews returned, though perhaps not in the same numbers, since many had moved to the more open and tolerant societies of equally Christian Eastern Europe, where they were welcomed as benefits to the local economy and society. Hence, he concludes, the *convivencia* ("living together") that Jewish memory ascribes solely to Spain before 1492, continued, in different ways and in different places, differently, in much of the rest of Western Europe.

More recently, Jennifer A. Harris has argued, I believe convincingly, that when looked at carefully, the Middle Ages was not a period of unrelieved negativity toward Jews and Judaism. Her essay, which cites Elukin among other Jewish and Christian scholars looking at the period today, argues that supersessionism, the idea that God abrogated His covenant with the Jews in favor of a replacement covenant with Christians, was by no means universally accepted by Christian thinkers. She analyzes the works of four of them: Bede, Aelred of Rievaux, Thomas Aquinas, and Alonso de Cartagena. In each she concludes that an acceptance of covenantal continuity, not supersession, best describes their actual thinking on this key aspect of Christian-Jewish relations over the centuries.[39] Her citations of recent scholarship in the field are most encouraging.

This being said, the real radical change in European attitudes toward Jews came, I would argue, not with such currents in Christian history, but after the Enlightenment and the rise of the modern nation-state divorced church and state finally and effectively. This lead, beginning in the seventeenth century and the development of the slave trade, and the need to justify it, to the invention of a *novum* in European history (save perhaps for the period of the *limpia de raza* legislation in Spain and Portugal, against which the Jesuits, among others, fought bitterly) and racialism, against which the church fought fitfully but increasingly effectively, as in the works of Bartolomeo de las Casas. The historian Hubert Locke, a Black Protestant, who went on to become deeply involved in Holocaust studies, noted in a conference I helped organize at Sacred Heart Seminary in 1964, when I was a student there, that such Catholic teaching against racialism and the dehumanization of slaves greatly ameliorated the conditions of slavery throughout Latin America, so that the condition and situation of slaves in those Catholic lands was much better than their treatment in North America, where the British notion that slaves were subhuman chattel to whom one could do anything, thrived. The Jesuits (again) among others argued that once a slave was baptized, he or she became fully a Christian, so that the slaves must be taught to read in order to be catechized. This did not go down well with the plantation owners and the "Black Robes" often found themselves in conflict with the civil authorities over the issue.

If a European looked inward at Europe, of course, he or she found few Africans but many Jews. So the ideology of racialism was added to the traditional Christian "teaching of contempt" against Jews and Judaism, giving birth to another *novum*: modern racial anti-Semitism. Jews could throughout Christian history convert from their "curse" by accepting Jesus and baptism, and by and large be accepted into Christian society. The racial theorists of the eighteenth century, however, denied this "cure," leaving only genocide as a "solution" to what they, in another discontinuity with European history, felt to be "the Jewish problem."

Teaching Christianity in Jewish Schools

As I have indicated above, studies of the teaching of Christianity and Jewish-Christian relations over the centuries in Jewish schools presents a problem mainly of omission rather than commission. Little is said beyond the barest of outlines. So, many Jews in this country gain what they think is an understanding of Christianity mainly from the media or stories handed down from the shtetls. One result of this is that, for many, time is frozen and there is an inability to accept the fact that *Nostra Aetate* really worked, and that the teachings of the Council have not yet penetrated down to the grass roots.

Studies of Catholic textbooks, however, such as my own doctoral dissertation for New York University and the 1992 follow up study by Philip Cunningham, have shown that what is taught in Catholic schools and religious education programs today has changed profoundly since the Second Vatican Council. The heart of *Nostra Aetate*, its twin affirmations that Jews cannot be considered in Christ's time or now to bear collective guilt for his death and the enduring nature of God's covenant with the Jewish people, have indeed permeated our Catholic classrooms, so that Catholic students, reflecting their teachers, have a far deeper and much more positive understanding of Jews and Judaism than not only their predecessors of the 1930s but also than the average graduate of public high schools in this country. What, I ask, can be more "grassroots" than our classrooms?

An ironic test case of the proposition that the Catholic Church has changed dramatically and irrevocably since the Council came with the release of Mel Gibson's *The Passion of the Christ*, which was nothing more than a glorified pre-Vatican II Passion Play. I agreed fully with Zev Garber at the time about the flaws of the movie, a position he articulated well, doubtlessly wearing jeans, as I do while writing this. Passion Plays over the centuries were the triggers that shot of the guns of pogroms over the centuries. Well, Mel pulled the trigger, but the gun did not go off. The teaching of Vatican II has indeed permeated all levels of the Catholic Church worldwide. Education, then, works.

If Jewish education in the United States is important for framing the attitudes of Jews toward Christians, how much more so is it crucial for framing the attitudes of Israeli Jews toward the tiny Christian minority in their midst, over whose lives Jews have, appropriately, full control. A recent study of Israeli school teaching about Christianity[40] contains some disturbing results which confirm those of Rabbi Ronald Kronish in the late 1980s. Israeli schools, like American Jewish schools, teach virtually nothing about Christianity. While "secular" (i.e., non-Orthodox) Jews, who make up the majority of the Jews of Israel, have relative positive attitudes toward Christians, the religious, Orthodox Jews have startlingly negative attitudes toward and laughably ignorant misunderstandings of Christians and what Christianity actually teaches. This, of course, is to be expected, since Orthodox students are much closer to the medieval traditions of the shtetls than are Jews in general. But it is something that the Israeli Jewish majority needs, I believe urgently, to correct. They have but to ask Rabbi Kronish for teaching materials and he will, I can assure the reader, provide them.

Conclusion

There remains much to do, the work of generations certainly among Christians, to repair the damaged relationship between Jews and Christians. We are only, as Cardinal Walter Kasper of the Holy See's Commission for Religious Relations with the Jews has pointed out, at the beginning of the beginning in working our way through the agenda set for all of us, Jews and Christians, by the Second Vatican Council. Setbacks seem as persistent as progress in this on both sides (e.g., the nonimplementation to this day by the State of Israel of the terms of the 1993 Fundamental Agreement between the Jewish State and the Vatican).

Both sides, I believe, are called by God to work together to pursue this God-given task. This is our joint mission in the world, to prepare the way for the coming of the Malchut Shamayim/Reign of God, which will, we equally believe, be inaugurated by the coming or return of the Messiah of Israel.

We may not be able to finish the task in our lifetimes. But as the rabbis ask, "If not us, who? And if not now, when?"

Discussion Questions

1. Is Christianity, as developed especially in the writings of St. Paul and St. Augustine, inherently and necessarily antisemitic? If so, why so, if not, why not"
2. What are the differences and/or similarities between Christian and Jewish asceticism?
3. Is it valid to speak about Christianity in general, or, like Judaism, must it be considered within its own internal pluralism? Give examples.

Notes

1. Eugene Fisher, *Faith Without Prejudice: Rebuilding Christian Attitudes Toward Jews and Judaism*, 2nd. ed. (New York: Crossroad, 1993).
2. Amy-Jill Levine, *The Misunderstood Jew: the Church and the Scandal of the Jewish Jesus* (San Francisco: HarperSanFrancisco, 2006).
3. Once in a while a classmate would slip and let loose a disparaging comment about the goyim, then look at me belatedly, realizing I was one and that he or she had forgotten. I considered this a compliment and said so, referring to the fact that God had the temerity to call Abraham a "*goy gadol*," so I could hardly take umbrage at the term! That usually broke the ice.
4. Eugene Fisher, "Typical Jewish Misunderstandings of Christianity," *Judaism* 22, no. 1 (1973): 21-32.

5. Promulgated on October 26, 1965, the title is derived from its first words in Latin, which are translated as "In Our Time" or, as many Jews preferred, "It's About Time!"
6. Naomi W. Cohen, *What the Rabbis Said: The Public Discourse of Nineteenth-Century American Rabbis* (New York: New York University Press, 2008) shows that this assertion of the ethical superiority of Judaism to Christianity was a major theme of rabbinical discourse in the late nineteenth and into the twentieth century. This is not surprising since many of the early rabbis were trained in Germany.
7. Julius Wellhausen, *Geschichte Israels* (1878) published in 2nd edition (1883) as *Prologomena zur Geschichte Israels.*
8. Given the reliance of *Nostra Aetate*, no. 4, on especially the new understandings of St. Paul in Romans 9-11, it can be stated unequivocally that without Pius XII the new understanding of Judaism that came out of the Second Vatican Council would have been impossible. The chief drafter of *Nostra Aetate*, of course, was Augustin Cardinal Bea, who was a close confidant of both Pius and John XXIII and who was a biblical scholar. *Nostra Aetate* was noteworthy among conciliar documents in not referencing the Fathers of the church but going back directly to the New Testament and its key passage on how Judaism is to be understood *post-Christum*. See Eugene J. Fisher, "The Impact of Christian-Jewish Dialogue on Catholic Biblical Studies," *Studies in Christian-Jewish Relations* 3, no. 1 (2008): Article 20, CP-1.
9. The reaction of Christian polemic was only one pole of the motivation behind the Science of Judaism. Deeper was the need for new definitions of self-identity in the face of the dangers of assimilation. See H. M. Sacher, *The Course of Modern Jewish History* (New York: Dell, 1967) and David Rudavsky, *Emancipation and Adjustment* (New York: Diplomatic Press, 1967). Ahad Haam's essay "Imitation and Assimilation" in Leon Simon, ed., *Selected Essays of Ahad Ha-'Am* (Cleveland: World Publishing, 1962), 67-79, illustrates the difficulties of the period.
10. Immanuel Wolf, "On the Concept of a Science of Judaism," trans. Lionel Kochan, *Yearbook 11* (1822; London: Leo Baeck Institute, 1957), 194-204.
11. Cohen, *supra*, records the leeriness of American Jews, especially Reform Jews, about Zionism, e.g., the Pittsburgh Platform.
12. One can find an excellent summary of the reflections on the death penalty in rabbinic Judaism over the centuries and the much more recent rejection of it by the Catholic Church in the 1999 statement of the Consultation between the National Council of Synagogues and the US Conference of Catholic Bishops on the website of the USCCB, http://www.usccb.org/comm/archives/1999/99-288.shtml.
13. See, for example, such disparate writers as Isidore Epstein, *Judaism: A Historical Presentation* (Harmondworth: Penguin Books, 1959), 12 and Julius Guttmann, *Philosophies of Judaism* (New York: Anchor, 1964), 3-19.
14. E.g., Max I Dimont, *Jews, God and History* (New York: Simon and Schuster, 1962). The pervasiveness of such views can be seen from the fact that this work was a best seller. Dimont's *The Indestructible Jews* (New York: World, 1971) echoes Geiger in speaking of a Jewish "manifest destiny" which moves in three "acts" coached by a divine director. "Whereas each sunken civilization remains submerged, the Jews emerge time and again from seeming doom, riding the crest of a new civilization rolling where the old one once flowed."
15. Henry Siegman, "Dialogue with Christians: A Jewish dilemma," *Judaism* 20, no. 1 (1971): 93.

16. The Bishops' Clarification can be found on their website www.usccb.org. The 2002 statement "Reflections on Covenant and Mission" can be found on www.bc.edu/cjlearning. Berger was quite right to raise concerns about the 2009 statement, which raised more questions than it answered and was itself very ambiguous in many ways.
17. Cited in Jacub R. Marcus, *The Jew in the Medieval World* (New York: Atheneum, 1969), 422-24.
18. Trude Weiss-Rosmarin, *Judaism and Christianity: The Differences* (New York: Jonathan David, 1968), 142.
19. S. Giora Shoham in *Valhalla, Calvary & Auschwitz* (Cincinnati: Bowman and Cody, Tel Aviv University: Ramot, 1995), while providing fresh instights and perspectives on a number of issues, ascribes to the "Christianity as Hellenized Judaism" model, though he reserves the "other-worldly" category to Catholicism and adds a notion I had never heard before, that Catholicism views labor as evil, stating that "we have ample proof that Catholics' other-worldly orientation and their conception of labor as a curse and a corollary of original sin . . . make them less achievement-motivated than Protestants" (16). While Genesis does portray labor as more difficult outside of the Garden of Eden (and childbirth more painful), the long line of social encyclicals by the popes starting at the turn of the twentieth century clearly extol the dignity of labor and the worth of the laborer. Nor is it accidental that the labor movement in the United States was largely a Catholic-Jewish enterprise. So while there is truth to the Protestant work ethic notion that Shoham evokes, this resulted in an intensification of achievement orientation, but Catholicism has never really taught that labor was or is evil in itself.
20. Ahad Haam, "Flesh and Spirit," in *Selected Essays of Ahad Haam*, trans. Leon Simon (New York: Meridian, 1962), 152.
21. Bahya b. Joseph ibn Pakuda, *Duties of the Heart*, vol. 2, trans. Moses Hyamson (Jerusalem: Feldheim, 1970), 288-90.
22. Ahad Haam, "Flesh and Spirit,"139.
23. Nedarim 10a; Sifri, Naso # 30 (ed. Friedman, p. 10). See *Yerushalmi Kiddushin* IV, end.
24. Matthew V. Novenson, "The Jewish Messiahs, the Pauline Christ, and the Gentile Question," *Journal of Biblical Literature* 128, no.2 (2009): 357.
25. Harris Lenowitz, *The Jewish Messiah's from the Galilee to Crown Heights* (New York: Oxford University Press, 1998), 7.
26. Michael J. Cook, *Modern Jews Engage the New Testament: Enhancing Jewish Well-Being in a Christian Environment* (Woodstock, VT: Jewish Lights, 2008)
27. Leslie Dewart, *The Future of Belief* (New York: Herder and Herder, 1967).
28. Eliezer Berkovits, "Death of a God," *Judaism* 20, no. 1 (1971): 79.
29. "Pastoral Constitution on the Church in the Modern World," in *The Documents of Vatican II, Translated from the Latin,* ed. Walter M. Abbott and trans. Joseph Gallagher (New York: Guild Press, 1966), 199-200.
30. Martin Buber, *Two Types of Faith* (New York: Harper Torchbooks, 1961), 34. Buber's approach is essentially an existential version of that of Mendellsohn and the Science of Judaism. He states: "The difference between 'It is true' and the other 'we believe and know' is not that of two expressions of faith, but of two kinds of faith. For the first, faith is a position in which one stands, for the second, it is an event which has occurred to one, or an act which one has affected or affects, or rather both at once" (35).

31. In his preface to *Two Types of Faith*, Buber mentions four Christian theologians as influencing the development of his theory: Rudolf Bultmann, Albert Schweitzer, Rudolf Otto, and Leonard Ragazo. Note the German Protestants. Soren Kierkegaard was another strong influence. And Kierkegaard was definitely strongly ascetic, otherworldly and committed to a blind faith (the "leap") approach. Buber's error was in failing to view these men in the context of Christianity as a whole, rather than equating it with them.
32. Rudavsky, *Emancipation and Adjustment*, 124.
33. See Gershom Scholem, *Major Trends in Jewish Mysticism* (New York: Schocken, 1961), 289-99.
34. J. Dillenberger and C. Welch, *Protestant Christianity* (New York: Scribner, 1954), 41.
35. Paula Frederiksen, *Augustine and the Jews: A Christian Defense of Jews and Judaism* (New York: Doubleday, 2008).
36. Robert Chazan, *European Jewry and the First Crusade* (Berkeley: University of California Press, 1996).
37. Jonathan Elukin, *Living Together, Living Apart: Rethinking Jewish-Christian Relations in the Middle Ages* (Princeton: Princeton University Press, 2007).
38. Yosef Hayim Yerushalmi, "Response to Reuther," in *Auschwitz: Beginning of a New Era? Reflections on the Holocaust*, ed. Eva Fleischner (New York: KTAV/Cathedral Church of St. John the Divine/Anti-Defamation League, 1977), 97-108. It is ironic to note that Reuther, who bemused most Jews, except scholars such as Yerushalmi, with her sweeping statements condemning Christianity, went on to write *The Wrath of Jonah: The Crisis of Religious Nationalism in the Israeli-Palestinian Conflict*, (Minneapolis: Augsburg Fortress Press, 2002), which has become a classic in the field of pro-Palestinian, anti-Israel, anti-Zionist literature of the period.
39. Jennifer A. Harris, "Enduring Covenant in the Christian Middle Ages," *Journal of Ecumenical Studies* 44, no. 4 (2009): 563-86.
40. "Should Christianity be Taught in Israeli Schools?" YnetNews.com: Israel Fax, February 25, 2009.

Section 3

Teaching, Dialogue, Reclamation: Contemporary Views on the Jewish Jesus

How Credible Is Jewish Scholarship on Jesus?

Michael J. Cook

This essay explores the problem of the methodological credibility of Jewish scholarship on Jesus. My prism will be a number of "favorite" Gospel topics toward which Jews most often gravitate:

- Jesus' Last Supper
- his Sanhedrin trial
- his "blasphemy" verdict
- his pairing with Barabbas
- his Jewish opponents
- his partiality for the "lost sheep . . . of Israel"
- his Jewish observances
- his Passion-week outline
- his intent to "fulfill" the Law

I am often asked by Christian scholars why Jews overly accept the Gospels' basic historical "facts" about Jesus. They ask also in writing—for example, Donald Hagner: "modern Jewish scholars . . . on the whole . . . surprisingly tend to ascribe more reliability to these materials than do many of the more radical non-Jewish critics."[1] Some Jews have agreed—for example, Samuel Sandmel: "I am sometimes aghast at the amateurishness of Jewish scholars in Christian literature," at "the almost fundamentalism of some Jewish scholars when they approach the Gospels"[2]; also Trude Weiss-Rosmarin: "Jewish historians tend to accept the Gospel data on Jesus as basically factual. . . . They take issue with the Gospel accounts of his trial and death as if they were history."[3]

If we Jews predicate our analyses of Jesus on events about whose very occurrence many Christian scholars entertain doubts, I feel not only that our credibility in their eyes suffers but also that the closing of this chasm devolves upon us, and via three avenues: 1) fuller exposure to Christian scholarship; 2) fuller sensitivity to the problems the Gospel writers felt constrained to address; and 3) fuller recognition of the techniques early Christian writers applied to resolve those problems—techniques I have named "Gospel Dynamics."

Giving Christian Scholarship Its Due

When we Jews by-pass Christian scholarship and plunge directly into Gospel studies, we can appear to commit trespass—securing entry without paying our admission fee. Given the long and enormous accrual of Christian scholarship, the Gospels appear an ever-enlarging smorgasbord of contrasting "data," with different Jesus profiles proliferating depending upon how selected passages are arrayed. Hence the mushrooming of creditable (although not uniformly respectable) Christian efforts showing Jesus to have been a pacifist or militant, prophet, apocalypticist, Pharisee, reformer, liberator, Essene, charismatic, magician, healer-exorcist, cynic-philosopher, savior, even pure myth (or combinations of these). Thus multiple Jesuses are projected simultaneously on the same screen, frustrating confident retrieval of the original. Another impediment is that peculiar tendency of different generations of Christian researchers to reconceptualize Jesus more as they are than as he was (likened to peering down a well at the "person below," really one's self-image reflected).[4]

If there are cogent reasons why Christian scholars themselves have reached this impasse, then should not Jewish scholars become fully versed in how this predicament evolved? Most rewarding is an immersion in the history of Christian scholarship commencing with early nineteenth-century writers. For it has now indeed been over 200 years that brilliant Christian minds have refined methods to determine who the historical Jesus was only to see findings by one generation of scholars significantly modified, even overturned, by some succeeding enterprise. That Christian "quests" for the historical Jesus—spurts of research extending decades at a time—are numbered signals that interim periods have been essentially calls for "time-out," for giving up the venture altogether, or possibly for reversions to earlier conventional views. But the inevitable effect of reading these past giants is not simply deepening our knowledge but what is even more impactful still: altering our very thinking patterns. Thus, while the conclusions I will impart in this essay are Jewish as well as original, my process of reaching them I owe to the absorption of Christian scholarship.

Given that almost all Jewish scholars are far less steeped in Gospel scholarship than are our Christian counterparts, why presume that we can succeed where they have admitted limited, even no, success? We may bear special expertise (e.g., in rabbinics) or, seeing matters from different vantage points, feel we have something distinctive to contribute. But inevitably, if we are perceived as cutting corners, then analyses we offer will seem suspect.

Giving Early Church Problems Their Due

Gospel traditions became reshaped, even invented outright, to solve problems arising for Jesus' followers between his death and the Gospels' completion. Respecting many Gospel texts, Jews often fail to ask: does this tradition reflect factual history or, instead, early Church problem-solving? I categorize such problems (with some examples) as follows:

Some Problems Internal to Early Christian Communities

a. Discomfort over perceptions that Jesus had died a victim
b. Pressure to redefine "Messiah" in view of Jesus' crucifixion
c. Impatience, frustration, or doubt over delay in the second coming
d. Anxiety over betrayals of Christians to Rome

Some Problems External to Early Christian Communities

Vis-à-vis Rome

e. How to stem Roman persecution of Christians
f. How to disassociate Christians from the image of Jewish rebels (66-73 CE)
g. How to persuade Rome that Jesus' crucifixion should not stigmatize his later followers as seditionists
h. How to shift blame for Jesus' death from Rome to another party (the Jews)
i. How to convey that Jesus was condemned only for "blasphemy" (of no concern to Rome)

Vis-à-vis the Jews

j. How to establish that Jesus was the Messiah despite claims that he failed to fulfill Jewish expectations
k. How to account for why Jews rejected the very Messiah who came for them
l. How to demonstrate that Jewish scriptures predicted Jesus
m. How to show the applicability of Jewish festivals to Christianity
n. How to refine the chosen people concept so as to incorporate Gentile Christians
o. How to justify departures from the Law of Moses by Gentile Christians
p. How to refute Jews' denials of Jesus' resurrection
q. How to cope with ejections of some Jewish Christians from the synagogue

Vis-à-vis Others

r. How to compete with the rival John the Baptist movement
s. How to counter gnostic denials that the Christ took on flesh

Giving "Gospel Dynamics" Their Due

I have coined the umbrella term "Gospel dynamics" to designate those skillful techniques by which early Christian writers came to refine their conceptualizations of Jesus himself so as to address the very type of problems enumerated just above—problems germane to the authors' later day but less so, if indeed at all, to his. I name sixteen such techniques: aggrandizement, attenuation, conformance, improvisation, reinterpretation, retrojection, theologizing demography, theologizing geography, typology, and so forth.[5] Whenever we have good reason to suspect that given Gospel traditions, ostensibly about Jesus, instead enlist him primarily to address problems arising only after he died, I contend we are then on the trail of Gospel dynamics. Vigilance in spotting the underlying operation of Gospel dynamics is a key to enhancing Jewish credibility in Jesus research.

Selected Analyses

Respecting those nine favorite Jewish subjects that we will examine now, I showcase in the first five the Gospel of Mark—whose determinative impact I believe many Jewish scholars severely underestimate. (Readers who wish to scrutinize my reasoning here in further depth may consult my volume, *Modern Jews Engage the New Testament.*[6])

The Last Supper and Passover

All four Gospels fix the Last Supper on Thursday night, with Jesus' death on the following Friday afternoon. But they disagree over when the Passover meal itself fell. Mark (14:12-16), upon whom Matthew (26:17) and Luke (22:7) depend, sets the Passover meal Thursday night, coincident with the Last Supper; but John distinguishes the two meals, setting the Passover meal the following night, Friday, directly after the Passover lambs' sacrifice that Friday afternoon (13:1-2; 18:28; 19:14, 31-36). In Paul's sole Last Supper allusion (1 Cor. 11:23), he designates the bread that Jesus broke as *artos*, the term normally understood to mean "leavened."

Understandably, Jewish scholars interested in whether the Last Supper was a Passover observance are eager to determine whose chronology is correct: the Synoptists' or John's. But careful analysis of Mark alone reveals how off the mark many Jewish studies on this question may be, since the difference in reportage by Mark and John is purely theology and not at all, as we may misassume, history.

The entire Last Supper-Passover problem pivots on but a sole five-verse paragraph, Mark 14:12-16:

> And on the first day of Unleavened Bread, when they sacrificed the Passover Lamb, his disciples said to him, "Where will you have us . . . prepare for you to eat the Passover?" And he sent two of his disciples: . . . "Go into the city, and a man carrying a jar of water will meet you; . . . wherever he enters, say to the householder, 'The Teacher says, "Where is my guest room, where I am to eat the Passover with my disciples?"' And he will show you a large upper room furnished and ready; there prepare for us." And the disciples . . . went to the city and found it as he had told them; and they prepared the Passover.

I contend that Mark himself crafted and inserted this unit into the original written tradition he inherited, with Matthew and Luke, knowing no differently, dutifully replicating what Mark had done. Only consider these four major anomalies in Mark's brief account—I term them "anomalies" because Mark's Passover paragraph does not sit well with the surrounding material.

> Anomaly 1. Rupture in the story line: In Mark 14:2 ("not during the feast"), the authorities intend to dispose of Jesus before the festival. Yet, in 14:12, the feast has already arrived when the Last Supper (here, a Passover meal) commences. If something went amiss with the original planned timetable to arrest Jesus, then we should expect to be told what went awry. If nothing went amiss, and Jesus was indeed arrested before the feast, then clearly his Last Supper could not be a Passover meal. Instead, however, Mark leaves these two chronologies unreconciled, a confusion which has spawned imaginative (but ill-advised) proposals that Jesus' group followed a calendar different from that of the establishment—for example, that at Qumran.[7]
>
> Anomaly 2. Unnatural concentration of all Passover material: All Passover material found in Mark is unnaturally compressed into but this one paragraph (14:12-16). Nothing outside verses 12-16 hints that the feast has yet arrived. Had the Last Supper genuinely been a Passover meal, allusions to Passover's arrival should recur throughout the encompassing narrative.
>
> Anomaly 3. Telltale omissions: Curiously unmentioned in Mark's Last Supper account are constituent elements of Passover observance: the Exodus, bitter herbs, lamb (the main food), even matzah (only regular bread[8] is present; see also Mark 14:22; 1 Cor. 11:23).
>
> Anomaly 4. A mathematical error: In verses 12-16, Jesus sends two disciples from Bethany to Jerusalem to prepare the Passover meal. When Jesus himself comes, only ten disciples remain available to accompany him. But in verse 17 "he came with the twelve," even though the two who went to Jerusalem do not appear to have rejoined the group. While "the twelve" could here be but a formula meaning members of Jesus' inner circle irrespective of the exact number present, Matthew and Luke themselves conclude that Mark made a subtraction error. This is why Matthew adjusts Jesus "came with the

twelve" to "sat at table with the twelve" (26:20),[9] and why Luke changes "he came" into "the hour came" (22:14).

All four anomalies are instantly resolved by one simple recognition: that Mark has folded a single Passover Meal paragraph (14:12-16) into an earlier story line that was resistant to it, a new-time line (introducing the Passover meal) superimposed upon the original (devoid of one). Thus, if we delete the Passover Meal unit (12-16):

1. we no longer wonder why the plan to arrest Jesus before the feast failed because, without these verses, the plan succeeded;
2. we understand why all Passover material is concentrated into but one paragraph—because Mark himself inserted this extraneous paragraph as a filter through which he wanted us to understand the Last Supper;
3. we can explain why the meal lacks Passover motifs (lamb; matzah, etc.)—because in transforming the Last Supper into a Passover meal, Mark forgot or did not know to include the key components;
4. we can solve the mathematical anomaly since, without this paragraph, there was no Passover meal to prepare, and consequently no sending of two disciples ahead to prepare it—so when Jesus arrived for his Last Supper (now, only an ordinary meal) he could indeed have come "with the [literal] twelve," as per verse 17.

While the clues from these four anomalies are enough to crumble the entire case for the Last Supper as a Passover meal, here are three more. Anomaly 5: Mark's chronology sets Jesus' Thursday night trial on the first day of Unleavened Bread (Nisan 15). This oddity—a capital case on a Jewish holiday—vanishes once we excise 14:12-16, for then the trial would precede Passover. Anomaly 6: the wording of Mark 14:12 is odd ("And on the first day of Unleavened Bread, when they sacrificed the Passover Lamb"). Here Passover's one day, Nisan 14, appears absorbed into the seven days of Unleavened Bread, Nisan 15-21. Is this a telltale clue that the Passover paragraph was composed after the Temple's destruction in 70 CE, which ended the sacrifice of lambs? Anomaly 7: why is the verb here incorrect, since the lamb was "eaten" on Nisan 15, not "sacrificed" (which would be the late afternoon of Nisan 14)?

Even if we demote anomalies 5-7 to second rank,[10] all seven point to the same solution: Mark has inserted a single paragraph (14:12-16) as a theological lens through which he wished the story of Jesus' Last Supper now to be understood. As for his motive, I believe he wanted to correlate Passover, festival of freedom for the Jews, with Jesus' death and resurrection, bringing freedom for humanity. Meanwhile, John's twenty-four hour disjuncture between the Last Supper and the Passover meal is likewise theological: to present Jesus' death as coincident with that of the paschal lamb.[11] Since the lamb had to die before the Passover meal, this required John to set the Passover meal on Friday night, after Jesus' death that previous afternoon.

These two options, Passover meal (Mark) or Passover lamb (John), were mutually exclusive, so only one could be incorporated by any evangelist: Jesus as the paschal lamb (in John) could not be alive at the Passover meal Friday night, so his Thursday night Last Supper had to be but an ordinary meal; or, if he did attend a Passover meal (as in Mark), he could not be identified with the paschal lamb which had to have died beforehand.

The bottom line is that this kind of analysis is more credible than those Jewish treatises on the Last Supper which presume Mark conveys actual history instead of theology. The error that much of Jewish scholarship most consistently commits is approaching Gospel events as if they were history.

Jesus' Sanhedrin Trial

On no other Gospel subject has Jewish scholarship generally gone more awry than on that of Jesus' supposed trial. In Mark 14:53-72, Jesus undergoes a night-time Sanhedrin trial headed by the high priest, with the jurors consisting of "chief priests, elders, and scribes." When Jesus affirms that he is "the Christ, the Son of the Blessed," the high priest decries this "blasphemy." The Sanhedrin then condemns Jesus as deserving death.

I submit that the proper place to begin treating this subject is with what I term the two "delivery" texts in Mark 14:53 followed by 15:1. Each relates Jesus' delivery to an authority figure. The first (14:53) shows an arresting party on Thursday night capturing Jesus in Gethsemane and then delivering him to the high priest Caiaphas[12]; the second (15:1) relates how, Friday morning, Jewish authorities held a "consultation" and delivered Jesus to the Roman prefect, Pontius Pilate.

Note how much of the entire Passion story line these two delivery verses capture and convey: "And they led Jesus to the high priest. . . . And as soon as it was morning the chief priests, with the elders and scribes, . . . held a consultation; and they bound Jesus and led him away and delivered him to Pilate."[13] Nothing yet establishes that these two delivery passages were once juxtaposed (i.e., connected). But observe how the story they relate effectively proceeds with no Thursday night Sanhedrin trial at all! Further note how the function of any Thursday night trial is here seemingly already co-opted by Friday's morning's "consultation"—which could have been redundant had a Thursday night trial genuinely transpired. For after a full-fledged night trial what precisely remained to consult about the next morning and why is the full complement of the same personnel required to attend again?

Starkly, put, all these curious factors converge: Thursday night's trial could be duplicative of Friday morning's consultation. The two delivery texts alone likely convey an earlier skeletal story: on Thursday night, Caiaphas received the captive Jesus, and nothing more occurred; then on Friday morning, he convened a (mere) "consultation" to report on this to the not-previously present "chief priests, with the elders and scribes." Thereafter Jesus was delivered to Pilate.

As for the personnel needed to staff the invented Thursday night trial, Mark borrowed "the chief priests, with the elders and scribes" from Friday morning's "consultation" (15:1)—extending their hours of service back into Thursday night, early enough for them to be on hand when the captive Jesus arrived for trial. Note that, of Mark's mentions of this triad (8:31; 11:27; 14:43, 53; 15:1), only in these two (14:53; 15:1) do the "elders" occupy the second slot of the three groups—possibly a telltale clue that Mark drew these personnel from the second delivery text (15:1) back into the first (14:53).

The fiction of Thursday night's full trial was triggered by the Gospel dynamic I term "aggrandizement." Theologically, how woefully inadequate, even insulting to the Son of God, was a mere "consultation" Friday morning without his speaking (or even his presence?). Nothing less than a full-fledged trial before the supreme court of the land could possibly suffice and also more clearly implicate the entire Jewish nation in his death! Thus was Friday morning's "consultation" trumped by its aggrandized but wholly fictional counterpart version, which was invented and inserted between the two delivery texts—with the story of Peter's denial later sandwiched around it.[14] The primitive story line simply had progressed with no Thursday night Sanhedrin trial at all.

Pointing in the same direction is the sheer skimpiness of the purported trial (14:55-65) which betrays its makeshift construction. Essentially we have here but a crude mosaic of five accruing and rather incohesive layers:

- Layer A (55-56) shows the Sanhedrin as predisposed to condemn Jesus.
- Layer B (57-59) virtually repeats the previous verse. Because verse 56 neglected to specify the content of the false witness, layer B now provides it.
- Layer C (60-62) seeks to supply words that were ascribed to more important persons, Jesus and Caiaphas.
- Layer D (63-64) conveys Mark's key message: that Jesus' strident response to Caiaphas constituted blasphemy (not sedition, which would have been Rome's chief concern).
- Layer E (65) concludes the episode.

Respecting the high priest's two queries, Mark drew their cadence and format from the two speaking parts he assigns Pontius Pilate roughly a dozen verses later. And the clashing demeanors of Jesus' two Sanhedrin responses—silence, then stridence—result simply from Mark's harnessing Jesus to two clashing proof-texts: the silence of Isaiah's Suffering Servant (53:7: "he opened not his mouth"); and the stridence of the apocalyptic "Son of man" text from Daniel 7:13 (aided by Ps. 110:1).

In sum, like the Passover unit, the Sanhedrin trial unit is constructed to address Mark's own purposes: replacing Rome with the Jews as the villains of the piece; replacing Pilate with the (Jewish) high priest as determiner of Jesus' death; and replacing a verdict of sedition (a crime of great concern to Rome) with blasphemy (a crime of no concern to Rome). Yet although the Sanhedrin account is not reported but only created history, not science but only art, how many Jewish scholars have written reams about an actual Thursday night trial that appears never to have happened, and then embarked on the standard but irrelevant practice of heaping up literally a score of procedural discrepancies between Jesus' Gospel Sanhedrin trial and Talmudic capital cases. Such analyses hardly redound to our credibility. (In 1988, even the conservative National Conference of Catholic Bishops expressed doubts concerning the trial's historicity.[15])

Condemnation for Blasphemy

Many Jewish scholars pursue whether Jesus could have been guilty of committing "blasphemy" at his trial. Here the chief preliminary bypassed (besides failing to confirm that there was a trial) is the Gospel dynamic of "retrojection": Christians of the Evangelists' post-70 age, hearing themselves maligned by contemporary Jews as "blasphemers" for exalting Jesus as more than human, naturally presupposed blasphemy as the charge of which Jesus himself was likewise accused. That, hardly genuine history, is how the "blasphemy" motif came to culminate the fictional trial-narrative. Further, with the placard on Jesus' cross reading "King of the Jews" (signaling sedition), later Christians, wary of being so stigmatized, could displace sedition with "blasphemy" (of no concern to Rome).

Observe how Mark extends chapter 14's "blasphemy" pronouncement back twelve chapters to the healing of the paralytic opening chapter 2: "Some . . . *scribes* . . . questioned . . . 'Why does this man speak thus? It is blasphemy!'" Christian scholars already nearly a century ago[16] recognized that Mark here inserted an extraneous five to six verses that lack thematic connection to the surrounding paralytic story. My explanation: Mark wanted to get "blasphemy" on stage as early as possible, and to have it verbalized no less than by Sanhedrin personnel themselves ("scribes"), so as to foreshadow the verdict Mark intended for the trial in chapter 14.

Pairing with Barabbas

Jewish scholars are understandably exercised by the account that Jews as a mob demanded Jesus' crucifixion. We are told, first in Mark, that Pilate offered the Jewish crowd release of a criminal of their choice: either Jesus or Barabbas (an insurrectionist). Exhorted by their priests, the Jews opted for Barabbas, demanding that Pilate crucify Jesus. Disposed to free Jesus, but wishing to appease the crowd, Pilate consigned Jesus to the cross. Thus all blame for Jesus' death falls upon the Jews. (Here is where Matthew inserts 27:25, the infamous blood curse: "his blood be on us and on our children!")

As with the inserted Passover, Sanhedrin, and blasphemy units, the Barabbas episode (15:6-15a) likewise appears anomalous in context. Besides the lack of evidence confirming any such prisoner-release custom, it is inconceivable that Pilate would tolerate a process (freeing the insurrectionist Barabbas) that could compromise law and order. Further, what logic was there in arresting the popular Jesus—recall his Palm Sunday entry (11:8-10)—thereby guaranteeing him as an odds-on favorite for release but several days later? Mark himself, noticing this discordance, requires the chief priests to stir up the Jewish crowd against Jesus.

Some scholars will insist that the crowd before Pilate was different from that welcoming Jesus on Palm Sunday. Again, this penchant for assuming, and then finding the means for defending, Mark's historical reliability can be our undoing. We have here the same Markan editorial fingerprinting as in the Passover, Sanhedrin, and blasphemy units: Mark has inserted a Barabbas unit between 15:5 and 15:15b but neglected to smooth out the inconsistencies he thereby introduces. Omit Barabbas (15:6-15a) and our problems vanish: the illogic of arresting a popular candidate just in time for a supposed popular-criminal release, and the absurdity of Pilate's freeing an insurrectionist (a custom for which we lack all evidence in any event). Only note how smoothly the narrative reads once we excise Barabbas: "But Jesus made no answer, so that Pilate wondered, and having scourged Jesus, he delivered him to be crucified" (15:5, 15b).

As with the previous examples, once we mistake fictional Gospel data for genuine history, and then base our lectures and publications thereupon, we compromise our status.

Jewish Leadership Groups

Controversy traditions between Jesus and Jewish leaders (scribes, Pharisees, Sadducees, chief priests, etc.) obviously interest Jewish scholars attempting to define pre-70 Judaisms and Jesus' distinctiveness therefrom; and in tracing escalating hostilities between Jesus and his opponents. Yet always overlooked is this preliminary: the peculiar choreography of the groups' placement throughout Mark's Gospel. Five Jewish leadership groups share the desire to have Jesus arrested and executed. Why then are they compartmentalized into two utterly separate camps?

1. Chief priests and scribes and elders
2. Pharisees and Herodians.

Never in fourteen appearances[17] do the chief priests, in one camp, encounter, much less conspire with, either Pharisees or Herodians in the other. Elders as a leadership group never meet Pharisees or Herodians. In twenty-one appearances, scribes are never mentioned with Herodians nor with Pharisees either, aside from two incidental exceptions which I argue[18] reflect Mark's editorial need to bring Jerusalem-based scribes into Galilee (7:1,5; see also 2:16).

Aside from these camps' radical segregation are the rigid partnerships of the members within each grouping: Herodians never act or appear independently; their partners, the Pharisees, are always bracketed with them. If elders are mentioned, one will find the chief priests mentioned in the same breath, and usually the scribes as well. Not even the powerful chief priests appear alone; nine times they are bracketed with one or both of their usual allies, scribes or elders; and the five instances when they seem independent are only illusory.[19] But scribes are a different story: they appear alone eight times (1:22; 2:6; 3:22; 9:11, 14; 12:28, 35, 38). How do we explain why they are the sole exception?

Thus, before accepting them as genuinely historical traditions of Jesus' encounters with these enemy groups, Jewish scholars should see in the above odd schematization a cause for pause. The sole solution I can devise here is that Mark drew upon, and manipulated as he saw fit, three written collections presenting Jewish leadership groups:

- An early Passion Narrative informing him about "chief priests, scribes, and elders" in Jerusalem (underlying 14:1-2, 43; 15:1, 3-5, 15b, 21, 26, 34, 37).
- A collection concerning scribes only, set in Jerusalem or assigned there by Mark (underlying 12:18-34a, 35-40; 9:11-12a, 13ab).
- A collection involving Pharisees and Herodians, either set in Galilee or assigned there by Mark (underlying 7:1-2, 5; 2:15-3:5; 12:13-17, 34b; 3:6).

Such origins would help explain why all the Gospel writers themselves (including John) are so unclear concerning who these Jewish leadership groups actually were in Jesus' time: these authors did not adequately define and describe them or distinguish among them because they could not. "Chief priests," "Herodians," and "elders" are merely amorphous constructs and, except for "Pharisees," not one of these groups was likely active post-70—and even about the Pharisees themselves Mark seems but skimpily informed (7:3-4).

Matthew and Luke, wholly dependent on Mark for all the groups, cannot discover what distinguished scribes from Pharisees because it is not evident from Mark whether anything did. Hence Matthew 23's peculiar repeated bracketing of "scribes, Pharisees, hypocrites!" and Matthew's occasional substitution of Pharisees where Mark has scribes[20]—all because Matthew cannot, based on Mark, differentiate one group from the other. Luke, meanwhile, figures out what they have in common and thereby adds to the mix two additional groups: "lawyers" (10:25; 11:46,52) and "teachers of the law" (5:17; Acts 5:34).

I believe that Mark derived "Pharisees" from one of his three sources but that in his other two sources this same element was called by an earlier term, "scribes." Is this analogous to the rabbinic term, sopherim ("scribes"), who often appear as predecessors—in their essentially equivalent duties—to *perushim* ("Pharisees")?[21] In any event, not realizing the equivalence of the two groups ("scribes," "Pharisees"), Mark misunderstood this one essentially self-same element as, instead, two distinct societal components and this is what prompted the confusion by Matthew and Luke in distinguishing them.

No more, then, should Jewish scholars triumphantly remark on the absence of Pharisees from Mark's Passion Narrative—for are not scribes present? Further, can Jewish scholars in all confidence now discuss any of these groups as they appear in the Gospels, once realizing how tenuous the underpinnings of such traditions actually are?

"Lost Sheep of . . . Israel"

Cited with extraordinary frequency by Jewish scholars are the two dramatic passages, unique to Matthew, which cast Jesus as concerned not at all with Gentiles but solely with the Jews. When his disciples embark on their mission, Jesus charges them: "Go nowhere among the Gentiles, and enter no town of the Samaritans, but go rather to the lost sheep of the house of Israel" (10:5-6)—that is, the lost sheep who constitute the house of Israel.[22] And when implored to heal the daughter of a Canaanite woman, Jesus intensifies this warning: "I was sent only to the lost sheep of the house of Israel" (15:24)—not simply to the Jews primarily but to the Jews alone.

I believe that most Jewish scholars quote these two texts without due regard to how these originated or why such a consideration would matter. If, yes, Jesus genuinely did utter them, he could thereby be affirming his personal commitment to fellow Jews. But if these passages arose instead from a Jewish Christian wing of a church pressing its interest against some rival Gentile Christian element, then these two texts might not characterize Jesus himself at all. Or if it was Matthew's final redactor himself who gave rise to these statements, they could reflect his attitude towards the Jews but not necessarily that of Jesus. Also, possibilities can be combined—for example, this editor could advance personal views to which the historical Jesus might also have subscribed.

In any event, are we seriously to entertain the bizarre notion that, had Jesus not issued this kind of directive, his disciples would of their own accord have embarked upon evangelizing Gentiles? Only well after Jesus' ministry was the idea of recruiting Gentiles introduced to Jesus' Jewish followers—and it then evoked consternation from the "pillars" of Jerusalem's church (see Gal 1:18-2:21). Further, at our current stage in the story line (reflected by Matt. 10 and 15), the Jesus movement is only fledgling. Jesus' disciples are unsophisticated (4:18-22; 9:9; see also 10:1-4). Could they intelligibly articulate a message of a coming kingdom to Gentiles in terms that could be comprehended, let alone be found appealing? During Jesus' ministry itself, "a more unnecessary prohibition [than going to the

Gentiles] can hardly be imagined."[23] Why, then, do Jewish scholars so confidently cite these texts as if Jesus himself uttered them?

Given this predicament, a yet more vital preliminary can go overlooked in Jewish scholarship: the question of whether the intent of these two passages may be precisely the opposite of what Jewish scholars often presuppose. That is to say, these texts may appear "pro-Jewish" but Matthew intends them to function as "anti-Jewish."

Suppose that, by the time of this Gospel's final editor (ca. 85), the ranks of his church had assumed so Gentile a cast as to prompt him to account for what otherwise could appear anomalous: that since the Messiah concept was originated by the Jews, who then is responsible that Jews themselves have failed, overwhelmingly at the least, to accept Jesus? The blame could not possibly lie with Jesus who, after all, had (supposedly) insisted that he "was sent only to the lost sheep of . . . Israel." The fault, by default, can lie solely with the Jews themselves who rebuffed, and thereby forfeited, Jesus' partiality for them. Against such a backdrop, these two ostensibly "pro-Jewish" passages were devised or applied in an "anti-Jewish" way—so as to account for why Christianity's sustaining membership, by Matthew's day, had come to depend mostly on a Gentile influx—this was the fault of the Jews, not that of Jesus.

Observe this unmistakable progression in Matthew. It begins with the ostensibly sympathetic "lost sheep" passages yet transitions into how "great is . . . [the] faith!" of one Gentile woman (15:28). Six chapters later, 21:43 warns that "the kingdom of God will be taken away from you [Jews] and given to a[nother] nation [by definition Gentiles[24]] producing the fruits of it." This is then reinforced by 22:8 where, while "the wedding is ready . . . those invited [the Jews] were not worthy," so that others (Gentiles) should be invited—not in addition to Jews but in their stead.[25] Then Jesus laments in 23:37, "O Jerusalem . . . how often would I have gathered your children together as a hen gathers her brood under her wings, and you would not [accept me]!" This progression culminates in Jesus' Great Commission to his followers, in 28:19, to "go and make disciples of all nations," or, alternatively, and I believe correctly, "go and make disciples of all Gentiles."[26]

This would mean nothing less than that the editor recasts Jesus' ministry now to conform to developments that had emerged over the decades: "historically, the community failed with its mission to Israel; then the whole course of the story of Jesus told in the Gospel lays the foundation for this fracture."[27] The thrust in Matthew, then, is that, because Jesus initially presumed full acceptance by Jews, he limited his mission to them alone. As for what had gone wrong, Matthew tells us that it was the Jews who had gone wrong. The lost sheep texts therefore are but the beginning of a sustained anti-Jewish polemic so Jewish scholars should simply stop quoting them altogether as reflecting the historical Jesus.

Jesus' Jewish Observances

Luke poses a particular attraction for Jewish scholars because he furnishes details about Jesus' religious observances conveyed by no other writer: that the infant Jesus was circumcised (2:21) and was brought to Jerusalem's Temple for a redemption of the firstborn ceremony "according to the custom of the law" (2:22, 27); that the holy family journeyed to Jerusalem for Passover—one trip culminating in Jesus, at age twelve answering the sages, the central fashioners of Judaism, and in the Temple (2:41-51), Judaism's central institution; and that the adult Jesus taught daily in the Temple (19:47; 20:1; 21:37) and regularly "in their synagogues" (4:15)—note in particular his (anachronistic?[28]) *haftarah* exposition in Nazareth's synagogue (4:16-21).

The oft-overlooked preliminary here? While ostensibly plausible, these Jewish observances are only makeshift ("window dressing") devices of Lukan theology: they reflect not Jesus genuinely but Luke's own day and needs. Because Luke-Acts is one extended work by the same editor, it is legitimate to search out what Luke does with Paul's image. The parallels with the Lucan Paul force us to devalue Luke's portrayal of the historical Jesus to the point that Jewish scholars should entirely cease citing Luke concerning Jesus' pattern of Jewish observances.

Compare what Paul tells us about himself in his genuine Epistles with how Luke revises that profile. Luke shifts Paul's upbringing from the Diaspora to Jerusalem (the center of Judaism), and diminishes Paul's disaffection with the Law by recasting him as a kind of proto-rabbinic Jew. Only Acts (not any Epistle) reports Paul's training at the feet of the chief Pharisee, Gamaliel I (22:3), and gives Paul a Hebrew name, "Saul" (13:9),[29] and facility in the Hebrew language (21:40; 22:2)—even though biblical quotations in Paul's own Epistles reflect Greek translations, not the original Hebrew. I contend that Luke manufactures Paul's willingness to circumcise Timothy (16:3) precisely to neutralize the genuine Paul's flat-out refusal to circumcise Titus (Gal. 2:3).

Directly analogous to what Luke does with Jesus, he places Paul also regularly in synagogues: "as was his custom"; "every Sabbath"; "for three months" (Acts 17:2; 18:4; 19:8); and also places Paul in the Temple where he happens to be when he is arrested (22:17; 26:21; see also 24:12). This also explains why the Lukan Paul, when reciting his autobiography (26:4-5), stresses that "my manner of life from my youth . . . [was] spent . . . among my own nation and at Jerusalem" and "according to the strictest party of our religion I have lived as a Pharisee."

Examining Luke's treatment of Paul, therefore, is a key preliminary to what should be our take on Luke's presentation of Jesus. Luke's improvisation of "Jewish" motifs for Jesus (as well as Paul) is not factual reportage but only a theological dynamic—to persuade readers of the ultra-Jewish religiosity of Jesus (and Paul). Luke thereby wishes to establish that the Christianity of his own day (as the extension solely from Jesus and Paul) constitutes the sole genuine extension of authentic Judaism. Accordingly, Jews who reject Jesus thereby have orphaned themselves from their own legacy. How telling, and compelling, that Luke ends his two-volume work on precisely this note: that "this people . . . shall . . . never understand . . . never perceive."

Jesus' Passion-Week Outline

For all the Jewish studies of Jesus' Passion, the preliminary most often bypassed is the Gospel dynamic of "typology," the conformance of Jesus by Christian tradition to match Jewish biblical imagery. The most powerful example involves Jeremiah. The description I craft for Jeremiah could easily be mistaken for Jesus:

> Long ago, there lived a righteous Jew who spoke for God. Defying the religious establishment, he aroused enmity from Jewish priests (Jer. 26:11). Demanding that they amend their ways, he threatened destruction of the [First] Temple ("a den of robbers" [Jer. 7:11]). The priests threatened him with death (Jer. 26:8, 11). He warned that they could bring innocent blood upon themselves (Jer. 26:15). The vacillating civil authority (Jer. 38:5) summoned him (Jer. 38:14) and, pronouncing him innocent, expressed reluctance to heed his accusers' demands but capitulated to them out of fear (Jer. 38:19). As the just man warned (Jer. 7:14), the Temple was later destroyed.

Not necessarily knowing details of what had befallen Jesus or not finding those details that they did know sufficiently inspiring, would not earliest Christians naturally have reconceptualized Jesus in terms of their own biblical models such as Jeremiah (much like Isaiah's Suffering Servant, etc.)? Compare the inquiry convened for Jeremiah (26:10) with the Sanhedrin convened for Jesus (Mark 14:53); how the priests said Jeremiah "deserves . . . death" for words that "you have heard" (Jer. 26:11) with the Sanhedrin's pronouncement that Jesus "deserves death" (Matt. 26:66) for words that "you have heard" (Mark 14:64); Jeremiah's "you will bring innocent blood upon yourselves" (26:15) with Matthew's "his blood be on us and on our children!" (27:25).[30]

Fulfilling the Law of Moses

Almost all Jewish reconstructions of Jesus highlight Matthew 5:17: "Think not that I have come to abolish the law and the prophets; I have come not to abolish them but to fulfill them. . . . Whoever . . . relaxes one of the least of these commandments and teaches men so, shall be called least in the kingdom of heaven." But surely typology should be a problematic concern here too, because of Matthew's extraordinary commitment to presenting Jesus as the second Moses. This commences, and then branches out, from the infancy narrative where Jesus equals Moses; Herod equals Pharaoh; Bethlehem's innocents equals Egypt's Hebrew infants; the disobedient magi equals the disobedient midwives; Jesus' leaving Egypt equals Moses' exodus therefrom; and Jesus' return toward home equals Moses' return home (Exod. 2:23; 4:18). Then ensue broader parallels still: Jesus and Moses cross water (Matt. 3:13-17; Exod. 14:10-31); undergo wilderness temptations (Matt. 4:1-11; Exod. 16:1-17:7); give a Law (sermon?) in five divisions on a mount (Matt. 5-7; Exod. 19:1-23:23); are transfigured atop a mount (Matt. 17:1-9; Exod. 34:29-35); and commission successors (Matt. 28:16-20; Deut. 31:7-9; Josh. 1:1-9).[31]

The pertinence here is this: since Matthew so thoroughly conforms Jesus' image to Moses, how do we know that Matthew is not doing exactly the same here in 5:17-19, that is, assigning Jesus a "Moses-type" promulgation? We must note that these words in this particular form—indeed, the entire Sermon on the Mount, for that matter—appear solely in Matthew. Why is that if, as we may uncritically assume, they authentically go back to Jesus?

Matthew's emphasis on Jesus as a law-giver seems a deliberate countering of Mark's own emphasis on Jesus as a law-breaker, and is also the very antithesis, for that matter, of Pauline theology. Is the function of Jesus' words in 5:17-19, then, rather than a faithful recall of the historical Jesus instead a reflection of a Matthean polemic? The peculiarly pointed and seemingly unnecessary words, "whoever . . . relaxes one of the least of these commandments and teaches men so, shall be called least in the kingdom of heaven," whether by coincidence or deliberately, match Paul exactly. As for who is to be "least" in the kingdom of heaven, Paul (in 1 Cor. 15:9) terms himself "least of all the apostles" (the two renditions of the Greek word are identical in form).

Before our automatic recourse to Matt 5:17-19, then, Jewish scholars should ponder how much of Jesus' ostensible affirmation of the Law in Matthew—especially in its present formatting—could constitute Matthew's attempt to neutralize Paul's influence and not have originated with the historical Jesus at all.

An Alternative Proposal

I have not meant to suggest, in this essay, that there is nothing Jewish scholars can confidently say about the historical Jesus, only that the obstacles are so overwhelming that whatever can be said will bring us but little academic mileage. After all, judging by the volume of the topics Jews have treated the most frequently, I selected nine themes that Jewish scholars deem among the surest bets for productive research on Jesus. Yet I demonstrate why I feel we should have no confidence in a single one of them. If the Last Supper, Sanhedrin, and Barabbas units or even the "lost sheep of ... Israel" and "fulfilling the law" texts and so on, fail to pass muster in this regard, what then of genuine substance may we hope to glean from lesser bets?

I myself do believe that Jesus taught provocative parables defining in radical ways what it meant to be truly righteous, but there is no demonstrable way of confidently isolating the genuine core of such parables from later church accretion,[32] or even for gauging the original context in which Jesus may have delivered them. Yes, Jesus may indeed have felt a kind of messianic mission generated by his conviction that the end of the world order was imminent, and he may have interpreted his personal assignment as being God's last envoy to promulgate what was impending. Indeed, it is also likely that he was arrested because his preaching God's kingdom was construed to threaten the Roman and Jewish establishments.

But in the grand scheme of things, I foresee Jewish scholarship as essentially recapitulating, on a much delayed basis, the ultimately disappointing "quests" already undergone by our Christian counterparts. Jewish scholars will advance what they feel are exciting theories in Jesus study. But these will inevitably be subjected to rigorous and effective rebuttal, and this will be true even regarding applications of rabbinics which, while always assumed a fruitful area of exploration generally, I consider a veritable methodological minefield if applied to historical Jesus research.[33]

This is why throughout my career I have implemented, and here continue to recommend, an alternative approach that shifts gears from a type of knowledge that we can never secure to another type proximate, promising, and productive. This approach proceeds as a *via negativa*: researching and teaching what little we can as to who Jesus was but much more so as to who he was not. We can do this best by focusing on the "Gospel dynamics" which altered his profile—those skillful techniques by which early Christian writers came to refine their conceptualizations of Jesus himself so as to address challenges germane to their later day rather than to his.

I urge this alternative also out of responsibility to the Jewish populace at large. For although the New Testament has exerted the most harmful impact on the Jewish people's history, Jews have always opted to remain ignorant about it. This policy, initiated by our ancient Talmudic sages, has been the glaring exception to the time-honored Jewish approach to problem-solving, which is to amass—not shun—knowledge. As a result of not knowing how to engage the New Testament, our people have allowed problems that began after the mid-first century not only to recur frequently but also to intensify and fester. These problems have persisted into modern times, continuing to destabilize Jews' well-being on a communal as well as an individual basis.

Increasingly, but only gradually, Jews are coming to recognize how opting for ignorance about the New Testament indeed has been to their detriment. We Jewish scholars now have it in our power to accelerate this reversal of an age-old aversion, essentially to declare that ancient directive by our sages of old as no longer sage advice for Jews today.

We cannot accelerate this reversal by teaching about Jesus per se, for not only is no definitive portrait of him retrievable and or even reconstructible but, as a function of our history, too many Jews will always simply recoil at the mere mention of his name. If we wish to change this last circumstance, the most effective route will be indirect: by revealing the Gospel dynamics that resulted in the alteration of his image away from who he genuinely may have been.

The excitement that this alternative kind of teaching can engender among our people is beginning to become documented.[34] It is also energizing because the ability of Jews to detect Gospel dynamics, to explain these to themselves and their children, and ultimately to articulate them to Christian friends and to a broader Christian society is what will enable them to exchange their sense of victimization by the New Testament for a strong sense of confidence that they now knowledgeably control this literature and are thereby free from it. That is indeed the paradigmatic Jewish way of problem-solving, and will enhance the credibility of Jewish scholarship.

Discussion Questions

1. What are the key avenues to closing the credibility gap between many Gospel analyses by Jews and more substantive treatments by Christian scholarship?
2. What fundamental preliminary questions should Jews ask before examining any Gospel tradition?
3. How can Jewish scholars help their populace at large to exchange a sense of victimization by the New Testament for confidence that they can knowledgeably control this literature and thereby be free from it?

Notes

1. Donald Hagner, *The Jewish Reclamation of Jesus* (Grand Rapids: Zondervan, 1984), 67; see also 33.
2. Samuel Sandmel, "The Jewish Scholar and Early Christianity," *Two Living Traditions* (Detroit: Wayne State, 1972), 16; see also Samuel Sandmel, *We Jews and Jesus* (1965; repr., Woodstock: Skylight Paths, 2006), 63-64.
3. Trude Weiss-Rosmarin, *Jewish Expressions on Jesus* (New York: KTAV, 1976), ix.
4. Thus, confident times for world improvement spawned Jesus the social-reformer; World War I, Jesus the apocalypticist; the Six Day War, Jesus the militant; oppressive class struggle (Latin America), Jesus the liberator.
5. My "Gospel Dynamics Index" lists these types with 100 examples: Michael J. Cook, *Modern Jews Engage the New Testament: Enhancing Jewish Well-Being in a Christian Environment* (Woodstock: Jewish Lights, 2008), 352-54.
6. See preceding note; also the review by Zev Garber, *Shofar* 27.4 (2009), 146-49; http://www.case.edu/artsci/rosenthal/reviews/NewTestament.htm.
7. Annie Jaubert, *La date de la Cene* (Paris: J. Gabalda, 1957); in English, Annie Jaubert, *The Date of the Last Supper,* trans. I. Rafferty (Staten Island: Alba House, 1965).
8. The generic, "bread," could encompass unleavened. But Hebrew Scriptural texts on this festival routinely specify "unleavened bread."
9. In Matthew, Jesus sends all of his inner circle (not two) to prepare the meal; Luke retains Mark's sending of but two.

10. I forgo anomaly 5 since I dispute the historicity of Jesus' "trial," and anomalies 6-7 because of possible quibbling that Mark's readership might not know that Jewish days began the previous evening.
11. See also John 19:36 with Exod. 12:46; Num. 9:12; Ps. 34:20(21). Paul also applied "paschal lamb" imagery to Jesus (1 Cor. 5:7).
12. Mark never names "Caiaphas" (supplied by Matt. 26:3), which I use here for convenience.
13. Ellipses reflect excision of material that I believe Mark added editorially.
14. Cook, *Modern Jews*, 134-47, 274; see also 185, 272, 322 n. 5; 322-23 n. 11. Since I assign "Peter's denial" to Mark's latest stratum, I see it as not "in position" to receive the trial insertion (189-90; see also 153, 324 n. 11).
15. "The historical and biblical questions surrounding the notion that there was a formal Sanhedrin trial argue for extreme caution and, perhaps, even abandoning the device [in Passion productions]," *Criteria for the Evaluation of Dramatizations of the Passion,* Bishops' Committee for Ecumenical and Interreligious Affairs, National Conference of Catholic Bishops, 1988, # C.1.c.
16. E.g., Benjamin Bacon, *The Beginnings of Gospel Story* (New Haven: Yale, 1909), 24, 26; W. Bousset, *Kyrios Christos* (Nashville: Abingdon, 1970) first published 1913, 77-78; Rudolf Bultmann, *History of the Synoptic Tradition*, trans. J. Marsh (Oxford: Blackwell, 1963) first published 1921, 15; E. Klostermann, *Das Markusevangelium* (Tübingen: Mohr, 1926), 25.
17. Mark 8:31; 10:33; 11:18, 27; 14:1, 10, 43, 53, 55; 15:1, 3, 10, 11, 31.
18. Michael J. Cook, *Mark's Treatment of the Jewish Leaders* (Leiden; Brill, 1978), 58-67; and "The Distribution of Jewish Leaders in the Synoptic Gospels: Why Wariness Is Warranted," *Soundings on the Religion of Jesus: Jews and Christians on the Jesus of History.* Edited Bruce Chilton, Anthony Le Donne, and Jacob Neusner (Minneapolis: Fortress, 2012), forthcoming.
19. Ibid., 30 n. 12.
20. Matt 12:24; 22:34, 41 (see also, respectively, Mark 3:22; 12:28, 35).
21. See Sanh. 88b; Kid. 17b, 39a, possibly 30a; Suk. 28a; R.H. 19a; Yev. 20a.
22. The "lost sheep" balance out "Gentiles" (10:5-6), so entire peoples are meant.
23. F. W. Beare, "The Mission of the Disciples and the Mission Charge: Matthew 10 and Parallels," *Journal of Biblical Literature* 89 (1970): 9.
24. The judgment of Joachim Jeremias, *Parables of Jesus* (Englewood Cliffs, NJ: Prentice Hall, 1979), 70; Charles Dodd, *The Parables of the Kingdom* (New York: Scribner's, 1961), 99; J. Dominic Crossan, *In Parables* (Santa Rosa, CA: Polebridge, 1992), 90; Charles Carlston, *The Parables of the Triple Tradition* (Philadelphia: Fortress, 1975), 44; Douglas R. A. Hare, *The Theme of Jewish Persecution of Christians in the Gospel According to St. Matthew* (Cambridge: University Press, 1967), 153.
25. In this parable all the Jews are already killed, leaving only Gentiles.
26. While the Greek *ethne* can be rendered either way, "Gentiles" better fits the progression. (Also, in Hebrew Scriptures, the analogous *goyim* most often means "Gentiles.") Douglas Hare and Daniel Harrington, "Make Disciples of All the Gentiles," *Catholic Biblical Quarterly* 37 (1975): 359-69; Kenneth Clark, "The Gentile Bias in Matthew," *Journal of Biblical Literature* 66 (1947): 165-72.
27. David Balch, "The Greek Political Topos *Peri Nomon* and Matthew 5:17,19 and 16:19," in *Social History of the Matthean Community,* ed. Balch (Minneapolis: Fortress, 1991), 79.

28. Luke casts Jesus as reciting messianic texts from Isaiah, but we have no reason to believe that prophetic selections (the *Tanakh's* second division) played any liturgical role already in Jesus' day.
29. I submit that Luke improvised this name from Philippians 3:5, where the genuine Paul identifies himself as "of the tribe of Benjamin" (whose most famous namesake was "Saul"; see 1 Sa 9:1-10:16).
30. Cook, *Modern Jews*, 126-27.
31. Dale Allison, *The New Moses* (Minneapolis: Fortress, 1993), 268.
32. Most likely underlying versions of the Prodigal Son (Luke 15:11-32); the Unmerciful Servant-Creditor (Matt. 18:23-35); the Good Samaritan (Luke 10:30-35); the Talents (Matt 25:14-30) or Pounds (Luke 19:12-27); and the Laborers in the Vineyard (Matt. 20:1-15).
33. See Michael J. Cook, "Jesus and the Pharisees," *Journal of Ecumenical Studies* 15 (1978), specifically 456-58; "Rabbinic Judaism and Early Christianity," *Review & Expositor* 84 (1987): 201-21; and *Modern Jews*, 5-6, 14-15, 49, 275-76.
34. Detailed in Cook, *Modern Jews*, xvi-xvii, 9-11, 17, 75-91, 288-99.

Taking Thomas to Temple: Introducing Evangelicals to the Jewish Jesus

Christina M. Smerick

The Judaism of Jesus of Nazareth provides a challenge to most American Christians of any denominational stripe, as typically this Judaism is not emphasized in religious education or in religious services or sermons. While I currently teach at an evangelical Christian college in the United States, I was raised in the Roman Catholic tradition and can state unequivocally that I did not receive a robust education with regard to Jesus' Jewish faith in my CCD[1] or catechism courses as a child. Jesus, for most Christians (if I may be so bold), seems to be an exception to his culture rather than an active participant in it. A naïve reading of the Gospels provides modern Christians with a Jesus who argues with Jewish teachers, who challenges their authority and scriptural interpretation. For one who does not know the history of the times, this seems evidence enough that Jesus was not a fan of Judaism and indeed came as a challenge to it. The triumph of the church under Constantine simply cemented the previous rifts that quickly formed between the Jewish Christians and the larger Jewish community in the Second and post-Second Temple eras. What most modern Christians inherit, then, is a Gentile church that formed itself in many ways in opposition to the Judaism in which Jesus actively participated. Counteracting this triumphant attitude is certainly a challenge to any church or religious institution. Thus, this study aims to describe how one such religious institution—in this case, an evangelical Christian college of the Free Methodist tradition in the rural Midwest—wrestles with the Judaism of Jesus both in and out of the classroom, and the particular challenges we face with regard to the preparedness, or lack thereof, of the student body to this new information.

This paper first aims to provide a snapshot of the student body at Greenville College. It then moves to professor interviews, in which professorial observations regarding the challenges they face in teaching these ideas to a largely unprepared student audience are articulated. This is followed by a descriptive section of the other experiences and events that Greenville College students have the opportunity to participate in that emphasize the importance of Judaism to the person of Jesus, and thus to the Christian community. Finally, an analysis of a focus group event and survey is provided, demonstrating that the observations of professors are largely accurate, but that real change seems to occur amongst our student body after exposure to the Judaism of Jesus in our courses and extracurricular activities. Finally, I provide some final reflections as to the current challenges faced by American Christianity with regard to this issue, and some possible causes for it. Some caveats are in order: first, this is a profile piece, and therefore the data and information here cannot be generalized to include all Protestant colleges, all evangelical colleges, or even all Free Methodist colleges and universities. Second, this is not a sociological study; the entire populace at Greenville College was not polled. What this work attempts to do, rather, is to provide a snapshot of how the topic of "the Jewish Jesus" is addressed at one, rural, evangelical Christian college, the challenges we face in doing so, and the reactions of students in response to such information.

Greenville College is a small, Christian, liberal arts college in south central Illinois, a rural area east of St. Louis, Missouri. Our student population of traditional, undergraduate students ranges from 1000-1200; additionally, we have a number of adult education and graduate programs that, for the purposes of this profile, are not included in the data. Greenville College is affiliated with the Free Methodist Church, an evangelical denomination in the Wesleyan tradition[2] that emerged in the 1850s. The Free Methodist Church first became a separate denomination in response to both the practice of charging money for pews in Methodist congregations (the breakaway Church opposed this, thus labeling themselves the "Free" Methodist Church) and the practice of slavery (the Free Methodist Church took an abolitionist stance relatively early on). Thus, the Church itself has its roots in the Wesleyan Holiness movement, which originally was characterized as much by its commitment to social justice as its emphasis upon a passionate and engaged Christian life.[3]

However, most of our students now come from self-described "nondenominational" churches, a recent phenomenon in American Christianity (18.3% of those identifying religious affiliation as incoming freshmen prefer this label). Such churches tend to be generically Calvinist and "evangelical," without adhering to a specific denomination's statement of beliefs or doctrine. They may range from small gatherings in someone's home to mega-churches with congregations numbering in the thousands. The reasons for forming a nondenominational church are varied; some are formed as breakaway churches from an established denomination; some view denominationalism as a divider of the Christian community. Some criticisms denominational churches have of this movement stem from the lack of systematic training for nondenominational pastors—since the churches do not hold to a specific denomination, their pastors may not have seminary or theological training. What this means for a Christian college is that a significant portion of our population comes from churches that may not have a structured catechism or theology. Thus, we cannot assume that they are familiar with the history of Christianity or with orthodox Christian beliefs.

Second to the nondenominational category in our student population is the Baptist denomination (10.8%), which has many subparts (Southern, American) that can differ greatly from one another.[4] However, in general, our Baptist students come from conservative churches that lean toward fundamentalism, a moniker best described as a position that takes a fairly strong stance for biblical inerrancy and against modern science, particularly evolution. Scripture is the central focus of such churches, with an emphasis upon a literal interpretation.

It is fair to say that most of the students who come to Greenville College do not have a strong grasp on the Judaism of Jesus of Nazareth. As we will see later from the focus group and survey, most students have not been exposed to a historical examination of Scripture, nor has Scripture been placed in historical context. Jesus as a Jew does not seem to serve as a regular topic in their Sunday school or church experiences. As such, Greenville College strives to introduce students to the Judaism of Jesus via a variety of courses.

Professor Observations

In order to paint a fuller picture of the challenges facing a Christian college that seeks to educate evangelical students with regard to the Judaism of Jesus, I interviewed a number of my colleagues who teach courses that address the subject. All of the following professors are in the Religion and Philosophy Department at Greenville College. All have taught multiple sections of our Scripture courses over the years, and have thus had firsthand experience with the questions and struggles students have and go through when confronted with an unfamiliar history of their Savior. In the following, I have summarized the subject matter covered in their various courses, and the unique difficulties such content gives students. I have also included the professors' observations as to the causes of such difficulties, and how they attempt to overcome or mitigate them.

Ben Wayman[5] teaches New Testament Survey and Synoptic Gospels, both of which deal directly with Jesus' relationship to Judaism. Professor Wayman observed that most students seem to have a "generic Christian faith," in which the particularity of Jesus does not factor. He uses their generic love of Scripture (see introduction for a description of the emphasis on Scripture in most churches) as a way to discuss the fact that the Old Testament is cited and appears throughout the New Testament, and that therefore one cannot know of Jesus or of the Gospel without knowing and thinking carefully about the promises and significance of the Old Testament. Thus, he provides historical background, demonstrating that Christianity began within Judaism, as a renewal movement, not as a separate religion. To reject the Judaism of Jesus, or indeed of Christianity, can have horrible ramifications (indeed, Wayman sees a connection between precisely this nonhistorical attitude that reduces God to a "cloud of love" and the radical failure of the German church to respond appropriately to the Nazi agenda—the appropriate response being one of defiant rejection and protest rather than meek acquiescence). In the class itself, he has not witnessed a lot of "push-back" against these notions, but he is unsure as to how to read that lack of response. It is difficult to tell if they are rejecting this notion, or simply thinking about it. (One could write an entire paper on the polite passivity one finds in the Midwest.) Wayman observes that, upon coming into his classes, students tend not to consider the Bible as a continuous story, in which the intelligibility of the New Testament is narratively dependent on the Old Testament. Ironically, the first bit of work he must perform in the courses on the New Testament is to get students to understand that without the Old Testament, the New Testament makes no sense. Both Jesus and Paul consistently and constantly refer to Old Testament passages, demonstrating a deep and thoroughly familiar relationship with their Scriptures. Thus, the students themselves need to know the whole story, which does not begin or end with Jesus' birth and death.

Brian Hartley[6] teaches a number of disparate courses for the college. The topic of Judaism with regard to Jesus and Christian history arises predominantly in his Pauline Epistles course, which focuses upon the writings of Paul in the New Testament of Christian Scripture. While the Judaism of Jesus is a secondary topic in the course due to the emphasis upon Paul, Hartley finds that emphasizing Paul's Judaism is also a challenge to the students. One of the topics that students wrestle with in the course is the Pauline notion that Judaism is not to be rejected, but rather that Christianity is grafted onto the "trunk" of Judaism. This is difficult for students to grasp, given the fact that for 1700 years the Christian church has been dominant, and thus they are exposed and take as fact the "triumphant" Gentile church as the norm. Thus, most students have an ahistorical attitude toward Christianity, and tend to assume that, if anything, Christianity should be the trunk. They are used to thinking of Paul as a man who turned his back on Judaism upon his conversion, and thus miss the subtlety and indeed the inner conflict that Paul expresses in his writings regarding the relationship between Christianity and Judaism. Therefore, while the Judaism of Jesus, specifically, does not arise much in the course itself, the subjects of Judaism and the Jewish roots of Christianity do, and can lead to some cognitive dissonance as students struggle to reconcile this new information with what they have been told thus far in their churches.

Ruth Huston[7] teaches Pentateuch, Old Testament Survey, and Wisdom and Poetic Literature. Since our students are predominantly Christian, courses on the Old Testament also lead to questions about Jesus' relationship to it and to Judaism. Thus, she works on having students learn to read the Old Testament with both Christian and Jewish eyes, requiring students to study rabbinic literature on the books studied. In fact, she encourages them to not use Christian commentaries at all when studying the Old Testament, in order to expand their understanding, however slight, of the thoroughgoing Judaism of the texts. In Old Testament Survey, she works to persuade students that they cannot be Christian without starting to understand the Old Testament or the Judaism of Jesus. As such, she spends the first three weeks of class teaching the students about ancient Jewish history: the languages, social structures, and geography of the ancient Jewish world. Only then do they approach the Scriptures themselves. Students, she observed, seem grateful for the information; sometimes their reactions are along the lines of "Why didn't my pastor tell me any of this?" (a question for the ages, surely). She pushes them to avoid reading the Old Testament as Christian allegory, and instead encourages them to fully face its true religious roots, and thus, Jesus'.

I, as the Shapiro Chair of Jewish-Christian Studies, teach History of Judaism, World Religions, and Jews, Christians, Muslims. In History of Judaism, a 300-level course that is cross-listed as a History and as a Religion course, we cover the time period beginning with the Babylonian Exile (586 BCE) through the fall of the Second Temple in Jerusalem (70 CE). The rise of the Jesus movement within Judaism occurs, of course, within these parameters and thus is explicitly discussed in class. Since the course is upper division, students have usually had some exposure by this point to the notion of Jesus as Jewish; however, they do not have a solid grasp of the history of the land itself or of the other sects of Judaism that were prevalent at that time. Thus, the course attempts to guide students into understanding that Jesus was not one who, culturally or religiously, was departing radically from an already determined and unified Judaism, but rather was living and preaching during a time where various Judaisms were alive, well, and engaging in ferocious debate. Emphasis is placed upon the history of the Pharisees (in order, in part, to counteract much of the prejudice students carry toward this religious group due to the pejorative descriptions of them found in the New Testament), Sadducees, and Essenes, so that students might be better able to place Jesus' messianic message in context. Furthermore, students learn of the various other messiah figures (for example, Simon bar Kokhba) who were active at roughly the same time period. This can be challenging for students, because one of the most consistent messages from the church is that Jesus was exemplary and utterly unique in his work and his message; that he stuck out like a sore thumb, so to speak, and presented a radical break from the Judaism of his day. Historical and even scriptural evidence reveal the inaccuracy of this depiction, but the historically Gentile church has portrayed Jesus as far more of a Gentile or radical outsider than as a participating member of the Jewish community.

One of the issues that tend to arise is why Christianity became a separate religion of its own, one that subsequently developed an attitude of persecution and violence toward its parent religion. Most students by this point feel a strong connection with the history of Judaism and its traditions, and seem to experience a sensation of mourning at the loss of a relationship between Judaism and Christianity. Students do struggle a bit with retaining a sense of Jesus' uniqueness within this historical context, and wrestle with how Christology developed from such humble beginnings. This presents an opportune moment to discuss the role of faith with regard to history, such that students may begin to understand that, similar to the sacred interpretations the Jewish people developed regarding their history, so too has Christianity developed sacred interpretations of historical events, interpretations that ground our faith "in things not seen," rather than a mislabeled "faith" in evidence demonstrated.

In Jews, Christians, Muslims and World Religions, common issues that arise have more to do with Jesus' relationship to Judaism as it is presented in the New Testament. Students struggle to understand how one who challenges the Law on so many levels nevertheless participated actively in the following of that Law. There is an over-simplification of Jesus' teachings that leads students to assume, without realizing what they are doing, the false doctrine of supercession that has haunted the Christian church for centuries. One of the challenges in these courses is to gently separate students from this doctrine without shaming them. The orthodoxy they are left with is a far more complex and complicated one, and many students find this exhausting, especially when the Christianity they had been raised on prized itself on simplicity. Invariably, students leave the courses with a deeper appreciation for Judaism; however, the repercussions of such an appreciation upon their own faith still continue and often remain unresolved.

From the interviews with the professors on the front lines, one can draw a number of conclusions. All observe a deep-seated naïveté in our students when it comes to knowledge of the history of Christianity, or indeed of Scripture itself. All feel that there is work that has to be done in the classroom of a preparatory nature before they can actually start to discuss the material around which the course is organized. Disabusing students of their preformed opinions is a difficult and delicate task, and all the professors recognize the need for a balance between challenging our students and nurturing them—between providing information that contradicts or defies what they have heard from pastors and parents alike, and making sure students feel listened to and supported through the process. As such, teaching these courses is not simply about providing information or material, but involves spiritual as well as academic guidance. Without such guidance, students can find themselves cut adrift, having neither the faith of their families and churches nor a renewed or deepened faith to draw upon. The wonderful aspect of this process, however, is that students of this age group are in a rather open and flexible state of mind, and many find the new information to be deeply satisfying and heartening, rather than destructive. We will see the latter trend more clearly in the section that describes how students feel about the subject matter in their own words.

Extra-curricular Experiences

Of course, a college is not simply a series of courses and classrooms. In fact, extracurricular events and activities provide much-needed concrete experiences that help to orient students to the information received in their coursework. As such, Greenville College provides a number of events that focus upon Judaism, and thus the Judaism of Jesus, in order to help students gain a richer understanding. This is in line with the aforementioned "Wesleyan Quadrilateral," which emphasizes the role of experience as a source of truth.[8]

All students at Greenville College are required to take four core courses and a number of distributed courses as part of the General Education Program. Of the four core courses, the one that corresponds to the interest of this study is COR 102: Christian Thought and Life, typically taken in the second semester of the freshman year. An integral part of the course is the Chicago trip, in which every student is taken to Chicago for a weekend in order to visit and participate in a variety of religious services. These include a variety of non-Protestant Christian services (Greek Orthodox, Roman Catholic), a visit to a mosque, and a Shabbat service at a synagogue. For most students, this is the first exposure they have had to any religion other than their own; for many, it is the first time they have witnessed something other than a Protestant religious service. The Shabbat service provides them not only with the experience of a Jewish worship service, but with question-and-answer time with the rabbi and other congregants. In many cases, this is the first conversation students have had with a Jewish person, and one of the elements of the discussion is an emphasis upon the Judaism of Jesus. Thus, students are exposed to an alternative understanding of the person of Jesus and begin to wrestle with the notion that their religion—Christianity—is not the religion that Jesus practiced. (This may seem obvious to academics and well-educated laypersons, but often comes as a dawning revelation to students who have never thought about the issue before.)

Other extra-curricular events available for students are organized by the Shapiro Jewish-Christian Studies Program, which is a general education program that provides courses and events designed to educate the community regarding Judaism and to promote interreligious dialogue between the Jewish and Christian communities of faith. Given the relative naïveté of the student body regarding other religions, these opportunities tend to reinforce what is learned in courses and provide students with real-world experiences that go beyond the classroom.

The Shapiro Jewish-Christian Studies Program hosts a biennial lecture series named for Samuel Sandmel.[9] For this series, a prominent Jewish scholar who is well-versed in Jewish-Christian dialogue comes to campus to speak in chapel and at an afternoon colloquium, as well as in various courses according to his or her schedule. This event has provided much food for thought for students as they are confronted with a passionate and engaged person of Jewish faith who challenges them regarding Christian misunderstandings and attitudes toward both Judaism and their own faith tradition. Recent Sandmel Lecturers have included Marc Bregman (University of North Carolina-Chapel Hill), Rabbi David Sandmel (Chicago Theological Union), and Zev Garber (Los Angeles Valley College).

The Jewish-Christian Studies Program also provides other events throughout the year, including a Yom Kippur Reflection service, which seeks to educate students regarding the high holy day of Yom Kippur and its significance; occasional Holocaust survivor colloquia, in which a local Holocaust survivor tells his or her story on campus; a trip to the St. Louis Holocaust Museum and to Sha'are Emeth synagogue in St. Louis for History of Judaism and Jews, Christians, Muslims students; and a Jewish Literature series sponsored by NextBook, which focused on prominent twentieth-century Jewish novelists and their work.

All of these events seek to further students' understanding of and appreciation for Judaism, and explicitly do so by reminding students that by all accounts, Jesus of Nazareth was a devout and practicing Jew. Again, emphasis is placed upon the cohistory of Judaism and Christianity, on the indications in Scripture of Jesus following Torah, as well as on the many persecutions suffered by the Jewish people at the hands of Christians throughout history. The goal of these extra-curricular activities is to link the real world with the subjects students are engaging in the classroom, and thus provide a more holistic approach to the task before us, of orienting students to a deeper understanding of their own faith and its relationship with other faiths and peoples.

Student Data[10]

As part of this study, I held a focus group to discuss the notion of Jesus' Judaism, and to learn from students about their previous exposure to this subject and their current views. The focus group was pulled from the History of Judaism course, and consisted of 10 students. A focus group interview was conducted, followed by a survey to quantify the data. I discovered that by and large, the professors' assumptions and observations closely matched how students described themselves, especially with regard to previous exposure to the Judaism of Jesus. The following is a summary of the quantitative survey data.

Of the 10 students surveyed in the focus group, six were Religion majors, one was a Youth Ministry major, one was a Contemporary Christian Music major, one was a Biology major, and one was a History major. Four were seniors, two were juniors, and four were sophomores. Four declared themselves denominationally affiliated as "none," "N/A" or "ain't happening." There was one Free Methodist, one United Methodist, one Southern Baptist, one nondenominational, one Christian Reformed, and one Evangelical Free (a denomination, not a wish!) in the group. Knowing the student group, I would interpret those answering "none" or "N/A" as meaning nondenominational.

The following charts represent the quantifiable data with regard to the questions indicated:

Chart A. Answers to the question, "How much emphasis was placed upon Jesus' religion and/or culture in your religious experiences before Greenville College?"

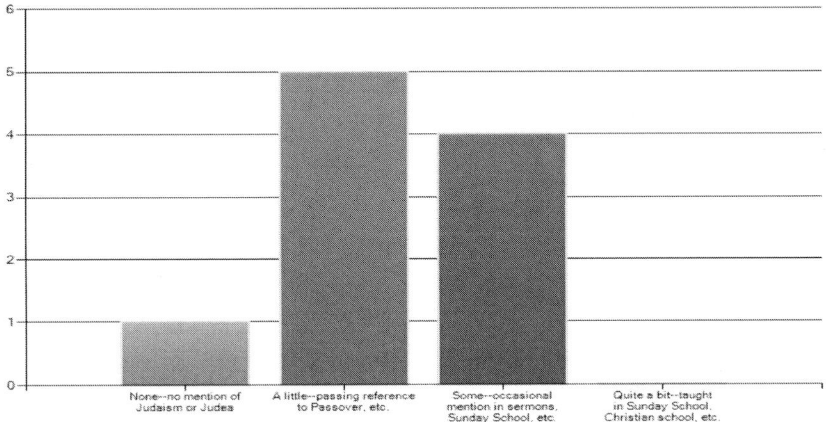

Chart B. Answers to the question, "How important is Jesus' religion/cultural background to your religious/spiritual life now?"

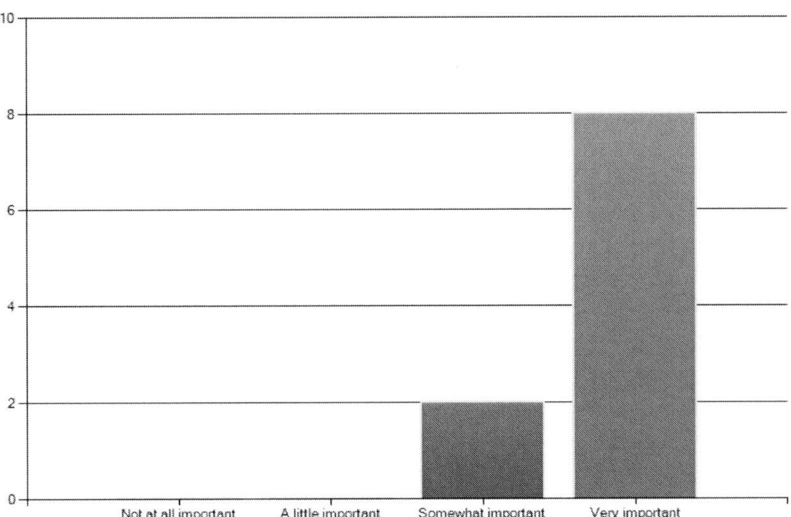

Chart C. Data derived from the question, "Please rate the following GC experiences/courses regarding their contribution to your understanding of Jesus as Jewish."

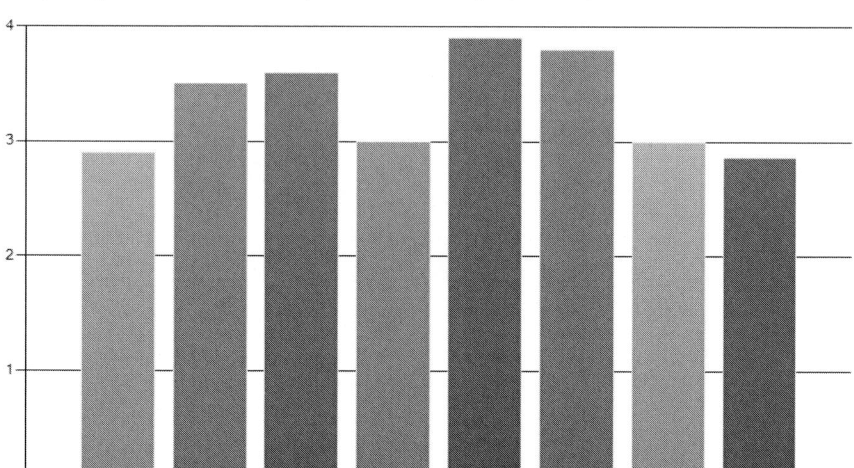

Chart C represents how many students felt that each course/experience contributed to their deeper understanding of the Judaism of Jesus.

The next set of questions were open-ended, and asked focus group members to articulate why learning about "the Jewish Jesus" was important to them, what courses or experiences at Greenville College helped in their understanding of Jesus as a Jew, and what courses or experiences we could offer in the future that would help students to understand and appreciate this topic. Finally, they were asked to articulate, as if to a fellow student, why or why not studying Jesus' culture and religion is important for Christians. The table on the following page represents the themes present in the answers given to the questions addressing both the students' personal feelings about the importance of the Judaism of Jesus, and how or if they would articulate that feeling to other students. The table provides samples of actual student comments that correspond to the themes.

Summary of Student Responses

Student responses to the focus group and survey were remarkable consistent both with each other and with professors' observations. Most students had little exposure to the Judaism of Jesus prior to coming to college. Passing reference to the Last Supper as a Passover meal seemed to be a common experience, but a sustained lesson or sermon on the Jewish practices of Jesus was not experienced by any of the focus group within a church setting. Some students had parents who were interested in Israel and thus introduced their children to Judaism, but

Themes	Student Comments
How Jesus lived is crucial knowledge for Christian faith	• Our faith today stems from Jesus' faith and life when he lived. Knowing what his faith, life, and religion were like is crucial to understanding our faith, because our faith stems from him. • Jesus is a complex figure who lived in a complex world very different from ours. He grew up a Jew, and he taught as a Jew. Judaism is a window into that world… • We shouldn't follow Jesus' teachings without knowing who he was in his time. There is truth in the statement "Everyone is a product of their past", and Jesus, being fully human, was no exception. • Jesus was not a white American. As we seek truth, it is important for us to learn about Jesus' context so that we can better understand the meaning of the life, death, and resurrection of Christ.
Combating Anti-Semitism in the Church	• The history of Christianity is stained with anti-Semitism; therefore, it is important for us to learn how to appreciate Jesus as a Jew in the hope that appreciating Judaism may help the church repent of its anti-Semitic past. • Judaism is a window into that world, and the more we interact with Jews the more we can come to understand Jesus, our own faith, and help define ourselves without being disrespectful to a very important group of people.
Helps us understand Jesus' teachings	• Studying Jesus in his religious and cultural background is important because it gives us something to relate his teachings and methods to. Deeper than that it reminds us of Jesus Christ's own belief system, as well as what he means to his followers at that time. • Studying Jesus' cultural/religious background is important to practice because, just as we wouldn't follow the teachings of Carl Marx without first knowing something about him, specifically his background and such, we shouldn't follow Jesus' teachings without knowing who he was in his time. • Jesus' Jewish background is important for contextualizing the message of the gospel that the church believes, teaches, and confesses today.
The relationship between Christianity and Judaism is important historically and today	• Christianity evolved right out of Judaism. Jesus was Jewish, and he grew up immersed in Judaism. Its history holds in it the beginning of the history of God's relationship with people, which is important to me because God is important to me. • The land and the people shaped him, many of the contexts Jesus experienced are still contextual to Jews who practice today.

again, this was not typically in any sustained fashion. Students expressed frustration upon looking back at their religious education and experiences prior to college, with the most common expression of this frustration being, "Why didn't we learn about this?" All the students involved in the focus group and survey expressed that studying Judaism and understanding Jesus in a Jewish context was important to very important regarding their religious life and faith. Most of them emphasized the important of context in understanding both Jesus himself and his teachings, and thus felt that a deep Christian faith required a better grasp of the culture and history of Judaism. With regard to courses and experiences had at Greenville College, more emphasis was placed on speakers and experiences than courses, thus suggesting that students felt that real-life interaction with those of the Jewish faith was more helpful than simply studying Jewish history or Scripture. Regarding what courses or experiences Greenville College could offer students that would educate them more thoroughly on the Jewish Jesus, students wisely suggested a course on the Judaism of Jesus.

Reflections

What conclusions can one draw from a profile of a single evangelical Christian college with regard to the Judaism of Jesus? Obviously, no valid sociological data could be determined about evangelicals in general or even Christian higher education in general. However, there are some broad themes that emerge from this specific study which can be articulated, with proper caveats in place.

First, there continues to be a rift between the academy and the church. This is the subject of many a conversation at Greenville College. What occurs in our churches—the lessons taught, the emphases placed—can conflict with what academics teaches, which causes tension both within the student and between, generally speaking, pastors and laypeople and academics at Christian institutions. There can be a lack of trust expressed by laypeople and clergy regarding scholarship practices, particularly with regard to Biblical Studies. The rise in importance of the historical-critical method of biblical scholarship in the early twentieth century produced among Protestants in the United States a significant response, best expressed by the book *The Fundamentals*, which was a series of five volumes published between 1910 and 1915 by the Bible Institute of Los Angeles. In particular, this issue of proper biblical study methods created a rift between the scholars who seemed, to the layperson, to be persons without faith subjecting Scripture to secular standards, and clergy, who felt that the Bible needed to be treated differently than other texts.

This problem is exacerbated by the fragmentation of denominations that we see in our students' religious experiences. Common religious educational experiences like catechism study are not typically present in nondenominational churches. As such, students come to us from a variety of faith traditions within Christianity, but not necessarily with a religious education accompanying such traditions. Indeed, even the use of the word "tradition" is problematic, as many evangelical churches of any stripe have moved to a more contemporary worship service style that de-emphasizes the reading of sustained Scripture in place of a more emotive worship style. Finally, Bible Studies, which remain popular among Protestant Evangelicals, are sometimes unguided by any sort of Biblical scholarship, or are undertaken individually, thus failing to provide the kind of checks and balances regarding Scriptural interpretation that is so needed by a faith community. These issues, coupled with a wariness expressed by clergy regarding academics in religion, can create an atmosphere of distrust and ignorance that is very tricky to navigate.

However, our students both hunger for and wrestle with new information about Jesus and the history of their faith; and thus we as professors have to consider how much we challenge and how much we nurture. All changes are difficult, and none so much as a change in what one believes to be true. We seek to strike a balance between the challenging and nurturing aspects of this transformational process, but it would be naïve to think that this tension would be resolved finally. Discovering Jesus' Jewish faith presents a real challenge for students who have an ahistorical view of Jesus as an outsider to the Jewish culture of the time, as one who stood out and criticized rather than a teacher who circulated and interacted with other Jewish teachers of the time. We must balance our students' hunger for information with their accompanying fears, and continue to work to find a balance between challenging our students' assumptions and providing them with the necessary reassurance and structure so that they do not feel lost or abandoned by their faith.

Third, as both Huston and Wayman observed in our interviews, there is a changing climate among evangelicals in general, not just our student body: many evangelicals are profoundly ignorant of the history of Christianity, particularly as it relates to Judaism, yet many are hungry for this information. One can attribute the lack of knowledge, perhaps, to the aforementioned rejection of the historical-critical method of biblical scholarship, which arose in the early twentieth century. Many evangelicals found it to be more critical than historical, and used as a tool to dismantle or reject Christian doctrine rather than deepen and enhance it. The tide is turning, however, and the younger generation of evangelicals seems to be not only returning to notions of social justice, but to a desire to know more and appreciate more deeply the history of their faith. This gives us hope that the future of Jewish-Christian relations may take on an adult character, in which Christians are neither ignoring Judaism altogether, nor "fawning over" Jewish ideas without any sort of engaged response.

Thus, it is crucial for contemporary Christianity to focus on a number of steps that need to be taken. First, we must provide a robust foundation of historical accuracy to the study of Jesus and the early church. The twentieth century saw a rise in anti-intellectualism amongst some Protestant groups, which led to a glorification, in some cases, of willful ignorance regarding the origins, history, and doctrines of Christianity. This trend leads people to have what many have called a "thin" Christianity—a religious faith that is grounded primarily in the repetition of key phrases and terms, but is lacking any deeper sense of the meaning and origins of such terminology. This leads to the reification of merely temporary, and often unorthodox, beliefs, and can lead as well to mistaken assumptions regarding, for example, Judaism and the Jewish people. Indeed, in the most extreme example, some Aryan Christian groups deny the Judaism of Jesus altogether; while in more benign cases, Christians may assume that the Pharisees represented all Jews; that Jesus was "against" the Pharisees; and that therefore Christianity has superceded Judaism in the mind of God. Such beliefs, as we all well know, have led to crimes against the Jewish people throughout history. Education to the deep Jewish roots of Christianity and the Judaism of Jesus can help to mitigate these beliefs and hopefully dispel them.

Second, we need to work on interreligious dialogue with members of the Jewish faith in such a way that we remain honest and true to our own faith traditions, yet open and flexible regarding alternative understandings and interpretations. Christians can only do this once they feel properly grounded in their own faith and history; otherwise, defensiveness or feeble capitulation is the best we can hope for. However, ideally this conversation should not remain at the level of academics and clergy, but should extend to the body of believers on both sides. A grounded and educated Christian of deep faith is a boon to both Christianity and to the world; a Christian who does not know her own roots or traditions can be at best an ineffective interlocutor and at worst a bigot. There is a way to understand Jesus as a Jew without dismantling Christianity; a way to appreciate and inform ourselves about Jewish history and faith without either misappropriating it or "losing our religion." I firmly believe that Christians can come to a far more robust and complex devotion to Christ precisely via a better understanding of his life and context. Thus, even at a small, rural, evangelical college, we work to make this vision of a complex Christianity that has embraced the Jewish Jesus, a reality.

Discussion Questions

1. What social and economic explanations are there for the evangelical rejection of academic methods of biblical study? What factors, besides those covered in this essay, may have led to such a position?
2. Should the Jewish community be concerned about the lack of understanding that may persist among evangelicals regarding the Jewish Jesus? What implications does it have for interreligious dialogue or current political and social issues?
3. What is an appropriate relationship between the academy and a religious community? Are there tendencies among academia that are of legitimate concern to religious communities, and how do we foster communication between said groups?

Notes

1. The Confraternity of Christian Doctrine (CCD) is the religious teaching program of the Catholic Church. These classes are taught to school age children to learn the basic doctrines of their faith.
2. The Wesleyan Holiness tradition began in the eighteenth century as a reaction to the rigid formality of many church services. Emphasis was placed instead on the "baptism of the Holy Spirit," in which a person's whole being, especially the emotions, would come into play. John Wesley was an Anglican who, along with his brother Charles, began the Methodist tradition (not denomination). Of note here is the emphasis in Wesleyan churches and colleges on the "Wesleyan Quadrilateral," which emphasizes that truth comes not only from Scripture, but via Reason, Tradition, and Experience as well. This structure informs much of what we do at Greenville College, and is in contradistinction to the Calvinist emphasis upon "sola Scriptura," i.e., Scripture alone, as the source of truth.
3. For more information on the formation and history of the Free Methodist Church, see Wilson T. Hogue, *History of the Free Methodist Church in North America*. (Chicago: Free Methodist Publishing House, 1915).
4. There are dozens of churches in America that claim the "Baptist" name; however, not all of them are affiliated with the Southern or American Baptist denominations. Thus, while a student may call himself Baptist in our demographic data, his church may be more nondenominational in structure. For more information on the Baptist denominations, see Bill J. Leonard, *Baptists in America* (New York: Columbia University Press, 2005).
5. Wayman, Benjamin, M.Div., Duke University. Interviewed by the author. June 9, 2009.
6. Hartley, Brian, Ph.D., Historical Theology, SLU. Interviewed by the author. May 5, 2009.
7. Huston, Ruth, M.A., Asbury Theological Seminary. Interviewed by the author. June 9, 2009.
8. See Hogue, *History of the Free Methodist Church*.
9. Samuel Sandmel was a pioneer in Jewish-Christian interreligious dialogue. He wrote, among other things, *A Jewish Understanding of the New Testament* (Woodstock, VT: Sky Paths Publishing, 2005), a ground-breaking study of New Testament literature from a Jewish perspective. A rabbi and scholar in Cincinnati, Rabbi Sandmel became good friends with Bishop William G. Black, the Episcopalian Bishop of the Arch-Diocese of Cincinnati and an alumnus of Greenville College. In his honor and memory, Bishop Black funded the biennial Lecture Series.
10. Summary data in its entirety is provided in the Appendix to this essay.

Appendix: Taking Thomas to Temple

Method: Ten students who had self-selected to take History of Judaism served as the focus group. A two-hour session was conducted, for which the following questions were asked. As a follow-up to the focus group, a survey was sent out using SurveyMonkey.com. Questions for the survey were derived from the focus group discussion. The survey served to quantify some of the qualitative data and gather some demographic information on the participants. All participants signed a waiver indicated that they knew that information from the session and the survey were going to be published in a study on the Judaism of Jesus as taught at an evangelical Christian college. Anonymity was guaranteed.

Focus Group Questions:

Chart 1. Year of graduation of students surveyed.

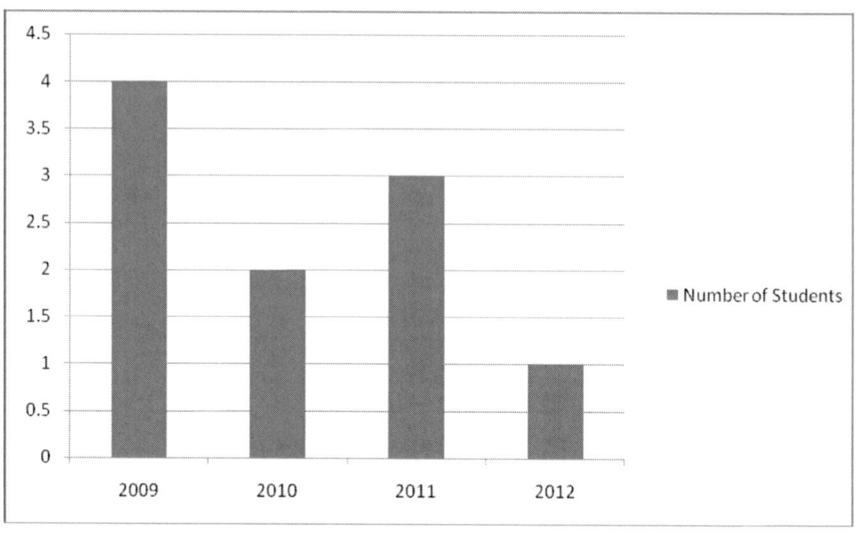

Chart 2. Majors of the students surveyed.

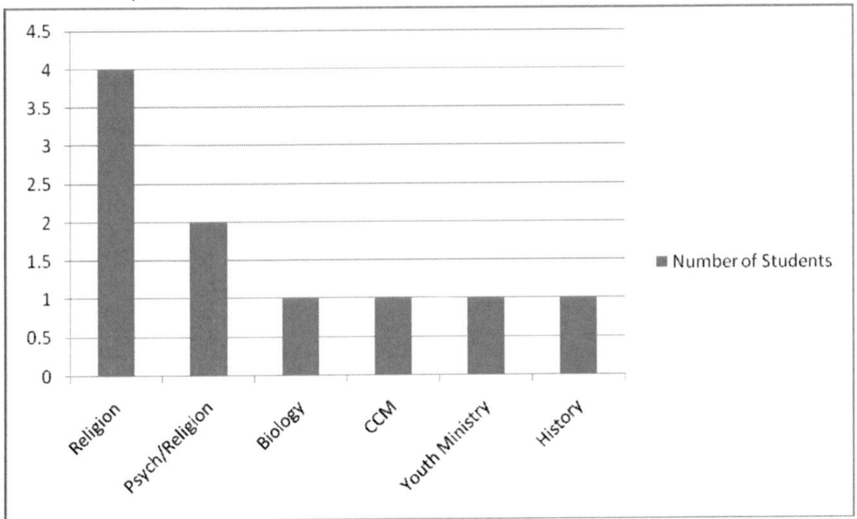

Chart 3. Student Christian denominations.

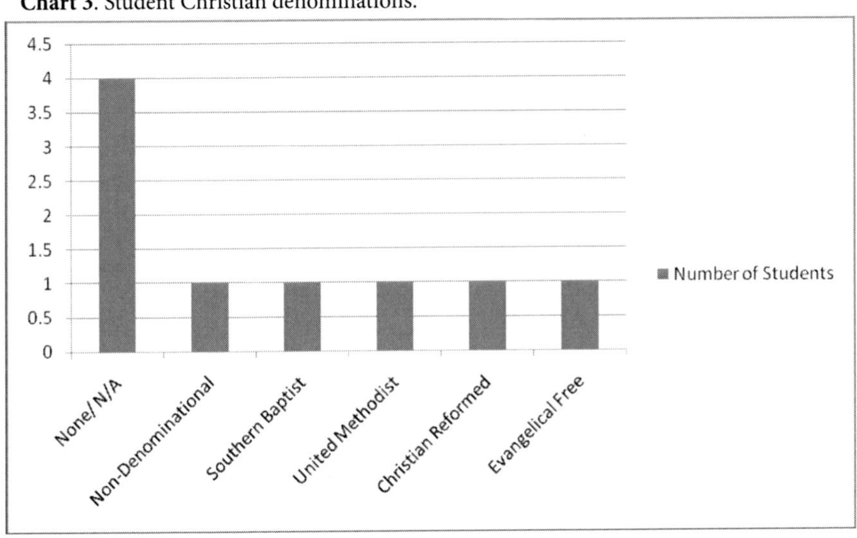

Chart 4. Level of exposure to the Judaism of Jesus before college.

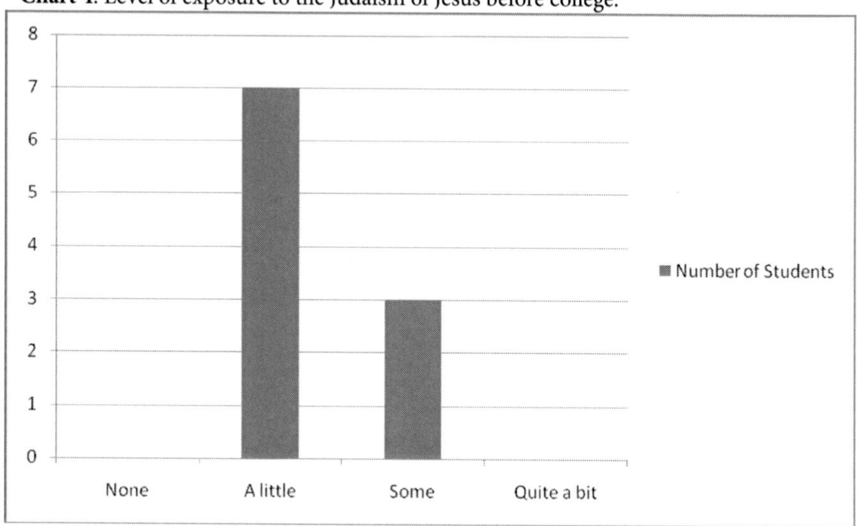

Chart 5. Sources of information regarding the Judaism of Jesus prior to college.

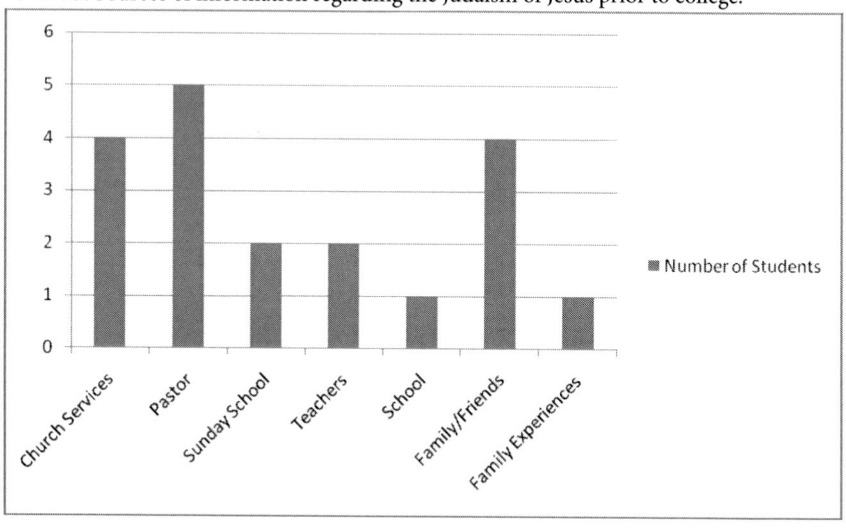

Chart 6. How important is Jesus' background/religion to your religious life now?

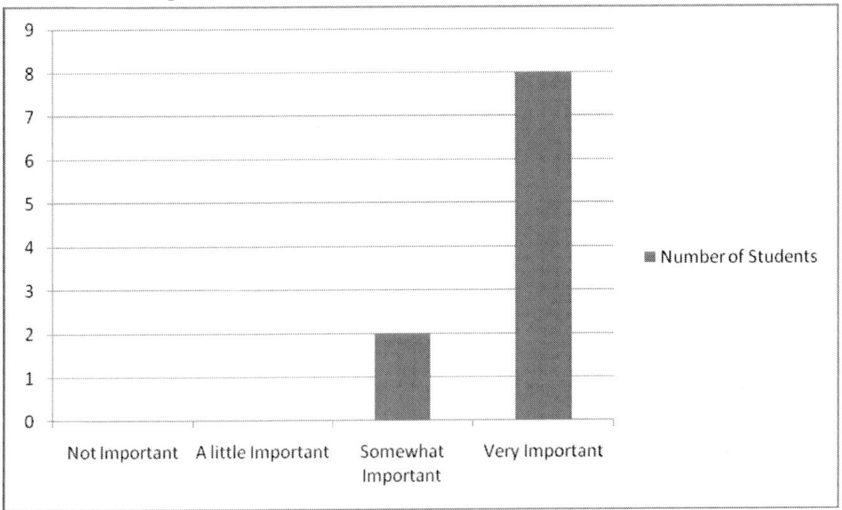

Chart 7. (from SurveyMonkey): Rate GC experiences regarding their contribution to your understanding of Jesus as Jewish.

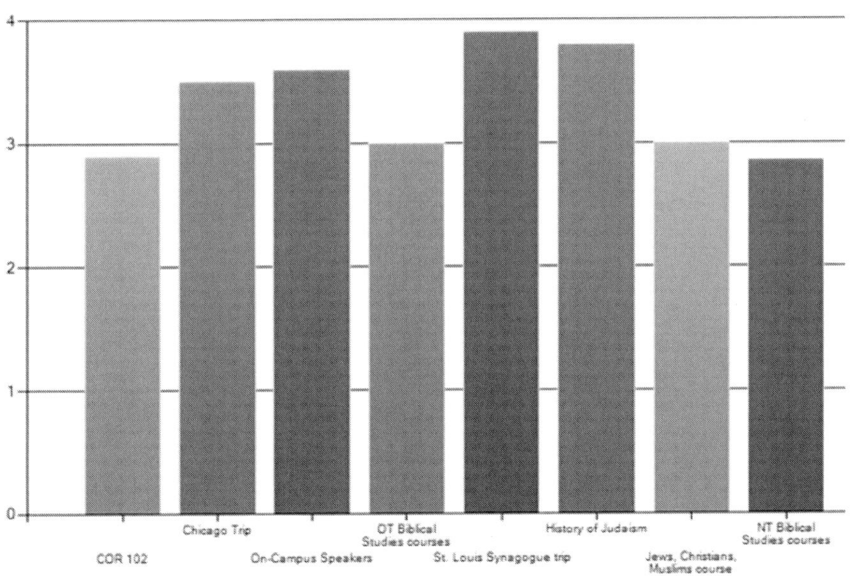

Table 1. Answers to the question, "What experiences could Greenville College provide that would provide a more comprehensive exposure to Jesus' cultural/religious background?"

- A course on Jesus as a Jew or a course in Hebrew.
- Possibly a course focused on the Contextualization of Jesus. Although courses like History of Judaism, Jews-Christians-Muslims, and even some NT Biblical Studies courses like Pauline Epistles do a good job at this.
- Maybe another history of Judaism class with the focus just on Jesus.
- Wilson R. King taught a class called "the Life of Christ" for many years when he was a professor at GC. Check the GC Catalogs in the Archives from the 1940s for a course description. I believe that the Life of Christ class was transformed into today's Synoptic Gospels class. Perhaps it would be beneficial for non-religion majors to take a freshman/sophomore level class about the life of Christ that would fulfill the Biblical studies component.
- Maybe a history/religion course on 'Understanding the Jewish Jesus'.
- I think Greenville does a good job of exposing us to stuff like that, but I think we as students don't take enough of the responsibility to learn what we are being taught upon ourselves.
- Jesus' Cultural/Religious background 101.
- Dr. Smerick could give a talk in the COR 102 classes after the Chicago Trip, helping to integrate a foundational understanding of Judaism.
- Could this be an extension of the Jewish studies program here? A specific class that would address this topic more thoroughly. Otherwise, I think it could be emphasized more in History of Christianity.

Table 2. Replies to the question, "Please explain, as if to a fellow student, why or why not studying Jesus' cultural/religious background is an important spiritual practice for Christians."

- The faith that we understand as Christianity is so influenced by the Catholic faith and is far from where it first started and pulled along by society that there is so much that is missing and forgotten from where we started out from. That is why we need to know and understand where Jesus came from and so we can get a better grasp of who he was and why he taught the way he did.
- Studying Jesus in his religious and cultural background is important because it gives us something to relate his teachings and methods to. Deeper than that it reminds us of Jesus Christ's own belief system, as well as what he means to his followers at that time. Studying Jesus as Jewish is simply one of the most integral parts in truly understanding Jesus Christ as who he was, a man who came to breathe hope into his people, and not to start a newer religion of Christianity.
- Because if not how are you going to understand why Jesus was so important in his time and why he was killed and how he affected the Jews.
- Jesus was not a white American. As we seek truth, it is important for us to learn about Jesus' context so that we can better understand the meaning of the life, death, and resurrection of Christ. In addition, the history of Christianity is stained with anti-Semitism; therefore, it is important for us to learn how to appreciate Jesus as a Jew in the hope that appreciating Judaism may help the church repent of its anti-Semitic past.
- Studying Jesus' background is important on many levels. its first important to compare/contrast Jesus with the religious people of his day. this helps one see how radical Jesus really was. it's also important just to become familiar with the land and civil structure that was present during the first century. this helps to form an idea of the authenticity of Jesus.
- Studying Jesus' cultural/religious background is important to practice because, just as we wouldn't follow the teachings of Carl Marx without first knowing something about him, specifically his background and such, we shouldn't follow Jesus' teachings without knowing who he was in his time. There is truth in the statement "Everyone is a product of their past", and Jesus, being fully human, was no exception.

- I would like to reflect more on this topic, more so with Rick McPeak, but as can be seen in question # 8, i haven't concluded enough to think straight and/or know what I am talking about.
- Jesus is a complex figure who lived in a complex world very different from ours. He grew up a Jew, and he taught as a Jew. Judaism is a window into that world, and the more we interact with Jews the more we can come to understand Jesus, our own faith, and help define ourselves without being disrespectful to a very important group of people.
- Our faith today stems from Jesus' faith and life when he lived. Knowing what his faith, life, and religion were like is crucial to understanding our faith, because our faith stems from him.
- Embracing the Jewish character of Jesus seems to encourage a more holistic perspective on what Christ exemplified within Judaic society and why Christianity is in close relationship to Judaism.

The Historical Jesus as Jewish Prophet: Its Meaning for the Modern Jewish-Christian Dialogue[1]

Sara Mandell

Although considering the historical Jesus a Jew is a common, but not universal academic tenet, it is not so perceived by those albeit rather limited segments of the lay public whose anti-Judaism causes them to separate Jesus *the* Messiah from his Second Temple Jewish background.[2] For the most part, the great majority of lay Christians, who have no anti-Jewish feelings, do not pay attention or simply give lip service to the historical Jesus' Jewishness because it is only slightly if at all relevant to their faith and/or theological precepts.

On the other hand, there is a growing movement by lay Christians to pay attention to Jesus' Judaism. This occurs because fundamentalist Christians believe that Jesus will return when the Jews return to Israel, thereby presupposing a core connection between the return of the Messiah, namely Jesus, and that of the prophetic spirit,[3] with Jewish History past, present, and future;[4] and, some Christian sects are influenced by the Jewish-Christian dialogue, whose focus is on commonalities —whether or not their shared origin from Second Temple Judaism is acknowledged— rather than differences. Since this dialogue is evolving into a strong religious force,[5] it is bringing the lay into the academic arena.

Although at least as a theological dictum lay Christians and Jews today do not think of Jesus as if he were a prophet,[6] it is likely, provided the earliest manuscripts of the Gospels were in accord with whatever manuscripts may have been handed down,[7] that some or even many of Jesus contemporaries did consider him one (see, for example, Matt. 21:46).[8] For example, in some villages, the people identified Jesus as John the Baptist, Elijah, or a prophet (Mark 8:27; Luke 9:18). The delineation of Jesus as prophet is indicated by Jesus' use of Old Testament themes regarding the torture and death of prophets as we see in Matthew (23:34-39).[9] We also see this in the "woe" oracles (Matt. 23:13-33), which deeply reflect prophetic pronouncements. Jesus clearly shows himself to be a prophet,[10] as evidenced by his comments regarding a prophet's acceptance or honor in his own country (Gos Thom. 31:1;[11] Matt. 13:57; Mark 6:4; Luke 4:24; John 4:44).[12] Moreover, the "crowds" in Matthew (21:11) and Luke (7:16, 24:19) explicitly call Jesus a prophet. He is deemed a great prophet (Luke 11:16). Most importantly, he self-identifies as a prophet (Luke 13:33). The understanding that Jesus was a prophet remains part of the Muslim conventions (Q 2:136), but, it has not continued to be given consideration in nonacademic, lay Judaeo-Christian traditions.

There are various reasons that the historical Jesus' prophetic nature, which is part of the academic understanding, is not part of the modern lay Judaeo-Christian dialogue. The latter is only beginning to deal with the historical *realia* pertinent to core beliefs, rites, and practices, and to very specific parallels found between Old Testament/Hebrew Scripture and New Testament texts.[13] Rather, the differences between the two perspectives are related to the albeit conceptually or theological evolved focus of those beliefs, rites, and practices. The lay understanding views the New Testament text only as it pertains to modern Christianity or Judaism: in other words, it revolves around what is pertinent to the respective believer without regard to the historical validity. On the other hand, the academic understanding concerns itself with historical validity, and it looks at what we believe was pertinent to the respective believer in Jesus' own time as well as that in which the canonical text was composed.[14]

Christians have, as the core of their faith, Jesus, who had been born as king of the Jews (Matt. 1:1; Mark 1:1) and who is also the anointed one, the Messiah or Christ (Matt. 16:16; Mark 8:29; Luke 9:20; John 1:41, 4:25).[15] Surprisingly, therefore, it is only in John 4:26 that Jesus self-identifies as such.[16] However, since John is patently influenced by middle Platonism, this attribution may simply be a differing delineation of what was clearly understood by Jesus' followers, including the authors of the Synoptic Gospels. From the Easter faith perspective, the messianic persona of Jesus is founded and based on the resurrection (Acts 26:23; Rom. 4:24, 8:11; Gal. 1:1; Eph. 1:20),[17] specifically by the holy spirit (Rom. 8:11)[18] or by the father (Acts 2:32, 3:15; Thes. 1:10; Gal. 1:1; 1 Cor. 6:14; Rom. 4:20-24; Eph. 1:17-20). However the messianic persona also embraces Jesus' virgin birth (Matt. 1:18-25); his status as Son of Man and Son of God;[19] his suffering and death for mankind's sins (Matt. 26-27; Mark 14-15; Luke 22:23; John 12-19); his status as one who himself has been raised (1 Cor. 15:12, 19:3-4) and will come again (Matt. 24:27; Mark 13:24-27; Luke 21:25-28); and, one who not only has the power to raise others from the dead (Mark 5:35-43; Luke 7:11-15; John 11:1-34),[20] but will raise up or bring believers to eternal life (John 5:21; Acts 26:8;

Rom. 4:17; 2 Cor. 1:9) although it is not clear if it is God the Father or Christ who is the efficient cause.[21]

When modern lay Christians consider Jesus and prophecy, they generally do so in regard to Yahwistic prophecy that is deemed to foretell Jesus' coming. They only deal transiently, if at all, with the prophetic persona of Jesus.[22] This does not mean that those who knew or dealt with the historical Jesus also disregarded his prophetic nature. Being Yahweh's anointed and a prophet are not mutually exclusive.

Although Jesus' prophetic nature is not relevant to contemporary Jews, it may well have been relevant to some sects of Jews during the late Second Temple era and shortly thereafter. So, given the theological precepts of some of the Dead Sea communities as well as the ways in which their practices differed from much but not all of what was practiced in the Temple State of Judah and Jerusalem, it is not surprising to find references in their literature to Old Testament prophets as anointed (CD 2:12, 5:21-6:1; 1QM 11:7, 8).[23]

Insofar as his messianic status is concerned, it is Jesus as the Messiah, be it eschatological or political-military, not the idea of a messiah that has been and still is rejected by many rabbinic Jews from the end of the Second Temple era onward.[24] During the Second Temple era, the expectations of an eschatological messiah may have been slight and limited to certain sectarian groups in Jewish Palestine,[25] particularly those in Qumran; nevertheless, it was continuing to develop.[26] During the period extending from 200 BCE to 100 CE, messianic references were "used only infrequently in connection with agents of divine deliverance expected in the future."[27] This deliverance may or may not have been considered imminent in the Temple State of Judah and Jerusalem, but were clearly thought of as imminent in the Qumran communities.[28] Furthermore, in Judah and Jerusalem itself, we know that R. Akiba considered bar Kochba, who led the Second Jewish revolt against Rome (132-135 CE) to be a messiah, if not the Messiah. Significantly, by the end of the second century CE and beginning of the third, we see an expectation of a world to come for all Israel (*m. Sanh.* 10:1); and, in the sixth century CE, we find in the Bavli an expectation of a suffering messiah (*b. Sanh.* 98a-b). Even today, a cup for Elijah is placed on the Seder table and the door is left open so Elijah can enter and drink in accord with the prediction found in the late fifth century BCE prophet Malachi (3:23-24 [NRSV 4:5-6]) that Elijah will return "before the great, horrendous day of the Lord."

Amongst lay Jews today, there are various expectations or lack thereof for a future Jewish messiah, be he predicated on Scripture, Jewish mysticism, or modern sectarian beliefs and practices.[29] Just as some rabbinic Jews believe that the term "anointed" in Scripture can, but rarely was used to refer to a future eschatological savior or redeemer, others, particularly Hassidic and Orthodox, await the coming of such an eschatological messiah.[30] Some members of different Jewish affiliations await the coming of a political-military one. But, for the most part, we do not hear many lay Jews expressing any messianic expectations.

Regarding eschatology, today Jews do not theologically reject the idea of resurrection, and it was certainly not rejected during the period between the composition of the Deuteronomistic History and some time well after the end of the Second Temple and even of the early rabbinic era.[31]Although in most modern sectarian groups within Rabbinic Judaism, resurrection is not usually a topic of discussion either amongst the lay public or the rabbinic establishment,[32] this is not the case in Hassidic (in particular) and Orthodox Rabbinic Judaism. What is historically significant, here, is that either R. Judah the Prince or the framers of Mishnah maintained a belief or at least a dialogue regarding a belief in resurrection. It is stated that those denied a portion in the world to come are the ones who deny the attestation of the resurrection of the dead in Torah (*m. Sanh.* 10:1).

There is no denying that in Primary History there is at least one explicitly noted instance of death and resurrection, in which the Deuteronomistic Historian reports about the ecstatic-shamanic prophet Elisha's resurrection of the Shunenite woman's son (2 Kings 4:8-37).[33] However, the tradition clearly does not treat this as anomalous since even contact with the dead Elisha's bones could revive the dead (2 Kings 13:20-21). But, the circumstances in which such an act occurs are extraordinary in general, and are considered limited to the actions of the shamanic prophet, Elisha, whom Yahwah possesses.[34]

Elisha had various shamanic characteristics that are also basic to and paralleled in, albeit with modifications, the Jesus traditions: for example, Elisha caused multiple jars of oil to come from one jar (2 Kings 4:1-7); he was able to feed a number of men from only a small amount of food (2 Kings 4:42-44); he both cured (2 Kings 5:1-19) and made sick with leprosy (2 Kings 5:20-27). As Elisha had caused multiple jars of oil to come from one, Jesus caused multiple jars of wine to come from water (John 2:2-11). And, he performed other miracles that were similar to those of Elisha: for example, he fed thousands from seven loaves of bread (Matt. 15:32-39; Mark 8:2-10); and again, thousands from five loaves and two fish (Matt. 14: 13-21; Mark 6:35-44: Luke 9: 10-17: John 6: 1-15); he healed the sick (Matt. 4:24-25; 8:14-17; 9: 20-22; 12:13-14; Mark 1:29-31; 3:1-5; 5:28-31; Luke 4:38-41; 6:8-10; 8:43-48); he revived the dead, on various occasions (e.g., the dead girl [Matt. 9:24; Mark 5:35-39], the dead woman [Luke 8:52-3], the Widow's son [Luke 7:11-1]), the boy [Mark 9:26], whom the crowd believed dead, but who may have been simply possessed; and, most notably, Lazarus [John 12:1-17]). Moreover, he considered John the Baptist to have been risen from the dead (Matt 14:2).[35]

These attributes, abilities, and miracle workings which the historical Jesus shares with the allegedly ninth-century BCE shamanic prophets,[36] at least as depicted by the late sixth- to early fifth-century BCE Deuteronomistic Historian,[37] complement the suffering and rejection that he shared with eighth-century BCE writing-prophets,[38] thereby forming a paradigm that demands he be classified as a prophet just as the author of Acts (3:22-26) describes him. Not only does Jesus share some characteristics with the allegedly shamanic Elisha, he also shares a few characteristics with the allegedly thirteenth-century BCE Moses,[39] whom Jews consider a prophet and whom Christians believe prophesied the coming of Jesus as Messiah (Acts 3:22-26). Jesus, like Moses and the other prophets does speak directly with Yahweh. Moreover, Yahweh speaks through Moses, the shamanic prophets, the writing Prophets, and Jesus. Yahweh also possesses the shamanic prophets, and some but not all the writing prophets (at least when they receive their "call"), and possibly sometimes Jesus as well.

So, it is meaningful that, as de Jonge points out, Elisha is the only Old Testament nonregal prophet who is specifically noted by the Deuteronomistic Historian as being anointed (1 Kings 19:15-16); but, de Jonge also points out that this is not mentioned in his call narrative,[40] which is significant. However, there is at least one (Saul) and possibly a second (David) Old Testament ecstatic prophet who is anointed albeit because of regal rather than prophetic status. When Samuel anoints him king, Saul prophesies (1 Sam. 9:26-10:16; see esp.10:1-2 for anointing and 10:6-7 for Saul as ecstatic). When Saul sends messengers to seize David, not only do they become possessed by God's Spirit (1 Sam. 19:20-22), but ultimately so does Saul himself even prior to meeting Samuel (1 Sam. 19:23). When Saul does find Samuel, he not only undresses himself, he raves: in other words as depicted by the Deuteronomistic Historian, he either acted insanely or ecstatically, for the second time. This was so characteristically ecstatic that Saul's actions elicited the question "Is Saul also among the prophets." So, the Deuteronomistic Historian (1 Sam. 19:23-24) makes it clear that King Saul was also an ecstatic prophet be it for a limited period or not. Two Samuel portrays King David as acting in a like manner. When David dances naked before the Ark as it is entering Jerusalem (2 Sam. 6:14),[41] he is acting ecstatically. This indicates some relationship to the ecstatic, that is to the shamanic prophets. This relationship is particularly definitive from the Deuteronomistic Historian's vantage point since, as Keil and Delitch point out, David wore a white ephod, which "was, strictly speaking a priestly costume" and "the dress which denoted the priestly character of the wearer."[42] However, what we know about the priestly dress may be late.[43] So again, we must question the veracity of the interpretation. Although both Saul and David were anointed kings, the narrative clearly relates these actions to prophetic status.[44] Because Jesus is presumed to consider himself king of the Jews, and believed by many of his followers to be king, the concomitant prophetic and regal status of Saul and David, however limited it may be, is particularly pertinent to the Jesus paradigm.[45]

Rabbinic Jews categorically reject Jesus as the, much less a messiah, and they deny that he was ever the king of the Jews, but do not deny his being of the Davidic line.[46] From a rabbinic perspective, the lack of any tradition of Jesus having been anointed to office with oil,[47] as is demanded for high-priestly or regal status but not for prophetic, may itself disqualify him.[48] Although early Christian writings show him to have been anointed with the spirit, clearly a different type of anointment, this is not relevant to Judaism today; but, it was relevant to some sectarian groups during the late Second Temple era.[49]

It is notable that, during the Second Temple era and for some time after, there were multiple Jewish messiahs, some of whom even then were deemed false, of whom Jesus was just one.[50] Additionally there is a tradition of priestly anointment (2 Macc. 1:10). However, there were various sectarian expectations regarding the type and delineation of the messianic prophet who was to come.[51]

In Primary History, the kings of Israel and Judah are anointed as are some high priests,[52] namely Aaron, his sons, as well as Zadok (see, e.g., Exod. 29:1-7; Lev. 4:3-5, 6:15 [NRSV 6:22]).[53] Royal anointment is most notable: and, the greatest number of royal anointment citations refer to David, however there are quite a number for Saul, who is called Yahweh's anointed at least nine and possibly more times.[54] There are somewhat less for Solomon, Joash, Jehoahaz, Absalom, and Jehu.[55] One non-Yahwist, Hazael, is called anointed (1Kings 19: 15) along with the two Yahwistic shamanic prophets, Jehu and Elisha (1 Kings 19:16-17). But, this is the representation of the Deuteronomistic Historian,[56] whose work is very late. So, we cannot assume that the traditions he reports and stories he tells have any historical validity.[57]

In Primary History, with the exception of Hazael, non-Yahwists are not usually called messiah even though we know that anointing was part of the royal ascension process, the enthronement ritual, in the Ancient Near East.[58] In Exilic literature, there is an example of a non-Yahwist, Cyrus, whom Second Isaiah (45:1) deemed messiah.

Christians today categorize Jesus as the Messiah for five interrelated reasons: 1. Jesus was accepted by his followers as the Christ,[59] whether or not he acknowledged his kingship; 2. every king of Israel and Judah had been a political-military messiah; 3. according to the canonical Gospels, Jesus himself almost, but does not quite acknowledge his kingship both in the garden (John 18:1-11) and when questioned by Caiaphas (Mark 14:53-65; Matt. 26:57-68; Luke 22: 63-71; John 18:20-23),[60] but he does acknowledge his Christhood (Mark 14:62); however, when questioned by Pilate, who asked him if he were the king of the Jews, Jesus obfuscates and tells Pilate that he (Pilate) says it (Matt. 27:11);[61] 4. the soldiers mocked him as king (Matt. 27:29; Mark 15:18; Luke 26:36); 5. moreover, the people who mocked and attacked Jesus as king of the Jews when bearing the cross to Gethsemane understood him to have believed he was king (Matt. 27:42-43).

Although it was Roman policy to side with the pro-Roman faction, usually the upper classes, in provincial administration, we cannot conclude that Pilate was functioning as an arm of the high priests and the Sanhedrin per se. Rather, or at least more importantly, he was acting in accord with Roman interests and law when he asked Jesus if he were king of the Jews. Nobody could become king in a Roman client kingdom, much less the Roman imperial provence into which the Temple State had been incorporated and which was directly under imperial rule, without pre-approval by the Emperor.[62] Pilate was justified in questioning Jesus since some considered Jesus their king. Since Jesus was not a priest, Pilate may well have understood the kingship implicit in Jesus being deemed messiah. The fact that the Gospels depict Pilate as asking Jesus if he were king of the Jews, but not asking him if he were the anointed one, the Christ, suggests he understood the correlation. We cannot presuppose a lack of understanding: rather, Pilate would have known that anointment was required of a legitimate Yahwistic king.[63]

Jesus reply that Pilate was saying this merely shows Jesus understanding of Roman law in regard to this matter. Jesus could not acknowledge kingship since that would have both indicted and convicted him of treason against Rome,[64] insofar as arrogating for himself the kingship of Judaea without Roman permission or appointment. Most importantly, Jesus' Christ-hood was an extremely dangerous idea in Roman eyes. The self-or popular deification of a ruler, that is in this case someone deemed messiah, would have placed such a person over and against the deceased, but self-divinized founder of the Roman Empire, Augustus, as well as his son Tiberius.

Before Jesus, it is likely that each Jewish messiah was considered human,[65] which is what Son of Man often means.[66] However, Jesus, in the Gospels, is denoted as "the Son of Man,"[67] and the articulation clearly indicates some type of divinity. Here, then, it is used analogously with Son of God.[68] By the late Second Temple era, an expectation of an eschatological as well as a political-military messiah had come into being,[69] hence Jesus' classification as *the* Son of God. This is an ambiguous designation which might denote a deity, as is the case in many of the Graeco-Roman traditions that were becoming well known in Jewish Palestine; or like Son of Man, it may also designate a human being insofar as it denotes being a follower of God as many others have noted.

Those who accept Jesus as the Messiah draw on the prophetically announced paradigm, particularly that of the four Servant Songs in Second Isaiah (42:1-4; 49:1-7; 50:4-11: 52:13-53:12). These Servant Songs are still and have been interpreted by Christians,[70] from relatively early times until the current day, as prophesying the coming of Jesus as eschatological messiah and, therefore, as the "Suffering Servant of Yahweh" as well as the Son of God.[71] Consequently, they interpret his delineation as the Son of God unambiguously as a sign of divinity. Actually the designation is ambiguous and can denote both the divine and human, and thereby define him as both.[72] For Christians, the depiction of Jesus as a Son of Man and the (only begotten) Son of God is congruent, but capable of being differentiated. So, the perception of Jesus as the king of the Jews as well as the one foretold by the prophets does and must rest on that of Jesus the human Jew, be it acknowledged or not. This does not deny his divine status, but rather signifies the regal ties to the human individual.

There are several interesting aspects to this. For example, nowhere in the Gospels does Jesus refer to himself as king of the Jews, although Matthew considers him born to be king of the Jews and Jesus concurs. Whether Jesus' guardedness is for safety's sake so as not to be categorized as treasonous by Roman Law (above) or because he did not think of himself as king of the Jews, which is unlikely given the near admissions, is impossible to determine with only the extant biblical and extra-biblical writings. On the other hand, the superscription over Jesus on the cross reads "the King of the Jews" (Mark 15:26); or "This is the King of the Jews" (Luke 23:38); or "Jesus of Nazareth, the King of the Jews" (John 19:19-20); or "This is Jesus, the King of the Jews" (Matt. 27:37). These superscriptions show that the Romans crucified him for the treasonous act of assuming kingship whether or not he had admitted to this when questioned by Pilate.[73]

Additionally, there is the matter of the Suffering Servant of Yahweh paradigm found in Second Isaiah, which Christians posit as anticipating Jesus.[74] However, it is highly possible that Second Isaiah may not have construed the Servant Songs as prophesying a future messianic figure. Rather, as is most likely, just as First Isaiah was reflecting on the birth of King Hezekiah (7:14) in a statement later taken to prophesy the birth of Jesus,[75] Second Isaiah in the Servant Songs may have been reflecting on the suffering of First Isaiah. That is, it may really have been referring to the eighth-century Isaiah of Jerusalem, who like other eighth-century prophets of whom we are aware,[76] was a despised pariah in his own day.[77]

The correlations are strong. Precisely because First Isaiah's form of Yahwism was decidedly different from what he attributes to his contemporary Judahites, and particularly to the Jerusalemites, he was quite rightly scorned by his contemporaries. His practices, according to his own testimony (Isa. 1-39),[78] albeit demanded by Yahweh, were anomalous, at least in the society for whose sake, but at the same time, against which he preaches. It is he, not those he carps at, who is different. Most importantly, his preaching about the sins of the Jerusalemites in chapters 1-6 is vituperative.

Likewise, Jesus' preaching (e.g., the Beatitudes [Matt. 5:3-12; Luke 6:17, 20-23]) goes beyond what insofar as we know was practiced in the Temple State, and it was often out of accord with the priestly doctrines (Matt 5:17-48). Jesus' attack (Matt. 5:1-7:27) on the religious practices of those in the Temple State is analogous to First Isaiah's attack on the daughters of Jerusalem. His attack on the money changers and others in the Temple (Matt. 21:12-13; Mark 11: 15-19; Luke 19:45-48; John 2:13-22) is perhaps the high point of his attack on the Temple State, particularly the Jerusalemite establishment. But, significantly, when Jesus is asked why his disciples transgress the elders' traditions (Matt. 15:1-6), he responds (Matt. 3-9:1; Mark 7:1-23) by telling the Pharisees and scribes that they give priority to their traditions rather than to God. In justification, he cites First Isaiah (29:13). Like Isaiah, it is Jesus and not those he carps at who is different. As to nastiness, it must be noted that Jesus made it clear he did not come to bring peace, but to set one against the other (Matt. 10:34-36; Luke 12:51-53), and he treats those whom he believes are violating his father's house and laws with vituperation. Moreover, in Matthew, he speaks of himself as having come with a sword. Both First Isaiah and Jesus intend to bring dissension to change the religious practices of the people.

The hatred and scorn for First Isaiah clearly came about for several interrelated reasons. First Isaiah violated Judahite customs or sense of morality: for example, he followed Yahweh's instructions to remove his sandals and sackcloth, in itself not the customary dress of upper-class Judahites except those in mourning, if we can trust 2 Sam 3:31,[79] and to walk about naked and barefoot (Isa. 20:2). Perhaps he had only removed an outer garment, and therefore acted out of accord with custom rather than violating morality, which Keil and Delitch offer as a possibility. Should that have been the case, this too would not have endeared him to the Jerusalemites.[80] More importantly, he offended the Jerusalemites by telling them they were violating a religion of which, ironically, they were either then unaware or did not think pertained to them. In fact, he was doing more than that: he was preaching a new type of Yahwism that countermined what had hitherto been practiced. Likewise, Jesus was preaching a different type of Yahwism, which clearly was offensive to the scribes and Pharisees. It was also offensive to the Sadducees, who did not believe in resurrection.

First Isaiah preached the worship of Yahweh alone, thereby treating the commonly practiced Cult of the Dead as anathema;[81] and more specifically, he condemned the prevailing religion in which Yahweh was deemed first among the gods rather than the only god, thereby accusing the sons of Israel of violating true Yahwism and consequently to be punished. First Isaiah (chaps. 2-4) pronounces "Judgment on Israel and Jerusalem in ways reminiscent of Amos." Likewise, he condemns both the "civil and religious leadership" of Israel and Judah (Isa. 28-33).[82] This naturally led to the martyr-like status of First Isaiah. Jesus told his disciples and followers to practice and observe the teachings of the scribes and Pharisees, but not to emulate their actions (Matt. 23:1-12; Mark 12:38-40; Luke 20:45-47), and he condemned them in a series of woes (Matt. 23:13-36).

It is notable that First Isaiah's Yahwism, the cult in which Yahweh is deemed the only god, like that of other eighth-century prophets, was not accepted by the majority of the sons of Israel until Josiah's reform of 622 BCE or possibly subsequent to that reform, even as late as the Babylonian exile, and possibly even later.[83] Isaiah and others do assume that Hezekiah, the king, did, however, accept Yahweh alone rather than Yahweh as first among the gods. Likewise, Jesus' Judaism, which predicated Father, Son, and Holy Spirit, was not accepted by the leadership and, insofar as we can tell, the majority of Jews from Judah and Jerusalem.

Like First Isaiah, Jesus violated the accepted norms of Second Temple Judaism as practiced in Judah and Jerusalem.[84] For example, Jesus forgave sins (Matt. 9: 2-6; Mark 2:5-8; Luke 5:20-21); he ate with sinners and tax collectors (Matt. 9:10-11; Mark 2:15-16; Luke 5:27-30), he reaped on the Sabbath (Matt. 12:1-2; Mark 2:23-25; Luke 6:1-2); and when questioned about his and his disciples' lack of observance of the traditions of the elders (Matt. 15: 1-2; Mark 7:1-5), he cited First Isaiah (29:13). Jesus frontally attacked the established order when he entered the Temple and drove the buyers and sellers out as well as overturned the moneychangers' tables (Matt. 21:12-17; Mark 11:13-19; Luke 19:45-46; John 2:13-16).

Clearly, Jesus the Jew may be modeled on the paradigm of First Isaiah via the Servant Songs of Second Isaiah.[85] Although this is in contradistinction to the accepted dictum that, in these songs Isaiah prophesied Jesus' suffering for Israel, it does not mean that both could not be true. Moreover, although some such as John Drane think that Jesus actually modeled himself, rather than having been so construed by followers, on the Suffering Servant of Second Isaiah,[86] this is unlikely. Scholars believe the term "messiah" is not to be found in the hypothetical Q document, which if true means that his early followers had not heard him declare himself messiah; and, the Gospels show Jesus as reluctant to be called messiah.[87] Clearly, however, like First Isaiah, Jesus had picked up the prophetic mantle. And, like many prophets, Jesus was a suffering servant of Yahweh.

Conclusions for a Modern Jewish-Christian Dialogue

Jesus' Jewishness is acknowledged by some Jews today, mainly academic, and tacitly accepted by most Jews, both lay and academic. Except for the Jews for Jesus, modern Jews do not consider him either a prophet or messiah.

On the other hand, lay Christians for whom Jesus is both the political-military, that is, the kingly leader in battle[88] and eschatological messiah do not consider him a prophet, whereas some academics see him as both prophet and messiah. As I have already noted, only a few do not accept that he was a Jew.

The lay public often does not understand that a prophet was a pariah or at best out of touch and hated or scorned by his contemporaries. This may be why Jesus is rarely categorized as a prophet, and Isaiah himself is not viewed through the lens of First Isaiah, but rather intertextually through the lens of Second and Third Isaiah.[89] It also may explain why most lay Jews and Christians look at what the prophets preached rather than how those against whom they preached viewed what was being preached. So, their sympathy is with a prophet like Isaiah and others who preached Yahweh alone rather than Yahweh as first of the gods, particularly since the prophetic perspective colors and strongly influences modern theology. The approach is clearly one sided.

The matter is more complicated in the case of the academic community's understanding of either Isaiah or Jesus. Since it is now rare for academics, even those who wish to view the biblical text from a New Critical perspective and thereby disregard the temporal differential of composition, to disregard the different nature of the prophetic voice respectively in the three Isaiah's, there does not seem to be any problem in delineating the prophet as hated and scorned by his contemporaries where it is text appropriate. However, if we wish to understand why Jesus the Jew was a prophet for his time, we must see him as *the* Suffering Servant of the Lord,[90] with the full panoply of hatred and scorn directed at him.

Moreover, in pursuit of our understanding of commonality, we must try to understand how, why, and under what circumstances the lay perception regarding the historical as well as the temporally developed nature of Jesus, which the faithful deem unchanged (e.g., in the doxology, "as it was in the beginning, is now and evermore shall be") differs from the academic at the same time as we focus on the history of prophecy and prophetic movements.

Generally, the lay perception of Jesus or of a prophet is not relevant to an academic study, even when the academic understanding of his prophetic nature is discussed; and the lay perception is either omitted or summarily dismissed. But, when it comes to the perception of who and what Jesus was, how he as well as other Second Temple era prophets were viewed,[91] as well as how Israelite and Judahite, most notably the eighth-century prophets were viewed by their contemporaries, it may be useful to take a fresh look. In the process, we must examine both the academic and lay perception, respectively, so as to see how they differ from and how they coincide with one another. Differentiating what is faith based and what is an (albeit attempted) historical analysis will enable us to learn how the one influenced and has continued to influence the other. We may then see how the analogies between Jesus and the eighth-century prophets in particular have influenced our modern perception of Jesus with the result that we have lost sight of the historical Jesus.

It is easy to grasp how the understanding of the prophets as beloved of the people developed when we look at portions of Second and Third Isaiah. Likewise, it is easy to ignore the expressed hatred and scorn for Jesus, which is attributed to specific sectarian groups without regard to its members' social status,[92] so as to see him as beloved by the people in New Testament. It is not so easy to see the same thing when we read prophets who lived after the eighth century, such as Ezekiel or Jeremiah or even Jonah, either through the lens of an understanding subsequent to their preaching or via a modern critical analysis of the respective texts in their historical context.[93] To understand fully the transformative phenomenon involved, we must analyze their works from a socio-, a literary-, and a theo-political perspective. That is, we must look at it comparatively, that is in its own historical milieu, rather than in a historically chronological one by category.

It is also easy to understand how the perception of Jesus as non-Jewish developed. Once Paul brought his new religion to the Gentiles, Gentile Christianity began to dominate the religious practices, at least insofar as our historical traditions suggest. However, because of Paul's influence, the sectarian nature of very early Gentile Christianity differed from that of Second Temple and early Rabbinic Judaism. Christian sectarian differentiation, which was ostensibly but not really lost when Constantine declared Christianity the religion of the Roman world, reflected the nationality vis-à-vis the polis or in some cases the broad based nation of its practitioners. This, however, was not determinative in bringing gentile Christianity to the fore and relegating Jewish Christianity to an ever dwindling religion. What matters is that the influence of early gentile Christianity is such that it is perceived as the true Christianity, and Jewish Christianity is treated as an anomaly. This, of course, leads to some of the problems inherent in defining the true Israel as well as the historical Jesus.

On the other hand, the influence of early Rabbinic Judaism, which like Christianity is a daughter of Second Temple Judaism, also has led to the Jewish lay perception that there is no real distinction between Second Temple and Rabbinic Judaism, which in rabbinic ideology form a continuum. Likewise, it has reinforced the rabbinic belief that Jesus was a radical Jew who separated himself from his own true religion. This may have led to the perception that somehow or other, Jesus was not Jewish: a not surprising development since Jesus lived at a time when there was great social and political unrest in Jewish Palestine. Moreover, it was not to the benefit of any school of early Rabbinic Judaism to treat Jesus as "traditionally" or "normatively" Jewish.[94] So, he is at best ignored. If at all regarded, he is treated as a renegade Jew or a heretic or somehow or other dissociated from Judaism. Interestingly enough, he was never deemed a half-Jew as were the Samaritans.

Consequently, even those Jews who acknowledge that Jesus was born of Jewish parents, and Christians who acknowledge that Jesus was born by virgin birth from a Jewish mother frequently treat him as other than Jewish. Perhaps they view the later evolution of Christianity as reflective of its origins rather than as something derivative of them. This, of course, presupposes that Second Temple Judaism and Rabbinic Judaism alone form a continuum in accordance with Rabbinic dicta. In fact, like Second Temple Judaism and Rabbinic Judaism, Second Temple Judaism and early Jewish Christianity also form a continuum. Rabbinic Judaism and early Jewish Christianity are siblings, each born of the same parent.

Perhaps some type of gentile anti-Judaism or even anti-Semitism, be it acknowledged or not, influences a limited group's understanding of Jesus' Jewishness. Or perhaps some type of Jewish anti-Christianity leads some groups to the desire to dissociate the origins of the Christian faith from the history of Judaism. Granted this, whence comes the perception that Jesus was a Jewish prophet? From a Christian perspective, we have Luke's Gospel, in which Jesus' prophetic nature is "the epistemological center" and "the essential kerygma."[95] From a Moslem perspective, it is a way of co-opting Jesus and subsuming him into the theological lineage of Mohammed so as to present Islam as superseding Christianity.

For Judaism, however, the matter is more problematic. Most Jews do not think of Jesus as a prophet. Although scholars think we know what his contemporaries believed, we only know what the extant sources want us to know. Early Christian literature tends to present late Second Temple Judaism as monolithic, which we know is not the case, and as antithetic—which it may or may not have been—to Jesus as Christ. Early Rabbinic literature treats Rabbinic Judaism, albeit with more than one school, as the only form of Judaism, ipso facto denying the prophetic nature of Jesus much less his Christhood. On the other hand, pre-

Constantinian Graeco-Roman data, including literature, for early Christianity tends to present Christians as revolutionary and thereby treasonous whereas, in fact, it was the treatment of Jesus as king of the Jews, not its revolutionary nature, that made Christianity treasonous. For there to be concord, we need to analyze and understand the differences as well as the commonalities. This is the difficult task that faces Christians and Jews who are now in dialogue.

Discussion Questions

1. Why do we focus on the prophetic nature of the Servant Songs in Second Isaiah as predictive of Jesus, and ignore the parallels between First Isaiah and Jesus?
2. Why is it important to understand the relationship between the lay participants in the Jewish Christian dialogue and academic studies of New Testament and the historical Jesus?

Notes

1. In discussing the historical Jesus, we are limited by the relative lateness of even the earliest texts such as the genuine Pauline letters, which are contextually Hellenistic, with a non-Judaean focus despite Paul's Jewish ethnicity. The Gospels are later than Paul. And, although Q is considered to reflect the sayings of the historical Jesus, it is as yet hypothetic. So, although the Synoptics are Judaean and Matthew and Luke are believed to be derived from Mark and Q together with other albeit lesser oral materials, we can only be sure of the Markan derivation. We do not know to what extent they, or any extant writings, reflect the historical Jesus.
2. The distinction between the proper noun, Messiah, and the common noun, messiah, is significant.
3. For the Jewish expectation that "the return of the prophetic spirit was inextricably related to messianic times," see Franklin W. Young, "Jesus the Prophet: A Re-Examination," *Journal of Biblical Literature* 68 (1949): 285-99. Franklin's hypothesis makes it clear that there is a tie between Jesus as messiah and as Jewish prophet.
4. Although this is generally presumed to have been, and may currently be a belief in a return of the Jewish people to "the Land," Israel, there is another interpretation that must be considered. If the Christians are *verus Israel,* it is possible that at one time it was believed that the return to Israel referred to the conversion of the Jews to the true Israel, not a return to "the Land." For an understanding of this, see Marcel Simon, *Verus Israel: A Study of the Relations Between Christians and Jews in the Roman Empire (AD 135-425*), trans. H. McKeating (Oxford: Oxford University Press, 1986).
5. Note, in particular the International Center for Christians and Jews (*ICCJ*); the Council of Centers on Jewish-Christian Relations (*CCJR*); and their constituent groups, of which there are many.
6. Perhaps this confusion arises because, as Amy-Jill Levine, in *The Misunderstood Jew: The Church and the Scandal of the Jewish Jesus* (San Francisco:Harper, 2006), states, "Jesus does sound like a prophet" (110). But, according to Levine, this is mitigated by the Gospels, in which he is regarded as "more than a prophet" with the context

disrupting "the prophetic analogy." However, Levine also views Jesus as part of the continuum of Jewish teachers (rabbis) and prophets because of the commonality of their worldview (20).

7. Levine, *The Misunderstood Jew,* 104-05 is in accord with the consensus opinionis, pointing out that we have no autograph copies of the canonical Gospels; we don't really know who wrote the Gospels or where; but what we have comes from around 200 CE.
8. Paul E. Davies, in "Jesus and the Role of the Prophet," *Journal of Biblical Literature* 64 (1945) suggests that a growing "interest in Christology" was being accompanied by a "slight reference to Jesus' work as a prophet" albeit with limitations (253). Despite the growth of Christology today, studies of Jesus' prophetic nature are still limited; but, they are growing and have become part of the academic dialogue.
9. P. Oxy. 2683 (which, being mid to late 2nd century, predates the earliest MMS of the Canonical Gospels), has a large segment of Matt. 23-30. But Matt. 23:34-35 is missing, so we can draw no inference from it. All citations of Papyri in this paper are from: Philip W. Comfort and David P. Barrett, *The Text of the Earliest New Testament Greek Manuscripts* (Wheaton: Tyndale House/Libronix, 2001).
10. David L. Turner, "Matthew 23 as Prophetic Critique," *Journal of Biblical Studies* 4 (2004): 23-42, see esp. 25-33; Susan Rieske, "Jesus' Use of Old Testament Themes in Matthew 23:34-39," *Journal of Biblical Studies* 4 (2004) at journalofbiblicalstudies.org, n.p. Moreover, Davies, "Jesus and the Role of the Prophet," suggests that the references to false Christs and false prophets in combination (Mark 13:22) may be "suggestive" of Jesus' "self-designation" as the true one (242). Significantly, J. Severino Croatto, in "Jesus, Prophet like Elijah and Prophet-Teacher like Moses in Luke-Acts," *Journal of Biblical Literature* 124 (2005) points out that the messianic designation obfuscated the lay awareness of Jesus as prophet, which role is central to Luke (451). Most importantly he states the prophetic viewpoint in "Jesus' activity is so intense in the Lukan magnum opus that it is astonishing that it could be replaced by the messianic readings" and that this became the focus of the text to the virtual exclusion of the prophetic interpretation (465).
11. The citation in the Gospel of Thomas is very significant since this work may be very close to what we call Q.
12. John 4:44 is found in the mid-second century Bodmer II + Inv. Nr. 4274/4298 papyrus. William John Lyons shows that this is not just a commonly quoted proverbial statement by Jesus in "A Prophet is Rejected in His Home Town [Mark 6.4 and Parallels]: A Study in the Methodological (In) Consistency of the Jesus Seminar," *Journal for the Study of the Historical Jesus* 6 (2008): 59-84. He speculates that the idea that Jesus' own ministry is the basis of the saying (82-83).
13. P. E. Davies thinks that our customary messianic nomenclature for Jesus actually obfuscates his prophetic nature ("Jesus and the Role of the Prophet," 254).
14. Based on what we know of oral transmission, it is probable that the two not only may have, but most likely differed.
15. There is an enormous body of literature dealing with Jesus as the Messiah. Despite their age, Tryggve Mettinger's *King and Messiah* (Lund: ConBOT 8, 1976) and Sigmund Mowinckel's *He That Cometh: The Messiah Concept in the Old Testament and Later Judaism* (Grand Rapids: Eerdmans, 2005) are still relevant. For problematics regarding Second Temple messianic figures, see Jacob Neusner, *Messiah in Context: Israel's History and Destiny in Formative Judaism* (Philadelphia: Fortress, 1984); see

also, *Judaisms and Their Messiahs at the Turn of the Christian Era*, ed. Jacob Neusner, William Scot Green, and Ernest Frerichs (Cambridge: Cambridge University Press, 1987).

16. For an earlier witness (mid-second century CE) than the earliest MS of the canonical text to John 4:26, see P. Bodmer II + Inv. Nr. 4274/4298.
17. Joseph Jensen, "Prediction-Fulfillment in Bible and Liturgy," *Catholic Biblical Quarterly* 50 (1988): 656. Whether resurrection was bodily is a matter of debate. George W. E. Nickelsburg, in "Resurrection," *Anchor Bible Dictionary*, ed. David Noel Freedman (New York:Doubleday, 1992) says that such traditions suggest some type of "apologetic tendency" (5:691). F. W. Horn, in "Holy Spirit," *Anchor Bible Dictionary*, notes that the raising of Jesus from the dead "is expressed in some of the oldest Christian formulas" (3:267).
18. See 11Q Melch 18, where the herald of the end time is referred to as "anointed by the spirit" (משיח הרוח). See, for example, Adam Simon von der Woude, "Messianic Ideas in Later Judaism," *Theological Dictionary of the New Testament*, ed. Gerhard Kittel and Gerhard Friedrich, trans. and ed. Geoffrey W. Bromiley (Grand Rapids: Wm. B. Eerdmans, 1964), 9:517.
19. New Testament repeatedly uses these terms in reference to the historical Jesus or the eschatological Christ. For an overview, see George W. E. Nickelsburg, "Son of Man," *Anchor Bible Dictionary* 6:141-50. For the "Son of Man" and for the influence of Enoch on the delineation of Jesus, see G. W. E. Nickelsburg, "First and Second Enoch: A Cry against Oppression and the Promise of Deliverance," in *The Historical Jesus in Context*, ed. Amy-Jill Levine, Dale C. Allison Jr., and John Dominic Crossan (Princeton: Princeton University Press, 2006), 87-109; see esp. 89-92. For a comprehensive discussion of their messianic and human meanings and usages respectively, see Adela Yarbro Collins and John J. Collins, *King and Messiah as Son of God: Divine, Human, and Angelic Messianic Figures in Biblical and Related Literature* (Grand Rapids: Eerdmans, 2008). Crispin H. T. Fletcher-Louis, in "Jesus as the High Priestly Messiah: Part 2" *JSHJ* 5 (2007), shows the term Son of Man to be used in referring to Jesus as "king and priest after the order of Melchizedek" (57-79, esp. 57). Fletcher-Lewis notes that John (Rev. 1:13-16) "sees Jesus as Son of Man" with the appropriate high priestly garments (59). J. Andrew Overman, in *The New Oxford Annotated Bible:NRSV with the Apocrypha*, 3rd ed., ed. Michael D. Coogan, (Oxford:Oxford University Press, 2001) notes the Greek use of Son of God to denote either a leader of some kind or a divine entity (32 [New Testament] *ad* Matt 16:16).
20. Belief that the dead can be raised can be traced from antiquity onward. Most notable in the New Testament is the raising of Lazarus. We see the raising of the dead in the Ante-Nicene Fathers. See, e.g. "On the Resurrection of the Dead The Treatise of Athenagoras the Athenian, Philosopher and Christian" in *Early Church Fathers 1.2.4.2.0.0: The Ante-Nicene Fathers 2*, ed. Alexander Roberts, James Donaldson, and A. Cleveland Coxe (Grand Rapids: Eerdmans/Libronix, ND), 149-62.
21. For these and other traditions and terms related to Jesus' designation as prophet, which, unlike Son of Man or Son of God, may be "an irreducible minimum," see P. E. Davies, "Jesus and the Role of the Prophet," 24. That "Sons of the Father," the equivalent of "Sons of the Prophet," may be used more explicitly than "Son of God," is very important. See, for example, James G. Williams, "The Prophetic 'Father': A Brief Explanation of the Term 'Sons of the Prophets,'" *Journal of Biblical Literature* 85 (1966): 344-48. J. Severino Croatto, in "Jesus, Prophet like Elijah," 453, calls the term

Son of God "polysemic and ambiguous." He treats "the tradition of the 'sons of the prophets' in 1 Sam.10:5; 19:20-24; 2 Kgs. 2:3; Joel 3:1-5" as referring to the ecstatic. On the other hand, this understanding may be early.

22. This ignores the fact that when Jesus states what will happen, he is acting as a prophet. It may, however, be related to the debate regarding the existence of prophecy in the Second Temple era. For a discussion of the continuation of prophecy in the Second Temple era, see Benjamin D. Sommer, "Did Prophecy Cease? Evaluating a Reevaluation," *Journal of Biblical Literature* 115 (1996): 31-47. Although Sommer concludes that Second Temple Jews did expect prophecy to be renewed with the advent of the Messiah (47), I believe Second Temple era history suggests this was a sectarian based outlook. For a discussion of Second Temple history in general, see John H. Hayes and Sara R. Mandell, *The Jewish People in Classical Antiquity: From Alexander to Bar Kochba* (Westminster: John Knox, 1998).
23. CD 5:21-6:1 refers to Moses and the holy anointed ones as givers of commandments. For the prophets as being spirit anointed and seekers of truth, see Michael A. Knibb, *The Qumran Community* (Cambridge: Cambridge University Press, 1988), 27, *ad* II.11-13. See also Marinus de Jonge, "Messiah," *Anchor Bible Dictionary* 4:782; Emil A. Wcela, "The Messiah(s) of Qumrân," *Catholic Biblical Quarterly* 26 (1964): 340-49. It may be significant that Ps. 105:15 uses "anointed ones," having as its antecedent the patriarchs, and "prophets" in parallelism.
24. We must remember that Rabbinic Judaism is itself a late development, perhaps but not necessarily beginning as a continuation of Pharisaic Judaism after the fall of the Temple. For the possible Roman understanding of this, see Sara Mandell, "Who Paid the Temple Tax when the Jews were Under Roman Rule?" *Harvard Theological Review* 77 (1984): 223-32. For the restoration of the king's portion (*m. Sotah* 7:8), and the "Messiah, who in Jewish eyes, would be a fully functioning Jewish King in the political sense," see Hyam Maccoby, *Early Rabbinic Writings* (Cambridge: Cambridge University 1998), 106.
25. See, for example Richard A. Horsley, "Like one of the Prophets of Old," *Catholic Biblical Quarterly* 47 (1985): 435-63.
26. For a rise of messianic expectations in this period, see John J. Collins, in Collins and Collins, *King and Messiah as Son of God*, 45-46.
27. de Jonge, "Messiah," *Anchor Bible Dictionary* 4:777.
28. Joseph Fitzmyer, in "The Aramaic 'Elect of God' Text from Qumran Cave IV," *Catholic Biblical Quarterly* 27 (1965), notes the messianic expectations in Qumran starting sometime during the Hasmonaean era (352). See, for example, 1QSa 2:14, 20 for the eschatological messiah (anointed one); 1QS 9:11 for the future prophet and the messiahs (i.e., military and eschatological); 4Q Test 5-8 for a prophet; and, 4Q Flor lines 11-12 for the Davidic messiah who will come forth at the end of time. See esp. 11Q Melch 18-19 for "the anointed one of Spirit," which is particularly interesting since it clearly serves as a prototype for Jesus' anointing.
29. Even some Jews who reject any form of religious practice, but love Israel, still hope for a political-military leader, who will save Israel from her enemies. They might not consider this a messianic expectations, but by definition it is so.
30. See, for example, the listing of Hassidic opinions on the web at *truthnet.org*.
31. David J. Bryan, in "The Jewish Background to The Resurrection of the Son of God by N.T. Wright," *Journal for the Study of the Historical Jesus* (2005), notes Wright's observation that there are biblical exceptions to the Old Testament perspective that

death is final: namely "Enoch (Gen. 5), Elijah (2 Kings 2) and Moses (Deut. 34)" (156). I see no justification for including Deut. 34, however. In any case, Bryan follows through with "the emergence of hints of hope for the dead" and following that the "'awakening' of the sleepers." For late Second Temple Jewish sectarian differences in belief about resurrection, be it of Jesus or others, see, for example Acts 17:32, 23:6, 24:21;1 Cor. 15:3-4, 21, 29; Eph. 5:14.

32. In the Mourners' Kaddish, Jews praise God for all eternity without mentioning death.
33. I use the terms shamanic and ecstatic synonymously. In any case, here Elisha is also called the man of God. The articulation may be significant.
34. The group of which Elisha was the leader has been compared to a "possession cult." See, for example, R. R. Wilson, *Prophecy and Society in Ancient Israel* (Philadelphia: Fortress, 1980), 202. See also Keith W. Whitelam, "Elisha," *Anchor Bible Dictionary* 2:472.
35. Notably Jesus justifies his ministry to the gentiles (Luke 4:27) by virtue of Elisha's healing of Naaman; see Whitelam, "Elisha," *Anchor Bible Dictionary* 2:472). For Jesus' baptizer, John the Baptist, as a restored Elijah, see J. Severino Croatto, "Jesus, Prophet like Elijah," 454.
36. Jesus has been well recognized as an Elijah figure. See for example, John A. T. Robinson, "Elijah, John and Jesus: An Essay in Detection," *New Testament Studies* 4 (1957-58): 263-81. J. Severino Croatto, in "Jesus, Prophet like Elijah," points out that "Luke collects a series of miracles 'imitating' parallel miracles of Elijah and Elisha" (456).
37. The lateness of most of DtrH, with the exception of several poems, is well established. Despite the belief of many scholars that there were earlier traditions on which portions of DtrH rest, with the exception of Judges 4 which is a late and variably interpolated presentation of what is in Judges 5, the existence of prior narrative material is currently unprovable and therefore must remain hypothetic. Moreover, since the Elijah and Elisha cycles are not amongst the exceptions, we have no way of attributing any historical veracity to the narratives. Meaningfully, Susanne Otto, in "The Composition of the Elijah-Elisha Stories and the Deuteronomistic History," *Journal for the Study of the Old Testament* 27 (2003): 487-508, dates three of the Elijah-Elisha stories as being composed not long after 562 BCE, and the remaining Elisha stories as fifth-century BCE and even post-Deuteronomisitic (see esp. 497). Otto's view that most of the Elisha stories are based on "an older collection of miracle stories" (505) is unsubstantiated, and notably, she does not date that collection. Although she may be correct in asserting that 1 Kings 19:1-18 was inserted into DtrH as an attempt to validate the importance of prophecy, which had been demoted in support of the primacy of Moses and the Pentateuch (507), this would have occurred at a later date, since it was Ezra who divided the Old Testament of the earliest Bible into the Pentateuch and Prophetic corpus. See David Noel Freedman, "The Formation of the Canon of the Old Testament: The Selection and Identification of the Torah as the Supreme Authority of the Post-exilic Community," in *Religion and Law: Biblical-Judaic and Islamic Perspectives*, ed Edwin B. Firmage, Bernard G. Weiss, and John W. Welch (Winona Lake: Eisenbrauns, 1990), 317-18, 324-326.
38. Here I include Elijah since, in Luke, there is also an implicit tie to Third Isaiah as well as Jesus. However, we do not see the same correspondences occur as those between Elisha and Jesus. For Elijah imagery in Luke 4:16-30 and its relationship to Isaiah 61:1-2, see John C. Poirier, "Jesus as an Elijanic Figure in Luke 4:16-30," *Catholic*

Biblical Quarterly 69 (2007): 349-63. Poirier does not consider "the Elijah and Elisha analogy" to be a "stray logion" (363). Significantly, Poirier notes that it is most likely that Elijah was anointed although there is no explicit statement regarding this (353). This is a clear correspondence with Jesus, who is deemed the Lord's anointed, but there is no representation of traditional anointment with oil.

39. Given the lateness of Primary History (= Genesis through 2 Kings MT), and particularly DtrH and P, with the latter most likely dating from the early Second Temple era, our picture of Moses, who may or may not have existed, is itself quite late.
40. de Jonge, "Messiah," *Anchor Bible Dictionary* 4:778.
41. Since "all Israel" was unanointed, it is unlikely that the sons of Israel acted ecstatically when, if we can trust any unsubstantiated portion of Dtr as historical, they danced with David before Yahweh (2 Sam. 6:5). However, since the anointed David was clad in the priestly ephod when he danced before the Ark (2 Sam. 6:14), he is acting as both king and priest, and was clearly ecstatic.
42. For a differing perspective, rejecting the relationship between kingship and prophetic status, see trans. James Martin, "Isaiah," in C. F. Keil and F. Delitsch, *Commentary on the Old Testament* (Edinburgh: T. & T. Clark, 1866-1891), 7:119-644.
43. My primary source is Exod. 28, with additional information in Exod. 29:2-31; 39:28-29; Lev. 8:7, all of which are most likely P. Since P most likely is very late, either exilic or more likely early Second Temple era, we cannot assume that the priestly dress as described reflects earlier traditions. Although the ephod has been cultically linked to the sanctuary at Shiloh (1Sam. 2 2:18-19,28; 14:3), 1 Samuel is part of DtrH and therefore so late that we cannot presume any historical basis resting on earlier sources. Although some believe parts of DtrH do rest on earlier traditions, this cannot be substantiated. Although the Chronicler mentions David's bringing of the ark (1Chr. 15:25-28), his description is limited, simply stating that David wore fine linen and a linen ephod (1 Chr. 15:27). Since we cannot attribute the traditions used by the Chronicler, who was writing during the Restoration or early Second Temple era, to any time much earlier than that of Dtr, his description is basically irrelevant.
44. Nevertheless, it is interesting that the term "my Chosen One" is used for Moses (Ps. 106:23), the Suffering Servant of Yahweh (Isa. 42:1), and Jesus, who is called the Son of God (John 1:34). This usage was noted by J. Fitzmyer, "The Aramaic 'Elect of God' Text," *Catholic Biblical Quarterly* 27 (1965): 370 in a different context.
45. So, it is particularly notable that the first reference to "The Kingly Messiah," who may have been called the Messiah at least once, is 1QSa 2:12 from Qumran. See A. S. von der Woude, "Messianic Ideas in Later Judaism," *Theological Dictionary of the New Testament* 9:516.
46. This demands that he be loved. For Yahweh's love for his anointed, David and promises regarding his line, with hints at a Suffering Servant tradition, see Ps.18:50; 89:20, 37-38, 51: 132:10,17. For the messiah as a king "who would come to continue the Davidic dynasty," see Pheme Perkins, "Messiah," in Paul Achtemeier, ed., *Harper's Bible Dictionary* (New York: Harper and Row, 1985) 630. But, Perkins points out that that the term "messiah" is not used by the prophets to denote a "future king."
47. His anointment by Mary cannot be construed as being done to elevate him to office. Matthew (26:6-13), Mark (14:3-9) and John (12:1-8) make it clear that he is being anointed for burial.
48. Clearly this would not have disqualified him in Qumran (11Q Melch 18. See above).
49. The idea of the Holy Spirit may have been borrowed from Qumran usage. See F. W. Horn, "Holy Spirit," *Anchor Bible Dictionary* 3:261.

50. For a discussion of the multiple sects of Jews with differing views regarding the idea and definition of a messiah during the Second Temple era, see Neusner, Green, and Frerichs, *Judaisms and their Messiahs*. See, however, J. Jensen, "Prediction Fulfillment," 656 n. 33 for the perspective of several articles in this edited work as indicating that first-century Judaism had "no general unified expectation of a messiah." During the second century CE, Bar Kochba was deemed messiah by Rabbi Akiba, as I have already noted. It is possible that during the second century BCE the Teacher of Righteousness was considered a messiah. But Joseph Fitzmyer, in "The Aramaic 'Elect of God Text from Qumran Cave IV," *Catholic Biblical Quarterly* 27 (1965), believes that the Teacher of Righteousness did not consider himself a messiah: rather, he was "a leader in the line of the prophets like Moses" (351). Moreover, Fitzmyer does not see it as self-evident that "Elect of God" meant messianic in Qumran.
51. See, for example Richard A. Horsley, "Like One of the Prophets of Old," *Catholic Biblical Quarterly* 47 (1985): 435-63. Horsley notes that the evidence is limited regarding Jewish "Expectation of an Eschatological Prophet" (437-43).
52. This is of particular significance, since Jesus lived during the late Second Temple era, and historically, the high priesthood is itself a very late Judahite, and possibly an Exilic or even Second Temple era development. This does not mean that there was no priestly caste earlier, but rather that P does not serve as evidence for it unless we can prove P itself rests on earlier traditions, something for which there is no current evidence.
53. These are Priestly (P).
54. What is interesting is that Saul is never simply called anointed, but rather Yahweh's Anointed. See Franz Hesse, "משח and משיח in the Old Testament," *Theological Dictionary of the New Testament* 9:502.
55. See for example, F. Hesse, "משח and משיח in the Old Testament," *Theological Dictionary of the New Testament* 9:497. Hesse also points out that "Anointing is strongly attested only in relation to the Southern Kingdom of Judah and with ref. (sic) to David and his successors."
56. For our argument, it does not matter if there is more than one Dtr. That is primarily important in regard to his/their dating.
57. Anyone who has played the childrens' game "Telephone" knows how unreliable oral tradition really is. The theological stance that the redactions of Old Testament were based on accurate or even real reports of events or that Rabbis received and handed down their traditions unerringly, (see for example, m Pirqe Abot), is a theological posture that bears no relationship to reality. There is a great body of literature, both supportive and opposing, dealing with the transmission of oral traditions in the creation of the Pentateuch as well as in that of the Homeric Epics. Most importantly, PH does not have the formulaic nature that characterizes and is necessary for such transmission on a continuous basis. Since most of what we do have rests on not datable myths and legends, the most of what we can say about them is that they may have become demythologized. For the most part, we can not even speculate about any basis in historical reality.
58. Which, despite the lateness of its representation may be whence the Judahite tradition springs although, historically speaking, we would more likely expect it to have been an Israelite development and therefore not linked to the David traditions.
59. With few exceptions, most attestations come from early Christian literature.
60. In fact, he responds in much the same way as he does when questioned by Pilate.

61. We have no way of knowing if Pilate understood that a political-military messiah and an eschatological messiah may, but need not be found in one person. For an esoteric discussion between Pilate and Jesus regarding Jesus' eschatological kingship, see John 18:33-38. What would have mattered to Pilate, in any case, was the possibility that, as king of the Jews, he was a political-military messiah, thereby standing in a treasonous relationship to Roman rule in Judaea. Two expected figures are noted in DSS: one priestly, anointed of Aaron, and one kingly, anointed of Israel (1QS 9:11; 1QSa 2:14, 20; CD 20:1; 4QP Bless 2:4; 4Q). For the "branch" of David, who will save Israel, see 4Q Flor 1:11-13. See also M. A. Knibb, *The Qumran Community*, 261 for this as being the Davidic Messiah. See also P. Perkins, "Messiah," *Harper's Bible Dictionary* 630.
62. Even the appointment of the high priest and the supervision of his robes was a Roman prerogative (see Hayes and Mandell, *The Jewish People*, 154).
63. The fact that we primarily hear about it in relationship to the Davidic line may well reflect the enmity between Judah and Israel even though, insofar as we can tell, both nations were Yahwistic. (This is not the place to debate the Minimalistic position, with which I agree.) But, more likely, it may reflect the fact that what was practiced in Judah and Jerusalem held to postulated Southern, that is Davidic authority. Particularly given the anti-Northern, non-Davidic bias of primary history or the traditions within the Temple State, Pilate may not have been aware of any other perspective.
64. During the late Republic and early Empire, crucifixion was only imposed for treason. In some cases, rebellion or sedition might be considered treason and its leaders were crucified (e.g., Spartacus), but there is no indication that Jesus was deemed rebellious or seditious by Pilate. Rather, he is brought before Pilate for having committed treason per se. Because Judaea was an imperial provence, it was solely the Emperor's prerogative to appoint or at least approve of Judaea's king. If Jesus had acknowledged kingship, he then would have committed treason. Jesus' refusal to acknowledge that he was king of the Jews is why Pilate found no fault with him.
65. And subsequently, in Rabbinic Judaism, the expectation that Elijah will come again or that he had been taken to heaven alive does not divinize him.
66. For a discussion of the implications of Royal Ideology in Old Testament and ANE, and the possibility that the king may have been divine, see John J. Collins in Collins and Collins, *King and Messiah as Son of God*, chs. 1-4.
67. See, George Nickelsburg, "Son of Man," *Anchor Bible Dictionary* 6:137-50.
68. Today, in the doxology, the two are used parallelistically.
69. Most notably in Qumran, but perhaps amongst certain sectarian groups in the Temple State. The following Jesus attracted may show that some of the perspectives we attribute to those in Qumran may have been more widespread than the extant writings suggest.
70. Jensen, "Prediction-Fulfillment," 658 notes the lateness of Jewish "identification of the Suffering Servant with the Messiah" as not being found prior to the fourth century CE. See also J. A. Fitzmyer, "Jesus in the Early Church through the Eyes of Luke-Acts," *Scripture Bulletin* 17 (1987): 32.
71. Richard T. Murphy, in "Second Isaiah: The Servant of the Lord," *Catholic Biblical Quarterly* 9 (1947): 269, notes that it was the controversy with the Christians that caused the rabbis to identify the Suffering Servant with Israel rather than with an expected Messiah.

72. As suffering servant, he could be Son of Man or of God. But, as an eschatological Suffering Servant, he can only be the Son of God. For the Son of God as different from its honorific usage in Hellenistic circles, see Paul J. Achtemeier, "Mark, Gospel of," *Anchor Bible Dictionary* 4:551.
73. This raises the question of the validity of the report in the Gospels that Pilate had found no fault with Jesus (above).
74. Moreover, Sirach (48:24) says of Isaiah, "By his dauntless spirit he saw the last things," which Christians would view as predictive of Jesus.
75. So, it is significant that Sirach (48:22-25) describes Hezekiah's actions as king as being in accord with Isaiah's teachings.
76. Since 1Qp Hab 2:9 refers to God's servants the prophets, it is a logical conclusion that First Isaiah is or at least could be the Suffering Servant Second Isaiah describes. For this usage, see 2 Kings 17:23, 21:10. Benjamin D. Sommer, *The Jewish Study Bible* (Oxford: Oxford University Press, 2004) 867, *ad* Isa. 42:1-9, states that Ibn Ezra considered the servant to be Isaiah. However, in his commentary on Isaiah, ibn Ezra interprets the servant as being Israel.
77. For Isaiah as well as other prophets being "present" in both Second and Third Isaiah, see Christopher R. Seitz, "How is the Prophet Isaiah Present in the Latter Half of the Book? The Logic of Chapters 40-65 within the Book of Isaiah," *Journal of Biblical Literature* 115 (1996): 237-38.
78. Although there are later additions to the text, it is primarily First Isaiah.
79. Although sackcloth is also worn by prophets, all attributions of this are late: 2 Kings 1:8; Zec. 13:4; Matt. 3:4; Mark 1-6.
80. A. R. Fausset's suggestion, in "Isaiah" (in *A Commentary, Critical and Explanatory, on the Old and New Testaments*, ed: Robert Jamieson, A. R. Fausset, and David Brown, [Eerdmans, 1935: www.libronix.com: Libronix] 1871), that he only discarded his outer garments is debatable and not fully warranted by the texts he cites. Sackcloth could be worn in two ways: with nothing under it or as an outer garment. For a debate regarding this conundrum regarding Isaiah's state of dress, see for example "Isaiah" in Keil and Delitsch, *Commentary on the Old Testament*, 7:119-644. Notably, Keil and Delitsch also think that he may not have been naked. However, they cite 2 Sam. 6:20 for this regarding David.
81. For the Cult of the Dead as treated with "pejorative overtones," see for example, Theodore J. Lewis, "Ancestor Worship," *Anchor Bible Dictionary* 1:241.
82. Joseph Blenkinsopp, "Isaiah" in *The New Oxford Annotated Bible:NRSV* (Oxford: Oxford University Press, 2001), 976.
83. Even as late as the Second Temple era, some Jews were not monotheists. For example, the Samaritans, whom the Temple State Yahwists arrogantly deemed half-Jews, ultimately dedicated their temple to Zeus. And, the Yahu coins have a picture of a male deity who looks decidedly like Zeus.
84. The practices of the various sectarian groups in Qumran and thereabouts are separate from what was practiced in the Temple State of Judah and Jerusalem. Likewise, those of the Samaritans were also separate.
85. Dtr. (2 Kings 21:16) notes that Manasseh was responsible for great bloodshed. Josephus (Ant. 10.3.1) adds to this his slaughter of the prophets. So, it is notable that the albeit late "The Ascension of Isaiah" treats his death as a martyrdom (see Asc. Isa. 5:1b-14).

86. John Drane, *Introducing the New Testament,* rev. ed. (West Oxford: Lion Publishing, 1999), 72.
87. Perkins, "Messiah," *Harper's Bible Dictionary* 630.
88. It is currently not fashionable to think of Jesus as a military figure. However, until recently, Christians acknowledged Jesus to be their leader in battle. See, for example, such hymns as "Onward Christian Soldiers," "Stand Up for Jesus," "We all do extol Thee, thou Leader in Battle," "The Battle Hymn of the Republic," "Soldiers of Christ, Arise," etc., which continue to be sung today. As the (only begotten) son of the Father, Yahweh Elohim, which Christians believe him to be, whose origins are as a warrior god, it is logical that Jesus, like his father, is a warrior.
89. We have no way of knowing if Second or Third Isaiah were accepted by their own contemporaries. What we do know is that they were held in esteem by later generations although we cannot establish when this began.
90. So, Richard T. Murphy's observation that the servant will be a prophet ("Second Isaiah," 263) is very important.
91. It is an unprovable theological construct that prophecy had ceased in the Second Temple era.
92. We cannot presume that by the late Second Temple era all Pharisees or Sadducees, respectively, were of the same social class. But, in the New Testament, there is no distinction between the leadership and the "people" who belonged to either of these sects.
93. Given their condemnation of the sons of Israel, it is hard to believe that any of their contemporaries cared for them.
94. Modern scholars have debunked the theory that there was some type of normative Judaism. This, however, does not deny that it was a clear theo-political posture, something made quite clear in the Mishnah's precept (in *m. pirqe Abot*) that Oral Torah had been handed down from Sinai, and it reached them through a chain of believing Jews.
95. J. Severino Croatto, "Jesus, Prophet like Elijah," 452.

Before Whom Do We Stand?

Henry F. Knight

> Know before whom you are standing when you pray. (*Berachot* 28b)
>
> And the Sovereign will answer them: "Truly I tell you, just at I you did it to one of the least of these who are members of my family you did it to me. (Matt. 25:40)
>
> But Jesus said, "Let the little children come to me and do not stop them; for it is to such as these that the rule and realm of heaven belongs. (Matt. 19: 14)
>
> "You're wrong," Pedro said. "The way is no less important than the goal. He who thinks about God, forgetting man, runs the risk of mistaking his goal: God may be your next door neighbor." Elie Wiesel, *Town Beyond the Wall.*

Before whom do we stand?[1] After the Holocaust that question, echoing the instructions of Rabbi Eliezer to his disciples, that they know the One before whom they stand when they pray, calls Jews and Christians to reexamine their understandings of each other and of their own grounding traditions. In the reflections that follow, I explore this question, particularly as it is refracted through artist Samuel Bak's iconic image of the Warsaw Ghetto Boy [2] and Elie Wiesel's character, Michael, from *Town Beyond the Wall.* Bak has captured with his brush the image of his murdered friend's face and, in multiple renderings, portrayed it in the iconic form of the Warsaw ghetto boy. His painting of Samek as a crucified child puts a face on Rabbi Eliezer's text that challenges both his tradition and mine. In similar fashion, Elie Wiesel's story of Michael in *Town Beyond the Wall* approaches other implications of Rabbi Eliezer's admonition. As I wrestle with Bak's image and Wiesel's stylized story, I am also cognizant of two other texts that represent the confessional ground on which I stand as I undertake this task.

Those texts, both from the Gospel of Matthew, are familiar to Christians and non-Christians alike. One expresses how Jesus identifies with the other in his life and expresses the significance of his relationship even to the least of others in his and his followers' lives. The second text represents how Jesus perceives the significance of children in God's and our ways with the world. I invite my readers to join me in my wrestling as I seek to make sense of these various texts, my place before them, and my place before the Jewish figure who stands at the center of my wounded world.

A Wounded Ark and A Defaced Summons

One of the artifacts on display at the United States Holocaust Museum in Washington, DC, is a disfigured lintel that once framed the ark of a synagogue in Nenterhausen, Germany. Carved across the top in Hebrew text are the words, *Da lifnei mi attah omeyd*: Know before whom you stand. The lintel and these words overlook a glass display case that houses Torah scrolls that were defiled during the November pogrom of *Kristallnacht*. The words are Rabbi Eliezer's instructions to his students from centuries earlier. They are recorded in the Talmud (*Berachoth* 28b) and have lived on in Jewish communities throughout the world, linking study with prayer and guiding the lives of Jews of every nationality. These

The wounded lintel above a Torah ark from a synagogue in Nentershausen, Germany—damaged during Kristallnacht.

wounded words invite visitors to the museum to enter into relationship with the human beings who experienced this atrocity.

Rabbi Eliezer's admonition is often carved or painted above the arks in synagogues and temples, marking the space set aside to house the sacred words of Torah. His words continue to reach out across the generations to teach new congregations. Their people face them each time the ark is approached. They greet whoever may be ascending the *bima* making his or her way to read or to take their place in the community. These words hold, like a Kiddush cup, the responsibilities human beings have to God and one another, the ties that bind us to each other and to all that we honor as sacred in our lives.

And those ties, like these words, were betrayed on Kristallnacht. They were desecrated, along with the trampled Torah scrolls in the facing case. Physically, the words were cut and gouged, most likely by a bayonet. Close inspection reveals that the word *lifnei*, constructed from the Hebrew word for *face*, was literally defaced. Its message, especially now when we look back using this wounded ark as our lens, is profound and tragic. Since every human being, every child of Adam, bears God's image, God and God's children have been tragically, catastrophically assaulted.

While explicitly Jewish, this text signals a broader invitation to any person of faith, or otherwise secular soul. The exhibit reframes Rabbi Eliezer's admonition to his followers and later generations of Jews into a question for those who makes there way to this symbolic crossroads in the museum: Before whom do we stand? The reframing is rooted in the defaced expression of Jewish identity. To borrow terms from midrashic hermeneutics, the Jewish character of this wounded text is an essential feature of the *peshat* of the exhibit, its plain meaning, calling out to be faced responsibly and explored respectfully.

This wounded frame—a mantle in more ways than one—is an apt metaphor for my entrance into and engagement with life lived in the shadows of the longer night of the Shoah. As the Museum's Permanent Exhibit suggests, Eliezer's desecrated words speak to more than just its Jewish victims, however powerfully they speak for and to them. In that added regard, they speak to and for me as a Christian who stands before a Jewish child of the covenant who is for us not just a figure of history but our burning bush. Like the burning bush of Moses, Jesus of Nazareth is not consumed by the revelatory power that he embodied and still does for his followers. Among other things, that means he remains a bar mitzvah who would have been murdered with the others who were betrayed by their fellow human beings during this twelve-year time of terror. That human being, his six million brothers and sisters from that time, as well as myriad other siblings past and present, stand before me as I stand before them—not unlike how all Israel stands before Sinai. I stand before this central figure in my life fully aware that while he remains a *bar mitzvah* while I am not, or at least not in the way that he is. I am a Gentile follower of his ways, and we Gentile believers have adopted and adapted what Jesus brought and still brings in ways that distinguish us from our Jewish siblings. Tragically, many of those adoptions and adaptations have contributed to the wounding reflected in Eliezer's defaced admonition.

The Crisis in Covenantal Theism

The difficult history and the contending relations between Jews and Christians, Judaism and Christianity, are familiar. They provide the context in which I offer these reflections. As I view it, we can identify several interrelated crises present in this complex trajectory: a crisis of credibility regarding covenantal theism, a crisis of credibility regarding Christianity's espoused values, and a crisis of integrity regarding essential features of Christianity's historic identity. In the latter case, whether or not Christianity faces an identity crisis similar to the one it experienced in the Reformation will depend on how the church and its representatives see and respond to this difficult history and the place of Judaism and other traditions in it.

The crisis in covenantal theism is a matter that confronts Christians as well as Jews, albeit the crisis for Jews is existentially more acute, since that crisis unfolds at their expense. Two names stand out among the Jewish teachers and scholars who have given articulate expression to this matter for me: Elie Wiesel and Richard Rubenstein. While Wiesel and Rubenstein find very different ways of responding to this crisis, they each provide memorable articulations of it. Wiesel, in *Night*, re-enters, in midrashic fashion, the historic question of the Passover Seder, by turning it on its head. Why is this night different than any other night? The story he recounts is both his personal narrative and that of myriad others who share his identity as a Jew. It is a recounting that in stylized ways layers his personal account with that of all those who entered that night with him, forming what Lawrence Cunningham has called a negative *haggadah*.[3] Where, after all, is the God who acts in history to deliver to sustain creation and deliver Israel? What has happened to the covenant? Where is the God of life who creates life in the divine image?

Rubenstein, in *After Auschwitz*, provides a more theoretical account, as he explores the theological significance of Auschwitz for a people entrusted and burdened with representing God's covenanted ways with creation. In a 1961 conversation with Pastor Heinrich Gruber, Rubenstein captures what is acutely problematic with the logic of covenantal theism as he relates Gruber's confident belief in the providence of God as the sovereign of history active in the affairs of the world. Even though Gruber was an active resister of the Nazis and rescuer of Jews, he could not avoid concluding that the destruction of the Jews during the horror of Nazi persecution was God's will, and, therefore, that what happened to them was an expression of divine judgment. Rubenstein recognized the empathy of Gruber for his people at the same time he could not escape the consistent logic that Gruber had espoused. The crisis was clearly framed and Rubenstein rejected the logic of covenantal theism that Gruber embraced as an act of theological and personal integrity.[4] Wiesel, on the other hand, followed a logic of resistance rooted in the hasidic traditions of his world, as well as in a somewhat mystical appropriation of midrash, a way of expressing the theological contradictions he faced without having to give in to them. Though with great respect, Rubenstein saw Wiesel's path as problematic and charted a more radical course. Regardless of their very different strategies, their questions continue to haunt any person of faith who allows the beliefs and assumptions of covenantal theism to engage the realities of the Shoah, especially what happened to the 1.5 million children who were executed for the singular crime of being born a Jew.

Children Defiled

Rabbi Irving Greenberg, a prominent Holocaust scholar and theologian, has captured the implications of this post-Shoah knowing with his now familiar criterion for post-Holocaust faithfulness: "No statement, theological or otherwise, should be made that would not be credible in the presence of the burning children."[5] Greenberg's words have been instructive for me. As a post-Holocaust Christian, I have learned to pray with the psalmist: "May the words of my mouth and the meditations of my heart be acceptable in your sight, O God, my rock and my redeemer." And, then, to add, "May they be credible in the presence of the

Iconographic image of the Warsaw ghetto boy.

burning children." To say "Amen" to that amended and compounded prayer is one way I attempt to *know before whom I stand.*

Artist Samuel Bak has given this summons visual expression using the figure of the iconic Warsaw ghetto boy as a base text. The image of that child is familiar.

A young boy, perhaps eight or nine, is standing in a crowd as a nearby soldier holds the child at gunpoint. The little boy, wearing shorts, knee-high socks, a hat, and a fine, buttoned coat has both his hands raised in surrender, as if he were a criminal under arrest. Bak renders a version of this child in numerous paintings, often depicting his upraised hands with nails piercing his palms. The symbolism is inescapable. A Jewish child is being crucified. Often, as in *Study I*, the face Bak paints invokes that of his childhood friend Samek Epstein, who was murdered by the Nazis when he was eight. Bak's young friend was executed and then left in a pool of his own blood to intimidate other Jews who might try hiding from the Nazis, as Samek had done.[6]

To stand before Bak's little boy is another version of Rabbi Eliezer's summons: Know before whom we stand. Indeed!

But we have to be careful in this regard. It would be easy for Christians like me to project the image of Christ onto crucified Jewish children. However, that would be another violation of those children and an inversion of Green-

Samuel Bak, *Study I 1995*, Pucker Gallery.

berg's searing hermeneutical principle. Instead, the power of these juxtaposed images works in the other direction. Over a million children under twelve were murdered by the Nazis or by their collaborators. Thousands were tortured. None were given a choice about how they might live their lives. Their suffering challenges any assertion Christians might make about the scope of what Jesus experienced. He chose his cross, or at least he chose to risk it. He offered up his life. The children did not. Emil Fackenheim's thoughtful commentary underscores the importance of this distinction: "Christians have always known how to acknowledge sin, including the sin of crucifying Christ all over again. However, the crucifixion of Christ-in-general is one thing; quite another is the crucifixion-in-particular of six million human beings, among them the helpless children, their weeping mothers, and the silent *Muselmäner*."[7]

When we Christians free ourselves from imposing messianic meaning on Bak's iconic child, we are able to grasp that crucifixion is a form of state-sanctioned cruelty. The execution of Bak's friend Samek, like the murder of so many other children, was not simply an act of passion. These children were killed with cold premeditation, no matter what delight their killers may have taken in their deeds. Bak's crucified child, like myriad others, was an instrument in state policy. His execution was a message of fear to communicate terror to other potential victims. To be sure, this image and what it represents places us before another covenantal crisis—this one with our assumptions about civilization and our obligations to those for whom Jesus said the rule and realm of heaven were given. We who lift high the cross stand in the presence of a heinous act that we cannot diminish by forcing the suffering of others into our interpretive needs. Are we really prepared to know before whom we stand? We need to ponder that question carefully, just as we should pause before Bak's image of the crucified boy.

How we treat every human being takes on added significance in this light. In one sense, nothing has changed. We have, as Rabbi Eliezer's words challenge us to understand, always stood in God's presence when we face another human being. Jewish teachers—and my Christian teachers—have taught us all this truth. Each human being, each son of Adam, each daughter of Eve, is a reflection of the One who gives us life. That truth has not changed. On the other hand, everything has changed: how we understand God, our bonds to one another, the urgency of what lies at stake in every relationship—in our politics, in every dimension of our lives, in Christianity's relationship to the people Israel; how we understand suffering; how we understand choice. All of it has changed. We live *after*. Charlotte Delbo, a French, Gentile survivor of the camps put it profoundly: "I know the difference between *before* and *after*."[8] We live *after*—after the Shoah, after the destruction, after the disfiguring assault on God's presenting face. Life, the world in which we live, the face of the other before us—they can never be the same.

Faces Beyond the Wall

I first came to confront this truth reading two books by Elie Wiesel: *Gates of the Forest* and *Town Beyond the Wall*.[9] One of the books was for a course in college, the other two years later, in seminary. I read *Town* again this fall for a course I was teaching with a colleague at Keene State College. The story begins in the confines of an interrogation room in which a Holocaust survivor by the name of Michael is being tortured and questioned. Later, the account continues to unfold in the cell in which Michael is confined. The story occurs some 20 years after the conclusion of World War II. Michael has returned to his hometown of Szerencseváros, which now lies behind the Iron Curtain. His goal: to confront a bystander whose impassive face has haunted Michael ever since this so-called neighbor—who lived across the street from the synagogue—failed to register any response to the removal of Michael and his family along with the entire Jewish community of the town from their homes.

A number of themes interact in this richly constructed story as the reader enters the chaos of Michael's confinement and pain. The tale unfolds in the midst of Michael's ordeal and shifts through various flashbacks to assorted times before his capture, recalling encounters between Michael and important people in his life, including Pedro, a Gentile smuggler who helped Michael return illegally to his home town before being caught. To the authorities, Michael is an intruder and is being interrogated to find out why he had sneaked into their city. Even though the authorities claim otherwise, Michael is clearly undergoing torture. His captors have devised a means of questioning that forces a prisoner to stand facing a wall without moving for hours and days without end—except for those occasions when they take the prisoner to a place to relieve himself.

In a cruel act of irony his captors have named each segment of this activity a prayer. (Never mind that in the aftermath of the Shoah prayer may have become torturous in a different way.) The physical pain is caused by the accumulated effect of continuous standing. Blood gathers and pools in Michael's legs. Slowly Michael is being reduced to his bodily reality—his legs—to become one with his pain. To endure, he commits himself to standing firm just long enough for his friend Pedro, a nonreligious Communist and criminal, to have time to escape. That act, a commitment to friendship with a person whom all his social conventions would identify as an outsider to be shunned, enables Michael to hold out, to stand the pain, long enough to save his friend's life. What could be a traditional stumbling block for Michael has become his cornerstone—but not in the Christological form familiar to Christians, nor in any other conventional sense.

Eventually, Michael passes out and is subsequently placed in a cell with three other prisoners. Like him, his cellmates are each wounded persons, each one traumatized by what has happened to him. One, a pious, young Jew named Menachem, engages Michael in probing dialogue about himself and the meaning of his commitment to Pedro. Another, a disturbed and frantic man, is constantly searching for a missing letter that exists only in the man's imagination. And the other, a silent, unresponsive young man, is nearly beyond reach. Each one inhabits a corner of the cell, dwelling as far from the others as they can manage. Though no longer physically being tortured, Michael faces another ordeal and yet another wall—this one less visible, separating him from the others in the cell. Knowing that his sanity, indeed his soul, may be at stake, Michael turns his attention to those with whom he must share this situation. He makes connection with Menachem, but eventually Menachem is removed from the cell. So Michael turns to the Impatient One, as he calls him. Before he can establish meaningful contact with him, he too is taken away leaving only the silent one, indifferent to life and any self-initiated presence whatsoever. To retain his sense of relational wholeness, even in—especially in—his life-denying circumstances, Michael must find a way to reach out and make contact with this unresponsive figure of a human being.

As Michael struggles to penetrate the wall of silence his cellmate has erected around himself, he continues to reflect on what is at stake. When we reach out and pass on our stories to another, we establish a chain of testimony. We enlarge memory and our worlds; we extend life and pass on our names. Pedro passed his name and story on to Michael. Michael passed his on to Menachem and tried to do so with his other cellmate. And now Michael hopes to reach the one who is beginning to respond in the most elemental of ways. Finally, in the closing scene of the book, Michael and the reader discover the name of the silent one who shares the cell with him: Eliezer, which the narrator explains, means "God has granted my prayer"; and which we know is the given name of the author.

Before whom do we stand? It is not only Michael who must discover how to respond to that question. For in telling this tale, as I have in this commentary, I give voice to Michael's story and bear witness to it, giving the silent presence of Eliezer (and myself, as the reader) a voice and role as well.

The richly stylized narrative of *Town Beyond the Wall* places me before Wiesel, before other survivors for whom prayer may very well be like torture. Such testimony helps me take my place before any who struggle to survive overwhelming trauma by reaching out to others to break through the solitariness—their walls—and to tell their story to someone who will listen. And in this case, Wiesel's story invites me to take my place before others who dare to listen and challenge the indifference of those who, for whatever reason, avoid caring.

When I first read *Town* (and *Gates*), I was profoundly moved and wanted to know the one before whom I sat when I read Wiesel's words. So I turned, as one would expect, to his memoir, *Night*. I've read and reread those words, in both English translations (as well as the French version) many times. And I have read his other books and most of his published articles. With each reading Wiesel helps me see more—more about myself, more about the world in which we live, more about what happened during that night that was different than any other night, and more about the people before whom I stand when I stand as a Christian before a Jew named Jesus.

In the fall of 2008, I participated in a celebration of Wiesel's eightieth birthday arranged by his colleagues and friends at Boston University. The occasion brought together a number of scholars who reflected on what Wiesel has contributed to his various publics and to his more circumscribed work with his students. Each of the presenters spoke as scholars as well as friends of Wiesel. They spoke about Jewish life, the Hebrew Bible, Talmud, Midrash, Eastern European Jewish culture. Some even spoke of Wiesel's impact on Christianity. As I listened, I realized how much I had learned from my friend of over 25 years. Again and again, I was reminded how, through study and friendship, I have been drawn to learn more and more about Judaism. Wiesel has helped me find my place in the study of the traumatic time we call the Holocaust or better, the Shoah, and its impact on my world as a Christian. In that regard, I am surely not alone. But he has helped me do more. He has helped me recognize the depth and power of the other Eliezer's words.

Clearly, sitting with a text can be a way of standing respectfully before the other. It need not be the dedicated study of scripture, though most assuredly, it is that. For me it has often happened with the stylized text of parable and fiction. Standing before the other is a world making matter, even in the solitude of study and prayer—but equally so in any setting, especially those in which we face our adversaries. Standing before the other is world-bearing and reveals rather poignantly whatever holiness we may honor in the world we face. As Wiesel's Michael reports, according to Pedro, "God may be your next door neighbor."[10]

The Promise and Danger of Midrashic Dialogue

In many ways, it has been my responsibility to initiate this kind of exploration. But it is an exploration I cannot do alone. Nor is it enough to have one or two mentors I know and read. Equally so, it is not enough just to rebuild a positive image of Jews and Judaism from selected sources, no matter how authentic they might be. J. B. Metz is right. For Christians, seeking to do theology with post-Shoah integrity requires doing it with Jewish others.[11] And if that work is going to repair the damage done by stereotype and caricature, is must be done with numerous others, individuals and communities, and in situations that are truly dialogical.

In this regard, I have been helped by good and generous friends who have made similar commitments to the repair of our worlds. The *Jesus Symposium* at Case brings several of us together and links us with other communities of dialogue in which I have learned about myself and our often contending traditions. Several of us have found friendship and respect across confessional boundaries and deepened our understandings of our own traditions in the process. Zev Garber, Steve Jacobs, Jim Moore, and I have shared in an eighteen-year midrashic dialogue in which we have taken Emil Fackenheim's observation that the way forward through the theological crisis of post-Shoah faith must be midrashic, holding our root experiences in creative tension with the unassimilated anguish of the Shoah. Indeed, as Fackenheim observes, the midrashic framework insists on a fully dialectical, yet creative tension between our grounding traditions and forms of human suffering that cannot be assimilated into them. That dialectic could just as easily be reversed to read that we interpret our worlds, holding our interpretations of them, even midrashic ones, accountable to our root experiences of human anguish.

We have added the dimension of dialogue to that interpretive activity and our tents of occasional meetings have added an additional other before whom I stand in their presence—the text or texts we face together. In our wrestling with them, they have become gardens of words and orchards of life entrusted to our care for the sake of others. I have learned to read on behalf of not only my own community of faith but also another that is more often taken for granted or buried in hidden assumptions that need to be unearthed and resisted, if not discarded, when I face these texts. Reading midrashically, we have learned to enter the textual domains before us alert to ways they speak to us as we wrestle with them while guarding against foreclosure and domestication of their otherness.

I share with my midrash colleagues another group, the Annual Scholars' Conference on the Holocaust and the Churches, under whose canopy we have met these past years. Its significance is especially poignant as I think of the witness and friendship of Franklin Littell who passed from us just two days ago. I give thanks for his life and his support of our work. I also share a dialogical community with other participants at this conference, Peter Haas and Rochelle Millen—The Weinstein, formerly Goldner, Holocaust Symposium—with whom I engage in similar projects, including a number of books we have written in dialogical fashion. And in my new base, Keene State College in Keene, New Hampshire, I host an interfaith midrash group that includes Jewish and Christian members of the college faculty who teach in our Holocaust and Genocide Studies curriculum as well as clergy from our local, New England community, most notably an Episcopal priest and the rabbi from our local Reconstructionist synagogue. Our dialogues are rich and making a difference in each setting. I participate, as well, in a regional interfaith dialogue group based in Manchester, New Hampshire along with others at the American Academy of Religion. One of the latter, the Scriptural Reasoning Group, pursues similar encounter with and through sacred texts from the three Abrahamic traditions, in addition to theoretical reflections about such work. That ongoing conversation is distinguished by its being composed of Jews, Christians, and Muslims.

Each of these groups and the individuals who make them work are vital to my dialogical experience. Whether we call it midrashic thinking or scriptural reasoning, engaging in dialogue across confessional boundaries deepens our understandings of ourselves and of the ones with whom we engage in that searching exploration. Each holding the other responsible in the light of their sacred texts illumines both the human other and the other's sacred texts we face together. Likewise, the Holy Other whom each tradition knows in and through the texts being discussed is disclosed in ways appropriate to those traditions. Not surprisingly, Eliezer's words reach into such richly textured settings as these with life-shaping power.

Even so, the midrashic imagination is not restricted to facing and interpreting scripture nor limited to extraordinary painters, biblical scholars, or professors of religious studies. For church and synagogue alike the primary texts of ministry are often the situations of human anguish and trauma that call us out of ourselves into presence for and with the other before us. The midrashic imagination offers a way of holding fast to the very grounding traditions that are often shattered in these kinds of circumstances when we give ourselves wholly to the other before us who has dared to trust us with the loss of their world. The midrashic way can distinguish ministry with families traumatized with the death of young children when their suffering simply does not fit into any framework of meaning. It can guide pastors and rabbis sitting with victims of violent crime or caring for families who have had a loved one murdered. The human anguish and the trust of those who need not to be alone become the *peshat* of that ministry. Just as a midrashic framework is not limited to reading written texts, neither is it restricted to reading only experience laden with Shoah-determined issues. Midrash's logic of plenitude and dialectical commitments to root experiences and the full anguish of our wounding world can be utilized in ministry, teaching, and many forms of public dialogue. Paul Ricoeur explored the matter of interpreting significant social actions as texts in his reflections on practical hermeneutics several decades ago in his essay, "The Model of the Text."[12] Applying his insights to the hermeneutics of midrash and using them to engage the challenges of responding to meaningless suffering provides a way of doing ministry that takes human anguish with great seriousness. Both church and synagogue can benefit from an interpretive model that sacrifices neither the root experiences of one's tradition nor honest encounter with the kind of trauma that resists domestication of any kind.

To be sure, the associative logic of the midrashic imagination can also be misused. Its power to utilize figurative ways of seeing and thinking the other can draw on the mythic power of stereotypes and prejudice as well. A great deal of Nazi propaganda tapped this dimension in the public media of the time. In this regard, the stories of historic Midrash reveal Judaism's wisdom in reserving communal judgment regarding the wisdom of any particular interpretation, even those with apparent power to evoke a sense of the holy. The story of the *bat kol* makes just this point and records the community's role in hearing and judging the credibility of any interpretation—even in the face of others that are ordained by heaven itself. The importance of this dimension can be seen when very real opponents of Israel, for example, are cast as Amelek and mythologized in such a way that any future breakthrough in conflict resolution is foreclosed ahead of time. Communal discussion of the configuring dimensions of mythic discourse keep such interpretation open to examination and critique.

There is another, seductive danger in my turn to the hermeneutics of the midrashic imagination to describe how the work of interpretation more generally grows out of such sensibilities. As with Bak's use of crucifixion to frame the tragedy of his friend Samek, and all other Samek's with him, there is the risk of theological theft when Christians like me embrace the hermeneutics of our Jewish siblings. Granted, I argue that the dynamics of midrash are present in my own sacred texts. More significantly, many key passages in my own scriptures could and should be understood as midrashic constructions. Still, the danger, to put it midrashically, is that of the younger brother once again usurping the birthright and blessing of the older sibling. If I am going to be faithful to the midrashic way, I must acknowledge this danger and guard against the misappropriation of it.

Any talk of adopting the terms of study and prayer of others to speak of one's own vocation is bound to evoke the deep memories of prior acts of theological theft that punctuates the historic relationships of Jews and Christians. Much too often Christians have co-opted the heritage of their covenantal siblings with little or no regard for how it is understood nor lived by the other members of their Abrahamic family. When Christians seek to come to terms with these matters, they inevitably evoke a dark and difficult history that from its earliest days has treated Jews and Judaism with disdain and contempt. Even when the intent is otherwise, that troubling dynamic will be present. Facing that history and its tender dynamics will be a necessary part of the dialogue.

The Displaced Other

The way forward places Christians like me to come face-to-face with a history that from its earliest days has treated Jews and Judaism with disdain. The beginnings of that contention are rooted in the intense competition between two rival Jewish sects seeking to gain leverage and influence among competing forms of Judaism, and later to assure survival and fidelity in the wake of the destruction of the Second Temple and its sacred city. With the influx of Gentile believers the conflict between the sects became acute. Polemics grew stronger and worsened. On the Christian side the disdain was often vitriolic. Eventually even theological positions were adopted to justify, on the Christian side, Jews' negative role in the overall make up of Christian identity and purpose. Christian preaching and teaching promulgated disdain in mythic proportions and anti-Jewish sentiment grew deeper and stronger. The story continues, of course, in ways most of us know well. The point of these comments is to underscore that the crisis of credibility vis-à-vis the Shoah is not met by dealing simply with the twelve-year history of Nazi Germany. What happened then could not have happened without the anti-Jewish sentiment and history of contempt cultivated in the heart of Christian culture. Christians who face this history confront issues much like those who have grown up in the southern United States with its history of racism and segregation. The reality of anti-Semitism, like the reality of racism, is bigger and deeper than individual prejudice. The violence is also structural and often covert, hidden in plain sight. Of course, like racism, anti-Semitism can be expressed behaviorally in very dramatic and dangerous ways. Its attitudes are more than behavioral and have to do with who non-Jews, especially Christians, are with others who challenge, for whatever reasons, their place in the world. For Christians like me, facing up to this thread in our identities is a matter of coming to terms with ourselves, and how we structure our worlds of meaning and value. We who claim to love our neighbors like we love ourselves must ask if that really means we can only love our neighbors if and when they are like us. That is a question of integrity and the doorway through is more often shame than guilt.[13]

I have learned through dialogue with Jewish colleagues to recognize an underlying dimension that I am confident I would have overlooked without their help. That crisis is more difficult to address because it is deeper still. It turns on whether or not Christianity requires a Jewish other over against whom Christian truth is triumphant or more adequate. This question came to vivid clarity at a previous gathering in this same location a few years ago. My colleague, Peter Haas, was hosting a discussion of scholars, Jews and Christians, working on these very issues. We had committed to work in dialogue with each other on a book that focused on God, evil, and the Holocaust as a project of the former Goldner Holocaust Symposium. Peter had drafted a chapter in which he reviewed three Protestant theologians and their attempts to construct a positive Christian theology of Judaism. I was a respondent. Peter's analysis explored how even the most positive attempts to portray Jews and Judaism in a reconstructed Christian theology faced two major tasks: how to portray Jews in positive regard without turning them into monolithic and unrealistic figures and how to develop a form of Christianity that provided a legitimate place for Jews and Judaism in its world without losing what is distinctive about Christian identity. In the process of offering his critique, Haas made the observation that he did not think that Christianity could be nonsupersessionary without giving up what is distinctive about being Christian. Later, in a different context altogether, I encountered David Novak arguing similarly—that Christianity was inherently supersessionary and that the real issue was to distinguish between what he called "hard" and "soft" forms of supersessionism.[14] Of course, the core question they each raise is whether or not Christian identity is essentially supersessionary.

Among other things, supersessionism is a belief or attitude that one's truth or identity builds on and surpasses any claims and foundations shared with others. According to Regina Schwartz, the problem underlying supersessionism is a fundamental mindset that Christianity as a monotheistic religion shares with Judaism and Islam. In her book, *The Curse of Cain*, Schwartz identifies two primary ways of construing the world, what she calls "logics" of interpretation. Each of the three monotheistic traditions of Abraham, she observes, tends toward the excluding logic of scarcity in contrast to a present, but often obscured, logic of plenitude.[15] Schwartz posits the idea that a hermeneutic of scarcity is employed by each of the monotheistic traditions to protect fundamental truth claims. If God is one and Truth is one with God, then the revelation of that Truth should be one. The alternative lens, what she calls a logic of plenitude, is rooted in a sense of the richness of creation and its abundant gift of life. Accessible through such practices as midrash for Judaism, parables for Christianity, and Sufism for Islam,[16] the logic of plenitude provides an alternative mindset that may also be encountered in each of the traditions. Of course, the power dynamics among the three and between Judaism and Christianity have made a frightening difference in how these choices have been made and embodied over the centuries. And in the secularized eyes of the Third Reich, supersessionism reappears in the guise of Social Darwinism. To complicate the matter, Schwartz describes the resultant identity produced by scarcity thinking as being agonistic. That is, such an identity is constructed over against a competing other who contends for the identity or truth that cannot be shared. If Schwartz is right, and I think she makes a strong case, then underlying attitudes of Christian contempt are rooted in using a construct of Jewish identity as a negative significant other against whom one interprets his or her mission, purpose, truths, and so on. Supersessionist thinking, therefore, depends on an other whom it displaces and discounts for its sense of self.

As Regina Schwartz makes clear, facing the displaced other with post-Shoah responsibility calls for coming to terms with the agonistic history in which one's own identity is constructed. Until we learn to face the signifying others in our lives in their otherness, they will remain less than who they are. They will be projections of our own interpretive needs even if or when we convert disdain to honor.[17] That is, the matter is thoroughly hermeneutical at the same time it is deeply personal and relational.

When we face the displaced other with renewed respect, we confront our own agonistic history of displacement and supersessionism, coming to terms with how we have used this other as a negative signifier in our lives. In other settings[18] I have focused on the chastening character of this extended encounter, likening it to Jacob's encounter with the *'ish*, the other before whom he stood, with whom he wrestled, as he returned from his twenty-year exile. He faced himself, his history with an estranged brother and his deceptive relationships with his parents. And in all that he also faced the God of his forebears. We know the outcome of that struggle—a new name and a limp thereafter. That deep confrontation was a wounding affair that marked his walk in the aftermath with humility and must distinguish my sense of midrashic awareness. To move forward with positive regard we pass through a similar struggle and, certainly in my case, are wounded by what we learn about ourselves and the identity we have constructed with our Jewish siblings, not to mention myriad others. Reconfiguring that identity in a nonagonistic way means making room for this essential other in our lives that allows for the other's full otherness. That is, we must learn to incorporate a fundamental sense of hospitality to and for the other at the heart of who we are.

Sacrament of the Other

In the aftermath of the Shoah, Irving Greenberg reminds us that the dignity of every human being is secured by remembering that each of us reflects God's regard for the other.[19] Therefore, each act whereby we stand respectfully before another person is a sacred act. When we face the other, who reflects in his or her image the loving presence of God, we stand before the One who gives us life. In the aftermath of the Shoah, Rabbi Eliezer's words are therefore *limned*, charged with meaning. Know before whom you stand. Indeed.

According to Emmanuel Levinas, the human face is the fundamental datum of our embodied existence. Levinas, a survivor and witness to the atrocity that befell his people, tells us that the human face speaks to each of us with its presence calling us to be present in response. Its appearance can be, a theophanic moment, a burning bush, as it were, declaring "Here I am," and asking at the same time, "Where are you?" But we have to have the eyes to see and the heart to comprehend such a moment—a moment that is as true in the beginning as it is *in extremis*. In other words, the human other is a sacramental presence, to use a more Christian metaphor, if we dare to pay attention.

To represent this turn and responsibility in our lives I propose that post-Holocaust Christian communities consider adopting a new, Levinasian sacrament, the Sacrament of the Other. Unlike Baptism or the Eucharist, this sacrament cannot be administered by the church, as church. Indeed, such a sacrament can only be administered to it, received in and through the recognition of its otherness. While most often offered outside its boundaries, this gift can, nevertheless, be received inside its own house of faith and at its doors, if the hosts in such houses embrace the other's presence with hospitality and respect for his or her otherness. In other words, whenever such a sacrament is converted into a veiled understanding of Christ in our midst, it ceases to represent the otherness of the other. Still, it can be an expression of the otherness of Jesus that remains undomesticated by the church. That otherness is surely embodied in his Jewishness as Christians recognize that his place in the Shoah would have been with other Jewish victims. The distinctiveness of his identity would have been subsumed in the Nazi need to eradicate the challenging otherness of this child of the covenant. Indeed, Christianity has known this kind of logic before and glimpsed it in Kierkegaard's meticulous unpacking of the command to love the stranger in *Works of Love*.[20] In that extended meditation, Kierkegaard explained that when Christians love the stranger as a stranger, they do so because they were commanded to, and in doing what is commanded, they honor Christ. But if they do so because they wish to love Christ in disguise, they do not love the stranger at all. They reach out to one they think they know, loving the one they know, not the one who is unknown and other. Consequently, they fall short of the command to love. After the Shoah, this careful and differentiating logic becomes radically significant.

So, here we stand before the other represented by the pluriform presence of Samuel Bak's crucified child, Wiesel's narrative of a Holocaust survivor's attempt to return home to a town that remains beyond reach on the other side of an historically constructed wall, and Jesus' admonitions about the significance of children and others who stand before him and his followers. Their distinctive features pose for us a deepened understanding of Rabbi Eliezer's admonition, *Know before whom you stand.* Their individuated presence turns Eliezer's words into an embodied question before which we stand whether as Christians before a Jewish figure at the heart of our confessional lives, or as Jews before the Holy One of Israel, or as confused souls confined to a world of strangers. To explore that question is the urgent task we face together. Before whom do we stand?

Discussion Questions

1. How does the question "Before whom do we stand?" capture the multiple crises of credibility, integrity, and identity that Jews and Christians confront when they seek to come to terms with the Holocaust and its impact on the world they share with each other?
2. How does a more honest encounter with the Jewish otherness of Jesus of Nazareth lead Christians into new confessional territory after the Holocaust?
3. Is supersessionism an essential feature of Christian identity or an inescapable one that Christians must re-examine if they are to be faithful to Jesus of Nazareth after Auschwitz?

Notes

1. These reflections develop and expand an earlier exploration of these issues published in *No Going Back:Letters to Pope Benedict XVI on the Holocaust, Jewish-Christian Relations and Israel*, ed. Carol Rittner and Stephen D. Smith (London: Quill Press, 2009), 28-31. The expanded reflections were first offered in a lecture given at Elms College in Chicopee, MA during the fall of 2008, prepared in honor of Elie Wiesel's eightieth birthday. They were later reworked and expanded further into the present form for the conference at Case Western Reserve University.
2. Samuel Bak has rendered a number of works utilizing the iconic image of a Nazi soldier holding a young child from the Warsaw ghetto at gunpoint while invoking the face of Bak's eight-year-old friend, Samek Epstein, who was murdered by the Nazis. Bak's paintings were exhibited by the Pucker Art Gallery under the rubric, *Icon of Loss*, and a catalog for that show can by obtained by contacting the gallery in Boston. The painting referenced in this essay, *Study I, 1995*, is reproduced with commentary

in Danna Nolan Fewell and Gary A. Phillips, "Bak's Impossible Memorials: Giving Face to the Children," in *Representing the Irreparable: The Shoah, the Bible, and the Art of Samuel Bak*, ed. Danna Nolan Fewell, Gary A. Phillips, and Yvonne Sherwood (Boston: Pucker Art Publications, 2008), 95.

3. Lawrence S. Cunningham, "Elie Wiesel's Anti-Exodus," *America*, April 27, 1974, 325.
4. See Richard L. Rubenstein, *After Auschwitz: History, Theology, and Contemporary Judaism*, 2nd ed. (Baltimore: The Johns Hopkins Press, 1992), 3-13, 157-209.
5. Irving Greenberg, "Cloud of Smoke, Pillar of Fire: Judaism, Christianity, and Modernity after the Holocaust," in *Auschwitz? Beginning of a New Era*, ed. Eva Fleischner (New York: KTAV, 1977), 23.
6. Fewell and Phillips, "Bak's Impossible Memorials," 95.
7. Emil Fackenheim, *To Mend the World: Foundations of Future Jewish Thought* (New York: Schocken Books, 1982), 281.
8. Charlotte Delbo, *Auschwitz and After*, trans. Rosette C. Lamont (New Haven: Yale University Press, 1995), 258.
9. Although I speak primarily about *Town Beyond the Wall* in this essay, *Gates of the Forest* could be characterized as a stylized meditation on Rabbi Eliezer's admonition. The main character of the story, Gregor, raises and explores the questions posed by these reflections in intriguing ways. Indeed, *Gates of the Forest* ends with Gregor taking his place in a *minyan* to say *Kaddish* on the occasion of an unnamed person's *yarzheit*. Along with Gregor, the reader is invited to ponder, informed by the complex narrative that precedes this moment, what it means to know before whom, for whom, and with whom we stand.
10. Elie Wiesel, *Town Beyond the Wall*, trans. Stephen Becker (New York: Schocken Books, 1964), 115.
11. Johann Baptist Metz, *The Emergent Church: The Future of Christianity in a Postbourgeois World*, trans. Peter Mann (New York: Crossroad, 1981) 17-33, esp. 18, 30.
12. Paul Ricoeur, *From Text to Action: Essays in Hermeneutics*, vol. 2, trans. Kathleen Blamey and John B. Thompson (Evanston, IL: Northwestern University Press, 1986), 144-67.
13. See my essay, "From Shame to Responsibility and Christian Identity: The Dynamics of Shame and Confession Regarding the *Shoah*," in *Journal of Ecumenical Studies* 35, no. 1 (1998): 41-62.
14. See David Novak, "The Covenant in Rabbinic Thought" in *Two Faiths, One Covenant?* ed. Eugene B. Korn and John T. Pawlikowski (Lanham, MD: Rowman & Littlefield, 2005) 66.
15. Regina M. Schwartz, *The Curse of Cain: The Violent Legacy of Monotheism* (Chicago: The University of Chicago Press, 1997), 1-13.
16. The interpretive role of these distinctive hermeneutical practices reflects my own reading of these rhetorical strategies. In various ways they express a logic of plenitude or abundance.
17. I am profoundly indebted to Peter Haas for helping me see the significance of this matter. I am convinced that Schwartz's distinction between the logics of scarcity and plenitude provide helpful guidance in moving forward in this regard.
18. See Knight, "From Shame to Responsibility," among others.
19. Greenberg, 42-45.
20. Soren Kierkegaard, *Works of Love*, trans. Howard and Edna Hong (New York: Harper, 1962), 34-57, 153-96.

Edith Stein's Jewish Husband Jesus

Emily Leah Silverman

Edith Stein (1891-1942), a philosopher, mystic, and Jewish Carmelite nun, had a queer relationship to Jesus in that her personal religious framework was simultaneously Jewish and Roman Catholic. Her relationship to Jesus was unusual and out of line within the context of Carmelite spiritual practice. She saw Jesus as a Jew before Christian theologians took this fact seriously, but her mystical marriage to him reveals that she advanced in her interior life an unambiguous supersessionism that demands the replacement of Judaism with Christianity. For Stein, this interior devotion to her husband, Jesus the Jew, was a form of spiritual resistance to the destruction by the Nazis of her people, the Jews, in the outer world. However, no normative Jewish position accords with Stein's religious claims to Jewish identity.

In this chapter, I will examine how Stein viewed Jesus as a Jew just like herself through her writings, actions, and religious practice. We will see what it meant to Stein be a Catholic Jew, who felt directed by God's will to become a Carmelite nun in order work for the end of the suffering of her people. Stein believed that this deliverance required that the Jews accept one of their own as their Savior. For Stein, it was she who truly understood that only a fellow Jew could fully practice the *imitatio Christi* through a sacred marriage as a Carmelite to transmute Jewish suffering. Her Carmelite practice opened her to offer herself as a sacrifice for her people as the Jewish Jesus had done nearly two millennia before. This self-sacrifice was part of her Carmelite theology.

Born and raised a Jew in Breslau, Germany, Stein was the first woman to receive a Ph.D. in philosophy 1916 from Husserl, from whom she learned the phenomenological philosophy that enabled her to forge a Catholic-Jewish identity.[1] She converted to Catholicism in 1922, and subsequently worked in 1933 as a docent at the Catholic German Institute for Scientific Pedagogy in Munster. With the rise of the Nazis, Stein lost her job because she was born a Jew. Stein saw this loss as a divine sign of God's will for her to follow her true vocation and become a contemplative and was accepted into the Cologne Carmel as Sister Teresa Benedicta of the Cross. In 1938, she was forced to move to the Echt Carmel in Holland and in 1942 she was deported with her Sister Rosa to Auschwitz.

After the loss of her Munster job, events in Stein's outer world gave her a powerful sense of meaning, and ultimately an experience of divine love and union with God. Stein's reflections in her story "How I Came to the Cologne Carmel," which she wrote just before her forced emigration to the Echt Carmel in Holland on 18 December 1938, point to her inner certainty regarding her spiritual path. From the moment Stein converted to Catholicism in 1922, she had wanted to become a Carmelite contemplative. "For almost twelve years, Carmel had been my goal; since summer 1921, when the *Life* of our Holy Mother Teresa had happened to fall into my hands and had put an end to my long search for true faith."[2] On 16 February 1930, Stein wrote a letter to a friend and former philosophy student, Sr. Adelgundis Jaegerschmind, with a foreboding sense of her Divine mission.

> There is a real difference between being a chosen instrument and being in the state of grace. It is not up to us to pass judgment, and we may confidently leave all to God's unfathomable mercy . . . After every encounter in which I am made aware how powerless we are to exercise direct influence I have a deeper sense of the urgency of my own *holocaustum* . . . .
>
> However much our present mode of living may appear inadequate to us—what do we really know about it? But there can be no doubt that we are in the here-and-now to work out our salvation and that of those who have been entrusted to our souls. Let us help one another to learn more and more how to make every day and every hour part of the structure for eternity—shall we?[3]

Let us note how Stein referred to her sense of urgency in the presence of God. It was uncanny that Stein had such a strong sense of her own self-sacrifice that she used the Latin word *Holocaustum* three years before the Nazi Reign of Terror. *Holocaustum* comes originally from the Greek, and means "burnt offering." A *holocaustum* was a burnt offering that was totally consumed by flames. What did it mean to Stein to live with a sense of being a burnt offering? If one felt the urgency of sacrifice, then it demanded a total presence in the here and now at every single moment. We connect to the eternal through the here and now. We have no control over whether God will choose us or, in other words, if we will receive the gift of God's grace. This means expressing or having an epiphany, a revelation that comes to a mystic. A mystic recognizes her powerlessness before God, but also knows that the only way to be connected to God, to the eternal is through the here and now. If one can focus on the here and now, one has the potential to be granted grace and truly connect to a state of divine union. Sister Teresa Benedicta of the Cross writes in her 1936 philosophical magnum opus *Finite and Eternal Being*, about the meaning of Divine union: "Despite this fleeting being, I am; from moment to moment I am being held in being and in my fleeting being I am fastened to an enduring Being. I know that I am being held and therein I find calm and security."[4]

Stein recognized that being in communion with enduring being from moment to moment gave her an inner sense of calm and security that helped her confront the horror of what was happening to her nation, to her own chosen new religion, and to her community of origin, the Jewish people. Stein's awareness of the demand to be present in the here and now gave her an extraordinary perception that most Germans—Jewish or Christian—were not fully able to share: the extent of the impending danger when the Nazis took power on 30 January 1933. It was exactly because of Stein's straddling the two worlds or simultaneously being both from the Jewish community and a devout practicing Catholic, who had lived in and taught in Catholic religious institutions, that she could see the impending Holocaust. This was long before German Jews could even comprehend the looming catastrophe of their situation in Germany. In her urgent sense of now, she saw the oppressive political situation very clearly; and this enabled her to take a drastic action that became a major form of resistance.

Shortly after the Nazis' rise to power, Stein had a deep insight in a conversation with someone who did not know she had been a Jew. She chose not to reveal herself as one, and their discussion turned to the topic of American newspapers' reports about the precarious situation of Jews in Germany. Stein writes of this conversation: "True, I had heard of rigorous measures against the Jews before. But now a light dawned in my brain that once again God had put a heavy hand upon His people and that the fate of this people was also mine."[5] Stein realized even then that being a Catholic was not going to save her from the Nazis. She would share the same fate as her people, a fate she links to Jesus' own Jewish blood. This epiphany leads her to her first act of resistance, outward protest, and to another realization.

In April 1933, she had just visited her spiritual director, Archabbot Raphael Walzer, during Passion Week in Beuron. While attending evening services on the Friday of Passion during the first week of April, she was called by her Lord the Savior. Stein writes about this calling:

> I talked with the Savior and told Him that I knew that it was His cross that was now being placed upon the Jewish people; that most of them did not understand this, but that those who did would have to take it up willingly in the name of all. I would do that. He should show me how. At the end of the service I was certain that I had been heard. But what this carrying of the cross was to consist in, that I did not yet know.[6]

What did Stein mean by saying that the cross was now being placed upon the Jewish people, who were also her people? Did the Savior's cross represent the suffering of the Jewish people in the same way that Jesus had suffered at the hands of the Romans? Was Stein equating Jesus' suffering with Jewish suffering? Did this mean that someone who was born Jewish like Stein but who recognized the Lord as the Savior, the Son of God, had an extra special responsibility because they could see the whole picture from the perspective of the passion of Christ? Did Stein see that the Jewish people were about to go through unbearable agony and suffering and that no one was trying to stop it or intercede on their behalf? Stein had this conversation with her Savior during Passion Week, which commemorates the suffering, death, and resurrection of Christ. Was Stein in a position to do something about the suffering of her people that no one around her was able to do because of her unique identity claim of being a Jew, like Jesus, but also realizing that he was the Savior?

This was not the first time that Stein viewed Jesus as a Jew. She had told her Jesuit confessor, Father Hirschmann, "You don't know what it means to be a daughter of the chosen people—to belong to Christ, not only spiritually but in the flesh."[7] Stein's connection to Jesus was one of flesh, which meant to her that he was no different then her own Jewish family. Stein's union was unique among her Carmelite sisters, because she had the same physical flesh of their sacred husband and Lord. While Stein's transgression of Jewish-Catholic boundaries in her mystical marriage to Jesus the Jew is a synecdoche of her hybrid religious identity, her self-understanding reinforces ethnic boundaries as significant. For other Carmelite nuns, Stein's position implies, mystical marriage to Jesus is a kind of intermarriage in a way that it is not for Stein. This sense of family connection also gave her a deeper sense of radical urgency in her contemplative work on behalf of the Jewish people.

Her emphasis on her ethnic ties to her mystical spouse, Jesus, is especially significant when one considers that her romantic interests were for non-Jewish men. Stein had strong feelings for two non-Jewish men before her conversion to Catholicism. In 1917, she developed an affection for the Catholic phenomenologist Roman Ingarden; based on the fact that Stein requested that Ingarden burn their letters, Stein's niece speculates that there was a romantic attraction.[8] According to Hedwig Conrad-Maritus (1888-1966), Stein's spiritual godmother and philosophical colleague, Stein was very interested in their mutual friend the phenomenologist Hans Lipps (1889-1941). He was a German Christian and Stein would have married him, if he had asked her, instead he married someone else in 1921. Maritus explains,

> She loved Hans Lipps . . . I am also certain she would have married him if he wanted it. But he did not want to. . . . I had a talk with her—concerning the photograph that, all by itself, still stood on her small desk in our Bergzabern home. I said to her that it didn't seem right to surrender totally to God and

> to want to dedicate oneself to him and yet keep on the table the picture of a man who didn't want to marry you . . . She was deeply affected and shortly thereafter, perhaps even immediately, the picture disappeared from her desk. . . . I believe for certain that this profound disappointment of her life contributed . . . to her conversion baptism, yes, even to her cloistered life.[9]

Lipps asked Stein to marry him in 1932 after the death of his wife, but she said it was too late, she was already on her path to a cloistered life. Stein would have married Hans Lipps before her Catholic conversion in 1922. It is ironic that Stein wanted to marry outside of the Jewish fold but instead converted and married one of her own people in a divine marriage within a perceived Jewish community. In any case, the opportunity for her to become a Carmelite nun put her in a position to experience the divine mystical union of a contemplative to her Lord.

Spiritual Resistance in Carmel: The Way of the Cross

Stein entered the Carmel two days after her 42nd birthday, on 14 October 1933. She was finally able to serve her Savior. What did it mean for her to be a Carmelite? Sister Teresa Benedicta of the Cross gave the answer in a newspaper article titled "Before the Face of God: On the History and Spirit of Carmel," published in March 1935 in the *Augsburger Post*: "To stand before the face of the living God, that is our vocation. The holy prophet [Elijah] set us an example. He stood before God's face because this was the eternal treasure for whose sake he gave up all earthly goods."[10] A Carmelite takes vows of poverty, obedience, and chastity upon entering the order. Stein explains that "The vow of poverty opens one's hands so that they let go of everything . . . [It] is intended to make us carefree as the sparrows and the lilies so that our spirit and hearts may be free for God."[11] Once we let go of desire and wanting things in the material world, it frees the soul to receive from God. The vow of obedience was to make one free to follow the will of God: not one's own personal will that was ruled by emotion and reason, but God's will. The vows of obedience mean self-denial in order to serve and obey the Lord. "Therefore the obedient person . . . recognizes . . . how many small sacrifices are available daily and hourly as opportunities to advance in self-denial . . . because doing so deepens the burden, the conviction of being closely bound to the Lord, who was obedient to death on the cross."[12] Obedience was another way to bind one to the cross and to the Lord. Finally, the vow of chastity "intends to release human beings from all the bounds of natural common life, to fasten them to the cross high above the bustle and to free their hearts for the union with the Crucified."[13]

The practice of these vows and the willingness to freely choose suffering was the meaning of the cross, the very way to take it up. This was exactly what Stein wanted to do, for she saw this as the way to spiritually resist the evil going on around her and as an action that could transmute the evil. For when Christ died on the cross for the sins of humanity, he was transmuting evil and offering himself up as a sacrifice to God. Christ's suffering on the cross showed humanity the path back to God. Those who were accepted into a life of contemplative practice were taking the path of Christ for the sake of the sins of humanity. This was the way to prepare oneself to be open for receiving and uniting in God's divine love.

These vows guide the sisters of Carmel to experience the love of the cross, the face of God, and atonement. As Stein explains, these three vows lead to what the Prophet Elijah experienced:

> Elijah stands before God's face because all his love belongs to the Lord. He lives outside of all natural human relationships. His "relatives" are those who do the will of the Father . . . Glorifying God in his joy. His zeal to serve God tears him apart: " I am filled with jealous zeal for the Lord, the God of hosts" . . . By living penitentially he atones for the sins of his time.[14]

The statement that Elijah "lives outside of all natural human relationships" shows that Stein is working with a strictly Carmelite, not Jewish, interpretation of the biblical prophet.

Stein clearly recognized when she entered the Carmel of Cologne in 1933 that there were intense sins in her time that needed be atoned for. The way of the cross transmutes the sins of the times. These sins were clearly those of National Socialism, which she called the Antichrist, and those of the Jews who did not accept Christ as the Savior. Stein fled to the Echt Carmel in Holland in 1938, and preached to her new Carmel community about the renewal of their vows on 14 September 1939. "The world is in flames," she says, "the battle between the Christ and the Antichrist has broken out into the open. If you decide for Christ, it could cost you your life."[15] Carrying the cross did cost some sisters their lives. Sister Teresa Benedicta's life, however, would have been taken regardless of whether she was carrying the cross or not. Sister Teresa Benedicta knew Catholicism was not going to save her from Nazi violence, but she believed that faith in Jesus was a way of resisting the Holocaust.

Sister Teresa Benedicta understood that she did not have to live in the world, for behind cloistered walls one could take on spiritual suffering even more intensely. She explains exactly why she was offering herself up to Christ:

> The world is in flames. The conflagration can also reach our house. But high above all flames towers the cross. They cannot consume it. It is the path from earth to heaven. It will lift one who embraces it in faith, love and hope into the bosom of the Trinity.
>
> The world is in flames. Are you impelled to put them out? Look at the cross. From the open heart gushes the blood of the Savior. This extinguishes the flames of hell. Make your heart free by the faithful fulfillment of your vows:

> then the flood of the Divine love will be poured into your heart until it overflows and becomes fruitful to all the ends of the earth. . . . You can be at all fronts, wherever there is grief, in the power of the cross. Your compassionate love takes you everywhere, this love from the divine heart. Its precious blood is poured everywhere—soothing, healing, saving.[16]

The blood with which Sister Teresa Benedicta identified so intensely as a Jew was the precious blood pouring from the Jewish body of Christ—divine love that flowed everywhere and soothed, healed, and saved. In her description of it extinguishing the flames of hell, we can grasp why being both a daughter of the Jewish community and a daughter of the church had so much personal meaning for Stein. It gave Sister Teresa Benedicta's suffering double meaning. Christ's blood was her blood; she was the same as Christ when she bound herself to him with her Carmelite vows. The Jews' precarious state was similar to Christ's suffering, and now she, one of Christ's own flesh and blood, was able suffer as he did. Her contemplative practice showed her the way.

Carrying the Cross for Atonement and Redemption

Stein explicitly states that the way of the cross, which was Stein's atonement and reason for dying, addressed the sin of the Jews who did not accept Christ. Similarly, her dying was an atonement for the Germans; she was offering her life up on the cross for world peace and all humanity. This was Stein's way of resisting oppression. And more than offering herself up on the cross, it was a way to let divine love flow into the world through this suffering. She expressed this intention in her last will and testament, and in her recurring image of Queen Esther redeeming her people for the Lord Jesus.

Lucy Gelber explains the interior religious life of Edith Stein, which guided her in becoming a contemplative, and what the love of the cross and atonement meant for her:

> The first was love of the cross, which gives our being, unstable because of change and transience, an ultimate security in the constant primal Ground of eternal Being. The other is atonement, which breaks the disastrous and endless cycle of our own and others' debt of shame in the face of God's goodness and justice and so achieves reconciliation and peace.[17]

When Stein was deported, her behavior did in fact demonstrate her inner primal grounding in eternal Being. Stein saw that her ultimate act of bearing the cross and suffering would lead her to be able to see the face of God, achieve peace, and advance justice. Stein felt that if she could take this on personally as a contemplative she was literally offering herself up as a *holocaustum* to somehow assuage the madness of the Nazi war against the Jews and against all of humanity.

Stein wrote about the meaning of her future death in her last will and testament, composed on 9 June 1939: "I pray to the Lord that he may accept my living and dying . . . as an atonement for the Jewish people's unbelief and so that the Lord may be accepted by his own and that his reign may come in glory, that Germany may be saved and that there be peace in the world."[18] Sister Teresa Benedicta was atoning for the Jews, praying for them to accept their own fellow Jew, Jesus, as the Messiah, so that he might return again and bring world peace in with his reign. By this means, Germany would be saved.

Sister Teresa Benedicta repeated these sentiments in a dialogue she wrote entitled "Conversation at Night," composed to honor the prioress at the Echt Carmel, Mother Antonia.[19] It was the vision of a mystic, but reiterates Stein's reason for suffering and atonement. In this dialogue, written a year before the end of her life, Stein records an image of herself as Queen Esther delivering her people to the Savior. In passing, it is interesting to note that the Book of Esther is a point in the biblical canon where Jewish and Catholic textual variants make visible the tensions of a Jewish-Catholic identity.[20]

The dialogue opens with a stranger in conversation with the Mother, representing Mother Antonia, the prioress. The Mother asked, "Who are you?" The stranger explains that she is not the Holy Mother Mary, but she does serve her. "I am of her people, her blood, And once I risked my life for this people . . . My life serves as a image of hers for you"[21] The stranger who turns out to be Queen Esther identifies herself of Jewish lineage just as the Holy Mother Mary. Queen Esther risked her life to reveal herself to be a Jew to her non-Jewish husband to save them from Haman. In this case Queen Esther establishes that her people are again in danger.

Sister Teresa Benedicta reinterprets the Esther story and puts it in the context of a Catholic story of the redemption of her people through conversion and acceptance of their Lord as one of their own. This reinterpretation illustrates perfectly Stein's sense that her interior devotion to Jesus is an act for the deliverance of the Jewish people in the outer world. In the "Conversation in the Night," Sister Teresa Benedicta reveals that she is Esther, reappearing this time to save her people. In this dialogue we can see Sister Teresa Benedicta's deep sense of her mission as a contemplative and the meaning of her offering up her life on the cross while the world was in flames. Queen Esther was delivering the Jewish people to her redeeming God, the Lord Jesus, and this would bring about his second coming. However, the deliverance Queen Esther offers is not only a spiritual conversion, but it also addresses the immediate historical crisis. The Mother asks Esther, "And today another Haman has sworn to annihilate them in bitter hatred. Is this, in fact, why Esther has returned?'[22] This Haman was Hitler, who was in the process of annihilating the Jews with his final solution. In June 1941, the Mother may not have known how literally true her statement was to become.

In June 1941 the Nazis had just invaded the Soviet Union, and the special SS units called *Einsatzgruppen* had followed the German army during the invasion. The *Einsatzgruppen's* job was to exterminate complete Jewish populations, along with Gypsies and communists, in the towns of the Ukraine. The SS first attempted to do this by group massacres, using firing squads on Jewish communities; later in 1941, they used mobile gas units. In the winter of 1942, the major concentration camps, such as Auschwitz, were in full operation, systematically gassing the Jews and carrying out the Final Solution. Jews from all over Europe were concentrated in ghettos or interim prison camps, then directly deported to the extermination camps. When she was deported, Edith Stein was first taken to the holding camp at Westerbork, only to meet her fate in the summer of 1942 at Auschwitz.

In the midst of this catastrophe, Queen Esther explains why she has returned to Earth. She tells the Mother that she had died a normal death: "To the place of peace I found rest in Abraham's bosom with its ancestors." Queen Esther was also received into the heart of Jesus. Once she had entered there, she had seen the Holy Mother, the Virgin Mary. Queen Esther explains to the Mother: "I saw the church grow out of my people, . . . The unblemished pure shoot of David. . . . I saw flowing down from Jesus' heart, the fullness of grace into the Virgin's heart. From there it flows to the members as a stream of life . . . But now I know that I was bound to her. From eternity in accordance with God's direction—forever. My life was only a beam of hers."[23] Sister Teresa Benedicta was in a state of divine union with the Holy Mother and God. The church had grown out of the Jewish people, who were the same flesh as Sister Teresa Benedicta. She knew that she was a beam of light coming from the source of light. She had literally seen the face of God and was now returning to save her people. Queen Esther had been sent as an emissary of the Holy Mother to gather up her people like a shepherd and bring them back to her and to the Son of the Lord: "The Mother ceaselessly pleads for her people. She seeks souls to help her pray. Only then when Israel has found the Lord, only then when he has received his own, will He come in manifest glory. And we must pray for this second coming."[24] We see the Holy Mother trying to rescue her people, the Jewish people, with the help of prayers from the ones who are bound to the Lord and know that he is the Redeemer. Sister Teresa Benedicta was bound to Jesus through the radiating beam of light, which flowed from him to Mother Mary and branches out to her disciples in the Carmel. Sister Teresa Benedicta explains in an earlier letter to Sr. Agnelle Statdtmuller that we are branches that extend from a root like a grapevine. "Our roots are in the heart of Jesus"[25]

Queen Esther states that once Jews have found the Lord, they can return to earth at the second coming, and all suffering will end. The reason Queen Esther has appeared to the Mother prioress at this moment is to ask for help and prayers for the redemption of Jews, to return to the Lord so that they can be saved from annihilation through the Lord's redemption. The hearts of those cloistered in a contemplative order offered the best chance for the prayers of Queen Esther to be heard. The Mother responds to Queen Esther: "Where else was she [Holy Mother Mary] to find hearts prepared if not in her quiet sanctuary? Her people [the Jewish people], which are yours, your Israel, I take up into the lodgings of my heart. Praying secretly and sacrificing secretly, I will take it home to my Savior's heart."[26]

This was Stein's way of asking for help from the spiritually strong to pray for redemption. Stein showed that the task at hand was to pray for the Jews to come to Jesus the Savior. As Queen Esther, she conveyed the message that this work was to be done contemplatively and secretly within the heart through prayer and sacrifice. It was truly a way for Stein to show mystical resistance. After the Mother responds that she understands why Queen Esther has appeared to her, Queen Esther replies, "You have understood and so I can depart . . . We will meet again on the great day, the day of manifest glory. When the head of the Queen of Carmel [Holy Mother Mary] is loved, the crown of stars will gleam brilliantly because the twelve tribes will have found their Lord." With her dialogue, Stein transforms Queen Esther from a woman who comes out of hiding as a Jew to save her people from physical and spiritual annihilation to a mediator of a replacement theology, in which acceptance of Jesus fulfills Jewish messianic claims, negating two thousand years of Jewish self-definition.[27]

Just before the Gestapo came to arrest all the Catholic Jews in Holland, Sister Teresa Benedicta completed her last manuscript entitled "The Science of the Cross," which examined the writings of St. John of the Cross. She had drawn an illustration, a cross with flames all around it. On 26 July 1942, a protest letter against the deportation of the Jews was read from the pulpit in the Catholic Dutch and Dutch Orthodox branch of the Protestant Church during Sunday morning services. Following this, all Catholic Jews, including monks and nuns living in cloistered convents and monasteries, were rounded up on 2 August 1942. Sister Teresa Benedicta and her sister Rose were among them. Stein's predictions, going all the way back to 1930 and 1933, were being fulfilled.

Externally, she died no differently than any other Jew, identified by the Nazis and recognized by fellow Jews. In these circumstances, no one Jewish life was greater than another. Susanne Batzdorff, Stein's niece, writes:

> It was a fact that Edith Stein died in solidarity "with her people." Even though she had left the Jewish fold, she was finally, in an ironic twist, reunited with them in death. She was resigned to that fate, but she had no control over it. It was rather due to the Nazi definition of who was a Jew. It was because she was born Jewish, of Jewish parentage that she became a martyr in Auschwitz."[28]

However, in her internal sense of who she was, Stein died on a cross as a *holocaustum* to further the coming of her Jewish Jesus to save his redeem the suffering of the Jewish people. Stein tried in the interior realm to transmute their sins of unbelief into one of belief in her Savior, the Christian savior, who had Jewish blood like her.

Stein's self-understanding of her role in delivering the Jews contradicts every expression of Jewish self-determination since the rise of Christianity. In her mind, she was saving her fellow Jews, but to Jews she betrayed them as a people. Stein understood herself as dying on the burning altar, in a Holocaust for her people. The Jewish community died in the Shoah,[29] in an abyss, not as holy flaming sacrifice that would be redeemed by a savior Jesus Christ. Stein's view of her faith offends the Jewish community, because she was working to save them at the cost of their conversion to Christianity. This was a replacement theology.

Stein's understanding of herself as a mystic who was of Jewish flesh and in divine union with a Jewish Jesus of the same flesh opened her up to the path of passion of the cross and to the imitation of Christ. While *imitatio Christi* was a standard Catholic practice, what was unique in Stein's case was her perception of Jesus the Jew within the context of her Carmelite practice. She could not have had any other theological understanding but to redeem her fellow Jews through this practice. To her, offering her self as a sacrifice on the cross was one of eternal love and the only way she knew to deal with world that was in flames around her.[30]

Notes

1. See Rachel Feldhay Brenner, "Ethical Convergence in Religious Conversion," in *The Unnecessary Problem of Edith Stein*, ed. Harry James Cargas (Lanham, NY: London University Press of America, 1994), 78-79.
2. "How I Came to the Cologne Carmel," in *Edith Stein, Selected Writings: With Comments, Reminiscences and Translations of Prayers and Poems by her Niece Susanne M. Batzdorff* (Springfield, IL: Templegate Publishers, 1990), 17.
3. Edith Stein, *Self Portrait in Letters 1916-1942*, ed. L. Gelber and Michael Linssen, trans. Josephine Koeppel (Washington, DC: ICS Publications, 1993), Letter 52 to Sr. Adelgundis Jaegerschmind, Freiburg-Gunterstal, ST Magdalena Speyer, February 16, 1930, 60.
4. Cited by Antonio Calcagno in *The Philosophy of Edith Stein* (Pittsburgh, PA: Duquesne University Press, 2007), dedication page.
5. Stein, "How I Came to the Cologne Carmel," 16.
6. Stein, "How I Came to the Cologne Carmel," 17.
7. Joyce Averch Berkman, "The German Jewish Symbiosis in Flux" in *Contemplating Edith Stein*, ed. Joyce Averch Berkman (Notre Dame, IN: University of Notre Dame, 2006), 187-88.
8. Susanne Batzdorff, *Aunt Edith: The Jewish Heritage of a Catholic Saint*, 2nd ed. (Springfield, IL: Templegate Publishers, 2003), 185-86.
9. Hedwig Conrad-Martius, "A Great, Exceptional Personality: Edith Stein Remembered," in *Never Forget: Christian and Jewish Perspectives on Edith Stein*, ed. Waltraud Hebstrith, trans. Susanne Batzdorff (Washington, DC: ICS Publications, 1998), 265.
10. Edith Stein, *The Hidden Life: Essays, Meditations, Spiritual Texts*, ed. L. Gelber and Michael Linssen, trans. Waltraut Stein (Washington, DC: ICS Publications, 1992), 1.
11. Stein, "The Marriage of the Lamb: For September 14, 1940," in *The Hidden Life*, 99.
12. Stein, "The Marriage of the Lamb," 100.
13. Stein, "The Marriage of the Lamb," 100.
14. Stein, *The Hidden Life*, 2.

15. Edith Stein, "Elevation of the Cross, September 14, 1939. *Ave Crux Spes Unica!*" in *The Hidden Life*, 94.
16. Stein, "Elevation of the Cross," 95-96.
17. Lucy Gelber, "Editor's Introduction," in *The Hidden Life*, xiv.
18. Cited by Dorothee Sölle in *The Silent Cry: Mysticism and Resistance* (Minneapolis: Augsburg Fortress, 2001), 148.
19. Stein, "Conversation at Night," in *The Hidden Life*. Stein wrote the dialogue on 13 June 1941 in honor of the celebrations of Mother Antonia's birthday.
20. According to the Catholic commentary in the New American Bible, "The text of Esther, written originally in Hebrew, was transmitted in two forms: a short Hebrew form and a longer Greek version. The latter contains 107 additional verses, inserted at appropriate places within the Hebrew form of the text. A few of these seem to have a Hebrew origin, while the rest are Greek in original composition. It is possible that the Hebrew form of the text is original throughtout. If it systematically omits reference to God and his Providence over Israel, this is perhaps due to fear of irreverent response . . . . The Greek text with the above-mentioned additions is probably a later literary paraphrase in which the author seeks to have the reader share his sentiments. This standard Greek text is pre-Christian in origin. The church has accepted the additions as equally inspired as the rest of the book." http://www.usccb.org/nab/bible/esther/intro.htm. Accessed May 3, 2010.
21. Stein, "Conversation at Night," 129.
22. Stein, "Conversation at Night," 131.
23. Stein, "Conversation at Night," 132.
24. Stein, "Conversation at Night," 133.
25. Stein, *Self Portrait in Letters*, Letter 306 to Sr. Agnella Stadtmuller, OP, 313.
26. Stein, "Conversation at Night," 133.
27. On "replacement theology," see Krister Stendhal, "Qumran and Supersessionism—And the Road Not Taken," *Princeton Seminary Bulletin* 29, no. 4 (1998): 134-42.
28. Batzdorff, *Aunt Edith*, 205.
29. David Patterson, "Holocaust or Shoah," in *Maven in Blue Jeans: A Festschrift in Honor of Zev Garber* (West Lafayette, IN: Purdue University Press, 2009), 338. Patterson discusses the difference between the words Holocaust and Shoah and makes a strong point that the Jews died not as a holy sacrifice or burnt offering but in an abyss. To completely annihilate the Jews was the Nazi's point. This is the opposite of Stein's view of her own death.
30. I want to thank Dirk von der Horst, Ph.D candidate in Theology, Ethics, and Culture at Claremont Graduate University, for his insightful conversations about Stein's intermarriage and theology and for his wonderful editing. I want to thank Professor Zev Garber for inviting me to write a chapter.

Can We Talk? The Jewish Jesus in a Dialogue between Jews and Christians

Steven Leonard Jacobs

> "Truth must be distinguished from fiction and agendas (ecclesiastical, conspiratorial, feminist), realized or fantasized."
>
> —Zev Garber, "Reflections on Jesus"

> "Scholars not only need to recognize that they view Jesus through their own particular set of eyes but also to be on guard for how their interpretations might be (mis)perceived by others."
>
> —Gary Gilbert, Review of *The Historical Jesus through Catholic and Jewish Eyes.*

Introduction: A Vignette

In my previous career as a full-time congregational rabbi and part-time academic (what I now tell my students was my "second incarnation," my first being that of a high school teacher of English literature), I used to have any number of church groups (men's clubs, ladies guilds, youth groups, etc.) visit and sit in our sanctuary during an afternoon or early evening for an "Everything you always wanted to know about Judaism but never got around to asking" talk, with plenty of time left for questions and answers, and sometimes the Q & A lasting more than the original presentation. I distinctly remember one such visit by a ladies' guild, though I no longer remember the particular Christian denomination, when one of the elderly ladies, quite tiny (or is it now more politically correct to say "petite"?) summed up the entire visit with the statement, "Now after all, Rabbi, isn't

Judaism simply that branch of Christianity that doesn't believe in Jesus!?!" (It continues to remain one of my fondest recollections of that part of my career.)

Thus my aforementioned reference to the quoted comments of both Zev Garber, whose vision and insights have enabled us to contribute to this scholarly collection (with genuine thanks of course to our colleague Peter Haas and his wonderful team, and especially Linda Gilmore), and to Gary Gilbert for the second quotation.

There is no question that "out there"—in the so-called "real world" beyond the academy—the one question asked by genuinely interested Christian religious persons more than any others is "Why don't you Jews believe in Jesus?" And no matter what or how we choose to answer, the question remains and forms a foundational underpinning to all Jewish-Christian dialogical encounters. (Parenthetically, the Holocaust/Shoah and the State of Israel are equally foundational to all such contemporary dialogues.)

Let me, therefore, tell you how I used to answer that question and use that answer as the base on which to move the dialogue forward:

> We need to draw a distinction here, for we are talking both history and theology at the same time. If we are talking history, then the Jesus of the New Testament, our primary source of data, appears to be one born of Jewish parents (Yosef and Miryam) during the period of Roman oppression in Palestine at the turn of the millennium, seems to have had a reasonably good Jewish education, cared enough about his people to travel around both teaching and giving comfort to his fellow Jews who suffered, was arrested by the Roman authorities who saw his ability to attract increasingly larger crowds as potentially dangerous to their ability to maintain their control, and put him to death as was their way (with the support of a collaborationist Jewish leadership unrepresentative of the people). He was not a "rabbi" in the sense of receiving *s'micha*/ordination, despite the textual references, and, as a committed Jew and a rabbi, I have no difficulty in regarding him as a welcome teacher among many.
>
> But, truthfully, this is not the question being asked. For as a question of theological belief, it is your understanding that, whoever else he was and is, Jesus as the Christ is the merger of both the divine and the human into one being, and whose very willingness to offer up his own life in place of humanity "spared it further degradation in the sight of God and redeemed it from sin and death forever and all time."[1] That understanding I cannot accept as consistent with Jewish theological thinking regarding a fully human Jewish Messiah, and expressed in the writings of its greatest thinker Moses Maimonides (1135-1204), whose seven-fold summary of messianic responsibilities were neither completely fulfilled (word purposefully chosen) nor fully actualized during the life of Jesus, namely, 1. be a descendent of King David (a New Testament claim which may or may not be accurate),

> 2. gain sovereignty over the land of Israel (no), 3. gather the Jews from the four corners of the earth and restore Jewish political sovereignty (no), 4. restore the Jews to the full observance of Torah law through his own example (a possible journey in progress, granted, but problematic especially regarding the question of his self-affirmed authority),[2] 5. bring peace to the whole word (no),[3] 6. vanquish Israel's enemies (no, including the Romans, i.e., "fight the Lord's wars," not spiritual but physical and military), and 7. restore a destroyed Temple (not applicable during his life, nor since).[4] And while I did often quote from Maimonides' *Thirteen Principles of Faith*—"*Ani Ma'amin*: I believe in the coming of the Messiah and though he may tarry, I will wait for him on any day that he may come," I always closed with the following: "When the Messiah comes, you and I together will go and ask him, "Is this your first visit or is it a return visit?" Then we will know. Until then, however, let us respectfully agree to disagree. But let us also work together to create a world—free from hunger, free from poverty, free from want, free from war—of which he and we will be proud."

Taking the Dialogue to the Next Level: Four Questions

There is no question that *Nostre Aetate* ("In Our Age," affirmed 28 October 1965[5]) signaled a true sea change in Catholic- and later Protestant-Jewish relations based especially on two operative paragraphs:

> True, the Jewish authorities and those who followed their lead pressed for the death of Christ (John 19:6); still, what happened in His passion cannot be charged against all the Jews, without distinction, then alive, nor against the Jews of today. Although the Church is the new people of God, the Jews should not be presented as rejected or accursed by God, as if this followed from the Holy Scriptures. All should see to it, that in catechetical work or in the preaching of the word of God they do not teach anything that does not conform to the truth of the Gospel and the spirit of Christ.
>
> Furthermore, in her rejection of every persecution against any man, the Church, mindful of the patrimony she shares with the Jews and moved not by political reasons but by the Gospel's spiritual love, decries hatred, persecution, displays of anti-Semitism, directed against Jews at any time and by anyone.[6]

Subsequent Church documents—for example, *Guidelines and Suggestions for Implementing the Counciliar Declaration Nostra Aetate* (1984) and *Notes on the Correct Way to Present Jews and Judaism in the Teaching and Catechesis of the Roman Catholic Church* (1985)—have furthered the process of dialogue as have other denominational documents manifesting that same spirit, for example, the 1983 Resolution of the Lutheran Church Missouri Synod repudiating Martin Luther's (1483-1546) anti-Semitism and distancing themselves from it.[7]

Yet, despite all the progress that has been made over the last more than four decades of Jewish-Christian relations through the vehicle of dialogue (1965-2009)—and that progress is substantial, though not without recurring minefields both political (e.g., the Middle East Arab-Israeli-Palestinian conflict) and theological (e.g., restoration of certain Good Friday prayers to the Catholic liturgy)—there yet remain questions regarding this Christ which have not been fully addressed, to which I began giving voice in Berlin in 1994,[8] and to which I now return:

1. Is Jesus the Christ, the one and only begotten Son of God, only for those who accept him as such?
2. Or, is Jesus the Christ, the one and only begotten Son of God, for all humanity—including those who do not accept him as such?
3. What, then, about those who neither accept him as such, nor reject him outright, but stand in ignorance of him?
4. What then is the proper Christian response, first to the Jews and also to the Buddhists, Hindus, Muslims, and others?[9]

Questions 1 and 2

Theologically, and thus I would argue of dialogical necessity between Jews and Christians, these first two questions revolve around both the centrality of the question of "Christology" in Matthew—"But who do you say that I am?"—and the universality of the Christian understanding of this same Christ as reflected in John—"For God so loved the world."

As regards the first, we read in Matthew 16:

> 13. When Jesus came to the region of Caesarea Philippi, He asked His disciples, "Who do people say that the Son of Man is?" 14. And they said, "Some say John the Baptist; some Elijah; others Jeremiah, or one of the prophets." 15. He asked them, **"But who do you say that I am?"** 16. And Simon Peter answered, **"You are the Messiah, the Son of the living God."** 17. And Jesus responded, "Simon, son of Jonah, blessed are you, for flesh and blood did not reveal it to you, but My Father which is in heaven."

Thus, within this circle of those who affirm him, Jesus is their Messiah, their Son of God, and their knowledge, especially that of Simon Peter is gleaned, at least according to Jesus himself, through a (direct) encounter with God. Might this not present, then, a point about which Jews and Christians can enter into conversation: that for those who either have already had an experience of this Christ, or those who wish to do so, that Christ is indeed their Messiah, their Son of God? But for those who have not yet had such an experience, or who have no desire to have such an experience, this same Christ is not or not yet their Messiah, and while others may acclaim or proclaim him as their Son of God, respectful disagreement—the very heart of Jewish-Christian dialogue—remains in place.[10]

More difficult and more uncomfortable, to be sure, would be the possibility of a conversation, a dialogue, around John 3:16—the affirmation at the heart of Christianity—that "God so loved the world that he gave his one and only Son [alt. "his only begotten Son"] that whoever believes in him shall not perish but have eternal life." Here, too, conversation is possible, provided both come to the table comfortable enough in the other's presence and open to hearing what the other is saying. Such openness and presence is, of course, the result of a whole series of prior meetings, prior readings, prior discussions and prior conversations.

An example place to begin might be the following: Never in my growing up did I ever truly doubt that both my parents genuinely and truly loved me, and went out of their way to provide me with many, many opportunities—expressions of their love—to maximize my own potential. Of some I took advantage, others, for a whole host of reasons, I chose not to accept, though some, even now, remain and may still present themselves in my future. For religiously devout Christians and religiously devout Jews, thinking theologically about this Christ, the analogy remains: Christians are those who have already accepted this gift given in love and, while Jews choose not to do so (more on this in a moment, though I can already feel the Jewish angst beginning to surface), the gift remains available.[11]

Does such openness thus not open the door to conversionary efforts on the part of Christians to Jews? Yes and no—but only towards those who own the door and are willing to let others in. As I have previously written:

> Thus, religiously sensitive and knowledgeable Christians, morally and ethically aware of the Shoah and its effect upon Jews, must rethink and, ultimately, reject any form of missionizing whatsoever toward Jews. If the experience of the Christ . . . is *potentially redemptive* for all humanity, then Christianity is *potentially available* to all those who would choose to elect it, willing to explore its possibilities and come to it without coercion. To aggressively promote its proselytizing and conversionary activities as the only and exclusive way to experience the Divine-human encounter, however understood and interpreted, is to express no love or caring for Jews, to build no bridges between the two.[12]

Missionizing and proselytizing and openly sharing of the Christian faith with Jews, nonaggressively and nonthreateningly, is not an act of antisemitism, though given the sad and tragic history of these past two thousand plus years, it remains extremely difficult to engage in such a conversation, especially within the organized Jewish communities on this very issue. I do now find myself in agreement, however, with Amy-Jill Levine, who writes in her 2006 text, *The Misunderstood Jew: The Church and the Scandal of the Jewish Jesus*:

> Christian missionaries who seek to bring Jews "the good news of Jesus" do not do so because they hate Jews; they do so because they love Jews . . . Jews and Christians need to listen with each other's ears. Jews need to hear the sincerity in the Christians' message; Christians need to respect the integrity of the Jewish position . . . For Christians who feel compelled to evangelize—as they are commanded to do in Matthew 28:10, to "make disciples of all the nations"—the best means of evangelizing is to act, rather than to preach or go door-to-door.[13]

Questions 3 and 4

If what I am proposing in terms of moving the Jewish-Christian dialogue forward has any merit whatsoever, and the template suggested does indeed place these conversations about this Christ into an environment where Jews and Christians can truly talk to each other openly and respectfully about the very central thing which will always divide us—both communities fully realizing and understanding that there can, ultimately, be no resolution whatsoever of the divide (i.e., Christians cannot surrender any aspects of Christ's divinity while emphasizing his humanity any more than Jews can acknowledge or accept his divinity while de-emphasizing his humanity[14]; mathematically, positive one plus negative one equals zero, thus creating the null arena)—then, indeed, conversation is possible.

And, thus, parallel speaking, the aforementioned door now opens via questions 3 and 4 both to those who have never known of this Christ nor read the New Testament texts as well as to those already set within their own communities of faith. Respectful conversations on the part of those who come with a message to those who are themselves open to hearing the message. Respectful, too, of those happily embedded within their own faith communities with no desire to chart a new direction for themselves. Better to thus demonstrate commitment to one's own faith perspective through selfless action rather than further demonstrating again a too-real past history of callous disregard for the humanity of others and their religio-cultural systems and values, coupled with colonialist political, military, and economic agendas that bring honor to none and dishonor to all.

Such work as I have outlined would, of necessity, require a revisiting of those New Testament texts associated with both the so-called Great Commission and the so-called lesser commission, namely, Matthew 28:16-20, Mark 16:14-18, Luke 24:44-49, Acts 1:4-8, John 20:19-23, and Matthew 10:5-42, this last text addressed specifically to Jesus' fellow Jews. Whether or not the scholarly community weighs in on the issue of whether such missionizing obligations were indeed the actual words of this Christ or reflect the various Christian communities wherein these texts were first written is of secondary import to life outside the academy. They have been understood by millions of adherents throughout the last two thousand years by all manner of Christian denominationalists as legitimating their efforts to bring others under the banner of Christianity as well as behave badly towards those unwilling to come inside.

Thus, I would now suggest that such renewed textual work be done in the presence of Jews (not without a certain degree of chutzpah!, and not solely with Judaic scholars familiar with and conversant with these texts but Judaic scholars themselves comfortable with their own positive Jewish religious affirmations), following the insights of both Catholic thinker Johannes Baptist Metz (b. 1928) of Germany and the late Emmanuel Levinas of France (1906-1995), both of whom have strongly articulated and argued that such work requires after Auschwitz such presence. Dialogical interactions at the highest levels of solid scholarship are themselves a modeling how such things may very well be accomplished.

Enter Irving Greenberg and Jesus as "Failed Messiah"

Of late, at least in dialogical circles, much has been made of Irving Greenberg's (b. 1933) concept of Jesus as "failed messiah" (in the subsequent tradition of other failed messiahs) and as more fully explicated in his welcome collection of revised essays, *For the Sake of Heaven and Earth: The New Encounter between Judaism and Christianity*.

In two essays, Greenberg spells out what he means by a "failed messiah." In the first, "Toward an Organic Model of the Relationship," he writes: "A failed messiah is one who has the right values and upholds the covenant, but does not attain the final goal . . . The concept of the Second Coming, in a way, is a tacit admission that if at first you don't succeed, try, try again.[15]

While I fully appreciate what Greenberg is attempting to do, not only in this essay but throughout this text, and not only with this idea but, perhaps even more importantly, with his concept of "covenantal pluralism" in moving the dialogical encounter forward, I stand with others who have chided him for his word choice, and, as the second sentence quoted above indicates, a bit of flippancy which is decidedly unhelpful. Returning to Gary Gilbert's initial caveat that we scholars must be aware of how our interpretations and our words might be "(mis)perceived," it seems that Greenberg himself has fallen into that very trap, not theologically, but linguistically. If our intended Christian conversation partner hears "failed" with reference to Jesus, again outside the academy, based on my own observations and experiences, I am firmly convinced that the dialogue cannot proceed, for the word itself carries with it, not necessarily Greenberg's contention (although certainly a possibility), the idea of critique of the Christ and, by extension, of the very God to whom both religious Jews and religious Christians pay obeisance.

Before offering an alternative, however, let us turn to the second essay, "The Respective Roles of the Two Faiths in the Strategy of Redemption," for a somewhat lengthier comment which draws the distinction between "false messiah" and "failed messiah," and is truly the essence of Greenberg's thinking:

> The general Jewish position has been that Jesus was a false messiah. Why? Would it not be more precise to say that a false messiah is one who teaches the wrong values and who turns sin into holiness? A more accurate description, from a Jewish perspective, would be that Jesus was not a "false" but a "failed" messiah. He has not finished the job but his work is not in vain.[16]

In his own note to this paragraph, he states:

> Since the religion in his name persecuted Jews, spread hatred, and degraded Judaism, then the term *false* messiah was well earned. The term *failed* messiah recognizes that for hundreds of millions, Christianity was, and is, a religion of love and consolation, i.e. the right values. Use of the term also presupposes that the religion in his name stops teaching hatred of the Jews, and becomes a source of healing support for the Jewish people and a purveyor of respect for Judaism. If it continues to nurture stereotypes and hatred of Jews—or if it misuses these more positive views of Christianity in order to missionize Jews—then it proves that Jesus was a false messiah after all.[17]

Returning to the body of the essay, he goes on:

> Of course, Christians will hesitate to accept this definition—as will Jews, perhaps more so. Christians will be deeply concerned: Is this a dismissal of Jesus? Does this term demean classic Christian affirmations of Jesus' messiahship and the Incarnation? Jews will be concerned: Is this a betrayal of the classic Jewish insistence that the Messiah has not yet come? Does this term breach Judaism's self-respecting boundary that excludes Christian claims?

I believe that none of these fears are warranted. The term "failed messiah" is an example of the kind of theological language we should be seeking to develop in the dialogue, for it allows for a variety of Christian and Jewish self-understandings.[18]

Let me suggest to you—and to Greenberg—that such fears are not so easily dismissed or unwarranted. As noted, our English-language use of the word "failed" carries within it a conclusive critique that whatever energies had been extended in the past to accomplish whatever actions were desired, the actor has not accomplished them due to internal flaws or personal failures or the result of others' efforts. Either way, the mission was not accomplished, and failure remains a viable option even when considering another go-round. Not the best use of words to move the dialogue forward.

Thus, I would suggest—and have suggested—a far richer understanding would be to consider this Christ as a "potentially redemptive messiah," still here, still there, waiting for those either to experience him (I leave that concept purposefully open-ended.) or to enter into relationship with him. To wit: Theologically, it is logical to say that the world was, indeed, "redeemed" by the death of the Christ, but that the world, humanity, continues to ignore its own redemption? Or, is it more logical to say that the world was potentially redeemed by the death of the Christ on the cross, a potential that continues to exist for the world which, up to now, has refused to welcome that potential into its midst? A corollary to this alternative is that Christ represents, for those who choose him, the paradigmatic model of the very best of which humanity is capable. To surrender one's life out of love for another is an act which is found also among "righteous Gentiles" and Jews of the Shoah. From my perspective, the actual death of the Christ has not, either at that moment, or up to this moment, redeemed our world, but only opened the door to that possibility. But it was not then, nor is it now, the only possibility.

This understanding between Jew and Christian avoids what, historically, have been three of the most tragically difficult obstacles to such dialogue: 1. A rank ordering of the death of the Christ as the supreme event in all human history, all other deaths being of far less significance; 2. a kind of arrogant triumphalism which gives credence to this death and this death alone; and 3. a Jewish difficulty, given Jewish history, equating this death with world redemption and the realities of the Jewish experience.

To maintain the potentially redemptive death of the Christ allows for two possibilities essential to any fruitful Jewish-Christian dialogue: 1. that those who wish to consider themselves Christians are now free to draw from this moment that which gives meaning to their own lives, and 2. that those who do not wish to draw from this moment, in particular the Jewish people, are equally free not to do so.

Again, the potentially redemptive possibilities of the "Christ event" would seem best to address these questions for both Jews and Christians, as well as others. For those who accept Jesus as the Christ, there is no problem; for those who choose not to accept him as such, there is, equally, no problem. For those whose experience does not include even the most limited of encounters with Christianity and Christians, there is no problem.

Morally and ethically, post-Shoah, it is one thing to accept the limited and limiting experience of the Christ, letting it serve as a bridge to dialogue. It is quite another to profess the universality of the Christ for all humanity and the "arrogant triumphalism" noted earlier which, all-too-readily, historically (and contemporarily) has accompanied it and act in accord with that understanding.[19]

And thus I would suggest that it is possible for Jews and Christians to talk within the context of both Judaism and dialogue fruitfully and positively about this Christ, the heart of that which divides us, and that the challenge to this Church is three-fold: 1. to listen to what we elder brothers and sisters are saying about this Christ, and 2. to shore up the very foundations of Christianity which, like Judaism, remain in need of repair, and 3. that this dialogue poses no threat whatsoever to the faith and practice of either religious tradition, but may very well serve as the new way by which we go forward together.

In Conclusion: A Final Quotation

I began this conversation with two quotations, that of my mentor Zev Garber, and that of Gary Gilbert of Claremont-McKenna College. I close with a third, that of Yossi Klein Halevei (b. 1953), American-born Israeli author and journalist and author of a recent essay entitled "The Cross and the Crescent: Divergent Responses to Antisemitism in Contemporary Islam." Halevi writes:

> A penitent Christianity enables Jews to stop blaming Jesus for the persecutions of the past and appreciate his role in transforming humanity. Obviously, those of us who embrace Jesus as a long-lost brother relate to him in a particular Jewish way. For Christians, Jesus is the sacrificial redeemer who took upon himself the sins of humanity; for Jews like me, Jesus is a prophetic figure through whom faith in the God of Israel was [and is—SLJ] spread among the nations.[20]

And for Jews like me, he is worth talking about with those Christians for whom I am their brother.[21]

Discussion Questions

1. What is your answer to the question, "Why don't you Jews believe in Jesus?" How would you frame your answer so that it opens, rather than closes, the door to further dialogue?
2. What do you regard as the essential elements for any successful Jewish-Christian dialogue (or Jewish-Christian-Muslim trialogue)? Are there any public parameters for such successful conversation?
3. What answers would you give to the four questions in the section entitled "Taking the Dialogue to the Next Level?"
4. Construct a "dialogical event" where Jews and Christians read selectively passages from both the Hebrew Bible and the New Testament. A good place to begin would be James F. Moore, *Post-Shoah Dialogues: Re-Thinking Our Texts Together*.

Notes

1. Steven Leonard Jacobs, "Jewish-Christian Relations after the Shoah," in *War or Words? Interreligious Dialogue as an Instrument of Peace*, ed. Donald W. Musser and Dixon D. Sutherland (Cleveland: The Pilgrim Press, 2005), 65.
2. For an interesting "conversation" on this very point, see Neusner, Jacob, *A Rabbi Talks with Jesus: An Intermillennial Interfaith Exchange* (New York: Doubleday, 1993), 18-36.

3. See "The Messiah," Jewish Virtual Library, http://www.jewishvirtuallibrary.org/jsource/Judaism/messiah.html. Accessed 5 May 2009.
4. Maimonides, *Mishneh Torah, Section Hilkhot Melakhim Umilchamoteichem*, chapters 11 and 12:

   And if a king shall arise from the House of David, studying Torah and indulging in commandments like his father David, according to the written and oral Torah, and he will impel all of Israel to follow it and to strengthen its breaches in its observances, and will fight the Lord's wars, this one is to be treated as if he were the anointed one. If he succeeded and built a Holy Temple in its proper place and gathered the dispersed ones of Israel together, this is indeed the anointed one for certain, and he will mend the entire world to worship the Lord together, as it is stated "For then I shall turn for the nations a clear tongue, to call all in the Name of the Lord and to worship Him with one shoulder." (Zephaniah 3:9)
5. Somewhat jocularly perhaps, but not wholly without merit, Eugene Fisher, retired Associated Director of the Secretariat for Ecumenical and Interreligious Affairs of the (United States) National Conference of Catholic Bishops, Washington, DC, in his own presentation at the conference from which the articles in this volume were collected ("Jesus in the Context of Judaism and the Challenge to the Church," at Samuel Rosenthal Center for Judaic Studies at Case Western Reserve University, 24-26 May 2009), suggested another Jewishly meaningful translation for *Nostre Aetate*, "It's About Time!"
6. "Declaration on the Relationship of the Church to Non-Christian Religions—'Nostre Aetate'—Proclaimed by His Holiness Pope Paul VI on October 28, 1965," www.vatican.va. Accessed 5 October 2009.
7. "Luther's Anti-Semitism," www.lcms.org. See also "LCMS: On Martin Luther's anti-Semitic statements," www.appleofhiseye.org for a similar reprinting of this same statement.
8. Steven Leonard Jacobs, "Remembering for the Future II" (paper presented at Second International Holocaust Conference, Berlin, Germany, March 1994).
9. Jacobs, "Jewish-Christian Relations after the Shoah," 67-68.
10. Further fruitful discussion might also possibly ensue regarding the different understandings Torahitically, but post-textually as well, of the Hebrew phrase "son of God" (Hebrew, *ben Elohim*) and its reading as "human being" by Jews and "more than human being" by Christians. The whole notion of variant readings, interpretations, and understandings of the same texts has a long and while, at times, less than noble history, is equally worth exploring in a dialogical context. See, for example, among many, Andrew M. Greeley and Jacob Neusner, *Common Ground: A Priest and a Rabbi Read Scripture Together* (Cleveland: Pilgrim Press, 1997); Fredrich C. Holmgren and Herman E. Schaalman, eds., *Preaching Biblical Texts:Expositions by Jewish and Christian Scholars* (Grand Rapids: Eerdmans, 1995); Melody D. Knowles, Esther Menn, John Pawlikowski, and Timothy J. Sandoval, eds., *Contesting Texts: Jews and Christians in Conversation about the Bible* (Minneapolis: Fortress Press, 2007); and James F. Moore, ed., *Post-Shoah Dialogues:Re-Thinking Our Texts Together* (Lanham: University Press of America, 2004).
11. Jacob Neusner, pre-eminent Judaic scholar, articulated this same point in his Jack Chester Memorial Lecture Celebrating the 10th Anniversary of the Sue and Leonard Miller Center for Contemporary Judaic Studies at the University of Miami, FL, delivered 5 March 2009, and entitled "Transcending 'The Jewish Roots of Jesus'—

From Dialogue to Trialogue in Interfaith Relations," when he said: "But because in the Hebrew Scriptures, Christianity reveres the same Scriptures as does Judaism, I can learn from Christianity other ways of reading Scripture. Christianity and Islam reveal choices available to Judaism—roads not taken but logically available for consideration." *The National Jewish Post & Opinion*, 29 April 2009, 9.

12. Steven Leonard Jacobs, "Jewish-Christian Relations after the Shoah," 69.
13. Levine, Amy-Jill, *The Misunderstood Jew: The Church and the Scandal of the Jewish Jesus* (San Franciso: HarperCollins, 2006), 224. Her entire chapter 7, "Quo Vadis?" contains a explication of twenty-six suggestions designed to enhance rather than retard Jewish-Christian dialogue.
14. Some scholars have suggested that, perhaps, there may very well be room within the world of Judaic thought to incorporate Jesus' teachings and messages as well as those of Paul himself. See, for example, Michael S. Kogan, *Opening the Covenant: A Jewish Theology of Christianity* (New York: Oxford University Press, 2008); Martin Buber, *Two Types of Faith* (Syracuse: Syracuse University Press, 2003); Samuel Sandmel, *We Jews and Jesus:Exploring Theological Differences for Mutual Understanding* (Woodstock: Skylights Publishing, 2006); Richard L. Rubenstein, *My Brother Paul* (New York: HarperCollins, 1975). Particularly interesting was Byron L. Sherwin's essay, "'Who Do You Say That I Am?' (Mark 8:29): A New Jewish View of Jesus," *Journal of Ecumenical Studies* 31, nos. 3-4 (1994): 255-67; and my own response, Steven Leonard Jacobs, "A Jewish Response to Byron L. Sherwin's 'A New Jewish View of Jesus," *Journal of Ecumenical Studies* 32, no. 2 (1995): 263-67. Such scholarly rethinking, hardly filtering down into the pew, seems to me to parallel the work now being down to "re-embrace" the excommunicated but nonetheless important philosopher Baruch Spinoza (1632-1677). See, for example, Rebecca Goldstein, *Betraying Spinoza: The Renegade Jew Who Saved Modernity,* Jewish Encounters Series (New York: Nextbook/Schocken, 2006); Margaret Gullan-Whur, *Within Reason: A Life of Spinoza* (New York: St. Martin's, 1998); Steven Nadler, *Spinoza: A Life* (Cambridge: Cambridge University Press, 1999); Matthew Stewart, *The Courtier and the Heretic: Leibnitz, Spinoza, and the Fate of God in the Modern World* (New York: Norton, 2006); Yirmiyahu Yovel, *Spinoza and Other Heretics,* vol. 1, *The Marrano of Reason*; vol. 2, *The Adventures of Immanence* (Princeton: Princeton University Press, 1989); Harry Austryn Wolfson, *The Philosophy of Spinoza* (Cleveland: Word Publishing, 1961). Interestingly enough, I studied Spinoza as part of the graduate program in Rabbinics at the Hebrew Union College-Jewish Institute of Religion, Cincinnati, OH (1969-1974), and today teach a course entitled Modern Jewish Thinkers and Thoughts, examining the works of both Moses Maimonides (1135-1204) and Spinoza as foundational to all understandings of present-day Jewish thought.
15. Irving Greenberg, "Toward an Organic Model of the Relationship," in *For the Sake of Heaven and Earth: The New Encounter between Judaism and Christianity* (Philadelphia: The Jewish Publication Society, 2004), 153.
16. Irving Greenberg, "The Respective Roles of the Two Faiths in the Strategy of Redemption," in *For the Sake of Heaven and Earth*, 177.
17. Ibid.
18. Ibid., 178.
19. Jacobs, "Jewish-Christian Relations after the Shoah," 66-68. See also Steven Leonard Jacobs, *Rethinking Jewish Faith: The Child of a Survivor Responds* (Albany: State University of New York Press, 1994), 92-93. The whole of chapter 8, "Rethinking

Christianity: An Outsider's Perspective," 89-97, address a number of issues pertinent to any fruitful Jewish-Christian dialogue

20. Yossi Klein Halevi, "The Cross and the Crescent: Divergent Response to Antisemitism in Contemporary Islam," in *Not Your Father's Antisemitism: Hatred of the Jews in the 21st Century*, ed. Berenbaum, Michael (St. Paul: Paragon House, 2008), 157.
21. In response to this presentation at the "Jesus in the Context of Judaism and the Challenge to the Church" conference (see note 5), Professor of Judaic Studies Steven B. Bowman, University of Cincinnati, made two significant points: 1. Christians understand the act of Christ's death as that of redemption and resurrection as an act of affirmation (concepts about which Judaism has much to say, to be sure); and 2. the conference papers themselves, as well as the sources cited, in the aggregate reflect a Western Christian approach, and, therefore, to more fully enter into a dialogical encounter, one needs the benefit of an Eastern and Orthodox perspective as well. Both points are well-taken and much appreciated.

The New Jewish Reclamation of Jesus in Late Twentieth-Century America: Realigning and Rethinking Jesus the Jew

Shaul Magid

Jewish writing about Jesus in America that began in the mid-nineteenth century, with a few exceptions, ended after the "Jesus Controversy" in 1925. This controversy erupted in light of a sermon delivered by Rabbi Stephen Wise at Carnegie Hall in Manhattan on the occasion of the 1925 English publication of Joseph Klausner's Hebrew volume, *Jesus of Nazareth: His Life, Times, and Teaching* (1922). Although the discovery of the Nag Hammadi texts and other Dead Sea scrolls in 1947-48 reinvigorated the historical Jesus among many Protestants, American Jews didn't begin writing about Jesus again until the 1960s around the same time post-Holocaust theology began to emerge. Samuel Sandmel's important work, *We Jews and Jesus: Exploring Theological Differences for Mutual Understanding,* was first published in 1965 and in many ways inaugurated a new era of the American Jewish Jesus.[1]

In this essay I explore the new engagement with Jesus in the last three decades of the twentieth century and the first decade of the twenty-first century in an American religious culture informed by pluralism and multiculturalism as fundamental American values coupled with an American Jewish community more confident about its place in society than ever before.[2] Moreover, America at this time was no longer dominated by progressive and liberal Protestantism (Unitarianism was no longer the force it once was, even among intellectuals) and therefore questions of Christology and other doctrinal matters could not be ignored. I focus on four contemporary American Jews who have written about Jesus who will represent the postwar Jewish Jesus in America: Irving (Yitz) Greenberg, Byron Sherwin, Zalman Schachter-Shalomi, and Daniel Matt.

As much as Americans may be becoming more religious as evangelicalism continues to rise, this is not a return to any unreconstructed traditionalism.[3] New Age religion is implicated in this religious revival even for those who have no allegiance to the New Age per se. By that I mean we should view the "Jesus freak" movement focused on Jesus as liberation and self-discovery in the 1960s and early 1970s, surely a product of the American counter-culture and the New Age, as different in degree but not in kind from the conservative rise of evangelicalism in the 1980s to the present whose focus is on Jesus as "personal savior." Moreover, Thomas Jefferson's moral Jesus and Ralph Waldo Emerson's subversive message of "spirit" *contra* "religion" retain at least some cache in both of these Jesus movements. Yet the religious individualism and moralism of the Jefferson-Emerson outlook shares company with the miraculous Christ figure of evangelicalism as well as what Stephen Prothero argues is a Jesus who is a secular cultural icon, that is, a post-Christian Jesus.[4] Jews have to grapple with all these new American Jesuses in order to come up with one of their own. As American Christianity simultaneously experiences a born-again renaissance coupled with becoming unchurched, post-Protestant, or post-Christian, American Jews must confront their new status in a complicated multicultural postreligious (and post-secular) society.[5] As has been the case throughout much of Jewish modernity, Jesus plays a crucial role in American Jewry's own self-fashioning, especially in a country that increasingly defines itself as "Judeo-Christian."[6]

Much of the work on the Jewish Jesus in this period appeared in books of constructive Jewish theology or in theological journals such as *The Journal of Ecumenical Studies* or ecumenical collections such as *Jesus through Jewish Eyes*.[7] The purpose of these essays appears to be an attempt to renew the place of Jesus for postwar American Jews who, in some sense, no longer need him. For American Jews at this time, Jesus is no longer needed as a tool of acculturation for a fully Americanized Jewish audience. But in the wake of the counter-culture, Vatican II, and New Age religion, Jesus returns, no longer the epitome of morality but in a new role as spiritual master, personal savior, or cultural icon. Hence, the late twentieth-century Jewish Jesus will reflect that sentiment and respond with its own reconstruction. The continuing project of Jewish Americanization (also called Jewish identity) requires a new Jewish Jesus that can address the changing nature of Jesus in American Christianities.

Suffice it to say that the various postwar Jewish Jesuses (and more pointedly the post-1960s Jewish Jesuses) are products of postassimilationist and multicultural Jewish America.[8] Jesus is no longer the vehicle for assimilation or the quest for religious normativity in American Judaism he once was. Judaism is no longer only an "acceptable" religion in American because it resembles liberal Protestantism.[9] I agree with Stephen Prothero that Jefferson's theological project severed Jesus from Christianity long ago in America, and I extend that to suggest that this, in part, enabled Jews in America in the latter part of the twentieth century to experiment more freely with an adaptation of Jesus that is more deeply informed by their own theological tradition.[10] Alternatively, Jews can, and do, ignore Jesus completely, without paying much of a price. Except, that is, if one believes that Jesus has something to offer American Judaism's self-fashioning. Perhaps this is what distinguishes the late twentieth-century Jewish Jesus from the past; in the past Jews needed Jesus to be American. In the present, Jews want Jesus (or want to understand him in less than a negative light) because he adds something to Judaism that is lacking, thereby strengthening Jews' distinctive place in the multicultural world in which they live. Jewish leaders no longer fear American Jews will convert to Christianity in any significant numbers. The danger, rather, is apathy toward the Jewish tradition, replacing it with no religion at all.[11] Thus the competitive spirit between Judaism and Christianity (as earlier Jews envisioned it) has largely disappeared in this later period.

Yitz Greenberg and Byron Sherwin base their writings on Jesus on a more nuanced view of "the messiah" in Judaism that distinguishes between a penultimate and ultimate messianic figure, each serving a crucial role in the messianic process. Instead of simply rejecting the claim of Jesus as the Jewish messiah, each offers a more nuanced view, not of Jesus, but of the nature of the Jewish messiah. The bifurcated messiah is a notion that was developed in early rabbinic culture. The reasons for this dual-messiah doctrine remain in the realm of conjecture.[12] The dual-messiah principle assumes that the messianic drama unfolds in two distinct stages: the first is the culmination of the necessary wars that create the conditions for messianic peace; the second is the inauguration of the messianic age through the reestablishment of the Temple in Jerusalem and the in-gathering of Jewish exiles. These periods correspond to the prophetic position that the messianic age is preceded by "birth pangs" (*hevlei mosiah*) or "footsteps" (*ikvei de'moshiah*), a period of turmoil that serves as the final stage of purification before the redemptive era.[13] While some prophets speak of this proto-redemptive period without a messianic figure at the helm, the rabbis add to this prophetic vision a penultimate messiah descended from the House of Joseph who will lead Israel through the final stage of exile.[14]

Rabbinic and postrabbinic culture is generally divided between two distinct messianic visions; the apocalyptic and the naturalistic (with various gradations).[15] In the first case, the messiah will institute a spiritual transformation of the world, including the transformation or even erasure of the law and, perhaps, mortality itself. This is based on various intertestamental books and the concluding chapters of the biblical book of Daniel. It became popular in various works of Kabbala from the anonymous *Sefer Temunah* and *Sefer Peliah* to the Zohar, Sabbateanism, and beyond.[16] In the second scenario, the messiah's entry into human history will not result in anything other than "the Jewish liberation from servitude to the nations,"[17] usually interpreted as political and religious autonomy in a sovereign polity.[18] In the rabbinic imagination, the first messiah comes from the lineage of the House of Joseph, the second from the House of David. Both exhibit values intrinsic to the Jewish vision of redemption and both are dependent upon one another. In many versions the Joseph messiah will die (in some cases in the final battle of the apocalyptic wars) to make way for the Davidic messiah to enter human history and bring it to its conclusion.

Both Yitz Greenberg and Byron Sherwin use this model of a bifurcated messiah in different ways to suggest that Jews could, perhaps, accept Jesus as *a* "messiah" without agreeing with the Christian demands that he is the ultimate messiah. I will suggest that such a move is indicative of an American Jewish trajectory that seeks reconciliation with Christianity through a shared Jesus, not solely for the social benefit of Jewish acceptance into American society (which had largely been achieved by the time Greenberg and Sherwin were writing) but in order to reorient American Judaism in an era where the assimilatory project had largely run its course. That is, each in different ways view their social context as an opportunity to revise Jewish attitudes toward Christianity that had been corrupted as a result of centuries of persecution and exclusion. The fear of persecution and the competitive nature of liberal Christianity no longer colored the ways contemporary American Jews understood the relationship between Judaism and Jesus.

The Holocaust, Religious Pluralism, and a (Jewish?) Jesus: Irving (Yitz) Greenberg

Greenberg's thoughts on Christianity have been recently collected in *For the Sake of Heaven and Earth*, published in 2004. This volume contains essays published over three decades on three interlocking themes: the Holocaust, Israel, and Jewish-Christian relations. Greenberg's basic thesis is that the Holocaust was an "orienting event" that should evoke in both Christians and Jews a new sense of urgency regarding their tortured relationship. The Holocaust serves both as an occasion and a rupture in Western civilization for both traditions to explore their own failures in coming to terms with one another. "After the Holocaust, a model of the relationship of Judaism and Christianity ideally should enable one to affirm the fullness of the faith-claims of the other, not just offer tolerance."[19] This is combined with a post-Holocaust resurgence of Jewish "power" in the form of a sovereign nation-state. "Both religions have a major task at hand in the generation after the Holocaust. Both religions need to take up the charge of correcting their own deviations from the covenantal way. They need to overcome the denials of the Image of God in the other, which erode the religious power of each faith tradition . . . Both communities need the humility of learning from secularism and from each other."[20]

The premise in Greenberg's project is founded on the irony that the Jews most extreme experience of powerlessness in the concentration camps produced a world where Jews have unprecedented power in a Jewish state. The danger, of course, is to use the Holocaust as a justification for power, thereby maintaining the rights of powerlessness and power, using the former to justify the latter. Greenberg would like to see the Jews' return to power as a call for religious pluralism whereby each tradition can confront its own demons. Along the lines of Emil Fackenheim's post-Holocaust theory of the "voice of Aushwitz and the voice of Sinai," but extending the argument beyond the Jews, Greenberg suggests the Holocaust "was a revelatory event in at least two religions (Judaism and Christianity)."[21] This revelatory moment requires a renewal of the Jewish covenant, part of which is a reassessment of its relationship to Christianity.[22] My interest in Greenberg is quite narrow in that I am only concerned with one part of this larger project: his assessment of Jesus as a "failed" as opposed to "false" messiah, the coherence of that claim, and whether it contributes anything to the trajectory of the Jewish Jesus in American Judaism.

Greenberg begins by echoing something written in a letter from Franz Rosenzweig to Hermann Cohen that messianism in general is a sign of health for Judaism. "If Judaism did not generate messianic expectations, and did not generate a messiah, it would be a sign that is was dead. As long as Judaism is generating messiahs, it is faithful to its own calling."[23] It is not clear what work this statement is doing. On the one hand, it sends a message to Jews that the original Jesus movement among Jews that subsequently morphed into Christianity was not only integrally Jewish but a sign of the health of the tradition, even if the messiah chosen was a mistake. Hence, the roots of Christianity are an expression of a robust and passionate belief in the messiah in concert with the principles of Judaism. To Christians, it could be saying that however Christianity moved away from Judaism in subsequent generations (like many others, Greenberg blames this on Paul—a notion that has recently received critical reevaluation), the disciples of Jesus were acting in accord with Jewish principles and ideals. In this light, it is not merely that Jesus was "Jewish" but that the Jesus movement was a healthy expression of Jewish yearning. More broadly, failed messiahs are good for Judaism as long as they are acknowledged as "failed" if they do not fulfill the requirements dictated by Jewish tradition.

Greenberg asks Christians to recognize that Jews simply cannot accept Jesus as a successful messiah on historical grounds. "Given the facts on the ground, this person was no messiah. As open and anxious as they were for a new age, they heard no new signal of revelation. They were not deaf, but they heard a different call—to a greater level of participation in a new covenant."[24] He then claims that both Jews and Christians undermined the possibility of some form of reconciliation between "belief" and "history" at the outset by mistakenly positing a zero-sum game. That is, that the irreconcilability of nascent Judaism and what would become Christianity that has caused so much anguish to Jews over the centuries was the fault of uncompromising positions on both sides.

Unfortunately, Christians failed to reconcile their soul-searching fervor in generating a new covenental movement with the dignity and continuing vitality of the traditional people of Israel. And Jews were so enthused by the rabbinic renewal of their covenant that they could not imagine that a spin-off vanguard could be a second channel of God's blessing for the world.[25]

Setting aside the fact that Jewish Christianity in the early period did, in fact, claim to hold both precepts together (the law and Jesus as messiah),[26] Greenberg implies that a post-Holocaust world contains the requisite conditions to correct the error of Jews and Christians in the first century without undermining either tradition's fundamental commitments and principles.

While I sympathize with Greenberg's attempt to create conditions for pluralism as a foundation for a new Jewish-Christian relationship and commend his willingness to use Jewry's newfound power in the nation-state as a tool to cede ground to Christianity, both theologically and historically, I think that the false or failed messiah theory fails on two interrelated counts. First, it presumes that the messianic claims about Jesus constitute the very epicenter of Christianity, one that Jews must respond to with something more than outright rejection. Second, he maintains that Jews cannot accept the premise of Jesus as messiah yet can posit 1. the Jesus movement that became Christianity was a healthy expression of Jewish messianic yearning; and 2. that Jesus was *a* messianic figure who preached "truth" according to Jewish principles yet ultimately was not *the* Messiah because he did not usher in a new era in accord with Jewish belief. Hence, those who believed in Jesus as messiah in his lifetime (and, perhaps, Jesus himself) acted in concert with core Jewish values and beliefs and were not deviant in any way. This moves beyond the nineteenth-century and prewar rabbis and theologians in America who largely ignored the messianic question and focused on Jesus' ethical teachings in line with the historical Jesus school among Protestants.

It is worth asking here if according to Greenberg, Jesus (the little we know of him historically) was truly preaching messianic Torah (that is, he could have been the messiah), how can he justify those Jews who rejected him in his lifetime? That is, if Greenberg's justification for rejecting Jesus as messiah is solely on the criteria of history (i.e., his death and the unchanged nature of the world) shouldn't those Jews who rejected him be held accountable? Shouldn't the proper stance have been to accept him as messiah until his death? In another context, David Berger's polemic against Lubavitch messianism is not that the community held Menahem Mendel Schneersohn to be messiah while he was alive—this has been done numerous times in Jewish history—but that they continued to hold him as messiah after he died. At that point, Berger argues, Lubavitch moved beyond the boundaries of any viable Judaism in his eyes.[27] If Jesus' "failure" was only when he died, then when he was alive he was a true messiah and should have been followed. Greenberg himself makes this point in a footnote, in essence comparing the late Lubavitcher to Jesus in this regard.[28] According to Greenberg's logic, both Jesus and the Lubavitcher were "true" messiahs in their lifetimes. What then is the justification for not having followed them?

Greenberg sets the stage for his failed messiah position by suggesting that Jesus' ministry and the crucifixion took place in times so tumultuous that sound judgment was almost impossible, making the rabbinic (and perhaps early Christian) error understandable, if not excusable. Ancient Israelite society was experiencing the dramatic collapse of its entire civilization. The prophetic promises of return after the first exile were proving to be false. Hellenism had infected the very core of Israelite society; culturally, socially, religiously. In short, history as the verification of the Israelite covenent was being undermined. The covenant was failing and in dire need of renewal or re-interpretation. This is the stage that Greenberg sets to posit the rabbinic historical error and the Christian hermeneutical error. Regarding the rabbinic accusation of Jesus as "false messiah" Greenberg writes,

> The Rabbis perhaps erred here. Understandably, they did not do greater justice to Jesus because they were surrounded by an enemy (i.e., Christians) one hundred times larger than Jewry, aggressively proselytizing and persecuting the Jews in the name of Jesus claims. Out of defensiveness, the rabbis confused a "failed" messiah (which is what Jesus was) and a false messiah. A false messiah is one who has wrong values . . . a failed messiah is one who has the right values and upholds the covenant, but does not attain the final goal.[29]

This tacitly acknowledges the rabbinic error and offers a historical justification.[30] This contextualization works to create space for the correction Greenberg offers given the changed American environment in which Jews now live. But there is something fundamentally troubling here. First of all, the sages (call them Pharisees) who rejected Jesus as messiah in his lifetime (and even afterward) were not threatened by Christianity, which did not yet exist. And even if Greenberg is referring to the rabbinic sages in Babylonia and Erez Israel in the third to fifth centuries, they were not living under Christendom either. Peter Schaefer's study, *Jesus in the Talmud,* argues that while there are no overt references to Jesus in the Talmud there are enough suggestive puns and word-plays in rabbinic literature about Jesus to argue that they were aware of New Testament material in some (written or oral) form and, not feeling threatened by Christians in Babylonia, covertly mocked its claims.[31] As interesting for our purposes, most rabbinic literature is not very focused on the claim of Jesus as Messiah, the area where Greenberg puts his primary intention, but as a blasphemer or magician. Greenberg's comment can only apply to medieval Jewry which certainly did not initiate this false messiah position in Judaism but inherited it from a segment of their ancestors. And if we use Moses Maimonides (who lived almost his entire life under Islam) as an example, Jews in Islamic lands supported the false messiah argument just as stridently as Jews living in Christendom. Hence if Greenberg wants to maintain the false messiah error, it is an error that is not justified by the means he suggests. The failed messiah "mistake" needs to be explored more deeply inside the rabbinic construction of its political theology.[32]

Greenberg suggests further that Jesus is better depicted as a "failed" messiah because he died before completing his messianic task. He qualifies this by suggesting that "failure" is an attribute that applies to many well-meaning Jewish heroes including Moses, Jeremiah, and Bar Kokhba (and R. Akiva who supported Bar Kokhba as messiah). He then deploys the notion of the Joseph messiah as another example of a "failed" messiah. It is significant that while Greenberg uses the Joseph messiah model, he never claims, as Sherwin does, that Jews can envision Jesus as the Joseph messiah. Not without its problems (as we will see below), this step would be more of a substantive gesture to Christianity than Greenberg wants to make for various reasons. First, it would place Jesus solidly inside Judaism to this day; and second, it would require contemporary Jews to consider Jesus as an authentic voice in determining its covenental future. Rather, Greenberg posits the notion of messianic failure as an acceptable, even normative, category in Judaism that could include Jesus among its ranks. Jesus is legitimate for Judaism only in *potencia* but never in *actu*.

There are three points regarding the other characters on Greenberg's list as sharing Jesus' failed vocation. First, while it may be true Moses did not succeed in his mission accompanying the children of Israel into Canaan, he did get them to the very border, and his failure (if we can call it that) was divinely decreed (surely according to rabbinic tradition) long before his demise. It may be that his personal aspirations were never achieved but his collective responsibilities surely were. Second, while Jeremiah may have failed to convince Israel to repent, he did not fail to fulfill his obligation as a prophet, which is to convey God's word, not necessary to convince his audience. Third, I am not convinced the Joseph messiah fails in his task because he is killed. In fact, his death may be the completion of his task, as it makes room for the Davidic kingdom. Greenberg writes, "In the Messiah ben Joseph idea, you have a messiah who comes and fails—indeed is put to death—but paves the way for the final redemption."[33] If Greenberg would claim, as Sherwin does, that Jesus can be seen as the Joseph messiah, I would feel less uncomfortable with his argument. But he does not do that, at least not explicitly. For Greenberg Jesus fails because he does not complete what the messiah is supposed to do. He is thus not the messiah and, as such, is written out of Judaism because others believed he was. I submit that this is quite different than Moses, Jeremiah, or even the Joseph messiah in the rabbinic imagination.

Given that my focus is limited to the Jewish Jesus and not the larger question of Jewish-Christian relations, I ask what Greenberg has provided for us in his failed messiah model. He does not focus on the superior moral nature of Jesus' teachings as do early American Jewish writers. He does acknowledge the shared or at least overlapping qualities of his teachings and Judaism. For Greenberg, Jesus is a Jew and even a heroic Jew. But in the end he is a "Christian" messiah, a Jew who failed, failure defined by him in honorary and not derogatory terms. Yet Greenberg's attempt to soften Jesus' failed status by comparing him to other failed Jewish heroes in my view comes up short. While Greenberg claims Jesus shares this fate with the likes of Moses, Jeremiah, Rabbi Akiva and Bar Kokhba, he does not, from my reading, follow through with that assertion. For example, according to Greenberg, should Jesus' teachings like the Sermon on the Mount be taught in American Jewish Hebrew schools, the way Harris Weinstock suggested a century ago?[34] Should he be part of the canon of Hebrew heroes like Yosef Hayyim Brenner wanted?[35] That is, should Greenberg's Jesus become a part of Judaism (like Moses, Jeremiah, and Akiva)? Many nineteenth-century American rabbis thought so, as their projects were, in part, a reclamation of Jesus, not only for Jews but also for Judaism. As I read him, Greenberg has something else in mind. He is seeking to open lines of communication between Jews and Christians as two sovereign and distinct religions by enabling each to reassess their attitudes toward the other in order to produce a less contentious and even pluralistic relationship. In that I believe he succeeds. But Greenberg's Jesus remains outside Judaism. The failed messiah is a tool to soften the edges of the more offensive false messiah, thus enabling Jews and Christians to talk to one another on less contentious soil. Fair enough. On the question of Jesus' Jewishness and contemporary American Judaism, however, I do not see how Greenberg's failed messiah, who is then excluded from Judaism due to his failure, does much theological or, as important, corrective work for twenty-first century America Judaism. However, what Greenberg represents, if we read him in the larger context of earlier American Jewish writings on Jesus, is a move inside the arena of Christian doctrine that his predecessors intentionally avoided. For Greenberg, Jesus is a tool of ecumenicism, a means to cultivate a new relationship between Judaism and Christianity in a post-Holocaust world. He is not trying to reclaim Jesus as much as complicate the very notion of the messiah in order to meet his Christian interlocutors half way.

Jesus as the Joseph Messiah, or Bringing Jesus to the Center of Judaism: Byron Sherwin

Byron Sherwin's essay, "*Who Do You Say That I Am* (Mark 8:29): A New Jewish View of Jesus," originally appeared in 1994 in the *Journal of Ecumenical Studies*. It was subsequently reprinted in an edited volume by Beatrice Bruteau *Jesus through Jewish Eyes* in 2001. In many ways Sherwin's essay traffics between Martin Buber's assessment of Jesus as "a great brother" in his *Two Types of Faith* and Greenberg's attempt to reenvision a messianic vocation for Jesus that does not subvert Jewish theological teaching.[36] Writing in a late twentieth-century American context as both a rabbi and a scholar, Sherwin digs deeper than Greenberg, I believe, in searching for a Jewish Jesus that can address the new American Judaism in the fin de siècle.

The venue of the original publication of his essay suggests it is written for a Christian audience even as Sherwin writes, "the recovery of the Jewishness of Jesus may offer more of an opportunity for Jewish theologians than for Christian theologians" (36). Unlike Greenberg, for whom Jesus is a small part of larger project, and for whom the "Jewishness" of Jesus seems to matter little, Sherwin is committed to offering a Jewish Jesus that not only smoothes the edges of the conventional Jewish "error" of positing Jesus as a "false messiah" but more forcefully advocates for a contemporary "reclamation" of Jesus that implies an invitation for Jews to reconsider Jesus as part of their Judaism. In some sense, this echoes back to Jewish adaptations of Jesus in the late nineteenth and early twentieth centuries. However, Sherwin does not rest on the historical assumption of Jesus' "Jewishness" and the universal depiction of him as a master of universal morality. Like Greenberg, he attempts to justify Christianity's messianic claim within the confines of Jewish theological teaching. In my view, the weakness of Sherwin's argument is that he leans too heavily on Greenberg's failed messiah model. Yet in his advocacy of the failed messiah he writes, "my radical suggestion is that he may be considered a Jewish messiah, a failed rather than false messiah, part of rather than apart from the life of his people and their messianic hope." This last clause may take him beyond Greenberg in that for Greenberg the failed status of Jesus combined with his disciple's belief in his success excludes Jesus from the theological Jewish narrative, and thus excludes him from Judaism. Sherwin suggests this need not be the case. For Sherwin, "failure" is better understood as incompleteness, that is, Jesus' messiahship was "true" but he did not live to see its completion. And, by extension such an incomplete messiah he could still remain a legitimate messiah inside Judaism.

This is argued in Sherwin's central thesis that Jesus was the Joseph messiah who begins the messianic process that will be fulfilled after his death. While Greenberg alluded to the Joseph messiah in his essay as an example of a "failed" messiah, he did not identify Jesus as the Joseph messiah. The difference here is crucial. While Sherwin claims his interests are purely theological and not historical, he justifies his suggestion by citing the opinions of some historians (he does identify them) that "the idea of a Messiah son of Joseph was developed as an attempt to give Jesus a place within Jewish messianic theology. In this view, the idea of a Messiah son of Joseph was developed in order to try to convince Jews in the first few centuries who believed in the messiahship of Jesus that he was indeed a Jewish messiah though not the final Jewish Messiah."[37] Without entering into a discussion about the accuracy of such a historical claim, Sherwin deploys it to suggest that the Joseph messiah was invented as a tool to attract Jewish Christians back into Judaism—just as Paul was pulling the other way—by acknowledging Jesus' unique role but arguing that it did not require breaking with the Mosaic Law. In this sense, the doctrine of the Joseph messiah could be viewed as a rabbinic gesture to Jewish Christians.

By claiming Jesus to be the Joseph messiah, Sherwin suggests that he has a positive role to play in the continuation of that messianic process in contemporary Judaism. Citing Buber, he writes, "The Jewish community will recognize Jesus . . . not merely as a great figure in Jewish history, but also in the organic context over a Messianic development extending over millennia, whose final goal in the Redemption of Israel and the world. But I believe equally firmly that we will never recognize Jesus as Messiah Come, for this would contradict the deepest meaning of our Messianic passion."[38]

Sherwin concretizes Buber's notion of an "organic context" or Jesus as a "great brother" to refer to Jesus as an embodiment of the Joseph messiah (an idea Buber does not invoke), a Jewish prerequisite for redemption. This places Jesus solidly inside Jewish theology, bringing Sherwin to suggest that his theory "is virtually unprecedented in Jewish theological discourse." He may be correct. Although American Jewish thinkers examined in a this study made similar gestures earlier on, they largely did so without invoking theological categories.

I want to examine Sherwin's theory and try to view it in its American context around three questions. First, if Jesus is the Joseph messiah, how should Jews today relate to him (separate from the circle of Jewish-Christian dialogue)? Can one argue for the revival of a neo-Jewish-Christian movement whereby Jews believe Jesus was the Joseph messiah who inaugurates the redemptive process yet also remains bound to the law because that process is not complete? That is, can normative Judaism today bear the weight of a neo-Jewish-Christianity that would 1. not advocate Jesus' divinity and 2. accept Jesus' messianic status as penultimate, that is, as a Joseph messiah? Second, can Christians accept this by positing the notion that the Joseph messiah and the Davidic messiah, the messiah of Jesus' second coming, are really the same person (the genealogical incongruities can be worked out through creative interpretation)? Third, can Jesus be used by Jews today as a model of spiritual critique and renewal for their own Judaism and use him, as some Reform rabbis did over a century ago, to subvert the legalism and parochialism of their more traditional brethren?

If we follow Sherwin's view of Jesus as the Joseph messiah (he claims, with some others, that the Davidic lineage in Matthew is a later interpolation) it essentially means that while the person may not have completed the mission, the mission is true and lives on, or should live on, among contemporary Jews (and Christians). In that case, one could ask two things. First, should contemporary Judaism consider Jesus' criticism of the nascent Judaism of his time as still relevant and efficacious today? That is, should contemporary Jews view Jesus and his message as a legitimate critique of their own incomplete Judaism (the assumption here is that Judaism in exile is still incomplete in some substantive way and that exile is not simply the product of deficient observance). This would in some way echo Kaufmann Kohler's Jesus as one of the early Hasidim who offered a critique of mainstream Pharisaism. Second, should contemporary Judaism view Christianity and the embodiment of Jesus' message as true on Jewish theological grounds and, if so, how should that alter or revise the trajectory of Jewish theology? While we can, and should, scrutinize both religions in terms of deviations from Jesus' central message, the radicalism of Sherwin's claim is that, as the Joseph messiah, Jesus and his message should become the central pillar of both religions? Sherwin acknowledges that his theory "offers Jesus and Christianity not only a place but a messianic role within Jewish theology."[39] Echoing Buber but going beyond Buber's more circumspect and romantic assertion, Sherwin is suggesting not only bringing Jesus back into the Jewish fold (as was done by American Jews earlier) but giving him a messianic—that is, a central—role in the construction of Judaism for the future. This is more than reclaiming Jesus as the carrier of a Hillelite message and surely far beyond Greenberg's use of Jesus as a tool of religious pluralism. It is also, in my view, beyond Franz Rosenzweig's view of Christianity as sharing a messianic vocation with Judaism. It is, rather, a call for the acceptance of Christianity's messianic role and the figure of Jesus as a messiah in contemporary Jewish theology. The consequences of this regarding the serious study of the Gospel's in Jewish educational institutions remains a desideratum.

The Doctrinal Jewish Jesus: Revelation, and the Hasidic *Zaddik*: Zalman Schachter-Shalomi and Daniel Matt

Below I argue that the radical nature of Byron Sherwin's thesis is matched, if not outdone, by Zalman Schachter-Shalomi's new doctrinal Jewish Jesus. Schachter-Shalomi and, to a lesser extent, Daniel Matt present us with a significant development in the Jewish Jesus that has not fully emerged in popular Jewish writing in America until the end of the twentieth century: the use and adaptation of the Jewish mystical tradition as a template for the Jewish Jesus. While scholars have offered detailed studies looking at the historical depiction of Jesus among Kabbalists and the nexus between Kabbala and Christian doctrine—including, of course, Christian Kabbala[40]—few have deployed kabbalistic categories to offer a popular, and positive, Jewish Jesus that can be appropriated by American Jews.[41] This indicates the way in which Kabbala and Jewish mysticism have become part of the American Jewish mainstream due to various internal and external factors: the aftermath of the American counter-culture, the Americanization of Buddhism,[42] the success of Habad to alter the ideational landscape of American Judaism, and the commodification of Kabbala through the Kabbala Center and all its affiliates.[43] The deployment of kabbalistic and Hasidic rubrics to the question of Jesus enables Schachter-Shalomi, and to a lesser degree Daniel Matt, to engage the doctrinal principles of Jesus' divinity through a Jewish mystico-theological lens. In some sense, Schachter-Shalomi is offering a neo-Philonic rendering of Jesus. Philo described the Logos as the immanent dimension of the transcendent God. Although he was a Hellenized Jew living in Alexandria immediately before the Common Era, his writings were thought to be Christian until they were revealed as Jewish by the Italian historian Assaria de-Rossi in the sixteenth century. One reason for this is that his Logos theology in many ways conforms to early Christologies, even as those Christologies may have misrepresented what Philo may have meant (Philo, of course, wrote before Jesus).[44]

In any event, I argue that what Schachter-Shalomi offers is a kind of Logos theology newly refracted through the lens of what he calls the new paradigm "hasidic-kabbalistic" perspective. New Age religion equips Schachter-Shalomi to construct a Jewish Jesus who can be supernatural without being unequivocally parochial. He begins by criticizing two existing tropes of the Jewish Jesus. First, Jesus as moral teacher or, in his words "a teacher of aggadic (homiletic non-legal) Pharisaism who differed from other teacher of halakhic Pharisaism" undercuts Jesus' greatness.[45] Second, he considers the focus on Jesus as Messiah as a category error in Christianity's own understanding of Jesus' great worth and value and, in addition, contemporary Judaism's focus on Jesus as messiah. What is distinctive here is that Schachter-Shalomi wants to erase the messianic component of Jesus while retaining, and emphasizing, the doctrinal dimension of Jesus as the embodiment of the divine. Reversing the centuries-old attempt to give us a human Jesus without miracles (beginning in American with Thomas Jefferson) Schachter-Shalomi offers us a supernatural Jesus in line with his "kabbalistic-hasidic" new-paradigm Judaism and very much in concert with the New Age religion of his day.[46]

His first point exhibits his fin de siècle context. Whereas earlier (prewar) Jewish Jesus' were formed largely in light of liberal Protestantism's disbelief in the divinity of Jesus as Christ, Schachter-Shalomi writes at a time when the liberalism of Christianity has to some extent been eclipsed by a turn toward more devotional, Christological, and pietistic approaches. Schachter-Shalomi himself was a very much influenced by the Carmelite monastic order in Winnipeg Canada in the early 1960s and was a colleague and friend of Thomas Merton, the Trappist monk whose monastic humanism spurned a whole new approach to Catholic spirituality and social activism and contributed in bringing Catholicism into New Age religion.[47] In this light, Schachter-Shalomi writes, "But if the believer cannot assign the special unique creedal significance to his or her Christ who pales into one of the many teachers in the *Sitz im Leben* that the historian gives, then why bother believing? I cannot believe that just another rabbi teaching *aggadah* to fisherfolk would excite the regular Christian to participate in a Mass done in Jesus' 'memory.' So who is Christ?"[48] This question, "who is the Christ" is markedly different than the Jews who ask "who is Jesus?" It seems Schachter-Shalomi is subverting the entire project of Jesus' humanity as the template of his Jewish reclamation. He cannot accept the humanization of Jesus as the exclusive avenue of his Judaization because he rejects the fully humanized Jesus as the primary focus of Christian worship embodying, I believe, a new Christian spiritualism that comes from figures such as Merton. Jews must come up with a Jewish "Christ" or they will be hopelessly bound to a particular liberal depiction of Jesus that will not constructively confront the Christian believer or the new Jewish pietist, both of whom have moved beyond the belief in folding religion into ethics.[49] This "paradigm shift" Jesus not only breaks with Schachter-Shalomi's Jewish predecessors but with the entire Jefferson-Emerson trajectory of American religiosity. He is not returning to any fundamentalist model. Far from it. He is, like many other serious New Agers, trying to recapture a pietistic, and even doctrinal, past and rewrite it to conform to his humanistic and universal sensibilities.

Regarding Jesus' messianism, Schachter-Shalomi gestures toward the Joseph messiah espoused by Greenberg and more forcefully by Sherwin but he ultimately rejects the entire trajectory as unproductive. He admits that if (Jewish) Christians had designated Jesus as the Joseph messiah, "Jews would have been able to join Christians in the Good Friday lament and Jesus would have been one of the ten martyrs of the State and included his death with that of Rabbi Aqiba in the dirges of the Yom Kippur martyrology."[50] That is, Jesus as Joseph messiah may have enabled Jewish Christians to more easily remain inside the fold of Judaism. While this may be an exaggeration that does not consider how utterly marginal Jesus was in his time outside his small circle of disciples, it rhetorically works to criticize the audacity of Jesus' followers in their unwillingness to be more judicious in their evaluation of their teacher. In making such an absolute claim, they presented an either/or scenario to the Jewish authorities, leaving them little choice other than to react the way they did (all based, of course, on historical conjecture). Schachter-Shalomi posits that Jesus' disciples were "prisoners of hope" and chose to push their savior up to heaven, likening him to a New Adam and then interpreting him through his ostensible apotheosis while reality did not conform to the Jewish vision of redemption. Salvation was personalized and internalized to justify its unhistoricity. The greatness of Jesus, and here he means Jesus as "Christ," was not his humanity (moralism) or messianic vocation (as savior) but, according to Schachter-Shalomi, his being an incarnate of Torah.

Loosely gesturing to Franz Rosenzweig's tripartite model of creation, revelation, and redemption as the paradigm of all Jewish (and Christian) theological reflection, Schachter-Shalomi suggests that Jesus is better understood (for Jews? for Christians?) as "revelation" as opposed to "redemption." History simply does not conform to Jesus as Messiah (redemption) and yet to reject Jesus by rejecting him as Messiah is to miss a crucial opportunity to understand the deep idea of divine embodiment in the Jewish kabbalistic tradition.[51] What Schachter-Shalomi offers is not simply an affirmation of Jewish incarnationalism but a particular notion of incarnation as the embodiment of Torah, a Jewish Logos theology, the fusion of person and book, that he holds stands at the very center of kabbalistic and Hasidic *zaddikism*. The *zaddik* as *axis mundi*, the exemplar of God's word in a human body, "the *zaddik* as the archetypal model for behavior and anyone who will follow the *zaddik*—in the older sense of imitation—can also become a *zaddik*."[52] Here he seems to gesture toward the Eastern Orthodox notion of *theosis*, a process of individual divination through the sacraments. Except for Schachter-Shalomi this divinization, this becoming the *zaddik*, is (also) an act of *imitatio dei* inhabited via *imitatio christi*. This notion of the *zaddik* as "God's possibility for humanity in a physical body" can make sense for "Jews of a mystical, aggadic, kabbalistic-hasidic persuasion," that is, for Jews whose Judaism is infused with the postcounter-cultural religiosity of the New Age or perhaps the (neo) Hasidic approach of Habad. "True," he writes, "this aspect is far from the ken of the exoteric Jew but close to the esoteric one who is a hasid or one who follows the Kabbala." For Schachter-Shalomi, the kabbalistic world view refracted through the universalist nature of New Age spirituality and in celebration of religious experimentation in ritual and thought suggests that the Jewish mystical tradition, arguably the most xenophobic, insular, and Judeo-centric dimension of Judaism, provides the tools to reclaim Jesus not as messiah but as an dimension of revelation. His ability to do this is rooted in his adaptation of a form of Jamesian pragmatism regarding matters of the spirit.[53] Schachter-Shalomi gives us perhaps the first New Age American Jewish Jesus. Knowledge, practice, doctrine, and religious "truth" are products of the human struggle to articulate the experience of the world. His pragmatism comes through in the following: "What this calls for is a willingness to admit that all our formulations about God are nothing but tentative stammerings of blind and exiled children of Eve responding to the light deeply hidden in the recesses of their nostalgic longing for the untainted origin in which one needed not to look through the glass darkly but could hardly see."[54]

The mistake of what he calls the religion of the old paradigm is that it took "the ecstatic exclamations of the overwhelmed souls and [made] them numbered articles of creeds instead of acts of faith made in fear and trembling."[55] For Schachter-Shalomi, this is as true for the early Christian impatience regarding salvation and the Jewish rejection of Jesus as an exemplar of a *zaddik* as the embodiment of Torah. Truth is created using the tools of traditions and, in this case, he attempts to create a nonmessianic Christology that enables Jesus to be at the apex while not being the end.

Daniel Matt's contribution here is more modest and to some extent an extension of Schachter-Shalomi's more audacious project.[56] He offers a Galilean portrait of Jesus (not unlike many Jews before him), the product of a syncretistic and rebellious society, one that had animus toward Rome and was not under the watchful eye of the Pharisaic or priestly authorities. He claims Jesus' relationship to the law, as depicted in the Gospels, reflects a spiritual critique waged from within the Pharisaic context. For Matt, Jesus was not a moralist but a pietist who shunned convention, one who sought to "correct" the general Pharisaic world he belonged to in the spirit of the prophets.

Matt's depiction of Jesus is largely drawn from the scholar of early Christianity E. P. Sanders, who makes two observations relevant to the issue at hand. First, Sander's writes, "we have previously observed that explicit anti-law statements are hard to accept in view of the conflicts over the law after Jesus' death.

But the same arguments apply to explicitly pro-law statements. If Jesus was really on record as saying that absolutely all the law must be kept, Paul could hardly have persuaded James and Peter to sanction his mission."[57] Second, "we have found one instance in which Jesus, in effect, demanded transgression of the law: the demand to the man whose father had died. Otherwise, the material in the Gospels reveals no transgression of Jesus. And, with the one exception, following him did not entail transgression on the part of his followers. On the other hand, there is clear evidence that he did not consider the Mosaic dispensation to be final or absolutely binding."[58]

Sanders' position is that Jesus was an internal critic of the law and, through his critique, injected a notion, not uncommon in some Pharisaic literature of the period, that redemption presented the possibility of the transformation, or even erasure, of certain elements of the law but not the law itself. Matt draws from Sanders's historical analysis, translating it into the idiom of the modern pietism of Hasidism. Hasidism, especially as depicted by Martin Buber (who also serves as the source of the Jewish Jesus as pietist and not moralist) personalized and internalized the notion of redemption such that redemption was an existential category rather than historical reality, what Rivka Shatz-Uffenheimer called "self-redemption."[59] Matt suggests that Jesus was not claiming historical redemption in his kingdom of heaven as much as an internalized state of salvation. He argues that for Jesus the kingdom was "an immediate reality that could not be denied or evaded." The "here and now" of Jesus' kingdom was an ancient form of self-redemption that emerged later in Hasidism as it redrew mystical sources (rightly or wrongly) in partial response to the rigid legalism of its spiritual antagonists, the *mithnagdim*. The historical accuracy of the portrait of Hasidism is not at issue here. We are concerned only with Matt's construction of a Jewish Jesus and not the true nature of the Hasidic critique of rabbanism.

Matt builds on Sanders second observation that the Mosaic dispensation (in modern parlance, *halakha*) was not "absolutely binding" in the following way: "Like later Hasidim, Jesus felt it was not enough to follow the Torah: One must become Torah, living so intensely that one's everyday actions convey an awareness of God and evoke this awareness in other." This, of course, conforms to Hasidic depictions of their leader the Baal Shem Tov in two regards: 1. Hasidism's polemic against the *mithnagdic* position (real or imagined) was that the law as an end and not a means; and 2. early Hasidism's doctrine of *zaddikism*, that a holy person can absorb the Torah such that his will and the divine will (though Torah) become fused.[60] Thus, one reading of Hasidism (in line with a Buberean trajectory) could, perhaps, accept the legitimacy of Sanders rendering of Jesus as "not consider[ing] the Mosaic dispensation to be final or absolutely binding." Given that Hasidism was living in a highly charged traditional environment suspicious of such claims, partly as a result of the Sabbatean heresy that still loomed quite large at the time, this would need to be articulated in a more nuanced way. But the core argument that the law can be altered temporarily through spiritual practice without undermining its centrality exists in both Jesus teaching and some renderings of modern Hasidism.[61] Jesus is presented here as a Hasid in the full sense of the word, articulating the ideational center of the early movement.

Matt also offers us a slightly different use of *zaddikism* than Schachter-Shalomi.[62] For Schachter-Shalomi the notion of divine embodiment in *zaddikism* exceeds what normative rabbinic Judaism could tolerate. It is one of the cornerstones of what he calls a "hasidic-kabbalistic" approach to Judaism that could bear Jesus as "revelation" but not "redemption." The embodiment of Torah in a human becomes, for him, a shared idea that can then be deployed to understand the central focus of the other's perspective. Schachter-Shalomi implies that if Christianity can accept the notion of Jesus as an illustration of revelation, a revelatory embodiment of Torah, Judaism can accept Jesus as one of the greatest exemplars in their tradition. For him Jesus as a *zaddik*—in the ideational and not (merely) corporal sense—fits into his "hasidic-kabbalistic" Jewish paradigm.

The embodiment of the Torah in the *zaddik* is an idea that extends at least back to the Zohar and Abraham Abulafia in the twelfth and thirteenth centuries.[63] But it congeals in Hasidism in a particular way. Consider the following from Abraham Joshua' Heschel's essay "Hasidism as New Approach to Torah."

> Many aspects of Jewish existence which seemed petrified he [The Besht] suddenly made almost ethereal, or at least liquid; he liquefied them. To many Jews the mere fulfillment of regulations was the essence of Jewish living. Along came the Besht and taught that Jewish life is an occasion for exultation. Observance of the Law is the basis, by exaltation through observance is the goal.
>
> In other words, the greatness of the Besht was that he was the beginning of a long series of events, a long series of moments of inspiration. And he holds us in his spell to this very day. He who really wants to be uplifted by communing with a great person whom he can love without reservation, who can enrich his thought and imagination without end, that person can meditate about the life and being of the Besht. There has been no one like him during the last thousand years.[64]

This seems to capture Matt's use of the term *zaddik* or *hasid* (which in Matt's essay amounts to the same thing). What Heschel writes above about the Besht could, for some, describe Jesus quite well. In both cases (Jesus and the Besht) an individual arises and in a very short time fundamentally alters everything. He embodies a spiritual "event" that changes the very nature of all that comes before.[65] And the "personhood" of both live on to this day—and this is what really matters—to be the object of desire, not only admiration but, as Heschel writes, "[one] whom he can love without reservation." This is not speaking about memory. This Hasid can "meditate about the life and being of the Besht." "Unintentionally," Matt writes, "Jesus the Jew founded a new religion." This is in opposition to the Besht who, for Heschel, founded "a new approach to Torah." In some fundamental way, the two are not categorically different even as they are historically distinct.

The attempts by Schachter-Shalomi and Matt to take on these areas of Christianity that few before them would grapple with expresses a kind of confidence about the stature of American Jewry as the century (and millennium) came to a close. Moreover, introducing the "hasidic-kabbalistic" lens into the Jewish Jesus project opens new avenues of inquiry that offers new interpretive possibilities. This also brings the Jewish Jesus into the New Age.The underlying assumption here is that the mystical tradition of Judaism often came, perhaps unwittingly, quite close to certain dimensions of Christian doctrine.[66] Its focus on divine embodiment, the centrality of the *Zaddik* as both a transcendent being and mediator between the disciple and God, and its depiction of ritual as a kind of sacrament, all present potential areas of commonality with Christianity. Some of these commonalities have already been fleshed out in recent scholarship on Kabbala and Hasidism.[67] What Schachter-Shalomi and Matt accomplish here is the creative adaptation of these ideas now ground into an interpretive lens through which we can reread, yet again, a Jewish Jesus who reflects the sensibilities of a religious America that is firmly planted in a new age.

Conclusion

The history of the American Jewish Jesus in contemporary America is a curious phenomenon in part because many Jews who write about him do not see themselves following any historical trajectory. The figures examined in this chapter; Yitz Greenberg, Byron Sherwin, Zalman Schachter-Shalomi, and Daniel Matt seem oblivious to the vigorous writing about Jesus and Judaism in America from the mid-nineteenth century to 1925. The figures in this chapter are living in a Christian world very different from their nineteenth-century predecessors. Liberal Protestantism is no longer dominant, Jewish success, and acceptance, in America is more well-founded, the Holocaust created a new paradigm for Jewish identity and existence (as well as sympathy for Jews and Judaism more generally), Jewish theology has extended beyond acculturation and into the more creative, and precarious, realm of adaptation and experimentation, and Jewish tradition is less unstable due in part to the rise of Orthodoxy and Hasidic spirituality, in part refracted through postmodern and New Age lenses.

While Yitz Greenberg's "failed messiah" doctrine is part of his larger post-Holocaust project of ecumenicism, it is quite different than attempts by rabbis Kaufmann Kohler or Emil Hirsch to offer a Jewish Jesus that can bring Jews and Christians closer together. Greenberg offers a Jesus that is purely Christian. The doctrine surrounding him, that is, his messianic vocation, is one that Jews must reject but can do so in a way that is not offensive to Christians (or so the argument goes). Jesus is decidedly not the messiah according to any Jewish criteria according to Greenberg even but this rejection is not a rejection of his importance but only a rejection of the claims made about him. Byron Sherwin goes one step further in trying to reabsorb Jesus into Jewish theological thinking through his "Joseph messiah" doctrine. More courageous than Greenberg, Sherwin tries to find a place for Jesus as the (penultimate) messiah inside Judaism. For Greenberg, Jesus' death takes him permanently outside Judaism. In both cases, however, Jesus as messiah is fashioned on Jewish terms. The concept of shared ethical values between Judaism and Christianity, through the figure of Jesus that dominated the nineteenth-century American Jewish Jesus, is no longer operative.

Schachter-Shalomi and Matt move in a different direction entirely leaving the ethical Jesus and messianic Jesus behind. What is more salient for them is the notion of divine embodiment that stands at the center of Christology that they maintain has precedent in the Jewish notion of revelation through a "kabbalistic-hasidic" lens. This is one example of the maturation of (neo-)kabbalism as a new theology of American Judaism that emerges through the wide influence of Jewish Renewal. Christology can serve to reintroduce Jews to this largely mystical or pietistic idea that has been lost in the rationalization of Judaism in America. Here New Age religion plays a role in the American Jewish Jesus for the first time. Incarnation, as a form divine embodiment, an very idea that was thought to be anathema to Judaism, is suddenly reframed to cohere with the Jewish theological notion of revelation.[68] This is not to say Schachter-Shalomi and Matt accept Christian claims of incarnation at face value. It means, rather, that these "constructed truths" of Christianity (for Schachter-Shalomi, all truths are constructed) can inform new ways of thinking about Judaism in what Schachter-Shalomi calls paradigm-shift Judaism. Matt adds to this a correlation between the Hasidic *zaddik* and Jesus, both of whom serve as a kind of *axis mundi* for their respective religious communities.

What emerges from all this is that postwar Jewish theological reflections on Jesus in America illustrates a significant step in the theological "Americanization" of American Judaism. By mid-century the cultural Americanization had largely run its course. By mid-century a sizeable majority of Jews living in American were born there. I suggest that the success of the cultural project has begun to morph into a theological one. With the security and freedom to experiment natural to a native population coupled with successful acculturation and the disappearance of anti-Semitism as a threatening cloud, Jews in postwar America have begun to explore new Judaisms in conversation with other religious traditions. Here I used the postwar American Jewish Jesus among theologians as one example of how this process has unfolded.

Discussion Questions

1. What are some of the reasons that Jewish theologians in America began writing about Jesus again in the 1960s?

2. What are the implications of viewing Jesus "inside" or "outside" Judaism?
3. How can the renewed attempt to integrate in Jesus into Judaism today teach us about Judaism's own complicated notion of divine embodiment? Is it time we began to rethink the conventional distinctions between Judaism and Christianity is a world where Jews and Judaism have become an integral part of the American host culture?

Notes

1. See, Samuel Sandmel's important work, *We Jews and Jesus: Exploring Theological Differences for Mutual Understanding*, intro. David Sandmel (repr., Woodstock, VT: SkyLight Paths and Jewish Lights, 2006). Richard Rubenstein's *After Auschwitz* second edition (Baltimore, MD; John Hopkins University Press, 1996) perhaps the first systematic statement of post-Holocaust theology, was published in 1966 and Emil Fackenheim's first extensive post-Holocaust publication *God's Presence in History* (New York: New York University Press, 1970) was published in 1970 but was taken from the Charles F. Deems lectures delivered at New York University in 1968. The proximity of the new American writing on Jesus and post-Holocaust theology is worth further examination.
2. In general, see Paul Harvey and Philip Goff, eds., *American Religion after 1945* (New York: Columbia University Press, 2005), 479-533.
3. See, for example, Richard Wightman Fox, *Jesus in America: Personal Savior, Cultural Hero, National Obsession* (New York: HarperSanFrancisco, 2004), 15-17. Fox cites a 2003 survey that claimed four in ten Americans consider themselves "born again" and seventy percent consider "Jesus son of God and not just a founder of a great religion like Muhammad or Buddha." "Over two-thirds of the adults in one of the most modernized and industrialized countries on the world believe that a first-century Palestinian Jewish teacher and healer is the incarnation of God." (17). See also James B. Twitchell, *Shopping for God: How Christianity Went From In Your Heart to In Your Face* (New York: Simon and Schuster, 2007), esp. 1-60.
4. See, for example, in Robert C. Fuller, *Spiritual but not Religious: Understanding Unchurched America* (New York: Oxford University Press, 2001), esp. 13-44, 123-54; Robert Wuthnow, *After Spirituality: Spirituality in America Since the 1960s* (Berkeley: University of California Press, 1998), 9-18, 142-98; Mark Oppenheimer, *Knocking on Heaven's Door: American Religion in the Age of Counter-Culture* (New Haven: Yale University Press, 2003), 95-129; and Steven. Sutcliffe and Marion. Bowman, eds., *Beyond New Age* (Edinburgh: Edinburgh University Press, 2000).
5. On post-Protestant America, see Amanda Porterfield, *The Transformation of American Religion: The Story of a Late Twentieth-Century Awakening* (New York: Oxford University Press, 2001), 1-22; and R. Lawrence Moore, *Touchdown Jesus: The Mixing of Sacred and Secular in American History* (Louisville, KY: Westminster Press, 2003), 31-48. For a post-Christian America see Harold Bloom, *The American Religion: The Emergence of the Post-Christian Nation* (New York: Simon and Schuster, 1992), 21-76.
6. On a critique of the Judeo-Christian construction see Mark Silk, "Notes on the Judeo-Christian Tradition in America," *American Quarterly* 36 (1984): 66-85. There has been much that has been written for and against this idea in post-war Jewish

circles. In favor see Robert Gordis, *Judaism for the Modern Age* (New York: F. S. G., 1955), 216ff and idem. "The Judeo-Christian Tradition – Illusion or Reality," in his *Judaism in a Christian World* (New York: Mc Graw Hill, 1966), 154ff; Will Herberg, *Judaism and Modern Man* (New York: Meridian Books, 1951), 47-129. In stark opposition, see Arthur Cohen, *The Myth of the Judeo-Christian Myth* (New York and Evanston, ILL: Harper and Row, 1957). See also my discussion "The American Holocaust and and the American Jewish Dilemma," *Zeek Magazine*, March 10, 2009.

7. Beatrice Bruteau ed., *Jewish Through Jewish Eyes*, (Maryknoll, NY: Orbis Books, 2001). Another notable example is Bryan LeBeau, Leonard Greenspoon, and Dennis Hamm eds., *The Historical Jesus Through Catholic and Jewish Eyes*, (Harrisburg, PA: Trinity Press, 2000). This excludes the fascinating work on the Jewish Jesus done in the American academy by Paula Fredriksen, Amy-Jill Levine, Susannah Heschel, Daniel Boyarin, and Adele Reinhartz, among others. For a discussion of this phenomenon see Shaul Magid, *Jews, Judaism, and Jewishness in Post-Ethnic America* (Bloomington, IN: Indiana University Press, forthcoming)
8. For example, see Nathan Glatzer and Daniel Moynihan, *Beyond the Melting Pot* (New York: M. L.T. Press, 1966) and the important sequel, Nathan Glatzer, *We are All Multiculturalists Now* (Cambridge, MA; Harvard University Press, 1998).
9. On this we can consider the origins and meaning of the mainstreaming of the term the "Judeo-Christian Tradition" in postwar America. The term has its origins in Europe and more decisively in early twentieth-century America but it becomes as more commonly used term in the postwar period. Many Jewish intellectuals were highly critical of the term. For example, see Arthur Cohen, *The Myth of the Judeo-Christian Tradition*, (Evanston, IL: Harper and Row,), ix-xxi, 85-94.
10. See Stephen Prothero, *The American Jesus* (New York: F. S. G, 2004), 13, 14 and 19-32. For another discussion of Jefferson's Jesus, see Richard Wightman Fox, *Jesus in America: Personal Savior, Cultural Hero, National Obsession* (New York: HarperSanFrancisco, 2004), 160-72
11. On apathy and no religion as the overarching challenge of contemporary Jewish theology, see Arthur Green, "New Directions in Jewish Theology in America," in *Contemporary Jewish Theology: A Reader*, ed. Elliot Dorff and Louis. E. Newman (New York: Oxford University Press, 1999), 486-93.
12. On the dual messiah in classical Jewish literature see Joseph Heinemann, "The Messiah of Ephraim and the Premature Exodus of the Tribe of Ephraim," *Harvard Theological Review* 68 (1975): 1-15.
13. For some examples, see b. Talmud Megillah 2a; Midrash Tanhuma 58:3; and Yalkut Shemoni to Jeremiah 3:310.
14. For an examination of sources on the Joseph messiah see Joseph Klausner, "The Jewish and the Christian Messiah," in *The Messianic Idea in Israel: From its Beginning to the Completion of the Mishna*, trans. W. F. Steinspring, 3rd Hebrew ed. (New York: MacMillan, 1955), 519-31.
15. See an overview in Gershom Scholem's, "Toward an Understanding of the Messianic Idea in Judaism," in *The Messianic Idea in Judaism* (New York: Schocken Books, 1971), 1-36; and an alternative view in Moshe Idel, *Messianic Mystics* (New Haven: Yale University Press, 1998), 1-37.
16. See Gershom Scholem, *On the Origins of the Kabbala* (Princeton: Princeton University Press, 1962), 460-75. See also Idel, *Messianic Mystics*, 101-25.
17. See b. T. Berakhot 34b, Shabbat 151b, and Sanhedrin 99a.

18. See for example in Maimonides, *Mishneh Torah* "Laws of Repentance" 9:2 and "Laws of Kings" 12:2.
19. Greenberg, *For the Sake of Heaven and Earth* (Philadelphia: Jewish Publication Society, 2004), 146.
20. Ibid., 183.
21. See Emil Fackenheim, *God's Presence in History* (New York: Harper TorchBooks, 1970), 67-104; and Greenberg, *For the Sake*, 15.
22. On this see Hayyim Yerushalmi cited in Greenberg, *For the Sake*, 7.
23. Greenberg, *For the Sake*, 149. On Rosenzweig's comments see Nahum Glatzer, ed., *Franz Rosenzweig: His Life and Thought* (New York: Schocken Books, 1961), 350-51.
24. Ibid., 65.
25. Ibid.
26. See, for example, Oskar Skarsaune, "Jewish Believers in Jesus in Antiquity—Problems of Definition, Method, and Sources," in *Jewish Believers in Jesus*, ed. O. Skarsaune and R. Hvalvik (Peabody, MA: Hendrikson Publishers, 2007), 3-21; and Matt Jackson-McCabe, "What's in a Name? The Problem of 'Jewish-Christianity'" in *Jewish Christianity Reconsidered*, ed. Matt Jackson-McCabe (Minneapolis: Fortress Press, 2007), 7-38.
27. See David Berger, *The Rebbe, Messiah, and the Scandal of Orthodox Indifference with a New Introduction* (Oxford: Littman Library of Jewish Civilization, 2008).
28. Greenberg, *For the Sake*, 48, note 4.
29. Ibid., 153.
30. Ibid., 44. See also the review of Greenberg's *For the Sake of Heaven and Earth* by Reuven Kimmleman in *Modern Judaism* 27.1 (2007): 107, esp. 109. Kimmleman notes in numerous places in his review that it is often unclear whether Greenberg is writing historically or theologically (Kimmleman prefers "rhetorically" to theologically).
31. See Peter Schaefer, *Jesus in the Talmud* (Princeton: Princeton University Press, 2008), esp. 95-129.
32. On Maimonides, see his *Mishneh Torah*, "Laws of Kings," 11:4. See also Naomi Goldfeld, "The Laws of Kings, Wars, and the King Messiah According to Maimonides *Mishneh Torah*," [Hebrew] *Sinai* 91 (1983): 67-79; and Joel Kraemer, *Maimonides* (New York: Doubleday, 2008), 252-56.
33. Greenberg, *For the Sake*, 153.
34. Harris Weinstock was a mercantilist in California who, in 1899, presented a petition to institute the study of the New Testament and Jesus in Jewish educational programs because he believed Jewish ignorance of Christianity prevented the flourishing of Judaism in America. Almost a century later Roxanne Schneider-Shapiro, a graduate student at Hebrew Union College in Cincinnati, developed a survey she distributed to Jewish schools in the US regarding the teaching of Jesus in Jewish schools. For a brief discussion of both Weinstock and Schneider-Shapiro, see Michael Cook, *Modern Jews Engage the New Testament* (Woodstock, VT: Jewish Lights, 2008), 7-11. See also Prothero, *American Jesus*, 244-47.
35. On the Brenner affair, see Nutit Govrin, *Meora Brenner: Ha-ma'avak al hofesh habiyui* (Jerusalem, 1985) (Hebrew). See also Hoffman, *From Rebel to Rabbi* (Stanford: Stanford University Press, 2007), 90-116.
36. Buber's idea to refer to Jesus as a "brother" is echoed in Shalom ben Horin, *Bruder Jesus: Die Nazarener in judischer Sicht* (Munich: Guetersloher Verlagshaus 2005). Ben-Horin was a student of Buber's and founded the first Reform congregation in Jerusalem.

37. Byron Sherwin, "*Who Do You Say That I Am* (Mark 8:29): A New Jewish View of Jesus" in Bruteau, *Jesus through Jewish Eyes*, 39.
38. Ibid., 43.
39. Ibid.
40. See, for example, Gershom Scholem, "The Beginning of Christian Kabbala," in *The Christian Kabbala*, ed. Joseph Dan (Cambridge, MA: Harvard College Library, 1997), 17-54.
41. For some relevant scholarly studies that relate to the question of Jesus, incarnation, and Judaism, see Jacob Neusner, *The Incarnation of God: The Character of Divinity in Formative Judaism* (Atlanta, GA: Scholars Press, 1992); Moshe Idel, "Abraham Abulafia on the Jewish Messiah and Jesus," in *Studies in Ecstatic Kabbalah* by Moshe Idel (Albany: SUNY Press, 1988), 45-62; Moshe Idel, *Ben: Sonship and Jewish Mysticism* (New York: Continuum, 2007); and Daniel Boyarin, *Border Lines: The Partition of Judeo-Christianity* (Philadelphia, PA: University of Pennsylvania Press, 2004), esp. 89-147. Elliot Wolfson has written numerous groundbreaking studies on this question. Most recently and perhaps most comprehensively, see his *Language, Eros, Being* (New York: Fordham University Press, 2005), 190-260. See also Shaul Magid, "Ethics Disentangled from the Law: Incarnation, the Universal and Hasidic Ethics," *Kabbalah: A Journal of Jewish Mysticism* (Fall 2006): 31-75.
42. See, for example, Rick Fields, *How the Swans Came to the Lake: A Narrative History of Buddhism in America*, 3d ed. (Boston: Shambhala, 1992), esp. 168-94.; Amanda Porterfield, *The Transformation of American Religion* (New York: Oxford, 2001), 125-62; and Diana Eck, *A New Religious America* (New York: HarperSanFrancisco, 2001), 142-221.
43. See Jody Meyers, *Kabbalah and the Spiritual Quest: The Kabbalah Center in America* (Westport, CT: Praeger, 2004), esp. 1-32; Boaz Huss, "All You Need is LAV: Madonna and Postmodern Kabbalah," *The Jewish Quarterly Review* 95 (Fall 2005): 611-24.
44. Boyarin argues that the Talmudic rabbis also adopted a kind of Logos theology, albeit one that is incompatible with any incarnationalism. See Boyarin, *Border Lines*, 128-47; and Neusner, *The Incarnation of God*, 11-21, 82-100, and 165-98.
45. Schachter-Shalomi, "Jesus in Jewish-Christian, Muslim Dialogue" in Zalman Schachter- Shalomi, *Paradigm Shift* (New Jersey: Aronson Books, 1990), 33.
46. Schachter-Shalomi is not without support for his position that the messiah dimension of Jesus is overplayed. The question of whether Jesus considered himself the Messiah is, of course, a huge issue in New Testament scholarship. In 1901 German scholar William Werde makes a case that Jesus never considered himself the Messiah in his *Das messiasgeheimnis*. See Schweitzer, *The Quest for the Historical Jesus* (repr., New York: BiblioLife, 2009), 330-48. Isaac Mayer Wise also skeptical as to whether Jesus ever considered himself the Messiah or simply went along with the idea posed by his disciples. See Wise, *The American Israelite*, August 13, 1869, cited in Samuel Sandmel, "Isaac Mayer Wise's 'Jesus Himself'" in *Essays in American Jewish History*, ed. Jacob Rader Marcus (New York; Ktav Books, 1975), 341.
47. See Lawrence S. Cunningham, *Thomas Merton and the Monastic Vision* (Grand Rapids, MI: Eerdmans, 1999); and Robert Inchausti, *Thomas Merton's' American Prophecy* (Albany, NY: SUNY Press, 1998), esp. 63-70, 101-14, 131-40. On Schachter-Shalomi and Merton, see the interview with Schachter-Shalomi in *Merton and Judaism: Holiness in Words*, ed. B. Bruteau (Louisville, KY: Fons Vitae, 2003), 301-24.
48. Schachter-Shalomi, "Jesus," 33.

49. In the nineteenth and early twentieth century most Jews who sermonized and wrote about Jesus focused almost exclusively on his ethics. See George Berlin, *Defending the Faith: Nineteenth-Century American Jewish Writings on Christianity and Jesus* (Albany, NY: SUNY Press, 1989), 54.
50. Berlin, *Defending the Faith,* 35.
51. On the question of divine embodiment in Jewish rabbinism and mysticism see Alon Goshen Gottstein, "Judaisms and Incarnational Theologies: Mapping out the Parameters of Dialogue," *Journal of Ecumenical Studies* 39:3-4 (2002): 219-47; Alon Goshen Gottstein, "The Body as Image in Rabbinic Literature," *Harvard Theological Review* 82 (1994): 171-95; Jacob Neusner, *The Incarnation of God: The Character of Divinity in Formative Judaism* (Tampa, FL: The University of South Florida, 1992); Boyarin, *Border Lines*, 112-50; Elliot Wolfson, "The Body in the Text: A Kabbalistic Theory of Embodiment," *Jewish Quarterly Review* 95, no. 3 (2005): 479-500; Elliot Wolfson, *Language, Eros, Being* (New York: Fordham University Press, 2005), 190-260; Wolfson "Inscribed in the Book of the Living: *Gospel of Truth* and Jewish Christology," *Journal of the Study of Judaism* 38 (2007): 234-71; and Shaul Magid, "Ethics Disentangled from the Law: Incarnation, The Universal, and Hasidic Ethics," *Kabbalah* 15 (2006): 31-75.
52. Berlin, *Defending the Faith*, 35.
53. On Schachter-Shalomi's adaptation of Jamesean pragmatism, see "Pragmatism and Piety: The American Spiritual and Philosophical Roots of Jewish Renewal," in *Kabbalah and Modernity* (Leiden: Brill, forthcoming).
54. Schachter-Shalomi, "Jesus," 37.
55. Ibid.
56. Daniel Matt, "Yeshua the Hasid," in Bruteau, *Jesus through Jewish Eyes*, 74-80.
57. E. P. Sanders, *Jesus and Judaism* (Philadelphia, PA: Fortress Press, 1985), 266.
58. Ibid., 267. A similar opinion is expressed by Henry Cadbury in his *The Peril of Modernizing Jesus* (London: SPCK, 1962), 168 when he writes, "Of Jesus' ultimate view of Jewish law, two things must be said in this connection. The first is that the problem did not present itself to him in the abstract but in the concrete. He did not work out from an independent principle to its practical application. He worked rather from individual cases which came to his attention; he formed a judgment on those alone."
59. Rivka Shatz-Uffenheimer, "Self Redemption in Hasidic Thought," in *Types of Redemption*, ed. R. J. Zwi Werblowsky and C. J. Bleeker (London, 1970), 207-12.
60. For some examples see Moshe Idel, *Hasidism: Between Ecstasy and Magic* (Albany, NY: SUNY Press, 1995), esp. 189-209.
61. See, for example, Joseph Weiss, *Studies in Eastern European Jewish Mysticism* (Oxford: The Littman Library of Jewish Civilization, 1985), 27-46, 142-54, 209-48; Arthur Green, *Devotion and Commandment: The Faith of Abraham in the Hasidic Imagination* (Cincinnati, OH: HUC Press, 1989), and Shaul Magid, *Hasidism on the Margin* (Madison, WI: University of Wisconsin Press, 2003), 200-48.
62. For a precedent to Matt's connecting Jesus and Hasidism, see S. A. Horodetzky, "Rabbi Yisrael Besht," *He-Atid* 1 (1908): 123-25 (Hebrew), cited in Stanly Nash, *In Search of Hasidism: Shai Hurvitz and his Polemic in the Hebrew Press* (Leiden: Brill, 1980), 298. See also Hoffman, *From Rebel to Rabbi*, 109.
63. See, for example, Wolfson, *Language, Eros, Being*, 190-260 and Yehuda Liebes, "R. Shimon bar Yohai—Messiah of the Zohar," in *Studies in the Zohar* (Albany, NY: SUNY Press, 1993), 1-84.

64. Susannah Heschel, "Hasidism as a New Approach to Torah," in *Spiritual Audacity*, ed. Susannah Heschel (New York: FSG, 1996), 34.
65. The notion of the "event" as a truth category that alters all previous understanding stands at the center of the work of the contemporary French philosopher Alain Badiou. Close to our interests, Badiou uses this category to describe the resurrected Jesus in Paul's vision. See Badiou, *Paul: The Foundation of Universalism*, trans. Ray Brassier (Stanford: Stanford University Press, 2003).
66. This is almost always denied by many who work on ecumenical matters. Most recently see Zev Garber, "Reflections on Jesus: Review Essay," *Shofar* 27, no. 2 (2008): 8. Reviewing Amy-Jill Levine's *Jesus: The Misunderstood Jew*, Garber claims that "Mainstream Jewish tradition claims that there is one indivisible God (Deut 6:4): *there is no God before Him* (Deut 32:12,39; Isa. 44:6-8); *no likeness of Him possible* (Ex. 20:4; Deut.. 5:8) . . . And *no man can see me and live* (Ex. 22:30)." All this sounds pretty familiar. However, if one reads how the kabbalistic tradition reads these verses, and others like them, one will see that they can hardly be deployed as claims that are absolutely irreconcilable with some Christian theological tenets. It is not for naught that Christian mystics (and certain Jewish polemicists against Kabbala) saw in Kabbala a certain affinity with Christianity.
67. In particular see Wolfson, *Language, Eros, Being*, 190-226; Yehuda Liebes, "Christian Influences on the Zohar," in his *Studies in the Zohar*, 139-62 and his other studies cited there and Shaul Magid, "Ethics Disentangled from the Law: Incarnations, The Universal, and Hasidic Ethics," *Kabbalah* 15 (2006): 31-75. A very different approach is taken by Moshe Idel in his *Ben: Sonship and Jewish Mysticism* (New York: Continuum, 2007).
68. Resistance to this idea in the traditional world is intense. For example, see David Berger's case against Habad in his *The Rebbe, The Messiah, and the Scandal of Orthodox Indifference*. In addition there is a large and ever growing body of antimissionary literature written by Jews claiming the utter incompatibility of Christian doctrine and Judaism. Most work that seeks to narrow this divide is being done in the academy through the works of Jacob Neusner, Daniel Boyarin, Alon Goshen-Gottstein, and Elliot Wolfson, among others. Schachter-Shalomi and Matt are two nonacademic examples of constructive theology's contribution to this rethinking of the divide between Christianity and Judaism.

Annotated Bibliography

Basser, Herbert W. *The Mind behind the Gospels: A Commentary to Matthew 1-14*. Reference Library of Jewish Intellectual History. Boston: Academic Studies Press, 2009.

Emphasizing the Jewish roots of the Gospel of Matthew and accentuating the flexibility of the Jewish tradition, Basser takes the reader beyond approximately contemporaneous Jewish sources, such as the Dead Sea Scrolls and Tannaitic literature, into much later Jewish texts. In a fascinating leap, but based upon sound literary criticism, the author analogizes the scattered hagiography of the eighteenth-century mystic and rabbi the Baal Shem Tov (the Besht), considered by many to be the founder of early modern Hasidism, to the hagiography of Jesus. The author finds a rationale for extracting historical information embedded in Hasidic stories about the Besht and suggests that this process may be applicable to Matthew. This lucid commentary belongs on the shelf of anybody studying the Jewish context of the New Testament.

Batzdorff, Susanne M. *Aunt Edith: The Jewish Heritage of a Catholic Saint*. 2nd ed. Springfield, IL: Templegate, 2003.

Stein's niece Susanne Batzdorff describes what Jewish life was like in the Stein family. Batzdorff clarifies misperceptions by Carmelite biographers and responds to Stein's own autobiography *Life in a Jewish Family*, which had hurt the Stein family when it was published after the War. It provides a more balanced understanding of Stein's biography.

Berlin, Andrea M. *Gamla I: The Pottery of the Second Temple Period, The Shmarya Gutmann Excavations, 1976-1989*. IAA Reports 29. Jerusalem: Israel Antiquities Authority, 2006.

While this is a technical archaeological report, it contains a fascinating attempt to connect transformations and developments in pottery to changes in social, ethnic, and religious history.

Boyarin, Daniel. *Border Lines, The Partition of Judaeo-Christianity*. Philadelphia: University of Philadelphia Press, 2004.

Boyardin's book is a major intellectual history illustrating the influences of Jewish on Christian thought and vice versa within the religious and philosophical contexts of Late Antiquity and the Early Byzantine period.

Brandon, S. G. F. *Jesus and the Zealots*. New York: Charles Scribner's Sons, 1967.

The author explores the relationship between Jesus and the Jewish case against Roman occupation in Judea in the first century, including the Zealot movement. He provides a fundamental reinterpretation of a great part of the narratives of the Gospels as they were shaped by political and social forces two generations after the crucifixion of Jesus.

Bruteau, B., ed. *Jewish Through Jewish Eyes*. Maryknoll, NY: Orbis Books, 2001.

This is a collection of essays by contemporary rabbis and Jewish theologians about different aspects of Jesus, his relationship to Judaism, and ways Jews can engage Jesus as a figure relevant to cotemporary Jewish existence.

Chapman, David. *Ancient Jewish and Christian Perceptions of Crucifixion*. Wissenschaftliche Untersuchungen zum Neuen Testament 244. Tübingen: Mohr/Siebeck, 2008.

This book provides an excellent collection of ancient and late antique Jewish texts concerning crucifixion, including the Dead Sea Scrolls, works by the historian Josephus, and rabbinic literature. The author explores how perceptions of crucifixion affected Christian and Jewish views of the crucifixion of Jesus, in particular suggesting a trajectory indicating that early Christianity was influenced by Judaism.

Charlesworth, James H., ed. *Jesus and Archaeology*. Grand Rapids: Eerdmans, 2006.

This collection offers studies on various aspects of Christian archaeology of the land of Israel. While not systematic in presentation, it contains important studies on major sites associated with Jesus and includes discussions of archaeology and theology.

Chilton, Bruce. "The Transfiguration: Dominical Assurance and Apostolic Vision." *New Testament Studies* 27 (1980): 115-24.

Chilton provides an exegetical treatment of the transfiguration in Mark, the earliest written version of the story, on the basis of its connections to the mystical traditions of Moses and Elijah.

Collins, Adela Yarbr and John J. Collins. *King and Messiah as Son of God: Divine, Human, and Angelic Messianic Figures in Biblical and Related Literature.* Grand Rapids: Eerdmans, 2008.

This very important book is the most comprehensive modern text treating the New Testament usage of the terms "Son of Man" and "Son of God." As its title suggests, it draws conclusions regarding the relationship between Jesus' titles and his status as King and Messiah. Although it is a coauthored work, each author is responsible for specific chapters, thereby bringing his or her expertise to bear on the topic at hand. The book is suitable as a text for an upper level undergraduate course.

Eckardt, A. Roy. *Reclaiming the Jesus of History.* Minneapolis: Fortress Press, 1992.

This effort by one of the most important of the Christian post-Shoah thinkers reexamines critical questions for any Christian theology in a post-Shoah world. Eckardt's thinking about Jesus best exemplifies the effort in this context to reclaim the Jewish roots of Jesus as necessary for any authentic Christian theology.

Edelheit, Joseph. "The Messy Realities of Life: A Rereading of Numbers 19 and 20"; and James F. Moore. "Dialogue as Praxis: A Midrashic Reading of Numbers 19-20 and Hebrews 9." In Jacobs, Steven, ed. *Maven in Blue Jeans: Festschrift in Honor of Zev Garber.* West Lafayette, IN: Purdue University Press, 2009.

The first essay is Edelheit's contribution to the important volume, *Maven in Blue Jeans*, the festschrift for Zev Garber edited by Steven Jacobs. Edelheit's reading of the text of the Red Heifer is his challenge for any shaping of a Jewish post-Shoah theology which falls back into a model of victimhood, a model he is prepared to challenge. Moore engages Edelheit and extends their post-Shoah midrashic dialogue by discussing Hebrews 9 and Numbers 19

Ehrman, Bart D. "Christianity Turned on its Head: The Alternative Vision of the Gospel of Jidas." In *The Gospel of Judas from Codex Tchacos.* Ed. Rudolph Kasser, Marvin Meyer, and Gregory Wurst. Washington, D.C.: National Geographic, 2006. 77-120.

Ehrman provides a critical view of the Gospels and a highly revealing analysis of how Gnosticism contributed to the idea of the transcendence of Jesus the man to a higher deity. He sheds light on the role of Judas in theology in complementing Jesus in bringing about salvation.

Einbinder, Susan L. *No Place of Rest: Jewish Literature, Expulsion, and the Memory of France*. Philadelphia: University of Pennsylvania Press, 2009.

Einbinder's recent survey examines interesting medieval Jewish texts, revealing ways in which authors drew in from Christian and Islamic exemplars and recreated Jewish literature. It is mostly concerned with French and Italian sources.

Elukin, Jonathan. *Living Together, Living Apart: Rethinking Jewish-Christian Relations in the Middle Ages*. Princeton: Princeton University Press, 2007.

This work presents new insights on the history of Jewish-Christian relations, showing that in many places and during many times the treatment of Jews in Christian-dominated societies tended to be relatively decent, allowing for productive relations on all levels between the two groups. The significance of this is that most Jews today tend to the belief that relations were everywhere as bad as they were at their worst.

Enelow, Hyman G. *A Jewish View of Jesus*. New York: New Bloch Publishing, 1931.

Enelow offers a conventional but succinct Jewish view of the Jewish Galilean Jesus who opposed Roman rule and criticized Sadducee priestly decay. Unfortunately, few since Enelow have been able to fill in details of the Jewish life of Jesus and historical sources on the new movement he started and led during his lifetime.

Etkes, I. *The Besht: Magician, Mystic, and Leader*. Waltham, MA: Brandeis University Press, 2005.

The Besht is an introduction to the life and miraculous healings told about Israel Baal Shem Tov by his disciples and recorded 55 years after his death. In many ways his personality and teachings parallel those of Jesus.

Feldman, Louis and Gohei Gohei Hata, eds. *Josephus, Judaism and Christianity*. Detroit: Wayne State University Press, 1987.

Josephus, Judaism and Christianity is one of a multivolume set of excellent scholarly papers on Josephus through to modern times.

Fisher, Eugene J., ed. *Interwoven Destinies: Jews and Christians through the Ages*. New York: Paulist Press, 1993.

This collection includes essays by Daniel Harrington and Michael Cook on the Jewish context of the New Testament, Martha Himmelfarb and John Gager on the parting of the ways, Jeremy Cohen and Edward Synan on the medieval period, and Alice Eckardt and Arthur Hertzberg on the Reformation and the Enlightenment. The epilogue by the editor summarizes the six stages of Jewish-Christian history.

Flusser, David. *Jewish Sources in Early Christianity.* Tel Aviv: Mod Books, 1989.

Flusser offers an examination of parallels between the New Testament and rabbinic literature, which shows how Christian teachings had developed out of a Jewish background.

Flusser, David. *Jesus.* Jerusalem: Magnes Press, 1998.

Using biblical and rabbinic sources, this book by a traditional Jew and enthusiastic supporter of Jesus' wisdom illustrates that though Jesus was deeply involved in the first century BCE world of prerabbinic, Jewish thought, he was an independent, innovative teacher.

Ford, David F. *Christian Wisdom: Desiring God and Learning in Love.* Cambridge: Cambridge University Press, 2007.

This collection of insightful and probing essays explores an alternative, wisdom logic, rooted in traditions that have wrestled with significant forms of human suffering and trauma. Though he does not use Christian categories, Ford explores the potential of doing Christian theology utilizing a grounding hermeneutic that develops what Schwartz calls a logic of plenitude.

Frederiksen, Paula. *Augustine and the Jews: A Christian Defense of Jews and Judaism.* New York: Doubleday, 2008.

Frederiksen places Augustine within the context of the history and intellectual development of the Greco-Roman world from the time of Alexander to Augustine's own time. By showing what and who Augustine was arguing against and by carefully analyzing his key writings, she is able to explain to her readers why Augustine, against most of the Christian thinkers of his time, wrote not only in defense of the Jews but in such a way as to make it a part of canon law and papal policy to protect the right of Jews "to worship as their ancestors did," thus making the continued existence of Judaism, alone among all the non-Christian religions of his time, the only religion to survive Christian dominance.

Fredriksen, Paula. *From Jesus to Christ: The Origins of the New Testament Images of Jesus.* New Haven: Yale University Press, 2000.

Fredriksen conceptualizes the social and religious motivations operative in various early Christian communities. She then correlates canonical depictions of Jesus with these first-century dynamics.

Garber, Zev, ed. *Mel Gibson's* Passion, *The Film, the Controversy, and Its Implications.* West Lafayette, IN: Purdue University Press, 2006 .

This collection is an important text by seasoned Jewish and Christians scholars who expose the flaws of Gibson's cinematic Christ and suggest guidelines in understanding properly the scriptural Jesus in the Passion narrative.

Goldin, Simha. *The Ways of Jewish Martyrdom*. Trans. from Hebrew by Yigal Levin and ed. C. Michael Copeland. Turnhout: Berpols, 2008.

This is an excellent compendium of rabbinical thought concerning kiddush ha-shem, which compares it to Christian attitudes towards martyrdom. Though occasionally clumsy, the analyses are rich in contextual knowledge.

Goodman, Martin. *Rome and Jerusalem: The Clash of Ancient Civilizations*. London: Allen Lane, 2007.

Goodman's is a fine analysis of Roman and Jewish civilizations with a special section on the continuity of hostility into the Christian Roman Empire.

Hagner, Donald A. *The Jewish Reclamation of Jesus*. Grand Rapids: Zondervan, 1984.

Hagner offers a well-organized and amply documented analysis of twentieth-century Jewish studies of Jesus. While partisan (Evangelical), it spotlights areas of Jewish scholarship where Jews need to shore up their methodological credibility.

de Jonge, Marinus. *God's Final Envoy. Early Christology and Jesus' Own View of His Mission: Studying the Historical Jesus*. Grand Rapids: Eerdmans, 1998.

This is a major work by a leading European scholar that investigates the relationship between early Jewish and Christian teaching concerning the Messiah and Jesus' conception of his purpose.

Klausner, Joseph. *Jesus of Nazareth: His Life, Times and Teaching*. 1925. 2nd. ed. Foreword by Sidney B. Hoenig. New York: Menorah Publishing, 1979.

Jesus of Nazareth is a determined pioneering effort by a Jewish scholar, who taught modern Hebrew language and literature at the Hebrew University in Jerusalem, to reclaim Jesus as a Jew in the vital period of the "Parting of the Ways." The author portrays first-century Judaism as "a national world outlook with an ethico-religious basis."

Knibb, Michael A. *The Qumran Community*. Cambridge: Cambridge University 1988.

This is an outstanding resource for those who do read the original languages as well as those who do not. The translations are clear and precise to the extent that the material permits. The particular importance of this book is its commentary, which, on the one hand, is basic and therefore valuable to all who do research in the field, and on the other hand, is readily approachable so that it can.

Kogan, Michael S. *Opening the Covenant: A Jewish Theology of Christianity*. New York: Oxford University Press, 2008.

Opening the Covenant is a serious and well-written attempt by an academic philosopher to discuss both historically and contemporarily the ongoing question of whether it is indeed possible to construct a "Jewish theology of Christianity." Especially noteworthy is his second chapter on "The Question of the Messiah."

Krauss, Samuel. *The Jewish-Christian Controversy from the Earliest Times to 1789*. Ed. and rev. William Horbury. Tübingen: Mohr/Siebeck, 1996.

This book provides an excellent bio-bibliographical survey of the subject.

Lachs, S. T. *A Rabbinic Commentary on the New Testament: The Gospels of Matthew, Mark, and Luke*. Hoboken, N.J.: Ktav, 1987.

This verse-by-verse commentary to the Synoptic Gospels succinctly shows Jewish sources that are echoed in these Gospels. Lachs has many fine insights and his work is best used by those acquainted with the Talmuds and midrashim.

Levenson, Jon D. *The Death and Resurrection of the Beloved Son*. New Haven: Yale University Press, 1993.

Levenson's book is a brilliant analysis of child sacrifice in the ancient Semitic world, how it was transformed in Judaism and Christianity, and how the divergent transformations live on in contemporary religious life.

Lindner, Amnon, ed. *The Jews in Roman Imperial Legislation*. Detroit: Wayne State University Press and Israel Academy of Sciences, Jerusalem, 1987.

This book provides a useful assembly of Christian Roman legislation against Jews and Judaism, with extensive commentary. This legislation sets the path of legal rights and restrictions towards Jews in western and eastern Europe to the modern period.

Maccoby, Hyam. *Judas Iscariot and the Myth of Jewish Evil*. New York: The Free Press, 1992.

Maccoby presents the dynamics of the Christian use of Judas, symbolizing the Jewish betrayal of Jesus, the Jewish disbelief in his messianism, and the ensuing Christian retaliation. He also shows Hellenistic precedents in portraying the Jews as the source for all evil.

Meier, John. *A Marginal Jew: Rethinking the Historical Jesus.* Vol. 4. The Anchor Yale Bible Reference Library. New Haven: Yale University Press, 2009.

This volume is part of a series that investigates in a superb scholarly fashion details concerning the life of Jesus, in particular halakhic ("legal") questions. There are very few reliable sources attesting to Jewish law at the time of Jesus, but Maier combines statements and practices found in the Dead Sea Scrolls and other literature from the Second Temple period to provide the reader of the New Testament with highly credible insights. For example, the author demystifies some of the Sabbath observances recorded in the Gospels.

Meyers, Eric and J. Strange. *Archaeology, the Rabbis and Early Christianity.* Nashville: Abingdom, 1981.

Written by well-known senior archaeologists who also trained in biblical studies, this book explores how similar cultural stimuli affected two different faith communities in the early centuries of the common era and how each reacted differently to its cultural environment.

Moore, James, Zev Garber, Steven Jacobs, and Henry Knight. *Post-Shoah Dialogues.* Lanham, MD: University Press of America, 2004.

This text is a compilation of essays written over several years by the four authors. Each set of essays is an example of a dialogue built on basic principles, most especially the challenge to read texts together in a post-Shoah framework. The text also shows most clearly what is meant by a post-Shoah midrashic reading of texts.

Neusner, Jacob. *A Rabbi Talks with Jesus: An Intermillenial, Interfaith Exchange.* New York: Doubleday, 1993.

____. *Children of the Flesh, Children of the Promise: A Rabbi Talks with Paul.* London: Wipf and Stock, 2005.

Taken together, these two volumes provide a possible modeling for a "dialogical event" by helping the readers to imagine themselves actually in conversation with these two central persons of Christianity. Others with whom to engage in conversation by a close reading of their texts might be the (unknown) authors of Matthew, Mark, Luke, and John, and on the Jewish side, the (unknown) authors of the Five Books of Moses, the Prophets, especially Isaiah ("the messianic prophet"), and so on.

Pelikan, Jaroslav. *Whose Bible Is It? A History of the Scriptures Through the Ages.* New York: Penguin, 2005.

Pelikan undertakes to provide a readable history of Scripture from its existence as oral tradition to its current status as a book translated into many languages and found in many configurations. He examines the history of the canonization process for both the Hebrew and Christian Bibles and provides a compelling account of the effects of technology—the printing press, for example—upon Biblical study and academics.

Prothero, Steven. *American Jesus: How the Son of God Became a National Icon.* New York: F.S.G., 2003.

This book explores the phenomenon of Jesus as a figure who transcends Christianity and becomes a cultural icon in contemporary America. Chapters include "Black Moses," "Oriental Christ," and "Jesus Christ Superstar."

Reed, Jonathan L. .*Archaeology and the Galilean Jesus: A Re-examination of the Evidence.* Harrisburg, PA: Trinity Press International, 2000.

Reeds work is a standard presentation of Galilean archaeology, with very little in terms of material culture. He provides various attempts to understand the New Testament (and Q) in terms of archaeology.

Roth, Cecil, ed. *The World History of the Jewish People.* Vol. 9. *The Dark Ages.* New Brunswick: Rutgers University Press, 1966.

This volume of the *World History* series provides a number of popular chapters by seasoned scholars on the medieval period, with a focus on southern Italy.

Rubin, Miri. *Gentile Tales: The Narrative Assault on Late-Medieval Jews.* Philadelphia: University of Pennsylvania Press, 2004.

Gentile Tales is an important discussion of anti-Semitic libels in the fourteenth and fifteenth centuries, with carefully nuanced and well-documented distinctions between the blood libel, eucharistic desecration, and other Christian myths.

Rubenstein, Richard. *My Brother Paul.* New York: Harper and Row, 1972.

Rubenstein's book on Paul of Tarsus seeks to understand the life and thought of the first-century Jew who became one of the greatest Christian theologians of all time.

Sacks, Jonathan. *The Dignity of Difference: How to Avoid the Clash of Civilizations.* London: Continuum, 2002.

Sacks provides an important critique of the universalizing epistemologies of Western religious discourse and the need to develop ways of thinking that honor particularity and difference with respect and understanding. As a challenge to what he calls the lingering presence of "Plato's ghost," Sacks explores the promise of Jewish hermeneutics to seek the universal in the particular, honoring each in the process.

Sandmel, Samuel. *We Jews and Jesus: Exploring Theological Differences for Mutual Understanding*. Intro. David Sandmel. Repr..Woodstock, VT: SkyLight Paths and Jewish Lights, 2006.

This is the first book-length study on the Jewish Jesus in postwar America. Written by an accomplished Hebrew Bible and New Testament scholar, it explores the theological underpinnings of both early Christianity and late antique Judaism with attention to differences and potential for mutual understanding. David Sandmel, Samuel's son, includes a new introduction, bringing his father's work up to date.

Sawicki, Marianne. *Crossing Galilee: Architectures in the Occupied Land of Jesus.* Harrisburg, PA: Trinity Press International, 2000.

Crossing Galilee is an engaging presentation of life in Roman-period Galilee, combining the study of material culture, archaeology, anthropology, culture studies, and much more. While sometimes controversial, it is never boring.

Schwartz, Regina M. *The Curse of Cain: The Violent Legacy of Monotheism.* Chicago: University of Chicago Press, 1998.

Schwartz offers an exploration of the dichotomizing logic that characterizes the exclusivistic orientation of the monotheistic traditions of Abraham. She identifies a prevailing logic of scarcity operating in all three traditions of Judaism, Christianity, and Islam that she explores as fundamental expressions of violence to the other, which she contrasts with an alternative logic of plenitude that can be found in each of the three traditions as well.

Segal, Alan F. *Rebecca's Children: Judaism and Christianity in the Roman World.* Cambridge, MA: Harvard University Press, 1986.

Segal provides a succinct and compelling account of Second Temple Judaism by placing both Jewish groups and early Christian groups within a common social context. In doing so, he provides a rich context in which to understand the "Jesus Movement" alongside other political and religious movements of the time period.

Spiegel, Shalom. *The Last Trial.* Trans. Judah Goldin. New York: Schocken Books, 1969.

This is a brilliant study of the way history and legend interact in the story of the Aqedah and in the legends and commentaries that sought to comprehend it.. Spiegel also explores the relation of the Aqedah to the crucifixion and Judaism and Christanity.

Stein, Edith. *The Hidden Life: Essays, Meditations and Spiritual Texts.* Ed. L. Gelber and Michael Linssen and trans. Waltraut Stein. Washington, DC: ICS Publications, 1992.

This is a collection of Stein's shorter writings, which she composed while she was in the Carmel in Cologne and Echt. They reflect her thinking, practice, and vocation as a contemplative in Carmel and demonstrate how she saw her mystical life within the walls of the cloister. They are key to understanding Stein's calling to serve Jesus.

Stein, Edith. *Self-portrait in Letters, 1916-1942.* Trans. Josephine Koeppel. Washington, DC: ICS Publications, 1993.

These letters show Stein's life from her pre-Catholic days to just before she was rounded up and deported to Auschwitz. It is a rich source of Stein's evolution from a philosopher, scholar, teacher, mentor, and family member to a Catholic nun. It is a very rich source of the historical period and the philosophers, religious figures, and family around her.

Weiss, Zeev. "Jewish Galilee in the First Century C.E.: An Archaeological Perspective" In *Flavius Josephus, Vita: Introduction, Hebrew Translation, and Commentary.* Ed. Daniel R. Schwartz. Jerusalem: Yad Ben-Zvi, 2007. 15-60. (Hebrew).

Weiss's article is the best survey available today of archaeology and everyday life in first-century CE Galilee.

Wolfson, Elliot R. *Through a Speculum that Shines: Vision and Imagination in Medieval Jewish Mysticism.* Princeton: Princeton University Press, 1994.

Through a Speculum that Shines is an accessible yet critical and well-rounded discussion using phenomenological and critical historical tools, and covering Jewish mystical texts from late antiquity, pre-kabbalistic sources from the tenth to the twelfth centuries, and twelfth- and thirteenth-century kabbalistic literature.

Contributors

Herbert Basser was born in Toronto, attended Yeshiva University (B.A.), University of Toronto (M.A., Ph.D), and has taught at Hebrew University, University of California at Berkeley, and Touro College in New York. He has been at Queen's University in Canada since 1980. Basser, who was once a campus rabbi, is best known for his expertise in Talmudic and midrashic studies. He has been referred to as "the dean of contemporary scholars of the connections between the New Testament and rabbinic law." Among his ten books are *The Mind behind the Gospels: A Commentary to Mathew 1-14* (2009); *Studies in Exegesis: Christian Critiques of Jewish Law and Rabbinic Responses 70-300 CE* (2000); and *Midrashic Interpretations of the Song of Moses* (1984). Awaiting publication at present are his " Introduction and Annotations to the Letter of James," in Amy-Jill Levine and Marc Bretter, eds., *The Jewish Annotated New Testrament* (New York: Oxford University Press, 2011, forthcoming) and "Confirming that 'Tradition of the Elders' (*Paradosis*) refers to an Oral body of Law (*Masoret*)" (*Revue des Études Juives*). His conference talks have encompassed Talmudic studies and also the Gospels. He resides in Toronto with his wife and children.

Steven Bowman earned his Ph.D. in 1974 from The Ohio State University and is currently Professor of Judaic Studies at the University of Cincinnati. Recipient of several Fulbright and NEH awards, he was recently Miles Lerman Fellow at the US Holocaust Memorial Museum. His publications include *The Jews of Byzantium, 1204-1453* (1985, 2000); *Jewish Resistance in Wartime Greece* (2006); and most recently *The Agony of Greek Jewry during World War II* (2009). His annotated translation of Sepher Yosippon will initiate The Hackmey Hebrew Classical Library to be published by Harvard University Press and Tel Aviv University Press, and a monograph on this seminal medieval history of the Second Temple period is in progress. He is editor-in-chief of The Sephardi and Greek Holocaust Library, has edited eight Holocaust memoirs, and is the author of numerous scholarly articles on Byzantine and Modern Greek Jewry. He has been a visiting professor at Queens College CUNY, New York University, University of San Diego, Haifa University, University of California at Berkeley, University of Massachusetts, and Indiana University. He has lectured extensively in Canada, Great Britain, Greece, Holland, Israel, Japan, and the United States.

Bruce Chilton (Ph.D. from Cambridge, 1976) is a scholar of early Christianity and Judaism. He wrote the first critical commentary on the Aramaic version of Isaiah (*The Isaiah Targum*, 1987), as well as academic studies that analyze Jesus in his Judaic context (*A Galilean Rabbi and His Bible*, 1984; The *Temple of Jesus,* 1992; *Pure Kingdom*, 1996). He has taught in Europe at the Universities of Cambridge, Sheffield, and Münster, and in the United States at Yale University, as the first Lillian Claus Professor of New Testament, and Bard College. Currently Bernard Iddings Bell Professor of Religion at Bard, he also directs the Institute of Advanced Theology there. Throughout his career, he has been active in the pastoral ministry of the Anglican Church, and is Rector of the Church of St. John the Evangelist in Barrytown, New York. His most recent books are *Rabbi Jesus: An Intimate Biography* (2000); *Redeeming Time: The Wisdom of Ancient Jewish and Christian Festal Calendars* (2002); *Rabbi Paul: An Intellectual Biography* (2004); *Mary Magdalene: A Biography* (2005); *The Cambridge Companion to the Bible* (2007); *Abraham's Curse: Child Sacrifice in the Legacies of the West* (2008); and *The Way of Jesus* (2010).

Michael J. Cook is Professor of Intertestamental and Early Christian Literatures and holds the Sol and Arlene Bronstein Chair in Judaeo-Christian Studies at Hebrew Union College–Jewish Institute of Religion, Cincinnati Campus. His areas of interest include evolving Jewish views of Jesus and Paul, New Testament dynamics, images of Judaism in Christian Art, the history of anti-Semitism, and factors underlying Christian missionizing. His recent publications include: *Modern Jews Engage the New Testament: Enhancing Jewish Well-Being in a Christian Environment* (2008) and "Jews and 'Gospel Dynamics': Why Advice by Ancient Sages Is No Longer Sage Advice," *The Fourth R* (2009).

Eugene J. Fisher was Associate Director of the Secretariat for Ecumenical and Interreligious Affairs of the United States Conference of Catholic Bishops (USCCB), in charge of Catholic-Jewish relations from 1977 to 2007. He is the first layperson to have held such a USCCB post. His doctoral degree is in Hebrew Culture and Education from New York University (1976). He has served as a Consultor to the Holy See's Commission for Religious Relations with the Jews and as a member of the International Vatican-Jewish Liaison Committee He is an active member of numerous learned and professional societies and associations and has lectured widely throughout the United States, Canada, Europe, Latin America, and Australia. He has published twenty books and monographs, and over 250 articles in major religious journals, many of which have been translated into French, Spanish, Italian, Portuguese, Polish, and German for publication in Latin America and Europe.

Zev Garber is Professor Emeritus and Chair of Jewish Studies and Philosophy at Los Angeles Valley College and has served as Visiting Professor of Religious Studies at University of California at Riverside, Visiting Rosenthal Professor of Judaic Studies at Case Western Reserve University, and as President of the National Association of Professors of Hebrew. He is the founder and editor-in-chief of two academic series, Studies in Shoah (University Press of America) and Shofar Supplements in Jewish Studies (Purdue University Press), and serves as co-editor of *Shofar*. Author of many academic articles and reviews, his book publications include *Methodology in the Academic Teaching of Judaism*(1986), *Methodology in the Academic Teaching of the Holocaust* (1988), *Teaching Hebrew Language and Literature at the College Level* (1991), *Shoah: The Paradigmatic Genocide* (1994), *Perspectives on Zionism*(1994), *Peace, In Deed: Essays in Honor of Harry James Cargas* (with Richard Libowitz, 1998); *Academic Approaches to Teaching Jewish Studies* (2000), *Post-Shoah Dialogues: Rethinking Our Texts Together* (with Steven Jacobs, Henry Knight, and James Moore, 2004), *Double Takes: Thinking and Rethinking Issues of Modern Judaism in Ancient Contexts* (with Bruce Zuckerman, 2004); *Mel Gibson's Passion: The Film, the Controversy, and Its Implications* (2006), and *The Impact of the Shoah in America and in Jewish American Life*, USC Casden Annual 6 (2008). Finally, *Maven in Blue Jeans: A Festschrift in Honor of Zev Garber* was published in 2009.

Steven Leonard Jacobs holds the Aaron Aronov Endowed Chair of Judaic Studies in the Department of Religious Studies at the University of Alabama where he is an Associate Professor. Also an ordained Rabbi, his primary research foci are Biblical studies and translations, the Hebrew Bible and New Testament, and Holocaust/Shoah and historical and contemporary genocides. Among his most recent publications are *Maven in Blue Jeans: A Festschrift in Honor of Zev Garber* (2009); *Confronting Genocide: Judaism, Christianity, and Islam* (2009); and *The Jewish Experience: An Introduction to Jewish History and Jewish Life* (2010).

Yitzchak Kerem, Visiting Israeli Scholar in Sephardic history, American Jewish University of Los Angeles, 2008-2009, is a historian and researcher on Greek and Sephardic Jewry, Ottoman history, and modern Greek history, and a lecturer for the graduate-level Mekor Program in Sephardic Studies, The Hebrew University of Jerusalem. He was founder and past director of the Institute of Hellenic-

Jewish Relations, University of Denver, Denver, Colorado. He was contributor to Pinkas Kehilot Yavan, Yad Vashem, 1999; editor of the Greek section for *New Encyclopaedia Judaica*; past sub-editor of the *Encyclopedia of the Holocaust* (section on the Balkans), Yad Vashem. He was also contributor of numerous articles on Ottoman Jewish communities for the *Encylopedia of Jews in Islam*; contributor to *Larousse Encyclopedia of the Holocaust*, and Ben-Zvi Institute series on the history and culture of the Sephardic Jewish communities. Kerem was editor of the monthly e-mail publication Sefarad, the *Sephardic Newsletter*, radio moderator of "Diaspora Jewry," Israel (2004-2007), documentary filmmaker, and past acting mayor of Tzur Hadasa, Israel.

Henry F. Knight (Hank) is the Director of the Cohen Center for Holocaust and Genocide Studies at Keene State College, the first educational institution in the country to offer an undergraduate major in Holocaust and Genocide Studies. Knight teaches in the college's academic program and directs the Cohen Center's cocurricular programming. Knight is cochair of the biennial Steven S. Weinstein Holocaust Symposium (formerly the Pastora Goldner Holocaust Symposium) that he and Leonard Grob of Fairleigh Dickenson University cofounded in 1996. He serves on the Church Relations Committee of the US Holocaust Memorial Museum in Washington, DC and several other national and international advisory committees related to Holocaust Studies.

Shaul Magid is the Jay and Jeanne Schottenstein Professor of Jewish Studies and Professor of Religious Studies at Indiana University in Bloomington. He is the author of *Hasidism on the Margin* (2004) and *From Metaphysics to Midrash: Myth, History and the Interpretation of Scripture in Lurianic Kabbala* (2008), which won the 2008 AAR award for best book in religion in the textual studies category. His most recent book, *Jews and Judaism in Postethnic America: Becoming an American Religion* is forthcoming.

Sara Mandell, Professor Emeritus at the University of South Florida, earned her B.A. (Latin), M.A. (Latin), and Ph.D. (Classics) at New York University. Mandell studied Organ with Frederick Swann and Virgil Fox at Riverside Church in New York. She served on the Classics faculty of Emory University and subsequently both the Classics and Religious Studies faculty of The University of South Florida. Mandell won honorable mention in the Westinghouse Science Talent Search (now the Intel Science Talent Search) for research in Physical Chemistry. She is the recipient of NYU's Founders Day Award, two State of Florida teaching awards, and a USF Distinguished Service award. She has published numerous articles and book chapters and is the co-author of two books (one with David Noel Freedman and one with John H. Hayes). Mandell served as President of the South Eastern Region of American Schools of Oriental Research. She was on the editorial board of *USF Studies in the History of Judaism* and was Editor of its subseries, *The Hebrew Scriptures and their World.*

James F. Moore is Professor of Theology at Valparaiso University in Indiana. He is book review editor for the *Zygon Journal of Religion and Science*. He is author of *Sexuality and Marriage* (1987); *Christian Theology After the Shoah: a Re-interpretation of the Passion Narratives* (1993, 2004); *Post Shoah Dialogues* (2004); and *Toward a Dialogical Community* (2004) as well as numerous articles on Christian theology and the Holocaust, including a recent contribution to a new encyclopedia on religion and violence entitled *Christianity and Violence*. He is also on the board of the Center for Advanced Study in Religion and Science and is currently the chair of the transition committee for the Annual Scholars' Conference on the Holocaust and the churches.

Richard L. Rubenstein is President Emeritus and Distinguished Professor of Religion at the University of Bridgeport. He also serves as the Lawton Distinguished Professor of Religion Emeritus at Florida State University. The Lawton Professorships are Florida State's highest academic honor. He received the Master of Theology from Harvard Divinity School and the Ph.D. from Harvard's Graduate School of Arts and Sciences. He received his M.H.L. and rabbinic ordination from the Jewish Theological Seminary. Florida State has created the Richard L. Rubenstein Professorship in Religion in his honor. Rubenstein's first book, *After Auschwitz* (1966), is credited with having initiated the contemporary debate on God and the Holocaust. Among his other books are *My Brother Pau* (1972), a study of Paul of Tarsus, *The Cunning of History*(1975), *The Religious Imagination* (1985), a study of Jewish and Christian preaching and legend in the first three centuries of the Christian era, and *Approaches to Auschwitz*, co-authored with John K. Roth (1987, 2nd ed. 2003). His more recent works are *La Perfidie de l'Histoire* (2005), a study of the political, social, and religious consequences of the post-World War II mass migration of Muslims into Europe, and, most recently, *Jihad and Genocide* (2010), a study of the genocidal potentialities of jihad.

Joshua Schwartz is Professor of Land of Israel Studies and Archaeology at Bar-Ilan University, Ramat-Gan, Israel. He is also the Director of the Ingeborg Rennert Center for Jerusalem Studies and the Schulman Center for Basic Jewish Studies at Bar-Ilan. He has also served as Dean of the Faculty of Jewish Studies there. He has published extensively on the history and material culture of the Land of Israel in Second Temple times and in the period of the Mishnah and Talmud.

Emily Leah Silverman is a visiting scholar at Graduate Theological Union in Berkeley, California, where she received her Ph.D. in Interdisciplinary Studies of Religion. She received a Master of Divinity from Harvard Divinity School and a B.A. in the History and Philosophy of Science from Bard College. Her book, *Edith Stein and Regina Jonas: Religious Visionaries in the Time of the Death Camps* is forthcoming in 2011. She is editor of *Voices of Feminist Liberation: Celebratory Writings in Honor of Rosemary Radford Ruether*, also forthcoming. Upcoming articles include "'Halachic Treatise: Can Women Serve as Rabbis, (1930) by Regina Jonas" in *Landmarks in Feminist Thought*, edited by Tiffany K. Wayne and forthcoming in 2010. She serves as a peer reviewer for the *Journal of Feminist Studies in Religion* and sits on the board of the American Academy of Religion/Western Region, where she cochairs the Jewish Studies section. Dr. Silverman resides in San Francisco with her husband and their three children.

Norman Simms, born in Boro Park in Brooklyn, New York in 1940, has taught in New Zealand since 1970, with stints in France, Canada, and Israel. He is the author of hundreds of scholarly articles and books, the latest of which is *Morranos on the Moradas* (2009) and also of several books of poetry, aphorisms, and short stories, for example, *Half-Sour Pickles* (2010). He has also edited many academic and literary journals and reviews. He is now retired but hopes for visiting lectureships overseas where possible.

Christina M. Smerick is the Shapiro Chair of Jewish-Christian Studies at Greenville College in Greenville, Illinois. She received her Ph.D. in Philosophy from DePaul University in 2003. Her works primarily focus upon the intersection of Continental Philosophy with religion, particularly Judaism and Christianity. Her dissertation focused on the early writings of Walter Benjamin; her recent works have focused upon Sartrean ethics, and Christianity via the works of Jean-Luc Nancy (but not in the same article). Her most recent publication is "The Failure of Hate: Love, Hate and Hope in Jean-Paul Sartre" in *Philosophy Today*. She lives in Greenville, Illinois, with her husband and daughters.

Rivka Ulmer's research focuses upon midrashic literature; her book on *Egyptian Cultural Icons in Midrash* was published in 2009. She has published eighteen books, including: *Discussing Cultural Influences*, 2007 (ed.); *Recent Developments in Midrash Research*, 2006 (ed. with L. Teugels); *A Synoptic Edition of Pesiqta Rabbati Based Upon All Extant Hebrew Manuscripts And The Editio Princeps* (1997-2002), a three volume edition of a midrashic work that was republished in paperback (2008); *Turmoil, Trauma and Triumph: The Text of Megillas Vintz*, a Hebrew and Yiddish poem-song that describes a pogrom in Frankfurt in 1614; *The Evil Eye in the Bible and Rabbinic Literature* (1994), as well as more than sixty scholarly articles. Ulmer teaches at Bucknell University (The John D. and Catherine T. MacArthur Chair in Jewish Studies, 2002-2007; currently Associate Professor of Jewish Studies). Ulmer was a Visiting Scholar at the Center for

Jewish Studies at Harvard University. She is the co-chair of the Midrash Section of the Society of Biblical Literature and the Judaica chair of the International Society of Biblical Literature.

Ziony Zevit, Distinguished Professor of Biblical Studies and Northwest Semitic Languages and Literatures at the American Jewish University, is the author of *The Religions of Ancient Israel: A Synthesis of Parallactic Approaches* (2001). Currently he is engaged in a long-term project tracing the transformations of the beliefs and social loci of cult and practice characterizing Israelite religions of the Iron Age into those typical of proto-Judaisms during Late Antiquity. His study in this volume is part of that larger project.

Index